STANLEY D. WI

GROWING UP CHRISTIAN

Dear Al,

God bless your every breath & word for the Kingdom!

Stan Williams

PRAISE FOR
GROWING UP CHRISTIAN

"Stan, reading your book was like reading a movie or a sitcom script. I could see it all. And I could hear you tell these wonderful stories on stage. I laughed out loud so many times, it was great therapy. And your pearls of theological wisdom make this book a classic. I couldn't put it down. What a joy!"
— KELLY NIETO: Creator and Executive Producer, The Cross and The Light, Inspirational Speaker, Former Miss Michigan, Miss America runner-up, Mother of Five

"In Growing Up Christian, Stan Williams shares a beautiful and compelling story of his journey through the remarkable landscape of Christendom. With appreciation for the contribution each "tribe" made to his life, he eventually found his heart's true home in the Catholic Church. Regardless of your own faith tradition--or if you are not a person of faith--you will treasure this delightful book. Loved it. Of course, I knew so many of the people and places in it. Fond memories of my disastrous attempt at Bible quizzing where Bob Kenny was the LeBron James of Free Methodist Bible Quizzing. :)"
— LYN CRYDERMAN : Former Editor of Christianity Today, Former Publisher at HarperCollins/Zondervan, Publishing Consultant

"You can see why Stan is a brilliant screenwriting coach; his knack for getting to the heart of the matter, in any moment, is unparalleled. He could make a ham sandwich, and you'd have no idea how it was going to turn out... A pleasure to read."
— MICHAEL JANN: Senior Joke Writer, The TONIGHT SHOW with Jay Leno

"Hardly a page can be turned without laughing out loud or nodding over a similar experience or even blinking away a tear or two at God's tender mercy. An absolute delight to read! You write about your Christian life like a cradle Catholic; as familiar, heartfelt and close to home as a visit to grandma's house!"
— REV. JOHN BUSTAMONTE: Catholic Priest, Spiritual Advisor

"Written with keen insight and tender, oftentimes pointedly humorous wit, Growing up Christian takes readers on a delightful journey of faith even as it explores what it means to be a believer. Stan Williams' recollections from youthful days to more current stir the heart and soul, and will leave readers both chuckling to themselves while also nodding in agreement at the shared twists and turns of the always dynamic path of following Christ."
— **TAMERA ALEXANDER: USA Today Best Selling Author of** To Whisper Her Name **and** A Lasting Impression

"Stan Williams gives us a delightfully sentimental and insightful "romp" through Evangelical America in the 50s through to the 90s, and describes how he gradually came to believe in the truthfulness of Catholic claims. Stan (a filmmaker by trade) is a master storyteller, and that ability, as well as his propensity for always getting down to brass tacks and identifying both the fundamental errors and strengths of various Christian positions, make this book a pure pleasure to read, from start to finish. 5 stars!"
— **DAVE ARMSTRONG: Catholic Author , Christian Apologist at Patheos.com**

"Growing Up Christian is perhaps the most truthful book I've had the pleasure to read. My friend Stan Williams was, and still is, a very creative innovator and he continuously searches for better ways to communicate and teach. As a person reads about Stan's journey through life, they can understand how his Christian compass helps keep him focused and helps him maintain his values. This story is humorous, yet so painfully realistic that it would be hard not to see comparisons to one's own life."
— **ROBERT (BOB) KREIPKE: Corporate Historian, Filmmaker, Ford Motor Company**

"It's often said that converts make the best Catholics, probably because they tend to take a long, hard look down the path first, and then embrace the Faith with so much deeper appreciation. "Growing up Christian" is a cheeky romp across the landscape of Protestant Evangelical denominations. Even for non-Protestants it often strikes a familiar chord, underscoring many of the common experiences all Christians share while maturing in their Faith. The book is an entertaining read start-to-finish, full of the funniest anecdotes, and also delving deeper into Stan's lifelong analysis of Fundamentalism versus Catholicism."
— **RAY LONG, JR: Multimedia-Writer-Producer, Musician**

"From the first page, "Growing Up Christian" had me smiling and sometimes, I confess, laughing out loud. Stan Williams is a powerful storyteller, and his reminiscences of childhood mischief set the stage for the drama of discovery in his faith journey. When he wrote of attending his first Mass and being forced to abandon some life-long misconceptions about the Catholic faith, I wanted to cheer. Stan and his wife Pam now share their journey in a candid biography that's sure to plant the seeds of wonder in readers' hearts."
— **KATHY SCHIFFER: "Seasons of Grace" Blogger at Patheos.com, Former Network Radio Producer "**

Reads like pure Americana. So great that you are making the explicit, and universal, insistence that life is a storyline that is woven through family and other relationships into our stories."
— **MARY KOCHAN: Editor, Mother, Catechist**

"Colorful, alive and captivating to the point of disappointing when I had to stop and engage in some responsibilities around the church. The style of your introduction to your family and early childhood impressions have really brought life to this literary work. You have an appealing style with a strong moral imagination, humility, and humor. Dude, you are a hoot!"
— **C. LOUIS FETE': Catholic Deacon**

"I have started to read your book. It's hard to read without laughing! Even though I'm only in the first chapter, it's so funny to think about you walking to the zoo (alone at age 3), that your backyard squirrels were too fat (from feeding them too many crackers), and that your mom called the police on you (when you didn't come home at age 4)."
— **MARIA: Age Eight**

"A delightful read. Stan's story is filled with amusing anecdotes, poignant moments and moving examples of a faith filled Christian life. He takes his readers on an often charming and always inspiring journey."
— **MICHAEL (& DONNA) JONES: Vice President & General Manager at Ave Maria Radio**

"Growing Up Christian is a close up look at a long journey of faith. It is a study in how God can at times walk someone ever so slowly to His full truth. The powerful reasoning and logic that guided Stan, as he made his final faltering steps to the Catholic Church, is a story worth the price of the book all by itself."
— **DR. RAY GUARENDI: Clinical Psychologist, Author, Speaker, Television and Radio Host.**

"Master Storyteller Stan Williams raises the genre of conversion stories to the level of an epic. Growing Up Christian's rapid-fire chapters provides entertaining and insightful vignettes into growing up as a Protestant in the 1950s, the unfolding of his vocation to story writing and filmmaking, and his eventual entry into the Catholic Church. Intermixed with humorous anecdotes and comments, Stan gives the reader a front row seat to the intellectual and emotional struggles that eventually led him to discover that Protestantism just isn't workable, and that the last thing on earth he'd ever regard as a viable alternative, the Catholic Church, had the answers he was looking for. I highly recommend Growing Up Christian to Catholics and non-Catholics alike. It's a fascinating page turner, an epic adventure, and a conversion story on steroids... all wrapped up into one."

— GARY MICHUTA: Bible Researcher, Best Selling Author and Speaker

also by Stanley D. Williams

*THE MORAL PREMISE: Harnessing Virtue
and Vice for Box Office Success*
(Michael Wiese Productions, publisher)

The quintessential book on story structure for
screenwriters, novelists, and other storytellers.

<u>www.MoralPremise.com</u>

The most powerful tool in my new tool box.
— WILL SMITH

*The Moral Premise dares to suggest that movies might actually mean some-
thing. I recommend it for all those who want to bring depth and meaning into
their writing.*
— CHRIS VOGLER - Hollywood Script Consultant. Author, "The Writer's Journey"

*An incredibly practical and helpful tool that should be taught in every film
school. The Moral Premise is on the shelf right just above our computer.*
— MARIANNE & CORMAC WIBBERLEY, WGA
Screenwriters, the *National Treasure* Movies.

*Stan, You are a light and an incredible gift! Thank you for your insight and
innovation. The Moral Premise: It's Amazing!*
— DEVON FRANKLIN, Former Sony Entertainment VP, Executive Producer. Author,
"Produced by Faith."

*Should be required reading, retroactively, for every working Hollywood screen-
writer. A new bible for screenwriters.*
— BRIAN BIRD, WGA, Writer-Producer (Touched by An Angel, When Calls the
Heart, Step by Step.)

*Thank you, thank you, thank you for your wonderful Moral Premise, and for
all you've done for me and my writing, Stan.*
— TAMERA ALEXANDER, USA Today Best Selling Novelist

GROWING UP CHRISTIAN

*Searching for a Reasonable Faith
in the Heartland of America*

by
Stanley D. Williams, Ph.D.

with Observations and a Post-Script
by
Pamela S. Williams

Distributed by:

✓ineveh's Crossing

PO Box 29
Novi, MI 48376 USA
www.ninevehscrossing.com
www.GrowingUpChristian.us

ISBN-13: 978-0-9824058-8-8
ISBN-10: 0-9824058-8-X

Printed in the United States of America by McNaughton & Gunn, Saline, MI

First Printing 2015

Scripture quotations marked (NIV) are taken from the Holy Bible, New International Version®, NIV®. Copyright © 1973, 1978, 1984, 2011 by Biblica, Inc.™ Used by permission of Zondervan. All rights reserved worldwide. www.zondervan.com. The "NIV" and "New International Version" are trademarks registered in the United States Patent and Trademark Office by Biblica, Inc.™

Swirl Filigrees Copyright by Milen Kalachev (123RF.com). Used with permission. At times our lives seem complicated as they swirl in every direction. But looking back: "BLESSED BE GOD IN ALL HIS DESIGNS." (Fr. Solanus Casey, O.F.M.Cap.)

Tree graphic Copyright by Olga Nikitina (123RF.com). Used with permission. The roots of our lives are bigger than we are.

Possessive apostrophes on words ending in "s" are punctuated the way the word is spoken in the author's hearing. You'll find: Williams's and Walters'.

On the cover: Ronin does his first professional model job a day after his third birthday. Ronin and his shadow were photographed on his home driveway. In Photoshop they were separately cut out and dropped onto an extended NO PARKING Zone at Hillside Middleschool in Nothville, MI. Cameras: Canon PowerShotS5 and iPhone 5.

Cover photo, interior design and layout by the author. Body text: Minon Pro, Chapter headings: Bernard MT Condensed. Layout: Adobe InDesign.

FOR MY MOTHER
a better antagonist a boy like me could not have

FOR BEN WILLIAMS
EDITH WILLOBEE,
JOHN WILLIAMS,
& JEREMIAH WILLIAMS
teachers, missionaries, adventurers, evangelists
inspirations for a young mind

FOR PROTESTANT REFORMERS
without whom this book would not have been possible
in recognition of the
500th ANNIVERSARY OF THEIR REFORMATION
1517-2017

Contents

Do something concrete, that opens the possibilities. You don't know what God is doing on the other side, but He's doing something. You have to keep a sense of obligation on the one hand, and trust on the other.[1]

Mother Benedict Duss, O.S.B.
Foundress of the Abbey of Regina Laudis

1 Bosco, Antoinette, 2007. *Mother Benedict: Foundress of the Abbey of Regina Laudis.* Ignatius Press, San Francisco, p. 2-3.

Foreword

S TAN WILLIAMS, AGE three, opens his memoir moping around
the house, restless, bored with feeding the lazy, fat squirrels in his
backyard. Even then, he knew this was not the way things ought
to be: "Adventure" was already calling.

So he lifted the latch on the gate, stepped out of his yard and onto
the sidewalk. His three year old legs began an exodus to the promised
land of the Detroit Zoo. Only 9 blocks away, through city traffic, past
merchant stands, storefronts and hundreds of hurrying bi-peds, awaited sleek leopards, lumbering elephants and shiny cobras. Pumping his
stubby little legs, Stanley put the fat squirrels behind and pressed on to
the higher call of face to face communion with animal glory.

The quest started without incidence. But after turning a corner or
two, he stepped off the curb and was startled when an alert motorist
slammed his brakes. The well-meaning motorist gathered up the lad,
placed him on the sidewalk where he then had to choose whether to
help the tyke adventure on to the glorious Detroit Zoo or return to the
home of the fat squirrels. The squirrels won out.

Thwarted in this initial quest, Stan's (and, later his wife Pam's) longing for adventure, for spiritual reality, resembles the three year old's
zoo quest. Time and again, they dared to step out in faith, confident
that God was guiding. Time and again, they'd be thwarted by visionless
church leaders, depressed by congregational indifference, angered by
twisted denominational priorities and tempered in their enthusiasm
by their own musing about the will of God.

When the church he sought to serve had nothing to offer, Stan's talents were recognized by major corporations and his professional career flourished. His occupation would change; his vocation, not at all. His call to strengthen the plausibility of the Christian faith remained strong.

Stan Williams and I met in late 1978 when I began managing a Logos Christian bookstore on the corner of Telegraph and Eureka in Taylor, Michigan. Stan was one of those customers who would rather talk than buy. I was one of those managers who wanted the store to be an outpost filled with those kinds of customers. We were in the same age cohort, both low church, evangelical, Bible-only Protestants. Much of our conversation centered on the sad state of evangelical churches.

Stan wasn't subtle in his complaints: mopey worship services, unwelcoming congregations, mediocre music, boring, humorless, culturally irrelevant sermons, inane financial priorities, and a few lazy, fat ushers squirreling away nuts from the collection so Pastor Wannabebig could erect super church warehouses that were supposed to impress and attract the people whom he had failed to reach with his mopey services, mediocre music, etc.

Stan had seen a lot. At times, he resembled a highly discriminating suitor poring over his ecclesiastical dance card. He'd look down at the card to comment on all the fellowships and churches with whom he had tangoed, waltzed and rumbaed. Sometimes he seemed to prefer talking about churches to joining one.

But I didn't mind commiserating. After all, I was so dissatisfied that a few friends and I started a house church that we closed in about two years because we remained dissatisfied. And, though I attended church regularly, I had never actually signed up as a member of one until I was asked to pastor one years later.

I think I can say that we both thought the right church needed to be invented not discovered. Neither of us, I suspect, thought there was a divinely established Church to be discovered. So we had to adapt one as we went along sharing the gospel. Of course, inventors fail more often than they succeed. They are always fidgeting with one thing or another. Stan was no different.

Stan's restlessness was creative, a divine discontent. His expectations were not extravagant. They were legitimate because they were formed by his deep love of Scripture and his personal acquaintance with the God who promises the new wine of renewal and revival. Stan knew the reality of the wine; his problem was with wineskins.

- How do you sustain and distribute those moments of grace?

- How do you fashion a church structure that reliably transmits the Faith to the next generation without inflexible indoctrination?

- How do you fashion a church that meets the challenges of the changing culture by so fearing compromise that one separates from the world or by so lusting for relevance that one accommodates the faith so the church ends up indistinguishable from the world?

- How do you create a church that preserves the awe-inspiring, almost traumatizing, sense of the sacred and yet maintains the warmth of a family gathered for Thanksgiving meal?

THIS WAS STAN'S problem of wineskins. If wine isn't your spirit of choice then how about fire? How long can you keep the fire safely ablaze, serving hearth and home, without a functioning fireplace? How can the work of the Spirit achieve its goal if God's divinely ordained structure is ignored? These are the questions fermenting in Stan's soul and bubbling up through the pages of this book. .

Watching friends live out their experiments in faith can be a source of great joy or sorrow. This memoir shows the drama of wagering on one's experiment in living. Christian faith is never blind faith in the sense of being irrational. But it often has to operate blind, i.e., we don't know what God is doing and yet we must act faithfully. Stan and Pam more than once put their life and careers on the line in pursuit of what they believed, rightly or wrongly, was God's will.

Stan and I never spent a lot of social time together. Years could go by without a word. That's the way it was in late 1998 when I received a postcard out of the blue from Stan informing me that he and Pam had come into full communion with the Catholic Church. My first thought was, "Great. Welcome." My second was, "Uh oh." A band of gypsies had just decided to work for IBM or some other Fortune 500. Culture clash. I'd predict pain. Stan's restlessness, creativity, high expectations seemed a bad fit. Then there was his demand that church leaders should be quickly responsive to human need and cultural change. Yes, I predicted pain.

B UT STAN WAS not the man I met in 1978 or grew to know in 1982. Christ had been working his salvation in Stan through those years. Stan had remained faithful and growing. He had remained faithful in marriage, fathering and had already worked the Fortune 500 routine. The trajectory toward Rome was set long before I met him, wired by his intense hunger for the Church Jesus prayed for and his unwillingness to settle for imitations. *Growing Up Christian* tells the story.

— Al Kresta

Preface

ASIDE FROM THE narcissism, life-lessons and therapy involved in writing a memoir, an important objective for me was to avoid the on-set of boredom—not just for you, in its reading, but also for me, in its writing. Thus, I took liberty in fictionalizing ten-percent of what follows and exaggerating the other ninety.

Well, actually that's an exaggeration.

There are a number of chapters and anecdotes which did not require a rhetorical prostheses, so to speak. In fact, I've chosen to tone down some stories to make them believable. In particular, I am referring to those instances where my life rubbed against what I can only explain as mystical or supernatural dimensions of reality.

Hopefully, you'll recognize them without the need for an asterisk or footnote.

THE DIFFICULTIES IN *life I confronted were the ironic consequence of a blessing described in the underlined portion of this passage:*

> *I, the Lord your God, am a jealous God, punishing the children for the sin of the parents to the third and fourth generation of those who hate me,* <u>*but showing love to a thousand generations of those who love me and keep my commandments.*</u>[1]

That was true of my life. My ancestors were devout Christians—preachers, missionaries, prayer-warriors, and caregivers of the poor—

---

1 Exodus 20:5 (NIV)

who gave up their lives for the Gospel. Those were deep roots from which my life grew. God showered me with His blessings (the fruit of those roots) because those that preceded me had kept His commandments.

With such a blessing, however, came a responsibility that often overwhelmed me. I became obsessed with two of Christ's parables from the New Testament. The first was the parable of The Talents[2] and how a refusal to invest one's talents and generate a return for the King results in being thrown into the darkness "where there will be weeping and gnashing of teeth." The second was the parable of The Faithful and Unfaithful Servants. The unfaithful servant was unprepared for the King's unexpected return; so the King had the poor man "cut to pieces" without a second thought or a smidgen of remorse. So much for salvation by "faith alone." According to these stories, "works" were part of the formula. Christ concluded that parable:

> **God showered me with His blessings because those that preceded me had kept His commandments.**

> *From everyone who has been given much, much will be demanded.[3]*

FEARFUL THAT GOD would cast me into utter darkness or subject me to dismemberment, I frequently ran ahead too quickly. I often scribbled my first name in a rush. To me it looked like I had spelled SAINT...but friends would point out that I had scrawled STAIN. I could only hope that the errors in my life would be overlooked as typos. But alas, all too often they were real mistakes.

—SW

---

2 Matthew 25:14-28
3 Luke 12:35-48 (NIV)

Picture Gallery and more stories at:
www.GrowingUpChristianSW.blogspot.com

GROWING UP CHRISTIAN

*At 1 yr - Good natured, quick tempered,
a plunger—not cautious.*

*At 4 yrs - Same as at 1 yr +
determined to do what he wants to do
regardless of consequences
—will run away from home.[1]*

---

1 Mom's early notes.

Prologue: Raising a Red Flag

I T WAS 1960, and a hot, sweltering summer night. I was 13, in the midst of adolescence and attending an event that would be a sea change in my peculiar journey of faith.

Mom had me in a white shirt, tie, and creased, wool trousers. I matched Dad's getup except for the tie—his was wider and more colorful. Dad always wore his Sunday best...even to cut the lawn or take out the garbage. Not to be outdone, Mom was arrayed in her best flower-print, polyester dress and velvet hat with a fake flower pinned to the side and a fishnet veil pulled over her eyes.

We weren't in a fancy place, however. We were in a sawdust revival tent, and my goal was to get through another evening of fist-pounding, foot-stomping, hell-fire preaching without my Mom cuffing me for not being the ideal Christian kid.

I sat next to my 8-year old sister, Hope Ellen, her blonde locks in a curl hanging over her fancy Easter Sunday dress. She had learned, through my mistaken exploits, how to sit still, look pretty, and get Mom to beam at her.

The evangelist's lean face was red with emotion and wet from perspiration. After mopping his brow and neck with his white handkerchief, he'd wave it at his audience—trying both to air dry it in the humid August heat, and reinforce the point of his sermon: Our surrender to Communism if we elected John Fitzgerald Kennedy, a Catholic, to the U.S. presidency.

W E WERE SPENDING several weeks of vacation at our small cabin on the Free Methodist Church campgrounds, hidden in the woods just East of Jackson, Michigan. The campgrounds consisted of about 40-acres of woods on which were located several hundred lots organized along dirt roads and paths. Some lots contained small cabins--I recall helping my dad build ours--and on other lots trailers were parked, or tents erected. In the middle of camp was a large barn-like "tabernacle" that seated perhaps a 1,000 people on unfinished pine pews below bare hanging light bulbs pulsing with the beat of a hidden diesel generator. Meals were taken in a large WWII military surplus Quonset hut[1] dining hall, with food served up on compartmentalized metal mess trays. Each day of Family Camp was filled with Bible studies, youth meetings, prayer meetings, and swimming via a bus ride to nearby Gilletts Lake. The days concluded with a two-hour singing and preaching service in the tabernacle.

On a few particular nights in 1960, however, there was competition a few miles outside the camp on Jackson Road, near the Dome Ice Cream parlor. There, a traveling evangelist, Dr. Harvey H. Springer, had dumped a pile of sawdust next to the main road into Jackson, erected a modest tent over it, put up a canvas sign, and was preaching--not about God or Christ--but against Catholicism.

Historically (I'm old enough to feel the need to explain my childhood in such terms), General Dwight D. Eisenhower was completing his second term as President, and the Cold War was hot. Senator Joseph McCarthy[2] had died several years before, but McCarthyism's "Red" fear was very much alive, thanks to Soviet premier Nikita Khrushchev's rhetorical threat to take over the United States.

Khrushchev was reported to have said, "We will bury you." To which my very Christian, evangelical, Bible teaching, daughter-of-missionaries, mother would passionately respond, "I'd rather be dead than red."

She'd say this, and then ask if I didn't agree with her. I never did

---

1 A Quonset hut is a corrugated galvanized steel building where the cross section forms a semicircle.

2 Joseph McCarthy (1908-1957) was a Wisconsin Senator from 1947 until his death. He became infamous for his demagogic tactics of hunting down Communist sympathizers through the public Army-McCarthy hearings of 1954. His destruction of lives, companies and careers through public insinuation and his inability to substantiate his claims resulted in his censure by the United States Senate that same year.

know how to answer. Since she was the one that first taught me about Jeremiah's prophecies to the Judean king, Zedekiah, that it would be better to be alive and a slave in Nineveh, than dead and a snack for vultures in Judah. Yeah, yeah, yeah! I knew a lot about the Bible back then. But you have to remember, I was raised an Evangelical, not a Catholic... and Evangelicals go to Sunday School, every Sunday, all year long, their whole lives. We learned all about the stories and their meaning in the Old and New Testament. Hezekiah! We could even recite the books of the Bible—backwards.

It was the beginning of the 1960's—a sea change for American culture. The Kennedy-Nixon campaign of 1960 occurred during the pontificate of John XXIII, and, here in America, Catholics were busy having large families. We lived near the Divine Child parish in Dearborn, Michigan, and it seemed that every other household in the neighborhood was Catholic with 6-12 kids.

Some Protestants (like my mother) were afraid that Catholicism would take over America--not by killing people (like the Communists had threatened) but by having babies who would eventually allow Catholics to dominate the democratic process. She had not yet heard of the contraceptive pill, which would be made widely available to the public in a few years. Nor did she know that Catholic women would swarm to use the pill against the Church's prohibition. Mom might have been delighted had she known what the future held.

BACK IN THE sawdust revival tent, the perspiring Dr. Harvey Springer was waving his white handkerchief, and preparing yet another, but larger prop. I'll never forget the image or the "logic."

He had been railing, ranting, and raging for some time against Catholicism and Communism. The parallels were unmistakable (to him): (a) both institutions started with the letter "C" and ended in "ism"—suffixes that, by the standards of the English language, identified evil ideologies; (b) both Moscow and the Vatican were determined to take over the world, one by death, the other by having babies; and (c) both were in league with the devil--Communism outlawed God (neat trick), and Catholicism was the sinister front for the anti-Christ. Americans should fear both, he told us. "The facts spoke for themselves..." and my Mom, bless her rather-dead-than-red heart, joined the ever-louder "Amen!" chorus.

Then, it came time for the big climax, the coup-de-grace, the clincher. Springer selected two, good-looking pre-teen children from the audience, and led them onto the small wooden platform on which he stomped back and forth. The kids looked like shills—they were dressed, brushed, and combed for the part. Yes, in addition to knowing lots about the Bible, I was a cynic. I recall the girl was wearing a pretty white dress, with a bow in her curled blonde hair, like she had just posed for a shampoo ad. I really don't remember the boy. Hormones were in the process of permanently altering my interests.

Springer had the kids stand next to each other facing the audience, hands at their sides, idealistic smiles distorting their faces (they had done this before). Then with great pathos he intoned: "Men and women of America. I am warning you with God as my witness. If you elect John Fitzgerald Kennedy to the Presidency this is what will happen." And suddenly out of nowhere (okay, so I was distracted) he produced a HUGE red communist flag, and, standing behind the kids, draped it over their shoulders like a warm blanket on a cold night, pulling it tight around their necks, leaving only their faces staring sadly (as if on cue) at the audience like a mad Normal Rockwell painting.

The image was complete. The memory indelible.

My mother acquired one of the Harvey H. Springer, D.D., Th.D. pamphlets, CATHOLICISM IN AMERICA (see the on-line picture gallery), wrote my name on it and slipped it into my Memories Chest. I found it after I got married when she gave me the chest full of (her) memories from my childhood. The cover, under my name in my Mom's handwriting, pictures two dark clouds overshadowing a map of the United States. One cloud is labeled "COMMUNISM" and the other contains a crude drawing of John Kennedy with the label "CA-THOLICISM" written across it. Inside, many paragraphs are under-lined in pencil, and noted in my mother's handwriting are directions to "READ," and "Modern Day Persecution" detailing how the Catholic Church in Columbia, Latin America, in cooperation with the gov-ernment was killing Protestant missionaries, putting nuns in public schools in Ohio, and how Kennedy was taking orders from the Vatican.

Springer died at age 60, six years after my exposure to him. He was known as the "cowboy" preacher and was a former Communist before his late conversion to Christianity. I do not know if he is related to the infamous TV rebel rouser, Jerry Springer, but there was a similarity in their style and affinity for the sensational.

At 13, my mind wasn't on theological inconsistencies or political tyranny. Springer's stage theater did hold my attention, but I found Springer's pomposity and manipulation disgusting. Thankfully, I hid my feelings, because my head still ached from the last slap to the head I had sustained. Besides, Russia didn't sound like a good place to ask for asylum.

While I didn't believe Springer for a moment, my parents did and so it seemed did the rest of the audience—there were gleeful cheers, and boisterous affirmations while the stomping raised tiny clouds of sawdust. My mother indeed, much of her life afterward, would proclaim out of the blue: "I'd rather be dead than red."

Mom, the oldest child of adventurous American Missionaries, was born in India, the land of elephants, leopards, and cobras. She frowned on my own adventures as a kid, but I must have been born with her parents' persevering, damn-the-elephants-leopards-and-cobras spirit. And as she wrote in my baby book, I was "good natured, quick tempered, and a plunger."

Part I
ORPHAN

I DIDN'T FIT IN. During my years growing up, although I lived with my parents in an oddly functional and Christian home, I often thought of myself as a spiritual orphan.

My parents and all our relatives were Evangelical—a small, conservative part of Protestant Christianity. They found joy in conforming to a version of the faith that I found hard to understand.

While I never gave up on God or the Bible, I struggled with the variability found in American Christian culture. Deep within me there was a longing for a faith that avoided irrational ideology and embraced logic and reason.

The "orphanage" of which I became a part left me restless. For most of my youth it was as if I had been bundled-up in a thick wool sweater, a rain slicker and galoshes, then urged to hunker down in a church basement and pray for the cultural storm to pass. If we grew tired of praying, we could watch badly made Christian movies projected onto cinderblock walls. It was myopic, claustrophobic and irrational. Where was the faith that promised to teach us how to don swim trunks and navigate the shark infested surf? Where was life in all its fullness and adventure?

1
Visions of Adventure

IT WAS THE spring of 1950 and I was three. Hope Willobee, my Aunt who lived with us for the first eight-years of my life, says I never learned to walk—I went from crawling to running. As a toddler, I could not be kept in our fenced yard. It seemed that I was always trying to jump ahead, which explains a lot.

I had just gotten over my fear of our GE Monitor-Top refrigerator. A week earlier I came in from playing in our fenced-in backyard, opened the refrigerator, and grabbed a fresh glass of milk sitting there waiting for me to guzzle down. It looked so refreshing and cold. Except, once it hit my tongue I knew it wasn't milk. It was starch and water Mom had mixed for ironing Dad's shirts. Fortunately, not much got to my stomach before I coughed up the nasty stuff all over the floor. From then on, although the handle to the refrigerator was at eye level, I decided to keep my distance from the GE devil.

But spring was upon us, and there were things to do. Standing on the back porch, I girded up my courage, pulled open the screen door, walked into the kitchen, and stood next to the refrigerator where Mom was standing at the counter flipping green beans into a colander.

"Mom!" I said, in a loud voice. "It's spring. The sun is out and it's warm and lovely. Let's go to the zoo and see the leopards and elephants. They have cobras don't they?"

My mom's wrists flicked in a blur as her pairing knife cut the ends off green beans, diced the remainder, and dropped the good parts into the holey container.

"Not today, Stanley. We've got better things to do." She always used the plural pronoun when referring to herself.

As I gazed up at the bottom of the shiny colander, Mom's twitching wrists made short work of the veggies and I caught the reflection of my face. It was covered with tiny holes like I had just broken out in acne from the stress of the moment.

I slumped my shoulders and went back outside and stood on the porch. All there was to do was feed the backyard squirrels Ritz crackers. I love animals, but our squirrels were getting fat.

Suddenly, I realized that the Detroit Zoo was only nine blocks away and I knew how to get there. From our house I would head east along West Maplehurst, then turn north on Pinecrest Avenue, and in no time, the entrance to the Detroit Zoo and its landmark water tower would loom before me.

Enough of this waiting. Without a scruple, I lifted the backyard gate latch and walked to the front sidewalk, turned right, and I was on my way.

When I got to Pinecrest, I started across the busy street. Suddenly, a car screeched to a stop just feet from hitting me. The driver, a complete stranger, got out, took me to the sidewalk and asked if I knew where I lived. I told him I knew where I lived but I was on my way to the zoo. Much to my disappointment the man took me home, not to the zoo.

THEREAFTER, MOM KEPT me on a leashed-harness attached to a metal clothesline that ran down the center of our backyard from our back porch to the corner of the garage. On days when the laundry had to dry on the line I was restricted to the house. One day, when I was in my harness, I climbed the apple tree next to the garage. At one point I jumped off a branch into my sandbox, but I never made it. My leash had wrapped around a branch and my body was suspended a couple feet over the ground. No manner of trashing or squirming did any good. Not sure who rescued me.

When I was too big for the harness I made friends up and down the block, but refused to come home when I was supposed to. My mother had threatened to call the cops on me if I didn't come home on time. One day, late in the afternoon I knew I was gone from home much longer than I was supposed to be. I looked down the block toward my house and was shocked to see on the sidewalk a uniformed police officer walking toward me. It was the only time I ever saw a cop on West Maplehurst Ave. I panicked, ran into my friend's backyard, through the alley, to my backyard, up the back steps, and into my Mom's kitchen. She was there, wringing her hands in her apron, fuming mad at me for disobeying. Years later, she claimed she never called the cops on me, but I believe otherwise.

THE FUNNY THING was I wasn't the first person in my family to run for adventure and not come home when common sense suggested it. Later on I'll write about John Williams and Jeremiah Williams and their sense, or lack of it, for wandering and adventure. But the idea of getting away from normality and visiting wild animals in distant places came from my Grandmother, who coddled me as an infant in her arms as she swung from a hammock in our backyard.

In 1908 Edith Flesher (1880-1962), at 28-years of age, pushed aside the contemporary and vocal political milieu into which she was born—the U.S. Woman's Suffrage Movement—and followed a calling that instead battled patriarchy half a world away—in India.

After graduating from a Missionary Bible school in Iowa, Edith embraced poverty, and traveled alone half a world away on a slow steamer for the British colony of India, and the mysteries of a country one-fifth the size of the United States, yet home to 18 distinct languages and over 800 village dialects. It was in the Middle Province of India that she joined a small group of other similarly called men and women, members of the *Pentecost Bands of the World* missionaries, to care for the poor, the outcasts, the widows and orphans, and preach the Gospel.

A little over a year later, in 1910, a fellow classmate from the Iowa Bible School, Ross Willobee, followed Edith to India. Family rumor has it that Ross chased Edith there, but Edith's diaries indicate that the romance did not blossom until they were both in India. But, the Pentecost Bands board would not allow them to marry until Ross learned Hindi, which took him a year after he arrived.

They were married in 1911 and soon had three children: Ruth arrived in 1912, Hope in 1915, and David in 1919.

It's important to note, in charting Edith's persevering journey of faith, that when she came to India, getting married and having children was far from her mind. It can be inferred through her diaries that although she loved her children deeply and cared for them as best as the poverty conditions of India allowed, her first calling was to be a Missionary...to India.

Late in 1921, during an Indian famine, Ross returned exhausted from a week long conference. Overnight, he came down with black water fever (a form of malaria that turns urine black). Within two weeks, on Sunday, November 6, 1921, he was dead. As he died he called his daughters to his bedside, blessed them, and prayed that they would both get a college education that he and Edith had not been afforded.

Three days later, on Wednesday, their two-year old son, David, died of unknown causes.

Edith battled the local Raj (regional governor) and Hindi beliefs to have a Christian burial. The local custom, for sanitary reasons, was to either cremate the deceased or bury the bodies in shallow graves along a river-bed so that scavenging beasts or birds of prey could dig the bodies up and eat them. But Edith succeeded in convincing the Raj otherwise. Because wood was scarce, she tore out the interior doors of their small house that Ross had labored to install only months earlier, and built two caskets. Today their bodies lie next to each other in Ambagarh-Chowki, India awaiting the Resurrection.

After Ross and David's death, Edith had a nervous breakdown that put her in bed for six months. During her convalescence she came to realize that the American director of the mission was philandering with Indian nurses behind his wife's back. When he discovered that Edith knew his secret he threatened Ruth and Hope if Edith didn't quit the mission and return to America. But she refused to leave India.

Instead, one day in 1922, she rose miraculously from her bed, ordered two ox-cart covered wagons, and convinced two other missionaries, a native cook, a native Bible woman, and two drivers to help her plan an adventure. She had the wagons packed with tents and supplies, and with her daughters as singing evangelists and dialect translators, Edith and the "Willobee Sisters" spent 4-years traveling the countryside establishing six churches. Edith, too, plunged into things.

Each summer Westerners had to escape the simmering heat of the plains. Edith and girls went to a non-denominational missionary hostel in the small mountain village of Landour, near Mussoorie in the foothills of the Himalayas. The area used to be part of Nepal and Colonel Sir George Everest maintained a house nearby; he was the British surveyor of India after which Mt. Everest was named against his wishes. It was here, too, that Hope and Ruth attended the famous Woodstock International School that was visible from the veranda of the hostel and accessible by a mountain path that they used to get to and fro.

One summer at the Landour Hostel, Edith was diagnosed with

breast cancer. A British doctor told her she'd have to have a mastec-tomy to survive. Also staying at the hostel was a Catholic nun who prayed to the Blessed Mother to intercede with God for Edith's healing. Within a week the cancer miraculously disappeared. Edith never had a mastectomy and lived 37 more years.

In early 1927, Edith mounted a trip to bring her girls, now in their early teens, to the United States for education. The trip is documented in a detailed hand-written diary. They took ox-carts, trains, a ferry and finally two steamships. Along the way Edith parried with luggage thieves, ticket agents with sticky fingers, a dishonorably discharged drunken British soldier who decided to protect Edith and the girls, a sailor who courted my mother and bought her Amber beads in Port Said (we have the beads), and a determined Sheik, who, during the cruise from Ceylon to Tripoli, bargained with Edith for my mother, Ruth, to join his harem. Hollywood would demand the story be dumbed down for believability.

But Edith persevered, not without fear or prayer, but with surety of her calling and a bit of impetuousness. I admired her through the stories I would hear years later of these events, and her life gave me courage to persevere--and be a bit impetuous--as well.

In America, Edith set up the girls in a Bible boarding school in Tabor, Iowa. Then, she traveled the country speaking at churches and missionary conferences to raise money for the girl's schooling and for her own return to India.

> **My Mother as a major antagonist... prepared me to battle the misguided visions of others and the status quo.**

As soon as Ruth and Hope matriculated to Greenville College in 1936, Edith returned to India, like she had almost 30 years ear-lier, single and obedient, to help widows and their children trapped in poverty in the great country of India.

Hope and Ruth, while in college during weekends and summers, toured the country as *THE WILLOBEE SISTERS, SINGING EVANGELISTS,* which helped pay their way through school along with a few benefactors Edith had lined up. Fulfilling their father's deathbed blessing, Ruth and Hope graduated from GC in 1940, and both were hired to teach school in Romeo, Michigan.

A couple years later, the teaching positions ended for reasons un-known. They moved to Highland Park, Michigan (a city completely surrounded by the City of Detroit) where they found jobs. Ruth worked in a Chrysler plastics plant, and Hope became a fearless gun-toting Detroit policewoman.

That same year, in 1942 Edith retired from missionary service and came to live with her daughters in Highland Park. On weekends, the girls still sang together at church revival meetings and so they happened to discover and began attending the Ferndale Free Methodist Church, a small, white, clapboard affair with a modest steeple.

Their adult Sunday school teacher was Ben Williams, who had also attended Greenville College, but 26 years earlier. Ben was recently a widower; his first wife, Lucile, having succumbed to cancer in 1940. Over the next few years, Ben and Ruth became "acquainted" under the watchful eye of Ruth's mother and sister Hope. Then, in November of 1945, Free Methodist Bishop Leslie Marston, a classmate of Ben's from Greenville College in 1916, married them.

Edith must not have been too happy about the private wedding, which was held in their home and not at the church. Very few friends and relatives were invited. The formal announcement says, "Mrs. Edith Willobee announces…," but it's clearly not an invitation and there's no address as to the wedding's location. After the wedding, a news clipping describes the wedding as if it was in a fancy church with special music numbers and a full description of Mom's dress:

> *The bride wore a gown of ivory crepe accented with lace…a finger tip veil that fell from an orange blossom wreath…a bouquet of maiden blush roses and baby mums.*

But the news clipping finishes the description with this juicy morsel:

> *Mrs. Willabee (sic) chose a dress of black…for her daughter's wedding.*

Then there was this little note on the back of a wedding greeting card from Ruth's close friend Grace Hardee:

> *Your mother wrote to me about the wedding and said you looked very nice but I guess you had your troubles too didn't you? How do you like housekeeping for a job? Well, best wishes…" Lovingly, Grace Hardee.*

One can only wonder what happened. Perhaps it was an early edition of *Bridezilla*. At any rate, these should have been early signs of what was in store for Ben and their children, if they were to have any.

After the honeymoon in a cabin at Turkey Run State Park in Indiana, Ben and Ruth moved into the West Maplehurst address and Hope and Edith moved into the boarder's apartment on the second floor. From living alone for four years to suddenly having three women in the house, Ben must have been happy for the next addition to his household.

The next winter was cold and late, and so bundled up was Ruth when she attended church that no one knew she was pregnant until she showed up at church in April with me in her arms. That began a trend. As you will see, in the coming years I would continue to *surprise* people when I showed up in churches.

I'M NOT SURE exactly what my grandmother whispered in my ear during those lazy summer afternoons in the hammock, but I suspect they were full of adventurous ideas. For Edith was cut from a mold that defied safety and convention; and I was her grandson whom she helped raise during my most formidable years.

Edith's missionary adventures in a land of famine and oppression, with her young daughters at her side, were harrowing. They faced disease, danger and death. Their survival required an indomitable spirit and persevering faith—traits that to a lesser degree would animate my own life.

But these same traits, which teemed with virtue, would also set-up my Mother as a major antagonist for me. And as such, she trained me to understand who I truly was and prepared me to battle the misguided visions of others and the status quo.

In the end, what I remember most was this: As a family we visited the Detroit Zoo a lot. Seeing how the authorities kept wild beasts in cages was great preparation for the adventures that lay ahead for me, like when I met my sister.

2
Baby Mysticism

IN 1952, WHEN I was almost five, my Dad suddenly took off with my Mom and left me in the care of my Aunt and grandma who lived in the second floor apartment of our house. I had no idea what was going on. I don't recall Dad coming and going for the next few days, but he must have. I vaguely remember playing outside on a warm, sunny day in January.

I was throwing one of dad's white handkerchiefs up into the air. Onto the corners of the handkerchief I had tied some lengths of string and having cut the four lengths evenly (with Mom's heavy duty pinking shears that I was not supposed to touch), I then tied the ends to the shaft of a rusty iron bolt that I had requisitioned from a glass Mason jar on Dad's workbench in the basement. Provided I wrapped the handkerchief and strings just right around the bolt, and threw it up in the air at least as high as a tall mountain (as I recall), the invention would spread its wings and I'd watch my miniature parachute float to the ground. On the other hand, if I didn't wrap the handkerchief just right, the parachute would not open and the rusty bolt would hit me on the head.

It was after one of those failed test flights when I was rubbing the bump on my head that Dad's car drove into the driveway and stopped by the house. Dad got out and went to Mom's side of the car and opened the door for her. That was weird. Normally, Mom got out on her own long before Dad even opened his own door. Suddenly, Aunt Hope came running out of the house with her camera. *What's up?* I wandered over to the car, hoping Mom wouldn't ask how I cut the strings for my commando toy.

Mom was all smiles. She was carrying a bundle of blankets. As I approached, she crouched down and pulled back a corner of the blanket. It looked like a big parachute without any strings on the corners. Imagine my surprise when what I saw wrapped up inside was not what I expected—a big rusty bolt, but a pink baby.

I had no idea where my mother had gone. I had no idea where my sister had come from. It was a mystery. Of course, at five-years of age, the facts of life were supposed to elude me. But after growing up and learning where babies actually came from, my sister and I still found our existence a mystery. We had never seen our parents express any physical affection toward each other. How were we even possible, we wondered? Such was the time.

Suddenly being introduced to my baby sister was like being introduced to the mystical origins of humanity and the tentacles of the universe's ultimate authority. I had flashes of what later I would call omnipotence and omniscience…at least as far as I could possibly understand the two. Certainly, I was in no position to suggest an alternative. But mystery confronted me like a rusty bolt falling from the billowy white clouds overhead and putting a knob on my head. I was thunderstruck, bewildered, enchanted. Baby sis and the wonders of reality were here to stay.

> **Mystery confronted me like a rusty bolt falling from the billowy white clouds overhead and putting a knob on my head.**

Hope Ellen was named after Aunt Hope. To tell the two apart we began to call my sister by her first two names as if they were one, "Hope Ellen," and we called our aunt, Aunt Hopie (Hope-ē).

Hope Ellen must have been a quiet baby, or else I was not very observant because I remember little about her upbringing until she was 2 and I was 7. That's when Uncle Smith came for a visit.

3
Uncle Smith

IN JULY OF 1954 Uncle Smith and Deputy Minister, Raja Bahadu Binendra Singh from the Middle Providence of India came for a visit.[1] Their visit wasn't that unusual because Mom and Dad frequently hosted visiting preachers, bishops, and missionaries for Sunday dinners, sometimes overnight, and even longer, stays. I don't recall the Raja, but Uncle Smith left a lasting impression. He was a dark black man, born in Jamaica, who had been called by the Pentecost Bands to be a missionary in India. He lived and preached in India for over 50 years, where he took up citizenship, and where he died and was buried. His 1954 trip to the U.S. was to settle his mother's estate and I remember he stayed with us for several days. He was as a gentle giant of a man, who never stopped talking about Jesus.

During this stay Uncle Smith took the Bob-Lo excursion boat trip down the Detroit River to the Canadian island and amusement park of the same name. He used the hour layover at the island to go ashore and stop visitors along the boardwalk and with his Bible in one hand, and waving the other, talk to them about Jesus.

Back at my home, while carrying me on his shoulders down our back alley, and with Hope Ellen toddling along beside, he taught us to sing, "Jesus, Loves Me" in Hindi. To this day I can still remember parts of the Hindi lyrics.

Uncle Smith was instrumental in establishing Family Devotions at our house (about which I will say more later), a practice my mother favored but my Dad put off, until the authoritative Uncle Smith insisted upon it during his short stay. Thereafter, even into my adult years, my parents always celebrated evening Bible reading and prayers right after

---

1 My mother's guest book

dinner in the living room.

Uncle Smith wasn't anything like us or other visitors in appearance, speech or behavior. His erect, energetic posture and dark skin radiated life, his elegant speech and command of several languages was captivating, and his engaging personality made him the center of respect, grace and authority when he walked into any room.

I wanted that same exotic respect, So, shortly thereafter, when my Aunt returned from a trip around the world, she brought me a present that I was sure would command attention. Of course, my Mom had other ideas.

4
Chores &
Tigers

IN 1954 MOTHER determined that her only son would be a good soldier. Regimen, self-discipline, accountability, and self-initiative were values she had decided I would have before adolescence...or else.

I had just turned seven and was in first grade at Roosevelt Elementary, three short walking blocks north of our house. The brown brick, one story school was a bit schizophrenic. It sat on the boundary between two Detroit suburbs: Ferndale, where we lived, and Pleasant Ridge to the north. This was the perfect place for me to go to school, reasoned my mother. Since she was never quite sure exactly where I was at any one time it would be fitting if my earliest education experience matched my disorder.

Mom was three-fourths German, a stout woman with short curled blonde locks that were always in place, as was the rest of the house. Thus, the above virtues were in her nature, and since I was her natural child, she figured the task would be an easy one. In retrospect I'm sure both of us lamented that goal. Her regimen was only going to exacerbate what I popped out of her womb with—contrary *plungeresque*.

Nonetheless the task was at hand. It was a new moon, and Sunday, April 4, 1954 began the *third* week of Mom's boot camp. To track my progress she created a rubric[1] chart. There were ten rows and one

---

1 The term rubrics come from the Latin for the name of the powder grounded up to make red ink. The red lettering in liturgical texts directed the priest or people's posture during worship.

column for each day of the week.

There's no indication what score I had to obtain, one way or the other, to be awarded a punishment or prize. And, although I don't remember the rewards, the punishments are still fresh in my mind—no dessert, quartered to my room, and hard labor cleaning the house. This latter punishment would be short lived when I dusted--and *simultaneously busted*--a favorite vase.

One category of "chores" conspicuously missing, which I now find amusing, are rows for spiritual regimens—paramount necessities in our home. I can imagine my Mother adding a few more rows:

- ▶ Comes to Family Devotions without squabbling; prays with missionary zeal and conviction of heart.
- ▶ Confesses his sins to Mom or Dad on an hourly basis, regardless of promises of absolution.
- ▶ Can read assigned Scripture passages with the passionate pretense of a tent-meeting evangelist.
- ▶ Respects his Bible by not putting the fish bowl on top of it, or anything else.

We had just finished two weeks of trials, and I had not fared well. I'm not sure why a "Good Point" was denoted by a zero ("0"). It seemed to be at odds with society's concept of "points". Nonetheless, we began on a Sunday, Day 1. (See the actual chart on-line)

- ▶ Clothes put in right place: I remembered that my socks don't go on my ears. 0 points (which means "1")
- ▶ Bed Made on Sat. & Sun: There was really a streak of kindness in my German raised Mom. It seems I didn't have to do make my bed Monday through Friday. Getting the next two lines was more important. Score!
- ▶ Completely dressing self: I must have mastered this early in life for there were no demerits for the whole week.
- ▶ Getting to school on time: No school today...but then, no points either.
- ▶ Getting home on time: No school, no points. Few free passes with this woman.
- ▶ Practicing music: I think I'm going to like Sundays. Mom obviously considered practicing piano, work. I did too. And since Christians don't work on Sunday...no practice required. But, dang, no points either.

- ▶ Putting playthings away in-doors and out-doors: Clearly I didn't have many playthings, or Mom kept me too busy doing chores to get any toys out. I scored on this everyday. *Swift!*
- ▶ Helping care for our home: Which I interpreted as: "Don't stand on the coffee table and break it." (Check! Had been there, done that.) On Sunday when we were supposed to sit around, read and take naps, this was pretty easy. Another zero points for me. Other days would be different.
- ▶ Using good manners: What could have happened here? Was it snorting potatoes out my nose? Did I shake some old lady's hand at church just after passing said hand through my Brylcream-laden hair? I was never satisfied with just "a little dab." My first "X" for the day. Had I known my Roman numerals I would have argued for "10" points, but alas, my mother was German not Italian.
- ▶ Helping mother, daddy and sister: Another big "X," but I know what happened here. Hope Ellen didn't want my help, but I "helped" her anyway, and that was no help at all.

So, after my first day I had garnered 5 out of a possible 7 points. I was on a roll. But a dragon was about to blow smoke and a bit of fire onto my lucky start.

IT WAS MONDAY morning (Day 2 on my new Chore Chart) that I discovered "Clothes put in right place" had nothing to do with dressing but with the aftermath of undressing—where had I deposited my clothes the night before? I was blind-sided.

But it was another incident that tripped me up the rest of the week. My adventurous Aunt, who, you remember, lived in a second floor apartment with us, had returned from her trip around the world with the most incredible present for me. It was a colorful reversible satin jacket from Japan. One side was blue the other red. On the back of the blue side was an elaborately embroidered dragon. On the back of the red side was an huge embroidered Tiger. It was the most incredible gift I had ever received. I couldn't take my eyes off the detailed design and bright, shiny colors.

The catch was that I could not wear it to school. It was for Sundays and family outings. Like so many other tyrannical rules, I grumbled and wondered what use the jacket was if I couldn't show it off to my friends at school. I mean, I WAS A FIRST GRADER. Don't I get no rights?[1]

But I was clever, I knew how to do this—to get the jacket to school. My friends would be so envious. I would be so popular. I had a plan.

Number four on my mother's list was getting to school on time. This is how the Sunday evening conversation went as I boldly walked around the house with a tiger on my back, red side out, my favorite. Mom was doing something in the kitchen as I casually approached, grabbed a pop from the fridge and kicked back like a member of the Rat Pack.

"So, Mom, you know this chore chart thing we got going? I've got an idea how I can really get ahead and make you proud," I said.

Mom turned from the kitchen counter squinting her eyes at me as she held a meat cleaver in her hand and pointed it at me. "Careful son, I wasn't born yesterday."

"Right," I said, adjusting my stance. *Be more casual. Were my eyes blinking? Stare at the wallpaper across the room. Don't look at the cleaver.* I really want to get a lot of points, and I was thinking if you made my lunch, like tonight, I could leave early tomorrow morning and get to school on time. You know, number four, 'Getting to school on time?' You wouldn't even have to get out of bed."

Mom stared down at me and waggled the cleaver at me as if it was a washcloth and there was dirt on my nose. "I always make your lunch the night before."

"O, yeah, that's right," I flushed. Groan, this is not going to be easy. But she was right. My tin lunch box with Roy Rogers and his horse painted on the side was always waiting for me on the bottom shelf of the frig. Mom's regimen was so predictable I could find my lunch box in the dark. Okay Plan B. I turned to go.

"Young man," my Mom called me back within striking distance. "Time to get ready for bed. Be sure to hang up the jacket in your closet. Remember number one, 'Clothes put in right place.'"

I was so shocked that she could see right through me that I didn't get the gist of her interpretation of number one, and that night my underwear ended up on the floor and not in the clothes chute. Thus, the next day's demerit for number one.

The next morning I put Plan B into effect. I got up early. Dressed myself completely not even taking time to gloat over the accomplishment and another point scored: "No. 3 Completely dressing self". I listened at my bedroom door. All was quiet on the northern front.

---

1 With that kind of grammar, you didn't deserve any rights. (Ed.)

I looked down at my shoes and realized they made too much noise, so I took them off. Then in my stocking feet I carefully took down my dragon jacket, rolled it up carefully, put it under my arm, snuck downstairs to the milk chute (a hole in the wall where the milkman put the milk usually before we were up), removed the milk delivered in the wee hours of the morning, and stuffed my jacket in the chute, (it would now be accessible from outside the house). I took the milk up the landing steps and walked into the kitchen.

Surprise! Mother was standing there like a gargoyle...in her house robe and rollers looking down at me with suspicion. She always wore rollers in her hair at night. I figured they allowed cool air to circulate next to her hot head. I checked her right hand...no cleaver. Maybe I was safe.

"O, good morning, Mother. Here's the milk. Good Ol' Sealtest milk. Can I have some cereal?"

"Why are you asking? You've never asked before. Are you expecting me to put another row on your chore chart, 'Feeds self!'?"

"O, no, mother. I know how to feed myself."

"So, we've discovered."

I quickly put the milk into the fridge next to Roy Rogers lest the glass bottle slip through my sweaty palms and drop on the floor... something I had done more than once before to great effect.

Later, I timed my escape from the house so Mom and Dad would not be near the door when I left. Once outside, I quietly removed my jacket from the milk chute, scrunched it up in front of me and gave my back to the house as I headed for the alley that took me to Roosevelt Elementary, three short blocks away.

Once in the alley I put down my lunch bucket, unfurled the dragon jacket, careful to put the red side out, and strode toward school proudly wearing my Japanese work of art.

My ego soared. I imagined myself as a mighty dragon (or tiger) slayer as I walked briskly to school, along the gravel road behind fenced-in houses, and the large tin garbage pails that lined the alley like sentries

> **My challenge was to figure out which of their rules were Natural Laws and which were made by mankind for less than infallible purposes.**

standing at attention in honor of my regal passage. I was a sight to behold, resplendent in satin and oriental threads.

As I came to the end of the alley, I cut kitty-corner across the lawn of the Presbyterian church toward my school, still another block away. Maybe it was the presence of the church on my left, or perhaps it was coming out into the open after leaving the confines of the obscure alley. But suddenly, I felt horribly exposed and vulnerable. I stopped dead in my tracks and looked back. I felt as if I was being watched. Which was probably true, as not many first graders were likely sporting a fancy red satin embroidered tiger/dragon jacket along Pinecrest Road, which was flush to my right with rush hour traffic. I glanced at the crossing guard ahead...and...I panicked.

The pride of showing off my new jacket and its fearsome embroidery was swallowed up by the fear of being discovered by my mother back home. When I, a noted dragon master, ambled into school, I imagined my teacher making a fuss over how utterly beautifully I was adorned. Then there would be questions like where did the jacket come from, and the scariest question of all, "Why did your mother let you wear this to school, Stanley?" I was burnt toast. What to do?

I whirled around in the direction I had come and fixed my eyes on a tall wooden fence that surrounded a corner of the property at the end of the alley adjacent to a garage. There was a large mysterious fruit tree overhanging the solid fence in which was a gate opening onto the alley. I ran back to the gate in hopes of a quick obscuration. Reaching up and opening it carefully, I looked in. Old wooden chicken crates were stacked next to the fence below the apple tree. Garbage pails lined the wall along the garage. Between the two was a brick path leading to the house. Ducking inside the gate I took off the jacket, wadded it up as carefully as possible, and stuck it inside one of the crates, nestling it among the leftover white chicken feathers. I looked around for chickens, but didn't see any. Then, it was back out the gate, careful to latch it, and hustle to school on time in order to earn my No. 4 point for the day, "Getting to school on time."

What I didn't count on was how serious a failure I was going to be earning a point for No. 5 the rest of the week, "Getting home on time." I thought about my jacket all day and couldn't wait to get back to the chicken crate, retrieve it and then, somehow sneak it back into the house. If Mom ever found out my feathers would definitely be plucked. And being a skinny kid at the time, I didn't have many to pluck. I'd be cooked for dinner no doubt.

When school let out I rushed to the alley, opened up the wooden gate and reached for the door to the chicken crate that held my jacket. But there was no jacket. I looked through the slats of all the crates, but saw no jacket. My jacket was gone. My heart raced as I retraced my steps that morning and made sure I was in the right place. No doubt about that. I looked up at the house at the end of the brick path, but I didn't have the guts to go knock on the door and ask if they found a dragon jacket I had put in their chicken crates.

When I pulled myself home, mother didn't ask how my day went. She just said, "Stanley, why are you so late coming home? Did you get to school on time this morning?"

I don't recall what I told her, but do remember that I hoped she hadn't looked through my closet to see that the red and blue satin dragon jacket was gone. At least I was pretty sure it was. I went to my closet to see. Yep, there was the empty hanger.

For the rest of the week, Tuesday through Saturday, Days 3-7, I was always on time for school, but each day I was late getting home from taking time to look through the chicken crates in case someone put the jacket back. But they never did, and I never saw my colorful-reversible-satin-jacket, with an elaborately embroidered-dragon-and-tiger-on-the-back, ever again.

By the end of that week I had scored 42 out of a possible 60.

"You can do better," my mother would say.

I didn't always like Mom's rules and how she kept score. But her methods did teach me that authorities, right or wrong, infallible or not, would be offering to guide me to a happy life by following rules. My challenge was to figure out which of their rules were Natural Laws,[1] and which were made by mankind for less than infallible purposes.

And so, I searched for a reasonable faith. I wanted someone to look up to and idolize. You can imagine my excitement when my selected idol was scheduled to visit my elementary school.

---

1 Natural Laws are the unalterable physical and psychological rules of (a) human relations and the visible universe defined by the three-physical dimensions of space and the zero-dimension of time we live in; and (b) the invisible super reality of the multi-dimensions we cannot directly perceive. Man has no power or authority over Natural Law, regardless of government laws, or the spoils of war.

5
Rubbers
& Clowns

In 1955, a different kind of chore chart and authority began to emerge at school. Miss Kilgore was my second grade teacher at Roosevelt Elementary in Ferndale, Michigan. Every week she sent home with us children a behavior report to our parents...or, so I assumed because I was always taking a report home. The report was a simple grid-like calendar with the days of the weeks at the top and then in the rows below, a plus or a zero in the cells for each day of the week pertaining to three life skills: 1. Be kind to others, 2. Be helpful at school, and 3. Do good school work. A kid with perfect behavior could score a total of 15 pluses (or points) for the week. One particular hand-ruled report that Mom saved shows 6 pluses and 4 zeros in the first two rows, (she didn't score the third row). Not bad I thought, 6 for 10. But, Miss Kilgore, on the bottom and on the back of the report, in her perfect penmanship, wrote my parents this note:

> *Stanley is very careless when putting his rubbers in the closet. Monday he kicked them off & hit a girl in the face. Tues. he threw them in & hit two boys who were removing wraps. I have talked to him about being careful but it hasn't helped. Perhaps a word or two from you on the subject will help. --Miss Kilgore.*

Curiously, after my Mom had a "word or two" with me, the second report shows all pluses (10 points) with another note from Miss Kilgore:

Stanley has had an exceptionally good week.

In retrospect, the fact that these two behavior reports (and I only have two) were hand-ruled makes me now believe that I was the only kid that ever had such a report sent home. And on further reflection, the blue rubric lines and legend printing on Miss Kilgore's chart was identical to my mother's chore chart, except for Miss Kilgore's handwritten notes. Conclusion: My mom had given Miss Kilgore the chart to fill in.

There is no doubt that I kicked and threw my rubbers into the "closet"—which was more like a narrow hallway that ran behind a wall at one end of the classroom. Along the closet-hallway were hooks on one side for each kid's coat, space on the floor beneath for galoshes or rubbers, and a long shelf above for our lunch buckets. The hall-like-closet was closed off from the main room except for two openings at either end, which emptied into the classroom. This left a space of about 25-feet long and 3-feet wide that could not be seen from the classroom. You could see into the openings of the closet-hallway, but not down the center of it unless you walked into one of the openings, turned the corner, and looked inside. All of the rooms at Roosevelt Elementary (at least all the ones I was ever in) were designed exactly the same.

It was okay for my rubbers to go in the closet-hallway, but I wasn't going in there. No way. What Miss Kilgore didn't know, and what was still fresh in my memory, was what had happened to me two years earlier, in Kindergarten next door.

IN 1952, ON the Kindergarten day in question, all of us kids were sitting on the floor looking up at our teacher with great expectation and excitement. One of our television heroes was about to pay a visit to our classroom—Twin Pines' Milky the Clown. Twin Pines Dairy was the competitor to Sealtest Dairy that my father worked for, but that didn't matter to me. What mattered today was that Milky the Clown--clearly, the authority figure for the dairy--was going to visit us in person.

Milky was no doubt an out-of-work milk truck driver doing penance for backing into too many parked cars along his route. I know this because my dad was the safety and insurance director for Sealtest Dairy, and the company was shelling out a lot of money for such accidents. Dad thinks the cost of insurance is what drove Sealtest to get out of the route owning business and made drivers buy their own routes...

and insurance.

Anyhow, Milky had a television show that played movies. He wore a milk-white billowy clown suit with ruffles on ankles and wrists, a pointy white hat and completed the package with a white face. During commercial breaks he would crack jokes, perform magic tricks for the dozen or so lucky kids that got to be in his television audience, and pitch cottage cheese. This was 1952 live TV, in glorious black and white, which suited the white milk product Milky always drank on set. When television went to color, Milky was out of a job.

Nonetheless, Milky the Clown was about to make a personal appearance. What could bring more wonderment into the life of a Kindergartener?

Well, I'll tell you.

For some reason, I jumped up from my place on the floor and ran to the closet-hallway to get something out of my lunch bucket. I entered the doorway, turned the corner...and was about to take the last three giant steps to my bucket...when I stopped dead in my tracks.

There, not five feet in front of me, sitting on a tiny kiddie stool that made him look larger than life...was my hero and yours...Milky the Clown...in full white regalia, with the puffy sleeves, pointy hat and makeup. He glared straight at me with a threatening growl—like Godzilla ready to pounce. This was one unhappy clown. Why, I wondered? Then, it dawned on me. I caught Milky doing something that, at the time, was a career killing thing for a kid to see a TV hero do, especially a hero that stood for wholesomeness, goodness, health and a clean life.

Milky was dragging on a (white) cigarette and blowing thick "white" smoke out his nostrils like a dragon in heat.

I was stunned and scared. I had looked behind the curtain and I didn't like what I saw. Instantly, I knew, that the clown-man, who I idolized, the good guy whom I trusted, the white knight who made us laugh...was going straight to hell. I was mortified. I started to cry. And, I bolted from the closet-hallway in terror.

In short order my teacher soothed my tears and escorted me to the nurses office, where I'm sure they gave me some sort of experimental drug to calm me down and make me forget the breach in confidentiality.

I didn't forget. But, I did miss the show.

My idol in white, with billows of *incense* wafting over his head, was dethroned. But Mom was waiting in the wings with a replacement.

6
Religious Regimen

I N 1955 I became aware of the regimen that surrounded me. In Evangelical Christianity, ritual, liturgy and the rubrics that governed celebrations of worship were frowned upon, or so it was claimed. Free Methodists touted their "freedom" of worship. Structure was closely associated with Evangelicalism's anathema of cold formality and fear of an "empty liturgy." Liturgy, it was claimed, did not allow the freedom of the Holy Spirit and the extemporaneous nature of worship that validated such celebrations as true and genuine.

But I came to see this claim against liturgy as empty posturing. It was an example of the pot calling the kettle black. Evangelicals had highly ritualized worship, and they used rubrics; they were just a different color like my Mom's turquoise pen wasn't red.

I wasn't out of elementary school before I recognized the staid and predictable nature of the Free Methodist worship service—it was the same week-after-week, and not just at the church we usually attended, but also at every one of the many other Evangelical churches we visited in those years. They all contained significant liturgical elements, including:

► An unchanging order of service week to week that set a fixed pattern of prayers, hymns, offering, sermon, and the ubiquitous altar call.

► There were rubrics for standing, sitting, kneeling and singing directed from the pulpit and you would not dare sit if the

pastor said "stand."
► The recitation of The Lord's Prayer, the singing of the Doxology, and the responsive readings from the back of the hymnal.

I also began to understand that Evangelical criticism that high church liturgical services limited the Holy Spirit's presence in worship because the liturgy never changed, was like saying the Holy Spirit was limited in the use of the Lord's Prayer, the Doxology, and the Bible because they haven't changed from last week to this. To complain about ritual and rubrics is to complain about a parking lot because its parking spaces are marked with white paint, or to complain that there are rules that govern the safe transit of cars on a road.

As already indicated, the Bible held a special regimental place in my childhood home. We each had our own—a Bible that is, not a home. Mom's Bible was heavily underlined and annotated with sermon notes and favorite verses written on slips of paper stuck between the pages. The ink from underlined verses bled through the thin pages so badly she eventually had to buy a new Bible.

I still have Dad's KJV Bible which was rebound late in his life. Unlike my Mom who underlined many verses, Dad's Bible only seems to have a few verses lightly and very reverently underlined in light red pencil. (Is underlining favorite passages in a book a form of a "remember this" rubric?) Light red pencil can be seen under Dad's favorite verse, which he quoted often spontaneously whenever the spirit hit. Though a generally quiet and reserved man, to this day I can hear him boisterously proclaim:

> *Bless the Lord, O my soul: and all that is within me, bless his holy name. Bless the Lord, O my soul, and forget not all his benefits: Who forgiveth all thine iniquities; who healeth all thy diseases; Who redeemeth thy life from destruction; who crowneth thee with lovingkindness and tender mercies; Who satisfieth thy mouth with good things; so that thy youth is renewed like the eagle's.[1]*

Out of reverence for the Bible, in our home, nothing was ever placed on top of it, nor was a Bible to be put on the floor or someplace that suggested neglect. The Bibles in our home were sacred books. In later years I read how, in some cultures, the touching of a sacred book required the washing of hands after they were touched. But in

---

1 Psalm 103:1-5 (KJV)

our home, the attitude was to wash our hands before the Bible was touched. That wasn't a spoken rubric, but it was the idea.

At this same time, as a child in Sunday School, I was always involved in some sort of Bible memorization program, and have a couple of certificates to show for it.

Later, as a teen, I participated in a national Bible quiz program where a different New Testament book was studied each year to such an extent that the champion quizzers could quote nearly the entire book. I was not a championship quizzer, but I got to know a great deal of Scripture because of the program.

Winners of major tournaments were given red leather Bibles with their names engraved on the cover. During high school, when I first met Pam, my future wife, at the Dearborn Free Methodist Church, she had just such a Bible. I immediately asked her if she was "a quizzer". She said later that she had wished she could have said "yes," because she had a crush on me and wanted me to take interest in her. But she had to tell the truth. She wasn't a quizzer. And to tell the truth, I took an interest in her anyway. Today she claims it was her red Bible that got my initial attention. Such are the romantic benefits of carrying a (red) Bible.

> **Miraculous answers to prayer only had to happen once in a while to impress me that God and his angels were listening.**

Lastly, the Bible regimen and rubrics encouraged us, even as kids, to always have a Bible with us and to use Biblical premises and references in reports at school. After all, we were reminded, the Bible is the best selling book in the world every year...might as well cite it as authoritative.

Bible reading, and prayer were daily events at our house. We prayed before each meal, each of us sharing the responsibility meal-to-meal. At night one of our parents would always kneel or sit by our bed and we'd both pray extemporaneously.

The major event each day, however, was the Family Devotions that Uncle Smith helped establish. Each devotional time would begin by Dad announcing what Scripture would be read. We'd take turns night-to-night reading the passage. Often they were from the Psalms, which Dad loved.

After the passage was read, we might discuss it and share prayer requests with one another. Then we would turn and kneel at our chairs or couch and pray around the room by age. Sometimes starting with Dad, the oldest, other times with Hope Ellen. Dad and Mom's prayers were always very long—at times it seemed 15 or 20 minutes during which I would fall asleep with my head on the seat cushion. When it became my turn, Dad or Mom would poke me, and I'd wake up and pray for 3 minutes tops. I made 'em short, trying to get the hint to Mom or Dad to do the same. It seemed, however, that the shorter I made my prayers, the longer they made theirs. Parental unit compensation, I suppose.

The regimen of prayer and its power did make an impression on me, however, because of numerous dramatic answers that cannot be written off as mere coincidences. I'll relate several in this book. One evening at devotions Mom shared that earlier, about noon, she had an urge to pray for Rebecca (Becky) Bibbee, the missionary that essentially took over for my grandmother, Edith Willobee, decades ago at the India mission near today's Rajnandgaon. Mom did not know what to pray for, but felt it was for Becky's safety. So, she went upstairs to her bedroom, closed the door, and for perhaps 30-minutes asked God to protect the missionaries and the people they were caring for. That night in family prayers we all repeated a simple prayer for Becky's safety.

At the time there was no telephone service in Rajnandgaon and the only reliable communication was mail by boat that took about three weeks to get from Becky, in central India, to us here in Michigan.

About a month after we had all prayed for Becky, a letter arrived from India and my mother read it to all of us that evening. It detailed a frightful night for Becky and the people there, when a ravenous Tiger had stalked through the village looking for food. One of the men woke up, got a couple other men, and with sticks they chased the Tiger away, and no one was hurt. Becky had no idea that we were praying for their safety at that same moment on the other side of the earth.

Such miraculous answers to prayer did not happen every week, nor did the urge to pray regularly result in such a dramatic answer. But it only had to happen once in a while to impress me that God and his angels were listening to see if we were paying attention to their promptings. It was experiences like this that reinforced my scientific and empiricist conclusion that Christianity can be proven using the scientific method—an opinion I still hold, and that I discuss in later chapters.

But before we go there, my world was turned upside down. The old died off, or was cast off, and the new was ushered in. I was about to learn what the real world was really about.

7
The Big Move

B Y 1956 MY Aunt and Grandmother, Edith Willobee, had moved out of our send floor apartment and into their own home in Detroit where Aunt Hope, a Detroit police officer, was required to live.

Near to the same time as my Dad's retirement from Sealtest there was a big reorganization of the dairy company. Sealtest got out of the milk and cream home delivery business. Suddenly, all the home delivery truck drivers, for which my dad was the safety and insurance director, were to become independent. Not only did the drivers need to finance their trucks, but they also needed vehicle insurance.

Smart people that my parents were, they figured out how to convert dad's one income into three. First, Dad negotiated to become the independent insurance agent of record for all Michigan Sealtest trucks and drivers. He didn't have an exclusive, but he did have the inside track because of his existing relationship with the entire Michigan fleet. Being a licensed agent he would eventually round out his product offerings with homeowners and life insurance to anyone. But, if he earned too much in this new venture his pension and the new social security benefits would be curtailed. My folks didn't like that deal. They wanted to work more and earn more, not work more and earn less, which seemed to be the government's motive.

So, Mom disappeared for a month and went to school full time in Detroit to get her Michigan Insurance License. With her new license and for tax purposes, they put the business in her name; but Dad ran it.

Then Mom found a full time job teaching fourth grade in Livonia Public Schools, a suburb of Detroit.

To accommodate the new business they bought a huge old farm-

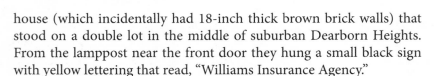

house (which incidentally had 18-inch thick brown brick walls) that stood on a double lot in the middle of suburban Dearborn Heights. From the lamppost near the front door they hung a small black sign with yellow lettering that read, "Williams Insurance Agency."

As a kid I earned extra allowance by organizing expiration notices, insurance certificates, and assembling mass mailings with 3¢ stamps. The one dark gray file cabinet Dad had then, I still use for old project files in my home office. Of the nine cabinets I have, its drawers roll out most smoothly.

But not everything in my young life was going to be as smooth as Dad's filing cabinet drawers. This was a new neighborhood and I had friends to make...some of which my parents weren't too happy about.

8
Catholic
Pagans

OR ME, THE 1956 move to Dearborn Heights wasn't retirement—
my life was just beginning, and it was time to make new friends.
Generally, that would not have been a problem, but perhaps
unbeknownst to my parents they had just moved into the shadow of
Divine Child—one of Michigan's largest Catholic parishes.

Most of the kids on the block were girls, Catholic girls. And since I
didn't like girls (they were a phenomenon that would encroach on my
consciousness later) my only chance at having a friend was with the
boy next door, who luckily was my age.

At first my parents thought Ned would be a good influence on
me—I wasn't that great of a student and Ned got straight A's. But with
all the studying he did he rarely had time to play. Maybe that was what
my parents had in mind—as to how they hoped Ned would influence
me. But that never occurred to me. Ned was out of my academic league.

Ned's dad was a beer-guzzling ex-marine with a huge gut and a foul
mouth. But he bought Ned cool stuff, like plastic model kits of every
tank, warship, bomber and fighter in the U.S. arsenal. Ned's room
and basement were showrooms of the U.S. military might, albeit in
plastic, with enamel paint and decals. Ned showed me how to put the
models together with just a little bit of the plastic cement on the end
of a toothpick. He also demonstrated his practiced steady nerves with
a hair-thin paintbrush to add the magic camouflage patterns to the
tanks and ships. But I wasn't much good on the nerves department,
and pretty soon I was relegated to breaking off the parts from the in-

jected molding sprue, and handing them to him for assembly.

The only thing I had up on Ned was that I didn't need eyeglasses and was a better baseball player. His glasses were an inch thick, and always had tape holding them together and a rubber band stretched behind his head to hold them on. The only way he got to play on the sandlot every summer morning was that his dad bought Ned the best gloves, bats, and balls. So, we let him play. In fact, because he had the only decent equipment on the block he was usually one of the two captains that picked sides; the other was Paul, whose dad owned the lot we played on.

D
URING THE SUMMER, we'd play baseball on Paul's back lot in the morning, and after lunch several of us would ride our bikes to the best swimming pool in the country. It was the Seashore Swimming Pool at Levagood Park in Dearborn, Michigan. It was round and huge. The perimeter was ankle deep and slowly got deeper to about five-feet at a fence that separated the shallows from the deep and the coveted diving tower at the hub. (There were water slides in the shallows and a kiddy's pool and plenty of cement and grass on which to sunbathe.) To get to the diving tower you had to enter through one of four gates at the points of the compass and prove to the lifeguard sitting on the stand at each gate that you could swim.

It was a big deal to swim to the tower for the first time. I can still remember getting up the courage to try. As soon as you entered the gate the depth fell off steeply to fifteen feet, all the way to the island. It was intimidating but a necessary rite of passage. I can still remember pushing off from the fence for the first time, under the watchful eye of a lifeguard, and stroking with all my might until I reached the tower's edge. It was exhilarating. I made it! Around the edge of the tower where four ladders that allowed you to climb out of the water. On the island were six diving platforms: two at three feet above the water, two at six feet, and two at ten feet—perfect for cannonball "dives." There were also two springboards. Over all this was a bevy of lifeguards looking down from above. It was the pool of a kid's dreams. And it was open to 10 p.m. every summer night.

As night fell large underwater lights, built into the island's foundation, illuminated the water all the way to the bottom. Swimming to the bottom at night was a mystical experience. There were also floodlights above the tower and around the perimeter. I spent many hours there as a kid, riding my bike home after the pool closed. As far as I can recall, my parents never brought me to Seashore, never picked me up, nor did they worry about me, even though I'd not come home until 10:30 at night on my bike. Those were different days.

T O GET TO Seashore from my house was a 15-minute bike ride. The short cut was through Divine Child Catholic Church's parking lot. And it was on one of these trips to go swimming, with Ned on our bikes, that I first entered a Catholic Church. As we cut through the Divine Child parking lot, Ned veered off, waved for me to follow, and we both coasted to a bike rack near the building. As we stuck our rolled up towels and bathing suits into our bike frames, Ned said he promised his Mom that before he went swimming he "would go to confession."

Up until that point I was only mildly aware of what a Catholic was, except that on display in the front yard of just about every other house in the neighborhood was one of those three-foot high Italian Florentine statues of Mary in the flowing pale blue robes. Ned's family didn't have one, so perhaps Mom and Dad didn't know their true identity. We were Protestant, so in our front yard was a three-foot concrete birdbath, with a broken edge so that there was never any water in it, which I suppose had some symbolic meaning about who we were.

So, there I was walking into a huge Catholic church that could easily have swallowed up ten of our church buildings. Ned immediately disappeared, so I just looked around. There was light streaming in through the south-facing stained glass windows that gave the room an eerie mystical quality; and there were candles burning everywhere. The cathedral-like space had an odor and haze that wasn't quite as pleasant or mythic as a campfire, but it was close. But what caught my attention was something else.

There were statues of men and women, everywhere. They were at the back, along the sides, and up front by the sanctuary. Each, seemingly full size, held something—a staff, a child, a book, a sword—as they looked down on you from their perches with eternal gazes as if they were busy reading your soul. Some

> **The cathedral like space had an odor and haze that wasn't quite as pleasant or mythic as a campfire, but it was close.**

were lit with spotlights, others had racks of small red candles in front of them; and in front of the candles a few people knelt and prayed. But the biggest statue of all was actually hanging on a huge cross up front.

It was a cross with Jesus hanging limp, even dead, on it. I'm not sure I had ever seen Jesus dead on a cross before. It was a bit unnerving. I knew he died on a cross, but usually the pictures of him in my church were of him smiling with a bunch of children or were very peaceful as in Warner Sallman's famous The Head of Christ painting.[1]

I was still taking this all in when Ned appeared at my side, and said, "Hey, I'm done, I just got to say some 'Hail, Marys.' Back in a sec." And, off he went to one of those statues, knelt, folded his hands, bowed his head, crossed himself and stayed there--transfixed--for a while. Weird!

It was probably then that I recalled riding with Ned in his Mom's car when we missed the school bus on occasion. One of the statues in the church looked like the little white plastic one stuck to the center on the car's metal instrument panel, just above the oval radio speaker. As Ned and I sat in the backseat of his Mom's new 1956 Ford Fairlane, I asked what that was and Ned whispered to me that it was St. Christopher, who allowed his Mom to break the speed limit and not get a ticket. Ned was joking, and I knew it, but I began to wonder what it was with all the statues.

Later that day I became intrigued with how trusting my otherwise strict parents were with my association with these Catholic pagans. Weren't they worried I'd come home with a miniature statue of someone, set up a shrine in my bedroom, and start burning incense? There was a perfect place behind the clothes in my walk-in closet. I had a big closet on the second floor next to the roofline. It having been a farmhouse, I imagined they needed someplace to keep the pigeons.

So, one day, as Mom husked corn over the garbage pail in the kitchen I went to her.

"So, Mom?

"Yes, Stanley.

"So, ah...the other day on the way to Seashore, you know with Ned, we rode our bikes like I told you. He had to stop at his church to see the pastor for something, and I went in with him, and..."

She interrupted. "There's no church on the way to Seashore." She paused to trace the route I had taken in her mind, then turned to me abruptly, "Was that Divine Child?"

"Yeah, I think so, why?" I had her undivided attention, now.

---

1 I thought The Head of Christ by Warner Sallman, which was in every church and home when I was a kid, was a very famous old painting. Imagine my surprise when I learned it was painted in 1941 and by the 1990's had sold over 500 million copies. (Wikipedia)

"Go on," she said even as she stared me down with suspicion.

"So...I noticed that all over the church were these statues, and candles, and some people were kneeling in front of the statues. Then I remembered that when Ned's Mom drove us to school last week, there was this little white statue on their dashboard. How come we don't have statues in our church and how come you don't have a little statue on your dash board?"

It was then that the real interrogation began. "What were you doing in the church again? Why was he there?"

I could sense that I was on the verge of something. "I think it was like what we do at our church when we 'go forward,' and get our sins forgiven. Except there was no altar call. But he said something about 'confessing'".

Mom did not husk any more corn that afternoon.

"So, why don't we have statues in our church?" I asked.

By now, Mom was staring at me with deep concern as she began to brusquely clean up the fallen husks and silk.

For the next several days I got lectures about how Catholics were pagan idolaters, because they worshipped and prayed to idols, how they broke the first two commandments, and how they didn't believe that Jesus rose from the dead because he was still dead on the cross in their church. When I asked how that could all be true if Ned had to get his sins forgiven, I was told that they may claim to be Christian but Catholics really don't know Jesus as their Lord and Savior, "anyhow"--and that is why they have to go to a priest to get their sins forgiven--but that doesn't work, "anyhow"--because they don't have a personal relationship with Christ for that to happen--"anyhow."

AFTER THAT, MY association with Ned and his family was restricted. If I wanted to play baseball I had to lie that Ned was not going to be there. And there was no way I could ride by bike to Seashore and have Ned ride along. If Ned and I missed the school bus, however, it was still okay for Ned's Mom to drive us to school.

My Mom reminded me, during the lecture series on Catholics, what I had told her about Ned and his family not praying before meals and how his dad smoked, drank and swore...although his Mom did none of those things. Mom would say, "Well, son, by their fruits you will know them."

After that, Ned's good grades mattered less to my parents.

An interesting observation I made at this time was that the statues in Ned's church were nothing like the idols and curiosities my Grandmother had brought back from India, which we had stored away in a box among other India memorabilia. The Hindu idols were fashioned out of mud and did not resemble humans but other-worldly deities. Ned's religion's statues looked more like the statues we saw all the time in parks like Belle Isle, the island park in the Detroit River. We visited Belle Isle often to watch freighters steam up and down the river, or we'd go there for picnics, or to hear the Detroit Concert Band. On the island were numerous statues to bring to our memory the soldiers of the Civil War and the Spanish-American War. There were also life-size statues of James J. Brady who, in 1914, founded the Old Newsboys Goodfellows of Detroit and Johann Friedrich von Schiller, a German poet, who wrote the lyrics to Beethoven's Ode to Joy, along with a larger than life-sized memorial to Union Civil War Major General Alpheus Starkey Williams astride his war horse.

But, I never saw anybody kneeling in front of these. I wondered why that woman was kneeling in front of a statue in Ned's church. Was my Mom right? Well, I never got a chance to go back and investigate. Mom and Dad found ways for me to be otherwise engaged.

ABOUT THIS TIME, while on my knees, I learned something about Hell...up close and personal. Fall was upon us and Dad and I were cleaning out the garage. We had one of those new gasoline powered push lawn mowers. Dad didn't want to leave gasoline in the small tank over the winter so he asked me to empty it out. I have no idea where he thought I was going to empty it. Probably in the dirt behind the garage. But I had other ideas.

> **About this time, while on my knees, I learned something about Hell...up close and personal.**

I had just read about things that go BANG!—like rocket ships that fail to get off the launch pad and collapse on themselves in a gigantic explosion. I wanted to learn more about that, and since experience is the best teacher, there was no better time than this.

I rolled the lawnmower to the street, found the sewer drain (a cast iron, rectangular 18 inch opening in the newly paved street), removed the cap from the gas tank, and tipped the lawn mower on its side so the half-gallon of gasoline remaining in the tank would drain into the sewer. Yes, this was long before the Federal or State governments had figured out that they needed an Environmental Protection Agency to protect the waterways from inquisitive idiots like me.

Having accomplished that, I put the lawn mower away and trotted into the house, my pulse racing with added excitement at what I was about to witness.

I pulled open Mom's kitchen junk drawer, rummaged around until I found a box of matches, stuffed the matches into my pocket and ran back to the sewer drain.

I knelt down next to the sewer with my knees on the grass. I was at least smart enough not to kneel in the street. Why a car could come along and hit me. I was an idiot, but not a complete one. Although, what was about to happen next puts that last sentence in grave doubt.

Peering into the sewer a foot above the iron grate I could see the gasoline swirling around on top of the water deep in the hole. It was mesmerizing, the volatile liquid catching light from the sky above my head, creating colorful refractions on the surface.

While still closely peering into the drain I retrieved the box of matches from my pocket, opened it, removed a single wooden match, and then was careful to follow the instructions on the cover: "Close cover before striking." I wanted to be safe, you see.

Now I was all set for the experience of a lifetime. While still watching the colorful sheen on top of the water I struck the match and tossed it into the sewer.

I have no idea what I was expecting. But Natural Law was not to be denied. The gasoline fumes in the enclosed sewer exploded like a rocket with a loud BANG!!!—engulfing my head and shoulders in the violent exhaust. Earth must have been shoved a few inches in the opposite direction, the blast was so terrific.

Needless to say, I was stunned, my hair completely singed, and my face and neck sustained second-degree burns. I spent the next two weeks in bed as mom nursed me back to health.

I'm sure my fear of hell came from that experience...along with a deep appreciation for physics and God's Natural Laws.

9
Show Business
& Dogs

IN 1957 MY 4th-grade teacher was Mrs. Richard—a science fanatic. She let huge garden spiders crawl over her arms spinning their webs as she stood in front of our class and talked about them. Her husband, Roger E. Richard, was an amateur radio operator with his "shack" just a block from my house. There I spent a few evenings with him talking to people all over the world via his call sign, W8IUA. And, perhaps, most importantly, she helped me discover the amazing gift of acquiring knowledge by reading *Science News Digest Magazine,* to which my parents subscribed at Mrs. Richard's insistence.

In the spring of 4th grade, Mrs. Richard asked if I wanted to be Master of Ceremonies for the lower elementary talent show. It would be held at Haston Junior High about a mile away, where there was a real stage. I didn't know what a Master of Ceremonies was, but she explained it and gave me a script for the 20 acts that had been selected. I had three weeks to memorize the short introductions. For reasons that seemed natural I took to the task with relish. I recall practicing my lines everywhere I went, especially in the back yard, trying to project my voice toward a small stand of trees as an audience.

About this same time my dad gave in to my request for a pet. We went to the dog pound and selected a feisty Jack Russell Terrier mix puppy. I immediately named the friendly dog, Cindy. The only problem was that neither my parents nor I were sure how to tie the pup up in the backyard during the day while I was at school. So, temporarily, I built a puppy bed out of scrap wood and an old army blanket and placed the bed under the basement stairs nearby dad's workbench. Then I secured Cindy to a 10-foot leash nailed to the underside of the steps. Each morning my job was to collect Cindy's overnight droppings she had dumped onto old newsprint, carefully wrap-up the papers and deposit the smelly mess in the outside garbage can. Coming back inside to the basement I would then spread new papers for her to poop on while I was at school. Unfortunately, this was not a neat or good way to housebreak the pooch.

Cindy was, nonetheless, a great joy to me, and when I practiced my lines for the talent show I'd take her outside, tie her to one of the trees, and pretend she was my audience. She'd sit alert on her haunches or stand up and bark happily at me. After I was assured that Cindy approved of my performance we'd take a short walk through the fields before coming in for the night.

I fed her canned dog food each morning that I'd spoon into her bowl, then set down next to her bed under the basement stairs. I loved watching her get excited when I brought her food. Her short brown tail would wag with glee and after she was done eating, she'd curl up in my lap as I sat in her makeshift bed and rubbed her tummy.

But Mom, being a very neat, tidy, and organized housekeeper, was never happy with our acquisition of a dog. Although remanded to the basement, Cindy's whimper and bark could be heard through the house, irritating my mom. Furthermore, to get to the clothes washing machine in the basement, Mom had to negotiate Cindy's smelly mess.

A few days before the talent show, which was at night, and required my Mom or dad to drive me to the Junior High School, I left for school before cleaning up Cindy's mess. When I got home the mess was cleaned up, and so was Cindy. She was gone. When I ran upstairs to ask Mom were Cindy was, Mom told me that she had called the pound to get her, because I forgot to clean up her poop before I went to school, and she (Mom) had no intention of doing it. The dog was gone, that was it...end of the matter...next time, she informed me, I would be more responsible.

I was furious and heartbroken. Dad was out of town on a business trip and I had no recourse to anyone for comfort. So, I went to the basement, curled up in Cindy's bed that Mom had not touched, and cried myself to sleep with the smell of my beloved Cindy fresh in my nostrils. It would be years before I could forgive my Mom for her heartless act. But it took mere hours for the anger I felt to overflow.

The talent show was two days away, and dad wouldn't be back until the weekend. Mom and I had words, and I lost my temper, telling her she was mean and I hated her. Evidently, that was okay by her. She clearly didn't like me much either.

But my insolence kept up for those two days and she finally had enough. She informed me, with only hours to spare, that she was not taking me to the talent show. I'd just have to miss the show for being rebellious and not agreeing with her—which I assumed to mean not agreeing with her reasons for getting rid of Cindy.

But there was a bigger issue at risk. It wasn't my pride, and it wasn't the idea of a variety show without Ed Sullivan, which clearly would not work. No, there was something else that was bugging me. It was something I decided that was more important than me, Mom, or even the talent show without a master of ceremonies. I had promised Mrs. Richards that I would do something. I had taken upon myself a responsibility and I was determined to be accountable...even to my detriment.

So, since I had never learned to walk, I ran to my room.

I put on a black suit of clothes, folded my well-marked-up script into a pocket, and without saying anything to my Mom, marched past her in the kitchen and out the door. As I was leaving she must not have noticed how I was dressed because she yelled after me. "Be sure you're back for dinner."

I wasn't. I was gone for the evening.

The walk of about a mile to Haston Junior High was invigorating. I was free. All the way there I repeated my lines over and over again, occasionally referencing my script. I was learning to turn my anger into something productive.

I still remember standing back stage and the stage manager signaling me when to part the curtains, walk to the microphone and introduce the next act. I probably made a few mistakes. But stage fright wasn't part of the game. After the show I remember, too, getting congratulated for a good job. No certificate, no award, nothing more than the satisfaction of at least one job that week well done. Mrs. Richards drove me home and found it sad that her pupil's parents had not shown up.

I UNDERSTOOD PUNISHMENT FOR things I had done wrong, but I also understood that punishment could be overdone. Around this time I would argue with Mom over verses in the Bible that warned parents not to discipline their children to the point of driving them to anger or bitterness.[1] Of course, my Mom reminded me that the verses preceding the ones I was quoting told children to obey their parents, which I was not doing.

There was a sense that my salvation wasn't anchored in faith, as my parents and pastors claimed, but in the works I did, or didn't do. In my mind, I started to extrapolate my Mom's chore chart into yards and yards of religious do's and don'ts. I concluded that it was impossible living up to their perfect expectations.

I hoped it wasn't true, but Mom sure gave me the feeling I was headed for hell. And, occasionally she found a way to remind me that my decisions had consequences. What she didn't realize was that what she called punishment, I often found empowering. (Yeah, she was probably right—I was headed for the fiery pit.)

---

1 Ephesians 6:4, Colossians 3:21

10
The Walk Home

A ROUND 1958, MY grandmother, Edith Willobee became bed-
fast with Parkinson's Disease. Aunt Hopie tried to take care
of Grandma in their new home in Detroit where she and
Grandma had moved after we moved to Dearborn Heights. But she was
a Detroit policewoman and couldn't stay home to care for her mother.
So the decision was made to move Grandma to Arnold Home, a home
for the aged about 12-miles away from where we now lived. Edith was
sad about the move and chastised her daughters for abandoning her.
But then, years earlier, Edith's call to India had forced her to abandon
her daughters in America.

Aunt Hope visited her Mom at Arnold Home during the week, and
my Mom, my sister and I would visit on Sunday afternoon. We did this
for years as was only fitting. Grandma's confinement was in the last bed
of a long narrow room on the third floor. You had to walk past the foot
of five other poor ladies who likewise hadn't moved from their beds in
years. It was a sad sight. But when we got to grandma she always put
on a thin smile and looked up with appreciative eyes.

She would raise a trembling hand close to mine so I could grasp
her Parkinson gnarled palm. She never said much; the disease had
made it difficult for her to talk. Yet, with sweetness in her voice and her
clear blue eyes she would look up at me and say, "I'm praying for you,
Stanley." I didn't fully understand or appreciate what that meant until
years later when I read her diaries and discovered the faith she put
in God to deliver her from the most trying of times. Her life demonstrated a *persevering impetuousness* that I was glad to make my own,
especially in matters of faith.

I liked seeing Grandma. She was a sweet woman, but after 15 or 20 minutes I couldn't think of anything else to tell her and since she could barely talk, and since she and Mom would start murmuring things to each other in Hindi, I'd go off exploring the large facility, both inside and out. My sister for the most part would sit in a chair near the window and read—a pastime whose pleasures I didn't discover until most of the way through high school. Mom would tell me when to return for our departure home...and I was gone.

I don't recall any of my explorations. Clearly there was nothing much to discover, but I do recall falling asleep in a veranda lounge that connected two wings of the large facility. Hope and I were always in our Sunday clothes for these visits, which were right after church and Sunday meals. I wanted to change, but mother would have nothing of it "on the Lord's day." There wasn't anything in the Free Methodist discipline about how to dress on Sunday except for keeping the habit of mod-

> **Her life demonstrated a persevering impetuousness that I was glad to make my own, especially in matters of faith.**

esty. But mother, having not possessed any good clothes until she was in America at age 15, was not about to let us look slothful. We didn't have rich clothes, but I did have a couple of white shirts, ties, and a blue plaid sports jacket that Aunt Hope had made for me.

On one particular spring Sunday, when the weather was fair and the buds on trees were in blossom, I woke from my veranda nap and dragged myself into Grandma's room. There was no one there, and Grandma was asleep. I hurried down to the entrance and out into the parking lot.

Now is probably the appropriate moment to tell you, my dear readers, that I had been frequently, if not habitually late in getting back to Grandma's room on time, and, as a consequence Mom had told me more than once, "Get back here on time, or you'll walk home."

Of course, I didn't really take her seriously...until this particular Sunday. Her 1949 Chrysler, with a trunk big enough for the Mafia's use, was nowhere to be found.

So, since it was a nice day I took off my necktie, and started the walk home—12 miles! Seven Mile Road west, to Evergreen Road south, to Outer Drive as it snaked through Rouge Park to Ford Road west, to Gully Road south the final two-blocks to our house. I was 11 and proud that I knew my way around the city. I enjoyed it, especially since Mom wasn't walking alongside hassling me about not wearing

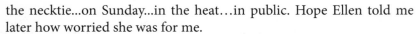

the necktie...on Sunday...in the heat...in public. Hope Ellen told me later how worried she was for me.

But that was just a warm up for the next summer.

11
Under the Bed

URING THE SUMMER of 1959, after 6th Grade and before Junior High, my family spent several weeks at the Free Methodist Campgrounds near Jackson, Michigan, where Dad had built a cabin.

Every night we were expected to attend the preaching services in the huge tabernacle that sat 1,000 on wooden benches. The rough asphalt floor sloped down toward the stage that dominated over the audience. Above the benches a hundred laminated wood beams arched the ceiling sixty feet into the air, and from those beams, bare light bulbs with reflectors dangled above the seated audience. A powerful public address system amplified the musicians and speakers. Although preaching by firebrand ministers was always the main event, the preliminaries included a 100-voice choir, trumpet-trios, and the talented young and beautiful pianist Gayle Moran, who later married jazz musician Chick Corea and consequently caused a scandal in the jazz-free Free Methodist ranks. When the tabernacle was empty it was fun to go inside, make a loud noise, or yell a word, and listen to the pronounced echo the room created.

During services, my parents, like most others, let their kids sit wherever they chose. Of course, some teens skipped the meetings and scared up mischief in the woods and swamps that surrounded the camp. But I dared not miss a meeting. And, neither did my nephew, Bob Kenney.

Bob requires a bit of explaining. Although Bob *really was* my nephew he was also six months older. It works this way…pay attention, even I find this hard to follow:

- ► 1918: Ben Williams (my Dad) marries Lucile Benjamin (not my mom).
- ► 1920: Benj and Luci have their only child, Dorothy.
- ► January, 1940: Lucile dies of cancer.
- ► June, 1940: Dorothy marries Oscar Kenney a Free Methodist minister.
- ► 1945: My Dad meets and marries Ruth Willobee.
- ► 1946: Dorothy and Oscar have a baby boy—Bob Kenney.
- ► 1947: (6 months later) Ben and Ruth have a baby boy—me.

So, I had a father old enough to be my grandpa and a nephew who was my senior. That should explain a few things about me, but as yet I haven't figure out what.

At any rate, back in camp, Bob's cabin was next to ours, and just a stone's throw from the tabernacle. All along the side of the tabernacle were crudely rigged, spring-loaded screen doors that SLAMMED mercilessly during a preacher's sermon like canon shots from hell. Such sounds reminded Bob and I to never venture into the woods during a preaching service. If we had, and if we had been caught (which we counted on) the punishment would have been three-times harsher than if the violators had been any other kids. Why? Because my dad was a well-respected lay-leader, and Bob's was a pastor.

So, one hot summer evening Bob and I showed up for the preaching service, rather than "gallivanting about" with the other riff-raff. We pretended to be the dutiful children of church leaders that we were, and sat in the front row of an otherwise vacant pew. In front of us, several strides, was the long prayer-bench where people, after hearing the preacher's hell-fire and damnation sermon, would scampered forward to kneel and get saved. Behind us were at least 800 people in their evening church duds getting ready to scamper forward. And above us, was the pulpit, which from the first row was a serious neck-craning- -probably why we had the front pew, made from roughed-out pine boards, all to ourselves.

As the service began we picked up a couple of the scattered paperback songbooks and sang old Gospel songs in time with the wild arm waving of the song leader backed up by choir, trumpets, and Gayle Moran's mastery of the ivories.

Every night was a big event with famous and not so famous speakers. But they were also predictable. We often sang the same songs, because people knew them, and at times, if the preacher wasn't too original, you could mouth-along the anecdotes and finish the clichés before the preacher could. He had to talk slower to accommodate the room's echo—"For G—Go—God—Goded, so lo—lov—love—loved, the wo—wor—worl—world"...and so it went for 60 to 70 minutes.

Consequently, the services were open to the appropriate and subversive mockery of adolescent boys sitting in the front pews, of which on this particular night there were only two. Behind these cut-ups sat a mass of camp goers. As the preacher of the evening got the congregation wound up, enlisting "Amens!" and "Yes, J-E-S-U-S!" and such required exclamations, these two particular pubescent adolescents, out of boredom from hearing this particular sermon a hundred times before, started flipping through the songbook.

In the preacher's defense, if the kids and the congregation had understood the sermon the first time and lived accordingly, perhaps the preacher might have felt compelled to advance to Step 2. But no, human beings, being what they are, sermons sometimes bore repeating...a hundred times.

Back on the front row, bored and looking for something to occupy their minds rather than the sins of the world...or their own, the preacher's kid (that would have been Bob) flipped open the hymnal and slid it to his uncle (that would be me), whispering: "Read the title, and then add 'UNDER THE BED' to it."

I'm not always sure why I did what my nephew suggested. Maybe it was because he was my elder, albeit of only six months. He was always getting into trouble and there I was with him on the front pew of this huge meeting with the preacher flailing his arms, and warning of hell fire and damnation. But I did it. I did what Bob in his adolescent wisdom asked.

"Just As I Am (UNDER THE BED)"...I smiled. Nephew Bob flipped the page for me.

"We Shall Go Rejoicing (UNDER THE BED)" (Flip)
"We're Marching to Zion (UNDER THE BED)" (Flip)
"Guide Me, O Thou Great Jehovah (UNDER THE BED)" (Flip)
"I've Pitched My Tent in Beulah Land (UNDER THE BED)" (Flip)
"Jonah and the Whale (UNDER THE BED)" (Flip)
"Touch Me Again (UNDER THE BED)" (Flip)

It was addictive...even as I write this. I keep wanting to add one more:

"Tho' He Slay Me (UNDER THE BED)..."

It didn't take long before we were hard pressed to restrain our giggles and body convulsions that were by now rocking the bench all along the front of the large meeting hall.

Suddenly, over the tabernacle public address speakers, the raspy voice of the revivalist preacher came to us like the wrathful voice of God.

> *BOYS! BOYS! YOU THERE IN THE FRONT. LOOK AT ME! LOOK AT ME AS IF YOU WERE LOOKING AT ALMIGHTY GOD WHO WILL JUDGE YOU TO HELL AND DAMNATION UNLESS YOU TURN FROM YOUR EVIL WAYS.*

We looked up in horror as the wirily evangelist poked his boney finger at us and shook it as if shaking off the flames of hell itself.

> *UNLESS YOU BOYS REFORM YOU'RE GOING TO END UP IN HELL. LISTEN TO ME AND STOP MAKING LIGHT OF THIS SACRED TIME AND YOUR ETERNAL DAMNATION. THIS IS NOT THE DEVIL'S SANDBOX.*

By now, all eyes were on us, including Bob's preacher father who was sitting on the platform. Needless to say after the sermon was over we went forward. We didn't need coaxing with six verses of "Jesus Will Walk With Me (under the bed)". The first refrain was all we needed, and we were on our knees at the prayer bench asking for forgiveness and begging to get saved...yet, again.

After the prayer service, of which Bob and I were central attractions, we were ushered off to our cabins and promptly fell asleep.

But I might not have slept so soundly had I known what the next morning would hold. It would be an extraordinary example of God's unmerited grace in my life... something that I would not recognize for years, but nonetheless told me that regardless of my mother's behavior at times, her prayers were always interceding for me.

12
The Ride Home

WHEN I AWOKE, it was still 1959 and I longed for it to be over. The morning after getting saved again for our "under the bed" exploits, I laid in my bed in my sleeping bag lined with bed sheets safety-pinned to the inside. It was an exclusive Mom-Design that I didn't like—the safety pins kept popping open and poking me in inappropriate places. I was surprised that she or Dad had not jostled me awake to get to the Dining Hall for breakfast and then on to the morning Youth Meetings with Bob and our friends. Instead I found my parents packing our car to return home, although camp still had a week to go.

This distressed me. Camp Meeting was a great time to be with friends from around the conference. There were dozens of kids my age and we had a great deal of fun from morning to night. It was also time to spend with Bob. In many ways we were like brothers who never got to live with each other.

The events of the night before had so infuriated my mother that there was no time to contemplate forgiveness or grace, or, God forbid, adolescence. We were not religiously rebellious kids, we were not doing drugs or fighting, we were...well, clearly we had come under the power of Satan and the surest way to protect me from hell was to get me away from Bob who was staying with his family for the rest of camp. Therefore we were leaving.

Dad drove our car out of camp before the morning services let out, to avoid further embarrassment. Mom rode in front with Dad, leaving me alone in the backseat. Hope Ellen luckily got to stay with the Kenneys and Bob's younger sister, Barb, who was Hope Ellen's age. I was jealous that Hope Ellen got to stay.

So, there I was alone on the trip home, still grinning at Bob's cleverness with the songbook trick. And I think that is what did me in. Because, finally, in the car driving along the newly minted Interstate 94, Mom turned to me in the back seat and angrily asked, "Stanley, just what was it that caused you to be so disruptive last night. What got into you?"

There have been times in my life where the concept of discretion vacated my lexicon. I've gotten in trouble far more times for telling the unvarnished truth (at least as I saw it) than I ever did lying. My problem was habitual honesty...but in the most dramatic, obnoxious terms I could conjure up. Hope Ellen, five years my junior, learned a lot from my ineptness. She would have been a good lawyer, politician or spy. How she managed in high school to go steady with a Catholic boy for years without any of us in the family knowing, especially our Mom, is a testament to her skill in discretion and the art of underground romantic intrigue. I wish she'd write at least a short story about it. I'm trying to imagine how that all happened with a German mother on her tail day and night. It seems to have all the makings of a tragic romance.

But, alas, I wasn't into discretion or intrigue, let alone romance. I was into bold face, suck-it-up, psychotic reality. Clearly I had not thought much of St. Paul's instruction of "be completely humble and gentle; speaking the truth in love...be patient, bearing with one another."1

So, when she asked, I told her. "We were playing 'Under the Bed,'" I said.

"Don't be smart with me, young man," she said.

"No really that's what we were doing." I smiled.

"What do you mean?"

"You take the hymnal, open it wherever, read the title, then add 'under the bed.'"

She looked at me dumbfounded.

So, I rattled off some examples: "*Just as I am*, Under the Bed; *O, Worship The King*, Under the Bed; *O Come, All Ye Faithful*, Under the Bed. Imagine that one, the whole tabernacle full of people crammed under the bed?" I giggled.

Mom was trying to process what I was telling her. I should have noticed the blood rising to her face and stopped. But no, not me. I started up again. "*I've Pitched My Tent in Beulah Land*, Under the Bed. What's Beulah Land by the way. That one wasn't as funny."

1 Ephesians 4:2

Mom interrupted my pitch, "And you thought this was funny, making fun of God?"

"We weren't making fun of God," I shot back. "We were making fun of the songs. Besides the sermon was boring."

"I'll tell you what won't be boring, son. Hell!"

"Give me a break, Mom. We got saved, again, didn't we?"

"I'll believe it when I see it. Stop being insolent. I won't have it, or you can walk home."

"That'd be a lot better than riding with you yelling at me."

There was only the briefest pause before she clenched her teeth and snapped at my Dad. "Stop the car, right now."

"Where?" said Dad.

"Right here!"

"Here? We're on a freeway, Ruth. I can't stop here."

"Yes, you can. Right now. I'll not have this boy sassing me all the way home."

"There's an exit in a few miles."

"I won't wait a few miles. I want him out now. Stop the car."

And my Dad did as he was told. We rolled to a stop on the shoulder and she told me to get out.

I was more than happy to oblige. Shutting the door behind me dad drove on...out of sight. She never looked back.

I walked for a mile or so until I came to a mile marker, did some arithmetic and realized it was a good 50 miles or more home. I had never hitchhiked before in my life, but had seen many others doing it. So, there on I-94, at 12-years of age, I stuck out my thumb at passing cars whizzing past at 60 miles per hour. It was overcast, but not rainy, not too hot. Actually, I was hot...emotionally so. I wasn't scared, but I was mad. So, I walked backwards along the shoulder with my thumb out, and prayed.

I didn't ask God for forgiveness, because in my mind I hadn't done anything wrong. I asked for protection and help to not be mad at my Mom. I talked to God a lot in my childhood, and still do today late in my sixties. I don't think of God as my friend or buddy, but there's truth to the old song, "What a friend we have in Jesus"...under the bed, or walking along side a busy freeway. I get plenty of ideas when I pray for answers. But deciding which one is from my Guardian Angel is tricky. There was one rule I applied to discerning God's will—it hinged on a door closing and another one opening.

About 20-minutes later a sedan pulled over ahead of me and the passenger door swung open. I ran to catch up. It never occurred to me to ask the driver a question or two to discern the wisdom of getting in the car of a stranger. Perhaps the ride that day was what convinced me to do so in the future, when I hitched a lot of rides cross-country during college. But that was then, and this was now. The door was opened and I jumped right in. "Thank you," I said.

"U're welcome, young man. How far ya goin'?" the driver said.

"Uh,...to Telegraph Road," I said. It just came out. I was surprised that I knew where I wanted to go, but figured I better act like I had a purpose.

"That's quite a ways, 'bout a hour. How come you're out here all by yer self on the side of the road like you was, if ya don't mind my askin'?"

As the car picked up speed, I kept close to the door and made sure I knew where the door handle was. This was before automatic door locks and seat belts. I studied the man. He was about 40-50, decently dressed in a clean brown suit, white shirt and tie; and the car neat. Nothing out of the ordinary. He was relaxed and kept his eye on the road.

I debated what I was going to tell him, but most of the stories that whizzed through my mind had little credibility. "Ah, we were coming home from camp meeting and my Mom and I got into an argument and she kicked me out of the car. Said I had to walk home."

"Camp meeting! Which is that?"

"Back a few miles. The Southern Michigan Free Methodist Camp Grounds, just this side of Jackson."

"Yer, comin' from a camp meetin'? And you get kicked out of yer mother's car?" He didn't sound that astonished, almost like he knew it before hand.

"Dad was driving," I said.

"That's too bad, young man. Can I ask your name?"

"Yeah. It's Stan."

He didn't say anything for a moment to two...then, "Well, Stan, that's all real interesting. Ya' see, I'm a preacher of the Gospel myself."

"Really?" I said to the man, whose name I don't think I ever asked. Thank you, God! I knew God answered prayers, but I had not been the direct recipient of anything quite so dramatic as this. It would be years before I figured my Dad, too, was also praying for me. I knew Mom's prayers were often answered, sometimes dramatically, but I'm not sure I wanted to know what she was praying for...or against...at that particular moment.

"You a Christian, then, Stan?" asked my driver.

"Trying to be," I said, keeping my eyes on the road.

"Stan, you know, one of the things that plagues a young man your age? It's something you have to be real careful about. And ask God to deliver you from."

Dang! I thought, here it comes: *Honor your father and your mother. Stop being so insolent to our parents. It's not right to argue with your mother who bore you. etc.*

But, no, that wasn't it.

I said nothing. I was going to find out without asking.

I waited. He passed a truck and pulled back into the right lane.

"Yes, sir. You gotta watch out for masturbation."

I stiffened...or was that a rock in the road we just ran over? *What did he say?!*

Then, as if he was reading my mind, "Yep. Masturbation is one of those things that can ruin your life."

For the next hour my eyes never left the road, although I kept him well within my peripheral vision. I was sure he was going to give me all the reasons for avoiding masturbation claimed by religion, ethics, morality, the Bible, and certain legalistic rules of a church, where the churches were brave enough to talk about it.

But, no, the reasons were all medical. Blindness topped the list, followed by my inability to have babies because all my sperm would be used up in my youth, I would be lousy at sports because my muscles would atrophy, I'd give my wife a disease, and ultimately I would suffer disfigurement and, for sure, eventual dismemberment of certain parts of my anatomy. I cringed at the thought. He never asked any personal questions, he just lectured me...generally...as one who should know...and as one who wanted to protect other young men, like me, from self-destruction. It was the only time in my life that anyone talked to me about...masturbation. And, here, I've talked about it too much already.

My "chauffeur" was deliberate, polite and respectful. As promised, he drove me to the Telegraph Road exit, where he pulled over to the side of the road and I got out, thanked him, and walked to the nearest gas station.

In remembering this day, I have always been aware of God's protective Providence—accessible, I believe, through my mother's intercessory prayers—especially in light of the perversion seemingly ubiquitous in society today. I have never taken God or the prayers of my ancestors for granted.

At the gas station's pay phone, I called home...collect. Dad answered immediately, asked where I was. Surprised by how close I was, he came immediately and picked me up.

When I got home, Mom said nothing. She acted as if the argument in the car had never happened, or that I had not just hitched a ride halfway across Michigan at 12. It was as if she knew I was going to make it home safely.

Everything returned to "normal," except every morning for weeks, upon waking, I checked my eyesight.

13
Rule of Law

A S I GREW into adolescence around 1959, and began to take a more active and intellectual interest in my Christian up-bringing. I asked more questions and often found reasons to debate my parents and others about Christianity as I was being taught it. A case in point follows. It's presented here somewhat didactically, but imagine it happening over a period of years and involving my parents and a pastor here and there.

My Dad was an active layman in the Free Methodist Church, one of a few denominations that have been historically categorized as part of the Holiness Movement.[1] Dad was one of the founders of Light and Life Men's Fellowship, the official men's club of the denomination. And, although Dad was not an obsessive follower of rules (he would often say to me, "Don't tell your Mom") Dad still followed a great many.

A set of those rules could be found in a book he kept on his desk—The Free Methodist Discipline—a small hardbound book that articulated the doctrines of the Church, directed how those doctrines should be lived out by its members, and how the church should be administered.

In its articles of religion, up front, and appropriately so, there are these two statements:

> 24. We are accounted righteous before God only for the merit of our Lord and Savior Jesus Christ by faith, and not for our own works or deserving; wherefore, that we are justified by faith only, is a most wholesome doctrine, and very full of comfort.

1 From largest to smallest the Holiness Movement consisted of: Church of the Nazarene, the Salvation Army, Church of God, Wesleyan Churches, and the Free Methodist Church.

25. Although good works, which are the fruits of faith, and follow after justification, cannot put away our sins and endure the severity of God's judgments, yet they are pleasing and acceptable to God in Christ, and spring out of a true and lively faith, insomuch that by them a lively faith may be as evidently known as a tree is discerned by its fruit.[1]

Here we read a clear delineation that faith saves us and that good works are not required, but are evidence of the faith.

But later we come upon a list of mandatory requirements that church members needed to live by or else they were "disconnected" from the fellowship. Here is the two-paragraph preamble to the list, which the reader will note places the list with "evil of every kind" (underline my own emphasis):

42. There is only one condition..."a desire to flee from the wrath to come, and to be saved from their sins." But wherever this is really fixed in the soul, it will be shown by its fruits.

43. It is therefore expected of all who continue [as Free Methodists] that they should continue to evidence their desire of salvation. First, by doing no harm, by avoiding <u>evil of every kind, especially that which is most generally practiced; such as</u>:

Below are a few of the items in the long list. I've taken the liberty to paraphrase some and omit many that were against a civil statue or law:

- ► Taking God's name in vain
- ► Working on Sunday
- ► Drinking or manufacturing alcoholic beverages
- ► Suing another Christian; driving a hard bargain
- ► Speaking uncharitably
- ► Wearing costly apparel, including gold wedding rings
- ► Belonging to secret societies
- ► Singing songs or reading books which do not tend to the knowledge or love of God
- ► Snuffing, Chewing, Smoking, growing, manufacturing or selling tobacco, or the habitual use of opiates

1 Doctrines and Disciplines of the Free Methodist Church of North America (1944), The Free Method Publishing House, Winona Lake, Indiana. p12.

To these my parents and some Free Methodist parachurch organizations added a few other restrictions that were not listed in the Discipline but might as well have been listed since they were preached against regularly:

- ► Recreational dancing (except for ballet and western square)
- ► Use of regular playing cards (but games with Rook cards were acceptable)
- ► Attending Hollywood movies (but watching them on TV was acceptable)

Then, to the above restrictions, these proactive works were listed in the Discipline:

- ► Do good to others as you have power.
- ► Feed the hungry, cloth the naked, shelter the poor, and visit those that are sick or in prison.[1]

And finally this warning about all these behavior requirements:

> *If there be any among us who observe them not, who habitually break any of them, let it be known unto them who watch over that soul as they who must give an account. We will admonish him of the error of his way. We will bear with him for a season. But if then he repent not, he hath no more a place among us. We have delivered our souls.[2]*

The interpretation of these passages from The Free Methodist Discipline is that we are saved by faith, but only through obedience to these rules can we maintain our salvation. This discredits "salvation by faith alone" (*sola fide*), although *sola fide* refers precisely to initial justification and not efforts afterwards to keep that justification valid. In my mind, however, there was no practical difference. You can argue all you want about initial justification, but works are still necessary, so both are required.

While this is just an account of Free Methodism during the time of my upbringing, it was also the commonly understood theology of all Evangelical-Protestants.

At the same time, my parents and other Protestants criticized Catholics over the Roman claim that there was merit in doing good. To me,

---

1 Ibid. paragraphs 43, 71, and 406.
2 Ibid. paragraph 46.

therefore, it was inconsistent that our Free Methodist preachers would proclaim that salvation was a free gift, and then demand a list of mandatory behaviors to maintain membership in the Church.

> **It was inconsistent that our Free Methodist preachers would proclaim that salvation was a free gift, and then demand a list of mandatory behaviors to maintain membership in the Church.**

Further, the Protestant claim that Catholicism teaches initial justification was possible through works, I discovered, was not true at all. Catholic theology taught that we are justified by faith, but that our good works, thereafter, did have merit in working out our eternal salvation. (That really was not much different from what Evangelicals practiced.) Jesus covered this in the Sermon on the Mount with His parable of the wise and foolish builders,[1] St. Paul talked about working out our salvation with fear and trembling,[2] and St. James said that faith without good works was dead.[3]

Compounding this basic Protestant belief in the necessity of good works, was the Holiness Movement's extension of it, made clear in this passage often quoted by my Mom:

> *Be ye therefore perfect, even as your Father which is in heaven is perfect.*[4]

I was also reminded as a member of the Free Methodist Church, that if I did not show a humble accommodation and true repentance in turning from such aberrant behavior as flaunting the rules of the Free Methodist society then "he has no more a place among us."

There were a number of concepts in the Discipline that were left up to interpretation, of course. One was, "habitually" and "We will bear with him for a season." But there was never any allowance for disagreeing with the rules per se.

I COULD EASILY TRUST a stable reality where the rules don't change. This is part of the mystery of God. I saw this stability in the laws of nature and in my nascent understanding of human psychology. My faith was in God's unchanging truth, and I came quickly to de-

---

1 Matthew 7:24-27
2 Philippians 2:12
3 James 2:14-26
4 Matthew 5:48 (KJV)

spise what my Protestant parents and teachers claimed were God's truths, but then changed them. You could not have faith in that kind of system, and I rebelled easily against it. As my Dad said of me, I was "impetuous and easily ruffled."

Whenever the church changed a rule, or my parents decided to ignore one of the rules, I would challenge them, and some level of debate would occur. In the late 1800s men could not wear neckties. But fast forward to the mid 1970s my mother didn't want me to go to Sunday evening church because I wasn't wearing a necktie. Growing up, my folks would not be caught dead with wedding rings; they were superfluous adornment. Yet this too became a moot point during my teen years. And, when Pam and I got married, in a Free Methodist church, my mother was upset that we were going to exchange rings, but our pastor did not hesitate to allow us to exchange them as part of the ceremony.

We called all of this evangelical-salvation-by-works-practice, "legalism," and it was emphasized much more than faith, as the Evangelicals defined it. And, it was this contradiction that began to drive my personality into something intolerable.

14
Impetuous and Easily Ruffled

I N 1957 DAD's description of me as "impetuous and easily ruffled" took on new meaning.

On Saturday morning, October 5, 1957, the Detroit Free Press ran a front page 3-inch headline that read SOVIET 'MOON' CIRCLES EARTH 560 MILES HIGH. It would be a few days before the media started to refer to Sputnik and the U.S. Explorer (launched February 1, 1958) as satellites. But my 5th-grade teacher, Mr. Jagodzinski, let the class bring in headlines and articles about the space race and assigned me to tape them to a wide paper banner that encircled the room above the blackboard. It was a very exciting time that thrived on my obsessive nature. I knew exactly how those headlines needed to be taped onto the large matrix I was creating, and became upset if someone tried to help.

During study period Mr. J. would play classical Long Play vinyl records on a small record player. The device was perched precariously on a desktop with the electric chord stretched across an aisle to the plug on the wall. One time I got up from my desk to sharpen my pencil. As I did, I scanned the perimeter of the room, examining "my" banner that ran around it, looking for any headlines that might have come untaped and were *falling out of orbit*.

This is where I reach for a metaphor. There were three things that were going around in circles at that moment and one thing that was not. Satellites were circling the globe, Tchaikovsky's ballet *The Nutcracker* was revolving on the record player, and my head was twisting on my shoulders. But my feet failed to gracefully pirouette along with everything else. I stumbled and fell across the electric chord, bringing the record player and *The Nutcracker* crashing to the floor.

Mr. J was not pleased with my ballet skills. But I, being as easily ruffled as a pink tutu, was upset that the chord had been strung across my path. It was like playing musical chairs with your teacher refereeing. The music had stopped and I was the last person standing. My punishment was to stay in from recess and write an essay on question number six in our workbooks.

When I got home that day I handed my mom a note:

> *Dear Mom. Today in school I blew my stack at my teacher Mr. Jagodzinski. He said either take number 6 or get out of school for 3 days. I was so mad I took the 3 days. I do not want to talk to anybody until tomorrow. Then and not to then will I tell you and the family what happen.*
>
> *Love, Stan*

I have good memories of Mr. J. He let me keep the newspaper roll of headlines, which for many years I saved in long, square corrugated tubes that I stuck in the rafters of my basement clubroom.

But the note I had handed to my Mom only foreshadowed what would happen in Junior High...a few chapters in the future.

15
The Telenews Theater

IN THE LATE 1950's television was the latest fad. We had a large Admiral black and white set, in a black aluminum cabinet that sat in our basement. But my Dad, who was born in 1894, kept to some old habits. Once or twice a month he would take me to the Telenews Theater in Detroit not far from his work.

Mom didn't like it because they showed movies occasionally, like *Old Yeller* and *Bambi*. She knew, somehow, that movies showed some bad stuff, like nudity. But Dad explained to her, as she must have remembered from their courtship, that the Telenews only showed newsreels with stories of world events, and family friendly fair. Mom was not convinced and put up a fuss. Hearing Mom's warnings, however, put me on high alert. And sure enough, next time we went to the Telenews, I saw it. Across the street and a block away was the theater my Mom must have known existed. It was a seedy and risqué looking affair. "Live Burlesque," read the marquee, with large posters underneath that left little to the imagination.

My Mom's aversion to movie theaters fit the Free Methodist profile for mandatory behavior. As I've already related, if you wanted to be a member of the Free Methodist church you were not allowed to attend movies, wear jewelry, go to dances, drink alcohol, crew or smoke tobacco, or, if you were a guy, wear thin monochromatic ties. Mom never wore makeup, and neither she nor Dad wore wedding rings—which were signs of secular materialism. But Mom and Dad "pushed the envelope." While Dad took me to the Telenews, Mom wore elaborate broaches at her neckline...to church. When I challenged her on them as jewelry, she explained that the use of a broach kept her dress together. I suggested a simple safety pin. She told me to go to my room.

The exterior of the Telenews was sedate by comparison. Inside there were no fancy ceilings or sconces. Checkerboard tile floors, not carpet. It sat about 500. The lights never came on, there was never a pre-show, and if they sold popcorn, Dad never bought any. The newsreels played continuously from two projectors above and behind the audience through two holes in the back wall. You could hear the projectors whacking away. I remember the first few times Dad took me, I was so curious about those beams of light that came out of the wall behind my head that I got a sore neck staring at the flicking beams and not at the screen. Once in a while when the reels would change I'd quickly look back and see the projectionist stick his head out a third window. I wondered how it all worked.

> **She explained that the use of a broach kept her dress together. I suggested a simple safety pin. She told me to go to my room.**

Even though the World War was over, there were still stories filled with violence and adventure on the screen. The cold war was ramping up, Fidel Castro was taking over in Cuba, there was fighting in Vietnam although the U.S. wasn't yet involved, there were race riots in the South as Southern Democrats tried to uphold the Jim Crow laws and keep blacks from the white only lunch counters. And, there was the cool stuff about the space race. Two years earlier I saw my first footage of a NASA launch of the Explorer 1 satellite at the Telenews.

But the behavior of society was changing. People stayed home more and watched the news on television for free. No more driving into town, paying for parking, walking down Woodward Ave in the cold weather, buying a ticket, and sitting with strangers in the dark. Television was just too convenient, and the Telenews died in 1960.

That was unfortunate, because that meant there was one less thing to do Sunday and Wednesday evenings.

16
Testimony Time

THERE WAS NEVER a chance, even when it was open, that Dad would have taken me to the Telenews instead of Sunday or Wednesday evening church services, wish as I might.

I liked going to church, but there were times when I wished there had been an alternative. It wasn't that I disliked God, the Bible, or the people. Far from it. It was because there was always the chance that as part of the worship service there would be a "Testimony Time." Actually, there was no "chance" of it happening. It always did, and I wanted to avoid it.

Testimony times were "opportunities" to stand from where you sat and extemporaneously tell the 50-100 people who had gathered, about the Lord's goodness in your life during the past week. Usually, spontaneous, one person after another would stand and share. Often it was an answered prayer request, or a spiritual insight from personal Bible study. Rarely did anyone monopolize the floor. The testimonies were generally short, humble, and personal.

So far, not bad.

Inevitably, however, there would be one or two in the group that would stand and share a testimony that we had all heard before...many times. It was always the same, word-for-word. Sometimes it came from a little old lady, other times from a nervous teen. As the person popped up and down as fast as they could, our lips would move in sync with the words they spoke:

> *I-love-the-Lord-will-all-my-heart-and-I-want-to-go-all-the-way-with-Him!*

Now reader, do not for a moment believe that I am ridiculing these dear people. My impression was that they were very sincere as they spoke clearly and deliberately. It was as if they were standing before the judge of the universe and asking for mercy, and indeed they may have felt that very thing. And from what I saw of their lives they were good Christians, if not imperfect humans, on a sincere journey of faith.

But I did not like to share. I tried to avoid it.

It wasn't that I was shy. Earlier, I wrote about my 4th grade appearance as the master of ceremonies for our elementary school talent show. I wasn't a performer, and I never sought the stage, but I can't ever recall having a case of stage fright. And while public speaking was never easy, it was a fun challenge

Nor did I avoid giving my testimony because I felt bereft of spiritual insights or prayers answered. In these I felt blessed. I lived in a home where there were many prayers sent aloft and many were answered. I had a relationship with God that allowed me to have the occasional spiritual insight that gave me encouragement. Although most of the time, due to my choleric-melancholy spirit, the insights were depressing.

No, it wasn't those things. I avoided sharing at testimony times for a couple of other reasons. First, I wanted to avoid the *Quadruple Guilt Whammy*. What is the *QGW*?

> **I avoided sharing at testimony times because I wanted to avoid the Quadruple Guilt Whammy.**

As I will detail later, during an altar call, amidst all kinds of promises that the sin or multiple transgressions you needed to confess were *just between you and God*, it was likely you'd get manipulated to come forward to the altar where you would tell an adult your sins. That was the *Single Guilt Whammy*. Yes, you're right, there was little apparent difference between this and my Catholic friends going to confession to tell a priest their sin. But as Free Methodists we claimed there was a big difference.[1]

And, the *Double Guilt Whammy*? After you got up from kneeling at the altar having confessed your sins you'd look up for the first time at the man who had come down to hear your confession and pray with you...and discover it was your girlfriend's dad. *Too late!*

This only had to happen once, however, before you learned to look at the person who you were going to confess to and make sure it wasn't either your girl's dad or some buddy of his. If it was your girl friend's dad (or his buddy) now you faced a *Third Whammy*: *In confessing my*

---

1 Actually, there was a big difference—the priest could give you absolution.

sins can I lie?

But *The Fourth Guilt Whammy* occurred moments after getting up from the altar. The pastor would announce a spontaneous Testimony Time to celebrate God's forgiveness (surprise!)—at which you'd be expected, *publicly*, to spill your guts. How often did I go forward to get "re" saved? I don't have the fingers and toes to count the times. But I do remember that I often felt manipulated and lied to, mostly by the preacher waving his Bible at the front of the church. I tried to pass the trickery off as part of the process—that whatever it took to get me to make a public confession of faith was justified. Yet, the feeling of betrayal never left. And, I lost more than a few girlfriends this way.

THE SECOND REASON for avoiding Testimony Time had to do with its practicality. The whole idea of having a Testimony Time was to help us Christians really be saved. You see, there was this verse in the Bible...well, actually it's still there, in Romans:

> *If you declare with your mouth, "Jesus is Lord," and believe in your heart that God raised him from the dead, you will be saved. For it is with your heart that you believe and are justified, and it is with your mouth that you profess your faith and are saved.*[1]

Now, this gets a bit tricky, so try to follow along. My mother had made me to understand that Evangelicals (and especially Free Methodists) were into salvation by *faith*, not by *works*. *Sola Fide (salvation by faith alone)* was our Church's rallying cry. As my mom explained, "Faith Alone" was an effort to separate us from those lost Roman Catholics who were all going to hell. Why? Because they falsely believed that *works* could somehow save them. One of the big differences (in the Evangelical mind) is that Catholics have to DO things to get saved, where Evangelicals only have to believe in their hearts to be saved, or so we were told.

Do you see where this is going? (I wasn't that smart, and yet I figured this out in Junior High...during one of those days I was suspended from school for bloodying up the halls.)

Testimony Time was supposed to do two things for you. (1) By confessing your faith in Christ vocally you would be saved. And, (2) giving vocal witness to your faith in front of the other members of the

---

[1] Romans 10:9-10 (NIV)

church would give you practice witnessing to your pagan friends who were not in church.

But for impetuous, rebellious youth like me, this didn't make a whole lot of sense. Oh, it made some sense, but I got hung up on a few things. (a) The Romans passage says very clearly that unless we confess with our mouth that "Jesus is Lord" we would *not be saved.* So, there was a "work" or something to "do" that was required, in addition to "believing." During the sermon we were told it was *only faith* that saved us, and then came the Testimony Time when *some work also* was required. Which was it, I thought? Just believing or did I have to do stuff, too?

> **As my mom explained, "Faith Alone" was an effort to separate us from those lost Roman Catholics who were all going to hell.**

And, if *good* works were not a part of our salvation then why did we have to confess the *bad* works? What we did outwardly seemed just as much a part of our lives as what we thought.

The other thing I got hung up on was this: (b) Everyone at church would understand what I meant, when I gave my testimony and used words like:

> *...the Lord...saving and sanctifying...his presence...a long journey...trusting in Jesus...to the end...heavenly reward...*

But talking like this at church didn't give me much practice for talking to my friends at school (or later at work) who were skilled at mocking my faith:

> *Lordy, Stan! If you want to get saved, stick in my presence and take the long journey to the bar after work where we can trust in a tall, dark cool one. That will be heavenly.*

Testimony Time only reinforced my reliance on Christian jargon that all too often never translated to the lives of my pagan friends. "You're insane," they'd say and then look at me as if to wonder what moon beam had vaporized my brain.

There was one Free Methodist pastor in our family, but before I had the chance to hear Oscar Kenney preach, give an altar call, or lead a time of testimonies, he died.

17
Playing Cards

REV. OSCAR KENNEY's death came in 1960, and it significantly affected our family.

My Dad's marriage to Lucile Benjamin had produced a daughter, Dorothy. In 1940 Lucile died of cancer when Dorothy was 20. A few months later Dorothy married Oscar Kenney, who was an ordained Free Methodist minister. But they didn't have children right away. Five years later in 1945 Dad married my Mom, Ruth Willobee, who was 18 years his junior. The race was on—who could produce the first kid? The Kenneys won. Their first child, Bob, beat me into the world by six months. Although we never lived together, neither of us had brothers, so we formed a brother-like relationship over the years and were the best men for each other's weddings.

The Kenney family moved around a bit, due to the short supply of Free Methodist preachers who were always in demand. For a time Oscar pastored a church in Texas and in letters and gifts to me, Bob took on the persona of a Texan, where everything was bigger and better.

In the late 50's Oscar was invited to be the pastor of the Wayne Free Methodist Church, in Wayne, Michigan, a suburb of Detroit. So, Oscar took the position and Bob and I began to see each other regularly now that they were only 30 minutes away.

In late 1959 Oscar was diagnosed with lymphoma and early the next year he died. He was 45-years old. It was a shock to the Southern Michigan Free Methodist conference where he and Dorothy were well-known and popular revival and camp-meeting speakers. Dorothy was an avid storyteller and used flannel graphs to tell Bible stories to groups of children. Oscar was a good amateur magician, and would use magic tricks in his spiritual talks. Bob later told me about one trick where his Dad would take a black velvet bag on a stick, and put into it a black cloth representing our sins. Then he would put into the bag a red cloth representing the blood of Christ's sacrifice. Then he would have a child from the audience stick their hand in the bag and pull out the only cloth inside. It would be white, representing how we are made pure by Christ's love for us.

Oscar's death resulted in what was said to be the largest funeral of the time within Free Methodism. The Wayne church was packed with other pastors from throughout Michigan. I remember the funeral cortège to the cemetery. As the car I was riding in, near the front, rose on a hill, I looked back. As far as I could see the procession snaked through town, the little black and white flags fluttering from the car roofs.

Oscar was buried in a Lutheran cemetery only a few miles from where I write this. Pam and I visited his grave-site recently. There are no monuments in this large, well-kept cemetery. All the markers are flat, below the top of the grass line. Dorothy chose this site because everyone was laid out equal in God's sight. There were no monuments to egos.

One of Bob's sons says that he wants to live by a cemetery, so on the day of resurrection, when the dead are to rise first, he can witness the sight. The inscription of Oscar's marker says, "For me to live is Christ, and to die is gain."[1] Thinking of Oscar as a magician I thought a second inscription might be appropriate, "Now for my next trick...the Resurrection. Romans 6:5."

To help his Mom decompress after Oscar's death, Bob came to stay with me. We put up a cot in my large bedroom and spent our spare time in my clubroom in my basement, which was the home's old preserves cellar. Bob and I had a common hobby; it was astronomy, and we called our club, with all of its two members, "The Star, Moon, and Planet Club." We stargazed and tried to build a 6-inch reflecting telescope. When that failed we wrote to observatories around the country and they sent us free 8" x 10" glossy black and white pictures of the sun, the moon, the planets and galaxies that we taped to walls. Far better than our 6-inch reflector could have taken with my dad's old 620-mm pinhole cameras. Over the main desk was a small certificate attesting our membership in the British Interplanetary Society, an organization founded in 1933 and which still exists to pro-

1 Philippians 1:21

mote the exploration of space. On the crude shelves were books, magazines, microscopes, and gear to do experiments with, like wiring your desk drawer so no one could open it up unless they have a magic piece of wire. And in the corner was a small stack of National Geographic magazines that I had culled from my parent's extensive collection elsewhere in the basement.

During the week Bob went to school with me at Haston Junior High. The school bus picked us up next door in front of Ned's house. One morning, before Ned came out to wait with us, I got up the courage to ask Bob a question I had harbored since the funeral. "Do you mind if I ask you stuff about your dad, I mean about his dying and all. We don't have to talk about it if you don't want to."

His answer surprised me, and has helped me at least a dozen times since when talking with the surviving spouse or child of someone who has died. "It's okay. Actually, I guess I want to talk about it. But everyone is scared to. Yeah, I need to talk about it."

I remember nothing else about that conversation. I was so surprised that he wanted to talk about his Dad, to whom he was so close. How close were they? Well, while Dad was taking me to forbidden newsreels in Detroit across from the burlesque house, Bob, at age 11, was driving his Dad's Oldsmobile across the plains of Oklahoma on the way to a revival speaking engagement, while his dad slept in the passenger seat. It just may be that Free Methodists, in a bid to be *Free* from the legalism that surrounded them, were all a bit rebellious.

Speaking of which, one day when Bob and I came back from school, Ned invited us into his house, and in the process of the visit loaned us a deck of poker playing cards. I trembled as I took them and stuck them in my coat pocket. I thought about the clandestine Superman comic books I had hid under my mattress at home. I made my own bed, so there was no chance Mom was going to find them. But what I now held in my pocket was more dangerous than the comic books, which I knew I'd get whipped for if my Mom ever found them. To Mom, Superman wasn't a metaphor for Christ, but the product of an idle imagination—an idol that replaced Christ. I took risks. But the playing cards were something else. The Free Methodist Church said that the use of playing cards was a sin. (They didn't say anything about comic books.) But Ned had an extra deck. Actually I think they were missing a card or two and thus were useless to the Catholics next door. So, I took them, and Bob's eyes dilated.

We walked next door to my house as if everything was normal. But rather than low-tailing it to the basement and our clubroom, we high-tailed it to the second floor and my bedroom...and shut the door. I had a study desk next to the double windows that looked over our dou-blewide yard to the South and Ned's house beyond that. We sat down opposite each other and started playing cards.

Now Free Methodists believed that playing cards were a tool of the devil that were closely associated with fortune telling, and games of chance like gambling, which imbued greed into the players. But the irony of the restrictions was not lost to Bob and me because the Free Methodist Church did allow the use of Rook playing cards.

> **Superman wasn't a metaphor for Christ, but the product of an idle imagination—an idol that replaced Christ.**

Parker Brothers game company intro-duced the 57-card Rook deck in 1906 as an alternative for conservative Christians who found the regular 52-card deck offensive. While Parker Brothers also introduced an original Rook game, the Rook deck was so similar in design that you could remove five cards and have a regular 52-card deck and play any regular card game, including poker. Bob and I knew a few games we had played with a Rook deck but we had never played them with a regular deck, so we were wound up with excitement at having a real deck of cards in our hands.

We unpacked the deck, tried shuffling them, looked at them with some level of curiosity and scrutiny, and started playing "Old Maid" where the queen of spades was the protagonist to be discovered or dis-carded .

Where Mom was pretty high strung and demanding, Dad brought some stability to my life with his quiet, steady ways. I recall my Dad only losing his temper one time in the 42-years I knew him upon this Earth. And that moment was upon me.

Bob and I must have been having a whale of a time because we never heard my father coming up the stairs, or the approaching foot-steps in the hall.

Suddenly, my bedroom door flew open, I looked up and saw my dad staring down at me, his 13-year old son, then looking over at the table with the playing cards scattered about.

Without saying a word, his eyes flared wide, his neck muscles pulled tight, and he exploded at the table with trembling arms. As fast as he could he frantically grabbed the cards out of my hands, Bob's hands, and off the table. Grasping the waste can near the door, he threw the cards into it, then glared at each of us, "Boys, you've done it now. This is serious business, and it will stop. Don't move, I'll be back."

And with that he left the room with my waste can...and this time we heard his pounding steps all the way into the basement. I never knew what he did with the cards.

A few moments later Dad came back into my room, "Robert, you go down to the kitchen right now and stay there. I'm going to have a word with Stanley, here."

Bob left. Dad's face was perspiring a bit, his lips were wet, and he dabbed at them with his ever-present handkerchief he kept in a hip pocket. He then closed the door.

"You knew this was wrong," he addressed me, his eyes watering.

"But, dad, we were just playing Old Maid, that's all."

"Where did you get those?"

I pointed at Ned's house out my window. "Ned gave them to us after school. We weren't playing for money or anything like that. What's wrong. It's the same game we play with Rook cards all the time at church parties."

"Don't sass me, son."

Now I was crying. I had never seen my dad like this before, and never did again. "I'm sorry. I really am. But I don't see anything wrong with it."

Dad swept his hand back through his gray hairs over his balding head. He was 66-years old, and by this time tired of battling things that he probably felt were over the top. "Son, there are many things in the world that seem right, but they can lead down paths of destruction. I pray for you every day that you'll do what is right. God will be your judge. But until then, your Mom and I have a duty to raise you right. Don't ever let me again see you doing anything that we think is wrong, under this roof. Do you hear me? I want you to promise me you won't do this again."

I nodded my head, but I wasn't so sure, with the inconsistencies of Free Methodist thinking and my parent's interpretation of the same, that I would always know what was right or wrong.

"Okay. Now listen to me. Your Mom's been out shopping. I'm not going to tell her about this. So keep your promise and stay low. Understand?"

"Yeah. Thanks, Dad," I said, greatly relieved.

"Okay, now. Go down to Bob and stay out of trouble."

Dad left the room, and in a few minutes after drying my tears I went downstairs.

Bob was sitting in the kitchen, hands folded in his lap. "C'mon," I said. "Let's go downstairs."

We went to our normal haunt, the "Star, Moon, and Planet Club."

We settled into our clubroom and wondered what to do. Bob casually picked up a copy on the top of my stack of National Geographic magazines and I stared out the window at the afternoon sun wondering if the sun was the location of hell.

> **I stared out the window at the afternoon sun wondering if the sun was the location of hell.**

"Wow!" said Bob, "look at this." I glanced down. Bob had opened an issue that featured a recent exploration of the New Hebrides Islands (now Vanuatu) in the Western Pacific. I had the issue in the clubroom because it was on the beach of Dillion's Bay of the island of Erromanga New Hebrides where on November 20, 1839 my missionary ancestor, John Williams, was martyred and eaten by cannibals.

But what Bob had found was not a bunch of natives sitting on the ground listening to a preacher...or eating him. It was a lineup of young women smiling at the camera. And except for one strategically placed piece of cloth on each, they were naked.

Mom wasn't home yet and I figured my Superman comic books would appreciate some female companionship. And while naked women and Superman were fascinating subjects, what caught my eternal imagination was the adventure of sailing to the South Seas. To me, the distant uncle was the real Superman.

Rev. John Williams (1796-1839)

OVER THE YEARS I've identified with John Williams. He's described in the oral tradition of my family as a distant uncle and an early missionary to the South Pacific. He was sent to the islands by the London Missionary Society in 1816, when the only mode of travel for such a long voyage was aboard intrepid sailing vessels. Over the short 23 years of his work he established churches throughout the islands and taught the islanders how to build sailing vessels for inter-island trade. From those adventures our family has a small collection of his curios, including a cannibal's ceremonial breastplate tanned from animal skin, on which were pained notches in human blood.

Going to the South Pacific in modest square-rigged sailing vessels was a great risk. The trips cost a fortune, and there were Christians in London, England who told him he shouldn't go. But his vision drove him toward his destiny regardless of the counter-arguments offered by otherwise good individuals. On Wednesday, Nov 20, 1839, and against the advice of his superiors and the ship's captain, Rev. Williams and an associate, Mr. Harris, went ashore at Erromanga. Their intent was to establish contact with the inhabitants and eventually preach the Good News.

Little did they know that earlier, abusive traders had pillaged the island of its valuable sandalwood, fruits, livestock, and killed many of the natives. In fear for their lives, and seeing that Mr. Williams and Mr. Harris were not armed, the natives ambushed the two men on the beach with spears and rocks. In full view of the crew on board the ship anchored at bay, the natives carried their bloody corpses into the bush never to be seen again.

Although he was martyred in the service of the Gospel, John Williams's work survives to this day with seven honorary chapels scattered around the South Pacific. After his death seven ocean-going vessels were built and commissioned, to assist Pacifica natives in their inter-island trade. Some were christened by Britain's royalty and carried the HMS[1] prefix. Over the years dozens of books were written about John Williams's life and his efforts to bring Christianity to the South Pacific. He clearly changed the religious landscape forever in that part of the globe.

I was never as adventurous or as risk-taking as John Williams, but I've discovered that in some ways I am like him. He was compulsive and impetuous, and frequently charged ahead when others told him to take the safer path. And in other ways I am far less his equal. He risked all in this life and lost it, but he gained everything for the Kingdom.

And me? I was scared of the natives at my junior high school.

---

1 It is His or Her Majesty's Ship John Williams (I, II, III,...VII)

18
Hallway Horrors

E NTERING JR. HIGH, in 1959, my problems were exacerbated by a health care experiment. I would only hope to survive. Here's what happened.

When I entered adolescence my dad had purchased a bottle of large, dark maroon, vitamin capsules called VM-22s. They were so huge dad had trouble swallowing them. So, in sixth grade, to prove my manhood, I started to take one every morning with breakfast. The consequences were immediate. In one year I grew 18 inches. When I started 7th-grade at Haston Junior High, I was 6-foot, 4-inches and skinny—clearly the tallest human in the building. It was strange.

But I kept popping the VM-22s. They were having an effect. Over the next summer I put on nearly 100 pounds. Now, I was tall, fat, un-coordinated and fatigued. With all the attention that sugary drinks, pizza, and burgers get today, I need to clarify that little of that stuff was in my diet. At our home we ate well; we had meat, potatoes, another vegetable, and dessert every night. Mom was a great cook, and I took advantage of it. I somehow knew that the college cafeteria with its mystery meat and extra bottles of ketchup on every table would be around the corner in a few years. So, during Junior High, I packed it on.

My growth spurt had some serious side-effects…aside from the stretch marks around my waist. In 8th grade I was always tired and found it difficult to walk without a spastic gait. I was the biggest dude in Junior High, in height and breadth…including the faculty.

Because of my size and awkwardness, I became the focus of jokes. My gym teacher gave me a girl's nickname that stuck—ammunition the bullies used to taunt me. I was twice their size but couldn't defend myself. They'd hit me and I'd swing back, but the momentum would trip me up, literally. It was a good day if between classes my books weren't knocked out of my hands, if I wasn't shoved over, or tripped-up to the laughter of my nemeses. They knew I had a temper and when I lashed back, they simply ducked and pushed me over one of their compatriots who had bent over behind me. Occasionally, I was lucky enough to connect and there'd be blood in the halls.

So, it was not unusual that I'd be hauled into the vice principal's office for a paddling. This happened enough that I've joked about adding a line to my professional resume: "Willingly bucks authority...over 274 hours of 'special' instruction. Can touch toes without bending knees." But the paddling got old too, and occasionally my Mom was called to pick me up and keep me at home for several days while the HAZMAT crews cleaned the halls.

One light-hearted event during this time occurred with my science teacher, Mr. Friend (his real name). I loved science and voluntarily sat in the front row. But, as I said, I was always tired. One day I fell asleep with my head resting on my arms. I can't remember falling asleep, but I do recall waking up. Mr. Friend, although he knew I loved his class, didn't think I was listening. Can't understand why. WHAM! He hit the top of my head with his oversized, teacher's edition of the textbook, *Science For You*. My head bounced off the wooden desk like a billiard ball off a table rail's bumper, and I don't think I ever fell asleep in his class again. Nice guy. This event would be repeated (sort of) during college, but with more dramatic results. Keep reading for that.

At the time of this writing in 2014, "traumatized" is probably an overly-used and excessive term to describe my 8th-grade in Junior High. But for 1960 and 1961 it describes my remembrance. Yet, I was not traumatized by the paddlings. They hurt enough to remind me to do my best and try to respect authority. I did not assign evil intent to the Vice Principal, Mr. Killbutski (our name for him). If I obeyed the rules I was given more than ample opportunity to better myself and prevent my butt from getting killed again. But I doubted there would be any justice in Junior High. So, my butt being whacked violently halfway up my esophagus became a metaphor for Mr. Killbutski's flawed judgments; he could not possibly know the truth although he wore omniscience like a judicial robe. He was operating under a number of fallacies categorized as "missing evidence."

In other words, I never started the fights but neither did I demonstrate any restraint in my efforts to end them. I refused to be bullied, so I jumped in and hit back...or at least *tried* to hit back. My physical condition, however, was not such that I could adequately defend my-self or end the fight on my terms.

I doubt that any teacher saw the beginning or middle of the hallway battles, but they clearly saw the remains at the end, and, at that point, there was no way to discern the truth of the matter.

Every time something like that happened, although I kept a stiff-upper lip, I would come home a psychological mess. I was humiliated that punks smaller than me could beat me up, I dared not tell my mother what happened unless I wanted more physical abuse, and I had no easy solution for my predicament.

After I had been sent home several times for three days to cool off--which was never a solution to me because my mother was waiting at home with her 15" biceps and a leather strap--the school came up with another solution that kept me out of the halls for an hour now and then, but that created a whole new set of problems.

19
Pervert Therapy

T HE HALLWAY BATTLES, paddlings, and suspensions from Junior High had a consequence. I was assigned to meet weekly with the school psychologist, Dr. Darling. (Trust me on this, that was his real name.) I was determined to make some good from it. My Christian faith was strong, but living it out in Junior High was hellish. I wanted to fix the disconnect and hoped the sessions with Dr. Darling would provide a solution, or at least lead to fewer blood transfusions. Yet, I privately hoped the sessions would allow me reveal the truth and send my antagonists on a one-way trip to wherever they put juvenile delinquents.

Thus, I was looking forward to my one-on-one meetings with Dr. Darling—a genteel man whom I instantly felt comfortable around. He was the antithesis of the Vice Principal with the paddle caddy woven into his belt. I imagined the two of them playing *Good Cop–Bad Cop* with repeat offenders.

But, alas, I was in for a surprise. The sessions were not one-on-one as I had hoped. It was group therapy with five other repeat offenders sitting around an old splintered, round wooden banquet table in a congested furniture storeroom, next to the boilers. It was the school's version of mass reconciliation and open confession, with a side door to hell.

I wanted to believe my summons to the sessions was for protecting my dignity, but it was probably more about giving the janitorial staff a break from cleaning up the blood-stained hallways.

And, who were these other juveniles in the room? None of them were the punks that had picked fights with me. These five, were... well...I discovered they had a different problem.

After each session, which did get me out of some unforgotten class, I came to understand that I had no doubt joined the F.S.O.A. club. (Future Sexual Offenders Anonymous). There could not be a more graphic way of learning the "facts-of-life." Thankfully, there were no visual aids to these sessions, and to his credit, Dr. Darling tried to offer only answers and advice about things adolescent boys wonder about. The descriptions came from the other five male, 7th and 8th grade commandos in the room. If I were to believe their stories, they had committed fornication with half the girls in school, and the other half were standing in line. I heard beat-by-beat accounts of consensual sexual encounters that, honestly, at the time, I found hard to believe.

Under the guise of education, Mr. Darling would occasionally (but not occasionally enough) interrupt the crass stories with benign questions: *"And what would you like to know? Do you have a question I can answer?"* Seemingly, to satisfy him into letting them continue, my "peers" would ask questions about the female anatomy or psychology that Darling would answer in as sterile and academic way as possible. I actually think I did learn some things from him, but I'm not sure I wanted to.

Today, when I hear school officials rant against home schooling because Christian students need "socialization" skills, I think back to Dr. Darling's therapy sessions and my hallway introduction to socialization.

I can only guess the administration's and Dr. Darling's rationale for holding such sessions. Perhaps they figured parents weren't doing their job in educating their children about the facts of life, which resulted in frustration with their identity and trouble at school. So, as a matter of public education, since the parents weren't doing their job, the school stepped in to help quell society's curiosity and unrest.

I remember one time having to attend after-school detention. There were twenty of us sitting at desks supposedly studying. We all had books, as I recall, pretending to do homework...except for one eighth-grade *dude* who had been held back for two years. He had greased back hair, leather jacket, tight jeans, and pointy boots with the polish worn off. He was doodling on a sheet of lined paper torn out of a three-ring binder. Hunkered over he worked furiously--a manic occupation. Although I sat slightly behind and to one side I could not see what he was drawing. After a while the male faculty monitor walked up the aisle behind him, stopped, and suddenly grabbed the artwork and held it up to look at. That's when I caught the glimpse of a most disgusting and explicit drawing of...well, it was something, ah, disgusting and explicit. A second later the teacher quickly folded the paper, grabbed the juvenile artist by the back of his leather neck, and forcibly hauled him out of the classroom, muddling something like: "This should put you in jail for a while."

So, maybe Dr. Darling's sessions were trying to help young men like the pervert in detention discover the benefits of a normal life. Did it help? I could only imagine...but refrain from doing so.

The other side of the story is that Dr. Darling's sessions filled in the knowledge gaps left by a scene in which I was the protagonist several years earlier.

D URING SPRING BREAK my family would sometimes travel to Chicago by rail, where we stayed in the loop, rode elevators up and down the fancy-to-us hotel, and took taxis to the fabulous museums Chicago is still famous for. There was always something wonderful to discover at the Field Museum of Natural History, the Adler Planetarium and the Museum of Science and Industry to which was attached a U-505—a WWII German submarine you could walk through. Oh, and then there was the Coal Mine tour accessible only through an elevator hoist that reportedly took visitors hundreds of feet below the city of Chicago. Scary stuff and perfect for kids like me.

For this particular trip, during spring break of fifth grade, I finally had worked up the guts to go on the mine tour into the depths of the earth. The previous year the elevator trip underground scared the heebie-jeebies out of me and I refused to get near the exhibit with its three-story hoist, cables and cacophony. This year, I couldn't wait.

But my industrious and ever responsible mother had other ideas. As I pulled toward the mine exhibit, and I'm pretty sure I was out of the harness by now, she yanked me by my leash into another hall on a nearby mezzanine to show me the large incubator from which little chicks were hatching from 100 or so eggs lying under heat lamps over a ventilated aluminum grid. Little kids, half my age, were pushing their pugs against the glass as I had done in years past. But by now, to a big strapping boy like me, it was boring. It took forever for these birds to beak out of their shell, only to lie there on the ventilated grate in their wet feathers to dry off over the next two hours. You've heard the expression, "watching paint dry"? Well, this was "watching feathers dry." It takes longer.

I looked at the chicks and the eggs for a moment, then craned my head toward the noisy and scary mineshaft. I was ready for the adventure of my life and wanted badly to descend into middle earth. But mother wanted to explain to me the adventure of life itself.

She pulled me into a dark mystically-illuminated hall with top-lit containers of clear liquid shining against a black wall. The exhibit went on forever, wrapping itself around a wall. Suspended in each of the containers was a chalk white human fetus. The first container held a fetus almost too small to see. At the other end of the hall was a fully developed fetus just before birth. I can remember Mom pulling me slowly along this eternal display--while, out of the corner of my eye, I watched dad take my five-year old sister closer and closer to the mine shaft elevator a half-floor below. Meanwhile, I was trapped on the balcony, held captive by my stubborn German mother. I would turn my head toward the mine exhibit, using my best mental telepathy to beg dad to come back and rescue me. But, no luck. Mom would take my head and forcibly spin it back to look at the next dead fetus, suspended in clear liquid like a horror experiment, back-lit against a morbid dark wall.

> **She pulled me into a dark mystically illuminated hall with top-lit containers of clear liquid shining against a black wall.**

I'm sure my mother was explaining to me, or trying to explain, the facts of life. But I cannot remember one word. Thus, I assume, providence stuck me in Dr. Darling's storeroom to hear what my mother had been saying. Except I'm pretty sure the words were different.

The fetus tour with Mom, and the story of life in a visually rich museum, was boring and forgotten. But the pervert therapy with Dr. Darling, in a sterile storeroom, and the stories told by my "peers" were shocking and memorable.

But none of this seemed to help me stay out of trouble. So, the school suggested Mom take me to a professional and check my wiring.

20
University Shrink

I'M NOT SURE what prompted it. Maybe it was Dr. Darling's concern over my lack of life-experience and "socialization skills," as it was obvious I was not "keeping up" with the other commandos in my group therapy. Perhaps, he may have suggested to my Mom, there was something really wrong with me and I ought to get checked out by professionals licensed to wear white coats.

So, one day in the winter of 1960, Mom took me out of school and drove to Ann Arbor in her black 1949 Chrysler with the huge trunk, which, I'm certain, she loaned to the Mafia on weekends.

After finding a parking space, which was much easier in Ann Arbor in 1960 than now, we walked to and entered a building with the promising sign out front: Institute for Human Adjustment. *I needed adjustment?* All I could think of was my Mom's car's trunk and how big it was.

I remember waiting a while and then being ushered into Dr. Shrink's interrogation room. There was a simple table and chairs, some benign pictures on the walls of cows grazing in a pasture, and on his desk a black dial telephone right out of Alfred Hitchcock's 1954 movie Dial M for Murder, which I had just seen on Sunday matinée television thanks to *Bill Kennedy's at the Movies*.

The shrink was unremarkable and barely memorable. A man, dark suit, thin tie, glasses over which he peered, between making marks on a clipboard. He hummed a lot, nodded while he wrote on his clipboard, and when we were alone, asked me dumb questions.

"So, Stanley, what do you like to do when you're alone? And don't worry, I won't tell your mother."

"I play with marbles. Sometimes I feed the squirrels, but it's winter now, ya know, and they're hibernating. And, ah...sometimes I watch lots of old movies about murder." I turned my head a little, hoping he couldn't see that I was staring at the black dial telephone. Luckily, it didn't ring right then. The interview continued.

"Is that something you're interested in? Murder?"

"Not really. Actually, I only watched one movie about it. It was on Bill Kennedy. He picked the movie, not me."

"Uh-huh. So you like school? "

"Not really."

"Why don't you like school, Stanley?"

"I get beat-up a lot."

"That makes sense."

"That I get beat-up a lot?"

"No! No! That you don't like getting beat up...a lot."

"Even once isn't fun."

"Yes, I guess that makes sense."

"Yeah. I try to fight back, but usually my fist misses and I hit the locker, cut my knuckle and there's blood all over the place. It's a mess."

"Yes, I can imagine so. How do you feel when you, ah, hit--a locker?"

"It's better than getting shoved inside one and the door slammed on ya. There's no handle on the inside, ya know. "

"That's happened to you?!"

"Naw. I'm too big."

"Yes, you are. That makes sense."

"It hurts."

"What hurts?"

"Hitting the locker with my fist. Isn't that what you asked, how does it make me feel?"

"Yes. Yes, it is. And...that makes sense...that it should hurt."

"Yeah, I guess so. Do you ever cut your knuckle and it bleeds a lot?"

"Actually, one time...ah, wait. I'm asking the questions, okay?"

"Yeah. Okay. I guess that makes sense."

Other than that nothing much happened and we drove back home in Mom's big Chrysler with the big trunk. I rode in the front passenger seat in case you were wondering. But something was up. Mom didn't make a peep all the way back. And, upon returning home, I kind of wished I had come back in the trunk. We were both headstrong, and while I was growing up we clashed a lot.

When we got in the house she was mad. And I hadn't even done anything, yet. She was mad because the doctor said I wasn't crazy. That everything seemed normal, except I was kind-of big for my age. Recall I was 6'4" and about 250 pounds.

Mom was 5' 8" and about 190. She was a big woman for her height. As soon as we got home she told me to go into the guest bedroom. I knew then what she meant to do and my heart started to race. It had been a long time since she had done this, and I wasn't sure I was ready. In the seconds that she was gone I figured out that my fighting in school embarrassed and infuriated her. I was her responsibility, and my behavior reflected on her and her parenting skills. Clearly she had not raised me right and the fear of God was not in me. In her mind this had to end. If the shrink had said I was mentally deranged she would have had an excuse, and perhaps room for some compassion. But the shrink told her I was normal. I was not crazy.

> **If the shrink had said I was mentally deranged she would have had an excuse, and perhaps room for some compassion. But the shrink told her I was normal. I was not crazy.**

I walked trembling with anger into the guest bedroom and waited for her. She strode into the room with my father's leather belt wrapped around her right wrist. She had it gripped so tight her fist was white. "Mom," I said, "you're not going to do this. I won't let you."

Her lips were drawn tight across her teeth as she ordered me to kneel down at the bed. In so many words she told me that she was not going to tolerate my rebellion against her any more. My fighting in school was going to end, and I would not sass her anymore. "Stanley! Kneel down!"

"No, I won't."

And with that, she started to swing the belt at me with a vengeance.

I put out my arms to protect my body. I got whipped a few times before I wrapped the belt around one of my arms, pulled her toward me and shoved her back onto the bed. She tried to get up but I shoved her back, again and again. When she stopped trying to hit me with dad's belt, I left the room. I told her then, as I told her many times before, that if she was a Christian I wanted nothing to do with it.

It would be hours before Dad or Sis came home. She said nothing more to me. I retreated to my room. I was shaking. I figured when dad came home, although he was no disciplinarian, there would be some consequences—Dad controlled my money, the car, and my time. But that night at dinner, although things were tense between Mom and me, nothing was ever said. Dad never said anything to me. For weeks I expected something to happen. But nothing did--except, that was the last time my Mom ever tried to whip me.

Little did I know it was time to move on and enter a special world that changed everything.

Part II
WANDERER

THE SEQUENCE OF disasters surrounding my introduction to adolescence—blood-stained halls and lockers, group therapy with perverts, and a session with a shrink posing as Alfred Hitchcock that almost resulted in a painful strapping by my Mother—motivated me to pray a lot more. I wanted out, but I had no idea where I could go.

I longed for a life where the practice of my faith was logically cogent and consistent, and where reason was part of my observance. I had no idea where to look and I certainly was too young to leave home and find my own way.

At the time, the way my parents practiced their faith only increased the depth of my dilemma. But I was soon to escape the ideological orphanage of my upbringing, and cross a threshold into a special world where I began to wander through a broader Christian subculture, looking for a spiritual home.

At the same time, I was tethered to a host of religious ideologies that I found at once comforting and disturbing.

21
Lutheran High

I N 1961, MY frustrated mother and dear father finally came to grips
with my sojourn through junior high. I wasn't crazy but public
school was more than I could handle.

So, they bit the bullet, opened their wallet, and enrolled me in Detroit's Lutheran High School West (LHW), about 20-minutes by car
from home. I was not Lutheran. I was Free Methodist. But my parents
hoped that the shift to a parochial school where there was more discipline and where the students were more likely to be from families
with Christian values, would help their oversized, vitamin enriched,
and only son survive high school.

My first day at LHW I was assigned a locker and locker partner.
Neither changed for four years. Phil Bray was African American, tall
like me, athletic unlike me, and easy going unlike me. I discovered
40-years later during lunch in Los Angeles where he now lives, that his
family was United Methodist. LHW administrators probably thought
we were from the same denomination. Little did they know just how
isolated Free Methodism was from the rest of Christianity.

Phil and I got along well, played football together, and I never recall
us having a disagreement. But Phil tells another story. As freshmen,
our physical education instructor was Dennis Toumi, a Michigan High
School Hall of Fame football coach. Toumi was one of those wonderful
mentors you'll never forget. He was built like a sturdy box with a square
bald head, a set of intense but friendly eyes, and an active R.G. Dunn
cigar in the corner of his mouth. Smoke constantly swirled around his
head. He looked like a professional wrestler, and in fact, he coached
wrestling, too.

Evidently, as freshmen, Phil and I had developed a grudge, although today neither of us can recall what it was about. Toumi, always on the lookout for a teachable moment, noticed our disagreement, dug through an old box in the equipment cage and found two pairs of boxing gloves. With a twinkle in his eyes he tossed the gloves to us, directed a couple students to lace them onto the end of our spindly arms, and proceeded to stage an impromptu grudge match during P.E. class.

Toumi got away with stuff like this because the school's Phys Ed room was off the school's radar. No one other than Toumi, his coaching staff, or us guys ever got into the room, nor would most want to. For one thing it was the only locker room in the modest Lutheran High building. Girls didn't do sports then…besides, the administrators probably figured the estrogen-challenged girls didn't need a locker room when they already had an oversized bathroom with wall-to-wall mirrors.

But the boys, well…testosterone-driven boys were different. So, they were assigned to meet in what was probably once a large store-room with a polished cement floor. Fixed to the perimeter of the three interior walls were dark gray lockers with dents in the doors from various "mishaps" that occur in such rooms. Dangling from a vaulted ceiling were a few off-colored florescent light fixtures. The fourth line of lockers, at the north end of the room, were set away from the exterior wall to create a space behind them we called "the weight room," with free weights, exercise equipment and a bench for taping ankles. The "weight room" was adjacent to the exterior double doors that led to the football field, which was next to the equipment cage with open racks of football pads and gear that always smelled of stale sweat from the practice or game the day before. Scattered around the walls were posters of famous athletes, dressed in colorful uniforms, each carrying their weapon of choice—a football, a javelin, a baseball bat, dumb-bells, etc.) And then there was Tuomi. Yes, he was part of the room. In actuality, he had a family that he went home to every night…or so the rumor had it. To us, this room was his den, his cave, his domicile, his abode of benevolent torture.

And, there was one more thing about the Phys Ed room. The doors that led us boys outside into the world, and gave access to the football gridiron around the corner, actually opened toward the field hockey pitch for Rosary High School, Detroit's only all girls Catholic High School. We were never sure if this was by design to get the Lutherans among us riled up at the papists across the fence, or to arouse us boys to act more like men when we ran out to the gridiron instead of the sorry wimps we were. We imagined that Rosary High probably had a locker room for girls, no doubt with posters of nuns in long black habits, white wimples, each carrying a heavy duty ruler.

But, enough of that - - we had a boxing match to attend to. Phil picks up the story:

> *Tuomi was all for the match. We had three one-minute rounds. In the first, I'm pretty sure you gave me a blow to the stomach that knocked me down. Then, in the second, I remember giving you a bloody nose with one of my Muhammed Ali jabs (of course we hadn't heard of him yet). Then, in round three, I remember us both being so tired that we couldn't lift our arms for the last 30 seconds. It seems a little sadistic that Tuomi would let us do that... It's not like the class was learning how to box!*[1]

AT THE TIME I was 14, fat and awkward. My hugeness suggested to the coaches that I should go out for junior varsity football. But, they had some doubts when they saw me try to run— when I pounded my legs and tried to sprint they weren't sure if I was moving forward or sideways.

In August 1961, we started two-a-day practices for several weeks before school began in September. I remember the fierce drills and wind sprints. Physical work like this was new to me and it was rough. At lunch I dragged my carcass up to a convenience shop and bought a half-gallon of orange juice. That would be my lunch routine for the next few weeks. But it was what I needed. I started the training period at 250 pounds, and by the end of the season I was down to 174 pounds and could run the 50-yard wind sprints faster than any of the other linemen on the junior varsity squad.

Half way through that improvement period, showing significant weight loss and increase in speed, my coaches wondered if, as a Freshman, I could move up to varsity and help out their otherwise middle-weight line. They decided to try me out.

I remember the day well. I was led over to where the varsity was practicing on a mud lot, the surface of which had been cratered by cleats from football drills and now was dried hard by the sun. It looked as if bricks had been jammed end-wise and randomly into the ground, their sharp corners sticking up, threatening pain to anyone who might fall upon them. I pitied the ball carrier that got tackled on such a

1 Phil Bray. Personal communications, 14 November, 2014.

surface.

They told me I was going to try out for varsity. I told them that might not be a good idea. They smiled…and in a flash of arrogance I imagined standing under the Friday night lights in my new uniform—Wow! Varsity as a freshman. But then, I took a look at the other linemen facing me on the practice field. I might have been taller than most, but I sure wasn't the meanest dude I had ever seen. Fear set in.

The try-out drill was very simple. I was told to get down on all-fours as if I was on the defensive line and then look up at the varsity's 200-pound star fullback squaring off at me fifteen feet away. I was told that the coach would flip the ball to the fullback who would catch it, and then sprint at me, his head down and the ball tucked tight.

Now, the purpose of a defensive lineman, the fundamental idea that is, and the only one that matters is really very simple: Stop the ball carrier, tackle him, make him wish he had never met you on the field of battle. Unlike the hallway drills in Junior High where I got paddled for smashing a guy into the lockers, now, I was given permission to smash this guy, and throw him to the ground. This could be fun. What's more, my opponent was required to run into me—I wouldn't be chasing him, or slamming my bare knuckles into metal lockers when he ducked. The fullback was not allowed to duck. He was mine. Or so I thought…ah, the foolishness and arrogance of youth.

It never occurred to me that the taller I was, the farther I had to fall…hard onto the jagged corners of the baked clay bricks that made up our practice field.

Coach flipped the ball to the fullback.

I jumped out of my stance and lifted a leg to take my first step… but I never had a chance to put my foot down and power-lunge into my adversary.

BAM! CRUNCH! PAIN!

A high speed locomotive hit me at full speed, knocked me flat on my can, left cleat marks on my chest, and dried mud cakes dangling from my face guard.

I looked up at my J.V. assistant coach, Ray Fix, who had come over to monitor the event. Ray was actually a senior whose nickname was "Bulldog" (an all-around good guy) who because of a football injury had to sit out the season, so he was helping coach us young'uns.

Ray yelled at me, "C'mon, Williams. Don't let that runt get the best of you. Let's do it again."

And so we did….again…and again…and again. I could not tackle the guy once. I was mincemeat for fullback cleats, not to say the laughing stock of the varsity backfield that had surrounded us for the "tryout."

Suffice it to say I did not make varsity that year. But I did play both ways, offense and defense, on the J.V. squad.

For the J.V. team I learned to punt. Long legs, I guess. Did pretty good. But I'll never forget the first time in a game I got the snap from center. I fumbled the ball; an opponent picked it up and ran for a touchdown. To this day I was surprised that they ever let me try to punt again. But they did, 15 minutes later. In four years I only fumbled that once. But I never forgot it.

By the time the end of the season came, I had lost 63 pounds, and weighed in consistently throughout the rest of high school and college at 174—not putting on a pound until Pam and I were engaged. But that's another story for later in the book.

The next year, as a high school sophomore, I made the varsity football team. Dennis Tuomi, and his assistant James Bales, were terrific coaches. Tuomi spent his entire career teaching and coaching at Detroit Lutheran High Schools. His election to the Michigan High School Football Hall of Fame was not honorary or accidental. He was a genius. Our squad, coming from a small parochial high school, could regularly beat larger schools. Tuomi and Bales devised a simple but clever all-numeric system for calling plays. With six numbers, like 626-134, everyone knew what to do. The first three digits dictated what the linemen were to do and the second three directed the backfield. It was all there—formations, cross blocking, traps, patterns, fakes, reverses, the works.

During practice, when we screwed up he'd come over to you, grab your face guard and blow R. G. Dunn cigar smoke in your face, and tell you what you did wrong and what you had to do right. The smoke would swirl around in your helmet for a bit. I can still smell it. But he never swore, never demeaned anyone, was never abusive, and smiled after he yelled at you as if to say, "I know you can do better. Now do it."

We knew this guy loved us, and we, in turn, willingly put our bodies and souls on the line for him. I played for him for three years. I wasn't the best player on the field by a long shot, but I earned my varsity letters all three years playing both ways. I have great memories of those days.

FTER MY FRESHMAN, J.V. football season, Coach Tuomi recruited me to wrestle for my winter sport. The theory was that in wrestling you learned to keep low, keep your balance, and get on top of your opponent, which was good for football as well. Seemed simple enough. We conditioned, lifted weights, and drilled our take-downs, escapes, reverses—all that good stuff.

But, my wrestling career, though memorable, was short. Halfway through my freshman season the LHW wrestling team went to River Rouge High School, a ruff and tumble downriver suburb of Detroit. I wrestled the 180-pound weight class, just under the heavyweights. My match was near the end of the meet and I watched my opponent as he warmed up the other wrestlers. He was a big guy, and kept his warm-up jacket on until just before we wrestled. When he took the jacket off, my eyes came out of my sockets. He was built like Adonis, and his chest looked like it was chiseled from marble. He had massive arms, a thick neck and bulging thighs. Just before we were called to the center of the ring to butt hands and begin, I turned to Coach Tuomi, with a look on my face that said, "Who's this?" Tuomi shrugged, "Oh, I didn't tell you? He's last year's state champ. Go easy on him." Tuomi backed away from the mat and let a smile creep across his face...terror crept across mine.

The referee called me to the center, I squared off with Champ, and the whistle blew. Champ and I grabbed each other's forearms, our heads side-by-side. Actually, that's not exactly true. My right hand tried to grab Champ's bicep, but I couldn't get a grip. His arm was so massive my hand was flat against its muscular bulk as if against a solid brick wall.

Champ pulled me in and dropped to his knees. Suddenly, I realized I had him in a perfect position to pancake his upper body and put his back on the mat. My arms were under his armpits, my feet were firmly planted and spread wide for support, and all I had to do was rotate- -he'd fall on his back, I'd drop on top of him, and... *Voila! I'd pin him.*

Wow, this is great, I thought. I'm on top, let's do it.

I started to rotate to the right. Nothing happened. *C'mon, let's go!* said my Guardian Angel, who, in such situations, was normally on vacation. I tried to rotate the other way. I'll pancake him to the left, I thought. Finally, something moved. He was turning. Amazing, I'm doing it. I couldn't believe my luck. This guy was going down.

But then I realized that although he was turning, it wasn't because of anything I was doing. It was because he was getting up off his feet.

What's going on? Your feet were planted wide, weren't they? I looked down. Indeed, my feet were wide, but now they were two-feet above the mat. Champ was hugging my legs and lifting my entire body straight up into the air. In less than a second he was standing straight up, and holding me above his head.

Did I tell you that in the months leading up to this match my Mom had taken me to the orthodontist to get an estimate of how much it would cost to fix my exceedingly protruding buckteeth? I sucked my thumb a lot as a kid, I guess. My two front teeth were sticking out at about 35 degrees to the vertical. When I smiled it looked hideous, like Bugs Bunny grinning at a juicy carrot. The estimate came back at $880. Now, again, recall, this is 1962. My folks did not have anywhere close to $880, which was like two months wages for my dad. So, nothing was planned other than having an airbrush artist, who normally worked on car hoods and drag-race spoilers, doctor my school picture. They figured that would only cost about $50. Expensive enough but they could afford that.

Now, before I continue with our hero (that's me up in the air), the other thing you need to know is that the rules of Michigan high school wrestling said that a competitor could only pick up and throw or drop his opponent to the ground if the thrower had his knees on the mat before the throwee (that's me) hit the floor. Champ clearly was familiar with this rule.

Before I knew it, I was turned upside down and thrown a good 10-feet toward the edge of the mat, face first. Meanwhile, while my body headed back to Earth from its sub-orbital arch, Champ calmly kneeled on the mat and watched me descend. Smart fellow, I thought. This is how he won at state, no doubt. Spent a lot of time on his knees? Pray much? I don't know about him, but I was…praying.

The first thing that hit, about 3-feet off the mat onto the hard gymnasium polished oak floor, was my two buck teeth. I heard…no, let's put it this way…I felt a loud C R U N C H as my teeth were rammed back into my gums. The rest of my 174 pounds came tumbling after me in a heap of arms, legs, and torso. For a moment, I just laid there afraid to move. Then, after a bit I felt something warm and sweet running into my mouth. I glanced over from whence I came and saw the floor covered with blood. Was that mine? Geez! What happened?

The next thing I knew the referee was looking in my mouth with our trainer, as Coach Tuomi helped me to my feet and stuck a bath towel into my mouth to stem the loss of blood. I looked over at Champ.

He was getting up off his knees as the referee walked over and held his hand in the air. Win by default.

I was rushed into a training room where I looked into a floor length mirror. The towel I was holding to my face was slowly turning red, but what shocked me more was the exposed parts of my body—my arms, legs, neck and face were now sporting an intense and dense, spotted red rash. My body was shocked so severely that my skin instantly erupted into a massive heat rash. An hour later, after a cold shower, the only thing still red was the towel jammed in my mouth.

Mom never came to any of my football games because they were too "pugilistic." But I never got injured at football, so I got to keep playing. Wrestling was something different. She refused to let me wrestle, even if my buck teeth were no longer a trip point and the incident had saved her and dad a small fortune. Dad did come to an occasional game, and was supportive in an agreeable way.

The good thing was that my teeth were shoved into place, and anonymous students stopped sticking carrots into my locker vent. One of my two front teeth regrew its roots and to this day is good, and the one tooth that died and turned black, was pulled out, and I was given a temporary silver retainer with a false tooth to fill the gap. It only cost my folks $88. Savings: $792. The pain? Priceless.

After that, the only thing to contend with were the weird stares from classmates as I sat in class and practiced retainer gymnastics—I had developed a nervous habit of using my tongue to flip my retainer over-and-over creating a clanging as it hit my real teeth. It no doubt sounded like a cyborg with a few nuts loose.

But even this was good, from my mother's perspective at least. It would be a long time before a girl would get close enough to the rotating metal in my mouth to kiss me.

AND JUST WHAT has all of this to do with my journey of faith? Are you kidding? Football and wrestling were more demanding than any religious experience I had known up to this point in life. Having a preacher yell at me was nothing compared to Tuomi grabbing my helmet's face guard and blowing smoke in my eyes— talk about a mystical experience. Football and wrestling with Dennis Tuomi required a religious dedication and ethic I never knew I had.

Ironically, there were some similarities between Mom and Coach Tuomi, other than body shape. Both were very demanding. Both followed rules religiously. And, from both I was the recipient of a fair amount of pain. But the differences were great. My mother's motivation seemed to be from the perspective of salvation through obedience to the law for the law's sake, but Tuomi was pure grace. When I screwed up he didn't discipline me out of spite, repression or to break my spirit. Tuomi, who always had a twinkle in his eyes, always had a rational reason for what he told me to do, for each wind sprint, for each rule, for each drill. Nothing was arbitrary. Nothing was legalistic. If a kid didn't understand why he had to do something he explained why in terms that made sense. And so the pain and suffering was worth it. And that's what I came to believe about Christianity. Correction, pain, suffering, self-discipline and hard work could make sense and strengthen your faith, not just in God, but also in those authorities over you. I was making progress toward a reasonable faith.

> **Having a preacher yell at me was nothing compared to Tuomi grabbing my helmet's face guard and blowing smoke in my eyes—talk about a mystical experience.**

But my parents weren't too sure. For one thing, they knew the Lutherans weren't big on getting saved and having altar calls. So I was always being pressured to attend revival services at our local Free Methodist Church or attend youth evangelistic rallies. There really was no escape, even when girls were somehow involved.

22
Is This Seat Saved?

O NE SATURDAY EVENING in 1962, during early high school, in the dregs of a Michigan winter, I attended a Youth For Christ rally at Masonic Theater in Detroit. These were large exciting affairs with the 4,000-seat auditorium filled with teens from all over southeast Michigan. The popular rallies featured special Gospel music groups, skits, comedy, singing, a sermon and an opportunity to meet a lot of kids your age from similar backgrounds. This particular evening I had come with a carload of other friends, but we were late and the place was full so we had to split up to find seats.

Suddenly, I saw a free seat on an aisle. I loved aisle seats because I was tall and had long legs. Actually, I still prefer aisle seats because my legs are still long. This particular seat had an added attraction sitting next to it. I leaned over and spoke to the fetching brunette, "Excuse me. Is this seat saved?"

She studied me curiously for a moment, no doubt evaluating whether or not I had just depleted my quiver of pickup lines, or if I was merely a nominal dweeb from the burbs. Finally, under the misguided perception that I was entirely harmless, she said, "No, but it's under conviction."

I noticed she was firmly holding the hand of the "dweeb" on the other side of her, but I took the seat nonetheless.

I contemplated her punch line. "Under conviction," pretty well summed-up my perception of Evangelicalism at the time. Even at the very fun YFC rallies, the songs, the teachings, the skits, and, of course, the sermons were all about being under conviction and getting saved. That was about it. Yes, there was chatter about sports, and dates with hot brunettes (at least the ones that weren't already holding someone else's hand), but generally Evangelicalism existed for the purpose of saving dweebs like me...so I could save other dweebs like you. It was very utilitarian.

There had to be more, I thought, as the rally song leader introduced the first song and the dweeb two seats over leaned into the brunette and put one on her cheek.

A S A CHILD, and then as a teen, my family went to church a lot. We attended church Sunday morning, Sunday evening, Wednesday evening, revival meetings, youth group meetings, camp meetings, tent revivals, and missionary convocations. In 90% of these meetings the goal was to save "the lost"--who just by accident, or "divine providence," happened to be present.

Here's how it happened, in seven steps.

Step 1

Pastor Randy Besiege had just finished an emotionally charged sermon on 1 Peter 5:7: *Casting all your care upon him; for he careth for you.* He had poured out his heart, begging us to humbly accept the love of Christ who cared deeply for us.

To help us understand, Pastor Randy spent time explaining the meaning of each word in the passage. He defined *casting* as what fishermen do when they throw nets into the sea—they have faith that fish will be caught, although they can't see the fish, and so we have to accept Christ's promise of salvation although it's not something we can see ahead of time. He talked about how *CARE* boxes are shipped to people in poor countries and are received with great joy, although the recipients know not what's in the box beforehand. But their joy is the result of faith in Christ's promises, believing that what's inside will save them from starvation and death. Pastor Randy talked about what it meant to be *upon* something—to actively pursue, Him—the one and only Son of God who loves us and cares—enough to die on a cross for us.

Why it would take a 50 minute sermon to communicate such a simple premise I could never figure out, except that the repetition of ideas did allow some of us to catch up on our sleep. Actively pursuing sleep during a sermon is a well-established tradition within Evangelicalism. Indeed, I have known several men who bragged for decades about how good the sermon was because they can sleep through it. This is no direct criticism of Evangelicalism, except that the preaching must be very ineffective or off target to cause such a thing to become an on-going joke within a large body of devout Christian people. And, yes, I have slept through more than one sermon.

Step 2

The sermon finished, Pastor Randy Solemn then would ask us to stand as the song leader led us in a slow, sad song about accepting Jesus into our sinful lives. Singing *Where He Leads Me I Will Follow* this particular night took 15-20 minutes. The song didn't take that long to sing. But the preaching between the verses did, thus justifying Pastor Randy's sanctimony and serving up a necessary wallop of salvation grace. After about 10-minutes I got weak in the knees and sat down. But Mom grabbed my ear and yanked me back up. "Don't be so disrespectful," she whispered in my ear. "This is Jesus we're singing about and your soul Pastor Randy is trying to save." She was right about one thing—I had lost respect for the beleaguered effort.

Step 3

During the break between verses 4 and 5, Pastor Randy Grave leaned into the microphone, lowered his voice and furrowed his brow: "Please, folks, in the quiet of yer own heart, ask Jesus to forgive ya for yer sins, right here, right now. Get rid of 'dem sins, folks, eternity is a'waiting."

He said this, I figured, to remind us of the point behind 1 Peter 5:7, which didn't seem at all to be about sin. I took a quick glance into my own heart. It wasn't that I couldn't think of a recent sin I had committed. That was easy. But, now I was worried and paranoia set in. Did I sleep through the part of his sermon about sin? What sin was he talking about? Had I just been sleeping through the part about sin? Had he seen me sleeping? Is he looking at me, now? If I slept through the wrong part of the sermon should I feel guilty? Naw, 'cause it all depended if I slept through what I already knew or if I slept through something I should know but didn't. But if you slept through it, how would you know it?

I was rattled…but not guilty. No, not me.

Step 4

As we finished yet another verse of what was feeling more like a funeral dirge, my reverie was broken when Pastor Insistence backed away from the microphone, raised his hand, and then his voice. "Now with e'ery head bowed and e'ery eye closed…which ones of ya just asked Jesus ta forgive you? Just raise yer hand so God can see it? I promise I won't embarrass ya by asking ya to slip out of yer pew and come forward. Everyone keep yer head bowed, now. If ya feel God tugging on yer heart, just lift a hand to Jesus."

Ah! I knew where this was going. I kept both hands in my pants pockets and leaned my wrists against the pew in front of me to keep them there. There was more to come and I had to stand strong. I put my full weight into the heavy oak furniture. Thank goodness the pews were screwed to the floor.

Step 5

Pastor Randy Serious now escalated the interrogation as he looked over his congregation. "Yes, I see that hand there in the back corner, in the crumpled trench coat. I see yer brother. Ya can put yer hand down, now. God forgives yer sins. Weren't that easy? Now the organ is goin' to keep playing, okay, and with all heads still bowed, and no one lookin' around, 'cause this is just between ya'll and God. Listen to the Holy Spirit speaking to yer heart. Yes, sister up here in the front row with the gardenias in yer hat, them is pretty, I see that hand. You can put it down, now. Jesus saves ya. I'm so glad to know that the Spirit of God is moving upon us tonight. No one looking around now…"

I was always tempted to look around, and often sneaked a glance; but I never saw a hand raised. But who's objecting? Me? —a rebellious kid sandwiched between parents with his arms burrowed so deep in his pants that his knocking knees are being dampened by perspiring palms?

The invitation went on for at least two more verses: *I can hear my Savior calling…Where he leads me I will follow…I'll go with him, with him all the way…through the waters…through the garden…to dark Calv'ry…to the judgment…*that we knew was coming, even tonight. But, my hands, by now, were making fists in my pocket. No way they were coming out.

Step 6

I wasn't the only one frustrated. There was Pastor Randy Renege who, trembling, said, "Folks. Ya could be driving home tonight and get in an accident, and meet yer maker. There, outside the pearly gates Saint Peter's going to ask ya for yer pass to get into heaven."

This woke me up a bit. Evangelicals didn't have saints. Who was this Saint Peter dude? Then, I recalled that in our KJV Bibles we had the Gospel according to Saint Matthew, Saint Mark, Saint Luke, and Saint John. I thought that was strange for all the angst my Mom threw at the Catholics for praying to their saints, which she said she didn't believe in. Hmmm!? But no time to dwell on that now, my soul's on the brink of hell.

Pastor Randy Persistence pressed, "Please don't leave tonight without making sure yer sins is forgiven. Ya'll that raised your hands, now listen to me, ya'll come down to the altar and let us pray with ya?"

I thought about the poor dude in the crumbled trench coat and the lady with the gardenia hat. I didn't want to be them. For, if by now I had been foolish enough to have raised my hand and didn't move down the aisle with all speed…like the crumbled trench coat evidently did not…I was in for a personal invite.

Step 7

Sure enough, Pastor Randy Warrior left the pulpit and came down the aisle and tried to usher Trenchy out of his pew with a compassionate arm, even as the song leader started verse thirteen. *He will give me grace and glory…and go with me, with me all the way.*

Now, dear reader, you may think I exaggerate. But…not really.

TWENTY YEARS LATER Pam and I were married and our third child was in the oven. We were living in a suburb of Detroit. It was Sunday evening and our older girls were feeling a bit under the weather so we didn't go to church that night…at least not as a family. I stayed home with the girls, and Pam decided, with her big belly, to take a stroll to the end of the block where there was a quaint little church with a long name of some reckoning that we had never attended.

She sat through the sermon and then the altar call. When it got a little long with the singing and the invitation, and she being pregnant, she sat down to rest. She has always been a prayerful woman and on this night, as she sat, she bowed her in head in prayer, seated as everyone else was standing. She must have been a pitiful sight.

Well, she must not have been counting because before she knew it the preacher had arrived at Step 7. His job was on the line because no one had yet come forward. Scanning the audience, he arrived at several conclusions. 1. The other thirty folks in the room were all saved by his recognizance. 2. There was only one person he didn't know—that woman there, seated with her head bowed. 3. The woman was clearly an unwed mother that had just wandered in off the streets looking for recompense and salvation. 4. Time to act.

> **Evangelicalism existed for the purpose of saving dweebs like me...so I could save other dweebs like you. It was very utilitarian.**

To him, Pam was sent there by the Holy Spirit, and there was no way he was going to close the service without ushering this soul into heaven. Next thing Pam knew the preacher had come down out of the pulpit, strode up to her, and laid hands on her head, praying for her deliverance.

When that didn't work he was tugging on her arm to get her out of the pew and come forward. Finally he leaned over and politely addressed the wayward unwed mother: "Sister," he said, "I see you seated there, in that seat that otherwise would have been vacant tonight. You're not here by chance. God has brought you here, to us. And, I know you're under conviction."

Pam looked up at him and smiled.

He leaned a bit closer to hear her confession.

But all she said was, "I'm not sure about the seat. But me? I'm saved."

It was all in a night's work for him, and it was no surprise to us.

I KNOW I'VE HAD a little fun with this chapter recounting one of the many, many times I sat through such a service. I know the pastors and others associated with these services meant well. They were doing their best to follow the leading of God in their lives and pass on God's saving grace to those in their charge.

But it really never made a great deal of sense to me...this continual, obsessive insistence with preaching salvation messages every which way to a group of people that had (really) all been saved.

Unless.

Unless every sin ever committed automatically knocked you out of the running for heaven and you had to *keep being saved.*

Later in frequenting Pentecostal services we'd see something similar, but then the emphasis was on being "refilled" with the Holy Spirit, with an ongoing utilitarian emphasis that we "Keep being filled. Keep being refilled."

After a few dozen such services I had my fill. My brain, my soul, my essence wanted to know God more deeply, more broadly. Somewhere in my heart I knew there was more to offer the God that created the universe and kept it spinning than just my soul. But it would be decades before I figured out what it was.

In the meantime, I found some spiritual repose in music.

23
Three Bassoons

L ET ME JUMP back in time for a bit and tell you about the three bassoons that kept me company from junior high through college.
When I was ten-years old, in 1957, I learned to sit still...for almost two-hours while Valter Poole sweated through his formal white dinner jacket. His white hair flopped about in sync with jerks of his head as if he were trying to avoid poking his eyes out with his wildly waving baton. That's the first memory I have of my exposure to classical music...it was ironically visual.

Mother had started to take Sis and me to the Detroit Symphony Orchestra's Children's Concerts held one Saturday morning each month during the winter at Ford Auditorium, which sat on the banks of the Detroit River. Valter Poole, the associated conductor of the Detroit Symphony Orchestra, in his white jacket and floppy white locks, was the Santa Claus-like conductor.

Sometimes the music put me to sleep, and often it was hard sitting still in an oversized, flip-up auditorium chair. As a tyke I could easily let my butt slide into the rear crack, have the seat fold up and let my legs jerk in the air as if someone had scored a touchdown—which is in fact what my butt was doing at the moment. More than once at intermission, after looking about to see where I had sneaked off to, Mom would find me half-eaten by the seat—crushed like an empty popcorn box—whereupon she'd pull me out onto dry land like a whale regurgitating Jonah. Only if they had served popcorn at Detroit Symphony concerts would it have been worth it.

In spite of my strangely creased dress pants, however, I felt important, just being at Ford Auditorium and listening to highbrow music that the fatherly Poole tried to make accessible to us.

Indeed, it was Poole's directing that mostly kept my attention. I wondered who laundered those white jackets after every concert, so laden with perspiration as they were. Thinking back, it probably was Poole's passion that actually intrigued me. Anyone that put such effort into something…well, it had to be good. Right?

At home I was addicted to an LP vinyl record that Mom would put on the Hi-Fi occasionally. It was called *Tubby the Tuba*—a musical story with narration and sound effects created by the instruments. It is a fun introduction for kids to classical music and the sound (and noises) the various instruments make.

TUBBY WAS THE story of a lonely orchestra tuba who never got to play a melody like the other instruments. He just played "OOMPH-PA, OOMPH-PA" all the time…unless, of course it was a waltz and then he got to change it up: OOMPH-PA-PA, OOMPH-PA-PA. Regardless, it was not a particularly creative existence.

One day, Tubby, quite by accident, tried to dance with the "pretty little tune" the other instruments were playing. At first, the Violins laughed with tremolo at his impulsiveness, the French Horns blew a snickering blast at his compulsiveness, and the whole orchestra broke out in trills of laugher at his naiveté. When rehearsal was over Tubby went to the river to sadly contemplate his sad "Oomph Pa" plight.

Until, that is, a friendly, precocious Frog who could sing, hopped up on a log and greeted Tubby with a melodious line or two of his "BARR-RUP, BARR-RUP, LOVELY EVENING, BARR-UP" song. After a slight misunderstanding, Mr. Frog explains that he understands Tubby's situation because no one listens to his barr-up either, although he sings it every night along the riverbank.

"Can you sing?" asks Tubby?

Whereupon the frog sings a lovely melody, figured by a duet between a bass clarinet and a bassoon.

"Oh, that's lovely," says Tubby.

The frog tells Tubby to try it. Tubby, excitedly does, and reprises the melody, intoned on the record by a real tuba, of course.

The frog compliments him, "You're a very fine tuba, do you know it, Tubby?" and goes on to suggest that Tubby try the melody with his orchestra some time.

Tubby says he will. He thanks the frog and runs off. Even though tubas don't have legs this never bothered me, as the bouncy notes of a tuba that played in the background pictured the scene perfectly for me.

At the next rehearsal, a new conductor, the great Seniore Pizzicotto, shows up, which creates a scurried excitement among the instruments. When Pizzicotto gives a downbeat, Tubby, with the aid of his newly acquired impulsiveness, plays his melody alone for all to hear.

The violins get angry and claim that Tubby will disgrace them. The trombones stick out their tongues with a menacing glissando, and the trumpets sneer like irritated horses.

But Seniore Pizzicotto says, "Tubby, I've never heard a tuba play a melody before. Let's hear the rest of it."

And so, Tubby, with great glee begins to play. The violins suddenly experience a "Come to Jesus" moment and call Tubby's melody "perfectly wonderful" and ask permission to play the song, too. After a few bars the violins are joined by a xylophone, the trombones, a celesta, a piccolo, and finally the rest of the orchestra joins in for a rousing coda.

Back at the river, Tubby is again joined by Mr. Frog who hops onto the log, "Well, we've done it, haven't we, Tubby? We have our points, too."

To which Tubby replies, "Oh, how happy I am."

N ATASHA KERN, A prolific book agent for women's fiction who has become an acquaintance, claims that a child's favorite storybook mystically foreshadows the person's natural personality styles, emotional disposition and motivational passions. Later in life the person may notice that their careers are somehow connected to the story they loved as kids.

I had two such stories. One was *Tubby the Tuba*, and the other was *The Little Engine that Could*. The first was about impetuously following your passion and the second was about a compulsive perseverance in the pursuit of your passion.

I think Natasha's insight about childhood stories is right. In several ways, my life has played out like Tubby's and the Little Engine. I would discover a "melody" and play it, but the rest of the "orchestra" would be embarrassed and refuse to play along. This is especially true in my journey of faith. I could only hope, through the exercise of perseverance, that others would eventually find my impetuous song melodious.

Passion and perseverance—that's what Valter Poole communicated to me. He gave fine art credibility, and that included the support mechanisms that I would professionally identify with more than the performers. For instance, although I was captivated by the musical talent of the people that performed, I recognized that their performance was made accessible and professional by hosts of others behind the scenes, from the ushers, to the music librarians, and to the stage manager who directed the arrangement of chairs and music stands. But I did admire the musicians and wondered if someday I might play an instrument half as well as they.

The Children's Concerts were only the tip of the iceberg in terms of my exposure to music. While there were always opportunities at church to hear keyboard and vocal soloists, one of the most exciting opportunities was our family's attendance at Detroit Concert Band Concerts under the direction of Leonard B. Smith, at the Fleming Band Shell on Belle Isle (the island park in the middle of the Detroit River). These were held at night.

> **I could only hope, through the exercise of perseverance, that others would eventually find my impetuous song melodious.**

We sat on long, green-slatted park benches, under the stars. Between 1960 and 1964, during these summer concerts, we could watch the U.S. Echo satellite passing overhead. Later, in high school, I managed to stop rotating my retainer long enough to get a date and take an unlucky lady on an dauntless canoe ride through the interior canals of Belle Isle to the Band Shell for a concert.

BY THE SUMMER of 1958, as an 11-year old, our family would frequent the Interlochen State Park of Michigan and attend concerts across State Route 137 at the 1200 acre National Music Camp. There, during eight weeks of the summer, over 1,000 young people (grades 3-12) from around the world converge to take music, dance and singing lessons and present nightly concerts outside under the stars, nestled between the pines and oaks of Northern Michigan. All the students wore sky blue shirts, red sweaters, and navy blue corduroy pants, or knickers for the girls with knee socks. The Northern Michigan outdoors was beautiful, and the talented teens only slightly older than me, were inspiring, especially if you spied them practicing their instruments in the woods. I especially liked the Gilbert and Sullivan musicals and the magic of the costumes, the lights, the dance, and the mystical music coming out of the orchestra pit. During intermission I would run up to the front and gaze into the pit orchestra and tried to identify all the instruments. The atmosphere and music was magical, and I longed to be a camper.

This conspired to set in my heart the bold goal that when I got older, I would attend the 8-week long National Music Camp. At the time I didn't realize that the goal might have had an ulterior motive—I would not have to contend with my Mom for an entire summer.

To attend Interlochen there were two requirements. One, you had to have real talent; and two, you had to be real rich. If I thought about either of those I got real depressed.

But, hey! I knew something about music. It may not have been "talent" but I knew the difference between a clarinet and a bassoon, although I had to be honest—I didn't know if a piano was a percussion instrument or a string.

Nonetheless, as I lay on my cot at night in our tent at the state park, and listened to the wind whistling through the pines, I began to strategize.

WHEN I WAS five, Mom started me on Kelly Kirby piano lessons. I did that for three years and hated every moment, except when someone that could play actually played the piece I couldn't...and then I was fascinated. At the heart of my problem was a very simple premise—although I had a tendency toward perseverance—I had no actual talent.

At eight, I decided that I needed more exercise. The fingers weren't enough. We frequently drove past a place called Modern Accordion Studios. I convinced Mom I was going to play accordion. But after a couple years I was just as bad as I was on the piano. Well, sort of. Lifting and squeezing a 20-pound instrument at least a third my size, kept me half-awake, and the rest of the time I was alert for fear of coming to the end of a phrase and pinching my nose in the bellows.

But, now, in sixth grade and still thinking about Interlochen, I noticed another problem—there were no accordions at Interlochen. My mother agreed. We had never heard a Mozart Concerto for Orchestra and squeeze-box.

AS FATE, LUCK, or providence would have it, in the fall of 1959 I started school at Haston Junior High. It would not be a good run as I relate elsewhere. But there was one bright spot: Band... and our director and instrumental instructor Stanley Roose, a gem of a man.

When my parents presented the Interlochen-Accordion dilemma to Mr. Roose, and that I was a miserable failure on the piano, he asked me if I had any interest in playing bassoon.

I perked right up. Bassoon! I knew what a bassoon was. I said, "Do you mean that solo instrument in The Sorcerer's Apprentice?"

"Actually," he said, "there is no solo bassoon in the Sorcerer's Apprentice. But there is a bassoon quartet made up of three bassoons and a contra-bassoon."

"Really?! Could I learn to play that?"

"Certainly!" he said without hesitation. "At least one of the parts at a time."

I tried to suppress the adrenalin rush that had kidnapped my heart and was jamming it up my throat.

I knew something about Paul Dukas's "The Sorcerer's Apprentice"[1] because it was the one orchestra piece at the DSO Children's Concerts during which I had not fallen asleep. In fact, no one sleeps through The Sorcerer's Apprentice unless they're already dead. It is also the music behind the famous Walt Disney *Fantasia* sequence where Mickey Mouse, playing the role of a wizard apprentice, battles a castle full of brooms that fetch buckets of water and threaten to flood the kingdom. The animation sequence and the music were both inspired by a Goethe poem written in 1797 by the same name.

"Why, bassoon?" my mother said.

Mr. Roose explained that Interlochen gives work scholarships out every summer to students who play rare instruments. He told us they almost never have enough bassoons, and I'd only have to be modestly good to get a scholarship and thus attend camp.

But the bassoon was hard to learn, and they were very expensive. Roose said, "Why not start him on clarinet, if he does well with that, then move him to bass clarinet, and if he progresses and demonstrates the discipline, then let's find him a bassoon."

So, that's what I did. I learned the basics on clarinet, and graduated to bass clarinet that first semester. In the second semester of my 7th grade, Aunt Hopie donated a new German-made Josef Püchner to the school (my first bassoon), and on Saturdays I started taking lessons from Lyle Lindsay, a bassoonist for the Detroit Symphony. Wow! This was cool!

The horn was difficult to learn, but I mastered the basics and by the end of 7th grade I could play most of the band music Stanley Roose put

---

1 The refrain to Johann Wolfgang von Goethe's poem, "The Sorcerer's Apprentice" goes like this: *Flow, flow onward/Stretches many/Spare not any/Water rushing,/Ever streaming fully downward/Toward the pool in current gushing.*

on our music stands.

But there was a slight problem. When conducting the band in rehearsals, Roose noticed that I was seriously distracted—I was always staring across the band at the drumline and rarely at him. He would say, "Stanley, look at me, not the percussion section." I had a crush on Janie, a pretty brunette who played drums. When I started on the bassoon Roose came up with the ingenious idea of moving my seat so the percussionists were behind me.

But I fooled him. In 8th grade I tried out to be student conductor and won the post. Now, when I got to conduct, I could stand on the podium and look right at Janie to give the downbeat. She'd smile at me, beat her drum and my heart would beat in rhythm. But, alas, the thing with girls would take another year to kick in. I don't think I ever had the nerve to talk to Janie, even once. At the end of the year in Honor Assembly I was given a certificate for perfect attendance. Didn't want to miss band, you know.

Roose had the last laugh, however. At the end of the 8th grade there was a Spring Band and Choir concert. As Student Conductor I got to conduct one number. Unfortunately I did not get to choose the music, Roose did. The number was called "Musicians Strike" by Philipp Fahrach and M.C. Meyrelles. It's a straight ahead military styled march but with a unique distinction. Half way through the piece band members begin to walk off the stage with their instruments, one-by-one, until it's just the conductor and a few drummers (cool), at which point the conductor cuts them off and walks off the stage himself.

Alas, that was the cue for Intermission.

ELSEWHERE IN THIS tome I relate stories about my transitioning from public Junior High in Dearborn Heights, to Parochial Lutheran High School West in Detroit. But here I'll continue on my bassoon adventure.

In her great generosity, in 1961, Aunt Hopie purchased yet another bassoon (my second bassoon) for Lutheran High West so I could play in the band and continue my musical education outside of school. Thus, I continued my instrumental lessons with Lyle Lindsay and became good enough in a couple years to audition for and play in the Dearborn Symphony Community Orchestra under the direction of Nathan Gordon, who was also the principal violist for Detroit Symphony. The highlight of playing with the Dearborn Symphony was sitting next to famed bassoonist Charlie Sirard for a few rehearsals and the concerts.

In their great kindness to me, and to save the orchestra's reputation, the Dearborn Symphony hired Mr. Sirard to play the principal bassoon parts that I could not touch. When we came to those parts I was told to fake it and watch his fingers. That I could do.

Finally, as a high school junior, it was time for me to send in an audition tape to Interlochen to see if I could secure one of the bassoon slots for the summer of 1964's national eight-week program. It was now or never. Lyle Lindsay convinced me to play the 2nd Movement (Andante ma Adagio) of Mozart's famous B-flat Major, KV 191 concerto for bassoon and orchestra. He didn't need to convince me not to stray into the Allegro or Rondo passages, which were from another dimension that I could not fathom.

The audition consisted of a tape recording that I needed to make with piano accompaniment. I got the piano music and gave it to my Mom, but one look at the score and she reminded me that unless the music was in a church hymnal she couldn't help. Mr. Lindsey gave me the name and phone number of a pianist in my neighborhood that might be willing to accompany me and make a recording at the same time. So, after preparing as best I could, I made the call and set up an appointment at a home not too far from my house.

I was expecting maybe a matronly woman with long gnarly piano fingers worn to the bone. But instead, when the door opened, I was greeted by the beautiful Karen Krisel, a high school girl my own age who attended Detroit's Cass Technical High School, the magnet arts school for the gifted. Karen was pleasant as she ushered me to her basement where she had what looked like a grand piano and small recoding studio. I was impressed. I set up my instrument, selected my best reed, and with her at the piano we ran through the music a few times. I was having a little trouble in one particular spot and she tried to be patient with me.

Finally, frustrated with my mediocre "talent," she got up from the piano, went into the other room, and came back with *her bassoon.* Let me repeat that for emphasis: she came back in the room *with her bassoon.* She sat down next to me, pointed out some things in the music, and then proceeded to play the passage flawlessly. Her tone and technique were perfect to my hearing. Then, she showed me how to play the passage with different fingering and demonstrated that as well.

Intimidation does not even come close to explaining the mortification I felt. I was truly awestruck, and it took a while before I could breathe again. I wondered why, on God's green earth, I had any com-punction to think I might get into Interlochen, when this stranger I just met—my piano accompanist—could play the bassoon so much better than me, and she wasn't even bothering to apply to the famed camp.

As I was writing this chapter I was able to track Karen down through the Internet and a short time ago enjoyed one of those conversations by phone from the past. It turns out that as a child prodigy she had a deep fascination with all the instruments of the orchestra, and determined to learn to play as many as she could.

Intimidation does not even come close to explaining the mortification I felt. I was truly awestruck, and it took a while before I could breathe again.

Indeed, Interlochen did offer Karen a scholarship to camp that next summer. But she didn't go. Here's what I imagined happened: Interlochen received my audition tape recording with Karen on piano, and correctly identified the bassoon player as mediocre, and the piano player as exceptionally talented. So, they reached out to the piano accompanist and offered her a scholarship on bassoon. That's how good she was.

Karen turned down the Interlochen scholarship because she had other plans. She was already playing her bassoon professionally in the Dearborn Parks and Recreational band and being paid a handsome sum each week of the summer. So, why go to camp and dream of being a professional, when you can jump straight to the gig?

I suspect, therefore, that Interlochen, having received Karen's rejection, caved and offered me the work scholarship for the 1964 camp season. Thank you, Karen!

In actuality, the scholarship Interlochen offered her was to come and play harp. Harp!? Her parents, recognizing her passion, perseverance and talent, and checking the balance at their bank, had bought Karen a harp a few years earlier to keep her bassoon, piano, and warehouse of other instruments, company.

Karen's talent reminds me of the high school phenom basketball coach Perry Watson from Detroit's inner-city Southwestern High School, who went on to coach at the University of Detroit. Watson's high school teams were so successful that nearly every year his whole team received full-ride basketball scholarships to college…including the water boys and the student managers! Well, that was Karen Krisel, I suspect, in the world of music.

I HAD A GREAT time at camp, with no tension from challengers below me, since I sat last chair the whole summer. And, to top it off, there was a consolation prize. I was the poster boy for the next summer's marketing campaign (see on-line gallery). Hey, maybe I couldn't play very well, but look at that embouchure.

What really shocked my mother, was the Camper Progress Report that was mailed to my parents a month or so after the eight-week camp was over. Unlike anything I had ever received, especially in contrast to my being suspended multiple times from junior high, my parents received this (underlining is in the original):

> *Camp Citizenship:* <u>EXCELLENT. Stan is an excellent camper.</u> *He is an active and socially responsible young man. For this reason he is discharging his duties as cabin social chairman very well. Stan's positive attitudes and good nature in regard to his relations with other campers make him an asset to the cabin. He is also responsibly discharging his cabin clean-up and cabin competition responsibilities well. Stan seems to find his time at Interlochen well occupied and will have many positive learning experiences to grow on. (Signed: Douglas Meyer, Counselor.)*

Joking aside, I need to give my German mother a lot of credit for this report, although at first she didn't believe it and thought I had somehow bribed the counselor. Mom so instilled discipline, rigor, and a work-ethic in me, that Interlochen, which did have plenty of rules and requirements, was a walk in the park. It also helped that I was "dating" a pretty flute player and if I wanted to see her in the evenings after classes, I had to be on my best behavior and avoid being grounded to my cabin.

But, Miss O, aside, I loved the music, the expertise of the conductors and instructors, meeting people like American composer Alan Hovhaness, who directed our conducting class one time, and Van Cliburn, who I met in a rustic wash room as we stood next to each other looking at the wall. There were also fellow camp-mates and acquaintances like Ani Kavafian, who became a world renowned violin soloist; I played in the accompanying Dearborn Symphony Orchestra for one of her early concerto performances, and cheered her on during her concerto debut with the Interlochen World Youth Symphony Orchestra (WYSO) in 1964. As I write this I'm watching YouTube of Ani playing a July 29, 2014 concerto with the same Interlochen WYSO 50 years later. Amazing talent!

AND THEN THERE was the amazing Charles (Chuck) Stokes, my bunkmate in Cabin 21. Chuck was from Coldwater, Michigan. He played trombone. Our cabin was near Duck Lake and one day as we left the cabin to walk the quarter-mile to a rehearsal, a speedboat cranked up and cruised across the lake at full speed. Chuck stopped and stared at the boat.

"What's wrong?" I asked.

"Dunno. But he's running that engine pretty fast. I've listened to him before, and usually it's pitched around an E-flat, but it's up around an F-sharp today. Must be in a hurry."

"Yeah, right," I said.

But Chuck just shrugged and started walking again.

After watching the boat zoom toward the other side of the lake, and listening more carefully to the sound of the motor, I caught up with him. "Can you tell what note that engine was making?"

"Yeah. And, the harmonics."

I was incredulous. But this was Interlochen.

A few days later I cajoled Chuck into an organ rehearsal cabin near ours to test his claim. There a two-manual Hammond B-3 was available in a large room. Chuck explained the stops and how to control fundamental and harmonic tones. He then stepped away and put his back to the organ. I pushed in all the drawbars except the fundamental, (to kill the harmonics), and played a B-flat.

"B-flat," he said. "But you can play more than one note at a time."

So, I played a C-chord in the second octave above middle-C.

"Stan, come on. I play trombone." He glanced back at me and smiled, "Use all ten fingers and don't play the only chord you know."

Okay, wise guy. I let him have it, I pulled out a little of the 12th (2 2/3') and 15th (2') drawbars for the lower manual, then randomly laid my ten fingers on the keyboard.

As soon as I did it, Chuck started in, "From the low octave up, "D, G-flat, B, D-flat, F, B-flat, D, F, and A-flat, and ah...D-flat, and you've got a little of the 12th and the 15th harmonics added."

"Why is everything flatted?" I asked. "Why not F-sharp, C-sharp and so on?"

"Because I'm not that sharp."

"Are we going out on that joke?"

"No, but we can do a reprise if you want."

He was dead on. I tried a few more tests and then resigned my claim. Chuck seemed normal, but from then on I knew he was some sort of savant from another planet who was planning on taking over the Solar System.

"So, Chuck," I asked on the way back to our cabin, "What do you want to be someday?" In my mind he could do anything he wanted.

Chuck, however, understood his gift.

"I'm going to be a piano tuner."

As I wrote this chapter, I tried to locate Chuck and discover what he ended up doing, but so far, no luck. *Hey, Chuck, you out there?*

Charles Stokes was a great bunkmate, and typical of the talented friends I made that summer of 1964.

In 1965, at the end of my senior year at Lutheran High West, I was asked to play a bassoon solo (with piano accompaniment) for our class's graduation commencement exercises. I don't need to tell you I hesitated—I didn't want my accompanist to stop in the middle of a performance in front of 1,000 people, take out a bassoon from under his piano bench, and show me how it was to be done.

The prospect was enticing, however. You see, the commencement exercises for Detroit Lutheran High West and our rival Detroit Lutheran High East were held together on the home stage for the Detroit Symphony Orchestra. (Ta Da!) Ford Auditorium. After attending years of orchestra concerts there, me playing a bassoon solo on that stage (with my Mom and Dad hopefully in the audience) would be very cool, indeed. Making the commitment to play for graduation, however, was difficult--unless I could find something easier than Mozart.

Mr. Lindsay suggested the Allegro from J.E. Galliard's Suite No. 2 for Bassoon and piano, which after practicing for several weeks, and recruiting fellow classmate Greg Palmer to play piano, I committed. Greg and I practiced a few times and it all seemed to go well. Greg was very good and the Allegro wasn't too fast for me.

The afternoon of graduation we had a run-through on the Ford Auditorium stage with both schools and all the program elements. As our classes filed through the two aisles of the auditorium to their seating on stage, the Lutheran East trumpet soloist and I stood in the wings with instruments and our accompanists. During the run-through the Lutheran East trumpet soloist went out on stage first. He left the wings awkwardly carrying his music stand in one hand, the trumpet in the other, and his music tucked under his arm. I was afraid he was going to lose that sheet of music into the pit and then drop his trumpet in order to retrieve it. If that was me, I'd be sure to drop my horn. I held my breath. After some awkward moments of watching him set up the stand, arrange the sheet music and begin his piece, I started looking for the stage manager. There was a better way to make an entrance.

But, there was still one more challenge that I nearly blew. During the rehearsal in the afternoon, I took note that the trumpet soloist played both an Andante and a Scherzo (a slow and a fast movement). But Greg and I had only practiced the Galliard Allegro movement. As a result, our musical presentation, was half as long as the East soloist's performance. Back stage, after the afternoon run-through, I turned to Greg and said, "We're playing the Adagio, first."

"No, we're not," he said.

"Yes, we are. We're not going to be embarrassed by East." I smiled. "The adagio is easy. Remember we played it once."

"ONCE IS NOT ENOUGH!" He nearly screamed, as his eyes shot nuclear missiles at me through his thick, black-rimmed glasses.

"Greg, you're ten times the musician I am. Let's not make fools of ourselves by taking a short cut."

"Stan, it's not me, it's you. You'll screw up. You're not that good. We'd have to practice a lot and there's no time."

"It's only 3 o'clock in the afternoon. We have until 6:30 or 7:00, no sweat. And, I've already played it, a lot. My problem is, the Adagio will put me to sleep, so let's play it faster than it's written. As soon as rehearsal is over we'll find a piano back stage and go over it, and I'll prove we can do it."

He glared at me.

On the night of graduation, Greg and I were on first. The stage manager proved flawless. While Greg and I stood ready backstage, the stage manager (I might add the Detroit Symphony Orchestra's stage manager) put my stand, music and chair in just the right spot between the concert grand and the lip of the stage, and he even placed Greg's music on the piano. Then, Greg and I walked out, and took our positions smoothly. Mother had not seen what had happened during the dry-run with the East soloist, but when I made my entrance I caught a glance of her clapping for me—a first.

It was a great experience as we played both movements. I even had time between phrases to sneak a look at the nearly 2,000 people in the audience and find Mom, Dad, and Sis. I smiled as my embouchure wrapped tightly around my double reed. It may have been the only time Mom was in a school audience for me, and she was smiling.

We did good, but I wasn't perfect. The last few notes of the Allegro, call for a quick arpeggio up to the high register of the bassoon before suddenly plunging to the bassoon's lowest note that was to be played double forte (very loud) along with Greg's final chords and stinger. I was so thrilled to have gotten through both movements without any major goofs, and without Greg getting up taking my horn and demonstrating the right way to play it, that I totally froze on the last note. I mean, I blew it. Let me be clear: I blew really hard…but absolutely nothing came out. Nothing. No double forte, just silence…and the only thing that was heard were Greg's final chords.

Later, Mom said she didn't notice anything wrong. "It sounded wonderful," she said. Finally, an attaboy!

M Y MUSICAL CAREER slowed down at Greenville College, a Christian liberal arts institution my folks had both attended and which I'll discuss later. As a freshman I signed up for a piano course, but the practice hours didn't allow time to eat. Further, I had to again face the facts that although most of my body could show up, my fingers never did. I dropped piano after a few weeks and never took another music course.

But, Aunt Hopie, bless her soul, wanted to buy Greenville College a bassoon, if I would play it. So, she did, and I did (my third bassoon).

The first year I played in the band, but it was pretty terrible, so I dropped out. There were special occasions like The Messiah concerts that I played in, but I needed something special to honor the beautiful horn my Aunt had purchased.

In my sophomore year there were three other students, (Peggy Kreh, Martha Tenny, and Tracy Lee) who all had an interest in forming a woodwind quintet, but with me that only made a quartet, and the missing instrument was an oboe. We asked around. Someone recommended we reach out to a local high school kid by the name of Glen Wilson. Glen met with us and was all for the endeavor.

> **Is it possible that the arts… are intended by God to make the unseen visible, and the mystical known?**

Glen was another musical prodigy that I was fortunate to meet. He started playing piano at five, oboe and harpsichord at 12. Two years later, at 14, he could play his oboe better than the rest of us could play our instruments, combined—or so was my impression of his skills. We enjoyed the rest of my sophomore year playing together, wrapping up our short time together at the all college Spring Concert in May 1967. A few months later, at 15, Glen left Greenville on an oboe scholarship for his Junior High School Year at the Interlochen Arts Academy. The next year he received a scholarship on harpsichord to the North Carolina School of Arts. At 17, he auditioned for and was awarded a scholarship at Julliard in New York. Two years later he was on his way to Europe to finish his solo harpsichord certificate in the Netherlands. Today, Glen lives in Bavaria where he teaches, has performed and conducted in over 30 countries with significant runs of an opera he produced and conducted in New York, Los Angeles, and Sydney. Glen Wilson has appeared as soloist or in chamber ensembles on over 50 CD projects for classical recording labels Teldec and Naxos, and is considered one of the great harpsichord talents of our day.

The point of all this? Before he moved to Europe and became famous, Glen played harpsichord at our wedding. Thank you, Glen!

M USIC WAS A big part of my life growing up. I was never talented enough to play professionally, but it taught me a lot about the mystical nature of humanity. Is it possible that the purpose of the arts, especially those created for sacramental worship as Bezalel crafted for the Tabernacle, are intended by God to make the unseen visible, and the mystical known? If so, why do we not use them more?

I'm not sure about that, but I do know that when my Guardian Angel talks to me, he sounds just like the bassoon in Tubby the Tuba.

24
Liturgical
Discoveries

IN 1961, I discovered that a small chunk of chalk, when thrown into the air, arcs through a parabola.

There was something wildly fanciful, restless, and impossible about it. The worn down piece of white chalk arched through the air and hit the top ledge of the wall-mounted chalkboard. It teetered for a moment, as if debating whether to land on the edge or fall to the tile floor of the classroom.

It fell.

The mastermind behind this oft-repeated, failed-feat-of-fancy was a restless short man with a swept-back, salt-n-pepper brush cut, thick-rimmed black glasses, a pointed chin and an unwavering mischievous grin. We always knew he was up to something, but he never let on as to what it was. Rev. Edward Williams wore a worsted gray suit dusted with chalk-dust. There was a debate among us students whether or not the suit, at one time, was black…as fitting the man's religious status. He was a Lutheran pastor who took up teaching part-time because he loved students, mathematics, and the daughter he wanted to put through Lutheran High.

Rev. Williams's daughter was Elizabeth Williams. Betty and I became friends because we had something in common and uncommon between us. The uncommon thing was that she was the shortest in our class, and I was the tallest. We could be seen occasionally walking down the hall with one another, me leaning over nearly horizontal begging her to grow a bit so I wouldn't hurt my back trying to be friendly. No one ever took us as related by blood, especially Betty, who was quite studious.

Rev. Williams taught algebra where, between pacing back and forth with his hands clasped behind his back, he wrote problems on the chalkboard for us to solve. They looked like this: $f(x) = 1 - x + x^2$, where $f(x)$ was called the "function of x,". His classroom windows faced the faculty parking lot, and out of habit he parked his car facing the classroom just ten feet away outside the window. One day in class, as we were silently working on a problem Rev. Williams had written on the chalkboard, one of my classmates piped up and said, "Hey, Rev. Williams, your car is a function of X."

We all looked outside to his Renault, the small, squarish car that you'd expect a pastor who sidelined as a math teacher to be driving. Sure enough the license plate on the front was FX-3492.

Rev. Williams, characteristically leaned forward, put his hands behind his back, walked deliberately to the window, and peered out at his car. Then he turned back to us, smiled and said, "And someday, if you pass this class, you'll discover that everything is a function of X."

With that he flipped a piece of chalk over his back toward the top of the blackboard. But it missed entirely, fell to the ground and cracked into several pieces. Wanting badly to cheer his success, we let out a collective grown. He smiled all the more as he crouched down to pick up the broken pieces with his hands and stuffed them in the pocket of his suit coat.

More than once while sitting in another classroom, we'd hear a class down the hall suddenly come to life with a roar of approval. We instantly knew what had happened—there had been a miracle in Rev. Williams's algebra class—another piece of chalk had taken up residence closer to heaven, albeit only on the top of a chalkboard.

If only we could be so lucky.

THREE TIMES A week we attended morning chapel in the Chapacafestuartorium[1]. Chapel at Lutheran High West however was different from anything I had experienced as an Evangelical. Entering chapel we each grabbed a hymnal and opened it to page 32—The Order of Matins, a combination of nighttime and early morning prayers, chants and songs that in monastic times was known as The Liturgy of the Hours or The Divine Office.

---

1 The nickname for the multipurpose room used for chapel, cafeteria, art, student lounge, and auditorium.

The very first time I attended Matins, however, I didn't do much praying, chanting or singing. I just sat there and tried to get my bearings. Three things struck me. First we weren't singing songs about Jesus like *What a Friend We Have in Jesus*; we were singing songs to Jesus like *We Praise, O Christ, Your Holy Name*. That was a switch that seemed appropriate, and I wondered why there was not more of that in Evangelicalism.

The second thing that caught my attention was that none of the prayers were spontaneous. They were all written, and deliberately so. Gone were the vain repetition of an Evangelical pastor's gap-filling expressions short on vocabulary and long on sincerity. In their place were words and phrases that sounded as if they came from the Psalms—a deep reverence minus the pathos.

The third thing was the singing, actually chant, with which Matins is filled. My favorite became *The Te Deum*. In Evangelicalism, when I sang, I focused a great deal on the music—singing on pitch, following a particular written part, or finding a stray harmony. But with chant I was forced to concentrate on the words.

> *We praise thee, O God:*
> *we acknowledge thee to be the Lord.*
> *All the earth doth worship thee:*
> *the Father everlasting.*
> *To thee all Angels cry aloud:*
> *the Heavens, and all the Powers therein.*
> *To thee Cherubim and Seraphim:*
> *continually do cry,*
> *Holy, Holy, Holy:*
> *Lord God of Hosts;*
> *Heaven and earth are full of the Majesty:*
> *of thy glory.[1]*

After a few months the formality of liturgical worship began to grow on me. I was surprised. I liked it, and I wanted to participate and stop sitting on my can all the time. But I had a problem—I was a freshwater Evangelical fish in a salty Lutheran sea.

Looking back, I wonder if my need to take a more active part in the service was some perverse need to be accepted by God through good works, or a narcissistic desire to be seen by everyone in the school, which Mrs. Richards (my 4th grade teacher back in chapter 9) had

1 The first lines of The Te Deum.

uncovered in me like Pandora's box and the evils of the world. In the end I think it was restless leg syndrome—I just didn't like sitting in a large group and acting like a lemming. Give me a broom and let me sweep the floor at the back. I'll hand out bulletins. *WHAT, no bulletins? Fine, give me a chisel and I'll scrape off the petrified gum underneath the folding metal chairs. I don't care, but don't make me sit still.* I began to wonder if I could toss chalk and so started looking around for a place to pace.

I needed to ask if there was something I could do. The services were led by one of the ministers on the faculty, usually the head chaplain, "Reverend D." Rev. Dequin was an authoritative, near-sighted, chain-smoking man of normal build except his right leg was six-inches shorter than his left, which required him to wear a shoe on his right foot with a six-inch sole. I felt sorry for him and tried to treat him with extra respect. But in these new surroundings I was thrown off my game and I wasn't sure what to ask. I noticed that during Matins there were no students on stage leading the singing, taking up offerings, or doing flannel graph presentations. There were ushers to control the orderly dismissal of the student body row-by-row. But I didn't like the idea of telling people when they could get up and leave their chair. It seemed rude considering I sure didn't want to sit there and wait.

I also noticed that students were the chapel pianists; and it was here that I made a discovery that's a testament to Lutheran-German family industry. At LHW nearly every male student I knew could sit down at a piano and sight-read hymns well enough to lead a church congregation in singing. This was astonishing to me. I concluded that there was a secret Lutheran rite, performed on the eighth day of a boy's life, usually in the morning at the family's home. It is then that they take their first piano lesson—as it is written: *This is a covenant, the covenant you are to keep: Every male among you shall learn to play the piano...any male who cannot play the piano will be cut off from attending Lutheran schools.* But alas, while this was an interesting observation, you, dear reader know, I was not going to be playing piano for chapel.

It was then that I discovered the acolytes. This was new to me. An acolyte used a long brass wand called a candle lighter. Before the service he would prepare the lighter by extending a slide along the side that pushed a wax wick out the far end. He'd light it with a match...or a cigarette lighter if Rev. Dequin was nearby. Then the acolyte would climb the steps to the platform on which the altar stood, reverently approach the altar, bow slightly to it, carefully light the two candles on either side of the altar, back off, extinguish the wick, bow, and leave the platform. At the end of chapel he would repeat the pattern but this time use the bell-snuffer on the other side of the same wand to extinguish the candles. You'll notice I used the masculine pronoun to describe the acolyte. Being an acolyte was exclusively a male occupation.

So, early in my Freshman year, I volunteered...and simple as that I was put in the rotation. I enjoyed being an acolyte—I figured it put me closer to God, and I was more active in the worship. But I had a lot to learn.

NOT EVERYTHING ABOUT Matins at Lutheran West was at odds with my Evangelical upbringing. There was one stark similarity—the interior walls. Both the inside of most Free Methodist churches and the LHW Chapacafestuartorium were cinder-block painted over with a pastel paint. Any number of single words could describe the environment: "Blah!" "Uninspiring" "Depressing."

Free Methodists had the excuse of avoiding "superfluous adornment" of bodily attire, a habit they carried over into their paint selection. In this respect Free Methodists were like Presbyterians who followed after John Calvin's abhorrence of stained glass and religiously inspired art that they saw as glorifying man (the artist) and not God (the Creator).

In the case of Lutheran High West, the reason was more practical. The chapel space was also used as a cafeteria, the art room, an auditorium and the occasional wrestling meet. So, applying German frugality, the stained glass was left to churches, and the schools got the cheap paint.

When I occasioned into a Lutheran church the real differences between Evangelicalism and Liturgical traditions became apparent. There was art everywhere. Not only did Lutheran worship spaces have real pipe organs, which I never heard or saw in any Free Methodist church, but there were elaborate mosaics, original paintings, stained glass, and inspiring sculpture. One such church that became a favorite to visit only a few miles from my home was Guardian Lutheran in Dearborn. Dominating the worship space was a 30 foot, polished, aluminum, steel tubular sculpture of a dove, representing the Holy Spirit, descending over the sanctuary's altar. What could have been left barren without anyone's complaint was a stairwell to the balcony. There on the landing halfway up the stairs was an eleven-foot high stone mosaic of Christ the King with gold-leafed-mosaic crown-stones for emphasis.

The comparison between Free Methodist to Lutheran worship spaces could be described as the differences between depression vs. exhilaration, homely vs. glorious, or repression vs. freedom. My mind was opened up. I never thought of God as depressed, homely, or repressive. I decided something had to change with how worship was conducted within Free Methodism.

UNBEKNOWN TO ME, however, things were about to change with how I was celebrating Matins at Lutheran High. One morning after Matins, at which I was acolyte and feeling good because of my participation, I carried the candle lighter into the faculty lounge that doubled as the sacristy. Rev. Dequin, as usual, was there and pulled me aside, "Stanley, I must talk with you," he said.

I stored the candle lighter in it's wall-mounted holder and joined Rev. Dequin at the side of the room.

He put out his cigarette, adjusted his glasses and looked up at me with a smile. "Stanley, are you a Lutheran?"

It's amazing how a simple question can suddenly shed light on circumstances and change one's life. I was about to discover that there were other similarities between Lutheran High West and my Free Methodist church other than the pastel painted cinder-block walls. There were rules. Sectarian rules.

"Not exactly," I said.

"Not exactly." Rev. Dequin repeated to himself. "What exactly does 'not exactly' mean? Might I inquire?"

I hesitated. "Well, I guess I'm not. I'm Free Methodist." Even as I said this I was wondering just where the line of truth in the sand could be drawn. I had come to a place where I wanted to be Lutheran, at least in terms of attending worship.

"Stanley. We do very much appreciate your service as an acolyte, but being an acolyte in a Lutheran service is something that should really be reserved for Lutherans. Do you understand?"

I was nearly heartbroken. "Yeah, I guess you're right. But I really like doing it."

"Yes, I can tell you do, and you're good at it, too."

I didn't know what to say. I shrugged my shoulders. *God! I'm trying, but I'm really not good enough, am I?*

"Don't lose heart," Rev. Dequin said. "But, I'm taking you out of the rotation."

I dropped my head and nodded. But I didn't lose heart.

Ironically, at the end of the year during the Awards Assembly, Rev. Dequin presented me (along with the "legal" acolytes) a Certificate of Award...for "Christian Service"...(Acolyte). So, not all was lost.

Friday, November 22, 1963

O N THIS FATEFUL day, I recorded the following in my diary:

It all started that Friday in school. I'm a Junior at Lutheran High West and student director of the band. Most of the morning was spent in anticipation of a film (CAROUSEL, 1965) most of the students would be allowed to watch after lunch as a reward for who had sold $10 or more toward the magazine drive.

This magazine drive was held to help fund the new track that circled the football field. It was gravel, and we hoped it could be running asphalt.

Band period was at 12:30 EST every day. On this particular day, I gave the downbeat for some warm up scales. Instead of a B-flat concert scale however, we played "Happy Birthday" to our band director, Harvey Hendrickson. The remainder of the period was spent in giving him silly gifts like a sponge cake with real sponges, and then a real chocolate cake and a cuff link and tie clasp set which was beautiful. The whole period was quite gay and it was topped off by the film which followed immediately, in the same band/choir room at 1:30 PM E.S.T. Little did we know that at that very moment, 1,200 miles away in Dallas, Texas, events had conspired to change our lives forever.

Everything seemed to be going great. I was quite surprised when I got to sit with a girl that I had had a secret crush on for about a month. And, so, the movie began. Carousel was a musical with a considerable amount of dancing and things like that. (My parents would not have approved.)

Then, not more than 15 minutes into the film, the projector was turned off and the lights were turned on. Rev. Franzen, a very emotional but good teacher (the choir director and New Testament instructor), asked for our attention for a very important announcement. His eyes were red, he was hiccuping, and gasping for breath now and then, and continued fervently wiping his face with a white handkerchief. Immediately I thought a teacher...no maybe a student, had died. Just his crying and emotional display drove many of the girls to tears before they knew what had happened.

Finally, in a stuttering and horridly tragic voice, Mr. Franzen said, "The president of the United States has been shot along with the governor of Texas..." and that was about all he knew.

I broke out in a cold sweat and half the girls broke out in fervent, terrified tears, as though this was the end of the United States, or even the world. Franzen led us in prayer. Lutherans usually read their prayers but not this one. It was quite evident that it was straight from Franzen's heart.

Mr. Franzen went out, and after a moment the lights were turned off, and the movie was continued. But not many were paying attention to it. We all continued to talk , murmur and cry...until Mr. Graminske (who taught History, Government, and coached the baseball team) came in. The lights were turned on first, even as the projector kept running. Instantly a dark quiet settled over the group. Not a noise could be heard except the projector, which then slowed down and stopped. The immediate second the projector stopped, Mr. Graminske said very quickly, in the subdued demeanor we had grown accustomed to during his classes, "The president is dead."

Great horror and confusion followed for a long while amidst our terrified amazement. Momentarily the room's public address speaker came alive with the announcement by our principal, Alvin Wied, of the John F. Kennedy's death. Rev. Dequin then came on the speaker and prayed.

The movie did not continue. For a while everybody just seemed to sit there in disbelief. Girls ran out crying and even a couple boys excused themselves from the room.

After the movie (which was very good) I spent the rest of the day listening to the radio trying to find out all I could about all that had happened.

And that's were I was on that fateful day. Where were you? And I have no recollection of who the girl was that I sat next to that day, or if I ever talked to her again.

Because the Lord is Always Near

IN THE SPRING of our senior year our class chose it's motto from Romans 8:31: "If God be for us, who can be against us?" The plan was for the class to sing a hymn at its Baccalaureate Services that somehow reflected that theme. Rev. Williams, our chalk tossing algebra teacher, was our sponsor. That was not so unusual since he was well-liked as was his daughter, Betty, who was in our class. What is a mystery to me is how I ended up being selected to work with Rev. Williams to find a hymn. I mean, after all, everyone knew by now that I had been kicked off the acolyte squad for failing the faith test. Perhaps they figured that this was an opportunity to be ecumenical and show deference, or perhaps it was because I was the student band director and they wanted someone to direct the class in singing the song.

At any rate I poured over the Lutheran Hymnal, since there were no Methodist hymnals around. (Surprise!) My friend, Greg Palmer, played a number of songs for me on the piano in the Chapacafestuartorium, and finally I found a song for which I liked the music. It was *O Christ, Our God in Years Now Past*[1] a tune in E-flat minor attributed to William Croft based on a St. Anne tune. But the lyrics, while nice, didn't quite fit our motto. I suggested to Rev. Williams that we rewrite the lyrics for the class. With a twinkle in his eyes he agreed, and together we set to work. I would go off and write a verse or two, bring it back to him for corrections and suggestions, and thus over a month of back-and-forth effort, we had a hymn.

But just to be on the safe side, in case Rev. Dequin found out I had mostly written the lyrics, we kept my authorship a secret until it was too late. Rev. Williams provided the theological imprimatur, and here are the lyrics to what I directed our class in singing at Baccalaureate… to St. Anne's beautiful tune:

---

1 Not to be confused with *O God, Our Help in Ages Past*

O CHRIST, OUR GOD IN AGES PAST

O Christ, our God in years now past
Great things thy guiding hand hath done
O Lord our God, we humbly ask
To guide our paths in years to come.

These past four years with Christ we've walked
Through times of turmoil, doubt, and fear.
We thank Thee, Lord, for time to talk
To Thee, forever nigh to hear.

Now bless us Lord as we prepare
To enter this world of strife.
And let us, Lord, Thy burden bear
In all we do throughout life.

We know our God with us will be
In all we do throughout the year.
For, now against us none can be
Because our Lord is always near.

During my four years at Lutheran High West, my perspective of worship, liturgy and liturgical art changed dramatically. I came to appreciate liturgical worship as more reverent, more deliberate, more contemplative, and more historically rooted than the informality of Evangelical worship. I also was drawn to the Lutheran's God-centered worship rather than the worship of my youth whose language was more us-centered. And, with the writing and singing of the class song, I had tossed my chalk into the air, and with Rev. Williams, the master chalk hurler at my side, heaven had caught my offering and allowed it to rest on the edge of life's chalkboard.

Now, if I could only do that with girls.

25
Other Women

BETWEEN 1961 TO 1968 (early high school and into college) I thought a lot about getting married. That's a conservative way of saying I had girls on the mind. After Dr. Darling's perverted therapy sessions in junior high I realized I needed some protective hedges and an honorable goal. Although, at first, I wasn't very serious at taking them to heart, I came up with three simple criteria:

> *I will marry a woman that:*
> *(a) is a Christian woman,*
> *(b) is a graduate of college; and*
> *(c) whose family I will have known for at least four years.*

At least that is what I told others.

Yes, it sounded noble and good and it was true...as far is it went. But if the truth were told, there was a bit more that was less good or noble. Nonetheless, my faith journey has been inextricably linked with the girls that were my friends. What's important to remember, for me at least, is that the journey, while it included some false turns and detours, was nonetheless guided by the Holy Spirit, and no doubt influenced by the prayers of my ancestors, my parents, and the woman who became my wife.

I DATED THROUGHOUT HIGH school whenever I could get my Dad to drive me on a date, or later loan me the keys to his pale blue Plymouth or Mom's bright red, stick shifting, sub-compact Chevy II. My first serious relationship, however, didn't require a car. It was with a flutist I met at the National Music Camp near Traverlers City, Michigan the summer between my junior and senior years of high school. Her name was Miss O, and she lived in Columbia, Missouri—a bit too far from southeast Michigan for a Friday night date once camp was over. When the eight week long summer camp was over both of our parents showed up to take their charges home. But before that happened the bassoonist among us managed to arrange a "Meet the Parents" ice cream social in the cabin my folks had rented.

When we sat down to dig in, the first question out of my mother's mouth was not, "So, how was your drive up from Missouri?" or "Is this your first visit to Interlochen?" No, that wasn't on her mind. Almost between gritted teeth she glared at the other parental unit and asked, "So, where does your family go to church?"

Dang! My heart sank. I knew the answer to that one, and it wasn't going to be one Mom liked. Miss O's family went to church, but it was a United Methodist church, not a Free Methodist church. And, in my Mom's mind, United Methodists were some variety of a pagan cult.[1] I need not explain further that the next 40-minutes was awkward, right up to seeing Miss O and her parents drive away in the dark.

After summer camp Miss O and I began to write each other almost daily. Coming home from school, if there wasn't a perfumed scented letter in the mailbox waiting for me, was a disappointment.

Dad seemed to understand the attraction better than Mom. So when school started up again in the fall, I began to work on Dad to take me on a 630-mile road trip during Thanksgiving Break, to Columbia for a visit. After some quiet diplomacy, Dad agreed, but at the same time said, "You know your mother won't like this one bit."

Of course, in my mind, I didn't understand why Mom needed to like it...liking it was my department. I found out later Mom campaigned behind my back to persuade my Dad not to take the trip. But Dad somehow managed to persuade Mother to lay-off because he would be driving and chaperoning the whole time.

Here's where I relay the all-important information that my mother was a prayer warrior, and that what she couldn't accomplish through earthbound methods of persuasion, she tried to accomplish by prayer.

On the appointed day, Dad and I packed up his pale Blue Plymouth. But Mother was nowhere to be seen as we started the journey.

---

1 Any church that allowed smoking, drinking, playing cards, dancing, going to the movies, and didn't have a weekly altar call to make up for all that sinning, was pagan...in my Mom's opinion. And the United Methodists were all that. It didn't matter that Free Methodists and the United Methodists were both descendants of John Wesley's Methodism; they just weren't our kind of people.

We had traveled a mile from the house and had just turned off Ford Road onto south-bound Telegraph Road when it happened. Dad's otherwise meticulously maintained three-year-old Plymouth sustained a catastrophic transmission failure. We noisily pulled over to the curb, called a wrecker and the trip was over. Just like that.

I found out the next day that my mother had fasted the day we left, against my father's decision to take me. When we pulled out of the driveway, she was on her knees at her bedside praying that God would stop the trip. Shortly thereafter, perhaps all of five-minutes, the breakdown occurred.

This was not the first or last miraculous experience I had as the recipient of Mom's prayers. What she lacked in some areas, she made up (mightily) through persevering prayer and faith.

Soon afterwards dad slipped me a note with this quote from an unknown source:

> *He knows, He loves, He cares;*
> *Nothing this truth can dim:*
> *He gives the very best to those*
> *Who leave the choice with Him.*

But I had not given up on getting to Missouri, at least not as long as the mail box was perfuming the neighborhood.

WHILE AT LUTHERAN High West, I had a very special English and Composition teacher, Miss Annette Schroeder. She was single, tall, large boned, gregarious, outspoken, very imaginative and a bit of a wacky rebel. She and I got along great. I wasn't that good of an English student, but she found excuses to give me passing grades. It probably helped that I was active in her afterschool drama club and was useful both on stage and as a technical director. She was so popular with the students that the drama club was three times larger than any other afterschool activity other than the sports teams.

Miss Schroeder's home was in St. Louis. She had five brothers: two became Lutheran ministers, one a printer, one a Naval flight instructor who later became a film director in Hollywood. Her youngest brother sadly was killed in a car accident while a student at Valparaiso, University.

In early April of my senior year, her father, Rev. Theodore Schroeder, the pastor of Mt. Calvary Lutheran Church in the St. Louis suburb of Brentwood, suddenly died.

At the end of the school year, because her brothers were no longer living at home, Annette moved back home to live with her mother, several cats, and a friendly German Shepherd named Sooty.

Later that fall, after high school graduation, my parents encouraged (read: "forced") me with financial support to attend Greenville College (GC), their alma mater. I was not initially excited about going to GC until I realized it was a lot closer to where Miss O was living and attending the University of Missouri in Columbia, MO. *Wow! That's only three hours from GC by "thumb,"* I thought.

Conveniently, in the middle of such a short hike was St. Louis where the Schroeders lived. Annette and her mother had invited me to visit when I was in the area. Being a former pastor's wife with five kids, Mom Schroeder made her home the way-station for a wide variety of friends and visitors who often would stay the night or even days on end. Their open-door home, which embraced the occasional foster teen or deaf student attending college nearby, was never dull.

So, I took up their invitation and made journeys by thumb to Columbia, with a stopover in St. Louis, where I was instantly put to work fixing doors and electrical outlets, carrying out the trash, and taking Sooty for long walks in the park across the street. The Sooty walks started after Mom Schroeder broke her arm in a tug of war when the 90-pound, overweight, neutered canine decided to chase a squirrel during one of its "walks."

Not having gotten along with my demanding mother back in Michigan, I found the Schroeder connection a good one, even after Miss O and I drifted apart during that first semester. In Annette's Mom, I found a compassionate mother, and in her home I found friendships with various guests and with Annette's brothers when they dropped by.

Then, there was Annette's friendship with Dorothy Fontana, a screenwriter in Los Angeles, who was known at the time as D.C. Fontana to hide the fact that she was a woman working in a man's industry. Dorothy was a prolific TV drama writer with dozens of credits for shows like Bonanza, Star Trek, Dallas, and The Waltons. She visited the Schroeder household one Christmas when the front door never seemed to close for the flow of visitors, boarders, brothers, church members and friends. The experience inspired her to write a Bonanza episode where the Ponderosa is overrun by brothers, relatives, friends and townsfolk who come to pay Ben Cartwright their Christmas respects. Thus, if you were in the Schroeder household when one of

D.C.'s episodes was airing, you were expected to sit reverently in front of the TV with the family and follow along with a copy of the script that D.C. had sent in advance. It was great fun.

The Schroeders were spiritually solid. They loved Jesus, and the liturgical nature of their faith didn't minimize in the least their spontaneous affection for evangelism or prayer. They revealed to me that Lutheranism was a lot more like my Evangelical upbringing than I thought. In fact, after she left teaching, Annette Schroeder made a long career of writing evangelization materials for the Concordia Lutheran Publishing house and Missouri Synod headquarters.

The one rule of the Schroeder household was that if you stayed over a Saturday night, you had to go to church with the family the next morning at Mt. Calvary, where Rev. Theodore Schroeder had pastored for 22 years before his untimely death. Mt. Calvary was, and still is, a modest but strikingly modern structure of white stone and stained glass. It was a beautiful church with great acoustics, set in the side of a small hill. Years later it would be the site of another turning point in my journey of faith involving my mother. But, I'll save that gem for a later chapter.

IN THE FALL of my junior year at college I dated, Lisa, a young lady whose parents had attended GC with my mother. Early in the relationship I had been invited to her parents home (who lived in Greenville) for dinner. After dinner I was shown a family picture album with a picture taken years earlier of me and their daughter, both of us two-years old, sitting on a blanket in the grass, oblivious to each other, grasping toys, chewing on crackers, and starring up at the camera. At first we thought the picture might have been an omen of our future relationship. Alas, it was not.

The breakup with Lisa stung a little, and I needed to get away. Although Miss O and I had broken up, we still wrote each other now and then. So, I called and asked if I could visit her for a day. I figured I needed to recharge my appreciation for the better half of the species. Although she was attached to a pre-med student at the time, she agreed to see me.

But to be perfectly honest I was impatient with God. In a prayer diary entry at the time I reminded God of the more detailed and less noble and good criteria for a wife that I had kept to myself: *"To marry a beautiful, talented, sexy, wonderful, persistent, even tempered, congenial, happy, funny, neat and tidy, Christian girl. She will be the greatest*

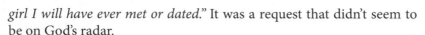

girl I will have ever met or dated." It was a request that didn't seem to be on God's radar.

So, I packed a bag and had a friend drive me out to the highway where I stuck out my thumb.

Many times while hitchhiking in the past, I would become impatient waiting for a car to stop, but wouldn't think of asking God for help. Yet, on this particular day, I became so impatient that I pleaded with God to send someone, anyone, and to send them quickly.

No sooner had I whispered that prayer than a car stopped, I hopped in and before I could take my next breath we were off. And then I took my next breath. Alcohol. And not just a little. The driver weaved all over the road and almost ran into a couple of trucks at 70 miles-per-hour. I quickly prayed another prayer to let me out and only about a mile later I was standing on the side of the road saying a big "Thank you, Jesus!"

> **If only I'd be patient, the Lord would send me someone that would take me to my destination and fulfill my heart's desires.**

It was then that I realized what the Lord was telling me about my future wife. It took me three more rides. Each ride took me a little further and closer, before the last one took me the final 100 to my destination. Was there a lesson in this? I wanted there to be, so I came up with this: *If only I'd be patient, the Lord would send me someone that would take me to my destination and fulfill my heart's desires.*

But, if I was honest, I spent a lot of time staring out of windows.

26
What Am I
Going to Do?

I HAD JUST TURNED 20, and my years as teenager had lapsed. In the spring of 1967, during my sophomore year at college, I found myself standing in my second floor dorm room gazing out the large window onto campus.

Absentmindedly I watched as students and faculty rushed to classes and staff hurried to meetings. Occasionally I'd snap out of the fog and notice that they were all going someplace. They had goals. And then I would think…where was I going? What was I going to do with my life?

Up to that point I rarely considered my future. But now it was time to make a decision…of sorts. I knew what I was supposed to do, or at least what my parents, teachers and my pastor thought I should do. Yet, I wasn't sure. You see, my ancestors were a peculiar breed. They were exceptional role models some might say, and, whether it made sense or not, I was expected to follow in their path. That was the assumption, that God's call upon my life would be the same as those that went before me.

That meant there was a bar to cross, and a cross to bear. The question evangelists and Christian speakers would often lob at us students was this: *"Are you willing to follow God's call upon your life? Or, are you determined to go your own way?"* That sounded like such a good and virtuous challenge. As kids we had been indoctrinated to believe that *if we liked something it was wrong.* And *if we didn't like something, that was what God wanted us to do.* There was this dichotomy established throughout Christian Evangelicalism that anything that was enjoyable was probably from Satan. After all, Christ died on the cross, so..."go and do thou likewise."[1] (You can prove anything with the Bible.)

It never entered my consciousness that if I happened to discover who God made me to be, that I might be happy being that *person*. If I developed my God-given talents into valuable skills, I might enjoy going to work. That if my motivations for getting out of bed in the morning were aligned with God's moral will, I might actually know that my life had purpose. But that was not the ideology I was brought up to understand. It was just the opposite: that ego was bad, and sacrifice was good, and never the two shall meet.

On a subconscious level I struggled a lot with these thoughts for several months, allowing them to become conscious only when I stood before that large window...and looked out. As I prayed I thought back to the lives and stories told of my ancestors: There was the adventurous missionary John Williams (a great uncle), who in 1839 was martyred by cannibals in the South Pacific; there was the post-civil war circuit rider, Jeremiah Williams (my paternal grandfather) who tangled with ruffians and "opposers" to the Gospel in the Midwest, and there was Edith Willobee (my maternal grandmother) who sacrificed much for the poor in India. And, finally, there were my parents, Ben and Ruth, who were passionate Christians who worked tirelessly in the church as lay leaders of one kind or another. Were their journeys of faith intended to direct mine?

The memories of my family legacy did, undoubtedly, mold my understanding of who I was and what I was called to do. There was some of John, Jeremiah, Edith, Ben, and Ruth in me. Like them, I was impetuous, easily took risks and was anxious to take up new initiatives. While all that sounded good, there was a downside. I was easily ruffled by rules, political inconsistencies, detours and the fear of a dark destiny—although I persevered, my *temperament* would often alienate and isolate me from others.

Nonetheless, the preachers, Sunday School teachers and other spiritual leaders in my formative years made it clear that my responsibility as a Christian was to follow God's call upon my life, and *that* meant one of only a few things: Be a preacher, a missionary, or Christian teacher... something that could be considered as "full time Christian service."

This ideology about the careers that Christians are allowed to pursue was pervasive in Evangelicalism. Over the years I've read and heard the stories of executives, athletes, politicians, Hollywood

---

1 Luke 10:37

craftsmen, and law enforcement officers who have left their well-established and successful careers to go into "full-time Christian work." When my children were attending a private Christian high-school, they were frequently lectured by the chaplain during weekly services that they were obligated to first pursue careers as pastors, missionaries or Christian school teachers. And only if they gave those choices the good old college try and failed at them, were they free to pursue another career.

But in 1967, although such pressure was strong, the glass I was looking through seemed smudged if not dark. Christ commanded us to be salt and light in the world. "Let your light shine before others, that they may see your good deeds and glorify your Father in heaven."[1] There were many ways to do that without being a preacher, missionary, teacher. I could be a builder of beautiful churches (the Lord knew the Free Methodists needed such a person). Or, I could be a ship builder that took missionaries to foreign lands, or I could be a writer of Christian Sunday School material, like Annette Schroeder. My mind swelled with ideas. It seemed I could honor God delivering milk, selling insurance, be a TV clown (that didn't smoke), or...I could be a mortician so I'd be sure to be near a cemetery at the Resurrection. With the limited direction we were given, there seemed to be a disconnect.

Growing up in Evangelicalism I saw a lot of Christian witnessing, but most of it was with *words* inside a church building or in an arena with Billy Graham's voice blasting over loud speakers. I saw very little witnessing or good deeds outside the church, unless you count the time I watched three Winnebagoes caravan at 3-mph down a dirt road next to a swamp in central Florida, blasting one of Billy's sermons over eternally mounted speakers. Every square inch of these lumbering motor homes was plastered with hundreds of brightly colored Gospel bumper stickers proclaiming: *"Jesus Saves!" "Repent, ye sinner." "The road to destruction is wide and narrow is the path to Salvation."*

And, Greenville College was an extension of that ghetto. It was situated in a small farming town, in a "dry" county. The school had rules that forbade students from darkening the door of the only movie theater in town unless Billy Graham's name was on the marquee. (It never happened.). Although I had never considered a career in the motion picture industry, I was sensitive to the hypocritical nature that such a taboo created. It was commonplace to hear Evangelical leaders pile mountains of criticism on Hollywood, yet we never heard of how

1 Matthew 5:13-16. NIV

Christians could let their light shine in Hollywood or make movies with redemptive stories, although it had been done many times before.

To me, Christ's words made sense: "Neither do people light a lamp and put it under a bowl. Instead they put it on its stand, and it gives light to everyone in the house..." It seemed to be that Evangelical Christianity was hiding under the bowl, afraid to light a candle and let it shine in the darkness. If the darkness was in Hollywood, then lighting candles in church basements was not going to help.

I might have seen myself cut out for radio. I loved my time producing radio shows and being on air at the college radio station, *WGRN, 89.3 F.M. "The ten-watt station that sounds like a million"*, I'd proclaim during a station break. My vision of a career in radio, however, was tainted by the time consuming task of preventing offending songs (sent to WGRN on promotional long playing vinyl records) from getting on the air by using a sharp instrument to scratch off the tracks. I never did discover who made the censoring decisions.

I wanted to be creative, not destructive.

Alas! The more I considered pursuing an "acceptable" career—that of a preacher, missionary, or teacher in a Christian school— the more the idea seemed inappropriate. I was well aware that I did not have the natural disposition that St. Paul describes to Timothy:

> *Whoever aspires to be an overseer desires a noble task. Now the overseer is to be above reproach, faithful to his wife, temperate, self-controlled, respectable, hospitable, able to teach, not given to drunkenness, not violent but gentle, not quarrelsome, etc..*[1]

Such a path was not for me unless I took sedatives. There had to be something else...some other way to serve God in a "normal" career.

Finally, one day in April, 1967, as I stood praying before my big window, pretending to be Daniel and telling God I would do whatever he asked of me...after a while...a wave of consolation, complete with tears and a cathartic release, swept over me. It was not a voice, nor a vision, but a deep satisfying realization that, unlike my ancestors, full time Christian ministry was not my calling. What a relief it was to know I could, and probably should, steer completely clear of so called Christian ministry.

But, did I listen? No...as later chapters will reveal.

---

1 1 Timothy 3:1

Luckily, I didn't know what mistakes lay ahead, but neither did I know what was I going to do. Thankfully, God soon sent someone to temper my spirits and help me on the journey.

27
Pamela Sue
to the Rescue

A MOMENT OF GRACE came the next year, in 1968. I was a junior in college. But to set the stage, once again I need to flashback.

As I've described earlier, during junior high, I ballooned upward and outward to the point that I was lucky if I could get to class without being the object of mockery. That didn't stop the hormones, however, and as I hit adolescence, my interest in girls became acute—distracting, difficult and unwelcome.

My weight, sloppy clothes and emotional confusion created an awkward combination that made me unpopular, and I knew it. I was an extrovert by nature, but my physical and mental status created chaos on the surface; I was like a rapidly flowing river current driving into the eye of a gale force wind. The results were big waves and a lot of surface unrest.

It became clear that I had to lose the weight, and get into some pants that were less than 46-inches at the waist. That would at least allow me to squeeze into a classroom without dislodging the door jams.

Thus, my timing in meeting my future wife was critical; but I can take no credit for it.

During junior high and the first semester of high school, I weighed in at over 250 pounds and was a social misfit. Twice each Sunday and once on Wednesday evenings my family drove 30 minutes one-way to the Free Methodist Church in Lincoln Park, Michigan. There were several Free Methodist Churches closer, but Lincoln Park was on the mend and they had requested Mom and Dad's leadership in a couple of lay-ministry roles. Mom taught Junior Church and Dad was the church Treasurer and helped organize the Men's Fellowship outreach, a national organization that he co-founded.

As I've already recalled, the first semester of high school playing football under Dennis Tuomi and Jim Bales solved my weight problem. By Christmas I had lost 76 pounds and bottomed out at 174, which I maintained for many years. This allowed me to wear regular clothes, appear athletic (although I was only a mediocre athlete), and gain some popularity with the ladies (or so I imagined).

My new found confidence sparked my campaign to start attending the Dearborn Free Methodist Church, which had a large and active youth group, a number of known high school athletes…and, you guessed it, a bevy of good looking girls. I figured this was an entirely reasonable campaign because (a) each Sunday and Wednesday we passed the Dearborn Free Methodist Church on our way to the Lincoln Park Church; (b) all Mom and Dad had to do was slow down a bit while I jumped out, and then hopped back in on their way home; and (c) several of Mom's college chums were helping to run the Dearborn Free Methodist church, including the superintendent of Dearborn Public schools at the time, Rod Smith. Wouldn't she want to hang out with them, while I hung out with the teens?

Mom and Dad had made a commitment of so many years to Lincoln Park, and they had several yet to go, but they realized that with my starting high school at Lutheran West I needed to make F.M. Christian friends that were a lot closer to home. Lincoln Park was too far away for me to attend social gatherings. During my freshman year of high school, Dad and Mom had already tried to drive me down there for mid-week youth events and the additional two hours on the road (one to take me and another to pick me up) was unreasonable and expensive. Dearborn was much closer. So, the summer after my first year at Lutheran West, on Sunday and Wednesday, they agreed to slow down to 10 MPH as they drove through Dearborn and let me jump out of the car—something I had practice doing, thanks to Mom.

Little did I know that my first jump from my Dad's new Plymouth was to land me within sight of my future wife.

The problem, however, was that my social "misfitness" had not entirely left my persona. It would be a few more years before my brain caught up to a level that would make me presentable to Pam and her parents. Consequently, I didn't have the sense to see what God was putting in front of me. Alas for her, Pam did. Bless her forever and ever.

It was probably the very first Sunday at Dearborn Free Methodist that I met Pam. She was tall, slender, and shy, but had a beautiful, innocent smile. I remember the encounter, but only vaguely. Thus, it's appropriate that I let Pam pick up the story that in retrospect worked out wonderfully.

PAM WRITES: *I remember seeing Stan for the first time as I walked into my high school Sunday school room. He was a tall, blonde, blue-eyed, broad-shouldered guy—one of the handsomest that I had ever laid eyes on. I immediately took notice of him. But, I was, though tall, not very striking, and very shy, so he did not seem to notice I was in the room at all. After class, when I got up to leave, he spoke to me...about my red Bible(!)—a gift from my parents who thought a red-letter edition should be bound in red leather, with my name embossed in gold letters at the bottom of the cover. Coincidentally, red-leather bound Bibles could also be earned through Bible Quizzing as a "trophy" for being on a Championship Bible Quiz Team—something very popular in Free Methodist churches nationwide. So, on that first day of our meeting, Stan very excitedly spoke six words to me. "Is that a Bible Quizzing Bible?" And I, very reluctantly had to admit, no...whereupon he raced out of the room to catch up with his same-age nephew, Bob Kenney, who was visiting that Sunday. I really didn't expect to ever see him again.*

But, I did see him after that, every time I went to church, because he and his family had moved to Dearborn from Ferndale, and they were Free Methodist. We both became very active members of the high school youth group at Dearborn FM, which included many social events like Caroling at Christmas, Car Wash fund-raisers, season parties, Progressive Dinners, and of course, Bible Studies and Youth Meetings. I found out from my girl friends that Stan asked them out for dates, but he never called me. I finally found out why. I was the fourth girl on his list. Only if the first 3 said no, would I ever get a call.

I'll never forget the day he did call. I was so excited and I wanted to finally have my dream date with him. But, when I did the obligatory check with my parents, my mom reminded me about the Social Studies report I had been procrastinating about all week. "But, it's Friday night, and I have all day Saturday to work on it," didn't work on my mom. I had to tell Stan no, and write my report first. I was pretty bummed. But, I also knew that my mom was right, so I got to work on my report right then, in case Stan should call again. He didn't.

But, I did get top grade in the class. I remember because my teacher bragged about it to the class the whole time he passed back each student's report, saving mine to last, which he passed to the wrong person...Pat Turner. I was Pam Turck. He didn't even know the difference. I don't even know if I got credit for the grade or Pat did, because I was too shy to correct him after class or speak up during class.

Stan did call me for a couple of dates, and that was enough to capture my heart...hook, line, and sinker. But, he was a year ahead of me and when he left for college I knew it was over, especially when I heard through his sister that Stan was steadily dating the daughter of the President of Greenville College. I couldn't compete with that.

So, when it was my turn to go off to college, I picked Spring Arbor—a "sister" Free Methodist College to Greenville, though several states apart. At Spring Arbor I could forget about Stan and I already knew many of my girl friends would be attending SAC, as well. I'd be able to concentrate on my studies more without the distraction of guys and dating. Fat chance! I actually had many opportunities to date, one being the brother of my college roommate, who fell for me and asked me to marry him. For awhile, I considered it, but when I knew I had to break it off and transfer to another college in order for the break-up to stick, I picked Greenville, and as God's perfect timing would have it, Stan had just broken up with the daughter of the Greenville College president.

It was between semesters of my sophomore year, and here I was, the new girl on campus and not knowing anyone. Stan became the perfect gentleman and showed me around. It was more like a big brother relationship, but it was still great fun. Stan knew everyone and was up on everything going on, proud to let his GC savvy show, so it was a win-win situation!

But, in addition to that, I put my own ingenuity into action. One of my new friends from my dorm had a job in the registrar's office, so I asked her to do me a favor and give me a copy of Stan's schedule for that semester so I could place myself strategically where he would be passing in or out of buildings to "accidentally" run into one another. Not only that, but Stan had become a regular host for the college Radio station (WGRN) where he was production manager. He was one of the AV nerds who set up microphones and film projectors for special events. So he had a master key to the main classroom buildings, radio station, and various AV and darkroom facilities on campus. He enjoyed showing me all the things he was up to and I was game to participate in anything that brought us together.

Then, in another strange turn of events, I made friends with a girl walking her horse through town past our dorm, and she thought I was experienced with horses by the way I made over hers, so she asked if I wanted to ride it. I did. So, on I climbed.

"Don't let him turn toward the barn, or you won't be able to stop him," she said.

About the time I asked her where the barn was, the horse took off. My shyness prevented me from warning her that I had never been on a horse before and I had no idea what to do. The horse raced through town, across busy streets. It was, at the same time, a scary and an exhilarating ride. But suddenly, I saw that we were going to attempt to cross the business bypass through the south end of town with a lot of car and truck traffic. The horse was not going to stop. So, at the last moment I jumped off. I was very fortunate that my feet came free of the stirrups, else I would have been dragged to my death.

When I fell, I broke a fifth metatarsal. Professor Phyllis Holmes,[1] one of my physical education instructors, was driving by at the time and she took me to the hospital. For the next six weeks I was in a cast from my foot to my knee.

This made Stan even more attentive to me. He came over to my dorm to serenade me with his guitar as we sat on the landing of the central steps and to keep me company while I had to have my leg elevated. We would have long talks about the papers I had to write for my philosophy class that he had already taken the previous year; he really helped me understand the purpose of the assignments. Our relationship went to a deeper level, and finally he asked me on a date.

That's how we ended up on the school bus to an away game in Fort Wayne, Indiana. I don't remember anything about the game, but I do remember the ride there and back talking and laughing and finally receiving my first kiss (from him) on the dark ride "home." By the end of that semester, as summer approached, I felt pretty sure we were headed toward romance. But, Stan had a summer job at a Jewish Day Camp in St. Louis—as Nature Specialist (where he caught poison ivy almost immediately) and I had a summer job at a Campfire Girls Camp in Holly, Michigan—on the Waterfront as a Red Cross (WSI) Water Safety Instructor.[2] So we went our separate ways. I had no idea if this absence

---

1 Phyllis Holmes was the women's basketball coach at GC. She also served as an assistant women's Olympic coach for USA basketball, and was the first woman ever elected President of the National Association of Intercollegiate Athletics (NAIA) basketball association.

2 Stan was a WSI, and in fact, taught and certified new WSI's. He thought I was in one of his classes, but I assured him I would have remembered *that*. He still thinks

would make his heart grow fonder or forgetful of me.

Little did I know that Stan was going to use this time away to date every girl under the sun (that he knew) to test whether what he was feeling for me was true love or just a relationship spawned by proximity and convenience. He had to be sure...

I THOUGHT I LOVED Pam. She had become my best friend. And there were definitely thoughts about marriage swirling around in both of our heads. But I had to be sure. We had not made any promises to each other about not dating other people during the summer, so I undertook a deliberate and delicate experiment, which if it worked, would give me assurances going forward.

The experiment was to stage some very nice dates with a number of lovely ladies I had known over the years or had met that summer in St. Louis. Throughout that summer Pam and I wrote each other about once a week but I didn't tell her what I was doing on the sly.

The consequences were remarkable. When I was at dinner with S____, at a fine restaurant, I wanted Pam to be there with me to share in the ambiance. During a walk with A____ through the Forest Park Zoo, I wanted Pam to appreciate the exhibits and displays. The melodrama farces on the Goldenrod Showboat docked on the Mississippi were hilarious, and T____ delightfully giggled as her blond curls bounced, but I longed to see the laughter in Pam's dark eyes. Even a canoe trip I took, with a Lutheran young adult group, I knew Pam would love being there because she loved physical activity and the outdoors. But, I didn't want her to experience the capsize and danger from which K____ and I had escaped. And, when I flew to New Jersey to visit N____, I had an enjoyable time meeting her family (also friends of my parents). We laughed our heads off watching THE GRADUATE, which had just been released, but there was a total absence of romance. Even the New Jersey family reminded me of Pam. N____ had a mentally and physically disabled brother, the same age as Pam's mentally and disabled brother, Tom.

Thus, in every situation, I missed Pam...a lot. Pam had become my best friend with whom I wanted to share all these special experiences. So, toward the end of the summer, having made up my mind, I decided I needed to make one final trip before school began. Here's how Pam describes it.

---

his signature is on my WSI card, if I could find it.

PAM WRITES: My family had moved to a larger home to care for my grandparents, and I was working full afternoon and evening shifts at the local Howard Johnson's Restaurant. It was mid-August and very cool for that time of year. The rain was coming down this one evening, and I dreaded the idea of getting off work and running through the rain to my Mom's car that was parked way in the back of the restaurant.

All of us waitresses kept an eye on the front door to be sure that new customers were not kept waiting. About 8-o'clock at night a tall handsome man with a big smile walked in wearing a trench coat and an Indiana Jones Fedora. I knew immediately it was Stan. I was in shock and I quickly walked over to him, brushing the crumbs off my uniform and pushing my hair out of my face. What was remarkable was that he had driven all the way from St. Louis, 10 hours in his 1960 Chevrolet Corvair that required he stop every 100 miles and feed it another quart of oil. The trench coat, and rain dripping off the brim of his Fedora was a scene out of a movie. I wanted so badly to hug him and kiss him for surprising me, but I held off. He was all wet, and I was supposed to be working.

"When do you get off?" he asked.

"As soon as I can," I said.

It was that night parked somewhere in his Corvair that he told me about his summer, his dates, his trip to New Jersey, and how he couldn't stop thinking of me the whole time. That night we made up for some of that lost kissing I had longed for since high school. But, just two days later, he returned to St. Louis, having to get back to work at camp, and finish a Calculus class at St. Louis University.

As soon as we returned to school in the fall of 1968 we started talking about getting married. That fall, at Thanksgiving, we made a trip to St. Louis to visit the Schroeders. While in St. Louis, we took time to walk the Galleria Mall, a beautiful atrium affair that even in winter is sunny and grand. Stan said he needed to visit a restroom, which we found on the second level next to the inside Foley Department Store entrance. I said, "I'll wait right here." He walked off, and I turned around and found myself inside Foley's facing a full display of wedding rings. Perfect!

By the time Stan came back and walked up behind me, and looked at what I was doing, he simply said, "See anything you like?"

AT CHRISTMAS BREAK in 1968 we both traveled home to Michigan. On Christmas Eve I took Pam to the fanciest restaurant I knew in Detroit—The Top of the Flame, which was on the top floor of the Consolidated Gas building, a Detroit skyscraper, that over-looked the International Waterfront with Canada—the only place in the world where Canada is south of the United States. You could see the building for miles, its top illuminated like a blue natural gas flame atop a stove.

That it was to be a magical night for us was foreshadowed as we entered the lobby and literally rubbed shoulders with world-famous magician David Copperfield as he and his entourage were leaving. It was romantic but not dramatically so, since she was the one that had picked out the rings. I didn't get down on one knee, but I did ceremoniously open the velvet box, take out the ring, reach across the table, and slipped it on her finger at 8:15 PM.

After dinner, we went home to her house, and then to my house, to show our parents what we had committed ourselves to. In our minds, engagement was not a test of our relationship, but a commitment to marry.

The next week was maddening as news of our engagement got out to our extended families. After our expensive meal in Detroit, we enjoyed invites to every known relative and many friends in S.E. Michigan for lavish brunches, fancy luncheons, and multi-course dinners. We both enjoyed the attention and the food…especially, on my part—the food.

In addition to the massive quantity of food intake, I also experienced a dramatic relief from years of psychological strain—I no longer had to worry about a date on Friday night. The search was over. *Done. Makellos. Finito. Fini!* And my whole body, mind, and soul took a rest.

As if I needed to be reminded that all actions have consequences, when we returned to GC after Christmas I had gained several inches around the waist and could not fasten or zip up any of the slacks in my dorm closet. For the next month until I could buy new clothes I wore sweat pants around campus. The trim 174 pounds I weighed for the past seven years was never to return. Luckily she still loved me.

We didn't set a date for the wedding except to say it would probably take place the summer after Pam's graduation in 1970. That was a long way off, almost two years, and neither of us liked the idea. While my parents had made it clear that they would stop paying for my college the day I got married (to ensure I did graduate), Pam's parents made it clear that even if we were to get married before she finished college, they would continue to pay for her education.

My plan after graduation, a year ahead of her, was to enter Physics graduate school. But the variables surrounding that were yet to be ascertained. I had not made application to any school, nor had I taken the

GRE's[1], and if the truth be told I had doubts that my grades were good enough to gain me entry to the lofty labs of discovery.

So, we didn't really know when we could get married, and we certainly didn't have any idea that God had a better and more reasonable plan.

---

1 Graduate Record Examinations.

28
Greenville
Revolution

F LASHING BACK A few years, it was 1965 and I was freshman in my first month at Greenville College. My roommate, Fred, and I had just returned to our room with towels wrapped around our waists from the showers on the third floor of Jansen Hall men's dorm. We entered our room and the door shut and locked automatically behind us.

Within moments, we heard a commotion of male students in the hall. Suddenly, they started to bang on the door demanding to be let in.

Shocked at first, I quickly knew what it was about. They were sophomores intent on enforcing "Freshman Initiation," something I had publicly ridiculed and in which I refused to participate.

Freshmen Initiation involved sophomores and other upperclassmen demanding that we, the freshmen, open doors for them, serve them in the cafeteria, sing the Alma Mater on demand, and, among other indignities, make and wear folded newsprint dunce caps around campus.

Because of my Junior High experiences, I developed a low tolerance toward any kind of harassment, which is how I classified Freshmen Initiation at GC. College was difficult enough for me, and the added distraction upon first arriving was unnerving. So I ignored their requests. That night they had come to teach me a lesson.

Fred and I felt we were safe in our room, but the sophomore Resident Assistant used his master key to unlock our door and allow the enforcers into our room. We tried to push the door closed, but we were no match for the group of them. I was incensed at the intrusion enough to grab an umbrella and thrust it into the crowd like a sword. One thrust caught one of the attackers badly in the eye. It didn't blind him, but he wore a patch for weeks after.

After a struggle, the gang forced me naked into a chair and brandished a couple pair of long, sharp scissors.

Mom's warning flashed before my eyes, "Don't run through the house with my good scissors." I always wondered if it was okay to run through the house with her *bad* scissors. Nonetheless, I crossed my legs and resigned myself as they took scissors to my blonde locks and hacked them to the scalp.

Their assumption, I suppose, was that their hack job was so ugly and disconcerting that I would be sure to wear my dunce cap to avoid public ridicule.

They didn't know me.

I never wore their dunce cap, and I never hid my head. This was their doing not mine. I was the belligerent victim.

I complained to the dean and the administration but there were no repercussions against the invasion of our privacy, nor was there any apology for the physical attack. The men's dean thought it was funny and that I should have complied with the initiation and thus saved my locks.

A couple of years later as a junior, I witnessed Freshmen Initiation again get out of control and posted my written dissent in the student union on a public discussion bulletin board called the "Wittenberg Board." It was Greenville's experiment with early social media, using paper and push pins. Other students and staff could post their rebuttals or write on your initial statement. I garnered remarks that both supported and derided my position against any type of initiation for the sake of dignity and respect. At the time I noticed that the student handbook for 1967-1968 had what appeared to be a new entry. It read this way (underline is mine):

> *Sophomores begin the year by conducting freshman initiation. This* is not hazing *in any sense of the word, but rather is intended to foster class and school spirit. Usually, freshmen are asked to "serve" the "aged" sophomores, juniors, and seniors by opening doors for them, taking their trays in the cafeteria, learning the alma Mater, etc.* There is no coercion of students to participate and it is understood that this activity will continue only as long as it is

genuinely Christian and wholesome.

How all this fosters class and school spirit but avoids class and school division and reprisals is beyond my powers of reasoning. Indeed the harassment continued until I was a senior and my nemeses had left the school.

I forget whether Fred was attacked that night, as the attention was on me. But the event did nothing to enhance his attitude toward the Christian school, even though he was a MK (Missionary Kid). For the rest of the semester Fred prominently displayed a number of Playboy centerfolds in our room. The presence of such materials on a Christian campus fell in the same category as drugs and alcohol. I wasn't into the latter, but neither did I take scissors to Fred's decorations and demonstrate my own lack of dignity and respect for the, ah…well, suffice it to say Fred left school after the first semester, along with the pinups.

I managed to stick around and find things to appreciate about my education at GC. But the lack of decorum and respect demonstrated by some students and the encouragement of the men's dean to further the disrespect and decorum lessened my view of the school. In the end I marked it up to two attributes of Evangelicalism: arbitrary rule-making and arbitrary enforcement of the rules.

There are good rules and bad rules, no doubt. But good rules, like all virtues when taken to extremes, do damage. Thus, courage in excess results in reckless abandon, and forgiveness in excess leads to the tolerance of evil.

Across the dorm hallway from Fred and me lived Henry, a gentle young man of spiritual mettle that we all so respected we elected him our floor chaplain. Like us, Henry was a first semester freshman. Fred and Henry could not have been more different in their faith. Fred was antagonistic to just about everything; his words were often denigrating and angry. Henry, on the other hand was a common man with a welcoming spirit and an

> **Courage in excess results in reckless abandon, and forgiveness in excess leads to the tolerance of evil.**

uncommon faith. When Henry inquired about you or spoke of God, his face would light up with evident joy. When one encountered Fred he was stuffing Playboys under his mattress…or someplace I never discovered. (Really, I looked.)

But there was also something else that worried a few of us. Henry would spend most of his day praying and reading his Bible. He wasn't trying to impress us; he didn't put a show on. But being across the hall we were close enough to notice that he rarely went to class. When we had floor devotions once a week, Henry read scripture, delivered a short devotion and prayed. He was good and I for one was in awe of his awareness and closeness to God.

When second semester rolled around, I was not surprised when my roomy was kicked out of school. But I was surprised when Henry didn't return...and he was missed. When I inquired of his roommate I was told that as spiritually minded and academically capable as he was, he skipped too many classes and missed assignments because he was compelled to pray and study the Bible.

Clearly, I do not know God's calling on Henry's life, but I've always been curious what happened to him. He was such a good person. But Henry's behavior was similar to what I had witnessed in some aspects of the Evangelical church. From my perspective Christians were too often hiding in church basements, afraid to confront the world or defend their faith. In an effort to avoid falling into sin they removed their salt and light from the surrounding culture.

I began to think that perhaps it was possible to study the Bible and pray too much. We were physical beings, living in the physical world. To me, that meant physical work. Was the purpose of faith to help us do the work? And if we put all our effort into faith and not into the work, would we be any earthly good? Faith without works seemed like an ironic death.[1]

ONE GREENVILLE COLLEGE rule was, "Thou shalt not consume alcoholic beverages." That made Bond County, where the school was located, a perfect location—it was a dry county— there were no bars, nor could restaurants even sell a beer. This rule, I discovered, was based on the Free Methodist infallible interpretation of John 3, where at the wedding in Cana, Jesus did not really make *wine* as the Bible claims, but rather 90-gallons of *unfermented* grape *juice* in stone jars...no doubt embossed with the Welches logo on the side. But, as the guys in the room next to mine discovered, you could buy cheap cider, store it uncapped in your closet next to your dirty underwear for a few months, and it's as good as having a still...or so my nose told me.

There were other rules, too. Although the town did have a movie

---

1 A sentiment also found in James 2: 14-26.

theater—The Bond Theater—students were not allowed to attend for fear, again, of exposure to the wickedness of the world. [We surmised that after college, graduates, in order to keep them protected, were to be secreted off to a protected domed city much as Truman Burbank (Jim Carrey) was "protected" in THE TRUMAN SHOW.] So, we missed a few of the James Bond films like DR. NO, which could have been a message from the F.M. bishops; and FROM RUSSIA WITH LOVE, definitely a device to seduce us into accepting Communism. GOLDFINGER would have fed the temptation, no doubt, to chase filthy lucre, and THUNDERBALL, well we could only imagine what that might be about.

My first semester in town, however, did reveal a weakness in the college's religious police. They didn't have any. At least there was no budget to stake out the theater with a surveillance team. I discovered, much to my surprise, that you could walk right up to the well-lit ticket booth on the West side of the town square, buy a ticket, go in, and leave, and no one would ever corner you, or raid your room at night with a pair of scissors asking for your ticket stub, or try to deprogram your experience.

That is probably why, in 1965 as a sophomore, on a double date with Pam, we bought tickets to DR. ZHIVAGO, the epic film based on Boris Pasternak's novel about World War I and the Russian Revolution. It was nominated for ten Academy Awards and won five of them. As I write this in 2014, it is the eighth highest-grossing film of all time, adjusted for inflation. But the movie did prove my parents and the college to be right in one small point. To this day I can still remember the scene

> **Was the purpose of faith to help us do the work? And if we put all our effort into faith and not the work, would we be any earthly good? Faith without works seemed like an ironic death.**

where Julie Christie's larger than life-size naked bosom was fully on display, although Pam remembers nothing of the moment. Hmm?!

I presume the college figured it could not enforce the prohibition on something that was not on campus, like the Bond Theater. But there was something they could enforce, and the Board of Trustees of the College insisted on it—no shorts were to be worn on campus ever, not even Bermuda Shorts, which were really knee length pants. In GC's eyes, shorts of any kind fell into the category of immodesty, a hold over from the 1930's and 40's when girls were required to cover their arms to the wrists, and their legs to mid-calf, all the time. After their graduation from GC in 1940, my Mom and Aunt, then new teachers in Romeo, Michigan, sent a picture to their mother in India of them standing next to their new car. In the picture, they are wearing short sleeve, dressy white blouses. The return letter from their mother chastised them for their immodest appearance, reminding them that they should fear hell.

In 1966, when I was a sophomore, the student council drafted a document they titled, "The Bermuda Resolution." It allowed students to wear Bermuda Shorts after 6 PM. Supposedly that's when visitors to campus would be hiding in their motel rooms and not be offended by the extensive display of faux pulchritude. Surprisingly, the Board of Trustees voted to accept the resolution. The buzz on campus was like WWII had just ended.

But change was in the air…or in the hair. The next year, in 1967, the student council decided to attack another sacred cow. For some time there had been a rule on campus that men could not wear sideburns, or facial hair, below the earlobe. This in spite of a portrait of the college's founder, John Brown, in the main campus building wearing a full beard, and across the hall from him a reprint of Sallman's The Head of Christ painting—also with a full beard. Yearbooks from 50 years earlier revealed that many men sported mustaches and many wore beards including the ministers that taught theology. But the current trustees saw facial hair as a rebellious, hippie thing that would not be tolerated.

The Student Association's resolution to drop the facial hair rule was rejected but a strange compromise was made. Men could wear mustaches. The rule read, "not below the upper lip." Thus, a new hairstyle was crafted with long sideburns that managed to slide across the face and join mustaches, creating a horizontal hairline from the corners of the lips to the facial horizon. It looked strange but those of us that could adopted the new motif.

During Pam's senior year, (we were married by now and living in town above the union hall. I car-pooled to St. Louis for work as Pam attended classes) the student body president was Glen Snyder, whose father was a respected Free Methodist medical doctor and missionary in Africa. Glen himself was considered a devout and conservative Christian who was respected by the school administration and the students. Early in the year, Glen and his council again approached the trustees with the hair resolution, but the trustees again soundly rejected it.

Now it's important to point out that the Student Association officers were charged with meeting and accompanying the occasional VIP visitor on campus, including political and guest lecturers. So it was, in protest, that Glen and the other four male officers shaved their heads. One of the six officers was a lady who (thankfully) decided to keep her hair on. The association officers reasoned, I suppose, that if long hair was a sign of evil rebellion, then no hair was obviously a sign of righteousness obedience.

Overnight the rule disappeared. Glen graduated with a full-beard as did other men. At the time, and to this day, the anecdote serves as an example of moral principal vs. arbitrary legalism.

O NE OF THE most colorful characters on campus at the time was history Professor J.W.T. Moody—a former Fulbright Scholar at the University of London. While in England he adopted a dress habit that he maintains to this day. Each morning, he'd attire his rotund frame with a black three piece suit, white shirt and black bow-tie—I said he was colorful—a silver chain slung from one vest pock to the other where he kept a pocket watch, and finally black, thick rimmed glasses.

I had Professor Moody for one history class, but I was terrible at history. Luckily, I didn't have to read the dense textbook on Western Civilization. All students had to do was remember what he told them in his very interesting lectures. He told stories. Grand ones. Long ones… with a touch of humor. The class began at 7:30 A.M. three days a week for a semester. I sat in the front row, in the middle (by choice), and took voracious notes. If I could remember what he said by deciphering my notes I'd Ace the course.

On Fridays he would brew a three-gallon jar of English Tea in the corner of his lecture room. If you brought a mug you could have some during class. I didn't own a mug. I never had any tea.

At the time I was the production manager at WGRN and I somehow ended up producing a weekly radio program with Professor Moody called Moody's Musings. I figured this was a way to help get history into my head and ensure at least a "B." The good thing was that his radio programs were, in fact, stories about famous moments in history, like The Naval Battle of Trafalgar (21 October 1805).[1]

As Moody told the story on-air, the battle was won decisively by the British, not so much because of Lord Nelson's unorthodox tactics,

---

1 I do recall some of this from Moody's Musings, but if truth be told Wikipedia helped out on this part, and Dr. Moody wrote to fill in detail.

but by a courageous crew of retired sailors who could not rest in the Old Salts Retirement Home in Kings Lynn, near Boston, England. The old salts, under the leadership of a Captain William Cyrus Moody had heard that Napoleon was going to invade England if Lord Nelson and his modest fleet of 27 warships could not stop Napoleon's French Navy that had joined up with the Spanish armada to form a fleet of 33 ships. Most feared among Napoleon's Combined Fleet was the *Nuestra Señora de la Santísima Trinidad*, which was the largest and most feared warship of the time. It had been expanded to accommodate an unheard of fourth gun deck, with a total of 140 cannon, and a huge stern to accommodate the name which made the Spanish Galleon nearly too wide to get out of the Bay of Cádiz. The weight of the additional guns, so high above her waterline, made her sail slowly and poorly, leading to her nickname, *El Ponderoso*.

Professor Moody tells the story of how these retired Old Salts outfitted a small six-gun sloop, named it the *Pickle* because that is what it would look like if demasted, and sailed into the shadows of the battle. There quite by accident, *Pickle* rammed the *Santísima Trinidad's* rudder, knocking it off, which put the mammoth warship out of commission and thus Nelson was able to win the battle and save England. After the battle, Pickle was rechristened *The Intrepid Pickle*, and ordered with all due speed to carry news of the battle's success back to England. Upon retirement a second time, William Cyrus Moody was given the title *Admiral of the Wash*, which is the name of the shallow bay the Old Salts rest home looked out on.

Years later, naval journals would record that the Santísima Trinidad was ineffective in the Battle of Trafalgar because it was unable to maneuver in the light winds. According to Moody's Musings, however, we knew the real story. And, as was true in all Professor Moody's tales, the real hero was one of his great, great uncles.

And that was the problem. I never knew what part of Moody's Musings was true and what part was fabrication. But they made great stories that you'd never forget.

Perhaps I should have read the textbook. As it turned out I couldn't read my notes…I earned a C.

I N SPITE OF my poor performance in his class, Professor Moody was determined to teach me at least one thing about history that I would never forget. Little did I know what I was in for.

We were studying the French Revolution. If you were half-a-better student of history than I was, you would know that at the on-set of the French Revolution political factions of the Third Estate began to guillotine anyone and everyone associated with Aristocracy. Charles Dickens's *A Tale of Two Cities* gives a vivid description of the period. Essentially, anyone that stepped out of line, even by the most innocent infractions, brought on calls for Liberty, Equality, Fraternity, or Death...especially death. The Revolutionary Tribunal had broad powers, and on a daily basis hundreds of heads met the edge of the guillotine. In ten months nearly 42,000 had been executed.

Back in GC, I was notorious for my own infractions. I was always late for class...which British schooled Moody began sharply at 7:30 AM, a bit too early as far as I was concerned. So, I'd saunter into the class about 7:40 and make my way past the class of 70 early risers, crash into other desks, plop down in front of the black & white suit, and start taking my notes, rarely looking up.

You may remember from an earlier chapter that sitting in the front seat of a class was an unfortunate habit of mine. I've already recalled how in Junior High I sat in the front of Mr. Friend's class and when I fell asleep I was rewarded with a lump on my head courtesy of the ten-pound teacher's edition of Science for You, (with a Special Teacher's addendum: *"How to Keep your Students Awake in Class"*).

> **His black and white outfit reminded me of the paranoia and legalism with which Evangelicalism (and Free Methodism), in their pursuit of a good society, was plagued.**

Falling asleep in Professor Moody's class was not a problem for me. Waking up from sleep in time to get there was. It seems I never learned.

As I was saying, the Professor was lecturing about the Reign of Terror and how those in control did away with people they didn't like. So, at the end of the one lecture he paused, put his hand into a brown paper lunch sack, looked at me and said, "Stanley. I am sick and tired of you always coming late to class. It's a disruption that is going to stop, today. The Tribunal has voted..."

Now up until that moment, as was usually my style, my head was bowed as I focused on my notes, writing rapidly the whole hour. When he said the above, I stopped taking notes and looked up. I still remember what I saw to this day. He stood behind his table-mounted podium not 10 feet away, withdrew his hand from the brown paper sack, and brandished a handgun. He aimed it directly at my face and pulled the trigger—BANG!

I can still see the bursts of fire that emanated from the barrel as the starter pistol's hammer discharged a blank.

He put the gun away and said, "I hope that cures your problem! Class dismissed."

And he walked out...never to be forgotten.

Professor Moody's tactics that day were all in jest, but the incident and his black and white outfit reminded me of the paranoia and legalism with which Evangelicalism (and Free Methodism), in its pursuit of a good society, was plagued. While they talked about the importance of faith, it was REALLY all about actions and works—if you didn't "get to class on time" you were literally "kicked out."

There were, however, two professors who, without resorting to gun powder, got my attention and altered my thinking about reality and what a reasonable faith looked like.

29
Stanley Walters

I T WAS MY sophomore year at Greenville College (1966-1967) that my religious journey of faith was substantially altered by two professors, Dr. Stanley Walters and Dr. Royal Mulholland.

Professor Walters was the head of the Religion Department and an ordained Free Methodist minister. Professor Mulholland was head of the Philosophy Department. Both men taught introductory courses in their discipline. Walters taught *Basic Christianity* (which I took in the fall of 1966), and Mulholland taught *Introduction to Philosophy* (which I took the following semester in the spring of 1967). Although I was majoring in Physics, Greenville was a Christian liberal arts college and these two courses were required of all students.

Basic Christianity, taught by Walters, used three small texts, which he heavily supplemented with handouts. The three texts were *Mere Christianity* by C. S. Lewis (a philosopher), *Basic Christianity* by John Stott (a theologian), and *The New Testament Documents: Are They Reliable?* by F. F. Bruce (a Biblical scholar). Complimenting these fine books was Walter's own background. A modern day Indiana Jones, Walters was one of a small group of biblical scholars who had deciphered and translated cuneiform tablets—"Assyriology being an underpopulated academic discipline."[1] As a busy professor and pastor he wrote many scholarly articles on Biblical exegesis but only one book, which was based on an archive of cuneiform tablets in the Yale Babylonian Collection—a book on irrigation in ancient Mesopotamia, *Water for Larsa* (New Haven: Yale). Forty-seven years after taking his course, Pam and I caught up with him for lunch near Toledo, Ohio. He's still researching and writing for Biblical journals.

---

1 Stanley Walters, personal communications, 8/28/2015.

The relatively short text books for Basic Christianity and Dr. Walters' handouts created for me a foundation for my assertion that I can prove Christianity through the scientific method—that sufficient physical evidence from both contemporary and historical sources, including special and general revelation, could be used to test the hypotheses of Christianity's claim. The course did not set out to demonstrate that Christianity could be proven by the scientific method, but it might as well have, and certainly my inclinations were reinforced by Lewis, Stott, Bruce, and Walters.

Here is an excerpt from the course syllabus, written by Walters; the underlining is mine:

> Biblical revelation acquaints us with *facts* about the universe of which we can become aware in no other way so well. In particular, these are *facts* about God, man, and the relationship between them....The student who is not acquainted with these *facts* and their implications for thought and life, is not fully prepared for life.[1]

While writing this memoir, Walters shared with me that his "strong rational" approach to Christian apologetics during his tenure there, was opposed by some at Greenville College. But, in the 1960's, as a physics major, hard, observable facts were important to me, and the connection between reason and faith that Walters made was a God-send that significantly reaffirmed my faith—faith actually meant something in the physical realm in which we lived. Faith could be backed up with reason!

Back in my dorm room, as soon as I cracked Stott's text, here is what I read: (underline mine):

> Is there any evidence for the amazing Christian assertion that the carpenter of Nazareth was the unique Son of God?...If Jesus was not God in human flesh, Christianity is exploded...But there is *evidence* for the deity of Jesus — *good, strong, historical, cumulative evidence*...
>
> To assent to his divine person, to acknowledge man's need of salvation, and to believe in Christ's saving work are not enough. Christianity is not just a creed; it involves

---

1 Stanley Walters, Course Syllabus, 1966, Greenville College, Religion 102: Basic Christianity.

action....we have to translate our beliefs into deeds.[1]

Now, isn't this interesting? Here we have an Evangelical Christian school that believes in *faith alone* and marginalizes any Christian teaching which claims good works have merit,...and yet the title textbook for a required course was written by an Anglican intellectual (John Stott) who endorsed the *merits* of physical evidence and good deeds to validate Christian faith.

> **The title textbook was written by an Anglican who endorsed the merits of... good deeds to validate Christian faith.**

But there was more. Not only was Stott an Anglican, so was C.S. Lewis. And F.F. Bruce, although he fellowshipped with Evangelical Open Brethren, he nonetheless lived, taught and wrote exclusively within the Anglican intellectual community of Aberdeen, Cambridge, Edinburg, Leeds, and Sheffield. So, perhaps unknown to Walters, and definitely unknown to the G. C. administration, Walters was teaching Anglican's and Catholicism's reliance on faith *and* reason, and *not* faith alone.

Walter's lecture hall (in LaDue Chapel in Marston Hall) and the entrance to the Physic lab (on the first floor of Hogue Hall) were physically only yards apart. I often walked out of Basic Christianity and into the exterior door of the Physics Lab. There, I learned how to form testable hypotheses to confirm or reject various theories about the natural world. Slowly it dawned on me that up in LaDue and in my reading for Walters I was learning how to form testable hypotheses to confirm or deny theories of the supernatural world—the theology of Christianity.

I needed physical evidence to make the scientific method work with Christianity. A hint of such came to me during a trip home for Thanksgiving and an incident that occurred with my mother...you knew we'd get back to my favorite antagonist, didn't you?

When I came home for Thanksgiving Break the fall of my sophomore year in 1966, I brought home a copy of C. S. Lewis's *Mere Christianity*. I laid it on the living room coffee table with every intention of reading it some evening...or starting to...or pretending to...should the mood strike me. Okay, truth be told I wasn't planning on reading it at all. But putting it on the coffee table in plain sight suggested I was studying it, and I figured my parents would be proud I was reading something so intellectual. (Can you get the gist that I was not a con-

---

1 Stott, John R. W. (1958). Basic Christianity. Eerdmans: Grand Rapids, p. 8-9.

noisseur of theology at that time?) Lewis was unique, however...he could be very convincing about the logical reasonableness of Christ.

But that is not what my mother thought. For most of us perspective is everything; and for my Mom, opinion was reality. She saw *Mere Christianity* on the table, picked it up and angrily demanded, "What is this? Why did you bring this into my house?"

I gazed at her hand that waved the thin green and white paperback in my face, "It's required reading for Basic Christianity," I said.

"Why would they tell you to read this?"

"It's one of the textbooks."

Now, I'm a slow learner at times. It never occurred to me that my mother would interpret the word "Mere" in its common derogatory sense of "minimal," "dismissive," or "inconsequential."

"Mom," I said, "It's by C. S. Lewis."

"I know who wrote it," she said even more angrily, "His name's on the cover."

I'll save you the debate. I was about to learn a bit of history on C. S. Lewis, whom my mother knew, in her time at Greenville in 1940, as an outspoken atheist, or skeptic at best. Lewis returned to his baptized Anglian faith in 1957 after a long conversation with J.R.R. Tolkien. Both men taught at Oxford and were members of an informal writing group called the "Inklings." Lewis's name, in my mother's memory, and the ironic title of my vacation reading, caused her to gravely doubt the wisdom of sending me to her Christian Alma Mater. It took a few minutes, and reading a few passages that I had already underlined, but she finally accepted that my homework assignment might have some benefit. But, alas, I had a secret: The underlined passages were not because I thought they were stellar examples of Christian apologetics, but rather because I couldn't understand the sentences. We had a case here of "snob appeal"—if you can't understand it, it must be of some value.

Again, I was a terrible religion student and earned a very modest C+ in Walters' class. But the course had a lasting impact on me seeing the revelations of God through nature and the written word of prophets (the Bible) as "facts" that could be handled in the same way I handled the facts from my study of physics.

A year later when Pam took the course, I got permission from Dr. Walters to tape record the entire semester of lectures, and I've kept all my class notes, handouts, papers and Blue Book exams. Pam has done so as well. One project I may attack someday, is to compile Walters' material into a book or audio lectures and make them available.

One final note about Dr. Walters. When Pam and I were planning our wedding we asked him to perform the wedding with our Free Methodist home pastor, Frank VanValin. At the time of the request we pleasantly discovered that Walters and VanValin had been roommates when they were students at Greenville College. One of our requests for the wedding ceremony was that Pam and I take communion during the wedding, but that the congregation not be served…for the sake of time. Walters refused because he knew that was a doctrinal injustice—everyone in the congregation should receive communion as a sign of the church's unity.

Today, as Catholics, we would agree, but that was then, and so only Rev. VanValin officiated at our wedding. Being a more loyal Free Methodist, and not one given to such a strong rational defense of Christianity as his roommate, he let us have communion, while the congregation did not. I'm sure God was merciful to us in our ignorance.

Professor Walters was down to earth and, as I've mentioned, spent some of his free time deciphering the meaning of cuneiform tablets from historic Babylon. Professor Mulholland, on the other hand, spent time deciphering the meaning of life by taking imaginary trips into the future and outer space.

30
Royal Mulholland

IN THE SPRING of 1967, Professor Royal Mulholland led a number of field trips to extra-solar planets where our class searched for extraterrestrial life. Such events took place in his Introduction to Philosophy, a required course I took the semester after taking Dr. Walters' required Basic Christianity. While Walters helped me see the rational evidence behind Christianity, Mulholland provided a key to interpreting my early frustration with Evangelicalism.

I always wanted to travel into space, and yes, my buddies in the Physics lab were jealous. But that was the magic of philosophy.

Now, before we blast off for Planet X, I need to explain that Mulholland was a *Christian Existentialist.*

Friedrich Nietzsche, the German nihilist philosopher, first developed existentialism as an *approach* of looking to our own experiences and observations for discerning what was true about the particular philosophical position a person happened to hold. Nietzsche set the stage, however, for existentialism to become its own *position* more commonly known as *moral relativism.*[1] More about that in a moment.

In preparation for our landing on Planet-X, Mulholland wanted to make sure that each of us was capable of experientially discovering, discerning and defining truth...through our personal experiences. Now in doing that the existentialist has a tendency to exclude the truth discovered by others.

However...

---

1 Moral Relativism (or Ethical Relativism) is the position that moral or ethical propositions do not reflect objective and/or universal moral truths, but instead make claims relative to social, cultural, historical or personal circumstances. (http://www.philosophybasics.com/)

The prefix Mulholland used, *Christian* Existentialism, claimed that while his philosophical position was "Christian," his method of collecting data was experiential. "Christian" meant that his value motivation was "others" centered as opposed to the "me" centeredness found in existential moral relativism. This allowed a *comparative* method of discovering truth. That is, the Christian Existentialist would openly consider, contrast and compare the truth he derived from experience with the experiential truth discovered and claimed by others. Christian Existentialists embraced both the importance of discoveries by others and themselves. Mulholland reasoned that if there was ultimately a truth that was reasonable, we could collectively discover it through a broadening of the data base.

If you haven't caught the drift, I'm writing about *evidence* based, *rational*, Christianity, as opposed to a Christianity based on an ideology of faith alone.

Here's another way of looking at how Mulholland wanted us to derive truth during our Planet-X expeditions. The Christian Existential process assembles a large database of perceptions from a variety of experiences (disciplines, personalities, histories, skills, lifestyles, measurements) in order to discover who we are and why we are here. When all the data is combined, a fuller understanding of truth emerges. But it comes principally from personal, individual, experiences...if not the personal experiences themselves, then the personal experiences of observing the data taken in and analyzed by others. Ultimately, Mulholland argued, all the data we take in was from our own sense perception, and not anyone else's.

When I thought about this it was clearly obvious, although to some Christians it sounded heretical. Christian theologians and Bible scholars want to put the entire onus on God, God's prophets and the Bible for special revelation. But no human can ingest any special revelation, regardless of its source without using his or her own senses. We must read the Bible with our own eyes, we must hear God's proclamations with our own ears, we must feel the waters of baptism with our own flesh. And we make the willful decision to embrace the Gospel with our own brains. It is then that a transformation occurs within our souls as the miracle of God. But none of that happens without the active engagement of our physical senses and mental processes. Thus, all revelation from God to humans is sensory...and personal.

So, as a class we blasted off for Planet-X. Yes, Mulholland was ahead of the pop-culture curve. It would be ten years later, in 1977, when

Hollywood director Steven Spielberg would catch up with Mulholland and direct CLOSE ENCOUNTERS OF THE THIRD KIND, and then five years after that, in 1982, Spielberg again surprised us with E.T. (the Extra-Terrestrial).

Mulholland was also interested in surprising us, not in an emotional sense, but intellectually. When we landed on Planet-X we began to search extra-terrestrial intelligence, and it was surprisingly easy. Indeed the first rock we hid behind and peeked over allowed us to witness (experience) something...something moving. Indeed there was more than one thing, there were many things...*and they were doing, well, ah...things.* From our hidden vantage point just below the top of a ridge, we looked down into a shallow valley, carefully observed, and took notes.

Strangely, the oxygen that supplied our spacesuits only lasted about the length of one class period, and it would take two days before our supplies for the next mission could be replenished.

Over the semester we thus made the trip to Planet-X every Monday, Wednesday and Friday from 10 AM to 11 AM. And on each trip we discovered a bit more about the things in front of us.

After several weeks of experiential observations we had discovered the following about the *things*...on the other side of the rock:

1. They were substance and physical and not spiritual or ethereal, for their bodies were always opaque and they could not move through each other or nearby objects.
2. They were living things and not inert things like rocks. They did not require external events like weather or earthquakes to move about. They appeared to have free will.
3. They were animals, not plants. Indeed they ate plants.
4. We discovered they were rational because they could reason out new solutions to old problems and did not incessantly make the same mistakes over and over.
5. The question of whether these things were moral or brutes was more difficult, for we could not read their minds. But we observed behavior that indicated some sort of fairness, justice, and punishment for bad behavior. We concluded they were moral beings, not brutes.
6. But whether they were eternal or terminal beings was beyond our sensory grasp.

Each trip to Planet-X forced us to think through the reasons why we came to the conclusions we did.

Of course, Mulholland was taking us through the classical onto-logical investigation of what it means to exist or what is the nature of being, devised by Greek philosopher Porphyry and today referred to as the Porphyrian Tree.

Each class was filled with lively discussion, debates and arguments. Mulholland seemed to love it when two of us in his class of 60-70 would argue with each other. He'd constantly be saying, "Okay, settle down now, and think this through..."

Pam particularly remembers the discussion where Mulholland de-scribed a difference in two groups of aliens. One believed in everything their leaders taught them, but no one in the group lived by the be-liefs they claimed. The other group did everything as if they believed, but their behavior didn't conform to their beliefs. Mulholland asked, which was the better adherent of their faith—those that *believed* or those that didn't believe? Those that *obeyed* or those that didn't obey? What constituted true membership in a group? Was it the mental as-sent to a belief system, or was it the physical adherence to it?

Such was our introduction into critical thinking. Being an exis-tentialist, he taught us to use our sensory experience and our personal insights to find what was true for us. But the "Christian" prefix taught us to contrast and compare "our truth" with what others were discov-ering, including the Revelations of God to those that came before us.

At the close of the semester a major paper was due, which theoret-ically combined this learning in a practical way. The assignment was to analyze a philosophy and compare and contrast it to Christianity. Here was my thought process in choosing my paper's topic.

First, I assumed that Christianity was an ideological, *faith alone* philosophy that rejected the validating evidence of personal experi-ence or any other kind of verisimilitude. That is, faith alone was free to reject what our senses perceived, if the perception appeared to conflict with an ideological tenet.[1]

Second, I asked, was there a diametrically opposed worldview that rejected the purely ideological faith position of Evangelical Christi-anity, but strongly embraced personal experience or an ideology that embraced physical reality alone?

---

1 It would be decades before I recognized the importance of FAITH and REASON to validate a philosophy. Faith can only exist through the application of reason, and reason can only operate with certain assumptions of faith.

Third, was such a philosophy subject to the extremes of existentialism (e.g. self-centered moral relativism) without the safeguards of *others-centered* morality, such as found in Christianity?

It took me a day or two, but I was reminded of Fred, my freshman roommate, who had decorated our room with Playboy centerfolds.

Available at the time, was a book edition (sans pictorials) of Hugh Hefner's *Playboy Philosophy*, which had appeared as a series of editorial columns in the magazine over a number of years. Since I liked taking risks I decided that this was as good a time as any *not* to ask permission but be prepared to ask forgiveness.

My final 5,000-word paper was titled "A Critical Analysis of the Philosophy of Hugh M. Hefner, editor-publisher of Playboy Magazine." No guts, no glory, they say.

The paper earned the highest grade in the class, 122 points out of 120—Mulholland gave me a couple of bonus points for guts, and verbally promised *not* to show it to the college president whose daughter I was dating at the time. (This was before Pam showed up on campus.)

Now, confession time. I recently read over the paper, and it does contain what you might expect from a student at a conservative Christian college trying to get a good grade—there's a lot of over the top Christian catch phrases and jargon pretending to sound philosophical and intelligent. I've made it sound very analytical and full of solid critical thinking, but it was more ideological than it was good.

During Mulholland's Introduction to Philosophy, I came to believe that Absolute Truth was knowable, and that it wasn't found in the concept of faith alone, or in Scripture alone, but also relied on the careful observation of the universe (i.e. Reason). Coming to this conclusion was like cement hardening. It seemed so obvious and it formed a defensible foundation for my journey.

I must have succeeded in making a reasonable case for faith and reason, or at least demonstrated I could bellow my way into making such a case. The next year Mulholland approached me and asked if I would do a little role-playing before his new Introduction to Philosophy class. He wanted me to pretend to be an empiricist, that is a rationalist or scientist. My task would be to give a short talk on why reason and empiricism were the best way to know what is real and true (aside from faith), then banter about Q&A with the students.

It occurred to me that such a position was probably not what Mulholland advocated (although I wasn't sure), but it was close to what I advocated. I wasn't a pure rationalist who discredited revelation, but verses like Hebrews 11:17 came to mind where it says, "He *reasoned* that God was able to raise even from the dead." Hebrews 11, where the faith of the ancients is celebrated, is often used by Protestants to advocate that Christianity is based on faith alone. But in Hebrews 11 and throughout the Bible, descriptions of faith are paired with terms that reference reason and action – terms like *evidence, universe, visible, sacrifice, taken up, (physical) salvation, generate, obey, acts, works, deeds, and wisdom.*

There was another thing that popped into my mind. Royal Mulholland advocated a very robust rational position to support Christianity, yet he could not explicitly take such a stand in an Evangelical school, so he recruited a student to take the fall—me. He probably figured I'd be gone in a year or two and he could then explain to the administration that my appearance in his class was an exercise in knocking my arrogance down a notch or two, while strengthening his class's *faith.*

> **I came to believe that Absolute Truth was knowable, and that it wasn't found in the concept of faith alone, or in Scripture alone, but also relied on the careful observation of the universe (i.e. Reason).**

No, I didn't think of all this at the time. What I was thinking was much more practical, observable, and involved verisimilitude. I was thinking how cool it will be to make an impression on the lady that would later become my wife—Pam—for she was a student in the class.

My talk before the class presented the evidence for Christianity as empirical evidence that could be discovered, measured and tested to prove the hypothesis that Christianity was trustworthy. In the process I did argue against "faith alone" and argued for the "scientific method."

In an attempt to undermine my position, a gal-pal of Pam's posed a question to me. She cast a sideways glance at Pam and said, "So, how do you prove love. You can't see love or measure it. How do you know your girlfriend even likes you?"

Pam arched her eyebrows at me as if to say, "Yeah, smarty pants, let's see you get out of this one."

My arrogance knew no bounds. "That's simple," I said. "Her love or dislike for me will be visible and scientifically verifiable. It can be hypothesized and repeatedly tested as physical evidence. Does she bake me cookies on Fridays and fill them with chocolate chips or Ex-Lax?

And on my birthday, does she know I love orange cake with butter frosting, or does she send me a box of rocks?"

PAM WRITES: Truly, the guy's arrogance knew no bounds. I had just done that. Not the rocks, but the cake...and I even baked the two layers in heart shaped pans. It didn't turn out so good, but he loved it. And he knew I loved him.

E ARLIER I DISCUSSED how in Introduction to Philosophy we spent some time observing alien life on another planet. Little did I know that a few years later I'd be doing it for real...or planning on doing it for real.

During the last semester of my college career, in the spring of 1969, Professor Mulholland announced an experimental philosophy class that would be open to second semester Seniors. They called it Interdisciplinary Issues Seminar. It was a senior level course offered by invitation only. The students were to be nominated by an informal committee of faculty from the various disciplines in which major courses of study were offered. Only one student from each of the college's departments was invited to participate. At the time there were 18 majors offered by GC and I was offered the slot from Physics.

The Interdisciplinary Seminar's goal was to prepare us to face a real-life moral dilemma later in our chosen field of work.

The class met only once a week, for three hours. Each week a different senior, from a different discipline, was to introduce a philosophical problem or occupational dilemma he or she expected to encounter during their career. Their assignment was then to engage the class in finding a practical solution that was philosophically consistent with the Christian faith.

I drew on my interest in astronomy and the country's manned space program. This was my question: *What should be our Christian response when humanity discovers Extra-Terrestrial Intelligence (ETI)?* At the time, SETI (the modern Search for Extra-Terestial Intelligence) had been going on for nearly a decade. SETI was partly responsible for the popularity of perhaps my all-time favorite motion picture, Stanley Krubrick's 2001 A SPACE ODYSSEY based on the novel of the same name by Arthur C. Clarke. Clarke was an atheist-physicist, who predicted the use of geo-synchronous communication satellites and the wide spread use of personal computers, some three decades before their existence.

2001: A SPACE ODYSSEY, although released the prior summer (May 1968), had developed a cult following and was still in one theater in St. Louis during the semester of the Interdisciplinary Issues Seminar. I had viewed the film five times earlier on and could not figure it out. It contained this intriguing mix of science, philosophy and art. I persuaded Mulholland and a few others from the seminar to secretly travel (against the school's movie prohibition) to St. Louis to see it with me...it would be my sixth time. Pam went with us.

At dinner after the movie, Mulholland explained that the prominent disorienting music later in the movie, *Also Sprach Zarathustra,* was written in 1896 by Richard Strauss as a tone poem inspired by a philosophical novel written by his friend, Friedrich Nietzsche.[1] The themes of the Nietzsche novel and the Kubrick movie were the same: (1) Eternal Recurrence, (2) The Superman (The Overman), and (3) The Will to Power. These themes conspired to push aside the morality of religion, especially Christianity (which Nietzsche heavily criticized), and elevate man to "super" status, giving him absolute freedom over any kind of universal morality. Nietzsche believed that the death of God would give man absolute freedom in the universe.

When revising this chapter I was struck by the irony that 2001: A SPACE ODYSSEY, which had clearly been a favorite movie of mine at the time, and still is today, resonated with me deeply. Even after Mulholland's disturbing explanation I went four more times to see the film, ten times in all. But I clearly did not espouse Nietzsche's philosophy. I wonder, now, if the movie didn't parallel my peculiar frustration with Evangelicalism. While the movie illustrated Nietzsche's view that man evolved from the ape to its current rational state, and was destined to evolve even further to become the super-being capable of instituting its own rules over the universe, could that be an outline for how Protestantism saw itself with respect to the Roman Church? Did Protestantism see Catholicism as an ape that needed evolving into a more rational figure (Protestantism), which then had the potential to evolve into a super church, rewriting moral laws to suit its needs? Is that what troubled me, that Protestantism rejected the Natural Law of the universe and the totality of God's special revelation, writing its own rules? Was the God of the early Christian Church dead, thus giving Protestantism freedom to invent it's own moral code? I would have to

1 *The Blue Danube Waltz,* which also features significantly in 2001: A SPACE ODYSSEY was written in 1866 by Johann Strauss II of Vienna, who was no relation to Richard Strauss, who was from Munich and Berlin.

think more about that.

W HEN MY WEEK to present my ETI paper came, I figured everyone would be pumped with the "reality" of human civilization having an encounter with ETI, like the evidence of one depicted in Kubrick's 2001. I provided a handout with the statistical evidence, produced a slide show with glorious pictures of deep space that elucidated (at least to me) the likelihood of humanity confronting such an ETI event. Then, I asked how I, as a Christian scientist, would deal with the discovery.[1] It was not up to each of us presenters to suggest solutions, but simply to present the problem and lead a discussion of the potential answers.

After my presentation, the subsequent discussion with my student peers was a disappointment—they never engaged the question. Instead, they questioned my premise. *How dare they?* They argued that ETI was not possible and that such an assumption, even for purposes of philosophical speculation, was a waste of time.

The "reason"? It was a matter of "faith." Their argument was simple enough: Man was created in God's image, the Bible said, and there was no mention of extraterrestrial life in the Bible. Therefore humanity, on earth, was unique. The universe was crafted exclusively for us, and that was it. The reaction to my premise came from an ideology that pushed aside reason.

At the time I didn't really care if ETI existed, but I thought the discussion of what to do if they were encountered would be a great intellectual exercise if only modestly practical. It was never to be. Intellectual pursuit gave way to ideological strangulation.

Christians are quick to criticize Nietzsche for his declarations that "God is Dead," reflected on TIME magazine's cover a year later,[2] "IS GOD DEAD?" But, it took *Christianity Today* 42 years to mount a rebuttal cover, "GOD IS NOT DEAD YET."[3]

Of this debate, my favorite was this doublet:

---

1 Although it would be ten more years before the release of Spielberg's CLOSE ENCOUNTERS OF THE THIRD KIND, the possibility had been explored by fiction writers for decades, perhaps most famously by Orson Welles's 1938 Halloween radio broadcast of "The War of the Worlds." Welles's effort, of course, was an adaptation of H.G. Wells's 1898 novel of the same name. Wells and Welles were not related.

2 TIME cover story 8 April 1966.

3 Christianity Today, July 2008.

"God is dead" — Nietzsche, 1893
"Nietzsche is dead." — God, 1990

At the age of 44 Nietzsche had a complete mental breakdown and died at 55 of syphilis and brain cancer. It seemed that Nietzsche had tried to adopt and promote an ideology that was far afield of reality, and he paid the price.

Clearly, Evangelical Christianity was nowhere close to such a nihilist worldview, nor did my Protestant associations disregard Natural Law morality. But there was a hint of Nietzsche's "go it alone" mentality within Protestantism, that prevented Christian unity and caused scandal; and about that I would struggle as I tried to figure out God's Plan for my life.

I N THE MEANTIME, the semester after Mulholland's Intro to Philosophy course, and during my 1967 Thanksgiving break, I wrote out a prayer in protest against two things: (a) The Free Methodist aversion to writing out prayers and reading them in services , and (b) the unrealistic expectation that once a person became a Christian, life was supposed to be free of pain and suffering. Surprisingly, our pastor at Dearborn Free Methodist let me read the prayer during the evening service following Thanksgiving. In the audience was Pam (who I was not dating at the time) and her family. I was sure reading the prayer would be provocative, but for years I had no idea how it contributed to changing my life.

An Existentialist's Thanksgiving Prayer

Dear God,
We never thank you for those things
Which so often we despise and reject
As the gift of a loving thoughtful God
But, today we'd like to go back and recollect
All those dreadful things
     and thank you
For the ineffectiveness of our lives
For the instability we often try to hide
For the insecurity too often realized
Lord, we thank you
For the let down of a friend
For the lamentations over a friend

for the loneliness without a friend
we thank you...   *for frustration*
              for failure
              for froth
For the evil in our hearts and mind
For the envy which we don't resign
For the egocentric life of mine
Lord, I thank you...   *for dissatisfaction*
              for disappointments
              for disrespect
For the unthankfulness of those we know
For the unrest from satan our greatest foe
For this unpeaceful restless life of woe
we thank you dear Lord...   *for desolation*
              for discontent
              for death
For the sorrow which today will bring
the sadness of tomorrow, and fling
the suffering of another in our ring
Lord we thank you
For the heartaches of a love once here
For the hindrances of a child so dear
For the hell on earth we often fear
Yes, Lord, we thank you.

Aside from the apparent blatant heresy such a prayer might bring to mind, there was forethought, which I tacked on crudely to the end, as if to justify my psychotic state of mind. It was this:

For we can rejoice
when we run into such
problems, trials, and temptations.
for they are good for us, we know
they help us learn to be patient.
For patience develops strength of character in us
and this in turn helps us trust God more each time
until finally our hope and faith are strong and steady.
For when that happens, we will be able to hold our heads high
no matter what happens and know that all is well,
for we know how dearly God loves us, lowly us!
and we will feel His warm love everywhere within us

because God has given us the Holy Spirit
to fill our hearts
WITH HIS LOVE (Romans 5:3-5)

Years later, well after we were married, Pam told me that hearing that prayer attracted her to me even more and was one of the reasons she tracked me down in Greenville a few months later. Her life had run into some difficulties and somehow she thought I was the solution. Little did either of us know.

31
Discovery Bound

I SHUDDER WHEN I look back to 1968 and 1969—my last year in college and the summer after. During those 18 months my conscious desire was to follow God's lead and subscribe to His plan for my life. But God didn't chase me around like a drill sergeant with a megaphone, although at times I think it would have helped. Although I believed in God's Providence when it came to who I was supposed to marry, what career I should pursue, or where should I live, the decisions were much more ambiguous and confusing. It would be decades before I found resonance in the words of Venerable Solanus Casey, "Blessed be God in all his designs."[1]

> I had a hard time telling the difference between God's "still small voice" and the rumble of my own heart.

The problem I faced during this time of transformation from child and student to adult and worker was that I was hard pressed to see any design in what was actually happening. Did God lead me? If he did, did I follow? If God nudged me in one direction, did I push back and go in another? If God spoke to me, did I ignore the call...or even hear His voice? I had a hard time telling the difference between God's "still small voice" and the rumble of my own heart.

I wanted to hear but feared I was deaf. I wanted to see but I balked at my blindness. My faith in God was strong, but I didn't trust myself.

Thus, the forces that pushed and pulled on my life decisions were

---

1 I frequently pray at Venerable Solanus Casey's crypt on which this quote of his is inscribed. It's located at the Capuchin's St. Bonaventure Monastery in Detroit, Michigan.

four...or, for the purposes at hand, I've limited them to four:

- ACCIDENTS, brought on by a convolution of Natural Law,
- FATES, brought on by mysterious supernatural operators or the occurrence of coincidence,
- DECISIONS, brought about by the exercise of my free will and reason, and
- PROVIDENCES, brought about by God's direct intervention in my affairs.

I suppose God can lead through any or all of these, but the lines of demarcation were blurred, and the process mysterious.

The irony of the journey, highlighted in the following chapters, is that while my goal was *security*, it seems that the only way I came to such confidence was by experiencing the *insecurity* of the times (e.g. the 1960's and the Vietnam War), exacerbated by my decisions, the happenstance of fate, and the inevitability of accident.

Oh, and then there were the prayers of my Mother.

32
Decision Bound

A	S MY SENIOR year at GC dawned Pam and I were steadies. After being separated from her the summer of 1968, I didn't want to leave her side, and as earlier related, we began to think about marriage. That meant I had better start thinking more seriously about my career and how I was going to support a wife and family.

Foremost in my mind was that Pam and I might never get married, unless some drastic measures were taken. It was the 14th year of the Vietnam War, and the United States government was in the final stages of starting up the military draft to supply more bodies for the killing fields of Southeast Asia. My roommate at the time, Richard Marcellus, was convinced we were going to end up in Vietnam as soon as we graduated the following June. It was fate, he implied, over which Providence had no control, although don't tell that to my mother.

The anti-Vietnam protests at universities across the country skipped Greenville's campus. As I recall, few of the guys I knew wanted to join up and go to war, but we weren't going to protest it either. In our eyes, the protesters were communists, political radicals, unemployed hippies posing as college students, or drug pushers looking for customers amidst the chaos.

I wasn't sure that was entirely the case, but in isolated Greenville we were much more intent on doing well in school than burning flags. Still, though we lived in a very small town, the war loomed large over our heads.

Drastic measures were called for. A friend of mine, who was also majoring in physics, persuaded me that if we didn't sign up for another branch of service we'd be drafted into the infantry. We figured planes were cool, and piloting an F4 with cannons in the nose, missiles on the wings, and bombs in the belly was better than crawling through rice paddies with a carbine.

So, early in October, 1968 my friend and I drove 90 miles south to Carbondale, Illinois and met with an Air Force recruiter. We figured, that being physics majors and in top physical shape, we would easily qualify for Officer's Training School (OTS) and flight school.

When we got there, the recruiter was overjoyed to see us. *What's with him, we thought?* He immediately helped us fill out applications, complete forms, take a simple physical, and then administered several fairly easy written and eye-sight tests. In all it took about 90 minutes. We returned to Greenville figuring we had beat the draft.

That we never heard from the recruiter again didn't seem to bother us. We had months of college to finish and we didn't really expect to hear anything before spring.

I had considered that my Mom would have been pleased with my signing up for the military. Throughout the last years of high school, she became so fed up with my insolence, that on several occasions she threatened to call the army recruiter and sign me up for basic training. *"The discipline would do you good."* I was too naive to realize she couldn't do such a thing without my cooperation, so I had tried to mend my ways, if only for a week or two.

After I returned from the Carbondale recruiter, I wrote Mom and told her what I had done. She'll be happy, I thought. But as I was to find out later, I didn't know my Mom very well…or should I say my Mom knew a lot more than I did.

ANOTHER OPTION WAS Graduate School in Physics, which would lead to a career in research science. I liked the idea of experimental physics, but the theoretical side scared me. Early in the fall of my senior year was the time to apply, so I sent off applications to seven graduate schools of modest distinction. I knew my grades were not good enough for the better schools. How to pay for graduate school, and how years of graduate study would allow me to support my wife, I had no clue.

One of the graduate school entrance requirements was the submission of a high score in physics and math on the Graduate Record Examinations (G.R.E). That I dreaded. Not only was theoretical physics not my forté, neither was taking written tests. I realized that the G.R.E. requirements proved that my bachelor degree didn't mean squat. I actually had to prove I knew something.

As a senior, this came as no surprise. I had been working toward this for nearly two years. The first semester of my sophomore year I flunked Calculus I. Now, don't get me wrong, it wasn't that I didn't fully understand it, well, okay, actually I didn't…but the excuse I've used for years was that the New Christy Minstrels were coming to campus for a concert, and I volunteered to run the student-side advertising and marketing for the event. Thus, in order to fulfill my self-imposed fiduciary responsibilities (to folk-singing) I skipped two weeks of Calculus right when the class began covering integrals. This was no accident, nor was it fate, or Providence. It was all me.

Suffice it to say, the New Christy Minstrels, who performed in the gymnasium, trashed the women's locker room that they used for a dressing room in retaliation for the Board of Trustees censoring the group's repertoire. *Verboten* were songs and lyrics that contained innuendos about sex, alcohol and general rebellion. In keeping with the New Christy Minstrel's behavior, I trashed Calculus. Missing those first weeks of Integral Calculus was terminal. I was never able to catch-up. Although I made-up the course during the summer at St. Louis University, I became well aware of my deficiencies.

Taking the G.R.E. was going to be bad enough, but submitting my transcripts gave me assurance that I'd never have to sit for the G.R.E.s. And, I was right. Out of seven applications submitted to middle of the road schools, I received seven rejections. What a relief; I didn't have to take the G.R.E.'s.

So much for will-power to direct my life. If I made many more decisions like the New Christy "*Mistrials*" I could forget asking God for help.

A S I'VE ALREADY described, near the end of the first semester of my senior year, during Thanksgiving, Pam and I purchased wedding rings in St. Louis. On Christmas Eve in Detroit we officially became engaged…and I went on an eating binge at multiple congratulatory dinners, thus requiring a new wardrobe when I returned to Greenville for my last semester of college. Now that I was engaged, it was time to focus on something else…like graduating. Thus, my last semester of college was particularly difficult. I took an overload of 19 credit hours in a last ditch attempt to graduate on time.

It didn't work.

33
Houston Bound

I T WAS LATE January 1969. I had just finished an intensive study of Atomic Physics during Greenville's month of special studies between regular semesters called *Interterm*. The next full-length semester, and my last, was going to be difficult. Pam and I considered returning to Michigan for a few days to visit our families. Actually, that was Pam's idea. My idea was *not* to go home and visit my parents. Dad and sis were okay, but I was always looking for a way to avoid being in the same room with my Mom for more than 30-seconds.

My salvation came in a phone call from my nephew, Bob *(under the bed)* Kenney. Having graduated a year before me, he was teaching in Jackson, Michigan and was on Winter Break. He pitched the idea of the two of us driving to the Manned Space Craft center in Houston, Texas. I'm not sure why I take his suggestions seriously; they usually end up with me being embroiled in some sort of disaster. But I was in a pinch. He offered to drive down to Greenville in his little Triumph, a two-seat sports coupe big enough for two sardines. If I could share expenses, we'd make it a week in the Lone Star state where he once lived. He wasn't really a Texan but he liked to pretend he was. (He would have made a great TV doctor.)

Now, it may seem odd for two college guys to waste a break on a visit to NASA rather than following other hormonally charged lemmings to the Florida beaches to cavort with bikini draped babes, tip some beers, and party through the night. The truth be told, neither one of us liked alcohol in any of its supposedly innocuous forms, nor were we into rogue parties that proved alcohol was anything but innocuous. It was true, however, we had no such aversion to girls…especially in bikinis.

But the attraction in Houston went back to our youth and our long interest in space travel. For in just four months NASA would launch Apollo 11, humanity's first attempt to land men on the moon, and return them safely to Earth. It was an exciting time for all space junkies. I even harbored the thought that Neil Armstrong and Buzz Aldrin might find an ETI, or a Kubrick-Clarke monolith on the moon like depicted in 2001: A SPACE ODYSSEY. Wouldn't that be interesting?

At least that was the excuse I gave Pam, who finally consented to my going when she realized that returning home without her fiancé in tow would start a rumor that we had separated. So, she stayed at Greenville to collect our mail and to study. (Study! Another reason she graduated with honors, and I…well, I graduated.)

Bob drove down from Michigan, I packed lightly for the trip (since the car was so tiny) and off we went to meet our destiny. Little did we know.

We drove straight through and found a cheap hotel near the Manned Spacecraft Center on NASA One Boulevard. The next day, we visited the Center's outdoor space museum, got pizza, watched movies in the Center's visitor's theater, got burgers, toured the Mission Control and Simulator buildings, crashed, and the next day headed off to repeat our vacation litany.

Now, you would have thought a couple of dudes who had been brought up in Evangelical Christianity, one being a P.K. (that would be Bob) and the other the son of an M.K. and P.K.[1] (that would be me), and both having attended church all their lives, and both having attended Christian colleges--would know when Sunday was.

But we were clueless until, that is, we turned into the Manned Spacecraft center for a tour and were told the Visitor's place was shut down on Sundays.

Duh!

Quick, find a church, we reckoned. But we were too late in the day for that.

So, we went for a drive toward Galveston Bay.

Just down the road a mile we drove past a little sailboat rental boutique on the body of water the map called Clear Lake. Hey we thought! Let's rent a sailboat.

We pulled into the parking lot and something didn't look right. First, Clear Lake was anything but "clear." It was, in fact, a wide, shallow muddy backed-up bayou from Galveston Bay. No doubt the city fathers

---

1 P.K. = Preacher's Kid; M.K. = Missionary's Kid.

that named the body of water felt guilty so they rectified their political correctness by naming the tributary that fed "Clear" Lake, something more truthful—"Mud Lake."

But we didn't really care. The temperature was in the high 60's— sunbathing weather for Michiganders. We pulled in, excited to take the plunge. But the rental office was closed. Why would it be closed on such a beautiful day?

We were slow. Go with the story.

But, there was a posted phone number. We found a phone booth and explained our plight to the proprietor—*two lost boys from Michigan in search of a good time.* The guy thought "we was nuts" insofar as it was *freezing outside* and…(drum roll please)…it was *SUNDAY.*

Duh!

But he was as hard up as we were and came down and rented us a sailboat.

It was great. There was a fresh breeze, as we tacked back and forth, heeled the boat over, came about, gybed, and generally had a blast for about 30 minutes.

Until…we capsized.

Fate? Providence? Accident?

More likely my stubbornness to think I could sail any boat in Clear Lake that looked like mud.

No harm done, the boats were designed for such schmucks as Bob (It's Sunday) Kenney and his faithful companion, "Stando."

Did I tell you the trip was so exciting we took pictures? I had this neat little leather-cased Instamatic camera. We went though all 24 pictures on the roll in two days. That was a lot of pictures back then, especially when you figured every picture was going to cost us about $2 for film, processing, and prints.

The sailboat proprietor took the last picture on the roll of Bob and me soaked in our muddy clothes grinning like idiots holding the remains of the sailboat we had managed to drag through the mud to shore.

We dried off, sort of, and shifted into high gear, and off we went in the Triumph down NASA Parkway back to our cheap-cheap motel. When we came to our first stoplight, I asked Bob "Hey, where'd you put my camera?"

"I gave it to you," my elder said.

"Yeah, but I put it on the top of the trunk…didn't you get it?"

"No," he said, "that's why I gave it to you."

"But I gave it back," I said.

"Sure you did, by putting it on *top* of the trunk."

He did a quick U-turn and in a minute we were back at the sailboat rental. We asked the proprietor if we had left our camera there. He said, no, but mentioned he did see something like the camera fly off the Triumph's trunk as we pulled out onto NASA One Blvd, and left in a cloud of mud. He said a Red Mustang stopped almost immediately picked whatever it was up (our camera) and took off after us. We thanked him, and off we went looking for a Red Mustang.

We drove through shopping center parking lots, up and down the Boulevard, and finally scooted down Upper Bay Road into the village of Nassau Bay and drove around, under and through garages of several apartment complexes, including one called The Balboa Apartments (remember that name).

We never found the Red Mustang, or the camera. (If anyone reading this had a Red Mustang in 1969, picked up our camera, and developed our pictures...how were the exposures? And...if the exposures were good, would you please send us copies of the pictures so we can prove to our significant ladies that we actually went to Houston? Thanks!)

All this may seem less interesting or important than swallowing a Life-Saver™ while sucking a lemon. But something was unfolding.

On Monday we got back to taking tours at the Manned Spacecraft Center. It was great stuff and we loved every minute of our time there. What an exciting place to work, I thought.

By Tuesday morning we were ready to head back home, having nearly run out of money. We checked out of the motel and did a little souvenir shopping, always on the lookout for a Red Mustang. Early afternoon we fueled up the car and our stomachs, and were ready to hit the road when I decided to call Pam's dorm and let her know I'd see her the next afternoon. We would drive straight through changing drivers while the other slept.

Once I got her on the phone and told her about our awesome trip, she told me that I had received a letter from the McDonnell Douglas Astronautics Company (MDAC) in St. Louis. She asked what that was about? I told her I had no idea, but that she should open it up and find out.

She did...and our lives changed forever.

In the letter, MDAC offered me a full time job as an Associate Electronic Engineer in the Astronautics Company at Lambert Air Field in St. Louis, at a decent salary (which worked out to $4.55/hour), to start as soon as I graduated from Greenville College.

The letter was totally unexpected. I had not made application for the job and knew nothing about it. There had been no interview, no letters, no phone calls. All I could assume was that GC's reputation for turning out science graduates preceded me. And, clearly, MDAC had *not* seen my transcript.

Pam read the letter to me three times as I stood in the phone booth, dropping quarters into the coin slots each time the operator interrupted our reverie.

> **There had been no interview, no letters, no phone calls... And clearly, MDAC had not seen my transcript.**

Nonetheless, in that phone booth, next to the freeway, just South of Houston, Pam and I decided that we would not wait until the summer of 1970 to get married. I would accept the job, and we'd get married later in the year. I have never accounted for this except by Providence. I knew it was not something I initiated, and I didn't want to think it was fate or simply an accident. Some would call it a lucky break, otherwise known as that moment when preparation meets opportunity. But I would be hard pressed to embrace such luck since my preparation was mediocre and I knew nothing of the opportunity to pursue.

Bob was waiting in the car, wondering what was taking me so long. With great excitement, I told him, and then in my enthusiasm I pushed aside Bob's magnetism for bad karma and asked him to be the best man at my wedding.

At the time I had no way of knowing that in two years time, as a MDAC engineer, I would be transferred to the Houston Manned Spacecraft Center to write flight procedures for Skylab[1] astronauts, that I would be working directly with astronauts training them in the simulator building we had just toured...and that Pam and I would move into the Balboa Apartments, the very place through which Bob and I had driven not an hour earlier looking for the camera. Was that just an accident, or Providential foreshadowing?

All of that notwithstanding, little did Bob and I know what was in our near future, and it wasn't bright.

---

1 Skylab was the U.S.'s first manned space station. Launched May 14, 1973, three crews occupied the station from 1973-1974. Skylab reentered Earth's atmosphere and disintegrated in 1979.

34
San Jacinto Bound

IT WAS ABOUT 3:30 PM when Bob and I left Houston's city limits behind, and sped North along the highway. Bob picked the first shift
at driving, while I folded my arms across my chest and fell asleep in
the passenger's seat of his fun little sports coupe.

The next thing I knew my rib was searing in pain, my head ached
something awful, I was dazed, and blood gushed from the bridge of
my nose. The car had come to a crumpling halt in the middle of the
highway. I pushed the door open, fell out, and struggled to breathe.
I recall stumbling away from the car and collapsing on the side of a
bridge in a daze. Blood dripped off my face onto the cement roadway.

Accidents happen.

What we suspect happened was this: A few minutes after I had
fallen asleep, Bob too fell asleep just as the speedy Triumph came to
the bridge over the West Fork of the San Jacinto River south of Conroe,
Texas. As his steering hand dropped into his lap, it tugged the wheel
to the right, causing the car to veer into the east curb and guardrail,
jostling the steering and waking him up. Grabbing the wheel in panic,
he over-corrected and the car, still going at highway speeds, suddenly
hooked to the left and hurled itself into the west guardrail, destroying
the front end and stopping the vehicle in the left of the two north-
bound lanes.

This was before seat beats were required and neither of us wore
one.

Dazed, I crawled out of the passenger's seat, and stumbled into the
middle of the road. As I did, I remember seeing a pickup truck stop
behind us. A man was getting out of it. I managed to crawl out of the
traffic lane, and to the west side of the bridge where I collapsed and

sat on the curb. My head drooped between my knees, blood dripped off my face onto the roadway, and my breathing was intensely painful.

Miraculously, no other vehicle or persons were involved. The pickup driver came to my aid. I looked around but didn't see Bob anywhere. The Triumph's driver car door was wide open, but he was nowhere to be seen.

Before I knew it an ambulance arrived and two EMTs (not to be confused with ETIs) were looking me over (who probably looked like an ETI). They tried to get me to lie flat on my back on a stretcher. But the pain of breathing was too intense so they finally allowed me to lie on my side in a fetal position. Moments later I was being rushed to the Montgomery County Hospital in Conroe, TX.

I asked about Bob. I hadn't seen him. The EMT's told me to relax, that my friend was alright and in a second ambulance.

My body went into shock and shook uncontrollably; my breathing was shallow and painful. I felt blood clotting in my eyes and nose. I gasped for breath. I struggled to get more comfortable, but the EMT's held me in place as the ambulance sped toward the hospital, its siren wailing.

I had time to think about what was wrong. I concluded that when my sleeping body flew forward into the car's dash, my right fist, which had been crossed over my chest, was forced against a rib that broke off my sternum. The loose end of the rib was digging into my left lung. There was also a huge gash on the bridge of my nose, and another gash several inches on my left side that was ripped open and also bleeding.

Once inside the emergency room I was given morphine as nurses and a surgeon began to clean my wounds and sew me up. Within minutes I started to feel better and my shaking lessened.

They wheeled Bob in next to me on a gurney. I said something to him, but he just stared at me blankly, totally disoriented. A doctor told me that a trucker had pulled Bob off the bridge railing as it appeared, in his delirium, he was about to jump into the San Jacinto River fifty-feet below. The river was currently at flood stage. Bob' s apparent disorientation was the consequence of a concussion that had left him in a state of amnesia. He didn't know who he was, where he was or anything about his life. The the EMTs had found his driver's license and registration and so the hospital knew who he was but they couldn't convince Bob of it. Ironically, Bob suffered no broken bones or cuts. It was just his mind; it had gone *kaput*. It was my job, the doctor's informed me, to talk him out of it, reiterating to him the events of the hours and days just past.

For the next few hours I kept telling him every little detail I could remember of our lives and especially the last few days. Slowly he started talking and making sense. But he had no idea what had just happened, where we were or why we were in Texas.

Later, when my vitals stabilized, we were admitted to the hospital and rolled into a room together. There we were given a mild sedative, and we got some sleep.

In the morning Bob woke up almost his normal joking self. Except the trip to Texas was erased totally from his memory, as it is to this day. But he knew me and began to crack jokes about being in a hospital. He was always fun to be around, and the more desperate the situation, the more ironic his jokes became. That he couldn't remember anything suddenly became part of his repertoire, and since then he's used that to his advantage: *"I had amnesia, what's your excuse?"*

For the next two days, every few hours, a pleasantly plump nurse in her fifties, with a round face, short curly blonde hair and red cheeks would come cheerily into our room to check our vitals and do…well, you know…nursey, cheeky stuff.

By the second full day Bob was in rare form and had me literally holding my stitched-up side with laughter as he found one thing after another strange or weird about our situation.

Mid-morning of day three, we lay in bed after eating most of our breakfast. Nurse Cheeky came into our room, plopped a couple of empty wide-mouth glass bottles on our bedside tables and said cheerily that she needed urine samples and that she'd be back in a few minutes to pick them up. Bob starred warily at the bottle and then at her as she left and swung the door shut. As soon as the door was closed, Bob asked me to hand him my sliced open grapefruit that sat uneaten on my breakfast tray. Warily I handed it to him even as I grabbed my bottle and slid it under the sheet in an attempt to do my duty.

But Bob had his own agenda. Taking his bottle he squeezed the juice from both his grapefruit and mine into it, then dutifully put it on the table.

Ten minutes later, like clockwork, Nurse Cheeky returned to collect our intimate samples. I was closest to the door, so she grabbed mine first and then walked around my bed to Bob's side and picked up his bottle.

"My, my," she said holding Bob's bottle up to the light. "A little cloudy today, aren't we?"

"Really?" said Bob, taking the bottle from her and looking at it closely. "Guess we'll just have to run it through again." And with that he promptly drained the bottle into his mouth and swallowed.

To claim that Nurse Cheeky screamed, would have been an understatement. For her it was the end of the world, if not her career. She exploded out of the room, and announced a Code Blue. Suddenly buzzers and klaxons were going off, and a stampede of white-robed medical personal poured into our room. And what did they find?

Bob, clearly pleased with himself, staring at them with a stupid *What me worry?* smile on his face like Alfred E. Neuman on the cover of a Mad Magazine.

And they found me, with blood pumping from my side like a mini-geyser. I was laughing so hard I pulled out my stitches.

Poor Nurse Cheeky didn't know what to do, pump Bob's stomach or wheel me back into emergency surgery.

The event convinced the hospital that we were actually well enough to be discharged, as soon as the vitals of the hospital staff returned to normal.

THERE'S ONE STORY about Bob that has nothing to do with my journey of faith, but perhaps it did for his. For a while after college Bob was on the staff of Youth For Christ in Ypsilanti and Ann Arbor, Michigan. One of his responsibilities was to help plan and stage the monthly assemblies at which hundreds of youth would attend. These were always fun as well as spiritual events that gave everyone associated with them a sense of belonging. For some reason on the afternoon of one of these assemblies, Bob and another YFC cohort rented a real lion (that came with a trainer) that would appear on stage that night for some aberrant purpose. In the meantime they wondered what to do with the beast. Their boss was Duane Cuthbertson, whose main task at this time in his life was to stay one step ahead of his staff—a difficult task when Bob was one of the instigators.

That afternoon, with the lion and trainer in tow, Bob, and another jokester, waited for Duane to leave his office for a break. Then, they took the beast into the office and got it to lie down on the couch. Quietly, they hid themselves behind the partially closed door of an adjoining room to witness their boss's reaction when he returned. A short time later Duane entered his office, glanced at the lion, and without missing a beat, walked to the door behind which his pranksters hid, knocked on the door and announced, "CHRISTIANS FIVE MINUTES!"

35
Graduation Bound

ACK AT SCHOOL I called McDonnell Douglas Astronautics Company (MDAC) and confirmed I would accept their job offer, but told them I could not start until July 14, 1969, because I had to finish up two all important classes to complete my degree. They said that was fine. I was glad they didn't ask what the classes were.

Then, they told me something I didn't want to hear. While the job offer was firm, they may not be able to offer me an occupational deferment from the draft, depending on which of the many projects I could be assigned to. That was the first hint that would lead to the common advice within the aerospace industry: *Make sure you have an avocation that you can turn into a vocation when you're laid off at the end of a government contract.*

The classes I had to finish in order to graduate were *Consumer Economics* and *Tennis*. Yes, that's right, a physics major required to take economics and tennis. That's because my physics degree was a Bachelor of *Arts*, a B.A, as opposed to the more common Bachelor of Science, or B.S. degree. The difference between a B.A. and a B.S., in my opinion, was that the B.A. required a great deal more B.S. The *Arts* degree required that I take courses in philosophy, physical education, fine arts, theology, and, of course, a sociology lecture course called *Marriage,* taught by an elderly man named Professor Wayman.

Professor Byron Wayman was a very neat and tidy Christian man who practiced what he preached. Students would regularly see him and his wife, both in their early 80s we supposed[1], holding hands like they were just out of high school. But there was something odd about

---

1 I'm not sure how old Prof. Wayman was. To us 19-year-olds, everyone over 50 looked like they were 80.

him. He had an aversion to chalk...or so we assumed. His *Marriage* course was filled with statistical sociological data about what made a marriage succeed or fail. At the front of the lecture hall was a black board that stretched the entire 30 feet across the front of the room. He would face the board and write across the board the information he wanted you to remember for the test, like the fact that in 1960, 80% of all adults ages 18 and older were married, but today only 72% were married. He'd then turn back to the class with a look on his face as if he had just given you the most important data in the entire world to help make your marriage succeed.

Anxiously, we would look at the board to write down what he had written. Invariably, however, there was nothing on the board. He had faced the board, moved his hands and arms as *if* he was writing with a stick of chalk, and in doing so walked clear across the front of the room constantly "writing" on the board the whole way. But when he was done there was no chalk in his hand, and not one chalk mark on the board.

We were continually dumbfounded.

Then again, perhaps more importantly, the dear man did not come home to his wife with chalk dust all over his hands. And as his reward, I suspected, when he got home from teaching, his wife would gleefully take his clean hands, press them between hers and lead him for a walk through town.

By the way, the man never smiled.

To shake up the lectures Wayman would occasionally role-play family situations. He would select a male and female student from class, call them to the front of the room, give them a moral dilemma to discuss as pretend husband and wife, and see if they could resolve the problem without yelling at each other.

One time Brad and Jane were asked to come up front. The problem they were assigned was a financial one. Jane wanted to spend more money than they had and it was up to Brad to convince her they didn't have the money to spend. Wayman stood aside and let Brad and Jane take their place at the front of the room. They started in. Jane insisted they had the money, Brad said they didn't. This went back and forth a few times until Brad turned to the black board and began to list their income and subtract from it the cost of the mortgage, food, gasoline and college tuition. He then turned to Jane and said, "Do you see this, darling? We have no money. Look at the numbers."

Jane looked at the black board. The class could not hold it in. Brad had not written a single thing on the board. "There's nothing," he said. "Look, sweetheart, there's nothing--left."

Jane lost it, too. She had no idea Brad was going to pull a *Wayman*, as we called the professor's vacuous mannerism. She started laughing so hard she got the hiccups and had to sit down...as did Brad.

And, Professor Wayman? He congratulated them on "A fine, fine job."

Class dismissed.

For me it was the perfect metaphor for a great deal of what I struggled with about American Christianity. You can argue, you can discuss, you can state perfectly logical propositions, and you can cite numbers. But if you can't see the tangible evidence you have to ask, "Is it real?"

NOT BEING ASSURED of an occupational deferment caused some tension. I looked back though my Air Force file, found the Carbondale recruiter's number and called. A clerk answered the phone, took my information, and looked up my file. Indeed, I had been turned down for entry in the Air Force. I asked why, but the clerk just said, she had no idea. Luck, fate... what was that all about? I thought I had a way out of the draft but evidently not.

> You can argue, you can discuss, you can state perfectly logical propositions, and you can cite numbers. But if you can't see the tangible evidence you have to ask, "Is it real?"

A month later Pam and I began to make plans for our life together. In mid-May we made arrangements to rent a sparsely furnished student flat above the union hall downtown on the square. There I would set up house after graduation, go to summer school, and then commute to MDAC in St. Louis, although my plan was to stay with the Schroeders most of the time until just before the wedding. Pam would go home for the summer to work and plan our wedding, which we set for August 30. Then it would be back to Greenville for her senior year as a married student. My graduation came and went at the end of May without much fanfare, if for no other reason than I had an asterisk behind my name on the program indicating that I had to successfully complete summer school to really graduate. Pam went home and I "knuckled down" in an attempted to cram a 4-month semester of Tennis and Consumer Economics, into 5 weeks.

Around the middle of June, half-way through summer school I received a call from MDAC that my job may disappear if Congress didn't pass the Anti-Ballistic Missile budget in August. In other words, I could start work July 14, but if the ABM didn't pass in August, I'd be laid off. I began to think harder about that avocation.

36
Air Force Bound

O N THURSDAY, JULY 3, 1969, I finished summer school, locked up our apartment, and drove to St. Louis where I celebrated Independence Day with the Schroeders. On Monday, July 7th, I went to MDAC to be processed, get my security clearance, get a tour of the building and be introduced to the group I'd be working with starting a week later, July 14. It was to be the aeronautics Collision Avoidance System (CAS) for commercial aircraft. That night I caught a ride to the other side of the airfield and hopped on a plane home to Detroit for a few days before I started work the next Monday.

On Tuesday, while at home in Detroit, I received another of those fateful calls from MDAC: There was a 99% chance that I would be laid off within a month of my starting work at MDAC. I needed to find another job. What I thought was going to be a relaxing week at home spending some time with Pam turned into a job hunting expedition.

My dad drove me around Detroit and I took about five interviews. The one I remember was again more than coincidental, but eerily Providential. I interviewed with a man named Andre Blay in a little office in a Farmington Hills industrial park. He was looking for a technician to operate and repair racks of videocassette recording decks onto which he was going to duplicate movies for sales to home videotape players.

I thought the man was nuts, movies on videotape in homes? Crazy! Remember if you can, this was the summer of 1969. Blay had founded a company called Stereodyne to duplicate 8-track audio tapes for use in car stereo systems that were popular from the late 1960's through the 1970's. But he was late into the game. So, he planned to leap frog the industry and introduce home video. He started Magnetic Video, where I interviewed, when he was putting the pieces together for the first ever videocassette duplication plant and sales distribution of the cassettes. No one had conceived the idea, yet. Except, Blay!

It was a fascinating but ridiculous idea I thought. And, he thought I was over qualified. No deal.

But in retrospect, there seemed to be a thread of Providence involved. Allow me to jump ahead to explain. The next year Andre approached 20th Century Fox studios and offered them $300,000 to license their old movies for *home video*. Fox thought he was crazy too, so they took his money, signed the deal, and then laughed all the way to the bank about the crazy guy from Detroit. Two years later Fox regretted their short-sightedness. When Blay returned for the home video rights to recent movies, the agreement was renegotiated. Blay now had to pay Fox an additional $500,000 a year for access to their library. To Blay it was still a steal. And Magnetic Video, located in the little industrial park north of Detroit, overnight, became the center of the world for videocassette duplication...with a high-end video editing facility to support the effort.

Five years later I was in Detroit making films and videos for Ford Motor Company, which did not have it's own state-of-the-art video editing suite. Guess where I went to edit my projects? Magnetic Video. In the same building I had been interviewed by Blay years earlier. At the time Blay was still in charge, but I found myself working with his manager, Steve Wild. A few years later Steve and I went to Eastern Michigan University night school together and got our Master degrees. Over the years I spent a lot of Ford's money at Magnetic Video.

Then, in 1979, Fox bought out Blay's business for a reported $7.9 million and put Steve in charge of a new facility down the street that was now relabeled *20th Century Fox Video* that provided expanded editing and duplication services.

In 1981 when I started Full Circle Productions, my production business in Dearborn, Steve extended to me production credits that allowed me to mount major productions with very little cash investment on my part. We worked together for years, and my production company was one of the first tenants in an office complex that he later formed when Steve and Harvey Grace bought out 20th Century Fox Video. Grace and Wild Digital Studios soon became the go-to production facility in Michigan, which included the largest film stage in the Midwest.

Was the full circle nature of my relationship with Magnetic Video and 20th Century Fox Video an accident, will power, fate, or Providence? I hold that sequence of vocational events in awe. It wasn't me, it wasn't accidental, and it wasn't the happenstance of fate.

G ETTING BACK TO the story, I still needed a job, because MDAC was going to lay me off in a month, just after I started the job, and just before I got married. Life can get scary at times, and Pam and I talked about putting off the wedding...for 10 seconds. I'd find something, we decided.

I flew back to St. Louis on July 12, settled in at the Schroeders, and started work at MDAC on Monday, July 14.

On Tuesday, July 22, I received notice from my draft board that I had been classified 1A, and among the first in line to be drafted.

On Wednesday, July 23, I called a St. Louis Air Force recruiter and tried again to get into the Air Force as a pilot. The next week I got a day off work, and went in to the recruiting station for testing and a flight physical. At first I thought it would just take a couple of hours and I'd be back to work in the afternoon, just like Carbondale. But my boss said to take the full day off.

He must have known something, because the tests and physical exams I took in St. Louis took all day. The Officer Training School (OST) entrance exams were difficult. They took most of the morning and included reading comprehension, geometry, physics, political science and geography. I was even given aerial recognizance photographs and asked to identify certain objects on the ground. In the afternoon the flight readiness physical exam took 5 hours and included a stress EKG, and detailed eye exam that required my eyes be dilated.

When I asked the recruiter what the difference was between Carbondale and this St. Louis exam he took some time to investigate. Turns out the recruiter in Carbondale had missed his quota of *enlisted* Air Force personnel. He had no pilot quota. So he tested us and put in our request of Air Force *enlisted*. We were turned down because of our college education, and we should have applied for OTS; we were overqualified. Of course, that is what my friend and I had thought we were doing. The Carbondale recruiter was using us against our will to meet his quota, and it didn't work.

Before I left the St. Louis recruiting station I found out that I had passed the OTS examination, I was 1/4 inch shorter than the maximum sitting height for an Air Force pilot, and that I had a small tooth cavity that had to be fixed before my application could be submitted to the Pentagon. Within the week, I had the cavity fixed, and an x-ray sent to the recruiter. Mission accomplished…or so I thought.

Later that week I found an excuse at work to visit the Phantom F4 factory that McDonnell Douglas operated on the North side of Lambert Field. I visited the line and watched the test flights of F4's taking off and landing. One time I watched as four F4's rolled down the runway together, lifted off in formation, and popped their afterburners climbing nearly vertical into the clouds with flames blasting out of their engines. *Incredible, invincible beasts and someday I could be flying one.*

What I didn't know was that Mom was praying for me *not* to join the Air Force. During high school she wanted me to join the Army in order to teach me discipline. But thinking about the possibility of Air Force officers coming to her house for a somber visit changed her mind. I didn't know (but she did) that thousands of planes were being lost over Vietnam, Cambodia and Laos, and thousands of pilots had become POWs.[1] I had no clue. Mom wanted me to develop some discipline, but probably not in a Southeast Asian jungle POW camp.

In the meantime, I was still looking for a more secure job. One possibility was with RCA in Indianapolis, Indiana, where I was interviewed for an electronic engineer position designing high-end RCA commercial television and video tape recorders. It was during that interview that I was asked the most perceptive and difficult interview question I ever heard. The elderly engineer behind the desk smiled and asked:

> *If a satellite is launched into an orbit that passes over Earth's poles and completes an orbit in one hour, what compass direction will it appear to be traveling if you observe it while standing on the rotating Earth below?*

It was a lovely question, but I couldn't figure out the answer in my head, and the interview failed. It was a good thing. Years later editing video programs for Ford and other companies, I would use the RCA machines and those manufactured by other companies in editing facilities around the country. The "quads," as we called them, were the first practical and commercially successful analog video recording machines. They used 2-inch wide video tape, the reels of which were over 12 inches in diameter and weighed about 20 pounds.[2] Nonethe-

---

1 In total, the United States lost in Vietnam almost 10,000 aircraft and helicopters. (Wikipedia: "Aircraft losses of the Vietnam War.)

2 Compare the size and weight of that 1 hour long quad tape to the digital tape

less, they were amazing creations, built by geniuses in my estimation. I was glad to be using them, and also glad I didn't have to explain how they worked.

My job continued somewhat tentatively at MDAC, and everyday I wondered if it would be my last.

---

cassettes that were professionally popular in the early years of 2000. The digital cassettes had the same 1 hour capacity, higher quality video but were only 2-3 inches in size and weighed 1.2 ounces. Then, a few years later, even higher digital quality, same capacity, stored on a 1/16-inch thin solid state flash card that weighted less than 0.1 ounce, became available. And, it only had to be that big so human fingers could grab it.

37
Marriage Bound

MCDONNELL ASTRONAUTICS HAD promised to lay me off a month after I began in July, 1969. But now it was August and I still had a job. Was that the consequence of fate? Certainly keeping my job was not the consequence of my own will. Was it God's? I knew that any day I could lose my job. So, I didn't want to push my luck.

But, in a few weeks, back in Michigan, I was supposed to get married...then there was the honeymoon. Having just started work, should I ask for time off? If I asked for too much, when I got back to St. Louis, although I'd have a wife, I might not have a job.

They gave me two days...Friday and Monday. I left St. Louis Thursday after work, and they expected me back on Tuesday morning. The wedding was on Saturday, the honeymoon would be short. But I decided I was not going to complain. I was getting married, and that was great!

Through letters and phone conversations Pam and I wrote pretty much all of our wedding ceremony, including our vows, with the advice and consent of our Dearborn Free Methodist pastor, Rev. Frank VanValin. The ceremony was to last but 30 minutes, too short I felt for the effort that was going into it all. So, Pam consented to letting me plan a prenuptial recital with some very talented musician friends.

Organist Tom Clark, flutist Althea Jones, soprano Rebecca Smith, and trumpeter Dave Hallmark were members at Dearborn F.M., and Glen Wilson flew in from North Carolina to play harpsichord.

Finding a harpsichord for Glen proved to be a challenge. Glen, who at the time was 17, traveled around Detroit with Bob (Grapefruit) Kenney for a place that would rent them a dual manual instrument.

The two didn't spawn confidence when they first walked into a store. Bob, although 23, wore a young mischievous grin that reminded some of Alfalfa from *The Little Rascals*. And Glen looked older than he was, but was clearly a teenager. Adding to the difficulty was that Glen, by this time, was taking lessons from some pretty famous musicians, and was due to start at Julliard in New York in a week; so not just any harpsichord would do. Store after store turned them down, *flat*. Finally, they walked into an upscale store in Birmingham, a posh suburb of Detroit, sat down at instruments in the showroom and started to jam, Glen on a harpsichord, and Bob on a nearby grand piano.

In spite of Bob's ability to get me in trouble, he was and still is an incredible pianist who has proven time and again his ability to adapt to any genre in the catalog on-the-spot. He couldn't keep up with Glen on the great classical works, but both of them knew how to jazz up and riff with the best. And that's what they began to do in the showroom of this ritzy establishment. Their pure musicianship got the attention of the proprietor who asked how he could help them. They informed him they wanted to rent the very expensive dual manual harpsichord that Glen had taken a shining to. Without hesitation, the owner said they couldn't rent it, but he would loan the instrument to them for free, if Glen was the one who was going to play it. All they had to do was pay a professional mover, which they quickly agreed to.

The prenuptial recital by our talented friends playing our favorite classical works went flawlessly. At the time, Pam and I didn't hear any of it, but we did have a very good recording made that has since been digitized and is now on our play lists.

Bob was my best man, and standing up with him was my physics chum and roommate for two years at GC, Alan Heath. Our philosophy professor, Dr. Royal Mulholland, who had profoundly challenged our thinking in college, stood behind Alan and then came our GC artist friend David Condon. David sadly passed away a few years ago, but two of his impressionistic acrylic paintings from his senior exhibit, *Warm Squeeze* and *Crabapple*, still grace the walls of our home.

Pam and I were also very glad to have photographer Robert Chi, who graduated a year beforemes, come and take black and white candids that we still cherish.

Standing with Pam as her maid of honor was her sister, Linda Turck, high school friend Patti Roy, Spring Arbor roommate Diane Hoopingarner, and my sister Hope Williams. At Spring Arbor College, Pam, Patti, and Diane formed a trio that was so good the college put them on the road many weekends singing at church events to promote the school. At the wedding, Patti, Diane and Becky (standing in for Pam) sang the final blessing for us.

After Rev. VanValin's homily to Pam and me, Rebecca Smith, accompanied by Glen on the "loaned" harpsichord, sang something that probably has never been heard before or since in a Free Methodist church. And that requires a short story.

ONE SUMMER, BEFORE Pam came to Greenville, I returned to the National Music Camp in Interlochen as a counselor. There I dated, Miss B., a young lady who worked in food service, although we actually met at a Bible study for camp staff. Miss B. was studying piano performance in Grand Rapids at Calvin College, a Christian Reformed school. There she sat under the instruction of Dr. Calvin Seerveld, a noted Reformed theologian. During a visit to Grand Rapids to hear her in recital, she took me to a special evening lecture by Seerveld, no doubt in an effort to *reform* me. It was an embarrassing meeting. I had just arrived in Grand Rapids exhausted from summer work and a long drive into the evening. So, during Seerveld's lecture, I promptly fell asleep. Miss B. was not impressed with such a demonstrative dismissal of her favorite theologian, and I think that ended the relationship. As sort of a consolation prize she sent me a copy of a Seerveld book that he wrote during a recent Fulbright Sabbatical. It was a translation of Solomon's Song of Songs in the form of an oratorio, with Middle Eastern styled music by Ina Lohr.

Seerveld's take on the *Song of Songs*[1] is the story of a love triangle, between KING SOLOMON who is attempting to woo the beautiful SHULAMMITE virgin into his harem of a thousand other beauties. But the woman is already betrothed to another man whom she truly loves. The tension Seerveld establishes is between Solomon's promiscuous lust and the pure celibate love of the Shulammite's LOVER. Unique to his translation is the addition of extra-Biblical character tags, helping the reader to identify which of the three characters is speaking.

I was never sure why Miss B. gave me the book, and I wondered if she thought of me more as Solomon or her chaste lover. Pam thinks she just liked Seerveld's theology…(!)

During our wedding, Becky Smith sang the difficult Middle Eastern melody pitch perfect, accompanied by Glen's harpsichord. It was their

1 Seerveld, Calvin (1967). *The Greatest Song*. Trinity Pennyasheet Press: Palos Heights, IL. p26-65.

own arrangement of several of the lyrical passages in Seerveld's translation and Ina Lohr's music. Perceptively, Rebecca and Glen omitted the lines Seerveld ascribed to lusty Solomon. Here are the lyrics transcribed from the recording with Seerveld's character tags.

HER LOVER: A-rise, beloved, my beautiful one,
Come wander away with me.
The winter is past; the heavy rains gone;
New flowers shoot forth from the earth,
The turtledove's coo is heard.
The fig tree colours its unripe fruit;
All vines are bursting with buds. O! The fragrance.
Arise, beloved, come wander away
My beautiful one with me.

HER LOVER: I come to my garden, my bride to be.
I gather my myrrh and spice.
I taste of the honey in my honey comb,
And drink deep of the wine and the milk.

HER LOVER: Hold me as a seal to your heart

SHULAMMITE: Keep me as a signet ring upon your finger.

HER LOVER: For love is as permanent as death

SHULAMMITE: aaThe passionate drive of love
As all consuming as the most terrible power!

HER LOVER: Its flames are flashes of fire

SHULAMMITE: A pure fire of the Lord God!

HER LOVER: Streams of water cannot put it out;

SHULAMMITE: Floods of water shall never quench the fire of love.

HER LOVER: If another man were to give all the treasures
Of his house for love–?

SHULAMMITE: He would be utterly despised!

SHULAMMITE: *Like the gazelle or a young deer,*
Take me quickly away, my lover,
Out to the sweet-smelling mountains.

SHULAMMITE & LOVER: *Ahhh....*

As I've been describing, there was an impetus within Evangelicalism to over spiritualize elements of Christianity. It verged on Gnosticism, where anything earthly was evil and only the spiritual component of humanity could aspire to heaven. If you've been raised Evangelical you were probably taught that *Solomon's Song of Songs* if anything, was an allegory describing the relationship between Christ and his church, or between God and Israel, where the divine is represented by the King (who is also the lover), and Israel or the church is the woman he woos to become his bride. For New Testament scholars this is reinforced by applying St. Paul's explanation in Ephesians 5 that a husband's love for his wife is to be modeled after the love of Christ for the church.

But Seerveld, while having no problem with such an exegesis, believed that the Bible has to be interpreted first literally and not sanitized to the point of missing the obvious. Seerveld describes his philosophy of translation as

> *...a deliberately chosen way of listening to Scripture, the scrupulously careful way urged by the Reformation with the formula* scriptura sui ipsius interpres *[Scripture is its own interpreter.]*[1]

Years later, I found these words curiously circular; and they illustrated my broader problem with Protestant theology. If Scripture, such as *Solomon's Song of Songs*, could interpret itself, then why was it necessary for Seerveld to re-stage, re-translate and re-interpret it in contradiction to centuries of theologians like Augustine, Aquinas and others who interpret *The Song of Songs* as an allegorical *dialogue* between just two people, the lover and the betrothed.[2]

I'm not taking sides here. I like both interpretations, the three handed love triangle of literal lust vs. love, and the allegory heavily laden with meaning for the church and Christ. But it made little sense for Protestants to say Scripture interprets itself and then in the same

1 Ibid, page 16. [I'm not sure phrasing this in Latin makes circular reasoning any more valid.]

2 Davidson, John (2005). *The Song of Songs: The Soul and the Divine Beloved.* Clear Books: Bath, England.

breath claim, "we need a new translation."

All of that aside, in the moment of our wedding, Rebecca and Glen provided an appropriate touch of mysticism and sexual tension to the ceremony celebrating our spiritual and physical union. I think it was also remarkable that we didn't have to convince VanValin that what Rebecca was singing was actually from the Bible.

S INCE THERE WERE no wedding vows in the Bible, we (as Sola Scritpura lovers) wrote our own wedding vows that we were supposed to memorize. I tried, but at Friday's rehearsal I could not remember a word. Rev. VanValin promised to keep a copy of mine hidden in his book…to prompt me. Nice guy. But I was determined, "C" student that I was. I stayed up half the night working on the,m pacing up and down in my home's basement. Next afternoon, happy to say, during the ceremony, I nailed them.

> **It made little sense for Protestants to say Scripture interprets itself and then in the same breath claim, "we need a new translation."**

After listening to the tape of our wedding that I resurrected after 45 years so I could transcribe our vows for this chapter, I had to call Pam to my aid. I couldn't understand a word she said on the tape. It's not her voice, it's my ears. I've grown deaf to the frequency of her voice. (Oooo! That sounds bad.[1]) Anyhow, here are our vows as delivered. First mine to Pam:

> *Pamela, with deepest joy I receive you into my life as my wife. As is Christ to his body the Church, so I will be to you a faithful sacrificial husband. Always will I perform my headship over you even as Christ does over me, knowing that his Lordship is one of Godly love and holiest desires for my life. I promise to you my deepest love, my unselfish devotion, and my tenderest care. I promise that I will live for Jesus Christ first rather than for others or even you. And I promise that I will lead our life always into a life of faith, hope, and love in Jesus Christ our Lord. Ever honoring God's guidance by this Spirit through The Word. Therefore, Pamela, throughout life, no matter what may come, I pledge to you my love, as a loving, faithful husband.*

---

1 In my sixties I began to lose my hearing in the high frequencies.

Pam, on the other hand, never had trouble memorizing anything.

Stanley, with deepest joy I come into my new life together with you. As you have pledged to me your life and love, so I too, happily give you my life, and confidently submit myself to your headship as to the Lord. As is the Church in her relationship with Christ, so will I be to you. I will live for you, loving you, learning from you and obeying you and ever seeking to please you. God has prepared me for you, so I would ever strengthen, help, comfort and encourage you. Ask me never to leave you nor to return from following you. For where you go I will go, and where you lodge I will lodge. Your people shall be my people, and your God my God. Therefore, Stanley, no matter what may lie ahead of us, I pledge to you my life, as a loving, obedient and faithful wife.

After we transcribed both of these from the tape and listened to them once again, Pam turned to me and said, "Boy, were we ever dreamers!"

"Yes," I said, "What were we thinking?"

Was our marriage an accident of love? Or was it a lovely accident? Those are good questions, especially considering what happened on the day of our wedding and the day after.

38
Accident Bound

OUR AUGUST 1969 marriage vows were not accidents, and neither was our marriage, but there were accidents. I'm reminded of the Proverb, "We can make our plans but is God convinced?"[1] And the day of our wedding provided four humorous examples.

ONE

August 30, 1969 in Dearborn was hot and muggy, so the church's head usher turned on the air conditioning. As the ceremony approached both Pam and I became nervous, about everything, and as the ceremony began both of us were covered in sweat. You can see it in the pictures. But the problem was not us. The head usher had turned on the *heat* by accident. He clearly was preparing me for the crucible called "marriage!"

TWO

That night Pam and I planned to treat our wedding party to a moonlight cruise on the Detroit River aboard one of the huge four-decker Bob-Lo boats. On board we would enjoy a live band, a dance floor (oops, we didn't dance. We were Free Methodists, remember?) and the cool breeze on the water as the boat plowed upriver into Lake St. Clair for a moonlight cruise and returned quickly to the dock.

Immediately after the wedding reception, as anxious as we were to secret ourselves into the Honeymoon suite at the classic Dearborn Inn where my parents had spent their wedding night, we had a debt to pay

---

1 Proverbs 16:1

to our guests. So, we quickly checked in, changed into less formal attire (Pam into a luxurious white pant suit that only made me want to get back to the hotel room sooner) and we were off to lead everyone to the boat docks. We got there just in time, met our wedding guests, and at dusk boarded the boat. As soon as the boat left the dock I knew something was wrong. The boat did not turn up the river toward the Lake, it went down river toward Bob-Lo Island, the popular amusement park that was open 'till 10 PM. I quickly found a steward and asked, "Isn't this the moonlight cruise?"

"No Sir Ree, Bob!".

I looked at him, "I'm sorry, I'm not Bob, that's Bob over there," and I pointed at Bob (piano man) Kenney.

The steward glanced at my nephew, "No, I was just sayin' a sayin'. "No Sir Ree, Bob" is just an expression. We's not going on a moonlight cruise. We's going to d'island, proper. You see. Why, yes sir'ree, you'll have the time of your life there. W'all be there two hours until the park closes. This is da last boat of da night. Plenty of time for you and your girlfriend here, all dressed up like ye'are, to have a gooood time. Yes sir'ree...," and he glanced over at my nephew and nodded.

"But wait," I explained. "It takes ninety minutes to get to the island, and almost two hours to get back against the current. That's..."

"Dat's seven and a half hours. For the price of one-and-a-half. That's a bargain, man. 'Dis here a great company ta work fer. Ya, need a job?"

My face fell as I glanced at the railing to see how far the boat was from land. *Could we jump?*

"What's wrong, sir, if ya don't mind me askin'? It's not like this was your wedding nite, all dressed up like..."

I glared at him.

He looked back at Bob who was escorting Pam's sister, Linda, who was also all in white, and the rest of the wedding party standing around, some of the guys still in their tuxes.

"Oh, no, man. Which one of you's just got hitched?"

Instinctively, Bob and I each pointed at the other.

"Well, might as well git comfortable," the steward said as he walked off, "'tis going to be a loooong, night."

THREE

Once on the island we tried to make the best of it. It was nice weather, the rides were all free, and we did have a lot of time to kill.

Pam and I tried to ride as many rides as we could. We needed to do something to take our mind off of not being where we wanted to be about now.

One ride was a large caged Ferris wheel, where the occupants of each cage could control the tumbling of their cage. When the giant wheel got to the top Pam and I had the cage tumbling upside down, where momentarily it hung, our heads pointed at earth 100 feet below. With all the screams, I didn't hear it fall, but out of the corner of my eye I caught sight of an object falling past my head. It had fallen out of a pocket toward the ground but was caught in the grating of the cage. Carefully, I reached down below my head, which was now pointed at the ground, grabbed the object and held on to it tight, afraid of putting it back into a pocket.

When we got back to the bottom and exited the ride the operator stopped me. "Hey, man, did you lose something up there? I saw something fall in your cage. Did you get it?"

"Yeah," I whimpered and opened up my shaking hand to show him. "This is the key to our hotel room. It's our wedding night!"

FOUR

We got back to our hotel about 2 AM. I had previously arranged for a bottle of champagne to be put on ice in our room about 8 o'clock, just before I figured we'd be back from the 90 minute moonlight cruise. When we got there the ice had all melted and the champagne was warm. Oh, well. We opened it up and poured our first ever taste of real, alcohol based bubbly. Neither of us, not being consumers of such things, were too impressed. My first impression was that an ice cold Pepsi would taste better. Together we drank about one glass and we'd had our fill. *Now, what to do with the rest of it?* The bottle was $15, which was about half the cost of the room. I sure wasn't going to throw it out. So, I stuffed the cork back in the top and packed it into my suitcase.

The next morning we checked out of the hotel, packed our suitcases into the trunk of the used Ford Galaxy 500 convertible that Pam's dad had given us for a wedding present, and headed for my house, where the plan was to pack the car with our stuff from both our parents' houses and drive toward Greenville.

Now, this is the place where I remind you that alcohol possession, in any form, within Free Methodism, was a serious hell-bound sin.

Having a few sips the night before in our room and then eating break-fast at the hotel would no doubt mask our breath and remove any smell of the forbidden bottle. But there was something we didn't count on.

When I got to my parents house, I popped open the Galaxy's trunk into which my family was going to pack bags and boxes of stuff. Not ever having a bottle of champagne before. neither of us knew that if you wanted to keep the champagne *in* the bottle, the cork alone was not going to do the trick. You also had to wire the cork in place around the bottle's neck. When I opened the trunk I was knocked over with the smell of champagne that I had packed inside my suitcase. Driving to my parents shook the bottle, causing the cork to pop and the bot-tled effervescence to erupt into my suitcase, thoroughly soaking my clothes, and dripping into the trunk. *The neighborhood would soon know,* I thought.

For the next two hours Pam and I worked hard to keep my Mom and Dad from approaching the car's trunk, which smelled like we had been running booze. (Did I tell you Dad once ran for Michigan Gov-ernor on the Prohibition ticket?) The suitcase and all my clothes were a total loss. (In case you're wondering, many cycles in a washing ma-chine with hot water and detergent does not remove the smell of cham-pagne.) Why is it every time I do something with Pam in Dearborn I have to buy new clothes when I get back to Greenville?

Accidents? Or did such events foreshadow God's leading under His grace?

39
Providence Bound

I T WAS NO accident that when I departed adolescence and started to notice how cool girls were, I somehow knew I was going to get married. (Priestly celibacy was never in the plan.)

Earlier I described how I had only three requests for a wife:

1. A Christian woman,
2. A graduate of college, and
3. From a family I would had known for at least four years.

But in the end, I think God had *also* read my prayer diary (also mentioned earlier) with the much longer list of wifely requirements... which was sort of the idea when you commit prayers to writing.

I still have to ask: Was my written prayer answered by coincidence? Accident? Willpower? Fate? Providence? I really don't know. But I do know that my prayer was answered: I married a beautiful, musically talented, sexy, wonderful, persistent, even tempered, congenial, happy, funny, neat and tidy, Christian woman, who loves music in all its genres, *would have* a college education in about 8 months (close enough), and whose family I had known for nearly eight years.

Better still, Pam was my best friend.

Our honeymoon consisted of one night in a pup tent on the Warren Dunes State Park in southwest Michigan on our way back to Greenville. We weren't complaining. At least not yet.

Pam started back to school, I commuted with a few other guys who lived near Greenville but worked at MDAC (it was an hour's drive one way), and I didn't lose my job. One day in October my manager, Wilbur VanFange said to me, "Stan, I have no idea why you're still here working. By all measures you should have been laid off weeks ago. But keep at it, you're doing fine."

A week later I was contacted by the Air Force. They apologized for taking so long to get back to me. Although I had passed the exams for OTS and Flight Training, the Pentagon rejected my application because I had reapplied within five years after being turned down once. The St. Louis recruiter was unaware of such a rule and it took an extra week to get confirmation.

That was it. I had no deferment, I had been classified as 1A, and even marriage would not keep one out of the army at this time in history.

On December 1, 1969 the new draft lottery system was established. All men born between 1944 and 1950 were eligible, which included me. It was a lottery-by-birthday drawing. The date of our birth was given a consecutive number, January 1 being No. 1, and December 31 was No. 366. (They include leap year's February 29.) These numbers, corresponding to the days of the year, were put into blue plastic capsules and the capsules into a large glass container that was then thoroughly mixed. The lottery then began as capsules were pulled one-by-one, and the dates corresponding to the numbers written in order on the Draft Registry. The first number pulled was 258, which corresponded to September 14, and so young men born on that date were first up for the draft. This continued through the evening until all 366 dates were recorded in the order of their drawing.

My number was 268th. As *fate* would have it, only the first 195 number dates drawn would end up being drafted. I was safe. It's been 46 years since that lottery drawing but I have always remembered my number—268.

Out of curiosity, I looked up the Draft Date of Pam's birthday. It was No. 2. Maybe we would have a life together, but I had no idea it would involve outer space.

THE EVENTS OF these last 18 months dramatically shaped the trajectory of my life. And, while I was praying mightily that God would lead me, I was only occasionally aware, at the time, of what was guiding my path. I wanted it to be strictly Providence. But, at times, it seemed that the dominant force was my own willful decisions, or some weirdness of fate, or some uncontrollable accident of nature. Is it possible that God used all four to lead my path? Am I in God's will now? I'd like to think I am, but humility before God tells me not to be so confident and keep listening.

One thing, however, is clear. There was a factor I normally never considered until afterwards, and that was the will of my Mother, expressed to God in prayer on my behalf. She kept me out of Vietnam.

But Mother's prayers were not always answered the way she had wanted. Such was the case when she came to visit us in St. Louis.

40
Mom Discovers
Lutheranism

AFTER PAM GRADUATED from college in 1970, we moved to St. Louis and bought a house in Berkeley, Missouri near my work at MDAC.

The house was near the landing pattern for the factory test flights of the F4 fighter jets that were being sent to Vietnam. Occasionally, on the way home, which was only a half-mile, I stopped at the end of the runway, and marveled at these loud machines as they took their maiden test flights, and I contemplated with a bitter sweetness that I was not flying one to Southeast Asia...on account of my mother.

One weekend, mother came to visit. It was a side trip from her 30th alumni reunion at GC. It was one of those events we'll never forget.

On Sunday, Pam and I took Mom to Mt. Calvary, the Lutheran Church Theodore Schroeder had pastored before he died, and where the Schroeders still attended. We had not yet settled on a church to attend full time, but we both enjoyed visiting with the Schroeders and we liked the worship at Mt. Calvary. This would be the first time my Mom met my St. Louis Mom.

Of course the worship at Mt. Calvary was not the simpler Order of Matins that occupied my high school days, but rather the full Divine Service. Mom was not anti-Liturgical as far as I could tell, but I was worried a little about how she might react to the use of actual wine rather than diluted grape juice during communion. I guess I would find out, or so I consoled myself. I needn't to have worried. We never got that far.

We arrived a bit early and in the lobby I introduced Mom to Verna ("Mom") Schroeder, and Annette who were the morning greeters. Annette had left teaching in Detroit to live with her mom, and was working as an editor at Concordia Publishing in St. Louis.

The narrow nave of the church sat 300 in parallel rows of dark walnut pews facing a simple but elegant altar area. Over the pedestal altar and elevated stone lectern to the right, green ordinary time vestments were draped. A small, polished brass baptistery font stood to the left behind the wood and aluminum communion rail. The whitewashed walls of cut limestone were unadorned and a colorful, abstract tapestry hung to the left of a 25-foot wooden and brass trimmed cross above the altar.

I led the way into a pew about halfway to the front, with Mom sitting next to me, and Pam on the center aisle. The congregation at Mt. Calvary was always reverent as it was on this day. The small pipe organ, in the balcony, played a soft prelude. An acolyte came and after bowing reverently, lit the two tall candles that stood on either end of the altar. Behind the altar, carved in a large stone was an inscription from Luke 22:19: "Do This In Remembrance of Me." As I studied the engraving, I remember Mom Schroeder sharing with me that every time she sits in the church and looks at the engraving she remembers her husband.

The Rev. Theodore Schroeder had been the congregation's second pastor and served it for 22 years. As the congregation grew they kept expanding until in 1964 construction began on the new and modern building under his guiding vision. But just weeks before the building was to be dedicated on Holy Wednesday, 1965, Theodore Schroeder suddenly died. He had built this church and he was hard to forget even to those, like me, who had never met him. And, indeed, in memory of him, a life-size relief of his bust is mounted in the building's foyer.

The Divine Service of Worship began with a processional hymn and we stood. Mother always loved to sing hymns and I noticed that this Sunday was no different although we were in a Lutheran Church.

As in many liturgical traditions the service began with a general confession of sins. It went like this.

> Priest: *If we say we have no sin, we deceive ourselves, and the truth is not in us.*
>
> Congregation: *But if we confess our sins, God, who is faithful and just, will forgive us our sins and*

cleanse us from all unrighteousness.

Priest: *(Facing the altar) Let us confess our sins to God our Father.*

Congregation: *Most merciful god, we confess that we are by nature sinful and unclean. We have sinned against you in thought, word and deed, by what we have done and by what we have left undone. We have not loved you with our whole heart; we have not loved our neighbors as ourselves. We justly deserve your present and eternal punishment. For the sake of your son, Jesus Christ, have mercy on us. Forgive us, renew us, and lead us, so that we may delight in your will and walk in your ways to the glory of your holy name. Amen.*

Priest: *(facing to the congregation) Almighty God in his mercy has given his Son to die for you and for his sake forgives you all your sins. As a called and ordained servant of the Word I therefore forgive you all your sins in the name of the Father and of the Son and of the Holy Spirit.*[1]

Suddenly, Mom reached for a handkerchief that she usually kept tucked up her sleeve. Tears came to her eyes and you could sense her agitation. She was still for a moment, but then leaned over, grabbed her purse, pushed past Pam, and wiping her eyes, bolted out of the church.

I was mystified. I looked at Pam, and she shrugged her eyes as if to say, "Par for the course, but I have no clue, either."

Mom didn't return.

After some time, when the congregation was again standing, I excused myself and went in search of Mom. She was sitting on a bench in the small picnic area next to the church. Her back was ramrod straight and she glared at me as if I had just given my soul to the devil. I knew the look, but I had no idea what had alloyed her spine into hardened steel.

---

1 This text is from LUTHERAN WORSHIP, (1982). Divine Worship II, First Setting, p 158. Concordia Publishing House: St. Louis.

I sat next to her. "Mom, what's wrong?"

With watery eyes, a stiff upper lip, and between gritted teeth she said, "You were never taught that you had to go to a priest to have your sins forgiven. You know you don't and shouldn't do that. You were taught to go straight to Jesus. I taught you different." She burst into a sob, wiping her face with her already tear-soaked hankie.

I was silent, and decided not to remind her that it was she who put me in with the Lutherans nearly a decade earlier, and that the liturgy made it clear *who* actually forgave our sins—Jesus—as we both believed.

> **Something was tragically wrong with the system that prevented Christians from being of one mind and worshipping together.**

At once I was mad, embarrassed, frustrated, and befuddled. The depth of my reaction is probably why, to this day, I can't remember anything else about her visit.

Sadly, I came to believe that many Evangelicals, under the guise of protecting their faith, closed their minds to even the slightest bit of evidence that might suggest their interpretation of things might be fallacious, or that some level of "reasoning" might impinge on their "faith alone" system of beliefs.

I did not understand all of this at the time, but I sensed something was tragically wrong with the system that prevented Christians from being of one mind and worshipping together. Subliminally, I registered not only my mother's reaction at Mt. Calvary Lutheran, but also to her reaction about United Methodists when we visited with Miss O's parents, and a few other denominations. Mom's rejection of Catholics, however, I didn't question. That made perfect sense to me.

Ironically, although Pam and I very much liked the Missouri Synod Lutheran Church, we were headed for an experience with Lutheranism that was not unlike my mother's.

41
Training
Astronauts

IN 1970, AFTER working at McDonnell Douglas Astronautics on the aircraft Collision Avoidance System, I was transfered to the Skylab engineering department. There I directed testing of the Skylab Space Station command and control electronics. A short time later I was offered the opportunity to move to Houston and write flight procedures and train NASA astronauts at the Manned Spacecraft Center. It was too good to pass up.

Since childhood I had wanted to be involved in astronomy or things involving outer space. Being an astronaut was a dream, and I had sent off for and received an application to enter the astronaut training program. But it was clear that my grades were keeping me from getting that advanced degree in physics, and at the time the astronaut corps was only open to the academically brightest. So, training them sounded like a great alternative.

Soon Pam and I were on a two-week holiday moving from St. Louis to Houston, by way of Cape Canaveral where, on January 31, 1971, we watched the launch of Apollo 14 from the VIP venue near the VAB building. As many will attest, the launch of a Saturn V rocket sending astronauts to the moon was an awe-inspiring, earth-shattering, adrenalin-pumping event, even from three miles away. [1]

---

1 The success of the Apollo Space Program, which sent the first men to the moon and back, is a bit incomprehensible when you compare Apollo's Guidance Computer (APC) to today's common smart phones. The APC weighed 70 pounds, computed at 1-MHz, had a 4-KB memory and cost $150,000. The iPhone 5 weighs 4-oz, operates

In early February we were 20 miles southeast of Houston, Texas, looking for a house to buy among the small communities of Clear Lake, Nassau Bay, and Seabrook that surrounded the Manned Spacecraft Center (MSC). But since we had not yet sold our house in St. Louis we had no down-payment, so we turned our attention to the overbuilt and under-priced apartments in the area.

As soon as we drove up to the Balboa Apartment complex I recognized it immediately as the place Bob and I had searched for our lost camera. The place was perfect. On Nassau Bay, the facility had a pool, tennis courts and new appliances. And it was just blocks from the main entrance of MSC, a shopping center, and a Lutheran Missouri Synod Church. So, we settled into a unit with a small patio on the edge of a Grasstex® tennis court.

M Y TIME AT MDAC's Houston Operations writing procedures and training astronauts lasted from 1970-1973. Although it was a dream job, it had a dark side. It was tedious and at times stressful. Wisdom also prompted many of us to develop avocations that could turn into new vocations when the government contracts were up and our jobs were eliminated.

My desk was in a two-story office building just outside the MSC gates. With seven other MDAC engineers, I poured over mechanical and electronic schematics, and met with designers in Long Beach, California, and St. Louis, Missouri to write two kinds of Check Lists: Normal Flight Procedures, and Malfunction Procedures.

MDAC's Skylab contract was for the design, construction, training and flight support of the Airlock Module, where the electronic and mechanical brains for Skylab resided. Each of us on the team was assigned systems to know better than anyone else on the planet, except perhaps the designers. It was our job to write flawless checklists and then test them with the astronauts on the 1-G (Gravity bound) simulators, which were real-hardware mock-ups of the space station constructed in the simulator building nearby. I was responsible for the Digital Command System (DCS), Intercom Communications (COMM), Video Recording (VTR), Caution & Warning (C&W), and Radiation Dosimeter Systems (RAD). I was also the backup trainer on the Electrical Power System (EPS) and Lighting (LTG) systems.

at 1.3-GHz, has a 64-GB memory and cost $400. That means our iPhones are 1,300 times faster and have 16,000 times greater memory than the APC. And what do we do with our iPhones? We play music.

On-site, at the Manned Spacecraft Center, we worked with our NASA counterparts on the second floor of Building 4 of the astronaut office building. The third floor contained the astronaut offices. The Apollo Astronauts often parked in front of the building in their red, white, and blue Chevrolet Corvette Convertibles.[1]

Throughout the building, posters drawn by Johnny Hart (of B.C. and The Wizard of Id fame) warned those of us who occasioned the building, that if we were the least bit sick to stay clear of flight crews. In 1972 NASA gave Hart a Public Service Award for outstanding contributions to NASA.

One day I was in the 1G trainer with the first mission crew: Pete Conrad, Paul Weitz, and Joe Kerwin.[2] We were stepping through a replacement procedure for one of the intercom boxes. Conrad was holding a screwdriver-like tool, when the next step that I had written told him to take hold of the box on the wall and remove it. He did exactly what the procedure told him to do. But to do it, he had to release the screwdriver. He did…and in the gravity of Earth the tool dropped through the grated floor and hit another astronaut on the lower level involved in a separate training session. I was reprimanded for not including an instruction line that said, "Screwdriver - STOW."

The Flight Check Lists we developed required that all verbs be capitalized. Thus "STOW" was not an acronym, but rather an instruction telling the crew member to "put away" the tool. Such was the necessity for every action aboard the spacecraft. Nothing was left to chance. Precision, including capitalization, of every word was important. We quickly became aware that equivocation of terms (using ambiguous language that could be interpreted in different ways) could endanger the crew and the mission.

Strange as it seems, writing such procedures helped me see a big part of the problem dividing Christianity. Different denominations would use similar terms but have different underlying definitions, or they'd use different terms but be talking about the same thing. No one, it seemed, wanted to take the time to define the terms, relying instead on churchy jargon, theological equivocation and forms of linguistic intimidation.

---

1 Since the beginning of the astronaut corps Corvette's were the vehicle of choice for many of the crew.

2 Pete Conrad flew on Skylab 2 (the first Skylab manned mission), Gemini 5 & 11, and Apollo 12 when he became the third man to walk on the moon. Weitz flew on Skylab 2, and STS-6. Kerwin flew on Skylab 2.

At NASA, the level of detail for the *Normal Operating Procedures*, however, revealed the dark side of being a flight crew trainer. A mix of anal attentiveness and paranoia often drove NASA to direct us to revise hundreds of pages of procedures and change a comma to a semi-colon, or re-capitalize the acronym for a switch from lower case [sw] to upper case [SW]. This required an untold number of hours that were littered with mistakes because everything had to be done manually with typewriters. Often a whole page would have to be retyped because of one comma. There were no computers, no word processing systems with search/replace functions and there was no ability to automatically search for the offending comma, or capitalization that had gone bad. Everything was manually written or marked up, then typed on an IBM Selectric Typewriter with a special "Title" type-ball.

Accompanying such changes were two other traits of the job that were nerve-racking. First, the changes often had to be made with ridiculously short schedules that were sure to generate mistakes; and second, there was insufficient time to check the procedures on the actual hardware. This was the reason that on May 14, 1973, during Skylab's unmanned launch, a thermal heat shield vibrated loose and subsequently so did one of the main solar arrays. Both the heat shield and the panel were lost. After arriving in orbit, ground control soon realized the extent of the problem—the temperature in the workshop portion of the station rose to 130 degrees. It was too hot for habitation. That's when they discovered that the second large solar array panel was jammed from fully deploying. This was the result of NASA by-passing launch vibration testing to speed the program along and avoid the expense.

The first manned mission was scheduled to take off the next day. But the problems delayed launching the astronauts until a fix could be devised. Ten days later the astronauts launched into orbit. Upon entering Skylab's workshop area, Joe Kerwin, Paul Weitz, and Peter Conrad deployed a package through a small scientific airlock. By pushing extension rods from inside the vehicle through the airlock to the outside, a mylar sunshade (or parasol) designed by NASA engineer Jack Kinzler, unfolded like an umbrella over the workshop portion of the station and the temperature began to drop. Two weeks later Conrad and Kerwin performed an EVA spacewalk and unjammed the remaining large solar array allowing it to deploy. This restored enough electricity to keep the entire Skylab mission on track.

MDAC would like me to point out that the solar panel arrays were the responsibility of another subcontractor.

In our case, the checklist mistakes would return time and time again, either because of monotony, or confusion from contradictory changes, or changes that put the procedure in jeopardy of an in-flight error. On one hand, we were commanded to make the change, and when we refused (because the change would cause an error) we were criticized by management for not following NASA's orders. I was told by management one time that my attitude had to improve and all I had to do was "simply make the changes NASA required." I remember one meeting involving all eight writers and our management. There was yelling, screaming, and the most senior and respected writer, a quiet man, broke down in tears. Much of this would be eliminated with the automation introduced by microcomputer and word processing technology. But, alas, that was years into the future.

The other situation was boredom. There would be weeks on end where there was nothing to do but wait for an opportunity to schedule the simulator in order to test the procedures. And yet, we were not free to leave the building or do something else, for fear NASA would call and we'd not be there. I remember one stretch of several days where I took hundreds of personal 35mm color slides to work to sort them into storage boxes--which I still have with the index I created at the time. It was a manic-depressive atmosphere.

WRITING THE SKYLAB *Malfunction Procedures*, however, was less stressful and more rewarding. That diagnosis portion of the process only had to be checked by the design engineers, not by astronauts. A malfunction procedure often resulted in a component's *Replacement Procedure*, which was very straightforward. It usually went something like: "1. Release the hand operated Calfax fastener. 2. Disconnect the wiring cable. 3. Trash the box. 4. Install new unit."

Because I was an Electronic *Systems* Engineer, I did not fully understand the component level operation of a device or how it might fail. To help me write procedures that foresaw what might actually go wrong on a component level, MDAC brought me together with a component design engineer from St. Louis named Chuck. We would hole up for weeks at a time in a conference room with schematics and a chalkboard. Together we'd study the schematics and ascertain what might fail with the in-flight system by drawing flow charts on the blackboard. We'd take pictures of the board with a Polaroid camera.

Later I would convert the photo into a Malfunction Procedure for distribution to other design engineers to check and test our conclusions.

It didn't take long for my St. Louis counterpart and I to determine that we were both Christians. So, often before we started work on a particular day we'd pray for the success of our work and the conversion of our bosses. It wasn't that our bosses were evil men, far from it; they were good and we respected them. We prayed for them simply because the Bible told us to pray for those in authority over us.[1]

Often, we can only discern God's will and plan for our lives, or the answers to our prayers in hindsight. Such was the case with my relationship with Chuck and the effect our prayers had long after he went back to St. Louis and we passed out of each other's lives. Before revealing the dramatic way our prayers for our bosses were answered, a few other situations were developing with unforeseen consequences.

---

1 1 Timothy 2:2

42
Photography

SHORTLY AFTER ARRIVING in the communities surrounding the Manned Spacecraft Center in 1970, Pam's parents sent her money to purchase a bicycle for her birthday. Since we had two cars, and a bicycle wasn't very practical for bringing home groceries, I persuaded Pam to pool the bicycle money with some savings to purchase our first professional 35-mm single lens reflex camera and an assortment of lenses. The camera was a Canon FT-QL and it served us well as you will soon discover.

Pam also let me set up a portable darkroom in one of the two apartment bathrooms. Thus, by 1971, working on weekends and evenings, I had established a small freelance photography business snapping shots for local news stories, and more formal work for model portfolios, business portraits, photo-journalism, fashion and forensic photography. I just had to be careful when washing the film, not to accidentally flush it down the toilet...an ever present danger.

All of this, of course, was to cultivate a future career if the unforeseen future required. And, to confirm the validity of the effort, I secured a photography pass to shoot publicity and business-related photography for MDAC at the Spacecraft Center.

About that time I joined with Bill Kinsey, another photographer in the apartment complex to form a company we called Nassau Bay Photography. Soon I was able to purchase some larger format cameras including a couple of twin-lens reflex Mamiya C330s for weddings, and a Calumet 4x5-inch view camera for more serious portraits as well as for perspective-controlled architectural work. In a short time I had amassed a sizable portfolio, and Pam had become competent using the Canon FT-QL for our casual family photography.

W HEN WE FIRST looked for a church to attend, we visited a Free Methodist Church about 15 minutes up the freeway in Houston. When the pastor there discovered we were brought up in Free Methodism and had both graduated from Greenville College, he made a concerted effort to gain our commitment. But his cinder block hovel of a church building had stiff competition.

Gloria Dei Lutheran Church, associated with the Lutheran Church Missouri Synod (LCMS), was a modern architecturally designed church just two blocks from our apartment. We could walk there is less than 10 minutes. The nave was small but constructed in the round with the sanctuary and altar in the center, and original art was scattered around the facility. Clearly, the church had been designed to communicate the Good News visually, just by its presence.

Rev. Leo Symmank was pastor and we liked him immediately. Although we weren't Lutheran (and Symmank and others knew that) we were approved to lead an informal youth group for the church that met in our apartment each week. The group called themselves "The Mustard Seed." We led Bible studies, prayed with the kids, and conjured up media projects that had some spiritual significance.

In July 1971 Pam and I caravaned a group of Gloria Dei teens, along with Pastor Symmank, to a 3 day weekend teen camp at the State Fair grounds in Waco, Texas. The event, called The Care Fair, was attended by 350 teens and about 60 adults. Enamored with the active and happy teens in a camp setting, I took hundreds of pictures. Back in our apartment's spare bathroom, I managed not to lose the film down the sewer and subsequently produced a stack of "8 x 10" glossies for which Leo wrote captions. We sent them to the Lutheran Witness, the national LCMS's monthly periodical.

The next month we were surprised to discover that the Texas Messenger (the state specific insert to the Lutheran Witness) was fully dedicated to our photostory about The Care Fair. Included were 26 of our photos and captions. Even more surprising, the cover of the national publication featured one of my photographs. It was a picture of 15 year-old Trudy Jander hugging her guitar. Symmank's caption read, "When photographer Stan Williams asked Trudy, "Do you love Jesus?" her face exploded in a joyful "Wow! Do I!" It was my first "cover photo." Trudy's picture and response to my question played significantly in our life a year later.

A few months later, in December 1971, Leo Symmank, in evidence of his interest in Youth Ministry, allowed The Mustard Seed, and yours truly, to rewrite the liturgy for the Christmas Eve divine service. I hesitate to reveal that instead of communion wafers Rev. Leo consecrated a birthday cake, and after the "communion cake" was distributed we danced around the altar to a Three Dog Night recording, of "An Old Fashioned Love Song." Here are the lyrics to the popular song:

> *To weave our dreams upon and listen*
> *To each evening when the lights are low*
> *To underscore our love affair with tenderness and feelings*
> *That we've come to know*
> *You swear you've heard it before*
> *As it slowly rambles on and on*
> *No need to bring 'em back*
> *'Cause they're never really gone.*
> *Just an old fashion love song*
> *Comin' down in three part harmony*
> *One I'm sure they wrote for you and me.*

Not everyone will read those lyrics like I did, but even today they seem to evoke the redemption of the world through the incarnation of Jesus Christ. Symmank, on the other hand, must have been counting on the 800 mile distance to LCMS headquarters in St. Louis to keep him out of trouble for consecrating Birthday Cake, even if it was Jesus's Birthday. (While preparing this section Leo told me he was pretty sure he did not consecrate birthday cake, but that bread and wine were on the altar, as well.)

Leo would later became the National Director for Youth Ministries for the LCMS in St. Louis. In publishing instructional material for the LCMS, he would work frequently in cooperation with Annette Schroeder (my high school English teacher), who by that time had become an editor for the LCMS' Concordia Publishing in St. Louis.

O NE MORE STORY about Leo, which fits chronologically at this point. Easter, in 1972 fell on Sunday, April 2. That was close enough for Leo to preach a sermon he had thought about since seminary. It was one of the most memorable because it was so surprising.

As a reminder, the seating in Gloria Dei's nave was arranged in roughly a circle around the large square altar that was slightly elevated circumferenced by a railing. On one side of the square room, the elevated pulpit displaced the regular arrangement of chairs, which in total might have sat 200.

It was a beautiful, mild and sunny day. Only 20 miles from the Gulf of Mexico, the area was blessed with fair winds—unlike the city of Houston 20 miles further inland that was always windless and muggy. The nave of the church was full that day, and drifting in from the halls were the smells of warm bean and bacon casseroles, and fresh baked goods. Now and then we'd hear the sound of cascading ice as it melted in beverage coolers. That day the much anticipated church picnic was scheduled in the park just down the street, immediately after the Divine Service.

Sermons in LCMS churches were not always short homilies that you find in higher-caste churches, especially if the pastor was good at telling stories, which Leo Symmank was. So, as Leo mounted the pulpit we all settled down for a long sermon and tried to ignore the wonderful smells that were filling the room.

"Today is Easter," Leo began. "It's a day of supreme celebration throughout the world, of our Savior's resurrection from the dead. The first Easter Sunday must have been a sunny day, not unlike the one we have today, with its warm rays of sun and cool gulf breeze. And among the apostles there must have been some anticipation about what was coming next."

Leo paused here, looked toward the hallway where the picnic foods were stacked on tables and the slow cookers were plugged into sockets near the floor. He looked down as this notes, shuffled them a bit, and then characteristic of him, suddenly looked up, pushed his black rimmed glasses back on his nose and smiled.

"I'm sure you're as anxious as I am to go outside and celebrate this wonderful day at our church picnic. So, what do you say we do just that? Let's dispense with the sermon and get on with communion."

And with that, he put his sermon notes away, stepped down out of the pulpit, and headed for the altar.

Boy, did we perk up. *This is great!*

Leo took four long strides toward the altar—he was a tall athletic man—and then stopped. He raised up, spread out his arms from which his robes hung, swept his arms left and right as if to include all of us and said in a loud happy voice: "April Fools!"

Of course, yesterday was April 1st, but it was close enough. He went on to tell us that Christ's resurrection from the dead was the best April Fool's joke ever perpetuated on mankind. The women came to the tomb, like Peter and John did later, expecting to find Christ's dead body. But the angel said, "April Fools. He's not here. He's risen."[1]

In 2005, Leo and his wife, Rose Merle, retired in the Nassau Bay area where they attend Gloria Dei, if he's not filling a temporary pulpit elsewhere. When doing research for this book, he told me that the April 1 sermon, which was preached only once in his career, is often brought up in conversation with parishioners at Gloria Dei that still attend there. The church is no longer comprised of the 100 or so families when we attended but has grown to over 1,000.

THAT SUMMER, FROM June 12-17, 1972, Pam and I took vacation time and traveled to the Campus Crusade for Christ Worldwide Explosion event in Dallas, Texas. EXPLO '72 was a highly publicized, week-long evangelistic conference that drew 100,000 Christians from all over the world. Major speakers were billed as attractions along with an all-star Jesus Music festival on the last day. At the time, Pam was four-months pregnant with our first child.

When we arrived at EXPLO '72 our intention was to shoot photos for several Christian publications that could not afford to send their own photographer to the event. When I applied for a Press Pass I was approached by Crusade staff and asked if I'd voluntarily help them cover the event since they were shy a photographer. Such an agreement would give me unprecedented access. They agreed to give Pam her own Press Pass. She would shoot for our freelance assignments and I would shoot for Crusade. I used a newer Canon camera body that I had recently purchased, Pam used our original Canon FT-QL, and we split up our compliment of lenses.

We stayed at a nearby motel, and at night bulk loaded film, charged our flash batteries, and logged our shooting notes.

On the last day of the event a large rally was to be staged in the Cotton Bowl where other evening events had been held for the 80,000-100,000 in attendance. But the final music festival rally drew 200,000 and the venue was moved to occupy a swath of land in the middle of downtown Dallas that had been cleared for building the Woodall Rodgers Freeway. The rally, which was booked as the Christian Woodstock, featured major Christian musical artists including Larry Norman, Randy Matthews, Kris Kristofferson, and Johnny Cash. The final "act" was a sermon by Billy Graham, who would be introduced

---

1 Easter was on April 1, in 1901, 1923, 1934, 1945, 1956, and will be in 2018, 2029, and 2040. Be sure to be in church on those days.

by Johnny. Only a bunch of quirky Christians would see a sermon as a grand finale, but we did.

For the final event I was assigned a front row, stage center position and was asked to take close-up head shots of those on stage with my long 350-mm lens. Pam sat to my left with shorter lenses and captured the wider shots of groups as they performed on stage.

The day went well. We took hundreds of photographs, and when it was all over I handed in my rolls of film to the photography office for overnight processing and proofing. Normally, I would see the results the next morning, but within an hour Pam and I were on our way home, back to Houston, where I was anxious to develop the dozen or so rolls of film she had shot for our freelance assignments.

We had no sooner entered our apartment than I received a call from John Crone, who was heading up the photography for Crusade. He asked if perhaps Pam might have caught the one image everyone was anxious to see and publish, but that so far, none of the rolls developed after the big music festival had revealed. Of course, I had no idea since we had not yet developed the film.

During that last day with Rev. Graham, there was a moment during the festival that ironically captured the event's nature. It was after Johnny Cash's set, when he introduced Billy Graham. Billy came on stage, put his arm around Johnny, and the two men raised their arms and pointed with their fingers to heaven—the sign that signified "One Way to God—through Jesus." The crowd of 200,000 went wild. I remember the moment but my camera, with it's long lens, only captured close-ups of the men's faces. And, evidently, the rest of the photographers scattered around the venue, were busy capturing the crowd's reaction. The question was, did Pam get the shot of Johnny and Billy with their fingers pointing to heaven?

Needless to say, I immediately began to develop Pam's film, with the utmost of care, making sure the temperature was right, the developer mixed properly, using the appropriate ratio of wetting agent to ensure the film was not scratched in the process, and taking extra care to close the toilet seat.

After an hour or so, I printed up contact sheets, and Pam and I studied the results of her work. And, there it was, a perfectly composed, exposed, and timed shot of the iconic moment. We called John back up, and told him we had the shot. The next morning we mailed the insured package with the negative off to Arrowhead Springs, and Pam's photograph was published around the world with her credit line. I was very proud that she had been such an important part of the project.

The week was so successful that soon after, I was recruited to leave my job at MDAC and join Crusade as a photojournalist at their headquarters in Arrowhead Springs, California. I'm pretty sure they figured they'd get Pam, too.

Seeing this as an opportunity to apply my avocation and be directly involved in Christian ministry, I began to pray earnestly with Pam for God's plan to be revealed. But I was torn, for in spite of the problems at MDAC, I was in a dream job working with astronauts and making decent money.

But, joining Crusade staff proved to be a long-drawn-out affair that will take the next four more chapters to explain. Surprises were in store.

43
The Institute

O NE THING THAT slowed us down from joining Campus Crusade was another trip to Dallas. Two weeks after EXPO, in August, 1972, my mother called and promised to pay all our expenses for "another week-long vacation." I was immediately suspicious.

Sure, enough, there was reason to question this sudden display of generosity. She wanted me to take *another* week of vacation time, travel with Pam back to Dallas, and attend a 30-hour lecture series presented over six days by a guy named Bill Gothard. It was an event called The Institute in Basic Youth Conflicts (IBYC) that we would attend with 10,000 other participants in an arena. It sure didn't sound like a vacation, although Monday through Friday the meetings were only in the evenings, and we'd be free to do whatever we wanted during the day.

The IBYC was really about family conflicts, not just youth, and Mom was right about one thing, she and I at least needed to resolve our conflicts, although I didn't see how. Nonetheless, in a weak moment, I agreed to waste her money and a week of my precious vacation.

After the first night, I had changed my tune. IBYC was memorable and worth nearly every minute, if only because the teaching was timely and practical. Gothard lectured quietly while illustrating his material with only black and white overhead slides. We were provided with a large three-ring binder filled with 160 pages of Gothard's overheads, except the key words on each page were replaced with blanks, which we were expected to fill as Bill revealed words, one-by-one, on the three-story high projection of his slides. The topics included:

- ► Discerning Levels of Conflict
- ► Acceptance of Self
- ► Family Communication Breakdown

- Removing Guilt
- Gaining a Clear Conscience
- Turning Bitterness to Forgiveness
- Transforming Irritations
- Eight Qualities Essential to Success
- Eight Callings in Discovering Life Purpose
- Friendships, and
- Successful Dating Patterns.

aNothing could sound more boring, and nothing was more exciting in all my years of listening to Bible teaching. After the first night we got to the venue at least an hour early to get the best seats (first row-center, first balcony). Gothard toured the country for decades giving these workshops to millions, and years later we'd send our teens and others with whom we had some influence.

The key to Gothard's success, I figured out many years later, was his ability to engage audiences by telling illustrative stories with well-placed, intriguing, narrative hooks. This discovery, and my experience attending IBYC three different times over the years, greatly influence my current work in motion picture story analysis. It was these narrative aspects of Gothard's technique, which he called "salting," that allowed him to intrigue his audience with cliff-hangers that he would eventually resolve with practical applications of Scripture.[1] It was a masterful technique that all successful storytellers employ to connect with their audiences. Thus, Gothard gained a good amount of my respect for his presentation techniques. But there were some issues.

> **The key to Gothard's success... was his ability to engage audiences by telling illustrative stories with well-placed, intriguing, narrative hooks.**

A FEW YEARS LATER after we had moved back to Detroit, I paid for and produced a documentary multimedia slide show that promoted the Detroit IBYC event, which I toured to local churches. When the IBYC team came to Detroit the local organizers wanted me to show it to Gothard himself. I agreed. But after I set up the gear for the private showing in a Cobo Hall Convention Center conference room, Dr. Gary Smalley showed up alone and said Bill

---

1 Today (2015), Bill Gothard's talks and many others can be viewed on-line for a small monthly fee at http://www.embassyinstitute.org

couldn't make it. At the time, Gary was Gothard's forerunner. Smalley watched the forty-minute show and afterwards politely thanked me for my effort. But then he confided in me that Bill would not have liked it.

"Why not?" I said.

"The music. It has a strong beat."

Gothard lectured against all music that had any kind of rhythmic beat, especially Christian rock music.

"But, Dr. Smalley," I said, "there is no rock music in the sound track. It, it's..."

"Stan, it has a beat, you have to admit that."

"Sorry, but the sound track is entirely from a 101 Strings album. There are no drums, guitars...not even a piano."

"There's a beat," Smalley insisted.

I replayed the music in my mind.

"You mean the pizzicato strings?"

"If that's what it is."

"The violins are plunking their strings. Bill would object to that?"

"Well, it's a beat."

Yes, that was the conversation. In Bill Gothard's lexicon, pizzicato strings—indeed, even walking down a street, if it was done at a regular pace—was just too much rhythm to be acceptably Christian.

This was the problem with many Evangelical churches, and like-minded para-church organizations like IBYC. Good *suggestions* for living a virtuous life could easily and quickly be elevated to the level of doctrine. A good thing taken too far becomes a bad thing...and a vice.

O NE OF GOTHARD'S week-long recommendations for a successful life was to memorize scripture—not a verse here and there, but entire chapters, so the context would be understood. This was not new to me, but in recent years I had spent little time committing even simple verses to memory, except my favorites from childhood days. So, after the week in Dallas, I decided to start memorizing Scripture again.

Gothard had warned that the intense memorization of God's Word would change our lives. Poor students would get better grades, torn apart relationships would be mended, and bad habits turned around. He made particular note that we might even experience nightmares as hidden evils which had taken root in our minds were loosed and expelled. I didn't take this latter claim seriously, but I believed (by virtue of personal experiences) the promises from Joshua 1:8, Proverbs 3:5-

10, and James 1:25 that mediating on and obeying Biblical teachings would bring success in both this and the next life.

I was also motivated by my seemingly insecure career as an aerospace engineer, and of becoming a first-time father in the next few months. I wanted to be better prepared for what lied ahead, so, I began immediately to memorize the first chapter of James, taking one or two verses a day.

About two weeks later, back in our apartment in Nassau Bay, here's what happened. One night we went to bed as usual. Pam and I shared a king-size bed and at the foot of the bed on the floor laid our dog, a German Shepherd mutt from college, named Jet—he was fast and he was almost solid jet black.

In the middle of the night I awoke from a terrifying dream and I had tried to exhale and yell but was unable to. When I awoke I was gasping for breath and there was an awful stench in the room. Pam, now nearly five months along in her pregnancy, did not stir.

I got up and looked for the source. Jet roused a bit, but stayed on the floor, his hind end was turned in my direction, and his tail tried to wag in his sleep. Staring at the barely wagging tail, I figured Jet had passed some gas. So I opened a window and aired out the room.

But when I laid back down I could not go back to sleep. So, I decided to open my Living Bible and memorize the next verse in James. In the days before, I had verses 1-20 down pretty good. So what was next was verse 21. Here's what I read.

> So get rid of all that is wrong in your life, both inside and outside, and humbly be glad for the wonderful message we have received, for it is able to save our souls as it takes hold of our hearts.[1]

As I went over the verse several times trying to commit it to memory, I recalled what Gothard had said about the consequences of memorizing large passages of Scripture. And, although I do not recall Gothard citing James 1:21, there was the claim: *Meditating on God's message would save our souls, take hold of our hearts, and get rid of what was wrong both inside and outside our lives.* Was the nightmare and my gasping for breath the minor exorcism of some entity leaving my body and fouling the room?

I do not recall wrestling with any grave sin or habit that suddenly

---

1 James 1:21 (Living Bible)

left me that night. I was pretty much the same lost sinner the next day, as best as I can remember. But I never forgot the night.

I RELAY THAT LAST anecdote for a couple of reasons. For one, it reinforces the physical evidence I inadvertently collected throughout my life for the viability of Scripture and Christianity. First, if you did certain things, with the right disposition of mind, certain other things would happen. And second, what Bill Gothard predicted may have just happened for real in my life. It was an anecdote, but it reinforced in my mind the Bible's trustworthiness. Those were the good lessons.

A virtue taken to extremes becomes a vice.

But there was a bad lesson to be learned in the coming month: A virtue taken to extremes, becomes a vice. Studying Scripture? A good thing. But, Studying Scripture too much, with the wrong frame of mind, could be a bad thing. If I had recalled Henry, my college hall-mate who dropped out of college because he spent all his time praying and studying the Bible and ignoring his education, I might have avoided what is described in the next chapter.[1]

---

1 For all the glowing things I say about Bill Gothard and the IBYC in this chapter, see the entry in my ACKNOWLEDGMENTS section for Bill Wiitala for an opposite (and I think, valid) reaction to Gothard's teachings.

44
Versification

I N LATE OCTOBER 1972, our first child was to be born. We decided that if it was a boy his name would be Kyle and if it was a girl, it would be Trudy, named after Trudy Jander, the effervescent teen who was our first covergirl...and who loved Jesus.

But we also needed middle names. So we let The Mustard Seed come up with suggestions. After 20 minutes of chatter while sitting around the floor of our living room, the group came up with "Jeffrey" (if it was a boy), and "Marcilee" (if it was a girl.)

On a Saturday late in October we helped the youth group with a paper drive. I borrowed a pickup truck and along with a large teen boy, Pam sat in the front seat as we bounced around the city collecting papers. Because of our broad shoulders that took up most of the space in the truck, Pam said she couldn't straighten up the whole day, which resulted in pressure on her womb, pushing the baby down.

Sure enough, early next morning, before the sun was up, Pam started labor. We got to the hospital in the middle of the afternoon and had time to take pictures of her hugging her Lamaze pillow by the Clear Lake Hospital sign.

Our girl was born that Sunday afternoon. Thus, Trudy Marcilee came, along with both her names directly out of our ministry with Lutheran teens. Ironically, it was this beautiful child that was going to force us to reconsider Lutheranism.

T O EXPLAIN THE problems we encountered with the Lutheran Church, I have to step back a couple months to early September 1972.

In the months leading up to Trudy's birth, our teen youth group and their parents became curious if we were going to baptize our baby at Gloria Dei of the LCMS. Doing so could force Pam and I to become "official" Lutherans. That didn't particularly concern us at the moment. We liked the Lutheran Church we were attending, and Leo Symmank, the pastor. But there was deeper concern. While Lutheran tradition required infant baptism, we came from an Evangelical tradition where infants were *not* baptized, they were *dedicated*. The situation was awkward, and we did not know what to do.

In early September this question prompted myself, along with two of my NASA friends, John Ritland and Bill Roeh, who *were* members at Gloria Dei, to meet with our wives (Susan Ritland, Beth Roeh, and Pam) and conduct a Bible Study on infant baptism. At the time Pam and I were the only couple of the three with a child (Pam was pregnant), and the only couple of the three that was not Lutheran. But that didn't matter. This couldn't be that difficult to figure out. After all, we were all "rocket scientists" (actually only John was). Nonetheless, in our confidence as smart adults devoted to God, we knew that by using only the Bible we were going to discover the infallible truth about infant baptism.

I noted that although we were going to get our truth *solely* from the Bible, we all immediately took stock of our Bible study aids—concordances, interlinears, study guides, and commentaries. We didn't just read the Scripture, we looked up everything, in these other books, which we read and debated. We even found supplementary materials from the LCMS that explained their interpretation of Lutheran doctrine. (I found out later there were over 100 different Lutheran confessions throughout the world.[1]) All of this we shared in multiple study sessions in the living rooms of our apartments where we took turns meeting together.

Perhaps you can see where this led.

We discovered that in the Zondervan NIV translation of the Bible there were 57 uses of the terms *baptism, baptizing, baptize,* and *baptized* in the New Testament. None of them make any mention of infants, babies, or children.

In argument *for* infant baptism we found verses that implied that generally everyone was to be baptized. Particularly, the Bible is specific that entire households were baptized:

Matthew 28:19 - Therefore go and make disciples of all nations, baptizing them in the name of the Father and of the

---

1 On-line, The Lutheran World Federation. www.lutheranworld.org.

Son and of the Holy Spirit

Luke 18:16-17 - But Jesus called the children to him and said, "Let the little children come to me, and do not hinder them, for the kingdom of God belongs to such as these. Truly I tell you, anyone who will not receive the kingdom of God like a little child will never enter it."

Acts 2:38 - Repent and be baptized, every one of you, in the name of Jesus Christ for the forgiveness of your sins. And you will receive the gift of the Holy Spirit.

Acts 16:33 - At that hour of the night the jailer took them and washed their wounds; then immediately he and all his household were baptized.

Then there were the arguments that compared circumcision (implicitly of little babies) to baptism.

Colossians 2:11-12 - In him you were also circumcised with a circumcision not performed by human hands. Your whole self ruled by the flesh was put off when you were circumcised by Christ, having been buried with him in baptism, in which you were also raised with him through your faith in the working of God, who raised him from the dead.

But while circumcision did not save you, Peter says baptism does:
1 Peter 3: 20-21-...in the days of Noah while the ark was being built. In it only a few people, eight in all, were saved through water, and this water symbolizes <u>baptism that now saves you also</u>—not the removal of dirt from the body but the pledge of a clear conscience toward God. It saves you by the resurrection of Jesus Christ...

In arguments *against* infant baptism we found verses that (only) those persons who believed were actually baptized.

Mark 16:16 - Whoever believes and is baptized will be saved, but whoever does not believe will be condemned.

Acts 2:41 - Those who accepted his message were baptized, and about three thousand were added to their number that day.

John brought his Book of Concord that explained historical Lutheran doctrine and that infants were to be baptized.

What do you suppose happened?

We argued…a lot.

Finally, we came to agreement about one thing, and two days before Trudy was born, I wrote my parents about our little group's discovery.

> *Dear Mom and Dad,*
>
> *Blah, blah, blah, blah...we made an intensive study...blah, blah, blah, blah...and are convinced that...*
> *blah, blah, blah, blah...the Lutheran Church is...*
> *blah, blah, blah, blah...irrevocably wrong.*
> *Scripture is clear...we now know this for fact.*

The letter goes on in some detail to describe the Biblical basis of why we had concluded that Lutheran doctrine was in error.

As I said, we worked with rockets and astronauts. We were smart and so were our wives (because they married us), and we were sure that our exegesis was flawless, infallible geeks that we were.

I ended the letter to my parents this way:

> *Question to my parents: Was I baptized as an infant? If so, why? What did it mean? What Scriptures were used to justify it?*

The letter archives I have of the event are absent my Dad's reply, although it says he sent one. But my Mom later told me, "You were *dedicated by sprinkling."* I challenge anyone to explain what that meant using Sola Scriptura.

Four days before Trudy's birth we had one of our final prayer and study meetings on the topic. I recorded a long written prayer at that meeting. In part it reads like this:

> *Lord, we feel so small and helpless, when confronted with what you have revealed to us tonite about baptism and its conflict with Lutheran belief...Bill who has been elected to the board of Christian Education at G. Dei and who is a member of the Lutheran Church Missouri Synod, and who has come to realize the Lutheran's error in their belief of the purpose of baptism...feels he should terminate membership... And John feels that unless the doctrine of baptism is*

*changed...they would have to terminate their membership
also, [although Susan is really Episcopalian so maybe she
doesn't.]*[1]

All six of us signed the prayer at the bottom in my prayer diary...
with great precision and penmanship, I might add, as if we were signing
an historic Protestant Confession that would irrevocably separate us
from Holy Mother Church. Never mind that we were already separated from Holy Mother Church once. I guess in our minds, another
separation between Protestants was par for the course.

Stanley David Williams
Beth Roeh
Pam Williams
Bill Roeh
John Ritland
Susan M. Ritland

All we needed now to make this official was the fancy signature of
the world's best known insurance agent, **John Hancock**.

I DON'T KNOW WHAT we were thinking. Our prayer, in all its sincerity,
was ridiculousness. Here we were, three insignificant couples in a
little Texas village acting as if 450 years of Lutheran confessions
was going to change because of OUR rocket-science insights. (Yes, yes,
only John was the rocket scientist. But we had all the books to certify
the six of us as theologians, by golly!)

Further John and Bill wrote a long paper to the Lutheran Church
Missouri Synod articulating their grievances with the doctrine of baptism as they interpreted the Bible. They later presented the paper to
the Gloria Dei Board of Elders. As you might expect the paper "was
received with cold interest."[2]

At the end of the presentation, Bill and John requested that Gloria
Dei submit the paper to the upcoming national synodical conference
for study. Symmank presented a rebuttal and turned down the proposal. There would be no such submission. Lutheranism would stand.

---

1 Author's diary entry, October 25, 1972.

2 I even made an audio tape recording of them reading their paper on audio
cassette tape so they could distribute it throughout the known world. Imagine Martin
Luther without a printing press...useless. But, the Three Rocket Scientists with an
audio cassette recorder? Priceless.)

A week after John and Bill's presentation, one of the members of the Board, the local head of the aerospace giant Lockheed-Martin, came to Leo and said, "That discussion we had over infant baptism got me to thinking. I don't see anything in the Bible that would prohibit any of the church's sacraments being kept from children, especially The Lord's Supper. If we as Lutherans are willing to baptize our children as infants, why do we wait until they're 12-years told or so to let them take communion?" Leo didn't have an answer.[1] The conundrum pointed not to the Bible (which gives no guidance on the matter), but to church elders and bishops who interpret the Bible.

Now you might think, so far, that the three of us were in one agreement about what Scripture taught.

Not so fast.

In fact, the three families did not arrive at a doctrinal consensus. (If we had polled our wives there might have been six different positions, but three was enough.) Each of us had interpreted the Scriptures differently through our own veil of experience and personality. Royal Mulholland, the Christian Existentialist, would have been proud.

And that's how we replicated Protestant history. We all came to such different conclusions that we all left the Lutheran Church and went in different denominational directions. John's family started attending a Bible Free Church, Bill's family became Quaker, and Pam, Trudy, and I headed off for Campus Crusade for Christ[2] (which was not really a church at all, and a story I cover in coming chapters).

Imagine this happening several hundred years ago when there would not have been such a selection of denominations scattered about town—we would have *each* started our own church, *each* convinced that *we* were right and our friends were wrong...each of us knowing *we* had the infallible truth revealed to us by the Holy Spirit, which meant the Holy Spirit was telling us each something different.

My problem? I just didn't believe that the Holy Spirit was schizophrenic; at least I couldn't find that in the Bible. So, this infant baptism episode bothered me for years.

---

1 Leo Symmank, personal communications, 2015.

2 In 2011 Campus Crusade for Christ changed it's name to "Cru. " (That's not a typo, look it up.)

L OOKING BACK, A technical way to describe our group's Biblical interpretive technique[1] is *versification*. Broadly defined, versification simply refers to the division of a text into verses for easy identification and location.

But more narrowly used, versification leads inevitably to misinterpretation. Since the verse divisions are not in the original text, modern day interpreters can divide the text into thought structures that are incoherent or inappropriate—ways not intended in the original. Verses become "paratext" elements, which allow interpreters to more easily focus on individual verses or groups of verses and ignore the text as a whole, which contributes to misinterpretation.

> **I just didn't believe that the Holy Spirit was schizophrenic; at least I couldn't find that in the Bible.**

Thus, regarding infant baptism, versification allowed each of our families to latch onto a particular group of verses where we felt the emphasis of Scripture should be placed. Given the differences in human nature from individual to individual, versification can lead to denominationalism, which Pam and I would contend with, and participate in, for many years to come.

In my job training astronauts, however, I learned that the interpretation of a text was *not* and *could not be* up to personal preference. To miscommunicate, to equivocate, or to make distinctions where there was no difference could easily become a life threatening issue and one of national concern.

Putting NASA check lists and national concerns for astronaut safety aside, there was still another force to be reckoned with.

---

1 Or, "hermeneutics" or "exegesis," the discipline of interpreting Biblical texts.

45
Mother's Prayers

WORKING AT MDAC and praying about the offer to join Campus Crusade as a photographer continued until March 1973. Pam and I figured we had to make a decision quickly to give us a couple of months to raise financial support for our "mission" and get to Crusade Staff Training at Purdue University by July.

Pam and I called our parents and asked them to pray for direction. We told them I was ready to quit MDAC, if for no other reason than to prove my faith in God.

But my Dad had other ideas. On March 4, 1973 he wrote me a classic and long letter. The advice was as good as I've ever received about determining God's will. Part of that letter reads:

> When the Lord wants to move you, or give you something new to do, He isn't going to rush you, but will give you time to be persuaded quietly and firmly, without any doubt about your decision. Here's how it came to me last night:
>
> 1. I feel that the Lord gave you that job at McDonnell's, when you consider all the circumstances how you got the job, and how you have been able to keep working.

He was speaking of how I dodged the draft and kept working at MDAC although they had warned me several times that I would be laid off as soon as I began.

> 2- So, you wouldn't want to quit the job UNTIL the Lord told you. Like the Israelites in the wilderness camped in one place until the Lord lifted the cloud, and then they moved on. You belong to Him, so you wait for marching orders-

UNTIL He moves you where He wants you to be.

3- So you stay put—at rest, content, just waiting his direction, and serving Him where you are, satisfied until He speaks. Remember you asked the Lord to make it real clear where and what He wills. That's the way I feel about it, but of course this is your decision and Pam's.

And then, in single spaced, carefully indented paragraphs Dad quotes the most encouraging verses from Scripture:

"In everything give thanks: for this is the will of God in Christ Jesus...Faithful is he that calleth you, you also will do it." (1 Thess. 5:18, 2 4.

"Giving thanks <u>always</u> for <u>all</u> things unto God...." (Eph. 5:20)

Psalm 3:3 TRUST in the Lord.....4 DELIGHT thyself also in the Lord...5 COMMIT they way unto the Lord...7 REST in the Lord, and waiting patiently...
23 The Steps of a good man are ORDERED

Psalm 84:11 "...no good thing will he withhold"

and m o r e and m o r e !

"Bless the Lord, O my soul..." Psalm 103:1-5

That was what my Dad's letters were like. Genuine epistles of hope.

A month later, it looked like we had to make a decision soon. During a telephone call Dad said again to me, "Don't leave it, boy, until God takes it away from you. Your mother will be praying for you." The key words in that last sentence, as I have come to appreciate, were, "Your mother..." Now to some "your mother..." sounds like the warm-up to a vulgar insult, but in my case it was the opposite: "Your mother..." Indeed! "...will be praying for you."

Of course Dad was praying for us, too. He was a man of his word, who read his Bible every day, prayed on his knees twice a day, was an active church leader, and contrary to my opinion about Mom, I never saw my Dad sin, as I understood sin. But here was the thing: Mom's prayers were answered even against the will of my Dad. Mom might have been ornery and mean at times, but she had a connection to God that got results. Don't ask me to explain it. That's just the way it worked.

So, on Thursday, April 5, 1973, Mom started to fast for our direction. Pam and I prayed, too, for guidance.

The next afternoon...*the next afternoon*...Friday, April 6, I was called into Earl Thompson's office. He was my supervisor's manager. He had me take a seat and closed the door behind me. Later on, "close the door" would become a signal that my life was about to change. But at the time I had no idea what was coming.

> **Mom might have been ornery and mean at times, but she had a connection to God that got results. Don't ask me to explain it. That's just the way it worked.**

Earl sat down and said something to the effect, "Stan, as you know, Skylab will be launching soon, and our role here in Houston will transition from procedure writing to flight support, and that requires fewer engineers. Unfortunately, you're the junior member on the team, and we're going to have to let you go. You won't be needed for the flight phase of the project, and there's no other contract available to absorb you either here or back in St. Louis."

I started to cry.

Earl was clearly taken aback by my emotional response. He tried to say how very sorry he was for the loss of my job, and if it was any consolation, I would be receiving some significant financial layoff benefits, especially since I had invested heavily in the MDAC stock savings plan.

It was clear that he was unaware of the reason for my tears. I explained to him that I was not crying because I had lost something valuable, a good job with a NASA contractor, but rather because it proved to be a miraculous answer to prayer...my mother's prayers no less. I explained how Campus Crusade had been recruiting me for the past year to work as a photographer at Arrowhead Springs, how my Dad had warned me not to quit a good job that had been given to me miraculously, and how the deadline was approaching for leaving Houston to raise support and get to Purdue University for Campus Crusade staff training. But the miracle was the timing. I told him that just yesterday Mom had started to fast and pray for direction for my life.

Earl was astonished. He stared at me wide-eyed, clearly affected by what I had just told him. I didn't know him to be a religious man, but there was nothing in his character to the contrary. At that moment I saw that he was aware of how God could work and lead in a person's life. He then told me that it was just yesterday that they had decided they had to lay me off. He was surprised, as well as I, at the timing. He then told me in a subdued and reverent tone that I was the only one being let go at this time from MDAC Houston Operations, a fact that in my mind solidified the event as miraculous.

MDAC gave me two weeks to clear out, which offered plenty of time to hand over my work to those that would be supporting the flight phase, pack up our belongings and put them in storage, sell a couple cars and buy a VW Westphalia Camper that we would use to travel around the country with our young daughter ,Trudy, and raise support.

And so, we left Houston for our job at Campus Crusade.

But that was not the end of the story.

Remember how Chuck and I had prayed for our bosses? Years later, Pam and I reconnected with fellow checklist writer Jim Arbet and his wife Shirley, who by the way was the delivery nurse at Trudy's birth in Houston. Jim told me the rest of the story.

Earl Thompson was so taken by how God had led me into and out of MDAC that he and his wife later decided to heed a long-standing call on their lives. Soon after Skylab, Earl and his family left MDAC and launched a career as Gospel Singers ministering at camp meetings and revival services. About the same time, and evidently also connected to my story, Earl's boss, Dana Boatman, left MDAC, attended seminary, and became a Presbyterian minister. I never again heard from Earl or Dana, and I've been curious about how their lives turned out. As for Pam, me and Crusade we--wait, that's the next chapter.

Suffice it to say, my situation, followed up by Earl and Dana's stories, pretty well confirmed that prayer works and God leads.

FRIDAY, APRIL 20, 1973 was my last day at MDAC and NASA. To pay my respects and see if I could produce a souvenir of my time in Houston, I visited the Astronaut Office Building and asked NASA's Book Manager, William Chanis, to sign my copy of the Final SWS Systems Checklist that I had helped write. As William signed my book, I expressed a desire to get the Skylab I crew's autographs as well. He checked the training schedule and told me they just happened to be finishing up a training session next door in the 1G Trainer. Since I still had my security passes, he said I should go over there right away and see if I could corner the crew before they left.

I did just that, and managed to catch all three of the Skylab I crew together. Graciously, Charles Conrad, Joe Kerwin, and Paul Weitz all agreed and signed my Flight Checklist, right over William's signature, like a seal of approval.

Happily, I headed back to Building 4 to show William how his suggestion had worked out. As he looked at their signatures in my book obliterating his own, I glanced out his second floor office window down into the astronaut's parking lot in front of the building. At that moment a pristine white Corvette Stingray pulled into the lot and parked in front of the building between two other Stingrays, one red and the other blue. The front and center parking spot was reserved for Chief of the Astronaut office. The driver was the first U.S. astronaut into space aboard a Mercury space capsule, Alan Shepard, Jr. I had never met Shepard, and I quickly realized this was my last chance to do so.

Saying my goodbyes to William, I retrieved my Checklist and headed for the front lobby. Avoiding the notoriously slow elevator, I leapt down the stairs two-at-a-time.

I entered the lobby from the stairwell just as Mr. Shepard entered through the building's front doors. Meeting him halfway next to the 1960's tubular chrome lobby furniture, I introduced myself, explained that it was my last day on the job, and would he sign my copy of the Final Skylab In-Flight Checklists that I had helped write? He graciously put down his bags and added his name above of the others, adding *"To Stan with best wishes..."* It made my day.

> **Words meant something, and their definitions and interpretations could not be subject to personal interpretations without endangering missions and lives.**

Later, on my way back to our apartment, it occurred to me, that as Pam and I started our NASA journey, we had watched Apollo 14 blast off for the moon with Alan Shepard in command. And, as we ended our NASA journey, the last person I would speak to, would be the same Alan Shepard, now Chief of Astronauts.[1]

My job with MDAC and NASA was short but memorable, especially because its beginning and ending were milestones of faith. But the long-term significance of the job was learning that *words meant something, and their definitions and interpretations could not be subject to personal interpretations without endangering missions and lives.* That became even clearer in our next adventure...that was never to be.

---

1 Alan Shepard was the only Mercury astronaut and the oldest astronaut to walk on the moon.

46
Jumping the Grand Canyon

FTER MY JOB ended at MDAC, Pam and I packed up and took off with our 8-month-old Trudy in our "new" VW microbus and began traveling the country raising financial support for our staff position at Campus Crusade for Christ. We first traveled to East Flat Rock, North Carolin,a where my parents had retired. My mother, the missionary kid from India, had grave doubts about our integrity as "missionaries" taking pictures out of a posh California resort headquarters called Arrowhead Springs. It was the antithesis of her idea of missionary work, and except for our immediate family she was sure no one would take notice, let alone support us.

During that week my parents, Pam and I took a day hike along part of the Appalachian Trail that passed nearby. On the trail we happened to meet the editor of the local paper on his mountain bike and struck up conversation. When he found out we were on our way to Crusade staff, he invited us the next day to his editorial offices, interviewed us, took some pictures, and wrote a long story for the paper that was published by the end of the week. Now, it was my mother's turn to be astonished that, indeed, God could lead in strange, back-woods ways.

We were modestly successful in raising support, and some funds began to trickle into the provisional account Crusade had set up for us. We never collected any of the contributions directly; they were all sent to Crusade, and after taking a small administration fee off the top, Crusade began to send us checks to pay for our expenses.

In July, 1973, we arrived in West Lafayette, Indiana, for Crusade

Staff Training that was staged at Purdue University. All Crusade Staff from all over the country convened for weeks of training that occurred in two stages. The first was called The Institute of Biblical Studies (IBS), and the second was staff Indoctrination. The month or so we spent in West Lafayette would be pivotal in our journey of faith. We thought we were headed for Arrowhead Springs and a photography ministry. How wrong we were.

THE FIRST WEEK of Staff Training, IBS, was exciting for me. Pam cared for our daughter, Trudy, and was excused from classes. I was told that I could skip the basic courses in Christianity, reserved for recent college graduates, because of the several courses I had taken in College, like Basic Christianity and Old Testament Theology. Thus, I signed up for a couple of weeks of advanced classes. One was under theologian Clark Pinnock for a class in Systematic Theology. We used his then recent book *Biblical Revelation* (1971, Moody). I recall being challenged and found Pinnock interesting to listen to, as I did the group discussions in the after class sessions. But several things stand out in my memory. First, Pinnock may have been a famous theologian and prolific writer, but he was no Stan Walters. Dr. Walters never claimed to be a theologian, but I took away more evidence and understanding about Christianity from Walters than Pinnock. Second, whereas I saved everything (notes, books and papers) from Walters, I threw away everything from Pinnock's class—including his book—during an early purge of my overgrown library. Books that I read I mark up with margin notes, and I found almost no margin notes in Pinnock's book. Third, and this was probably the most memorable, by chance, I sat next to Jesse James IV...yes, the great, great, grandson of the famous outlaw. Jesse was a few years older than me. He told me there were seven of his cousins and siblings with the name Jesse and one was his son, Jesse James V. He said his famous ancestor was clearly an outlaw but he didn't really know much about him. And that's what I remember about Systematic Theology. If Jesse had signed my copy of *Biblical Revelation* I might have kept it.

The other course I took was helpful, although afterward I wondered if the helpfulness was good. The class was an intensive three-week study of how to use Greek and Latin language reference books to unlock the meaning of Scripture. I kept those books and have used them often, the bindings of two being broken from use. For me, the most significant (and largest) was Strong's Exhaustive Concordance of the Bible. This impressive volume has no peer. If you're not familiar with the six-pound, three-inch-thick, 12" x 9" mammoth effort, The figure below shows how the title page reads…and it's all true…although, here, reduced in size.

THE

EXHAUSTIVE CONCORDANCE

OF

THE BIBLE

SHOWING EVERY WORD OF THE TEXT OF THE COMMON ENGLISH VERSION OF THE CANONICAL BOOKS,

AND

EVERY OCCURRENCE OF EACH WORD IN REGULAR ORDER

TOGETHER WITH A

COMPARATIVE CONCORDANCE

OF THE

AUTHORIZED AND REVISED VERSIONS,

INCLUDING THE

AMERICAN VARIATIONS;

ALSO BRIEF

DICTIONARIES OF THE HEBREW AND GREEK WORDS

OF THE ORIGINAL,

WITH REFERENCES TO THE ENGLISH WORDS

BY

JAMES STRONG, S.T.D., L.L.D.

S TRONG'S CONCORDANCE IS an impressive if not incomprehensible work. It does list every distinct word in the Bible and give each a unique number. In the back, there are two dictionaries, one Hebrew and the other Greek, giving definitions of each word in the Bible, along with a number assigned to their alphabetical order. Thus, the Hebrew dictionary lists 1 ('ab—*father*) through 8,674 (Tattenay—*a Persian*); and the Greek Dictionary lists 1 (a—*a*) through 5,624 ("ŏphĕlimŏs"—*helpful*).[1] The Hebrew numbers are normal, and the Greek words italicized to differentiate their use in commentaries.

These 14,197 words, with their unique numbers, allow Biblical language idiots like me to look up words by the numbers in other reference books to derive meaning and some cultural context. Thus, when I left IBS I also had copies of *The New Englishman's Greek Concordance of the New Testament* (Associated Publishers and Authors), an *Analytical Greek Lexicon* (Zondervan), and *A Manual Grammar of the Greek New Testament* (MacMillian) by H.E. Dana and Julius R. Mantey.

So convincing were the two instructors and the contents of these books, that after three weeks of instruction, I was ready to declare myself a Biblical scholar. Think about how wonderful these reference books would have been to the Early Church Fathers. They could have forgone all those eternally long ecumenical councils where debates waged for years about what was true and what was heresy. I imagined that if we had had this "extensive" training and these "exhaustive" reference books when we undertook the study on Infant Baptism in Houston, our small Bible study no doubt could have avoided all those arguments and stayed united. It was clear that with such reference guides on my bookshelf, along with every conceivable translation of the Bible (in English), I could start my own church. All I had to do, like any wannabe painter with no talent, was to follow the numbers. I can hear the radio commercial now:

> *Yes, you TOO can be a theologian and start your own church. Just follow the numbers and discover the truth of God otherwise hidden from mortal men. Be a pastor, a bishop, or even your own pope. It's all within your reach. Be STRONG and of good cheer. Buy STRONG'S today.*

---

1 A footnote to the Greek Dictionary tells us that due to "changes in the enumeration while in progress," Strong didn't have a word left for Nos. 2717 and 3203-3302. So, although 5,624 was the last number given the last alphabetical word, there are actually 101 words fewer, or 5,523. Before the age of computers I guess it was too difficult to change all those numbers once they were committed to printing.

THE SECOND HALF of Staff Training, appropriately called Staff Indoctrination, was to be a turning point.

The process started out with general orientation sessions about Crusade's administration and evangelism training. Most new recruits were fresh out of college and were not married. So, Pam and I, with one child, were an oddity and thus were matched up with another oddity, Dallas and Linda Strom, a couple who were a few years older than we, with three boys. They were there for friendship and to answer the informal inquiries we had about being on staff. But the more important aspect of staff indoctrination involved Pam and I taking psychological tests, and meeting at length one-on-one, and as a couple, with staff interrogators as I came to think of them.

It was during these latter sessions that we were told five things that put a serious damper on our call to Crusade.

ONE

As Crusade staff we would not be allowed to keep or use any copy of the Bible that included the Apocrypha (or Deuterocanonical) books. This came up because at the time my favorite translation was the Jerusalem Bible, which contained the Apocrypha. I remember our interrogator telling me, "Stan, there is some pretty weird stuff in those books."

"Well," I said, "I wouldn't know about any of that weird stuff you're referring to, since I haven't read any of the Apocrypha books in my Jerusalem Bible. But, have you ever read Revelation?"

As I recall that ended the conversation. But we were to rid ourselves of the heretical books.

TWO

We were told that we would have to be open to working on a college campus with one-on-one evangelism teams. I found this odd since we had been specifically recruited for the photography staff at Arrowhead. I also knew that my personality was not of the pastoral nature to be doing spiritual counseling on a university campus. But being assigned to a campus ministry seemed to be a firm requirement; for me it was a poor fit.

THREE

We were given a two page "personal testimony" of how to explain the Gospel to an unbeliever. Not only was memorizing anything by rote difficult for me, I found some of the phrases and logic in the canned presentation irrational or silly. The one line that I have always remembered was this: "Man can no more save himself than he can jump across the Grand Canyon *flat footed.*" I asked our interrogator if I could revise the line to read, "Man can no more save himself than he can jump across the Grand Canyon *given a running start.*"

I was told, "No!" I had to memorize it precisely as it was written because that is what Dr. Bright had determined worked best in talking with strangers. But it wasn't my "personal" testimony, I said, it was Bill Bright's. No matter, I was told. I would have to start with Dr. Bright's presentation, and when you get that perfected you can tell your own story. This was not personal evangelism. It was *plastic evangelism.*

FOUR

Related to the canned "Grand Canyon Jump" testimony, we were told how universally useful *The Four Spiritual Laws* were, and how they should be used whenever possible. *The Four Spiritual Laws*[1] were distributed by the millions in little booklets. You could carry around a dozen in your shirt pocket and share them with others, like you might business cards. Here's the abbreviated essence of the booklet, which includes Scripture and further explanations, with a prayer at the end to receive Christ into one's life:

1. God loves you and has a wonderful plan for your life.
2. Man is sinful and separated from God.
3. Jesus Christ is God's only provision for man's sin.
4. We must individually receive Jesus Christ as Savior and Lord to know God's love and plan for our lives.

The Four Spiritual Laws were too neat and tidy for me. In my young life I was always being reminded of the "cost" of following Christ, no doubt due to the many missionary stories I had heard growing up. This passage from Luke was foremost in my mind:

---

1 A small booklet Bill Bright wrote in 1956 for use in personal evangelism on how to establish a personal relationship with Jesus Christ. Millions have been printed in 200 languages.

*Large crowds were traveling with Jesus, and turning to them
he said: "If anyone comes to me and does not hate father
and mother, wife and children, brothers and sisters—yes,
even their own life—such a person cannot be my disciple.*

*And whoever does not carry their cross and follow me
cannot be my disciple.*

*Suppose one of you wants to build a tower. Won't you first sit
down and estimate the cost to see if you have enough money
to complete it? For if you lay the foundation and are not able
to finish it, everyone who sees it will ridicule you, saying,
'This person began to build and wasn't able to finish.'*

*Or suppose a king is about to go to war against another
king. Won't he first sit down and consider whether he is able
with ten thousand men to oppose the one coming against
him with twenty thousand? If he is not able, he will send a
delegation while the other is still a long way off and will ask
for terms of peace. In the same way, those of you who do not
give up everything you have cannot be my disciples.*[1]

Supplementing this was the encounter Jesus had with the Rich
Young Ruler to whom Jesus said, "Sell everything you have and give
to the poor...Then come, follow me."[2] According to the Four Spiritual
Laws none of these sacrifices were necessary.

Several years later, Wayne Rice satirized the Four Spiritual Laws
in the *Wittenburg Door* by rewriting St. Mark's story as an interview
between Jesus and Richard Ruler during which Jesus presents the Rich
Young Ruler with the Four Spiritual Laws. Rice's satire ends this way:[3]

JESUS: *Well, you simply pray the little prayer which I'll give
you here...*

RICHARD: *And that's it?*

JESUS: *You have to really mean it, of course.*

1 Luke 14:25-33 (NIV)

2 Mark 10:17-27 (NIV)

3 "You Can't Take it With You" *The Wittenburg Door*, February-March 1977
(p. 16-17). This is the issue with the long form, and very good interview, with Bill
Bright, founder and president of Campus Crusade for Christ, that *The Door* named
Evangelical of the Year.

RICHARD: And I'll have Eternal Life?

JESUS: That's the Gospel truth.

RICHARD: But there must be more. Doesn't it <u>cost</u> me anything?

JESUS: It's free.

RICHARD: You mean I can keep on being a rich young ruler?

JESUS: (Smiling) Absolutely. In fact, your testimony will be a real help to other rich young rulers.

RICHARD: What a relief. I had heard it was really going to cost a bundle.

JESUS: No, it's the "free gift of God." Just pray the prayer.

RICHARD: Far out!

As the curtain closes, Richard Ruler prays the prayer, and exits stage left happily ever after, for he had great possessions.

In the face of such criticism, however, Bill Bright defended the Four Spiritual Laws, in *The Door's* accompanying interview that honors Bright as Evangelical of the Year.

> *We believe the Four Spiritual Laws represent the distilled essence of the Gospel. We don't say that it's the best presentation...We [as Christians to grow into maturity] need to know a lot more than what is contained in the Four Spiritual Laws booklet.[1]*

To make the record clear, in spite of my differences with Crusade about these things (and another to come), I have always considered Bill Bright a man above reproach, and the Campus Crusade ministry a paragon of parachurch evangelization. If he were Catholic, I suspect he would have been quickly elevated to sainthood for his avoidance of all serious controversy and his disciplined and practical work for the Kingdom of God.

---

1 Ibid. p. 7d.

But there was one thing more.

FIVE

We were told that as Crusade staff we were not allowed to practice the charismatic gifts, like speaking in tongues (even in private), nor could we associate with Pentecostal or Charismatic Christians who spoke in tongues. Crusade found such activities and the promotion of the Gifts of the Spirit among Christians as divisive. How odd, I thought. In my interpretation, the Bible spoke of the Gifts of the Holy Spirit as tools to unite the Church.[1] We all had different gifts so we would be forced to depend on each other. But Crusade was convinced that tongues were not biblical, and that the Holy Spirit was not involved. Their evidence was that some Pentecostals were so pushy about how all Christians should speak in tongues, division was the result.[2] The solution, in Crusade's mind, therefore, was to *invoke more division: No tongues allowed.*

This presented several problems for us. Pam and I had a good many friends who were Pentecostal Christians who prayed in tongues, although up to this point in time neither Pam nor I had ever experienced the gift. After probing Crusade over this issue for several days, it was clear their policy was written in stone, and I came to the conclusion that I could never work for a ministry with such a divisive policy about something that was intended for unity. This was a serious blow to my confidence that God had led us away from MDAC to Campus Crusade. We had pulled up roots from Houston, voluntarily became temporarily homeless, struck out on the road toward this ministry, only to be told that *what the Bible claimed in I Corinthians was not to be believed.* I was incredulous. My sense of Crusade being in the center of God's will for our lives was destroyed.

The after-effect of these issues would haunt my Evangelical days for years to come. To me, Crusade, which was not really a church but an independent ministry, was demonstrating the dregs of denominationalism and something very contrary to the unity that Christ demanded. I was sent into a short depression.

What would we do now? Our short-term lease of five weeks was up in less than a week, and we had to go somewhere?…and find a job!

---

1 1 Corinthians 12 & 14
2 See explanation of how this policy came about later in this chapter.

THE ANSWER TO our sudden spiritual and practical dilemma came through a sad but ironic event involving our Crusade mentors, Dallas and Linda Strom, which also gave me pause about joining Crusade; you could enumerate this as point SIX.

Dallas and Linda were in their early 30's, about five years older than Pam and I. Married in 1963, they had three sons. In 1971, two years before we met them in West Lafayette, they had joined Crusade's Lay Ministry, and had been busy ministering with families in Minneapolis, Minnesota. There they were involved in a safe and loving Lutheran community. We found them congenial, smart, dedicated and family oriented.

Toward the end of the Purdue training period Dallas was rushed to the local hospital for an emergency appendectomy. A few days later their 13-year old son, Terry, cracked his head open in a serious swimming accident at the city pool. The injury required many stitches and lots of ice packs. Complicating the situation, Terry had entered adolescence and was beginning to resent the amount of time his parents spent in ministry to others. Linda had already been struggling with the amount of energy it took during the Purdue training to care for three male children and attend Crusade events. But now her husband was recovering from surgery and her oldest son from a serious injury. Guilt became a daily struggle. If she attended everything she felt guilty because of neglecting her children and husband, and if she followed her heart and stayed home she felt guilty because she was not measuring up as a member of Crusade staff. So, the night of Terry's accident, Linda and Dallas decided that Linda should stay in their rented apartment rather than attend the all staff assembly in the Purdue stadium at which Dr. Bright and Billy Graham were addressing the U.S. staff.

The following day Linda found herself, expectantly, in a meeting with her director. He told her that "Crusade calls couples, not individuals," and her decision to stay home with her son and not attend the Bright-Graham assembly "did not support Crusade's mission." She was questioned about her call to the work, and then informed that her excuse for missing the stadium event with Dr. Bright was "unexcused."

Linda says, she "was disillusioned and frustrated about being treated like an adolescent." Layered into Terry's run-in with the bottom of the pool and Linda's run-in with her director was another exacerbating issue that Crusade had created. Just before coming to West Lafayette, Crusade had transferred the Stroms from their close-knit community and support group in Minneapolis to a new work 300-miles away in Milwaukee, Wisconsin. In order to put their home on the market in Minneapolis and get to Purdue on time for training, they had rushed all their belongings into temporary storage. Still to come was house hunting in Milwaukee. And, since Crusade required all staff members to raise their own financial support, the move to Milwaukee uprooted the Stroms from many of their financial supporters. They were utterly in physical and financial limbo. As soon as staff training was over, provided everyone was healthy enough, Linda was anxious to get to Milwaukee, research the surrounding communities for a place to live, and then fulfill a critical goal—ensure that her boys were enrolled in a good school system and prepared for entirely new surroundings, friends and teachers. All of that weighed heavily on her mind.[1]

> **Bible studies, prayer meetings, and worship services are only worthwhile if they prompt us to lead better lives.**

But from my perspective, their experience confirmed that Crusade and I were no match. To my understanding rules, policies and doctrines of religious institutions had a purpose outside themselves. They were to guide us in how to live a more fulfilled *life*.[2] As soon as the ministry takes precedence over life, Pharisaical tyranny takes the lead, not grace. Bible studies, prayer meetings, and worship services are only worthwhile if they prompt us to lead better lives. Such devotional or obedience activities are not ends unto themselves. What Linda learned from Crusade was supposed to help her be a better person and mother, not be a more obedient staffer.

Afterward, although Dallas and Linda returned to Milwaukee and the Lay Ministry office there, the incident involving Terry and the missed assembly left a scab on their souls. The next year when Crusade again moved the Lay headquarters office, this time to Atlanta, the Strom's decided to stay in Milwaukee where their sons were doing well in school. They started an independent ministry named Discipleship Unlimited, that we helped support for years. Although Dallas died of cancer (after a five-year struggle) in 2008, Linda carries on the ministry today with 200 volunteers ministering to women in prison around the

---

1 Personal Communication with Linda 2/20/15. Today, Terry is on the staff of Discipleship Unlimited. His mom says of him, "He is a fantastic worship leader and leads recovery groups in prisons. God uses everything. He has made beauty out of ashes."

2 John 10:10, "I have come that they may have life, and have it to the full."

world. She is the author of *Karla Faye Tucker Set Free: Life and Faith on Death Row*, the gripping story of the first woman executed in Texas in over 100 years. Linda was Karla's spiritual advisor and close friend for eleven years and walked with Karla to her 1998 execution.

THERE IS ONE more inning to this chapter. It's something that quietly happened a few years after our Purdue training, and it confirmed our decision to avoid Crusade's policy entanglements and to follow God's personal and dynamic leading in our lives.[1]

In the early years of Crusade's worldwide expansion, there was no policy for or against charismatic phenomena like miraculous healings or speaking in tongues. But a Crusade director in Indonesia, claiming to have received the baptism of the Holy Spirit suffered some mental instability and subsequently contributed to the destruction of Crusade's largest international ministry. Crusade's board of directors held an emergency meeting and adopted a policy that said Crusade staff "may not speak in tongues publicly or privately or advocate doing so." This, they hoped, would prevent division in Crusade's goal of fulfilling the Great Commission.[2]

But, as time went on, myself and others bumped up against this policy. Some of these individuals where actually Crusade staff that kept their involvement with the Charismatic Movement a secret, as did Linda Strom.

Shortly after high school, while he was working on staff at Arrowhead Springs, Bill Bright's eldest son, Zachary, was invited by other Crusade staff members to attend a meeting at Calvary Chapel in Costa Mesa, CA. Calvary Chapel was Pentecostal yet did not practice the gift of tongues in their Sunday or Wednesday evening public meetings. After Zachary's exposure to the group, he came home one night claiming he had been baptized in the Holy Spirit and spoke in tongues.

Zachery's confession was a "coming to Jesus" moment for the Bright family. According to Crusade policy, Bill Bright could no longer fellowship with his teenage son. Bill tried to build bridges with Zachery, but Vonette Bright, his mother, insisted that Bill enforce Crusade's policies. So Bill handed Zachary a copy of Crusade's policy directives for his son

1 The information in this section comes from a variety of sources: Conversations with anonymous Crusade staff members (1973-1983), personal interviews with Zachary Bright (February 2015), Linda Strom (February 2015), and John G. Turner's *Bill Bright & Campus Crusade for Christ: The Renewal of Evangelicalism in Postwar America* (University of North Carolina Press: Chapel Hill, 2008).

2 Matthew 28:16-20.

to read. In the end Zachary lost his job at Crusade, moved out of the house and into a Christian community. Later, as a compromise with his parents, he attended the Pentecostal Four Square L.I.F.E. Bible College in L.A. (now Life Pacific College in San Dimas, CA). During that time his father saw that Zachary's interest in Scripture had not declined as a consequence of his Charismatic experiences, but rather became "more attentive to and engaged with the Bible." By the time Zachary graduated from L.I.F.E. Bill Bright told his son that Crusade's restrictions surrounding the association of staff with tongue speaking charismatics had been loosened. Zachary writes, "the deal was sealed, so to speak, when my dad was the commencement speaker at my graduation in 1979."

Within a few years Crusade no longer forbade staff members from praying in tongues privately, but to this day there is to be no "charismatic phenomena in their public meetings except for healing" (which ironically, if it actually occurred, would be much more dramatic and perhaps divisive than tongues.) Since the mid-1980's Crusade has also publicly cooperated with Pentecostal and charismatic groups. Zachary eventually earned a B.A. in Religion and Philosophy from Azusa Pacific University (a Free Methodist sister school of Greenville College) and an M.A. in Theology from Fuller Seminary in 1992. He has been a Presbyterian Church (USA) minister since that time (the denomination in which he was raised) and is also part of what was then known as the Charismatic Movement.

Years ago, when I first heard of how Zachary's experiences challenged Crusade's polices, I thought it was proof that God had a sense of humor. But reflection today suggests that in our fallible state, God's grace allows us to make decisions that have a place in time, but not in eternity. And, as God is eternally patient, He brings us gently around to greater wisdom and understanding, revealing His ever-present, providential guidance in our lives.

For years after the Purdue Training events, however, my thinking wasn't that clear or patient. Conflicting thoughts about the state of Evangelical Christianity swirled in my mind. One thing was clear, however: Even the best of Christians were fallible and could be misled. So, maybe I still had a chance to be the person God wanted me to be. After all, I had my *Jerusalem Bible, Strong's Exhaustive Concordance*, a *New Englishman's Greek Concordance of the New Testament*, an *Analytical Greek Lexicon* and *The Interlinear Greek-English New Testament* from Zondervan, *A Manual Grammar of the Greek New Testament* by Dana and Mantey, six volumes of *Clark's Bible Commentary*, a five volume set of *The Inter-*

national Standard Bible Encyclopedia, The Complete Works of Josephus (with "Enlarged Type and Illustrated"), F. F. Bruce's *The New Testament Documents: Are They Reliable?*, John Stott's *Basic Christianity,* C.S. Lewis's *Mere Christianity,* a shelf-full of different Bible translations, my *Latin New Testament* from Lutheran High...and my Mom's pamphlet (with my name inscribed across the top) on *Catholicism and Communism in America.*

How far astray could I go?

A few months later, when I tried to buy a new Bible, I was reminded of just how *wide the path that leads to destruction...*was.

47
It's the Bible
Jesus Used

I N 1973, AFTER our flirtation with Campus Crusade, we looked for
photography jobs with Christian publishers and organizations near
Chicago. In my naiveté I didn't know that publishers did not have
staff photographers, so, the search was a waste of time.

But there was one interview that intrigued me. I made a cold call
on Creation House Publishers (while Pam and Trudy stayed in the VW
camper in the parking lot). I was surprised to be ushered into the office
of the president. Cliff Dudley was a big, gregarious man with a broad
smile. On his perfectly large and polished desk was a huge open Bible.
Let me repeat, the desk must have been 8-feet wide, 5-feet deep, polished to a sheen, and smack in the middle of an otherwise empty desk
was an over-sized Bible with gold edging that made me squint from
the glare. Cliff sat behind the glare grinning like the Cheshire Cat in a
dark pinstripe suit. His arms rested on the desk behind the Bible. He
was ready for his portrait.

Mr. Dudley spent 30-minutes with me during which time he received my resume, asked about my background, we talked about the
Bible and my desire to find a job as a photographer for a Christian
organization. He looked at and made nice comments about my photography portfolio.

Then, out of the blue, he asked if I would consider ghostwriting the
biography of Olympic Gold Medalist Janet Lynn, the skater that had
dominated the ice-skating world the last few years. She was a Christian
and Creation House owned the rights to her story. They were looking

for a writer.

The request of my interest in the matter was a surprise. I had no writing samples. Did writing technical reports and spaceship check-lists qualify me to write an inspirational biography? I didn't think so and was glad to leave the interview.

While preparing this chapter I made contact with Dean Merrill, who wrote Janet Lynn's book. He started on the project on Monday, July 16...three weeks before my interview with Cliff!? No slouch, Dean completed the book and it was published before the end of the year... something I cannot imagine myself doing. Since then Dean has written over 40 books, many ghostwritten for Christian personalities .[1]

BACK TO REALITY, Pam and I headed back home to the suburbs of Detroit. My father-in-law, Bill Turck, an engineer at Ford Motor Company in Dearborn, tried to get me an interview at Ford World Headquarters' Photomedia Department, which did most of the photography and filmmaking for the company. But he was told they were in the midst of a division-wide hiring freeze.

Not one to give up so easily, Bill called a layman from the Dearborn Free Methodist Church, Jim Buick. Mr. Buick had not only been one of my Sunday School teachers in high school, but was also the comptroller for the Lincoln-Mercury division.[2] As you might expect, as someone who held the purse strings at a Fortune 100 Company, Mr. Buick had connections, in spite of having the surname of a competitive product for General Motors.

Thus, as soon as we arrived in the Detroit area and set up a temporary home in the Turck's basement (all our furniture was still in storage in Houston) I had an appointment with Photomedia's Wil Moellman who was in charge of all Ford in-house photography, film and video production. The department was located in the basement of World Headquarters...a matter that will be significant later.

Moellman was impressed with my portfolio and resume and shared with me his own. He was an excellent nature photographer, and often his background photography would appear in Ford advertisements behind the foreground of shiny new Fords shot on the large stage just down the hall.

---

1 www.DeanMerrill.com

2 Jim Buick left Ford several years after this and became President of Zondervan Christian Publishers in Grand Rapids.

WIL HAD IMMIGRATED from Germany after World War II. As a child he was forced to be in the Hitler Youth against the objections of his father, who had been wounded in the leg and sent home to the family farm not far from Berlin.

Near the end of the war, and when word came down that all young men Wil's age were to be constricted into the regular army, Wil's father, who was very much against Hitler and the Nazi party, took a great risk. In the dead of night, limping, and with his Army discharge papers in hand, he led his family and a team of two horses pulling a wagon piled high with their belongings. After daybreak they arrived at a bridge near Berlin. The German Army held one side of the bridge and the American's held the other. But the Germans would not let the Moellman family cross the bridge, claiming that the Americans would not want them. The excuse was that the stupid Americans would not understand a word of German. Wil's father persuaded the gatekeepers to let his young son, Wilfred, walk across alone and ask the Americans. The German's laughingly agreed, not knowing that Wil knew some English. After walking across alone, with his family under guard behind the German barrier, Wil spoke to the U.S. soldiers. Momentarily, the American barrier was raised and the G.I.s gestured for the Moellman family to come across. The disbelieving Germans relented and let the family pass to freedom, but not before confiscating both their horses and all their possessions.

INDEED, PHOTOMEDIA WAS not hiring full time. But Wil seemed to like me and gave me a long tour of the large department. I asked if there wasn't a place for me in one of the dozen darkrooms, which I could see were very busy with three shifts. But he shook his head laughing, and said I was over qualified for such work. When we got back to his office he told me he would very much like to hire me but he could not put me on salary under the current hiring freeze. Then he asked me to work freelance as a vehicle test photographer in hopes that when the hiring freeze was lifted, he might be able to find me a creative position.

I immediately agreed, and began working the next day shooting black and white, 4 x 5-inch graphic reflex photos of bumper crash tests. It was nearly meaningless, simple work, but it paid decently, the other photographers were congenial, and, more importantly, I was in the door at Ford.

In the meantime, Pam, Trudy and I needed a place to live and some more meaningful work if only part-time. Pam's parents attended the Taylor Free Methodist Church, which conveniently was looking for a Youth Pastor. The advantage of the no-pay, part-time position was that it came with a free two-story house located right on the church's property. There was a downside, however. The previous year the domicile had been the Youth Group's Halloween House of Horrors and the city had come close to condemning the property. While a Christian Youth Group sponsoring a House of Horrors did portend the challenge that awaited me, in our desperation we took the job and moved in. Little did we know…

OW THAT I had landed a position in real ministry, I needed the credentials. By credentials I don't mean a preacher's license or a degree from a Bible school. What I needed was a new Bible. My favorite Jerusalem Bible was just too small. If I was going to be a Youth Pastor, I was determined to have the best Bible available to assist in my new position, a Bible that would set an example for the youth. It had to be the biggest and most sacred looking Bible that I could carry into church, short of using a fork-lift. It would be the measure of my spirituality and my commitment to God. Now, that sounds sarcastic, but it wasn't far off from my mindset at the time.

Thus, a few days later I stood in the Inner-City Baptist Bookstore in Allen Park, MI, staring at a large wall of Bibles for sale. The titles were legendary to Evangelical ears: Amplified, J.B. Phillips, Thompson's Chain Reference, Nave's Topical, Revised Standard, New Revised Standard, American Standard, New American Standard, Holcomb, Living, and the ever-present King James Version (KJV).

I was surprised but delighted at the variety of Bibles for sale that came in every conceivable size, color and edition: pocket-sized, paper-back, soft-back, hard-back, simulated leather, Moroccan leather, imitation cow hide, authentic vinyl, blue denim, heirloom, and psychedelic--don't ask.

Equal in variety were the interpretive aids: red letters (for the words of Christ), concordances, maps, footnotes, endnotes, paintings, photographs, diagrams, charts, time-lines, cross-references, glossaries and sticky-tabs. The Thompson Chain Reference Bible was particularly impressive with its encyclopedic appendixes that rivaled the biblical text in length.

For a while I just stood there--soaking up the sacred vibes. This must be what heaven is going to be like…a wall full of Bibles. (Indulge me, that *was* sarcasm.)

This heavenly shopping moment, however, had a downside. The sole clerk, a distinguished, elderly lady with gray hair in a bun, spectacles drawn down her nose suspiciously, was glaring at me as if I was about to commit a crime.

Little did I know, that in her eyes I was about to do just that. I figured that I had better stop medicating[1] on the smell of the Moroccan leather--and buy something, fast.

I made my way to the checkout with a beautiful New American Standard Study Bible that must have weighed-in just under six pounds, and would compliment my Strong's Concordance in demeanor. I lowered it proudly onto the counter next to the cash register being careful not to pinch my fingers under its weight.

Now the conversation I am about to reveal, dear reader, you may think is one of the exaggerations I confessed to in the Preface for the sake of readability. But, unfortunately, in this case, truth was not just stranger than fiction, it was alien. This is a nearly literal recounting of what transpired.

My bespectacled clerk was aghast. "Why do you want to buy THAT?" she asked backing away, pointing at the Bible as if I had just found the snake from the Garden of Eden.

"What? Well, I need a Bible for the teen Bible studies I plan to be leading," I said.

"Buy a real Bible then," she charged.

"Huh? This IS a real Bible--isn't it?" She had me wondering.

"No it's not. The only authorized Bible we sell is the King James Version. It says so right in the front."

"I'm sorry, madam, but you're mistaken," I said, carefully. "The King James translation was completed in 1611 and was based on a variety of other translations that came before it."

She stared at me as if I was the devil incarnate or a bad replica.

I trotted back to the Bible wall, grabbed a copy of the Thompson Chain Reference KJV Bible, opened to the help section in the back and found the chart (No. 4220) that showed how the KJV was based on a number of earlier translations including the Bishops, Geneva, Tyndale, Wycliffe, and Vulgate versions. Back at the check out counter I explained the diagram to her.

She was unimpressed. "You can't fool me," she said. "That chart isn't 'in' the Bible. It's in the back. It's not part of the authorized Bible. You

---

1 There are times when medicating is similar to meditating.

can't believe any of it."

"Okay," I admitted. "But this Bible was authorized by King James--not Jesus Christ."

She laughed, conjuring up her experience with the First Century Church. "Oh, that's where you're wrong. The King James Bible is the only authorized version because it is the Bible that Jesus used."

At this point there was a long period of silence as I repeated her words to myself. Finally, I burst out, "WHO TOLD YOU THAT?"

Unruffled, she narrowed her eyes, stepped into my space, and pointed across the street to the large Inter-City Baptist Church. "Our pastor!"

To reiterate, dear reader, that is word-for-word, a true story. I did not exaggerate.

THE INTER-CITY BAPTIST Bookstore incident raised some critical questions about Christianity. Which Bible are we to believe? Are they all inerrant? The translations were all different, and not all were based on the same ancient texts. And then there are the footnotes, and other study helps that many users consider as inerrant as the text itself. But are they? After all, everything I had read or heard claimed that none of the earliest Biblical texts have survived. All we have are copies. It's not like there is clear, physical evidence to point to.

For many years after, I was unsure how to argue with such a sincere yet misguided person as the bookstore clerk. I met them occasionally--like the woman I know professionally who explained to me last week why she wasn't Catholic: "I know all about the Catholic Church. In college I did a term paper and I discovered that the Vatican owned two birth control companies as profit centers. They're just a bunch of hypocrites."

In the face of such ridiculous opinion it seems that all reason is washed away by the tsunami of irrationality. I was then, and am still today, clueless how to deal with such people. Perhaps there will be an instructional poster in Purgatory that will explain it all to me. I can only hope.

IN THE END, the clerk stubbornly sold me the NAS Bible. I used it for decades until the binding fell apart. But the incident has long reminded me that in some sectors of Christianity there are Christians who believe that before His ascension, Jesus supervised the writing of the KJV (in Elizabethan prose), oversaw its printing on imported India paper, and approved the first edition leather bindings, before letting the Apostles organize a book signing.

That may sound sacrilegious to some, but today, as I write this in 2015, on the campus of the Bible Institute of Los Angeles (aka BIOLA University), there's a beautifully realistic thirty-foot outdoor mural on the side of a building of Jesus doing just that. He looks down on the students that pass-by and holds out to them a thick leather-bound Bible…hot off the press.

From that day in the Inter-City Baptist Bookstore, I began to more seriously wonder where the Bible came from. There still seemed to be some unanswered questions from Dr. Walters' Basic Christianity and the books we read.

The experience also forced me to ask the question, "What version of the Bible DID Jesus use?" From my Evangelical training I believed the answer was the Greek Septuagint of the Old Testament. Later, I was to discover that the Septuagint actually included 52 books plus additions to Esther and Daniel. And, surprisingly, my prized, six-pound, New American Standard Bible had only 39 books in the Old Testament.

What was I to believe? Who could I trust?

48
Media Renewal

A s A FREELANCE still photographer for Ford (where I put in 40 hours a week) I was still looking for a salaried job with benefits near the end of 1973. With a B.A. degree in Physics and a resume as an electronic engineer working at NASA, I started putting out applications at the various divisions of Ford scattered around Dearborn.

One day I was invited to an interview at the Ford Environmental Testing Laboratories. The Federal Government was tightening emission standards on new cars and Ford was ramping up their testing capability. After the interview I was immediately offered a full-time position as a test engineer, where I would be partially responsible for designing environmental test programs to ensure that Ford met Federal emission standards. It sounded interesting, and I was tempted to take the position on the spot. But I told the men that interviewed me that, although I needed a salaried position for my family's sake, I honestly would rather be working for the Photomedia Department. My potential boss said he understood and agreed to keep the offer open for a couple weeks while I tried to negotiate with Photomedia.

The next morning I met with Wil Moellmann and told him about the salaried environmental engineering offer, but that I'd rather work for him in Photomedia. He didn't hold out much hope. I asked again about the darkrooms. He said there was no way he'd put me in such a dungeon. He explained that in my experience, which was evident from my portfolio, darkroom work was creative. But at Ford, the darkrooms were strictly production and creativity was done *in-camera*. He told me to hang tight for a few days

My parents and in-laws said they would pray, as did Pam, me. But special mention, again, should go to my Mom. Two days later Wil asked me to come in and meet his boss, John Mayberry. Mayberry essentially read me the riot act, and said that if I came to work for them they would "own me" and I'd have to agree to work whenever they asked me to, even on Sunday. I glanced at Wil who smiled and shook his head as if to say "don't believe it." Mayberry saw it and said laughingly, "I'm serious, I'm going to own your ass."

Wil rolled his eyes and in his thick German accent said, "Stan, we've only worked on Sunday maybe once in three years."

Mayberry no doubt challenged me about working on Sunday because he knew I was a part-time youth pastor at a church. But I also knew that he was responsible for a department of 200 men and women who turned out time-sensitive photography and marketing material that had demanding deadlines for every division of the company around the world. I recalled Jesus's comment about how if an ox fell into a well on the Sabbath it was entirely appropriate to work and pull it out. So, without much hesitation, I said I was agreeable to his demand, knowing that if push came to shove I could always quit and find a job as an automotive engineer.

So, miraculously I was offered a full-time job as the Assistant Television Technician in Ford Photomedia's new Television and Film Department. But, I would have the job title of Photographer, since Ford's personnel bureaucracy had no idea what a "Television Technician" was or did. I was also asked not to talk about being hired because there was still a hiring freeze in place. An exception had been made to bring me on board. I expressed my appreciation and loyalty, and started the next week at a salary that was equal to what I had been offered as an engineer. Who knew such a thing was possible. God, perhaps?

A S THE PART time Youth Pastor at Taylor F.M. I was suddenly in an official leadership position in the denomination in which I was raised. A number of people at Taylor knew Pam and me from either nearby Dearborn F.M. where we attended as teens and where we were married, or because Pam's parents now attended Taylor. We were warmly welcomed.

The cultural shift from Gloria Dei Lutheran and Campus Crusade back to Free Methodism was a mild shock for me. At Gloria Dei I enjoyed liturgical worship (in the round). Commissioned art decorated the interior of the church, and there was an acceptance of recorded music and photography for teaching and outreach. I previously mentioned the Christmas Eve service The Mustard Seed led where we had the congregation dancing in a circle around the altar holding hands to Three Dog Night's *An Old Fashioned Love Song...coming down in three part harmony.* My attraction to Crusade was principally their contemporary evangelical magazines that used bold photography and colorful layouts, and which embraced the breadth of Gospel music and Christian entertainment as demonstrated at Explo '72, the Jesus Music festival.

I marvel today at how we ended up back in the staid Free Methodist Church. But we were desperate for a place to live and for Christian ministry. And, perhaps I thought I could bring some renewal to the denomination's Southern Michigan Conference where I was known. But worship at Taylor was dull, photography and graphics were all but shunned, and the preaching was focused entirely on evangelism and not discipleship or maturing the faithful, something I felt I personally needed. So, I convinced myself to rise to the challenge and channeled my missionary-preacher-teacher heritage...to change the world, starting right there in Taylor, Michigan.

While I had the official title, Pam was every bit as active in leadership and together we did much. Along with regular weekly meetings and Sunday School for senior-high and post-high school teens and young adults, we started a teen music group we called "All God's Children," and we started Bible studies and Bible memorization programs. I was automatically on the Board of Christian Education and after a year unilaterally drafted a comprehensive *Philosophy of Christian Education* for teens through adults, and outlined a broad biblical curriculum that was inspired by our college level courses and those at the Crusade's Institute of Biblical Studies. I also developed comprehensive workshops on "Dealing with the Devil," "Applied Christianity," and (much later) "Personal Goals and Mission Statements."

I was excited about being a Christian, and all there was to learn and apply. But there was a general lack of enthusiasm for what Pam and I were attempting to do. The fairly easy Bible memorization program we promoted and for which I filled a cabinet with trophies (albeit cheap and plastic), had no takers and no interest, even after a couple of months.

The more I observed, the more I theorized that the lack of interest in spiritual matters had something to do with the methods of presentation. We had to bring it alive. The program for children in the church always included visual aids and crafts that helped reinforce the spiritual lessons. But for the teens and adults there was only the spoken or written word in Bible studies and sermons. So, the youth music group began to experiment with different ways to present the Gospel. I wrote short skits for the teens, and we drew colorful posters, and we learned songs. I persuaded the senior pastor, Rev. Ray Ellis, to let the youth lead one of the Sunday evening services with what we were preparing. He readily agreed. The night came and we performed our skits, sang our songs, and held up large posters to illustrate the evening's message on the fruits of the Holy Spirit. The teens bounced up and down as they sang and held their posters high, and were full of energy and enthusiasm in front of the modest congregation of perhaps 120 souls.

After the benediction, we asked the congregation for feedback on how they liked the service and if the various things the youth did found any resonance with the congregation. The room was quiet. Finally, one woman stood up and said, *"I found the entire evening disgusting, and disrespectful. And if I ever see any more dancing in church I'm going to leave and find a real Christian church. You should be ashamed."*

> **"If I ever see any more dancing in church I'm going to leave and find a real Christian church. You should be ashamed."**

Well, one bad apple isn't so bad, I thought. But, while we got a few nice comments, there was nothing so good as to offset the comment from Mrs. Bitter Sanctimonious. I was miffed.

My senior pastor was more encouraging but not overly so. Ellis told me to keep my head up, that the youth liked me and were getting spiritual good out of my work, even if the congregation didn't appreciate it. But the congregation's lukewarm response told me something deeper was amiss.

One of the things I came to realize was that among the dozen or so regular older teens that had graduated from high school, few were in college. In fact, the church's membership was mostly blue-collar workers with little natural affinity for the intellectual side of biblical Christianity I found attractive and had been promoting. That explained a lot to me, and caused me to doubt my capacity to raise the spiritual awareness of those in my charge. So, I took refuge in looking outside my own experience for an answer, and sought suggestions from the older and more mature young adults, some who were just turning twenty.

Out of those conversations, mostly at the recommendation and encouragement of the young adults, I continued the exploration of expressing Christianity through media and began reading about the broader Church Renewal movement, which was a hot topic at the time.

The exploration into media came naturally because I was now engaged full time as an assistant film producer and video engineer at Ford Headquarters. So, in the utility room of the old "White House", as we called the former House of Horrors we were living in, I built a large photography darkroom to support what I hoped would become part of my personal ministry and not just a hobby.

On the Church Renewal track I was introduced to a number of books that stimulated my imagination and hopes for the Free Methodist Church. The most exciting at the time was *The Problem of Wineskins: Church Structure in a Technological Age* by Howard A. Snyder[1], who at the time was the Free Methodist director of Light and Life Men's Fellowship, the international men's lay organization that my father had co-founded decades earlier. Snyder's message was that the Gospel of Jesus Christ was always producing New Wine, and that in turn produced change in the world. Thus the New Wine had to be contained in New Wineskins, not old rotten ones that would burst. While the Gospel's message never changed, the church structures that contained and carried that message had to be continuously updated. The book took direct aim at what to me were hot topics: the role of the Holy Spirit, the role of spiritual gifts, putting on the mind of Christ, and the role of small groups and community. During this time I had some written communication with Snyder, who worked at Free Methodist Headquarters in Winona Lake, Indiana. He lamented with me over the Free Methodist Church's refusal to update its methods of communication and broaden its approach, which risked the Church's future growth and moral relevance in the world.

There were many books I devoured during this time that broadened my understanding of what the church could be. The titles tell you what was happening in many other Christian denominations.

- ▶ *Full Circle: The Creative Church for Today's Society* by David Mains (Word, 1971);
- ▶ *Ask Me to Dance* by Bruce Larson (Word, 1972);

---

1 Intervarsity Press, 1975. Snyder followed *Wineskins* with a sequel two years later, *The Community of the King,* that focused on the empowering of the Church through the gifts of the Holy Spirit. It was significant to me at the time that neither book was published by the Free Methodist publishing house, but rather by Intervarsity.

- ► *The Comfortable Pew* by Pierre Berton (Lippincott, 1965);
- ► *L'Abri* by Edith Schaeffer (Tyndale, 1969);
- ► *The Church at the End of the 20th Century* by Francis A. Schaeffer (Word, 1969);
- ► *The Normal Christian Life* by Watchman Nee (Christian Literature Crusade, 1961);
- ► *Catch the New Wind: The Church is Alive and Dancing* by Marilee Zdenek & Marge Champion (Word, 1972);
- ► *Let's Quit Fighting About the Holy Spirit* by Peter E. Gillquist (Zondervan, 1974).

Such reading was irrevocably changing my vision of the church and how to make the Gospel relevant and evident. Yet denominations like Free Methodism, in my experience, were clearly afraid of breaking free from the barren, pale green cinder brick walls of the worship spaces and other status quo structures such thinly painted walls metaphored. I was intent on trying to change all that. Yes, I was enamored with the power of media, but my love was the Gospel.

I N FEBRUARY OF 1974 I persuaded Pastor Ellis to let me make a presentation to the Taylor leadership on how media could be used to enliven worship and make the Gospel more accessible and effective. Although Ellis and I didn't agree on everything theologically, the presentation went well and he passed on my outline to someone at Free Methodist headquarters in Winona Lake, Indiana. A few weeks later I received an invitation from Winona Headquarters to do something similar for its leadership. So, on May 5, I made a Sunday afternoon presentation to leaders and a few bishops under the auspices of Dr. George Ford's office of Information and Stewardship. Two weeks later I received a letter from Dr. Ford's office thanking me again for the May 5 presentation, and asked that for "Winona '74," the annual national conference of Free Methodist pastors and lay leaders, I would present a workshop on June 22 under the title "Your Church Can Use Multimedia."

For all these presentations I handed out a fill-in-the-blank topic outline. I used overheads that incorporated text and graphics. And, I made available a long bibliography of resources. I also explained the background and theory behind sensory aesthetics, and the importance of change to create intrigue that lengthens attention spans. The foundational concept behind the talk, however, was that God stimulated all six of our bodily senses when He communicated with us, so why shouldn't we stimulate all six, as often as we ca,n to pass on the Good News to others? (Can you name all six senses? Don't look at the footnote until you do.[1])

Today, in 2015 as I write this, the list of ideas I presented seems juvenile, considering the wide spread use of media in churches today and the explosion of the Internet and smart phones. But at the time, decades before even the personal computer came on the scene, many found my demonstration intriguing if not strange.[2]

Some of this rubbed church leaders the wrong way. Free Methodism, you'll remember, was built around the concepts of simple, plain, straight, narrow, solemn, and bare. Over the years, Pam became a talented artist in the creation of large, colorful worship banners made from burlap, linen and felt based on Scripture for special services. Her first large banner celebrating Christmas hung 6-feet vertically from a 4-foot wide pole. On a light brown woven burlap background she glued and stitched graphics and text in colorful felt cutouts. In the center was a large bright yellow circle with rays of sunlight radiating in every direction. In the middle of the circle in a bold, purple celebratory font, was the name "JESUS." Above, in bright orange, overlapping the rays of sunlight were the words, "THE REASON" and below "FOR THE SEASON."

The youth had a part in the Christmas Day program for families, which fell on a weekday. For the program we hung the banner on a front wall to one side of the pulpit. Pam received many compliments. She's always been very good at designing and crafting visual displays for her school classrooms. I was proud of her and certainly happy to see something visually attractive on the otherwise blank, pale green cinder block wall. But, on Sunday morning, when it came time for the morning worship service, the banner was gone. I couldn't believe it, it was so beautiful and this was the Sunday service we'd be celebrating

---

1 The sixth sense is not ESP, but simply *balance*.

2 Today's churches use Bible quizzing, Bible memorization programs, drama, mime, readers theater, dramatic readings of Scripture during worship, professional musicians, large scale photography, overheads of sermon outlines, audio recorded interviews and location reports from missionaries, professionally performed and recorded music (F.M. churches did not have pipe organs), song lyrics projected with 35mm slides, sermon illustrations with motion picture clips, 8-mm films of church events and location reports, telephone chains, long distance telephone hookups with missionaries and VIPs for live interviews, dial-a-prayer recordings, banners, guests artists that sing, act and draw, etc.

Christmas. The only other decorations were a few red Poinsettia plants on the platform. I asked my pastor where the banner was, and he said he wasn't sure, but that he felt it was inappropriate for a worship service. I was speechless.

There was something in place of Pam's banner, but I'll save that description for a subsequent chapter on the Church Growth Movement.

Later, I found Pam's beautiful creation rolled up and stashed on end in the janitor's closet soaking up a puddle of wastewater from a mop and bucket that was being used to mop up the wintry foyer of snow and mud that peopled tracked into the church. For years later, I hung the water-damaged banner in my workroom as a reminder of the distance the church had to go in order to respect art and the artists who worked in the service of their Creator.

> **I found Pam's beautiful creation rolled up and stashed on end in the janitor's closet soaking up a puddle of wastewater.**

THE FOLLOWING MARCH, on the first day of spring, our second child came a month early. We named our darling preemie, April Dawn.

Remarkably, her name would foreshadow the spiritual dawn of our lives as Christians. And although April exhibited some Special Education tendencies during her academic career, on many occasions she would prove to be more spiritually sensitive and insightful than her parents.

Thus, April's arrival in our lives corresponded to a significant dawn, or wakeup call, that became apparent by August. During this time period I finished reading a stack of books on Church Renewal and the work and gifts of the Holy Spirit in the church. The latter topic was one Free Methodists and Pastor Ellis seemed to avoid like the plague.

But events were afoot and our lives were about to change.

49
New Insight &
New Directions

THE LATE SUMMER of 1974 presented a series of quickly unfolding events that told us Providence was pushing our family in a new direction. Here is what our diaries document in just a few weeks:

Sunday, August 11: Todd, a visitor at Taylor F.M., introduced himself to me and showed some interest in what we're doing. On his way out he asked Rev. Ellis to preach sometime on the "Baptism of the Holy Spirit." Ellis hedged and demurred.

Wednesday, August 14: Todd came to evening Bible Study. Afterwards, he shared privately with me his Christian journey and how his life had been invigorated after being baptized in the Holy Spirit. He's looking for a church where he can grow spiritually.

Saturday, August 17: We staged a special Youth Prayer meeting and Gospel Concert in the evening at the church. Disappointedly, only about 13 teens showed up, including Todd. The band was "The Potter's Clay" on tour from Florida led by my nephew, Bob Kenney and his wife. Afterwards, Bob and his wife talked at length to Pam and me about the important role the Holy Spirit was playing in their Florida church, and how their fellowship was growing by leaps and bounds.

<u>Later That Same Night</u>: After reassembling the altar rail for church services the next morning, I repositioned the display-Bible facing the congregation on the communion table. I let the Bible open randomly on its display stand. It opened to Acts 2, the story of the Holy Spirit descending on the Apostles causing them to proclaim the Gospel in foreign tongues they had never learned. I took notice but didn't flip the page.

<u>Sunday, August 18</u>: Pastor Ellis, on vacation, gave his pulpit over to the Vice President of Spring Arbor College, Dr. Rev. John Newby (1928-2009) who preached on "The fullness of the Holy Spirit." I took copious notes. He had an altar call and Pam went forward and prayed to be filled with the Holy Spirit. A number of us knelt around her and prayed with her. It was not an emotional experience—she didn't speak in tongues, fall over backwards, or flop around on the floor. But afterwards she had a feeling that something had changed.

<u>Monday, August 19</u>: The next books on my reading pile were *True Spirituality* by Francis Schaeffer, and *Baptism and Fullness: The Work of the Holy Spirit* by John Stott. I dove-in and hoped to finish both by the end of the week.

<u>Thursday, August 22</u>: Cathy Fanto, one of the young adults, invited Pam and me and a few others to a prayer meeting in Ann Arbor. I was expecting 15-20 people. But this was something different. First, it was at St. Mary's Catholic Church. *Do Catholics even pray?* And, second, it was in the gymnasium, from which I heard the low roar of a vast crowd as we approached the room. We walked in and I was stunned. Over 1,000 University of Michigan students and adults were sitting on chairs in a large circle around center court. I had walked into my first (of many to come) Word of God Community public Prayer Meetings, and the beginning of the Catholic Charismatic Movement.

After the group was greeted by one of the leaders from (literally) the inner circle, the singing and worship began. I was in awe. It was like "being in heaven," (which was how my Dad described the Word of God prayer meeting I took him to several months later). The worship, led by a small group of guitars, violins, a cello and various woodwinds in the center, was joined by the crowd's enthusiastic voices. The songs swelled to a crescendo and then mellowed to a whisper and then silence fell upon the group. At times, a voice from the crowd would speak up and proclaim a word of encouragement that sounded like Scripture, as if God was speaking to the group. This was my first exposure to what charismatics called Prophetic Utterances.

The only tongues I heard were spoken quietly by a man near me during times when everyone seemed to be praying out loud at once, but with a quiet dignity. I found out later that although the gift of tongues was encouraged in the community, the gift was not to be used in public for fear of misunderstanding by the public in attendance.

The worship continued spontaneously for 45-50 minutes. It seemed like the epitome of praise and worship.

After the singing ended, one of the leaders (Ralph Martin) gave a teaching that lasted as long as the singing. Then, after another song, the meeting was over.

Pam and I were ecstatic all the way home. I was so stunned I did not realize until after that I did not sing a note all night. I just stood there in awe and soaked up the aura. It was the renewal I had been reading about and longing for.

Thursday, September 5 (two weeks later): With Ellis still on vacation, Pam and I took a number of other older teens to the Word of God Prayer Meeting. It was our second visit, and the time spiritually invigorated the young adults who came with us. This time I acquired a Word of God songbook and sang heartedly with everyone else.

Friday, September 6. Ray Ellis and family returned from vacation and learned of our outings to The Word of God Prayer meeting. What he knew, and I did not, was that the Charismatic Renewal was not favored by the Free Methodist bishops and the practice of tongues (publicly or privately) was forbidden.

The Death Knell fell when Ray Ellis came to our house unannounced and he told me to immediately stop encouraging the youth's participation in any charismatic activity. He told me I was leading them astray. [Pam later wrote in the diary that during the encounter Ray "became visibly shaken."] In my mind I thought this was Campus Crusade all over again—it was a bad sign. I tired to share Scripture with him, but who was I to do that to my senior pastor? I pulled back and told him perhaps Pam and I would get away for the weekend and read our Bibles and pray. He said that would be a good idea, he'd cover for me.

Saturday, September 7. In despondent spirits, Pam and I left in the morning for an impromptu break. We dropped Trudy and April off with Pam's parents and headed for Weber's Inn (a mini-resort of sorts) west of Ann Arbor, Michigan. On the way we stopped in Ann Arbor and visited the Logos Christian bookstore to pick up some reading material. Parking in Ann Arbor has been impossible ever since the University of Michigan and cars have co-existed. We drove around and around and backtracked until Providence, delaying us just enough, allowed us to find a parking space. On our walk to the bookstore the reason for our delay became evident. We "accidentally" and literally ran into Lillian Stratford Hawkins [1945-2009], an old friend from Greenville College. We had no idea she was living in Ann Arbor, nonetheless in the basement of the Methodist Church where her husband, Don, was the church janitor while they both attended graduate school. Before we knew it Lillian was bubbling forth about the gifts of the Holy Spirit and how her small community (not related to the Word of God) was growing. *What's going on here, Lord? We try to get away from all this charismatic stuff and you throw it in our face? Well, tomorrow we'll be holed up in a hotel where nobody can find us.*

Sunday, September 8. Pam and I hid out at Weber's Inn. We decided not to drive into nearby Jackson, Michigan for church, but stay in our hotel room and read. But at 9:00 AM the phone rang and (Surprise! Surprise!) my half-sister, Dorothy (Kenney) Hagey [Bob's mom...you remember Bob] was in the hotel lobby wanting to take us to her church. We still have no idea how she knew we were there.

We reluctantly agreed, hurriedly dressed and hopped in the car for what we thought would be a short drive further West into Jackson. But then I had forgotten about Dorothy's compulsive nature...it was legendary and worse than mine. She and Russell Hagey [her second husband, recall Oscar died some chapters ago] bundled us into the back seat of their very long and wide Oldsmobile that bounced on coil springs, and headed for Detroit, an hour East, and from where we had just escaped. After we hit the city limits, we drove for another hour, and ended up at the largest independent Church in Detroit at the time, Bethesda Missionary Temple. We discovered that this was Dorothy and Russell's "home" church, 2.5 hour drive one-way from where they lived in Spring Arbor. (I still want to know how they found us.) Oh, and here's the kicker, Bethesda Missionary Temple is Pentecostal. Oscar, the Free Methodist pastor must be holy-rolling over in his grave.

I T'S NOT TECHNICALLY accurate that Bethesda Missionary Temple was Pentecostal. The classical Pentecostals that emerged from the 1906-1915 Azusa Street Revival, split into various groups as the century wore on. One of these was the "Latter Rain Movement," that Bethesda was part of, although even that moniker has been dispensed with and today (2015) Bethesda considers itself part of the wider Charismatic Movement. But when we first attended, Bethesda Missionary Temple's interpretation of Scripture and the Gifts of the Holy Spirit, had been rejected by the Classical Pentecostals as *un-Biblical*. Yes, even Pentecostals, we discovered, couldn't agree on how to interpret the Bible. But that did not bother the 5,000 ecstatic congregants the Sunday we visited. Pam wrote in our diary about that day:

> *In Sunday School, we received a profound teaching from God through the senior pastor, James Beal. He taught on Hebrews 6:1-3 about laying the foundations of the church: (1) repentance, (2) faith toward God, (3) doctrine of baptisms (4) laying on of hands, (5) resurrection from the dead; and (6) eternal judgments...before we could go on to deeper spiritual matters. The Church worship service was much like the Word of God meetings. God seemed to be telling Stan and me that the church (our F.M. Church) had left its foundation especially in regard to the baptism of the Holy Spirit and the laying on of hands.[1]*

Needless to say, when we returned to Taylor a few days later, our sensitivity about the spiritual needs within the Free Methodist Church had not quieted, but had been enlivened. Ray Ellis was disappointed, and at an Official Board Meeting the night of our return, I gave an account of the Youth Ministry activities. I received some rebuke from a couple of the members and Ray about The Word of God events. I partially lost it, and exchanged harsh words with several of the members. The next day, I made the round of apologies, but I was restless and unsatisfied and the damage had been done.

A FTER SEVERAL MONTHS of study, in January of 1975, I wrote a 5,000 word white paper titled: *A Discussion on Tongues Addressed to the Free Methodist Church of North America*. Since I had not then or ever since spoken in tongues, I felt the paper was objective exegesis of Scripture and history. But after I gave him a copy, Ray Ellis, in an exchange of letters, had a different opinion and we

1 Personal diary entry Sept 12, 1974

agreed to disagree on how to interpret God's Word regarding the role of tongues.

Next, I wrote a long letter of my concern for renewal and the gifts of the Holy Spirit to one of the Free Methodist bishops I knew. Rev. Donald Bastian had been our college pastor in Greenville. I didn't send him the paper, but in his written response he was concerned that I had been caught up in the tongues movement and he warned me to be cautious.

AFTER MORE TIME, I saw no way out. My soul was thirsting to know God better, and my efforts at moving the church toward that goal were stymied by what I called at the time *a satisfaction with the status-quo*.

On April 6, 1975 I delivered a letter to the Taylor Official Board and resigned my position as Youth Pastor at Taylor Free Methodist and my membership in the Free Methodist Church. The letter cited five reasons, here summarized:

- ▶ I need to grow spiritually before I can effectively minister.
- ▶ No monies have been budgeted for Youth Ministries. All youth program expenses had been born by my family. (Remember too, there was no salary for the position, just the free house.)
- ▶ None of my program proposals have been accepted or implemented.
- ▶ My creative efforts with the Youth had been frequently criticized by parents and church leaders.
- ▶ The Church has rejected the world-wide out-pouring of the Holy Spirit and has separated itself from the charismatic renewal.

I made the resignation effective July 1, which gave me two months to wind down, plan my exit and move my family. But the Board accepted it effective the end of the following week.

We tried to buy a house in a hurry, but such things take time. At the end of June the youth group (who were sorry to see us go) helped us move out of the White House and back into my in-laws' basement.

PHYSICALLY, MY YOUNG family was technically homeless. But I wasn't lost spiritually, nor I did think God had abandoned me. I was upset with God, however, for the state of affairs I saw within Free Methodism, and I expressed that anger with God when we couldn't find or buy a house on short notice. And, when we moved back into my in-laws' basement with 80% of our belongings stashed in their garage I felt like a complete failure. Pam was okay with it, and so were the Turcks. But my pride drained me emotionally even while I "reasoned" that my humbling was exactly what God wanted. After all was said and done I prayed that God would be in charge. What I didn't like was how He did it.

Balancing out the disaster of suddenly being homeless was an awareness that I not only had a good job, but I was learning a level of professional media production I could not have dreamed about a year earlier. But what good would that do, I wondered? My real passion was to use media to promote the church's spiritual renewal, and it appeared that God had slammed that door in my face.

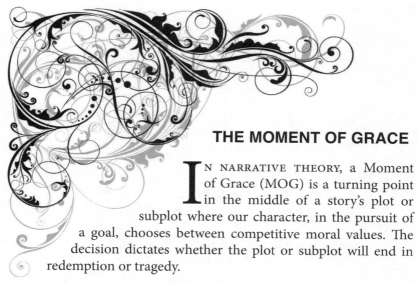

THE MOMENT OF GRACE

IN NARRATIVE THEORY, a Moment of Grace (MOG) is a turning point in the middle of a story's plot or subplot where our character, in the pursuit of a goal, chooses between competitive moral values. The decision dictates whether the plot or subplot will end in redemption or tragedy.

In this memoir there are many minor moments of grace, but only three *major* ones. (A) The MOG in the subplot about my love life was falling in love with and marrying Pam (Chapter 27). (B) The MOG in the main plot, relating to my faith journey, was leaving Free Methodism in Chapter 49, which you just finished. (C) The MOG in the subplot of my professional career, coming up in a few chapters, I'll leave to your curiosity to identify. See if you can spot it.

Moments of Grace are the great scenes in life where we face moral dilemmas. In each we make choices that dictate our future. When I faced such times growing up, my Mom frequently paraphrase Romans 8:28. Her words of advice have stuck with me to this day:

In all things, God works together with those who love (and obey) Him to bring about what is good.

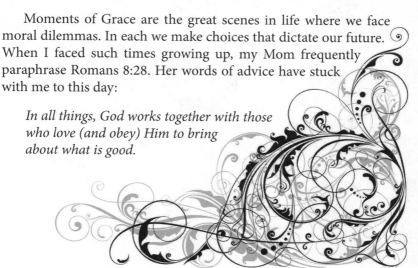

Part III
WARRIOR

L EAVING THE YOUTH Ministry and my position at Taylor Free Methodist was traumatic. For the weeks before and after my resignation I prayed unceasingly for wisdom and guidance.

In response to those prayers, my Guardian Angel reminded me that in high school I had spent time categorizing the citations of every verse in Proverbs onto 3x5 cards and placed them into a topical card catalog system. I dug out that little tin box and found dozens of cards with subject headings like *finance, family, women, children, obedience, wisdom, foolishness,* and even one on *bribes.* Beneath the titles were dozens of citations from Proverbs. I remember looking up many of those verses, and pouring over chapter after chapter hoping for some nugget of truth that would free me from my current situation.

But there was no silver bullet, just the dogged reminder to persevere as a warrior might in pursuit of a goal.

Later, I realize that leaving Free Methodism was a *moment of grace,* to use a term from the architecture of stories. For the first time in my life, I was unencumbered from any religious institution...except *my own interpretation of the Bible.* I could attend any church I wanted without approval or excuse. And, I was free to investigate or dialogue without explaining my actions to a pastor. But people change slowly, and Free Methodism was not yet out of my life.

50
League of Misfits

I HAD BEEN A pain to the pastor and other leaders at Taylor Free Methodist. This bothered my parents some, since the bishops of the national church knew Dad and Mom, both well-known lay leaders in the denomination. So, it was not totally unexpected that eventually I got a call from the office of bishops and was asked to come down to see them in Winona Lake, Indiana. *Here we go, again,* I thought, as I recalled my many trips to the Vice Principals office in Junior High. *They've figured out some ghoulish way to get me to touch my spiritual toes.*

But that wasn't it at all. Surprise! Instead, I was being invited to attend a leadership banquet at Headquarters and receive an award.

What!?

Yeah, I was as surprised as you probably are.

Here's what had transpired.

Within a few months of leaving Taylor and moving in my in-laws' basement, our family of four bought a house not far away. We moved out of the basement, and into our "new" older bungalow with four bedrooms and a full basement. One-half of the "new" basement gave me space to set up a production office and build a large darkroom. But what good would it do, I wondered.

No sooner had I gotten set up than Dr. J. Arthur Howard called and asked to stop by and pay me a visit. I didn't know Jerry (as he asked to be called) but soon found out that he was the project liaison for the Free Methodist Church department in charge of Missions and Stewardship. He and others had seen my Media in the Church presentation at Headquarters a couple years earlier and had also seen a slide show I had produced and was showing around that unofficially promoted Bill

Gothard's Institute in Basic Youth Conflicts. Jerry wanted to know, for his boss Dr. George Ford, would I produce a couple of training slide shows for the Free Methodist Church to promote Missions and Stewardship? They would pay me.

Whoa! That was new and different.

So, Jerry came by and we sat on two old wobbly kitchen chairs in my tacky but proud production facility…and talked. Come to discover, Jerry was also a fan of Dr. Howard Snyder, my Church Renewal hero who had authored the *Wineskins* books.

Jerry also knew how to cement common ground and gain my confidence. Once, after listening to some of my complaints about the church's archaic communication methods, he told me: "Stan, you and I are members of a very select group of human beings. Only 3% of the world population is in our league."

His statement made me feel important. Although, in retrospect, he never fully described the criteria for being in his unique 3% league of misfits.

The short of Jerry's visit was this: I started Full Circle Productions with two very creative multimedia friends, Bill Wiitala and Don Schendel. Over the next eight months we produced two elaborate, multi-projector slide presentations, with a fully produced sound track. It traveled all over the United States, and eventually was turned into a filmstrip presentation that went to every Free Methodist Church in the country.

WHEN PAM AND I attended the banquet in Winona Lake, Indiana, the bishop who got up to present me with the award was none other than my former college pastor, who had also counseled Pam and I before we were married, Rev. Donald Bastian.

He held a small plaque in his hand and to explain it to those in attendance (and to me), read something from the Bible I had never heard before, and something I never will forget.

> *The Lord said to Moses, "See, I have chosen Bezalel son*
> *of Uri, the son of Hur, of the tribe of Judah, and I have*
> *filled him with the Spirit of God, with wisdom, with*
> *understanding, with knowledge and with all kinds of skills—*
> *to make artistic designs for work in gold, silver and bronze,*
> *to cut and set stones, to work in wood, and to engage in all*
> *kinds of crafts. (Exodus 31:1-5)*

Then Bishop Bastian handed me the plaque and read the inscription, which he called the Bezalel Award:

PRESENTED TO
STAN WILLIAMS
MAY 14, 1976
IN APPRECIATION
FOR THE COMMITMENT OF HIS TALENTS
TO CHRISTIAN SERVICE
THROUGH SIGHT AND SOUND
BY THE FREE METHODIST CHURCH
OF NORTH AMERICA

I was very appreciative and a bit embarrassed. As I gazed at the plaque, I was contemplating the Exodus passage. I never knew that one of the gifts of the Holy Spirit might include the crafting of visual art. But there it was. I choked up. Before that moment my calling had been in doubt. Now it was assured.

But, of course, I jumped ahead, as was my nature having never learned to walk, and made the assumption that my calling was to do church media and get paid to do it. *Not so fast, Stanley,* my Guardian Angel whispered in my ear. I stuck a finger in my ear and flicked out the irritating gnat.

As a consequence of some modest marketing and sales presentations, our fledgling company had several requests from other Christian Church denominations for proposals to create various kinds of presentations. Although Bill, Don and I had not quit our day jobs, we were excited that we would soon be doing God's work full time.

Whoa, there!, my Guardian Angel kicked the backside of my eyeballs! I took two aspirins to quell the pain.

I wrote proposals, Don produced beautiful three-color stationary and business cards, Bill produced detailed budgets, together we laid out schedules, and I traveled hundreds of miles to make the presentations. We're in business. I was thrilled.

My Guardian Angel flew through my nasal passage, squeezed into my spheroidal sinus cavity, and screamed at my brain stem: *"Would you slow down and listen for a minute?"*

I ran to the drug store for decongestant.

Maybe you, dear reader, have been listening better than I was.

In each of the four proposals we wrote and I presented, we were almost laughed out of the room by the costs we quoted. When I asked how much they were prepared to pay, the answers, in every case, would not have even paid for our supplies. Not only would there have been no salaries or incomes, we would have been expected to actually pay a portion of the material production costs out of our own pockets. While the Free Methodist Church had not paid us an income commensurate with the hours we had spent, at least they had paid us for the supplies and equipment.

Lesson: *There's no business in Church business.*

But did I learn the lesson? Not really. I did, however, make a conscious effort from then on to stay in secular media and with my excess resources produce Christian related media. But I have never been very good sticking to the resolution and have been constantly on the edge financially. It has been rough emotionally and has stressed my marriage with Pam. Common sense should play a role in all this, but passion usually takes precedent. I'm convinced that the best businessmen quell their passions and manage by the numbers. But there's hope: When I drop dead I will have solved the problem. From the grave I can spend no more money. Alleluia!

> **My Guardian Angel flew through my nasal passage, squeezed into my spheroidal sinus cavity, and screamed at my brain stem: "Would you slow down and listen for a minute?" I ran to the drug store for decongestant.**

A few months later Jerry asked me to write a series of articles for the Free Methodist Pastor Newsletter on the use of Media in the Church. There was no money involved, but that was okay, since putting down my ideas on paper wasn't going to require cash. I wrote eight articles, which appeared in monthly issues starting October of 1976. They had titles like: "Jehovah, the Great Multimedia Communicator," "Art Communication in the Church," and "Worship, The Congregation on Stage." I had hoped the articles would stir up discussion about how to improve the church's communication model in support of the spiritual renewal that I knew was more important. To this day, I greatly appreciate Dr. Ford's office, Jerry Howard and the bishops for letting me get my message out, but clearly there was little grassroots interest. Except from Jerry's kudos, I received no feedback.

51
By The Numbers

IN JULY OF 1976, our third child (and first son) was born. I had always been enamored by the story of Moses when he sent 12 princes, one from each of the tribes of Israel, to spy on the Promised Land of Canaan. They were to scout out the land and bring back reports that would inform the Israelites how to conquer the land and what promises it held. After 40 days of crisscrossing the land, the 12 returned and brought with them some of the fruit of the land. It was indeed a rich land of soil and produce. But 10 of the 12 princes sowed discord among the tribes and grumbled against Moses, Aaron and God, saying "we will never conquer the land, we should have stayed in Egypt. The people of Canaan are bigger and stronger than we are; they are the descendants of the Nephilim."[1]

But two of the 12 disagreed and gave a positive report saying that if the people put their trust in God, indeed they would enter a land of promises and riches and conquer it.

To put it kindly, God was upset with the Israelites' lack of faith after He had done so much for them and saved them from slavery. So, He declared:

> *As surely as I live, I will do to you the very thing I heard you say: In this wilderness your bodies will fall—every one of you twenty years old or more who was counted in the census and who has grumbled against me. Not one of you will enter the land I swore with uplifted hand to make your home, except Caleb son of Jephunneh and Joshua son of Nun.*[2]

1 Numbers 13:31-33.
2 Numbers 14:28-30

With Pam's agreement, we named our first boy, *Joshua Caleb*, which just so happens to create the initials J.C. It would be a few years later that I came to understand that "Joshua" was the English equivalent of the Hebrew "Y'Shua"…but, more about that later.

PAM WRITES: One day our oldest child, Trudy (then 4 years old) asked me what I liked for names for the baby in my tummy. I said, "If it's a boy, I like the name, "Joshua." From that day on she went around prophesying, "My mom has a baby in her tummy and his name is Joshua!" This was before ultra sound so we had no idea if it was a boy, until he was born. But when he came, we were bound by our little prophetess, for Josh's first name.

On giving birth to Joshua, Pam almost died. A quick acting doctor saved her from bleeding to death when Josh's placenta refused to detach from her uterus. So, that was the end of children for us. Seeing what she went through I got a vasectomy. As Protestants, we had no qualms about self-sterilization. For the sake of Pam, I was through with growing our family.

B UT THE CHURCH we were now attending was obsessed with growth—numerical growth. As a kid I remember the Attendance Award Pins. You got your first pin the second year of perfect attendance. It was a small gold wreath, with a white background and a red Christian cross in the center. At the bottom it said in gold relief letters "Second Year." Then, each successive year of perfect attendance the pastor would call you up front and give you a charm that chain-linked to the bottom of the lapel pin. The charms read successively, "Third Year," "Fourth Year," etc. Linked together they hung down from one's coat lapel proclaiming how many years you had shown up without missing a Sunday. One old man had a pin with over 50 charms hanging down nearly to the floor. As he walked down the aisle his swinging badge of honor would flay anyone that got near. That's why he never missed a Sunday, no one would get close enough to give him a virus.

And there were contests. One summer I came in Second Place in a Vacation Bible School contest by bringing a few neighborhood friends. As a result I was presented with a beautiful shellacked wooden plaque of Warner Sallman's *Christ Our Pilot*. For years after I treasured the picture of Jesus guiding a young man at the wheel of a sailing ship in a storm and hung it prominently in my bedroom.

Our pastors would deny that such promotions had anything to do with numbers, but rather with saving the lost, including us. But every time you walked into the worship auditorium[1] of an Evangelical church and looked toward the front you'd see displayed prominently near the large cross, the pulpit, and the communion table…an Attendance Board. Evangelicals loved Attendance Boards. If you couldn't put your trust in the cross, or in the sermon, or the altar table there was the Attendance Board.

The Attendance Board, in bold black and white numbers, displayed how many people came to church "Today" and "Last Week." Some even told you how much offering had been collected the previous week.

LAST WEEK'S ATTENDANCE 344
TODAY'S ATTENDANCE 351
LAST SUNDAY'S ATTENDANCE 356
SUNDAY SCHOOL 412
OFFERING LAST WEEK $679
SUNDAY EVENING WORSHIP 120
WEDNESDAY PRAYER MEETING 55
ATTENDANCE A YEAR AGO TODAY 350

If the preacher was long winded, or if you didn't like something he said, you could always glance over at the Attendance Board for inspiration. Numbers never lie, you know. I would often try to do math tricks in my head. *Quick! What's $679 divided by 356. What?! Only $1.91 per person. Cheapskates!*

But sometimes the Attendance Board wasn't enough.

WE HAD RETURNED to our roots at the Dearborn Free Methodist Church, about 10 miles to the north of the Taylor church. At Dearborn we knew many people and some of our high school chums, now married, were attending there. It was like coming home, in some respects. Our former pastor who married us, Rev. Frank VanValin, had retired. In his place was Rev. S., a man of sincere spirit and modest but driven disposition. He seemed to fit well with the membership.

At this time, in the mid-1970s, the Church Growth Movement

---

1 Most would call the area of a church building where the congregation sits the "nave." But in evangelical churches there is no "sanctuary," or "chancel," because there is no altar or tabernacle. So, it's hard to imagine there being a "nave."

(CGM) was making serious inroads into Evangelicalism. As you might discern from the name, the movement's purpose was to increase the size of the church—your church, preferably. CGM's strategy was sociological, its tactic was marketing. In practical terms the CGM encouraged churches to program their activities and design their worship around the perceived needs of the populace. This sounds good because Christianity has always been about helping those in need. But, CGM introduced a fallacy into the equation by confusing the populace's true spiritual and physical *needs* with the populace's perceived cultural *wants*.

While the Attendance Board, by its placement, boldly announced its importance to anyone sitting in the pews, CGM took the awareness of numbers to a new level.

My first direct run-in with CGM was at Taylor Free Methodist when the pastor removed Pam's hand-made, burlap and colorful felt, celebratory, 6x4-foot Christmas banner, which read "JESUS IS THE REASON...FOR THE SEASON," and replaced it with mass-produced, paper, blandly-designed, 8x10-inch posters, stuck to the cinder-block walls with masking tape. The little posters beckoned us with "inspiring" slogans like: "THINK GROWTH," "PRAY FOR CHURCH GROWTH," and "CHANGE IS INEVITABLE, GROWTH IS OPTIONAL." None of them were God-centered; all were man-centered. I remember looking over at these sad little pieces of paper taped to the wall (which were nearly too small to read) and thinking that a 6-foot high stained glass images of Christ performing miracles might be more, ah,...inspiring!

Today, the Seeker-Church Movement, an outgrowth of CGM, meets the "needs" of seekers through on-stage rock bands that play popular music (with spiritual sub-themes), entertaining drama, and generally high quality media. Most of these churches have professional video crews that write, produce and package arresting elements that are sure to intrigue and communicate.

Ironically, what these seeker churches do today seems to be what I was advocating in the mid-1970s. But, in my mind, there was a big difference. While I was all for, and still promote, high-quality media targeted at society with the message of the Gospel, I always understood that worship was about the congregation being on-stage before God, not the pastor and worship leaders being on-stage entertaining the congregation.

My second run-in with CGM was at Dearborn Free Methodist on

Easter Sunday. It's always a joyous time when Christians celebrate the resurrection of the Lord Jesus Christ. That Sunday, the hymns were as you'd expect and there were Easter Lilies displayed on stands at the front of the auditorium. While not full by any means, there was a larger than normal attendance. The place would hold 500 packed tight; normally we'd have 300-350 for morning worship and this Sunday there were perhaps 400. Things went as expected until midway through the sermon.

Pastor S. began with an appropriate Easter passage of Scripture and talked about how...

> *...the church was able to grow in the First Century because Christ first rose from the dead. Yes, Jesus was the center of Christian worship. But the key to church growth was always new life.*

Where is he headed? I was soon to find out.

> *Christ was the center of the early church, and his resurrection ensured that the masses would be ushered into the Kingdom of God....For our church, today, to grow and bring people to Christ we have to resurrect our church. Imagine the power of a resurrected church.... The Lord has laid it on my heart that it is our time, too. It is time for our local church's resurrection and growth.*

And then Rev. S announced...TA! DA!...we were going to resurrect our church...*and build a brand new, and B I G G E R church building.*

My teeth began to grind. Layers of enamel fell from my mouth into my open Bible's binding.

This was not the first time I had heard a pitch for a building fund program. But this one was laced with the unusual logic that a larger edifice would attract a larger congregation, and thus more souls would be saved. Rev. S's building program wasn't necessary to accommodate over-crowding, or a deteriorating building. It was the *bigger-is-better-and-we're-not-good-enough-so-let's-get-bigger* plan.

I looked down at my Bible, flipped into my concordance, and finally, not finding this teaching in Holy Writ, looked to my infallible pew-mate. Pam just shook her head, as if a nut had lodged in her ear and she was trying to shake it out.

After the service, I held back in the receiving line to talk to Pastor S.

a bit longer than the obligatory handshake. When I finally approached, he smiled shook my hand and handed me a green-is-growth pledge envelope. I challenged him on the need to start a building program for a new church when on most Sunday mornings the auditorium was only half full. S. said (and this is almost verbatim):

> Stan, a pastor only gets a chance like this once in a lifetime. It would be foolish of me to pass it up.

I wasn't familiar with logical fallacies at the time, but it sure sounded like "the wrong reason."

After three more Sundays of listening to Rev. S. twist Scripture to support his plan for a new church building, I left the church, never to return. I'm not sure what Pam did with her Sundays, but I was out again gallivanting around the religious landscape looking for…some representation of Christianity that fit my interpretation of the Bible. That is, after I shook the enamel dust out of mine.

Within a year Pastor S. was asked to leave by the congregation. I never knew why, but at the time I suspected it was because of his push for the new church building. I was relieved. They surely didn't need it.

But I was wrong.

TWO YEARS LATER I was flying back to Michigan from a business trip. In that time, Pam and I had moved on to another denomination. On the flight back, by chance, I sat next to VB, a layman I had known at Dearborn FM. Our conversation was memorable in a way I could never have imagined. I made the mistake of asking VB what he was doing and what was going on at Dearborn FM. A polite, safe question I figured.

The answer? VB proudly told me he was the Chairman of the *New Church Building Committee*. [I kid you not!] Suddenly, he burst forth and told me about the bigger-and-better edifice they were building. He offered to show me plans. Would I like to see them?

I couldn't wait.

As he was digging out the drawings from his briefcase, I recalled Rev. S's words to me: "Stan, a pastor only gets a *chance* like this once in a lifetime." It was then that I realized the building program was not Rev. S's idea but the lay leaders of the church, and Rev. S had been more than willing to go along with it. It was his *chance*. It was *not his idea*.

Rev. S's sermon that Easter was still disturbing. You just can't twist scripture to rationalize building a bigger church to attract souls. Well, yes, I guess you can…at least the laymen at Dearborn FM certainly had.

VB told me that the Official Board had decided not to build on their existing property. It was too crowded with houses nearby and parking was mostly on the streets. So, they purchased new land a mile to the West on Telegraph Road, one of the busiest roads in the metro area, and construction was about to get underway. VB showed me elevation plans for the new church sitting 25 feet off the busy road. It was a huge three-story affair, dominated by a peaked roof that slanted down on the North and South sides to within -feet of the ground. The elevation facing West featured faux-brick arches built into plain vertical walls. Inside the arcs were opaque, black glass. The elevation facing East, where the parking lot was to be built, was more inviting and featured a bell tower (with no bell) but with a cross.

What you see today (in 2015), when driving along Telegraph, however, is not a tall, cathedral like "church" structure, but rather something that Pam describes as an "aircraft hanger." Gazing at the plans on the plane that day with VB, the building looked like a very large utility garage with a huge swath of brown shingles and roof vents…something you'd expect to see snow plows and garbage trucks drive in and out of from time to time.

But the height was impressive. I didn't see any windows on the upper stories, but figured they were on the other side of the drawings. So, I asked VB, "Wow, that's really big. What's on the second floor, Sunday School classrooms, like the old church?"

"Oh, no." said VB. "There's nothing up there. Just empty rafters."

"Empty? But it's so big. There must be 10,000 brown asphalt shingles on display."

"That was the plan," said VB. "We wanted to build a large church to attract people. It had to be big so they'd see it as they drove along Telegraph."

But it's so ugly. I was dumbfounded.

The lay leaders of this Free Methodist Church had bought into the Church Growth Movement's heresy that success is measured by numbers, and that you attract numbers by pretending you are successful. It was marketing on a "big" scale.

As VB chatted on about their "exciting" project, he informed me that the building would also be highly energy efficient…(drum roll please)...because the auditorium would have no windows. I looked past him and out the window as the plane cruised over the Appalachian Mountains. The shade was open and morning sunlight slashed across our seats. For a moment I recalled the old Dearborn FM church in which Pam and I were married. The old church had large arched-topped windows along both north and south sides of the auditorium, which let in plenty of light. The white pews were trimmed in teak-stained oak, giving the auditorium a simple but uplifting feel. A few candid black and white photographs of our wedding masterfully taken by Robert Chi, look like Norman Rockwell paintings with attendees backlit by the windows.

I can't help but compare the airiness and light of the old church with the new church, which I've been in a few times. Indeed there are the faux arches on the new church's exterior, but they are only visible on the outside. There are no windows that allow light into the auditorium. I don't know what is more depressing, the exterior that looks like a mausoleum, or the inside that reminds me of the shadowed interior of a pyramid—a tomb.

In 2013 the Dearborn FM celebrated its 75th anniversary. Average attendance? One-hundred-fifty—a 40% decline from when we met there for the first time as teens...in a building that was perhaps 40% larger.

Thus, I found it hard to put my trust in denominational institutions, and I kept coming back to the Bible. Until, that is, another memorable day at my local Bible bookstore.

52
The Holey Bible

(The title of this chapter does not contain a typo.)

I OFTEN SEARCHED FOR Christian truth in my local Bible book-store—one of a chain of Logos Bookstores nationwide. For a while in the late 1970's, a good friend, Dennis Stacey (1950-2011), managed one and I paid the store a weekly visit to browse the shelves of the latest released truth to hit Christianity. Upon seeing an attractive cover or enticing title like, *All Dogs Go To Heaven (All Cats Go To Hell)*, I'd flip the book over and study the 50-word biography-blurbs on the back. Invariably they celebrated the author's *unquestionable* pedigree and expertise, from universities you never heard. I'd asked myself, *Was this someone I could trust? How reliable was his authority?*

The more I read, however, the more I agreed with King Solomon:

> *"Meaningless! Meaningless!" says the Teacher. "Utterly meaningless! Everything is meaningless." Is there anything of which one can say, "Look! This is something new"? It was here already, long ago; it was here before our time. For with much wisdom comes much sorrow; the more knowledge, the more grief."* [1]

One day, the weariness of seeking biblical truth literally leapt off the biblical page. I remember it as if it was yesterday. That lightning didn't fall from the heavens, char Dennis beyond recognition, and obliterate his Christian bookstore is still remarkable. But then, God must have known the good that was in Dennis's heart.

To understand the impact of this story, you have to understand

---

1 Ecclesiastes 1:2,10, 18 (NIV)

how I, and many of my Evangelical friends, were raised. To us, there was only one thing we could do that would send us straight to hell: It was to sacrilege the Bible, even if it was a dog-eared paperback copy of Good News for Modern Man. There were many ways to disrespect a Bible—dropping it, letting it get wet, putting another book on top of it, laying it (even reverently) on the floor, or dropping pizza sauce in the binding.

One day, in the bookstore, I was standing behind the tape rack with a book in my hand reading the author's-blurb about the latest Christian truth she had discovered. I heard a commotion at the check-out counter and peered down the aisle toward the front. There, I saw Dennis holding court with an argumentative customer. A glass display case showing off the latest releases from an "I'm-holier-than-thou" jeweler and a cash register, kept the two burly men apart.

The rotund and jovial Dennis reminded me of Santa Claus except with thinning black hair and a thick rust beard. His sport was bookstore banter and debate, but always with a smile. His sparring partner on this particular night was a hardboiled, bald-headed Calvinist. Their "conversation" dealt with predestination and whether or not a Christian could lose his or her salvation.

Dennis teased his denominational opponent. "So, you're telling me a Christian cannot lose his salvation?"

Already boiling, Hardboiled turned up the heat with one Bible quote after the other, careful to throw in the citation for authoritative emphasis: "'And I give unto them *eternal* life; and they shall *never* perish, neither shall any man pluck them out of my hand.' John 10:28. 'For whom he did foreknow, he also did *predestinate* to be conformed to the image of his son...who shall lay anything to the charge of God's elect?' Romans 8:29 and 33. 'I will never leave thee, nor forsake thee.' Hebrews chapter 13 verses 5 and..."

"Whoa there!" Dennis said as he pulled in the reins. "Those verses don't guarantee to protect *you* against *yourself*. You're still a creature of free will. Dennis jabbed the man in the chest with a finger. "You can walk away from Christ. Geez, even run if you want."

"That's not what my church believes," Hardboiled cracked. "You just can't say that."

"Sure, I can say it. And you can, too," Dennis yelled back.

"But God is always faithful. You can't!" said Hardboiled.

Dennis paused for a moment to consider his next propositional statement. "God may always be faithful, but man isn't. Let me show ya something." At that point Dennis reached under the counter and pulled out a well-worn Bible, flipped it open, and laid it on the counter facing his opponent. After a few page turns, he again jabbed his finger, but this time into the Bible at a verse he read upside down. "'Not every one who says unto me, Lord, Lord, shall enter into the kingdom of heaven...' Matthew 7:21. What do you say about that?"

Hardboiled leaned over to scrutinize the verse where Dennis's finger was scrunching up the thin linen-fibered paper. "Well, I don't believe..."

"You don't believe the Bible?" said Dennis. His bushy eyebrows jumped. (Dennis had really thick, black eyebrows that he often used with great effect.) I could feel the WHOOSH 15-feet away.

"No!" Hardboiled confessed. "I don't believe what you're insinu-ating...ah...you see...what I mean is...Damn it! What translation is that, anyway? I just don't believe that."

Dennis suddenly brightened. "You don't believe that?" slamming his open hand on the open Bible.

Hardboiled stiffened his back and shook his head defiantly.

"Then, I got the perfect solution for ya," said Dennis. And, at that moment, Dennis, the beleaguered Bible bookstore manager, closed his fist on the tissue thin page of scripture and with a flourish, RIPPED out the 7th chapter of Matthew, wadded it up, and flippantly tossed it into the wastebasket.

"There, you don't have to worry about that verse a-n-y-m-o-r-e." Dennis closed the Bible and offered it the customer. "Wanna buy a slightly used Bible? You're sure to like it more, now that it's been con-formed to your personal beliefs."

I can still see the startled look on Hardboiled's face. He didn't know whether to yell or run away, believing as I did that lightning would strike any second. He left the store abruptly in *disbelief.*

Yes, that's a true story...one that gives a new meaning to the "holey" Bible.

On my visit to Dennis's story the next week I noticed a sign in the window: *FOR SALE: SLIGHTLY USED, CUSTOMIZED BIBLE."*

DENNIS STACEY WENT to be with his Lord, on November 3, 2011 after a two-year battle with skin cancer. His widow, Cheryl, whom I talked with during the final edit of this book, said of Dennis's homecoming, "He did it so well." He was jovial and teasing up to his final hours. He planned his funeral, and relentlessly teased

Cheryl about what she was doing to do about all the things in their life after he was gone. It took her three years to part with the boat. But he left her a beautiful house on a small Michigan lake that he had built and landscaped—his chosen profession the last decades of his life.

When I asked Cheryl about the truth of the story in this chapter, she howled over the phone.

> *Stan, he did that! I saw him! He kept an old Bible under the counter for that very purpose. But at the same time he sold more Bibles than any other bookstore in the Logos Bookstore chain nationwide. He put a table by the front door, and literally put Bibles in customer's hands to flip through. He said, "The best translation was the one people would read."*

Dennis's provocative Bible customizing trick made me think a great deal about how to interpret the Bible. I though, *Indeed! Where's the trustworthy authority to interpret the infallible Bible? Really! How do we know who's interpretation is right?*

Such experiences led to questions but no answers, so Bob (the prankster) and I did the next best thing. We invented a game.

> **Dennis's Bible customizing trick made me think — Indeed! Where's the trustworthy authority to interpret the infallible Bible? Really! How do we know who's interpretation is right?**

53
The Rapture Game

IN 1977, MY discontent with Evangelicalism morphed into satire. And who else to help me do that but my grapefruit-loving nephew, Bob Kenney. He was living in Florida now, but somehow we conspired to take a pot shot at an Evangelical sacred cow—The Rapture—and the Evangelical church's obsession with Church Growth.

If you're not familiar with the "impending Rapture" of the Christian Church, here's a shorthand version. In very general terms, the Rapture refers to an event similar to the second coming of Jesus Christ, but one in which Christ levitates the members of his church off the earth to join Him in heaven. This leaves chaos on earth as the non-believers are "left behind." Various apocalypse styled books and motion pictures have been made in an attempt to interpret the doctrinal theory.

While the Second Coming of Christ doctrine reaches back to the first century and Christ's teachings about His return to Earth, The Rapture, as a separate event form the Second Coming, is a fairly recent Christian doctrine that traces its origins back only to the 1500's at the earliest, and more popularly is found in the writings of theologians from the late 1700's and early 1800s. As you might expect there are various interpretations of when and how the Rapture will occur, which sets up more denominational differences.

Our response to the doctrine was somewhere between serious and satirical. And the result of our thoughts on the topic resulted in a board game, styled somewhat after Monopoly. Except in our game, the goal wasn't to get financially rich, but to store up treasures in heaven. We called it The Rapture Game and the idea was that when the Rapture Occurred (at a time in the game no one would know) the winner would be the player with the most living saints in his church. Where

Monopoly had CHANCE CARDS, the Rapture Game had CIRCUM-STANCE CARDS. One read:

> *Church sanctions high school class Ouija board experiments. 15 members go to the church on your left unless you have the gift of WISDOM, in which case take 15 from left-hand church.*

Where Monopoly had COMMUNITY CHEST cards, The Rapture Game had EVANGELISM and DISCIPLESHIP CARDS.

Writing the promotional flyer and instructions became a sort of spiritual outlet for my Evangelical Christian Church frustration, (and maybe Bob's as well). The flyer read:

> *THE RAPTURE GAME: IT'S AN UPLIFTING EXPERIENCE.*

> *RAPTURE is a tongue-in-cheek adventure into the throngs of church growth, trials, spiritual gifts and the end times.*

> *Build your church...but be watchful, because SUDDENLY the RAPTURE could occur. Would your church be found ready, or wanting...more points?*

> *Use the GIFTS OF THE SPIRIT to counter the most unbelievable trials and tribulations ever to hit the face of a board game...let alone a church!*

> *EVANGELIZE and add to the size of your church, but what kind of members did you get? Are they SPIRITUAL MEMBERS, CARNAL MEMBERS, OR HYPOCRITES?*

> *DISCIPLE the members of your church, and increase your church's spirituality. (These cards convert hypocrites to carnal Christians, or carnal Christians to spiritual Christians.)*

> *GO TO COMMITTEE and LOSE TWO TURNS, But don't lose your turn to get the RAPTURE GAME.*

> *GET IT TODAY, before it's TOO LATE!*

Yes, there were dice, saint-clips, which allowed you to occasionally take the spiritual Christians in your church and convert them (via Calvinism) so they were eternally saved, thus preparing your church to be raptured and win the game. The tokens were painted rocks, of course; plastic was not biblical enough for *this* game.

The game instructions also had provisions for:

> *SUNDAY OFFERINGS (Yes, there was play money to dole out)*

> *EARTHQUAKE or FAMINE (lose 1/2 your money)*

> *WAR (lose 1/2 of your money and 1/2 your members)*

> *CHURCH SPLITS (lose 1/2 your members)*

> *FAITH PLEDGES (a great way to increase revenue)*

> *GIFTS OF THE HOLY SPIRIT (which minimized the negative effects of certain Circumstance cards)*

> *REVIVALS (when you could take 20 hypocrites and turn them instantly into eternally secure saints)*

> *THE EYE OF THE NEEDLE (where, if you had more than $1,000 saved up, you would lose all your discipleship cards, but you get to keep the money. It's your only reward.)*

And then there was:

> *PASTOR'S RETREAT (if two rocks or player tokens land on the same space, both players get $50 from the bank, unless it happens in Committee...then watch out.)*

We manufactured 1,000 games in my basement, and sold most of them. A small time Christian publisher bought the rights, but then reneged on paying us.

Coming up with the Rapture Game was a wonderful relief to the frustration I was experiencing with my life as an Evangelical. I don't think it advanced my understanding of God, but it released a lot of tension through laughter...at myself.

Now, the Rapture, if it happens the way some think, will be a surprise. And if it doesn't? There will always be Paris...well, actually, it was Pittsburgh.

54
Pittsburgh?
Who Knew!

S HORTLY AFTER I turned 30, in the spring of 1977, Dad took me on a mysterious trip. My Dad, Benjamin Williams, was not a traveler by nature, and I can never recall him taking me alone anywhere except for a few hours to the Telenews Theater or a Detroit Tiger's baseball game...or the one mile we drove to visit Miss O is Missouri before Dad's car broke down. Out of town vacations were my mom's idea; she was the adventurous one. But this time, an out-of-state, overnight trip with Dad raised my antenna. I thought back to the Old Testament story of Abraham and Isaac on their way to Mt. Moriah. As we put our suitcases in the back of his Plymouth I checked the trunk for a bundle of wood. I didn't see any, so I figured I was safe unless the route took us into the Appalachian Mountains.

Dad told me it was time to meet my relatives...in Pittsburgh. I had relatives in Pittsburgh? Who knew this? I wondered, why now, at age 30, I was being introduced to the lost branch of Williams's? I knew Dad didn't think any of his brothers were Christians, but I had no idea if they were alive or dead or where they lived. I was intrigued, doubly so, because he was insistent on taking the trip on a particular weekend. I would not make sense of the trip for decades, but it explained a lot about who I was, and more remarkably it foreshadowed my later journey.

One of the reasons I knew little about Dad's side of the family was because Dad was not a talker. He was calm, and good-humored, but not confident at explaining things. One of his favorite sayings was, "I just don't know." And, he was sincere when he said it. One time, during college, I came home and got into a terrible spat with my mother and aunt. He later wrote to me about the tangle, but offered no criticism except, "I don't know what to tell you, son. It's beyond me." And, then, as he always did, he quoted Scripture, encouraging me to praise God in all things. At times like that, Dad's ignorance was an unfathomable virtue.

My mother, on the other hand, was supremely confident that what she knew of a situation was *God's truth*. To balance her ignorance of the facts she often held tightly to sarcasm. When caught in an entangling assumption, she'd turn away, grit her teeth and mutter, "I guess I'm just uneducated." At such times, Mom's knowledge was an unfathomable weakness.

D URING OUR DRIVE to Pittsburgh I learned a great deal about Dad's early life, his brothers, and his first wife. I hadn't thought about it much before our trip but my father was from another generation. He was born in 1894 during a time when most of civilization got around on horses or carriages pulled by horses; it was a time when airplanes were only figments of the Wright Brother's imagination. In short, Dad was old enough to be my grandfather. To me, as a young boy, he seemed to have been around forever. Because of my early interest in astronomy and space, he had once told me about seeing Halley's Comet in 1910 when he was 16-years of age. Then, in 1986 he saw it again at the age of 92. Although we were from different eras, we shared a similar love of the Bible and a thirst for God. I'm well aware that these were attributes he no doubt imbued in me simply by modeling them. Remarkably, I never knew my dad to sin openly. And, for that reason alone, he became my providential spiritual mentor.

He was "Benji" to his friends, the fourth of six children born to Jeremiah Emerson Williams and Emily Jane (Kane) Williams. Jeremiah was a circuit-riding Methodist preacher in Illinois, Indiana and Ohio right after the civil war. There were many stories about Jeremiah that seemed to me to come right out of the Wild West. He didn't carry a gun, but woe to those that did and opposed him.

As we accessed the Ohio Turnpike, Dad recounted one story that intrigued me. It was a haunting tale about my grandfather that occurred in Edgerton, Ohio, just West of where we got onto the Turnpike. As was his custom, when Jeremiah planned a weekday revival in a distant town, he'd arrange for the use of the local Methodist Episcopal Church building. But when he held services in Edgerton in early 1889, disgruntled church members opposed him. They were irritated because my grandfather was a *Free* Methodist, which made him a firebrand who was part of the rebellion that broke off from the Methodist Episcopal Church 28 years earlier. The local bishop had warned Jeremiah to preach only what was acceptable to the locals, or else he would be in trouble. But, Jeremiah, not one to be intimidated, told the Methodist-Episcopal bishop that he would preach what God led him to preach and nothing else.

The meetings, held at night, relied for illumination on oil lamps that hung along the walls and stood on either side of the pulpit. The "opposers," as Jeremiah called them, assembled in the building early and took the front seats. This forced those sympathetic to Jeremiah's version of the Gospel to the rear of the building.

In my preparation for this book I discovered the original handwritten calligraphy account of the meeting. Jeremiah wrote out the story in 1889 for use in *The Free Methodist Magazine*. Here is an except:

The Oil Lamps

I had an unusually close[1] time in preaching that evening and at the close I gave opportunity to any who so desired to speak or testify. Immediately one of the opposers arose to her feet, with her bible in her hand, also a sheet of paper on which she had written her references. Taking off her hood, she turned around to face the audience and began to show what false things (as she supposed) I had been preaching. At the same time the lamp on the wall just over her head went out. Then turning toward the lamp at the right of the pulpit, she again began to read, and that lamp began to flicker and puff, and someone (fearing it would explode) blew it out. The lady then took her position by the pulpit lamp, and it immediately began to go down until it gave no light. She then said, "I am very sorry you have no oil in your lamps to-night." But it was not for want of oil

---

1 careful, meticulous

that the lamp would not burn. Just then I reached over the pulpit to turn up the wick, but as soon as I touched the screw, the light went out with a flash.

After this the lamps were taken out and refilled, brought back and held for her to read by, but not one would burn.

Lanterns were next called for and brought in, but as soon as [they were] held up for her to read by, each one began to flutter and go down and fail to give any light. Finally she sat down in confusion and defeat. Her own lantern acted as bad as any of the others.

Her brother, who had been seated on the opposite side of the church, now arose and tried to prove that we were not working in harmony with the word of God. As soon as he started to read the lamp on the wall near his head went out with a flash.

Again they called for lanterns and one after another was brought in, but with the same result as before - not one would burn. Altogether a dozen or more lanterns were tried. He stammered and stuttered a little, and sat down in utter confusion.

We were left in almost total darkness, when one of the pilgrims began singing in the Spirit, and then jumping to his feet, he gave in a ringing testimony which seemed to set fire to all the saints.

One after another witnessed in the Spirit to the mighty power of Jesus to save, until every one in the house realized that God was present and there to defend his people and his truth.

At the time these two persons were talking, a number of trustworthy witnesses, both saved & unsaved, said that the wallpaper just back of where the opposers were sitting, seemed to change color,

*and to go in streaks and waves across the wall.
One wicked young man said to some one after the
meeting, "Either God or the devil is here tonight."
They were all frightened or amazed. After the
meeting was dismissed the lamps and lanterns
burned all right, and the next evening they seemed
to give a brighter light than ever before.*

*The enemy was defeated, God's children had
the victory and precious souls were gloriously
saved. Praise the Lord. Brother and Sister
Sheffield of Delta, Ohio were in this meeting and
they can witness to the facts herein stated. God will
not be mocked. May God help us that we be not
found fighting against Him.*[1]

Rev. Jeremiah Williams ("Uncle Jerry" to his spiritual family) eventually settled down to pastor a Free Methodist Church on the main road in Rocky River, Ohio, just west of Cleveland. Although of weak constitution, he was a fearless risk-taker, braving run-ins with bullies, thieves and ruffians to follow God's call, though to others his risk-taking and calling seemed foolish. I liked that, and whether for good or bad, I developed a rhinoceros hide that was fairly impervious to the criticism that came with the journey God has called me to.

PITTSBURGH WAS STILL four hours away, so I quizzed Dad about his siblings, my three uncles and two aunts. They were all natural children of Jeremiah and Emily. Dad described his mother as somewhat beleaguered, tending to her brood of six for months at a time while "Uncle Jerry," was off, on horseback, saving civilization.

Each of these individuals had an effect on my life, although I never met any of them. In fact, I wasn't even aware of their influence until I began reading the correspondence and diaries they left behind.

---

1 Jeremiah Williams letter dated April 1, 1889 of a meeting the previous winter.

Gertrude N. Williams (1886-1950)

Jeremiah and Emily's oldest child was Gertrude. Because my grandfather traveled so much she became my Dad's spiritual guardian. She never married, but was a lay Bible scholar whose voluminous notes on her studies filled a 4" x 7" notebook with single spaced typed pages. Most of her writing is about the risky life and missionary journeys of St. Paul, but articulated in the vernacular of her 19th century, Protestant upbringing. The notebook opens with a handwritten note that begins this way:

Some men seem to have been sent into the world for an express purpose in times of crises in history. In dark ages—men chained in superstitions—Luther, Knox, Calvin were simultaneously raised up in different parts of Europe to break the chains of superstition and the yoke of the Papacy...[1]

(There's that concern again about Catholicism.) The notebook reveals a woman whose heart—like those of the missionary St. Paul and her circuit riding father—sought after God, and celebrated those who took on risky ventures for the Kingdom. I have felt this same call to venture beyond what is comfortable and cannot shake the sense that I am a beneficiary of her risk-bearing prayers.

Gertrude spent her latter years caring for her aged parents, and died of cancer 4 years after her father passed.

As I've already pointed out, my father considered Gertrude the only one of his living siblings to be a Christian and how he had relied on her for spiritual guidance. Oddly, and it was true of our trip to Pittsburgh as well, Dad never spoke of the spiritual training he received from his preacher father or mother. It was Gertrude he looked to.

I was five when Gertrude died and I never met her. Yet, because of her spiritual heritage and the letters she wrote from her sick bed to my Dad, invoking prayers for "little Stanley," I've felt the impact of her life on mine.

As related earlier, Pam and I named our first child, Trudy, after Trudy Jander, a bubbly young lady I photographed at a Texas Lutheran Youth retreat. The picture of her hugging a guitar and exclaiming how much she loved Jesus ended up on the cover of *The Lutheran Witness*,

---

1 Gertrude Williams diary.

my first magazine cover. Thus, it was inadvertent that Trudy is also named after Jeremiah's first child, Gertrude. Yet, over the years, I've become aware how Gertrude's passion for God has been present in Trudy's life, who similarly has become a spiritual mentor for others. Is it just coincidence that Trudy shares Gertrude's name and passion for the things of God? No, I'm convinced it's evidence of Providence—Jeremiah's faithfulness flowed into Gertrude, who mentored my father and prayed for me. I've been disappointed that I never met Gertrude. But I've had the joy of knowing Trudy, my first born, and seeing in her the fulfillment of God's promise that He will show His love to a thousand generations of those who love him and keep His commandments.[1]

Burton Emerson Williams (1889-1954)

JEREMIAH AND EMILY'S second child, Burton Emerson (1889-1954), became a famous White House press photographer during the Truman presidency, which he covered for the Pittsburgh Sun-Telegraph newspaper. In 1945, after several years of correspondence with press photography associations across the country, Burt was one of the founders of the National Press Photographers Association (NPPA). He worked for 40 years as a professional photographer until health issues forced retirement. Sadly, he died in 1954 at the "young" age of 65, which was 23 years before our trip to Pittsburgh. To this day, each year, the NPPA presents the *Burt Williams Award* to select news photographers who have completed at least 40 years of service. My parents had a camera that they used for special occasions, but they exhibited no particular interest in photography or media production. So, when Dad told me this about Uncle Burton, I wondered if it was just coincidence or if there was some hereditary connection between Burton's career and mine.

Alice Rosella (1891-1895)

ALICE WAS JEREMIAH and Emily's third child, but she died at age four of an unknown malady. Unfortunately, nothing was recorded of her life or personality except that Alice had a weak constitution like her father.

What sadness her death brought to the family we will not know in this life. Gertrude was nine-years old when her younger sister died. No doubt they were growing close and Gertrude was helping her mother

1 Exodus 20:5-6

care for little Alice who was often sick. Imagine the emotional trauma Gertrude must have gone through when Alice died, and Gertrude's concern and wonder if Alice had gone to heaven.

The year before Alice's death, my Dad, Benjamin, was born.

Could it be that after Alice's death, Gertrude turned her attention to her one-year old brother, with the intention that if little Ben died he certainly would go to heaven...that is, if she had anything to do with it? Gertrude is reported to have doted on Ben and watched over him. As my Dad tells it, that was the reason his faith flourished.

There was something troublesome about how Dad's three brothers were raised. Although their father, Jeremiah, was a preacher of the Gospel, they all fell away from the faith. Was it because their father was so busy ministering to others that he failed to be a father to his own boys? Not only did Dad keep his faith but it overflowed. I cannot help but thank Gertrude for that. She seems to be the one that made the difference.

> **Could the strong faith, which my Dad's entire extended family enjoys today, be the consequence of the grace that came from Alice's death?**

There was a saying within Christian circles of the time that we are called by God to "sacrifice or service." I wonder if little Alice was called to exceptional Christian sacrifice, so as to enliven Gertrude's call to exceptional Christian service? Could the strong faith, which my Dad's entire extended family enjoys today, be the consequence of the grace that came from Alice's death? Surely, such sacrifice has occurred before...to the thousandth generation.

Benjamin Roland Williams (1894-1989)

MY FATHER, BEN, was born in 1894, just a year before Alice died. At 18-years of age Ben joined the Ohio National Guard. The next year, in 1913, he was called upon to guard the streets of Dayton, Ohio during the great flood there. Corporal Williams, in a letter to Gertrude, wrote of the anarchy that reigned during those days, how martial law had been declared, and how the Guard had been ordered to shoot looters on sight to maintain order. His letter describes the Guard's execution in the middle of a street of one looter. During our drive to Pittsburgh, Dad told me how scared he was of the whole affair and how thankful he was that although he shot at one looter, it turned out to be a shadow. He relied on the prayers of family during those times, and these stories of his faith bolstered my own.

Being from a poor preacher's family with a lot of kids, it took until 1915 when he was 21 before Dad finally pulled together enough money to attend Greenville College as a freshman. There, in the waning days of WWI, he organized a platoon of recruits that he marched in formation around campus and the farming town. Pictures of Capt. Williams marching the GC Military Company appeared in the 1917 yearbook.

His first semester, he met Lucile Benjamin, who had enrolled that same year in the college's Associate Theological Studies program. They became a number on campus and are referred to in the college yearbook as "Luci and Benji." Lucile's love of the Bible and her Christian faith contributed to the legacy of the journey I would undertake decades later.

In June of 1917, when Lucile ended her two-year certificate in Theological Studies, Dad, being short on school funds, and clearly head-over-heels in love, followed her to Detroit. Lucile's father, Oscar Benjamin, was the head and majority stockholder of The Detroit Brass Works that had been making munitions for the Department of Defense. But Oscar refused to hire Ben, not willing to make a commitment until it was clear that Lucile was going to make one as well.

> **Just before she died, "Her face glowed so bright I could hardly look at her. I didn't know what to think."**

So Dad made the rounds of the Detroit marketing and sales industry as a clerk and assistant to the assistants. He called himself a "Greenhorn" and how on his first job working for a large marketing firm he spent several days running around between departments and buildings tracking down a device his boss desperately needed—a "Left-Handed Paper Stretcher." In later years he told me how embarrassed he was to discover that there was no such thing, and the whole exercise was a ruse and a practical joke. But in the process, he learned where every department was, and the names of many department heads and supervisors, making him more valuable to his boss.

Ben and Lucile courted for a good year and Dad increased his network of business associates throughout the city. Finally, she said yes, and they applied for a marriage license on June 13, 1918 and were married June 28, 1918 by Ben's father, Jeremiah. It was then that Oscar hired my Dad as an Assistant Supervisor. After all, he had a family to support.

After World War I ended, the Detroit Brass Works fell on hard times, and Dad finally found a job as the Insurance and Safety Manager for Sealtest Dairies. After their only child, Dorothy, was born in 1920, Ben built one of the first houses in Ferndale, Michigan. Next door he built a second house for Lucile's sister, Mable, and husband, Cornwall Hart, a die maker from London, England.

But in the late 1930's tragedy struck, and Lucile was diagnosed with cancer. On a Wednesday, from her room at the Hotel Damon next to the Mayo Clinic in Rochester, Minnesota, she wrote Ben a letter. That day she was scheduled for another blood test. Then she was to check into the hospital across the street, where surgeons would attempt to remove a lump the next day. She hoped it would be "a dead lump." Here are excerpts from that letter written on Hotel Damon stationary, the underlines are hers.

> *My Dear Boy:*
>
> *How I would love to see you this morning, and sit on your lap awhile, yes, even if my bones did hurt you, but you are far away and I must be brave and make the best of <u>everything</u>, and trust the Lord to work it out for my good and His glory.*
>
> *I was <u>so glad</u> to get your letter, and have read [it] over & over. I will take this to the Post Office and then will likely get another one from my <u>good hubby.</u>*
>
> *You have been a <u>wonderful</u> husband to me, I could <u>never</u> have found one that would have babied me along like you have, and I know you have <u>always</u> done your <u>best</u> to make me happy, and I do appreciate your love and affection <u>for me</u>, you have always looked over my faults and failings (which have been many) and loved me <u>just the same</u>, and I believe if the Lord sees fit to spare me a few years longer, that we will have our second honeymoon, and enjoy our little home together. Not very many men would have been so consecrated to God's work to have spared their wives away from home to work for "others" and His cause,*
>
> *Now that I am facing an operation and*

realizing that I may go to Heaven from the operating table, I'm glad that I can look up to the Lord and tell <u>Him</u> I have done my best. I know I have made a lot of mistakes but God knows I have always wanted to do <u>His will</u>, and He gives me the assurance just now that I am <u>all his</u>, for "sacrifice or service."

Well, my dear. I'm expecting the Lord to bring me through, and I'm praying and holding on in faith that they will find this lump dead or something else, but if, — (Please let me say this without making you feel bad) I should slip away to Heaven don't feel too bad, my troubles and trials will all be past and I will forever be with Jesus. I have been homesick for Heaven ever since the Lord gave me a glimpse into Heaven, when little Kenneth[1] slipped away. Your loss will be my gain.

Bye-bye my dear, I do love you with all my heart. Lots of love and kisses, your own little girl,

Babe OOXXXX[2]

The date of the letter is unknown, although we suspect it was written only six months before Lucile died in 1940, at home, with Dad at her bedside. He told me that just before she died, *"Her face glowed so bright I could hardly look at her. I didn't know what to think."* When Dad told me that, I envisioned her in heaven looking down on others and me and praying for us that we also would be faithful to the end of our journey.

Lucile was buried in Northwest Detroit next to her parents in the Benjamin family plot. The marker reads "LUCILE B. WILLIAMS, 1892-1940." To me that reads: *Lucile Benjamin Williams*—oddly romantic.

Within months of Lucile's death, Dorothy convinced her dad to let her marry Oscar Kenney on June 22, 1940, a man recently ordained and pastoring the Free Methodist Church in Albion, Michigan.

Now, living alone, without even a boarder on the second floor of his home, Dad threw himself into church work. At the Ferndale Free

---

1 We do not know who "little Kenneth" was. Perhaps he was child of one of the families of the church to which Lucile had been dedicated in her ministry of hospitality to which she refers in her third and fourth paragraphs.

2 Lucile Williams, original letter in family archives, date unknown.

Methodist Church he became the Sunday School Superintendent, taught an adult Bible study class, and was the church treasurer. On the national level Dad joined with evangelist Rev. Charles W. Kingsley to found the Light and Life Men's fellowship. For years Dad was the organization's General Secretary and actively promoted the involvement and leadership of laymen and women in local churches. Today the organization is still active within Free Methodism but is known as Men's Ministries International.

As I've already accounted earlier in this book, Dad met my mother, Ruth Willobee at the Ferndale Free Methodist Church and they were married in 1945. But it was the first 50 years of my Dad's life which formed a spiritual bedrock for a faith upon which I was able to build my own.

Howard Russell Williams (1895-1980)

ANOTHER INTERESTING CONNECTION to my career path was my Dad's next younger brother, which the family called by his middle name. Russell settled in St. Petersburg, Florida and for many years owned and operated Ace Movie Productions, producers of "Ace Color Travelogues" and "Four Star News Reels." That Russell produced News Reels, which were shown in theaters across the country, may have been one reason my Dad and I occasioned the Telenews Theater. If so, Dad never said so. But, here was another strong connection to my career. Up until the time of our trip to Pittsburgh I had known nothing of Burton or Russell's involvement in visual media. While I relished the short descriptions my dad offered in the car as we drove, I was sad that we were not going to meet either of these men on our trip. Burton, of course had died, and Russell was in St. Petersburg, Florida.

Raymond Williams (1897-1990)

THE LAST OF my Dad's brothers was Raymond (1897-1990) who, I found out years later, worked and died at 93, in Cleveland, Ohio. Dad offered little information, and to this day I know next to nothing about him except what Ancestry.com hints at, that he was widowed and a machinist. I wondered what my Dad was thinking as we drove through the outskirts of Cleveland and he made no mention of Raymond nor did we make any attempt to look him up.

Most of Dad's family lived physically close to us. Indeed, Lucile's sister, Mabel and her husband Cornwall Hart, who also worked at Detroit Brass Works, lived next door to us in Ferndale. But I can only remember meeting them once, and that I knew next to nothing about them until I was thirty, created questions—the most prominent being: *Why were my uncles and their children, especially those in Pittsburgh, and some my age, kept from my awareness?*

55
Lost Clan

T HE ANSWER AS to why these relatives on my Dad's side of the family were kept from my awareness until I was 30, dawned on me slowly as we drew near Pittsburgh that spring in 1977. The only relatives I would be meeting were two cousins— two of the three children of Burton and his wife Marie: *Fran*, a ship construction engineer for Dravo Corporation, and his sister, *Patricia*. And who was the third child? Well, that was the surprise. To answer that takes us back to Burton's marriage to Marie Veronica Hennessey, who would be a harbinger of my own spiritual journey and who provided a clue as to the critical timing of this trip to Pittsburgh.

It was 1914 in Cleveland. Against the advice of his parents and my Dad and Gertrude, Burton fell in love with and married Marie Veronica Hennessey. Why would they oppose the marriage to such a lovely sounding woman? Simple. She was a devout Roman Catholic. The family was further distressed when Burton agreed to let all his children be raised Catholic. Imagine the shock waves that created for the Rev. Jeremiah Williams, a Free Methodist pastor, and his wife Emily. On our trip to Pittsburgh, however, Dad expressed to me his skepticism that Burton had actually been a Christian. So, the shock to the family of Burton becoming "Catholic" had been understood in the context of a non-religious man marrying a woman who was a member of an idol worshipping cult. Imagine the scandal.

The first child of Burton and Marie's marriage, who for some reason we would not be meeting, was Aldebert (Del) Emerson Williams (1915- 1986). Somewhere along the Interstate south of Cleveland, Dad told me that Del had become a *Catholic priest*. I still remember the shiver that ran through my body. *Holy Cow!*

My Dad's nephew and my cousin is a Roman Catholic priest! Skeletons! No wonder we're not going to meet him.

When I asked why we weren't going to meet Adelbert, Dad explained that after Burton's untimely death in 1954 at the age of 65, his wife, Marie, moved into the rectory with Del and worked at the church as an accountant and festival chairperson. That didn't answer my question, so I asked again. Then, Dad explained that (this weekend) Fr. Del and Marie were visiting Dad's other brother, Russell, in Florida, so we'd miss them. Ah, ha! I began to ponder the meaning of this.

As I write this, decades later, I imagine Marie Veronica, like the Biblical Hannah (see, 1 Samuel), dedicating her firstborn son to the Lord and his service. It must have worked to some degree. Adelbert had the reputation of being a devoutly religious man and often talked to his father, Burton, about the faith, trying over the years to get Burton to come to church. But, being raised by a preacher in a strict Free Methodist home where "newspapers, cards, smoking, drinking, dancing and other 'sins' were forbidden, Burton would later remark to his son, the priest, that by the age of 16 he had enough religion to last him for a lifetime."[1] There's a story in the family, however, that near Burton's death, he surprised his son at Mass by showing up, and received the sacraments (confession and communion), and continued to do so for several weeks before his death.

When the parish celebrated Fr. Del's 40th year as a priest (1941-1981), he sent my Dad a letter, enclosed a bulletin of the liturgy and hymns, and briefly described the event.

> *I was grateful that no one had made much of it...The*
> *parish had a dinner and about 225 parishioners were there.*
> *Fortunately, it was informal and there were no speeches or*
> *politicians.*

I thought more about the timing of our trip to Pittsburgh. I wondered if Dad's anxiousness about arriving on a particular weekend wasn't intended to avoid introducing his problematic son (me) to another set of "problems" in the family—Marie Veronica and Fr. Del. He may have come to the conclusion that Fran alone was the safer alternative. I imagined my Dad and Mom working out the details of the trip.

BEN: I think it's time to introduce Stanley to my

---

1 Biographical sketch written by Burton Emerson Williams's grandson, named Burton Edwin Williams.

relatives in Pittsburgh.

RUTH: You don't mean those Catholic heathens, do you?

BEN: Bunches, my Sweet! They're not heathen, they're just misled.

RUTH: Ben, you know better. You get letters from your nephew, the priest, all the time and they're filled with stories about playing cards, bingo, drinking beer, and he sends you cards with pictures of Mary on them with prayers addressed to her and not to God. How can you be so confused? This is Stanley's cousin. It's dreadful.

BEN: But, Pie Crust, my Darling! They're really sweet people.

RUTH: Sweet on hell, they are! But then, I guess, I'm just uneducated.

BEN: Well, I was thinking that I'd take him... Stanley, that is...down there on a weekend in May when Father Del...

RUTH   (interrupting): Call no man Father, the Bible says...

BEN: ...Yes, yes, I know. But as I was saying, I'll take Stanley down for a short visit when Adelbert and his mom are in Florida, visiting Russell.

RUTH: Who are you going to visit then, if they'll be sunning themselves down south?

BEN: Well, I thought we'd pay a short visit to Fran and Pat, they're nice folks. We won't stay long.

RUTH: Aren't they Catholic, too?

BEN: Well, I...I...don't know. You must re-member...well, do you remember that Fran has two middle names?

RUTH: Couldn't make up their minds, huh?

BEN: I don't know. But he has two middle names. They're Charles and Wesley. Francis Charles

> Wesley Williams. He can't be all that bad
> with a name like that.
>
> RUTH: Charles Wesley, huh? Should have been John
> Wesley. Charles died an Anglican.

And with that, mom let Dad take the risk and bring me to Pittsburgh, once he confirmed that Del and Marie would really not be around.

I'm guessing that when it came to naming Fran, Burton and Marie had a little disagreement as to whether or not to name him after a Catholic or Protestant saint. Protestants don't really have "saints," but if they did, Charles Wesley, who wrote over 6,500 hymns (166 of which celebrate transubstantiation in the Eucharist [1]), would be a good candidate, if the Presbyterians didn't let the Baptists have a vote. So, Fran's middle names "Charles Wesley" may have come from his mother's generous spirit to acknowledge Burton's Free Methodist upbringing. What my mom and dad didn't know (ignorance is bliss) was that Fran's first name invoked one of Catholicism's greatest saints, St. Francis of Assisi. If Dad thought missing the devout Catholic mom and her devout son (the Catholic priest), was going to avoid confronting Catholicism, he clearly misread Francis Charles Wesley Williams. [2]

We only visited with Fran a few hours. But in that time he spoke admirably of his mother, Marie, and the Church; introduced us to his son, Tim, who was starting Catholic seminary; took us on a tour of West Mifflen, including Fr. Del's Church, St. Agnes. Just before we left, he shoved into my curious hands a 31-page, single spaced, description of The Cursillo Movement, for which he was the lay director in the Pittsburgh diocese.

If you're not familiar with The Cursillo Movement, as I was not, its purpose is to enliven spiritual renewal within Roman Catholicism. It began in Spain as a local movement during the mid- 1800's. At that time it was an effort to prepare young people for their pilgrimage along

---

1 Rattenbury, Ernest J. (1996). *The Eucharistic Hymns of John and Charles Wesley* (2nd American Edition). OSL Publications: Akron, Ohio, 201 pages.

2 "Despite their closeness, Charles and his brother John did not always agree on questions relating to their beliefs. In particular, Charles was strongly opposed to the idea of a breach with the Church of England into which they had both been ordained...Prior to his death Charles said to the church's rector, John Harley: 'Sir, whatever the world may say of me, I have lived, and I die, a member of the Church of England. I pray you to bury me in your churchyard.'" (Wikipedia's article on Charles Wesley)

the Way of St. James[1] to the famous Santiago de Compostela Cathedral, the reputed burial-place of Saint James the Greater, which tradition suggests was the first of the Apostles to be martyred. Today, the Movement's worldwide focus is on discipling adult men and women into devout Roman Catholics. This happens through retreats (called pilgrimages) that focus on God's grace, Sacred Liturgy, the Church's Sacraments, and the movement of the Holy Spirit. The goal is nothing less than the candidate's total commitment to Jesus Christ as Lord.

I'm sure Francis Charles Wesley felt his mission was accomplished when my Dad did not object to my receiving the paper, whatever it was. As Dad drove on the way home, I glanced through the long paper that was titled, "A Remembrance of My Pilgrimage [from] The National Secretariat of the Cursillos in Christianity." But I found it dense and beyond my current interest. It was filled with catholic jargon like *pilgrimage, Holy Father, Cardinal, Viget Salubriter, patron saints, renovation of society, religious life, apostolic, cursillistase, Christian asceticism,* and *spiritual direction.* It also liberally quoted popes, and claimed that this or that pope were "the supreme authority in the Church." That did it for me; time to file the paper away. Surprisingly, I did not trash it, probably the consequence of Fran's graciousness and humility in asking me to accept it. Then again, my Guardian Angel had probably misplaced the wastebasket when I cleaned out my files.

While the trip was interesting, I didn't give Catholicism much credibility, and on the way home, I felt a little sad that these people were so lost. But a seed had been planted...even as I marveled at the revelation of the Williamses in Pittsburgh that dared call themselves Catholic.

Nine years later, on July 5, 1986, Dad received a call from his niece, Patricia, with whom, during our trip, we had spent perhaps 30 minutes in her home. She told Dad that Fr. Del had died. A week later a letter arrived from Fran thanking my folks for the flowers and describing Fr. Del's end.

> *Father Del's demise was a blessing. Your heart would have ached for him while he was in the hospital. I counted 8 intravenous plus 5 monitors and a tube down his throat and nose. His arms tied to the bed. We all feel that he is with the Lord now and that the suffering is over. At the funeral there*

---

1 See the movie THE WAY directed by Emilio Estevez and staring his father Martin Sheen. (Screenplay by Estevez from book by Jack Hitt.)

were 100 priests and 5 Bishops. He was layed (sic) in state
in the center aisle of St. Agnes Church with an honor guard
throughout the night before the Mass of Christian Burial.
Our numbers are growing small and you are the only Uncle
left so please, please take care of yourself and Ruth. God
Bless you and keep you in the palm of his hand.

Love, Marie & Fran

A week later, July 11, 1986, Dad sent me this last letter from Fran, with a note of his own. It is the only letter from the Pittsburgh clan Dad ever forwarded to me. However, going through his keepsakes years after his death, I found a small stack of other letters that have helped me write this chapter. Included in this last letter from Fran, were the first prayer cards I ever held in my hands. One featured a photo of Fr. Del, the dates of his life and this prayer on the back:

Grant, we beseech Thee, O Lord that the soul of thy servant,
ADELBERT Thy priest, whom in this life Thou didst honor
with the sacred office, may rejoice in the glory of heaven for
evermore. Amen. Sacred Heart of Jesus have mercy on him.

A second card featured a bishop's crosier and a waterfall surrounded by lush vegetation. On it was this Scripture:

Everyone who drinks of this water will thirst again. He who
drinks of the water that I will give him shall never thirst.
(John 4:13.)

And the third prayer card was heavily laminated (no doubt to pass through the fiery tribulation we dispensationalist Protestants feared). It featured a painting of Mary in the clouds of heaven, with rays of blessings extending from her finger tips down toward Earth, across which was superimposed an image of both sides of a Miraculous Medal commemorating Mary's immaculate Conception. On the back was this prayer:

Most merciful Father, we commend our departed into your
hands. We are filled with the sure hope that our departed
will rise again on the Last Day with all who have died in
Christ. We thank you for all the good things you have given
during our departed's earthly life.

*O Father, in your great mercy, accept our prayer that the
Gates of Paradise may be opened for your servant. In our
turn, may we too be comforted by the words of faith until
we greet Christ in glory and we are united with you and our
departed. Through Christ our Lord. Amen.*

Upon receiving these documents and reading the prayers, I do not
recall any dramatic thoughts like, *Wow, these must be people of strong
faith. How amazing!* But meeting the Pittsburgh Williams Catholics,
and my Dad sending this one letter from Francis (and including the
prayer cards) of Fr. Del's death, clearly signaled that the prejudices espoused by Mom and Dad years earlier no longer took precedence. It
was as if my parents (or at least my Dad) were telling me, "Hey look at
this stuff. I think they must be Christian, after all." I took note.

In my Evangelical mind-set, I thought that Adelbert, although a
Catholic, must have been a holy and good man, else-wise 100 fellow
priests and 5 bishops would not have attended his funeral. It must have
been an impressive event. I remembered that. It meant something. It
was the Christian existential testimony of others that told me truth was
lurking nearby.[1]

---

1 It may be that all diocesan priests traditionally show up for another priest's
funeral, but that didn't change my conclusion that truth was at hand.

56
Unconfirmed

I N EARLY 1977, after we left Dearborn FM over the impending aircraft hanger-mausoleum building-program affair, we tried to have
church at home. We herded our small children together, told Bible
stories, sang songs, and prayed. Around this time my Aunt who was
now married, tried to convince me that while the church was not perfect, it was still the best social institution on Earth. I agreed with her
on one level, but I expected the Church of Jesus Christ to be more...
much more. I had the expectation that anything founded by the per-
fectness of Christ Himself, had to be at least theologically perfect. I
compared the church I was looking for to the Bible. Fallible, sinful men
may have penned the Bible, but through the inspiration and guidance
of the Holy Spirit what it taught was considered inerrant and infallible.
Why couldn't the church be as much? I had no clue, but something told
me to keep looking.

Later that year, over the course of a few months, Pam and I received
several reports from friends and relatives that were very distressing.
At first I thought they were vicious rumors. But they were so specific
and involved such close friends from our past, I followed up with
each to confirm. As each report turned out to be true, Pam and I were
devastated.

The reports involved four of our very best male friends from high
school. Each had been a leader of our spiritually active Dearborn Free
Methodist Youth (FMY) group. To my great disappointment, all had
recently divorced their Christian wives.

One man, SB, had been president of our FMY group. After college
and seminary he became a forerunner for the Billy Graham Evangelistic Association and was the chaplain at a Free Methodist college. He

was now divorced and was still trying to hold onto his job as college chaplain. I told him he should find another line of work, since St. Paul says to Timothy that a Christian leader should have his family intact and be a role model without reproach.[1] But my friend disagreed.

I met with a second friend, AD, at his office in Chicago. He was the vice president of a large firm owned by Christians. He explained that his wife had been diagnosed with a debilitating disease and he was forced to divorce her so she could move back in with her parents and get more affordable health care. AD was in an executive position with a nationally known company, run by Christians. Clearly, I didn't know the whole story but I could not imagine divorcing Pam for any situation, least of all a financial one.

A third friend, NC, had married a Quaker, who probably met his desire for a peaceful marriage. Years after his divorce he told me that he had never, ever seen his Christian mom or dad disagree in the least way. While I found that nearly unbelievable, I knew his mom and dad as kind and gentle stalwarts of the church. So, when there were disagreements between NC and his wife, neither had a clue how to solve their problems. As a result, my friend had a nervous breakdown and spent over a year in a hospital, unable to care for himself. Although NC had been a confident star football player in high school and college, he was now a shell of his former self.

The fourth young man was probably my closest high school church chum. We had double dated with our gal pals numerous times through high school, although after high school we lost contact. After TL graduated from a Christian college, he was accepted at the approved Free Methodist seminary, and became a pastor at a Michigan church. I was not able to track LT down, but I heard multiple reliable reports that he had suddenly left his wife and two children behind in the church parsonage, withdrew his savings from the bank, and ran away with a girl from the church youth group who had presumably turned eighteen. For years I wanted to find this past friend and beat the dung out of him. (Note to editor: This line stays in.)

These four stories came to us within months of each other, although the events they describe had evidently occurred over a few years. Pam and I were more than sad. I entered into a depressed state for months. Our high school youth group was always praying for each other, studying the Bible sincerely, and trying to be witnesses for Christ within our respectful high schools. I could not believe such things

---

1 1 Timothy 3.

could happen to four Christian men that I thought I knew so well from high school.

After many weeks of prayer and frustration with these stories I put the blame on the church, for its relentless emphasis on evangelization and avoidance of spiritual growth and discipleship. Every sermon and worship service ended with an altar call, trying to find that one last soul in the congregation, weaken them down, and get them to kneel at the altar rail. The church memberships were small. Everybody I knew was already saved. I kept thinking, wasn't it time for preachers to put getting saved on the back burner and make spiritual maturity a priority?

> **Wasn't it time for preachers to put getting saved on the back burner and make spiritual maturity a priority?**

MY GRIEF OVER what had happened to our friends turned to fear. I came to the realization that Pam and I were not going to grow in our home-brewed church beyond our limited understanding. We both wanted to avoid what had happened to these others that we loved so much. We asked around, and discovered that the Bethesda Missionary Temple, which we had visited earlier with my half-sister Dorothy and her husband, held an in-depth Christian catechism class that met on Thursday nights. We got a hold of and scanned the textbook, *Understanding God.*[1] It seemed to deal with many of the topics that were missing from the Free Methodist pulpit. I was also glad to see that the teachings were not all going to be about the gifts of the Holy Spirit, which is what I half-expected from the large Pentecostal church.

The class lasted eight months. The teachings and discussions after each lecture were mostly good. At the end of the eight-months, we all lined up to be baptized...again. (My previous baptism at the Taylor Free Methodist Church after starting there as the Youth Pastor, was not recognized by Bethesda.) I lamented the division in Christian churches over something so basic as baptism. I wondered if every church we might attend in the future would require something different to secure our salvation? But, what did we know? Getting saved was important. Getting wet a few more times was a small price to pay.

The principle difference between Bethesda's doctrine and Free Methodism dealt with the Holy Spirit's *gift of tongues*. The Free Meth-

---

1 Gruits, Patricia (1975). *Understanding God*: Answering Vital Questions About God, The Universe, Life, Death and You. Whitaker House, Springdale, PA, 422 pages.

odists wanted nothing to do with it, yet Bethesda didn't think you were a Christian unless you got the gift and did, at least once, speak in tongues, hopefully right after you were baptized.

So, after we were baptized (by full immersion) and changed into dry clothes, we were hustled into a large second floor prayer room where the lights were turned low. There, the 200 or so that were baptized, plus many prayer counselors, were devoutly at work.

I was told to sit in a chair and soon two male elders approached. They laid their hands on my head, and with them I was instructed to pray for the Baptism of the Holy Spirit. Pam was not far away in another chair, surrounded with praying women.

According to Bethesda's theology and practice, I could not be *confirmed in the faith* unless there was evidence that I had experienced the Baptism of the Holy Spirit. And the conclusive evidence of that Baptism was that I "yield and speak in tongues," the unintelligible words of angels. In short, while justification was necessary and came first, speaking in tongues became the default requirement for Bethesda to confirm you in the Christian faith.

As we prayed, the hands on my head became heavier. One of the elders was praying in tongues, and the other in plain English: "O, Lord God, come down mightily on this young man and fill him with your Holy Spirit."

Now up until this point in my life (I was 30-years of age at the time), I considered myself to be a pretty good Christian. I cannot remember a time when I was not seeking God or trying to understand what was true about my life and the world around me.

While I sat there with my hands firmly clasped in prayer, my mind considered an earlier conclusion—that the Holy Spirit was already in my life, and had been since I had first accepted Christ as my Savior. As much as I disagreed with the Free Methodists because of what Paul wrote in First Corinthians 12-14 about the Gifts of the Holy Spirit ("Do not forbid speaking in tongues..."),[1] neither did I fully agree with Bethesda's conclusion that tongues were required as evidence of the same. To my way of interpreting the Bible, Paul was clear, as he rhetorically rejected the idea that all members of the church should have the same spiritual gifts. ("Are all apostles? Are all teachers? Do all have gifts of healing? Do all speak in tongues?"),[2] each question demanding ...a "No."

---

1 1 Corinthians 14:39
2 1 Corinthians 12:29-30

Still, I sat, respectfully, and let these dear men pray over me. Perhaps I was wrong. Perhaps I would speak in tongues. I was trying to be obedient to those under whose authority I had placed myself.

But nothing was happening. And the longer nothing happened the more urgent and insistent the prayers became. In their eyes I'm pretty sure I was like a pagan bump on the log, a hollowed-out knothole where only slimy toads would dare to dawdle. I wasn't jumping up and down. I wasn't crying. I wasn't even sobbing. A wretch was I. A hard case, indeed!

At last, a third prayer warrior came and put her hands on my back and shoulders. They would have pushed me over onto my face except that I was sitting in a steel chair, bent forward, with my elbows firmly pressed into the hollows behind my kneecaps.

Nothing was happening.

One thing that had attracted me to Bethesda was their attempt to thoroughly explain the Christian faith. Their catechism text,

> **In their eyes I'm pretty sure I was like a pagan bump on the log, a hollowed-out knothole where only slimy toads would dare to dawdle.**

Understanding God, was thick and appeared thorough. It was a collection of 856 questions followed by answers and scriptural references, broken into 10 topics. It was well cross-referenced with scriptural passages and contained a comprehensive index. It had all the markings of a good academic textbook on theology. I hoped it would satisfy my need for answers on a doctrinal level.

During the eight-month catechism course, *Understanding God*'s author, Patricia Beall Gruits, would present a 50-minute teaching on the night's topic. The class was about 300 strong. Then, we broke into small groups. Each group was led by a married couple who engaged us in discussion and answered our questions.

Except rarely could they answer mine.

Unfortunately, the thoroughness of the text and presentations lacked a level of logic and consistency. Often I had difficulty understanding how the cited biblical texts backed up the answers Gruits gives in the book. More than once I challenged the couple leading our small group to explain the logic or the contradictions with other Scriptures I had interpreted differently. Unable to satisfy my inquiry, they asked me to meet with a group of elders in a room set apart. It was like being sent to the vice principal's office, something for which I had a lot of experience.

It was in these meetings (with the elders, not the vice principal) that I began to see a problem between faith and reason. Bethesda's leadership had brought a lot of reason to bear on the Christian faith by attempting to logically explain the Gospel in their two catechism volumes. (The second book, *Laying the Foundation: Achieving Christian Maturity*, was written by Patricia's brother and senior pastor of Bethesda, James Lee Beall.) The vast majority of those two volumes still make sense to me—they're filled with explanations of basic Christianity that are rational and consistent. They even hint at a Catholic upbringing in the distant Beall past.

But there were these holes. Deep pungent holes, that caused me to conclude that Bethesda's theology was often based on personal experience, and that the interpretation of "relevant" Scriptures were conveniently stretched to justify the experience.

One particular exegesis that bothered me was their insistence that believers who were infilled by the Holy Spirit would be able to pray in tongues, or glossolalia. Their evidence cited Scriptural passages such as Acts 2 when at Pentecost the Holy Spirit descended on the Apostles and they miraculously were able to preach in languages they had never learned but that the foreigners around them understood.

Another passage was 1 Corinthians 12:10 when St. Paul describes glossolalia as a gift and evidence of the Holy Spirit.[1]

But when I asked my small group leaders or the elders for explanations of why St. Paul says there should be no division in the body of Christ regarding these gifts (1 Cor. 12:25), and that not everyone should have the same gifts so that Christians should be dependent on others with different gifts (I Cor 12: 19-30), and that tongues was considered the least of the gifts (1 Cor. 28), and that we should strive for the greater gifts (1 Cor. 31)...well, this sort of counter-evidence did not match their pre-packaged answers. Their response to my interpretation of Scripture was disappointing: I was told that *I had to take their answers on faith*.

I explained that I had no trouble 'taking on faith' *my* understanding of the Bible, but I did have trouble 'taking on faith' *their* understanding of the Bible. Furthermore, I pointed out, the issue of "faith" was with respect to Jesus for my salvation, not them for an interpretation of Scripture...without reason. Either they had to provide some rational connection between the two interpretations, or I was under no com-

---

1 Other passages that mention the valid gift of glossolalia are: Mark 16:17, Acts 10:46, and Acts 19:6.

punction to believe that Bethesda had a good handle on the Bible. "Test everything," St. Paul says. (1 Thessalonians 5:21)...a phrase that demands the use of reason.

My attitude and challenge didn't sit well. After all, they were the elders and I was the student, and an unconfirmed one at that. My frustration had its roots in the limits they gave to reason...limits which reason has for sure, especially in the light of supernatural revelation. But what I faced in this particular learning experience was that where reason and faith seemed to be at odds, Bethesda's elders assumed that reason had to be disregarded entirely, and blind

> **I had no trouble 'taking on faith' my under-standing of the Bible; but I did have trouble 'taking on faith' their under-standing of the Bible.**

faith took over. That made me uncomfortable. For me, it was logical that faith and reason had to come from the same place, and if handled correctly they would agree.

Back in the upper room, the elders, probably having given up on my Baptism in the Holy Spirit, had now regressed and were praying instead for my salvation. There was a real need, I'm sure they concluded, for the Holy Spirit to send faith searing through my soul. The problem was that each of us was defining "faith" differently.

It was much later before I understood that the linguistic fallacy facing us was something called "equivocation"--a term that means "equal vocalization". It's when a word, term or concept sounds the same, but the underlying definitions are different.

Here, Bethesda was defining faith as trust in Ms. Gruits's understanding of the Bible, and I was holding out for my understanding of the Bible, although we both thought we were having faith in the Holy Spirit.

I thought we were disagreeing about what the Bible taught, but in reality our disagreement was with our interpretations of what the Bible taught. And what good was that? It was almost comic in nature, like melancholy clowns in baggy pants chasing each other around a three-ring circus honking horns and squirting seltzer at each other, trying to scare the other into submission.

All of this was twirling around in my mind as the hands and the prayers pressed upon me. Finally, the humor of the situation got to me, and I started to chuckle if not giggle a little.

What a mistake that was.

Quickly I realized that equivocation was at work again. My laughter was being interpreted two different ways. I was humored, but those praying over me were convinced that I was going to burst forth any moment in wild angelic utterances.

I tried to control myself and quiet down. But it was no use. The more I laughed the more serious they became. Finally, I just had to rise up, catch their eyes, smile and say, "I'm sorry, but I'm laughing at this situation and how you're praying for something I think I already have. My laughter is not the Holy Spirit descending with holy laughter. I don't really think I'm supposed to speak in tongues to prove the Holy Spirit is with me."

That did it. They were not amused. No salvation for me that night.

And so it was that the elders of Bethesda Missionary Temple became convinced that I was not a Christian and they refused to confirm me in the faith.

Pam, however, experienced things a little differently. She's always had a more adaptive nature. I doubt she ever saw the inside of the vice principal's office except to collect for Girl Scout cookies. Evidently she gave forth a convincing utterance in the upper room. Later she was confirmed in the faith, and furthermore was asked to publicly give her testimony at the graduation banquet while I sat glued to my "agnostic" seat.

Years earlier, by faith, I had embraced Christ as my Savior, and I had labored well since then to secure my place in the Kingdom…although I frequently fell short. Finding forgiveness, rallying again to obedience, continually working, studying, and getting excellent counsel from pastors and friends, I slowly matured in the faith, thanks in a large degree to the Evangelical-Fundamentalist Christian Community. And when my Protestant pastors, teachers and elders either denied or ignored the counter-evidence to their position, doubts developed that gave me pause and confounded my pursuit of truth.

But I was just getting started.

57
Old-Time Religion

ROM 1973 TO 1986 I spent a lot of time searching for that Old-Time Religion...that was "good enough for me."[1] The problem *(with me)* was that each church I attended was never good enough...for very long. I dragged my dear wife and children from church to church looking for a church that fit *my* interpretation of the Bible. With the great variety to choose from, it was clear that churches, denominations, sects, fellowships, et al came and went...by the hundreds...or even thousands. But there was only one Bible, or so it seemed to me at the time.

I visited dozens of different Protestant churches. Here and there, with Pam and the family, we'd settle down and actively participate in the ministry. The fellowships we temporarily settled for, in order were:

1. Mount Calvary Lutheran (Missouri Synod) - St. Louis, Missouri
2. Gloria Dei Lutheran (Missouri Synod) - Nassau Bay, Texas
3. Taylor Free Methodist -Taylor, Michigan
4. Dearborn Free Methodist - Dearborn, Michigan
5. Our Home Church in Living Room, Michigan
6. Bethesda Missionary Temple (Pentecostal) - Detroit, Michigan
7. Northwest Church (Christian Missionary Alliance) - Southfield, Michigan
8. Redford Church (Non-denominational) - Redford, Michigan

---

1 "Give Me That Old-Time Religion...it's good enough for me..." is a traditional Gospel song dating from 1873. (See Wikipedia)

9. Fairlane Assembly of God (Assembly of God) - Dearborn Heights, Michigan
10. Highland Park Baptist Church (HPBC) - Southfield, Michigan (Conservative Baptist Association of America, an association not a denomination.)

In between the ten above, we visited a wide variety of other Christian fellowships, including: Church of the Nazarene, Wesleyan Methodist, United Methodists, Lutheran Church of America, Presbyterian, Evangelical Presbyterian, Episcopal, Charismatic Episcopal, the Word of God Community, Messiah Community of Detroit, Bible Churches, three different Seeker Churches, Church of God, Church of God in Christ, various churches that called themselves Baptists (all different), a few home churches, and one store-front entity. And, then there was the little church at the end of our street with a name so long the sign blocked the driveway; as a family we never made it there, only Pam paid a visit.

And while they didn't claim to be churches, there was also a host of parachurch institutions that had their own statements of faith, which disagreed with the statements of faith of other organizations. I've already covered the rift I had with Campus Crusade for Christ. But one of the better-known public breaches of Christian fellowship became known in the late 1950's and continues to this day. It was between the Billy Graham Evangelistic Association (BGEA) and fundamentalist organizations, particularly Bob Jones University. I first became aware of this in the late 1960's when Bob Jones University students would transfer to Greenville College.

The fundamentalists had a tendency to take a *descriptive* Biblical passage and interpret it as *prescriptive*. While Bob Jones did not consider himself racist, he did believe that the Bible "explicitly" taught that the races were to be segregated. Where did he get that? From here:

> *From one man he made all the nations, that they should inhabit the whole earth; and he marked out their appointed times in history and the* <u>boundaries</u> *of their lands. (Acts 17:26)*

Here, St. Paul is preaching to the people of Athens about their "Unknown God" and in the process describes how people of different nations (races) live under God's providence in different lands, behind *boundaries.* Jones interpreted this as God's will that the races should be segregated.

In like manner, Fundamentalists were convinced that the Bible required a very strict agreement on Bible teaching that went considerably beyond simple faith in Jesus Christ. Billy Graham, on the other hand, kept it simple and avoided the divergent views of the many denominations by staying strictly focused on faith in Jesus Christ. During his evangelistic crusades the Fundamentalists decried the BGEA involvement with a wide range of Christian churches. Sitting on the platform behind Graham as he preached were pastors from every conceivable Christian church in the area, including Roman Catholics. In 1993 Graham was labeled as disobedient to the Word of God for "his illicit affair with the Roman Catholic system."[1] Particularly egregious to the Fundamentalists was that the BGEA turned over decision cards (filled out by converts at Crusades recording their decision to follow Christ) to "pagan" churches like Roman Catholics.

> **Particularly egregious to the Fundamentalists was that the BGEA turned over decision cards ...to "pagan" churches like Roman Catholics.**

FOR THE MOST part, Pam and I steered clear of the Fundamentalist groups and gravitated toward Evangelicals, who usually were more tolerant of divergents like me. When we found a place that seemed to agree with our theology, we looked for some way to be involved in the ministry. I played guitar in the worship band, we both led youth groups, and taught Bible studies (from our interpretation of the Bible, of course).

One of the most satisfying involvements was at Northwest Church where I directed a couple of chancel dramas and then created and staged an elaborate musical based on the Jews for Jesus music *Y'SHUA*. For that 2-year effort, the Jews for Jesus sent us their unmixed musical tracks, we rented the local community college's stage and practically sold out 13 performances over two years with a cast and crew of 150.

When we changed churches (again) and started in at HPBC, Pam and I became adept at dramatic readings of Scripture for worship services, one time scoring the Scripture for Easter with an edited version

---

1 Wilson Ewin's prayer letter on his book *The Assimilation of Evangelist Billy Graham into the Roman Catholic Church*, January 1993.

of John Williams's music from an early Superman movie.

One Christmas, at HPBC, Pam was asked to dress up like the Virgin Mary to read Mary's Magnificat[1] just before the sermon. (Yes, this was a "Baptist" church.) Beforehand, the worship leaders directed her to stand before a microphone off to the side, which inadvertently was in a giant shadow. On cue Pam appeared in her flowing blue and white robes, and began to read. But after only a few sentences she suddenly stopped and walked off stage. I nearly panicked. I looked around. No one seemed to know what was going on. But the pastor, much to his credit, waited patiently in his seat for the longest time. Finally, Pam came back on stage, slipped on a pair of eyeglasses and said, "I know Mary didn't wear glasses but I really need mine." We all laughed. Then she finished reading the Scripture. Her reading of The Magnificat was magnificent.

> **Finally, Pam came back on stage, slipped on a pair of eyeglasses and said, "I know Mary didn't wear glasses but I really need mine."**

Pam later told me what had taken so long. Although she had memorized the passage, she had planned all along to wear her glasses to *read* the passage from a card she held in her hand, but when she came out on stage she realized she had left her glasses in the back-stage restroom. Realizing there were 500 sets of eyes on her, she decided that the "show" had to go on. So, she tried to quote the passage using the card as a crutch. But it didn't work. She didn't know the Magnificat well enough to quote it, and in the dim light her eyes couldn't focus on the card in her hand. So, she stopped trying, slipped through the stage door, and trotted to the restroom. When she got there, however, someone was using the small facility and the door was locked. Did I tell you that Pam is one of the most polite and patient persons on the face of the planet? Even though there were 500 people waiting for her to reappear, and among them was a nervous husband who was praying frantically that she hadn't been raptured, she waited for the person to finish their business and come out. When they did, she quickly retrieved the miracle that allowed her eyeballs to function and returned to the stage.

Years later as a Catholic, when Pam has recounted this story to friends, I have imagined that Pam, as Mary, had been assumed into heaven, and when she reappeared on stage it was really just an apparition.

---

1 Luke 1:46-55

I N SPITE OF all these great and fruitful experiences in the variety of churches we (or rather I) attempted to embrace, something within the church's structure or the pastor's teachings would invariably become a distraction and a point for contention between me and the leadership. Generally, my discontent circled around how to interpret God's word, the Bible.

On multiple occasions I met with pastors to discuss our different perspectives. I can never remember arriving at an agreement. The personal interpretation of scripture was clearly a very personal thing, and not an inerrant, obvious thing. Sola Scriptura became a joke to me because there were so many supposedly "authorized" ways to interpret Scripture.

Some of the churches we attended claimed that they theologically agreed with other denominations on the essentials of the Christian faith, and that the various denominations only parted ways on the non-essentials.[1] That led to the conclusion that if *it was the non-essentials that separated one church from another, then by extension, it was the non-essentials that prevented one Christian from worshipping with another. And, who decides what the essentials of the Christian faith are?*

Thus, the doctrinal discussions I carried on with individuals and pastors from these churches covered the gamut, from one side of the issue to the other.

1. Does faith alone, or faith plus works save a person?
2. Should babies be baptized or dedicated, or neither?
3. Does baptism free a person from original sin, or not?
4. Does a Christian even need to be baptized, if it's only symbolic?
5. Is there such thing as original sin, or are all persons born righteous?
6. Is there a distinct second filling of the Holy Spirit (Holy Spirit baptism) or does the Holy Spirit come upon us at the act of justification (conversion)?
7. Should a Christian be able to pray in tongues, or does the

---

1 The phrase that floats around Protestantism is "In essentials unity, in non-essentials liberty, in all things charity." It has been ascribed to St. Augustine, but this is doubtful because it seems to conflict with Catholic doctrine. The adage sometimes appears in Latin... [*In necessariis unitas, in non-necessariis (or, dubiis) libertas, in utrisque (or, omnibus) caritas.*] ...a tactic I suspect employed by non-Catholics who want to give some concept credibility by implying it came from the Vatican.

Bible forbid it?

8. Should the charismatic gifts of the Holy Spirit be taught as part of the Church's teaching doctrine, or were they only for the first century?

9. If God knows your ultimate eternal destination, is that the equivalent of predestination, and if we're predestined why are we bothering with evangelism?

10. Are the communion elements only symbolic of Christ's body and blood or are they his real presence in some way?

11. Is artificial contraception permitted or is it a sin?

12. Is abortion acceptable, or is it equivalent to murder?

13. Is practicing homosexuality acceptable, or is it a mortal sin?

14. Is smoking a cigarette acceptable, or is it destroying God's temple?

15. Is drinking any amount of an alcoholic beverage, even wine at a wedding, acceptable, or is it a sin that separates one Christian from another?

16. Is it acceptable to fellowship with other Christians if they don't believe exactly as you do?

17. Should women teach in a church setting, or be silent?

18. Should women be ordained as pastors and reverends, or banned completely from pastoral ministry?

It didn't take long before I began to ridicule the denominational claim that different Protestant churches agreed on the essentials. For me this became *the Scandal of Christianity*, and a great embarrassment. There was no way I could logically identify or even defend what was true. I didn't know. I had my opinion, but who was I to judge? At times I thought I was infallible, but wisdom would sneak up on me and remind me that my knowledge and experience were not omniscient and thus I could not determine infallibly what was true. People told me the Bible was the foundation for truth. But, if that was true, then why did so many churches use the Bible to defend their *differences* against other churches...that, at the same time, were using the same Bible but coming to different conclusions?

Here are a few examples I kept running into:

Hell. More particular to my experience, one Lutheran Church pastor refused to preach about hell because he didn't believe that Satan existed.

At the same time Evangelical churches demanded that their pastors preach about hell, fire, and damnation or get another church to pastor.

Altar Calls. United Methodists congregations would walk out if the pastor had an altar call.

But most Baptist churches rose up in rebellion if the pastor didn't have an altar call after every sermon.

Charismatics. The leaders at Taylor Free Methodist didn't like anything charismatic or even fellowshipping with the "gifted."

Yet, the Pentecostals at Bethesda Missionary Temple demanded everything charismatic or you weren't considered a Christian.

Church Growth. At Dearborn Free Methodist the pastor (and lay leaders) were motivated to build a new church building even if the auditorium was only half-full on any Sunday.

Meanwhile, a friend, who ran a store-front church, believed it was wrong for any Christian institution to own property at all, let alone a Crystal Cathedral.

Hierarchy. At Northwest Church the pastor decried the denominational *hierarchy* that kept his theology in check (according to their interpretation of the Bible). But he decided that the Holy Spirit was telling him something different, so he was forced out into a storefront ministry on his own. (The pastor was significantly influenced by John Wimber and the Vineyard Movement. We'll have another run-in with Wimber's Vineyard Movement in a later chapter.)

Related to hierarchy is this true story. Not two years earlier, one of the assistant pastors at Northwest was called to pastor a nearby independent Bible Church where there was *no hierarchy,* overarching denomination or accountability. So with enthusiasm he took the position as pastor. Two years after that, the cops descended on his study in the back of the little church building to find him counting the money from a bank heist. The police were tipped off by a pimp who revealed that the minister was renting cars from a dealership to cover his tracks, as he pulled off a series of bank jobs in order to pay the pimp for his girls' services. (There's a late, late night movie in that one.)

Infallibility. At Fairlane Assembly of God, our pastor, BJ, would yell and scream at the congregation for 20 minutes on end about what

God's Word was telling him to tell us "for our sake." It was hard to bear. One Sunday his Bible rant was directed at men and how we shouldn't yell at our wives…as he yelled at us. I wrote him a letter that included this line:

> I should have been a Bible bashing preacher like you. Then I could rant and rage for several hours a week and everybody would call me holy.

Another Sunday, after telling us how he was misquoted in the Detroit Free Press in an article that none of us had read, he raised his voice in a vicious rant, shook his big Bible in the air with rage, and told those of us *who disagreed with him*, that we should just tear those pages out of our Bibles. The implication? Rev. BJ's word was as infallible as Scripture.

That did it. I stood up in the middle of the congregation, faced him, raised my Bible in the air and waved it (with all the pages intact). Then I crawled over people in our pew and left the building, never to return. On my way out I wondered if he had been hiding in the bookstore like me when Dennis Stacey confronted that hard-boiled Calvinist?

That last Sunday I heard him preach was also the time he railed at the large congregation of well over 1,200 because some wanted him out as pastor. He assured us God had anointed his ministry, "Just look at the crowd that's here today," he crooned. He assured us he wasn't going anywhere. Then, three weeks after I walked out, he suddenly left for a church on the west coast with his family and the director of music in tow. There was no time for a transition—overnight he and his family were gone. Bam! Three months later we heard that his new congregation had him defrocked after catching him in immorality.

Baptism. In some Bible churches baptism was optional—it was only a sign of what had already been done when the person was justified in Christ.

In the Church of God in Christ you had to be immersed, completely under water, or baptism was ineffective. While they claimed it was only a sign, they ironically required immersion or salvation wasn't complete.

In Presbyterian Churches immersion was not required.

The Eastern Orthodox Church claimed you should only be baptized one time because the creeds mention "one baptism."

At one independent Evangelical assembly the pastor taught that baptism was required *every* time a Christian fell into mortal sin; and he was proud to have been baptized over and over again.

And there was our small group in Texas that split with the Missouri Synod Lutheran Church because of their "heresy" on allowing infant baptisms.

Presumption. Then there was the ever-present presumption of judgment. I've already written about how one Sunday evening Pam decided to take a walk and check out the service at the small independent church that hid behind solid brick walls at the end of our street. She was about seven-months pregnant with Joshua at the time. I stayed home with our girls. Pam was cordially greeted, but a *single* pregnant lady comin' to church was a clear signal to the preacher and deacons that the Holy Ghost was calling them to action. After the sermon and near the end of his altar call, the preacher came out of his pulpit, down the aisle and tried to herd Pam to the altar to get saved.

So much for the infallible moving of the Holy Spirit. That was the last time she visited any church without me...at least with a name like *The Original Primitive First Baptist Church of the Redeemed in Christ Sanctified*. Yes, it's true, the city had given them a variance to the sign ordinance.

Because of all these differences and the double talk about them, it was surprising to me that I didn't give up on God and the Christian faith all together. Many people have done just that, and now I saw with good reason why. They were pointing to a scandal within Christianity that I could not refute. Pontius Pilate understood the problem all too well when he asked Jesus, "What is Truth?" I was left *without* a logical apologetic defense for the faith. So, I stopped criticizing those who criticized Christianity. They had a point.

One of the reasons there was such theological confusion among denominations was because there was fundamental confusion of their source of truth...as my daughter, April, was soon to discover.

58
Why Catholics Added Books to The Bible

M Y COLLEGIATE DAUGHTER, April, came home for a mid-term break in 1993, with a problem. She was almost flunking Introduction to the Old Testament, a class at Grand Rapids Baptist College in Michigan (now Cornerstone University). So, the instructor gave her an extra credit project, a list of research questions, from which she needed to pick only one and write on it over the break. Here's the question she picked:

> *Why and when did the Catholic Church add seven books to the Old Testament?"*

Why indeed? It was an interesting question that as Protestants piqued both her curiosity and mine. I have a large library on Christianity and history, so she asked for help in finding references to read. We had no idea that the answer we found would signal a change in our perspective about the Bible and that "cult" called Catholicism. We were certain that the answer would be another proof that Catholics were not Christians. As Evangelicals we knew you couldn't mess with the Bible. We revered it, refusing to place another book upon it, or turn over a corner of its pages. Sacred stuff. So, how could Catholics so easily sacrilege God's Holy Word? It seemed unfathomable, so arrogant, so wrong. Adding books to the Bible was certainly proof that Catholicism was a permutation of Christianity that could not be trusted.

April's research question came to her before the Internet, so we began to scour through real books. (Yes, I know, those archaic devices of the devil.) We came across a little pale orange paperback book that I had never read that was hidden in the back of one of my library shelves. In fact, it always seemed heretical to even own it: *The Apocrypha: An American Translation by Edgar J. Goodspeed (Vintage Books, NY 1959).* The Apocrypha was, of course, the collection of books that Catholics had added to the Bible.

Cracking the cover we read together the opening sentence of Goodspeed's Preface. It was one of those moments when a few simple words would change forever my vision of the Holy Bible as a monolith of writings that Jesus must have pulled from his knapsack and handed over to the Apostles moments before his ascension: "Here! Read this. It'll help." *What was I thinking?* (This was years before I saw the mural on the side of the BIOLA University building, of Jesus offering a leather-bound volume to passing students.)

With 26 simple words, Goodspeed let his lead foot drop on history's accelerator as he laid rubber across my sanctimonious vision.

> *The Apocrypha formed an integral part of the King James Version of 1611, as they had of all the preceding English versions from their beginning in 1382.*

Whoa, there, Goodspeed! Slow down. This is not what I was expecting. He sped around the curve, screeching his tires as he went full bore:

> *They [the Apocrypha] were part of the Bible of the early church, for it used the Greek version of the Jewish Bible, which we call the Septuagint, and these books were all in that version.*

Tell me this couldn't be! How is this possible? For God's sake, what Bible did Jesus use? Then...

> *They passed from it [the Septuagint] into Latin and the great Latin Bible edited by St. Jerome about A.D. 400, the Vulgate, which became the Authorized Bible of Western Europe and England and remained so for a thousand years.*

Pages later we read how the Bible had remained essentially unchanged until 1827, when the British and American Bible Societies pressured Bible publishers to stop including the Apocrypha in their printings of the Bible. Only then did the Apocrypha books practically disappear from Protestant Bibles.

1827 !?

Good Grief! How could this be? Was Goodspeed pulling a fast one on us, staying true to his name? April and I hurried off to the local library, checked some other references and discovered that Goodspeed's account was true.

This totally unnerved me for two reasons. First, the Bible that I had revered my whole life suddenly wasn't the Bible that I had thought it was. In the college Bible classes I took at Greenville College, I learned how one could trust the accuracy of a translation in all its delicacies.

> **My trust in what Protestant Bible scholars had led me to believe for 40 years evaporated quickly.**

But, there was nothing delicate about totally deleting seven entire books from the Old Testament, which also included parts of my favorite Old Testament book of Daniel! My trust in what Protestant Bible scholars had led me to believe for 40-years evaporated quickly—as fast as a jet-fueled dragster can empty its tank—VAROOM!. *Goodspeed was behind the wheel.*

Second, I was unnerved because April needed a good grade on this paper to keep her G.P.A. up so she could stay in school. Certainly, if she told the truth about what she had found, she'd get a failing grade on the paper. The Bible teacher at the Evangelical college would never settle for what we discovered—that Catholics didn't ADD seven books to the Old Testament, but rather that Protestants took seven books OUT. Who could I trust...now...about the Bible?

A FEW YEARS LATER Pam and I took a break from our work, and caught a romantic train ride from Detroit to Chicago for the Valentine Day weekend. While in Chicago, we took a walking tour of The Loop and thought we'd drop in on art galleries and old bookstores. We found the art galleries, but the closest thing to an old bookstore appeared to be an old stately stone building with a sign in front that said it was a library. It was a cold, blustery day in Chicago, so we walked inside simply to warm up.

When we entered we were surprised to be greeted by a burly security guard behind a large round counter near a staircase; but no books. We probably looked a little dumbfounded.

The guard looked us over and asked, "Are you here to do research?" A sign caught my eye that explained that we were in The Newberry,[1] a privately funded research library open to the public but only accessible by registration. I straightened a bit and recalled that I had just recently earned my PhD and thus was *fully qualified* to call myself a researcher. So I pontificated in my best academic demeanor: "Ah, yes, we are."

"What century?" the guard asked.

I had no clue. In fact, I distinctly remember how I could never remember if we were in the 20th or the 21st century...or was it the 19th? Recovering, I declared, "Uh...the 1500s." I did a quick examination of conscience--I had not lied. Indeed, I was writing a documentary on the early 1500s.

The Guard pushed registration cards toward us, and asked for our picture I.D.'s. I glanced at Pam. She was intrigued. We had no idea what awaited us, but we were game. On the 6 x 8 inch cards we filled out our personal information and presented them with our picture I.D.'s to the guard. He checked them over, returned our I.D.'s and told us to take the elevator to the fourth floor where a librarian would meet us. I thought, *Wow, what service! I'll have to suggest this to the public library back home—personal librarians.*

When we stepped off the elevator, indeed, a neatly dressed lady with eyeglasses hanging around her neck greeted us. She asked what books we would like to examine. It now became evident that you didn't check books out of this library, but are given access to them for a short time in a supervised reading room.

I said, "Do you have any old Bibles?"

The poor woman must have known at that instance she was dealing with rank amateurs. She smiled as if to say, "This dear man doesn't realize that there's nothing on the fourth floor younger than 400 years. "Yes, we do, we have first editions, in fact." With that we followed her to a cabinet of perhaps 40 card catalog drawers. She pulled out one and set it on a counter so we could look over her shoulder as she flipped through the cards.

Thirty minutes later, in a reading room, wearing white disposal cotton gloves, our personal librarian placed on the table before us an *original* parchment from Guttenberg's first edition of the Bible (1455),

---

1 www.newberry.org.

a complete *original* edition of Myles Coverdale's (English) Bible from 1535, an *original* Martin Luther (German) Bible (1539), and a *first edition* of the King James Version (English) Bible from 1611...all 30 pounds of it.

The KJV was 5-inches thick, with elaborate hand-colored paintings that included Mary and the saints. (We were told that the coloring was done by a private owner, as the original KJV printing was in black and red.) Holding this very large and very heavy book in my hands was like being transported back in time; I wondered what personage from history had held this very book. Perhaps King James?

> **In the three first edition Reformation Bibles we examined, the 7 Apocryphal Books were in all three.**

And guess what? In the three first edition Reformation Bibles we examined, the 7 Apocryphal Books were in all three, although in a separate section between the Old and New Testaments.

Had they not been accepted as inspired, why were they in these Reformation Bibles? The Apocrypha was not missing, nor had it been removed, as some reports claimed. Protestants, indeed, had taken books out of the Bible, which had been in every approved translation of the Bible since the Council of Cathage issued its canon of the Bible on August 28, 396 AD. Catholics, true to their word, had defended the faith and kept it pure and true. It was a day Pam and I will never forget. We now had "first hand" experience with history.

APRIL WROTE HER paper and detailed what she had discovered in our book research: That the Catholic Church had not added seven books, but that in the early 1800's Protestants had removed the apocryphal books without the benefit of several Ecumenical Councils, which was how the original biblical canon had been initially validated.

What this all meant did not immediately hit me. I knew that the Biblical scholars who had taught me, and the authors of the numerous books on Biblical theology that I had read, had all forgotten more than I would ever know. So, I easily accepted their judgment on the matter.

Therefore, it was not immediately evident to me that:

1. The theologians that demanded the Apocrypha be removed from the Holy Spirit-inspired Old Testament

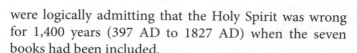

were logically admitting that the Holy Spirit was wrong for 1,400 years (397 AD to 1827 AD) when the seven books had been included.

2. If the Bible for 1,400 years was inerrant and infallible, then inerrancy and infallibility applied to the whole kit and caboodle, including those books some Johnny-come-lately (it was actually a Jerome-come-lately) theory wanted to discard. Either the whole Bible was inspired by the Holy Spirit or it wasn't. Pick one and live with it. But if you decide that 1,400 years of Christian teaching about the inspiration of the Holy Spirit was incorrect, then the foundation of the Bible's trustworthiness is undermined.

3. Sola Scriptura was suddenly a vacuous argument because you now had to differentiate which scriptural collection you were talking about, and in the process you had to justify the inclusion or exclusion of the seven books based *entirely* on Scripture.

4. But, there was no scripture that listed what books were to be in the Bible and which were not to be included.

5. The authority or process that determined which books were to be in the Bible must have been as infallible as the infallibility of books being selected. If the authority or process was not infallible then you have no guarantee that the books selected should be there in the first place.

6. Protestant theology was seemingly based on a 200-year old Bible, but Catholic and Orthodox Christianity were based on a 1,600-year old Bible. Which was more trustworthy?

These revelations rudely returned me to a state of spiritual adolescence. What they implied festered for a long time below the surface like bacteria infecting a host of facial pores. Slowly and assuredly, they worked their way to the surface, threatening any day to pop open like fully mature, logical zits.

Yet, through all of this, my faith in the Bible as the inspired, inerrant, infallible Word of God did not waver. I had enough personal experience testing and applying Scripture's truth to my life that it's authority was unscathed.

But, the discovery that Protestants removed seven books from a canon of Scripture that for 1,400 years had been considered whole, complete, inerrant, infallible and fully trustworthy...was subconsciously unnerving. Having someone misinterpret Scripture is sad. Being in Dennis Stacey's Bible bookstore and seeing him rip out a single page from the New Testament while arguing with a Calvinist was frightful. But here we're talking about removal of seven entire books that Christian doctrine told us were inspired by the Holy Spirit. That was something greater than frightful. It was inexcusable!

Strangely, at the time I never thought about knocking on Catholicism's door…far from it. I still figured that Martin Luther with his 95 Theses had done all the knocking (in 1517) that was required and the issue was settled—Catholics had lost their way. There was no need to include the other seven books, although I still treasured my Jerusalem Bible that included them. It was then that the "brilliant" idea came to me: *Maybe I should set aside some time to actually read them.* I had read the entire Bible several times all the way through, but I had never read the Apocrypha. What a novel idea? At least, then, I could come to some judgment of my own. Who else could I trust?

Oh! I guess this is important. April got an "A" on her paper and passed the course. The Baptist College professor had given her a trick question, and he congratulated her on discovering the truth.

You would think that my "instability" at finding a church would drive me to balance out my life by bending over backwards to keep some stability in my professional career. As I said, "you would think…"

59
Leaving Ford

My effort to discover a logical and consistent form of Christianity, or at least one I could call logical and consistent, took years. While I prayed daily for God's will to be done in my life, seeing and understanding God's will was an entirely different animal. I was looking for a 10-point trophy buck, clearly dead and mounted on my wall, something I could brag about choosing to hunt down. Yet, what God often sent was an angry, ferocious wolverine[1] that was hunting me. I thought God's will for my life was something that I came up with...and that I chose to pursue.[2] But, more often it was something He came up with and threw across my path to trip on. Over the short haul my progress was impossible to see. Looking back, the path wandered, jerked, jogged, and left me questioning if indeed God had a particular path he wanted me to follow.

> I thought God's will for my life was something that I came up with...and that I chose to pursue. But, more often it was something He came up with and threw across my path to trip on.

This was particularly true for the 17-years from 1981 to 1998. Perhaps I was "in training" for some great impossible mission. If that was it, however, God was good at keeping secrets, and I have never liked *not* knowing what was going on. I wanted to be as smart as others who I perceived as successful. But I wasn't...so I had to let my dogged

---

1 Wolverines are members of the weasel family, but look and act like small fearless and ferocious bears, thus being able to kill prey much larger than itself.

2 "God's Will" is still somewhat a mystery to me. Today, I believe that my passions and skills are God's gifts that I'm accountable to pursue and use rightly, as Jesus explained in His parables of the talents (Matthew 25:14-30 & Luke 19:11-27.)

perseverance make up the difference.

Thus, this chapter and the few that follow, relate stories that taught me a lot...about myself, the world, and how God was leading me. The problem was I saw none of it coming. I pretended I knew what was going on, but, when the water was chest-high and rising I couldn't find the plug to drain the swamp. I was forced, at times, to float on my back and stare up at the starry sky...but I'd only see clouds. Such a posture was difficult. I was lost without a goal and a plan of pursuit. Thus, I was cursed with episodes of divine narcolepsy...or, were they a blessing?

B Y 1980 I had earned a spot at Ford World Headquarters as one of their top producer-directors for corporate film and television production. I had won a number regional awards, and the honor of producing some big projects. But things changed dramatically in 1981, when there was a political battle for control over the film, video and staffing assets of the department of which I was a part.

My current big project at the time was the production and pro-gramming of Ford's first high-tech, interactive video LaserDisc (LD). This was years before the Internet came on the scene. LD offered stan-dardized, interactive video training and information at full broadcast quality in a virtually indestructible medium. The LD was a 12-inch diameter optical disc similar to the Compact Audio Disc (CDs) or Digital Video Discs (DVDs) we use today, except the data embedded in the disc was not digital 1's and 0's but something called Pulse-Width Modulation—a cross between digital's bits and analog's waves.

The laser discs were virtually indestructible. In a demonstration of the technology to Ford's Chairman, Donald Petersen, and the Board of Directors, I took the videodisc out of the player, put it on the carpet of the Board Room and wiped my feet on the disc, scratching it up pretty bad. Then, I put it back in the player, closed the lid, and almost instantly beautiful pictures re-appeared on the screen. Although the technology was initially developed by Netherland's Philips, marketed by America's Music Corporation of America (MCA), and built by Japan's Pioneer Corporation, Ford had latched onto the Sony Corporation derivative, pitched by the affable John Hartigan, a tall American who grew his hair long and gray and became one of Sony's very successful Samurai Salesmen. John was an immense help to me and my co-producer, Susan Hurst-Hopp, in producing Ford's first experimental LD for the Parts and Service Division.[1]

---

1 The first project was about the diagnosis and repair of Ford's new and complex

I had made the technology pitch in front of the Board of Directors at the request of Ben Bidwell, then Vice President of North American Sales and Operations. Bidwell wanted the Board to underwrite the plan to put a videodisc training system in every dealership in the country. It would be used for new car sales training, service technical training, and as a customer information kiosk. After Bidwell's presentation and my demo the Board voted to underwrite the effort with over a million dollars. The dealers would eventually subscribe and pay for the equipment and the production of discs they were to receive. In the coming years I would be privileged to produce over a dozen of Ford's first videodiscs on service training, but the department I was now in would only produce the first of those discs. Here's what happened.

Shortly after the Board's approval of Bidwell's project, the Public Relations (PR) division maneuvered to take over the vast video and film production facilities of the Photomedia Department of which I was a part. The take-over effort was one of corporate intrigue and one-upmanship, where one vice president was jealous of another vice president's holdings. I was part of the defense team for Photomedia, but the PR VP had the ear of the corporate president. It was a long battle, but one day all of the video and film facilities, including a large stage and all the high tech video editing facilities were under the control of Public Relations…including me and my fellow producers, directors, writers and support staff.

I had suspected that PR wanted control because the Board of Directors had just invested a million dollars in the videodisc technology that would be rolled out over the next year nationwide.

Boy, was I wrong.

Owen Bombard, the VP of Public Relations, called a meeting of his old and expanded staff. There was a pecking order. PR was located on the 9th Floor of Ford World Headquarters and we were scum from the basement. We often wore jeans to work with tennis shoes and baseball caps. (Hey, we were filmmakers who have to get down and get dirty.) They wore three-piece suits and were always in front of the press cameras. When those of us from the basement arrived at the meeting on the 9th floor, all the good seats around the mahogany table were taken, so we sat around the perimeter of the room with our backs against the

---

Automatic Overdrive Transaxle , the AOT. Where most interactive LD would have 1 or 2 program "dumps" to control the interaction of menus and Q&A, I persuaded Sony, with John's help, to place 12 dumps on the disc. It worked, and was a factor in selling Ford on the feasibility of the product.

wall. A few stood in the doorway. I managed to get toward the front of the room, but three rows back against a wall.

I can still remember the moment. Bombard was a big guy, given to cigars and posturing. He had a couple of "lieutenants" ,one who was WL, the guy who two-years earlier, had tried to get me fired. And, in that, there's a story.

IT WAS THE middle of the night before the Long Lead Press Conference announcement of the new, fully redesigned 1979 Ford Mustang. I had spent the last three months producing the show and was also directing the live event with a crew of 20. Involved were two-dozen 35-mm slide projectors and a motion picture projector displaying images on a 50-foot wide rear projection screen erected in the air on scaffolding, under which, on a curtained stage, we would reveal live cheerleaders, walk-on actors, executives, follow-spots, rotating cars, special effect lighting and fog, all to the accompaniment of a dramatic music track played through large Voice of the Theater speakers. We had everything except a marching band. It was pure Las Vegas stuff staged at the Ford Design Center rotunda for 300 international automotive reporters and perhaps 150 corporate Ford Motor brass. In the morning, about 8:30 AM, they would all file into the large domed room and sit on padded folding chairs that had been spaciously set on temporary risers so all would have a good view of the show.

Behind the audience and to one side, partially hidden by curtains, I would sit at a table with other crew and equipment, wearing a microphone-headset, and calling the shots as I followed my colorfully marked-up script.

As I said, WL was Owen Bombard's lieutenant, who was assigned to watch over my development and production of the event. Months before, I had been warned about his autocratic schizophrenic style that demanded revisions to projects that were often impossible to make within the schedule or budget. Early on, with weeks to go before the show, I found the time and shifted the budget to make his various changes.

But here we were. It was 3:00 AM in the middle of the night, during our all night preparation and rehearsals. We had six hours before the event, and WL decided he didn't like something. He told me what he wanted to change. Not believing what I was hearing, I asked him to repeat his request. He repeated it but this time it was a demand. Before I tell you what it was, you need to understand something.

At each of the dozen transitions in the show, hundreds of Mustang logos would flash sequentially across the 50-foot screen, introducing the next segment. The logos, each projected from a 35mm slide, were placed precisely among 1,920 other slides in slide trays mounted on 24 projectors, secured ten feet in the air on scaffoldings. The hundreds of logo slides were darkroom manipulations of the logo, so that they projected as Ford Corporate BLUE. My guess is there were about 288 of these slides among the trays.

WL decided, at 3:00 AM, with six-hours to go before the president of the company would walk onto the stage to welcome the press, that he didn't like Ford Blue...he wanted Scarlet Red. And he demanded I make the change before we did anything else. The technical checks were not important, neither were my planned rehearsals. The Blue now had to be Red.

I told him it couldn't be done...and that he should leave the venue until the show began. It was late, and I had no patience for fools, regardless of rank. He insisted. I lost my patience...chased him out of the building...then went back stage and had a good cry, under the exhaustion and pressure.

Sure enough, just as I had been warned, even though the show went flawlessly, thanks to my very competent union crew, WL was in my boss's office two days later ranting at my "unacceptable" behavior and demanding that I be fired. Amazingly, I only *heard* about *his* behavior, and I was never asked to defend myself or answer his accusations. Knowing about WL up front had prompted me to document every change he requested, and have my boss sign off on them. I had even documented his 3:00 AM demand and my response.

A month after the show, I was called into my boss's office and informed that my excellent job at producing and directing the '79 Mustang Long-Lead Press Conference had earned me a much belated *two-grade promotion*. I was no longer a video technician acting as a producer-director, I was now a "Producer-Director," part of Ford management, given a lease car, a huge bump in salary, and access to a few other perks like the management dining room...which was nice, but it cost extra, so I rarely used it.

I T IS NOW, two years later. WL and I were both sitting in Owen Bombard's big staff meeting in his conference room on the 9th-floor of Ford Headquarters. I looked across the table at WL, but he avoided my gaze. I wondered what it would be like to work with him in the same department.

Bombard began to detail his vision for his new and much bigger empire. He was feeling his political oats, and he had reason to. With the acquisition of our department he had just tripled his annual budget, and thus improved his status and power in the corporate structure. But, a great many of Photomedia projects dealt with training, not with public relations. In fact, the new videodisc effort that was on the verge of a national roll-out was 90% in-dealership training. The public information portion was very small. So, in one way, it was not surprising that Bombard announced to the room that this new merging of our departments would have nothing to do with the videodisc business. He said the technology was a big mistake, and it didn't offer the company any advantages. So he was not going to support it. I glanced at WL, but he didn't flinch.

You can imagine my thoughts. I was surprised to say the least. Just two weeks earlier I had been standing before Ford's Chairman, the Board of Directors and the President of the company giving a demonstration, after which, along with Ben Bidwell's business plan, the Board enthusiastically supported the videodisc effort with over a million dollars. *What was Bombard thinking?! Was WL behind this, trying to blackmail me and the whole LD effort?*

Evidently, I was not the only person in the room that had a thought like that. I looked away to my friend, and fellow producer, Bob Krepike[1] who was sitting at the back of the room. Bob looked straight at me with eyes wide open as if to say, "Did I hear him correctly? What are *you* going to do?" Then, I noticed a dozen other sets of eyes that were glancing at me for my reaction. I didn't say anything or ask any questions. No one ever did when Bombard was in a room standing at the end of a table, "holding court" as it were.

After the meeting on the way back to the basement I fielded a few questions from my friends. But I knew nothing more than what we had heard. *What was I going to do?* I had no idea. But I did know that there was going to be a huge demand for videodisc production and I knew that I was the only one inside Ford, at least, that knew how to do it, and in fact had already produced one disc for Ford Parts and Service that was being tested with good results. I had not considered, up to that

---

1 As I write this Bob, an extraordinary documentary filmmaker with whom I had the chance to work with on a number of his films, is the Ford Corporate Film Historian charged with maintaining the huge library of Ford Motor Company film archives.

time, starting my own company, but if ever there was an opportunity this might be it.

A month went by and I kept my head down, just to see what might actually happen regardless of Bombard's edict. Before the departmental shift to PR, Ford Division had arranged with my Photomedia bosses for me to make a tour of the country with Ben Bidwell and others to sell the video laser disc system to dealers at a half-dozen dealer conferences in places like Las Vegas, New York, Miami. We had our itinerary and plane tickets and were scheduled to depart in March of 1981.

I had a lot to prepare for. I was putting together a presentation for the dealer conferences that involved demonstrating the hardware and describing the training folios. I also had other projects that I had to delegate and tidy up, so our other client's efforts would not fall through the cracks. I was doing this in my office, a cubicle in the windowless basement of Ford Headquarters. It had always been a dreary claustrophobic location, but thankfully my job took me outside a lot, or onto a stage or into a recording studio or edit salon, so the cube wasn't that bad.

But on this day there was a small film shoot taking place in a cubicle nearby and the sound was so distracting that I couldn't concentrate, and I had to make some telephone calls where the background noise would have made it hard for the other party to hear me. I began to look for an empty desk where I could sit for a couple hours to make the calls, collect my notes and write my presentation. I could find nothing in the basement. Then I remembered a couple of empty offices on the 9th floor, with big windows (I like windows) that looked south over Ford's expansive holdings and the Rouge Plant along the Rouge River, a tributary to the Detroit River. So I took the elevator up to my new department's floor and found an empty office with a desk and a phone. Perfect, for a few hours, I thought.

My new boss's office was down the hall 50-feet, so I knew I was not intruding on any body's territory. Thirty-minutes later I was hunched over at the desk taking notes during a phone call, when my new boss, AM, strode into the empty office and stood before the desk I was sitting at. I cupped the phone and looked up at him. He said, "Come down and see me when you get off the phone." I nodded and he left.

A few minutes later I finished the call, made a few notes, and with pad and pen in hand went down to AM's office. I didn't know him very well, but that would change. He looked up at me from his desk and said, "Mr. Williams, that is NOT your office. Get your ass out of there and back to your own in the basement."

He didn't ask why I was there. He just told me what he thought, which was entirely within his right.

But his abrupt manner suggested to me that the videodisc fiasco with Owen Bombard (AM's boss) had come to a head. On my walk back to my basement cubicle I formulated a response. It was inspired by Henry Ford II's occasional response to the media when caught in a compromising situation.

I went to my desk and made a phone call to my coordinating contact at the Ford Division regarding our upcoming national tour. The call only took ten minutes. I then turned to my typewriter, wrote AM a short letter, and walked it back to the 9th floor. An hour after he had chased me out of the 9th floor and back to the basement, I walked into his office. He wasn't there, but I laid my missive on top of his other paperwork and left. It read:

Thursday, March 26, 1981

Dear A:

As the "Duke" said many times, "Never Explain. Never Complain." My last day as an employee of Ford Motor will be tomorrow, my birthday.

Stan Williams

I walked back downstairs to my office in the windowless dungeon, told my friends and old bosses what I had done, made a few calls to personnel and friends, and then packed up my desk. I wasn't mad. But, I was disappointed.

I was also very excited at what the future held. So, symbolically, I made a promise to myself that I've managed to keep all these years. From then on my office would always feature a large window. And, as I sit here writing this, immediately to my left is a large window-door-wall with another smaller window to the left—forty-two square-feet of windows looking out on a small green forest the other side of our driveway. Beautiful! (Okay, so I'd rather there be an ocean surf, but this is good.)

On Saturday, March 28, 1981, I got on a plane and sat next to a coach window, as I flew off with Ben Bidwell (who was in First Class) and others for the Ford Dealer Video Laser Disc Promotional Tour. It was my first job under my new shingle, Full Circle Productions.[1]

Although the previous business effort to do slideshow work for churches had long ago died off, I asked permission from Bill and Don to use the name and logo for my new videodisc production company. When the three of us produced slides in square frames, Don designed a logo of overlapping circles, which looked exactly like a stack of videodiscs. It was perfect.

When I quit Ford, I told Pam that I didn't know what the future held, but I was sure of one thing…that my risk taking would only drive me closer to God. I didn't then, and I don't now, have the confidence to think I can do any of this on my own.

W. Edwards Deming

IRONICALLY, MY FIRST big project on my own was for the very department I had just left. They hired me to produce a documentary about the work of W. Edwards Deming and the importance of Statistical Process Control techniques that were then being incorporated at Ford Motor.

> When I quit Ford, I told Pam that I didn't know what the future held, but I was sure of one thing…that my risk taking would only drive me closer to God.

Deming was the American statistician that tried to help American manufacturing turnout higher product quality. But they rejected him. Long story short, he went to Japan in 1950 and taught the Japanese manufacturing industry how to make things better and cheaper. He helped them create a revolution in quality and economic production that challenged the American manufacturing industry. In appreciation, the Japanese manufacturers created, in his honor, the annual Deming Prize.

When Japanese cars started to put American made cars out of business, Ford, General Motors and others apologized to Deming, and in his later years, hired him to teach them how to do what he had offered decades earlier.

---

1 I wrote my resignation letter on a Thursday the day before my 34th birthday. Exactly, to the day, 34 years later, also on a Thursday, I wrote the first draft of this chapter. I left Ford, the job that launched my professional media career exactly half my lifetime ago. If you're familiar with my book on screenplay and story structure, *The Moral Premise*, leaving Ford was clearly my ",", the mid-point in a story where things change for the good for the protagonist.

As part of the documentary I wrote, produced and directed, I interviewed many personages around Ford, including chairman Donald Peterson, and Deming himself, who was still bitter over his earlier rejection by the Americans.

When we finished interviewing Peterson on the 12th floor of Ford World Headquarters, in the board's Greenroom, we reset for Dr. Deming who was to arrive shortly. The Greenroom, was a lounge for presenters to wait before they were called to present to the Board of Directors. We had taken it over as a make-shift interview studio. Deming was a tall man, somewhat hunched over with age and a middle that protruded from eating too much pie, his favorite food. His reasoning was logical: "Why should I eat things I don't like, when I'm so old and have so little time left. I want to enjoy my short time here. Pass me that lemon meringue will you?" This is not a fabricated story. I watched one day in the Ford cafeteria as he left the line only with a small salad, a glass of water, and two large pieces of lemon meringue pie on his tray.

When Deming entered the Greenroom I went over and introduced myself. He was gruff and not happy about having to do yet another television interview. To him it seemed he did a lot of talking and repeating of himself over and over, and few people understood or did what he suggested. He had been at this for 50-years and was tired of the process.

Nonetheless my sound guy fitted Dr. Deming with a microphone, threading the wire under his suit jacket. When he was done I directed the famous statistician to a chair. Now, the chair was one of those low-slung pieces of furniture that did nothing good for one's posture. I did not like it for on-camera interviews. I wanted a chair that had the person on camera sitting up straight. We had looked all over the 12th floor for something better that wasn't on casters or looked like a cheap folding chair with peeling paint. Nothing. Deming obviously had similar thoughts. He took one look at the chair and said, "I'm not sitting in that. It will be uncomfortable."

Oh, this is going to be fun. I finally persuaded him that it was the only chair we had, unless he wanted to sit on an apple box, which my cameraman was using.

So, he sat down and we rolled camera and sound. The single camera setup was full-on Deming who looked at me balancing on a half-apple box just next to the camera lens.

I started in. "Dr. Deming, thank you for being with us today. Would you outline for us the fundamental concept behind statistical process control and why it's so important for manufacturers like Ford to adopt?"

Deming paused for a moment, looked at me carefully, then into the camera lens, and then back to me, and said, "No, I would not. I've already told them. They just need to do it. Can't they understand what I told them the first time? They should read my books if they don't get it. I've said all I'm going to."

And that was essentially the end of the interview.

I tried a few more times, but after about 3 minutes I motioned to my crew to stop the recording and asked my sound man (Ed Wolfrum, who appears later in this book) to take Dr. Deming's microphone off. We were all a little stunned, having never met anyone quite so resistant, especially since we were there to promote him.

But I knew how important this man was. I had read his material and had a copy of his next book, an unpublished manuscript, in my briefcase sitting next to the door. I decided that I would ask for his autograph, at least, and try to show him some respect. As the sound man untangled Deming from the microphone cable, I walked to the door and my map-case, pulled out the manuscript to "Management of Statistical Techniques for Quality and Productivity" by W. Edwards Deming. As the man walked toward me and the door I held out the manuscript and a pen and asked for his autograph.

Deming stopped dead in his tracks, looked up at me and then down at the looseleaf copy of the 352 page manuscript I held. He took my pen and the manuscript, sat down in one of those low-slung chairs and signed the cover. His handwriting was clean, even, strong, and legible with a classic slant.

I took the manuscript form him, looked at the remarkable signature for a man who feasted regularly on lemon meringue and said, "Dr. Deming, your handwriting is as clear and strong as your statistical theories. Thank you very much for your time."

At that point I expected a nod from him and his quick departure. Instead, from his slightly bent over posture, he looked up to my face and said, "You know. I didn't give you very good answers to your questions. I'm sorry. I think I could do better. Do you have time to try again?"

My eyes popped wide open and the crew froze in their places. "Yes, of course, we have the time, Dr. Deming," I said.

And without a complaint, the famous statistician was rewired for sound, sat down in the low-slung chair that we tired to make look decent by zooming in and avoiding his protruding stomach, and he gave us a solid 40 minute interview that worked perfectly into our documentary about him.

I can still recall the opening shot where he looks at me (just off camera) and says, as if God was his judge, "It takes just as long to make a good part as it does to make a bad part. So why not make a good one?"

M Y COMPANY, FULL Circle Productions, went on to produce the first 13 interactive laser video disc training programs for Ford Service Technicians, as well as other successful and cutting-edge interactive projects for Ford, General Motors and Chrysler. One of the more intriguing projects we produced involved the very same video group I had interviewed with years ago in Indianapolis, when McDonnell Douglas tried to lay me off before I had even started. Indeed, as you will soon see, things came full circle.

60
Technological
Fallout

A S I TOUCHED on in the last chapter, my production company, Full Circle Productions (later Full Circle Communications), produced a variety of media for the big three automotive corporations. We were relatively small—at the most we employed 12 full-time staff plus six freelancers. These talented individuals were producers, directors, programmers, artists, coordinators, sales representatives and support staff. Our specialty was custom interactive laser disc projects with touch screen interfaces for use in auto dealerships, corporate offices, auto-shows, and world fairs.

One year, when there were only seven of us, we flew everyone to Florida for a three-day exploration of the touch screen systems at Disney's EPCOT. We stayed in a cheap hotel, but gathered valuable design information from the most successful public interactive displays at the time. The outcome of that effort resulted in a Vancouver World Fair project for General Motors, that ironically, two years later, ended-up back at the GM display at EPCOT in Florida.

In 1984 we were approached by Chrysler Corporation to create a bank of interactive touch screen video displays that would feature their new cars for the big auto shows in Detroit, New York, and Chicago. We had done this before for Ford and GM, so we didn't anticipate any issues with either the hardware or the videodisc software. But after our proposal was accepted and we set to work designing the application, Chrysler requested a change to the project that threw us for a loop.

Ben Bidwell had recently left Ford and was now Vice President of the Chrysler Automotive Sales division working for his old buddy, former Ford president, Lee Iacocca. This was at a time when foreign imports, particularly from Japan, were chewing up U.S. automotive companies as if they were snacks for Godzilla. Like Americans who verbally order "American Fries" in order to punish the French, Bidwell wanted to punish the Japanese. So, we were handed an edict from Ben Bidwell that there was to be *no Japanese hardware or software in the Chrysler automotive exhibits.*

I told our client, George, who worked for Bidwell, that I totally understood why the request had been made, but that it was impossible to fulfill. (Visions of WL asking me change the color of slides at 3:00 AM for a press conference at 9:00 AM, filled my head.) Both the key video-disc hardware and the laser discs themselves were all manufactured in Japan. Phillips in the Netherlands may have invented the technology, MCA may be marketing it, but everything was being manufactured in Japan.

"Ah, that's not true, Stan," George said. "Mr. Bidwell is on the Board of Directors of RCA and they have a Capacitance Electronic Disc System (CED). We can use that. The players and the discs were developed and are being manufactured right here in the United States by the RCA Video division *in Indianapolis.*"

Shivers ran down my spine, and my body must of spasmed.

"What's wrong?" George said. "You look faint."

He was right. I felt the blood drain from my face as a dozen strands of hair suddenly up-rooted in rebellion, fell past my blinking eyes, bounced off my nose and were sucked into my gasping mouth. I coughed.

There were two reasons I felt faint and was now wheezing. First, I knew something about the CED system. It was one of those inventions concocted out of corporate pride and lousy science. Some considered it an embarrassment to American innovation. Second, I just realized that the CED "technology" was a product of the same RCA division I had interviewed with years before just out of college and before I started with McDonnell Douglas. Had I been hired by RCA, I might have been working on the CED project much to my everlasting chagrin. Yet, here it was, a piece of technology that was dead on arrival... and I was being asked to prove its market viability.

"Yes, George," I answered. "I am faint. And you will be too if you force us to do this."

"Get over it," he said. "Bidwell won't have it any other way."

"There will be a cost," I said, pulling out my Change Order Pad embossed in gold relief with dollar signs. "The CED discs are vinyl with a *physical* pickup device that actually rests on the disc like an old long play vinyl record's needle. They may be good for Pavarotti and Olivia Newton-John concerts[1] where they play like linear videotape. But they're useless for interactive projects because the stylus can't sit on a frame for very long without wearing out the groove."

"Yeah, yeah. I get that," George said. "Well, do what you have to, but be sure the computer and the keypad are made in the U.S. as well. And RCA disagrees with you. They guarantee that what you claim will not happen. They've been testing it for months. And of course you can't use Sony monitors. Use RCA TVs."

I cringed again. Video exhibits used discrete video level signals routed through dedicated coaxial cables to avoid electromagnetic interference. Televisions required video feeds via VHF converters tuned to a local unused channel on the VHF band and were susceptible to all kinds of radio noise. I didn't have a solution for the TV issue, but perhaps I did for a U.S. built computer.

As Providence would have it, Full Circle was a partner in a computer store that sold KayPro II portable computers. This was the precursor to the modern laptops and the PC competitor to the Apple II. The KayPro was an American made personal computer that weighed in at 29-pounds in its blue and gray metal box, the size of a small portable sewing machine, with a handle on top...thus it was deemed portable. I also had on staff two very technically astute electronic wizards. One was a programmer and the other a hardware guru who could hook up any fancy electronic device and make it work with another. We also found an American-made flat, numeric keypad for the visitor interface that could be mounted elegantly on the display.

The six systems were installed in a plywood and laminate display constructed by Chrysler's exhibit company, and made ready for the VIP reception at the International Detroit Auto Show. But we knew something was amiss when we got the shipment of CED discs from RCA.

Normally, on a *laser* videodisc, the menu that was displayed for the visitor was a video still frame. There were 30 of these frames in

---

1 The double irony of this was that one of the first CED demo discs, which sits on my desk as I write this, featured her hit single *Physical*. ("Let's get physical....") And that was the problem with the CED videodiscs...they required the player to get physical with the disc.

every second of video. As the disc spun at 1,800 rpm a red laser beam was reflected off oblong indentations (representing the video and audio) in one of 54,000 tracks on the shiny polycarbonate plastic. You could program the player to find any particular frame by number (e.g. 34,553) and the player would find that one frame in a second or two, decode the laser signal, and display the image at broadcast quality all day without damaging the disc. Because of its indestructible nature we would order just a few extra videodiscs, for souvenirs more than for anything else. So, when we ordered the CED discs for the display of 6 screens, we ordered 10 discs.

When the shipment of discs arrived from the Indianapolis factory there were 35 discs in the box. *What are all these for, I wondered?* But, I should have known.

That year at the auto show we had systems installed at both the Cadillac and the Chrysler exhibits. The Cadillac exhibit used Sony laser videodiscs, and the Chrysler exhibit used the six RCA CED videodisc players. We set up everything the morning of the Friday evening VIP reception. George kept a watchful eye on us during the setup. He and I both knew that Ben Bidwell and Lee Iacocca were going to show up about 6 PM to view the exhibits of cars and our information stations before the show opened at 7 PM for the black tie event. When everything was working to George's satisfaction, we left about 1:30 PM, and went back to our Dearborn offices, about 30-minutes from Detroit's Cobo Convention Center where the International Autoshow was staged.

At precisely 5:07 PM I got a frantic call from George. He sounded like he was in the middle of a cardiac arrest…deep breathing…and stuttering, incoherent speech. Through the phone, I could almost feel the spray of sweat off his brow.

"Stan! Stan! ALL THE SCREENS ARE BLACK! NOTHING'S WORKING. I MEAN EVERYTHING IS…IS…NOT WORKING. We cycled the power like you told us to, and like you showed us the systems should reboot and come up, but they don't. They make some noise and all. But…Oh, my God! Ben Bidwell and Lee Iacocca will be here in less than an hour. Please come down and fix this."

Indeed! Pray as hard as we wanted, God was not about to upset Natural Law for Chrysler. As my friend Dan Glovak told his daughter, Christin, and my son, Josh, when they started to date, "You guys can make any choice you want. Just remember. You have no choice over the consequences of your choices." Dan's reference was to Natural Law, and the adage applied fully to Chrysler and their choice to use CED.

In George's case, I knew exactly what had happened. And that is why I had stored the extra CED videodiscs in a cupboard at the exhibit. When I got there I didn't even bother looking at the blackened screens. I went to the cupboard, unlocked it, retrieved six new CED discs and then walked to the display where George met me. It as about 5:55 PM. I looked around for Bidwell and Iacocca but their entourage had not yet arrived.

I handed George the new discs, and told him to take out the existing discs, put in the new ones and see what happened. I let him do it because I knew he was going to have to do this two or three times a day during the run of the show. He did as I asked, and behold, the menus came back up as they were supposed to.

"What happened?" he said, holding the used discs in his hand.

"The menus wore off just as we predicted. Every few hours throughout the run of the show you're going to have to replace the discs in every machine. I'll call RCA and tell them to send a few dozen more. Collect the bad ones, and at the end of the show ship them back to RCA with a demand for your money back."

RCA, indeed, sent more videodiscs for George to change out during the rest of the show.

Before the Detroit show was over, George told us to refit everything with Sony laser discs and players for New York. But, we would need at least two weeks turnaround for manufacturing of the discs in Japan and the New York show was only a week away. So, the Chrysler interactive disc exhibit skipped the New York show and we refitted the entire exhibit out for Chicago (a month later) with laser disc. All went well.

Six weeks later RCA held a news conference and announced that they were exiting the videodisc business. The CED system was officially defunct. I breathed a sigh of relief. But I kept a few of the concert discs and the Chrysler Auto Show CED disc as mementos, inclining Olivia Newton-John's *Physical*.

MY EARLY FORTIES brought on a mid-life crisis. Full Circle, for a creative services production company, had a successful run. We were doing well over a million dollars in business a year with 12 employees. But, the investment in one-off, highly-customized, and expensive hardware and software systems that were obsolete in less than a year, had little financial return. That, and a failed investment in the computer store (mentioned in the last section) put

Full Circle in a cash strapped situation.

But what finally did us in was the Tax Reform Act of 1986 signed by Ronald Reagan. While the simplification of the tax code and the reduction of overall income taxes was good for the economy, we were hit hard. No longer would the interest on auto loans be tax deductible. That was one of the tax loopholes closed by the law that contributed to a $55 billion increase in revenue for the Federal government. But overnight we saw 60% of our business disappear. Our biggest regular client at the time was Ford Credit, the company that financed Ford car purchases. They saw their business shrinking dramatically and reasonably they cut back expenses. One of the things they cut was the production of interactive laser videodisc training for their 154 Ford Credit branch offices, which we had been producing. That and an overall recession forced me to close down Full Circle.

For me, it was a difficult time emotionally and financially. I spent hours praying for wisdom and direction. Did I hear from God? I'm not sure. I hated myself for not being more of a businessman and finding work to replace the lost contracts. The last thing I wanted to do was layoff my employees. So, I kept putting it off to the point that when I did layoff my friends I was unable to provide any severance benefits. My attorney told me I was under no legal obligation to pay severance in the State of Michigan, but I felt bad then, and guilt still haunts me. Being accountable for other people's lives in that way was difficult. I never felt I had the capacity or intelligence to establish a business robust enough to guarantee security. Since then, I've tried to avoid the ironic predicament of being successful to the point of having employees.

Ross ROY COMMUNICATIONS (an ad agency) offered me a job as the VP and Creative Director over all Chrysler Dealership interactive training. It was a short-term affair and I take pride that our team of very inventive and smart people accomplished some great things in those 18 months. But Ross Roy Communications was at heart an ad agency and did not have the mentality or patience to be a training company. When the company could not find someone to take the helm of the sales side of the training business, there was a reorganization. The training experiment was disbanded, my 30 plus staff was folded back into the ad agency structure. While the money was good and the projects challenging, I had grown weary of daily conference meetings led by cussing account executives who managed by intimidation. I was happy to leave.

I settled down poorer but more content as a freelance producer-director-writer. The timing was great, too, because it allowed me a flexible schedule to shag basketballs for Josh, my *up* and coming high school standout. And he stood out…at 6'10". During those freelance summers I never missed one of his games, regardless of the time of day, and I was able to travel with him to tournaments around the country with one of his two AAU teams. He was heavily recruited by universities, and I was thrilled when he chose the United States Naval Academy from which he graduated in 1999. (This is the place in my writing where I stop and thank all U.S. taxpayers for my son's college education. THANK YOU!)

AFTER FOUR AND a half years of freelance, and shagging balls for Josh, Sandy Corporation, one of my clients, asked me to join their agency as a Director of Operations for their client Harley-Davidson.

Harley had recently been bought from Brunswick by several officers of the company. They wanted to take the company public, but to do so required that their dealer network install cement floors in their service departments. That may sound like a joke, but it wasn't. Harley owners and the dealers were very proud to first be "riders" and "wrenches"[1] and only secondarily dealers and salespersons.

Sandy Corporation had made its mark as a business process improvement company. It would go into a corporation, find management and operation inefficiencies, and then implement interventions to turn the company around by improving customer satisfaction. So, Harley came to Sandy and said, what should we be doing?

After a year of poking around Harley's dealer network, Sandy recommended establishing what they called Harley-Davidson University, Dealer Operations Training (HDU-DOT). It was an annual business training conference for dealers and their department managers. After several successful years of operating the training event, I was hired to take over the year-long preparation of courses. We hired the best business and motivational experts and speakers we could find, prepared custom course materials and then hosted conferences in the winter at sunny locations in the southern states. Thousands of dealers, spouses and staff came from across North America.

Pam joined me on some HDU-DOT trips to places like Ft. Lau-

---

1 wrenches = mechanics and customizers

derdale, and to HOG[1] Rallies in places like South Dakota's badlands. We enjoyed being around the bikers who, for the most part, were attorneys, doctors, accountants and a few pastors, who dressed up like bad-guys out of the wild west. But we never rode bikes. I liked to say my brain was more valuable to Harley inside my head.

During my tenure on the project, I enjoyed meeting dealers and their managers from around the world, and even traveled to England to support the launch of Europe DOT. The long-term plan was for Sandy to run the DOT Conference for ten years and then hand it over to Harley's in-house training department. So, I inherited a wonderful job for six years, working with very smart people at both Sandy and Harley until Harley transitioned DOT into their corporate structure.

After Harley, I was chomping at the bit to be on my own again and head west...figuratively at least, since Pam wasn't going anywhere near California.

---

1 Harley Owner Groups

61
Masculine
Holiness

MY CAREER WAS coming to a dead end. I had done just about everything in the world of corporate media. I had produced hundreds of high-end and low-budget projects, won my share of regional and international awards, and held respectable positions at major corporations and agencies. But, by the time I had produced my sixth training video on *"How to Sell a Vehicle Lease to the Rich and Famous,"* I knew there was something better to do with my life.

When I shared my boredom with close friends and associates, a few suggested I go west and make feature films in Hollywood. But, I knew that making feature films was a world away from my corporate experience. I had a few distant acquaintances in the industry, had visited a few movie sets, and I had read a number of books about the business and creative challenges within the film industry. So, I knew enough to know that I didn't know enough.

But my motivation to make something out of nothing was driving me to produce something…as long as it wasn't nothing. I greatly appreciated the grand effort in the multitude of disciplines that came together to develop, fund, produce, edit and distribute a motion picture. When I was freelancing I usually had a few days between corporate jobs. So, I decided to write a book on a topic that had bothered me for some years—women. Or, more precisely, the role of men and their relationship with women. Still not sure what it was about? Well, that was sort of the nexus of my problem.

From my perspective, men did not pursue spiritual relationships the way women did. Recalling the many prayer meetings into the night I had attended with my family, most of the people in such meetings were women. I also noticed that on the bulletin boards at church where the names and pictures of missionaries appeared, there were easily three times more women than there were men. I would think often of my grandmother, Edith Willobee, starting churches in the middle of India, without the companionship of a husband. And, the current missionaries running the Wesleyan mission were two American women.

> **By the time I had produced my sixth training video on "How to Sell a Vehicle Lease to the Rich and Famous," I knew there was something better to do with my life.**

Even outside of the church there was this seemingly natural difference between men and women in terms of how they related to others. Women loved to get together and chatter, sew, cook, and shop…whatever it was, *as long as*, they did it with someone else. Men don't like to go shopping with their wives. I don't at least. Why? Because to a guy "shopping" means you go to the store, buy something, and get out. Women? Sure they buy stuff, but only after fingering everything in the store and holding it up to a mirror to see what it looks like. Can you imagine a man picking up a new hammer in a hardware store and standing in front of a mirror to see what it looks like as he swings it up and down, left and right, and maybe tries to holster it in his belt?

Of course, the reason women do all that primping is because they can ask the person with them, "What ja think? Is it me?" Men, when they get together don't chat, they grunt, or find trees that need watering at strange hours of the night. I can prove this.

ONCE, WHEN I was in Munich, Germany on a business trip, I visited a beer house during Oktoberfest. I don't drink beer, but friends told me that I should visit one of the beer halls or tents. So I did.

The large hall was packed with long tables and benches occupied by men and women who toasted each other with large mugs of gold brew, sang boisterous songs accompanied by a polka band, and enjoyed the kind of camaraderie that only inebriation allows. Young busty waitresses juggled an impossible number of overflowing tankards above their heads before arriving at the end of a table and shoving the steins down the wood planks to outstretched thirsty hands, like frothing jets landing on the deck of an aircraft carrier. Spilled beer was everywhere—on tables, on floors, benches, bibs and britches. The fragrant mix of warm hops and the musk of perspiration assaulted the senses. Standing near the entrance I marveled at the spectacle, but soon felt myself getting tipsy…without a drop of suds even grazing my tongue. Time to leave.

While inside, men and women sat together as one throng, outside, the differences were less egalitarian. Exiting the front door I turned right, then right again, when suddenly my eyes and nose were ambushed by a caustic stench. Carefully opening one eye to investigate the pungent odor's origin, I saw 30 or 40 men, lined up, facing the side of the building. They stood elbow-to-elbow like wobbling ducks in a shooting gallery. Their legs were spread, their heads down gazing at their…ah, feet, as they discharged what the waitresses inside had just served them. At the base of the building, running all along the side, was a galvanized metal gutter that carried the amber liquid away…but not before enough was atomized to saturate the air inhaled by every passer-by. The color of what was served inside and what was collected outside was identical. Only the nose knew the difference.

When I turned to go, my eyes caught a line of ladies nearby winding into a modest building. They chatted amicably among themselves, without anything untoward in their demeanor or behavior. Some minutes later, as I reversed directions to return to my hotel, I realized the women were waiting patiently to use a loo concealed inside the building.

I glanced back at the men's lack of dignity, even as they grunted and shoved for position over the gutter. Clearly, you would find no women standing anywhere close to those upstanding male citizens, not even a radical feminist who might fancy a urinal.

S OMETIMES NATURE HAD to yell to get my attention. The differences in behavior between the men and the women at Munich's Oktoberfest reminded me of Flannery O'Connor's oft quoted axiom for writers, *"To the hard of hearing you shout, and for the almost-blind you draw large startling figures."*[1]

The German men and women that day made it clear to me that

---

1 O'Connor, Flannery (1957). *Mystery and Manners.* Farrar, Straus & Giroux, New York, p. 34.

men could learn a few things from women, although, I frequently wished for the opposite—that Pam would think and act more like a man...in some ways. Rather than preach to the opposite sex about why they should be more like *men*, which was probably my real motivation, I thought I would be clever and write about something I knew—the foibles of my kind.

Then my genius really broke out. To further camouflage my intentions I would hide behind a cloak of spirituality, and ask, "Why could not men be more spiritually and relationally minded...like women?" As fodder I would draw on my experiences growing up in communities where women wore the spiritual pants.

So, the title of the book I intended to write became, *Masculine Holiness: Why Can't a Man Be More Like a Woman?* Can you imagine me pitching that title to a *Christian* publisher in today's gender-confused society?

My proposal did garner some interest and several publishers requested sample chapters and a chapter outline. The acquisition editor at Zondervan Publishing was Lyn Cryderman, a Free Methodist, and the son of one of the FM bishops. I had known Lyn somewhat, growing up, so he was kind enough to offer me some extended advice in a two-page letter that accompanied the rejection that I clearly deserved.

> *I resonate with much of what you had to say. In fact,*
> *I believe I could identify just about everyone you*
> *mentioned....However, the approach you've taken is a*
> *difficult one for an author who is somewhat new and*
> *unknown to a particular market.*[1]

Lyn offered many helpful suggestions for focusing the book's topic and treatment, and how to avoid the political suicide I was inviting by suggesting that men would be better off if they were more like women.

But what Lyn was really getting at was my need for *credentials*...so that readers would consider me an expert on the topic. He had mentioned that Zondervan's marketing department made the final decision on what books to publish. I recalled the bios of authors I use to read on the back of books at Dennis Stacey's Bible bookstore, and I cringed. Is that what I would have to do? Get a degree from some obscure Bible university and fake my education? *Sigh!* Lyn was right. Who would read such a tome on Masculine Holiness from someone like me, an

---

1 Lyn Cryderman, personal letter, September 10, 1992.

expert at transmission repair and automotive sales training? Certainly not me.

For days I stared at the open Masculine Holiness file drawer. Finally, but with a clearer vision, I filed the rejection letters, and closed the file drawer. It has remained closed until this day except to retrieve Lyn's letter.

K EEPING UP WITH my proclivity to avoid walking, I ran off in another direction—graduate school. Twelve years earlier I had earned a Master's Degree in Communications to help my credibility at Ford. Perhaps, now I needed a more advanced degree, something more sophisticated and intellectual to give me some credentials, which would help an "unknown" like me pitch and sell a book.

Except for a couple of courses in Physics, the only "A" I earned in college other than *Tennis*, was from Royal Mulholland for his *Introduction to Philosophy*. Royal had also kindly stood up in my wedding, so I phoned him and asked him what he thought about me earning my PhD in philosophy. I figured philosophy might be a good *generalist* degree that would apply in any number of fields of labor. No doubt, it would improve my thinking and credibility. For instance, if I had my Ph.D. in Philosophy I could persuade my automotive service clients to design a videodisc on Immanuel Kant's doctrine of transcendental idealism and teach technicians how to *intuit the metaphysical time continuum* of broken transmissions.

When I called, Mulholland was very generous with his time.

ME: Was I capable of such a degree?
    MULHOLLAND: No doubt. But you'd have to take a number of undergraduate credits before they'd let you into the PhD program. I think you only had two at Greenville.

ME: Would it help me?
    MULHOLLAND: That depends. I'm not sure how much Kant can add to the Zen of Motorcycle maintenance. But it'd make you a better thinker. Philosophy involves a lot of formal logic and stuff like that.

ME: What would I do with it?
    MULHOLLAND: You could teach or preach, but that's about it. Playboy has heard of you by now and they don't need a philosopher as a doorman.

Then without my asking, he offered up this spontaneous advice, which coming from an Evangelical was memorable:

> MULHOLLAND: *Wherever you go, if you do your work in philosophy, be sure it's a Catholic University, like St. Louis University, or Notre Dame. Catholics are the only ones that really understand philosophy in a Christian sense.*[1]

> **The Catholics are the only ones that really understand philosophy in a Christian sense.**

I began calling around to local universities, St Louis and South Bend were too far away. The more I called, however, the more I discovered that the number of undergraduate courses required was beyond my expectations and perhaps my capability. Maybe there was another major that would make more sense.

---

1 Royal Mulholland, personal communication, 1992.

62 Hollywood Calling

ABOUT THAT SAME time, I was hired, by one of my former employees, Paul Gustafson, as a freelance director to co-write and shoot a Chrysler documentary in Los Angeles. Paul was a Christian. When we got to L.A. he suggested we take an evening to join a gathering of Christians in Hollywood who worked in the film industry and met monthly for dinner and a talk. Would I like to go with him? It sounded interesting, so I agreed.

The Intermission Fellowship was a ministry founded by the late David Shaw under the sponsorship of the Hollywood Presbyterian Church. I expected to walk into a room of perhaps 30-50 people for dinner, light conversation and no doubt a Bible study. But my expectations were misplaced.

The Hollywood Presbyterian ministry to the Hollywood community was then, and continues to this day, to be wide and deep. Located just a block North and East of Hollywood Blvd and Vine St (the legendary center of Hollywood's downtown district), the church's campus includes three equity theaters that regularly receive excellent reviews from the secular trades. Their Henrietta Mears Center is a small conference center with a stage and dining facilities.

Our first night in L.A., after scouting locations and making arrangements for crew and equipment for the next day's shoot, Paul and I walked into the Mears Center and were shocked to be part of over 500 Hollywood professionals who had gathered for dinner and a talk by Glenn Keane, a chief animator for Disney on projects like *Beauty and the Beast, The Little Mermaid, and Aladdin.* (Glenn is the son of Bil Keane,[1] creator of the long-running, *The Family Circus* comic strip.)

Glenn's talk that night included clips from his films and how he had incorporated visual metaphors of Christian concepts in the animation of some of his characters. More importantly, he told the story about when he became a Christian he thought he should leave secular, evil Hollywood and become a preacher or a pastor. Luckily, some mature Christians persuaded him that he was needed as salt and light in the industry where he was at…and, that he could do much more good in his chosen field of work where he was revered by the entire industry and had a voice and a position that could reach millions.

Tears came to my eyes that night. I had been aware that there were a few Christians in the film industry, but I had no idea they could fill a room the size of the Mears Center. After Glenn's talk, the group stayed after to network. I found out that the attendees that night were only a small percentage of the many others God had called to work in an industry that had such a significant influence on culture.

Before we left I was careful to take a collection of brochures and flyers from the literature table that described a dozen different Christian organizations that worked to support the faithful in the industry.

I was shocked.

I pulled out a lime-green business card that I carried with me. It had a message on both sides that I had written years earlier. With tears in my eyes I read it again quietly to myself. In my travels, when I met another Christian who had interest in being salt and light to culture, I would give them this little card to prompt their prayers and involvement. Here's what's on the card, which to this day I carry with me.

Side One.

> *Consider a career as a* **Cultural Influencer.**
> *As a* **Christian** *you can light some candles in the darkness of our society. Prepare for a career in secular media or entertainment. Then, as you excel and gain recognition, use your influence to impart Biblical Christian values to the world. (over)*

Side Two

> *Pray for the* **Christians** *attempting to influence our society with Biblical values and ideas through their vocations in* **Television, Film, Art, Entertainment, Literature,**

---

1 "Bil" dropped one of the "L's" in his name to be distinctive.

Journalism, Education, Academe, Professional Sports and Politics. *God has called these individuals and gifted them* **like Bezalel** *(Exodus 31, 25, 36) to be Salt and Light in our culture. (over)*

I stood on the little mezzanine overlooking the banquet floor watching the mass of Christians in the heart of Hollywood, meeting and fellowshipping with each other. I had been praying for Christians in Hollywood for many years, but I had no idea there were so many. I felt overwhelmed by God's grace. My prayers had not gone unheard.

Traveling back from Los Angeles I thought more about the film industry and the Christians that were there as missionaries to give witness to the Truth. They were clearly lighting candles in a dark place. Was it possible to take the nascent call I had back in college and minister to the film industry in a way that extolled the truth like a missionary might to a heathen culture on an isolated island? I wasn't sure.

Back at Highland Park Baptist, I shared my vision of being a missionary to Hollywood with our missions pastor, retired missionary, Dr. Frank Allen. Frank had come to the Christian faith through the ministry of HPBC as young man, had served for decades in the Philippines and Asia as a missionary, and then retired back to HPBC as a pastor. He was a gifted preacher and had a compassionate heart. After church one Sunday soon after my return from Los Angeles, I shared my enthusiasm for the work as a missionary to the film industry. Rev. Allen looked at me stern faced, and simply said, "Get a life, Stan!"

He meant it as a stern rebuke. But I took it as a calling. Was I being called to "get a life" in Hollywood or to the film industry at large? Being a missionary to Hollywood certainly sounded sacrilegious to many in Evangelical Christianity, especially to those ignorant of the impact that art has on morality within society. But just how would I actually go about being a missionary to Hollywood? I had prayed for people in Hollywood for 25 years, never expecting I'd have any direct connection. Things were about to change.

63
Graduate
Research

F INALLY, THE PARTS of the puzzle came together—my love of stories and producing media, my boredom with making industrial
and corporate documentaries, Lyn Cryderman's implication
that I needed letters after my name, and my exposure to Hollywood
through Intermission...all led me to Wayne State University (WSU) in
Detroit, a half-hour drive from my home.

WSU was a well-respected research school located on a beautiful
campus in the middle of a downcast city. Because of my work experience in media and my earned Masters of Arts from Eastern Michigan
University, WSU graduate school admitted me on academic probation.
If I received a B+ or better in my first ten hours of WSU coursework, I'd
be accepted as a doctoral candidate. On May 11, 1993 I started classes
in the Film Studies Program of the Department of Communications.

On the surface, I went back to school in order to prepare me to
produce feature films, ostensibly in Hollywood. But there was a deeper
and more profound reason for working on an advanced degree. I had
a desire to bring intellectual integrity to the defense of Christianity
in an increasingly anti-Christian, self-centered culture. I had long argued that Christians needed to be more involved in public education
and not be cloistered away in the ghettos of private Christian schools.
Christians too often are non-factors in society, believing, falsely, that
their disdain and avoidance of culture is a virtue that will repress culture. But in fact, it's the avoidance of culture by Christians, it's their
refusal to be salt and light *in* culture, that allows evil to ferment. Where

light is absent, dark fills the void.

Thus, I felt at home at a secular university where my Christian witness would be sharpened through interaction with skeptics and agnostics. Although there was one type of person I did try to avoid, and luckily I only had one run-in with during my four years on campus. My avoidance of these folk was not without effort, and one time it came too close.

T HE WSU CAMPUS is in the heart of downtown Detroit, which is not the safest city in the world. As such, blanketing the manicured campus are 297 Emergency Telephones, 176 of these have an iridescent Blue Light mounted above their outdoor locations. Just the presence of these phones warn you of potential danger, especially at night.

One night after pursuing research in the graduate library, I left the building just as it closed at 11 PM. Ahead of me was a ten-minute walk across campus to a parking garage. The campus was usually void of people at such a time—there were no nightspots or hangouts. But there were strays like me who made beelines for their cars. I stepped off the library's portico, down a few steps, and walked swiftly across a stone plaza named Williams Mall. Still a bit paranoid from my junior high days when "Maul Williams" was a battle cry, I was always a bit squeamish leaving the library and entering the plaza.

That night, I had taken only a dozen steps when my eye caught the image of a young man in the shadows who was not making a beeline in any direction. Sure enough, he tried to flag me down.

"Hey, mister! Can you help me out?"

I turned only slightly to keep him in view, but I kept walking, sure not to slow my pace or change direction, which was away from him. "Yeah, What?" I yelled back at him.

"My car is broke down," he yelled back.

Grammar can be another hint that you need to walk faster.

Now, I have to pause here to relate a couple things. First, the main WSU campus is rectangular in shape about 1/3 mile x 3/4 mile in dimension. Except for service vehicles there are no cars on campus. Williams Mall is pretty much in the center of campus, and classroom buildings surround it, so there would be no cars (broken down or otherwise) for some distance.

I glanced at the guy, and realized that if his car "is broke down" he wouldn't be standing in the middle of a dark, vacant campus looking for help. I kept walking...away from him.

But he persisted, yelling after me, "My battery died or something over on Van Dyke. Can you give me a jump?"

The one thing about crooks is they are usually not very smart. They don't really think things through. First, it must have been obvious (to him) that I was not carrying jumper cables. Second, Van Dyke is a road that leads out of Detroit, but from Williams Mall its closest approach was a good four miles away.

Saying nothing, I picked up my pace and never let his shadow out of my sight.

But he persisted, vocally at least, for he was now standing still, too lazy to chase after me. He yelled across the increasing distance that separated us, "HEY! C'MON. I'M NOT A CROOK!"

That explained everything. I kept walking, keeping close to the blue light specials illuminating the walkways.

As I entered my car I said "Thanks!" to my Guardian Angel.

I DIDN'T AVOID OTHER students or faculty, but I was usually hesitant to enter into religious conversations with atheists, who I found irrational and polemic. By definition, atheism claims (omnisciently) that God does not exist. They know this (they "think") because their awareness and knowledge of the universe is "unlimited." (Can they be thinking anything else?) They practice an extreme variation of *arguing from ignorance*, a common fallacy. But I digress, somewhat.

One reason I went back to school was to become a better thinker and writer, and thus improve my ability to give witness to the Gospel. I believed that Christianity had intellectual integrity, but I felt inferior to the task of *proving* it. I should correct that last sentence. Dr. Larry Miller, a professor on my committee, was fond of scolding me, "Stan, you can't *prove* anything. All you can do is bring evidence to bear on the argument."

I am forever indebted to my chairperson for my attempt in confronting culture intellectually. Dr. Jackie Byars was a film scholar whose research examined the intersection of gender and culture. Her well-regarded book on film criticism, *All That Hollywood Allows*, examined how gender roles were depicted in motion picture melodramas of the 1950s.

Jackie referred to herself as a *feminist*. To me—a mostly cloistered Evangelical Christian—discovering that one of my key professors was a feminist was, at first, off-putting. For years, Christians from Evangelical and Fundamentalist camps had belittled feminist thinking as a rejection of God's moral will.

But I soon realized there were different kinds of feminists. In a general sense, feminism deals with the equality of the sexes and the appropriate social gender roles for women versus men. There were the *radical* feminists that thought women should be using men's urinals. There were *moderate* feminists who sought equality with men politically and economically. And there were *liberated* feminists who accentuated their femininity as a means of emancipation from male dominance and even as a way to win control over their male counterparts.

I came to realize that not only was my grandmother, Edith Willobee, a moderate feminist, but that I, too, was a feminist of sorts. I saw women as different, distinctive, but of equal importance to men. Then, it occurred to me that Jesus Christ was very much the same kind of feminist.

So, I wrote a heavily footnoted, 7,500 word essay for Dr. Byars' class in Feminist Film Criticism titled *Male Representation in anti-essentialist, Post-structural Feminism and Classical Biblical-Christianity: An examination of how the portrayal of gender roles in episodic television constructs gender egalitarian culture norms and traits that has its roots in Biblical Christianity.*[1] (It was my ability to come up with titles like that that earned me a Ph.D.) The paper compares and contrasts the feminism in episodic television programs like *Home Improvement* and *Joe's Life,* with Biblical teachings on gender roles…or at least how I interpreted the Bible on the subject.

Writing this paper within a secular academic environment was a milestone in my journey of faith. I was forced to realize that there was a difference between what Christian doctrine taught and what Christians often did. Christians often have a hard time defending Christianity against those that would ridicule it because some Christians act hypocritical, or, in fact, may be CINO's (Christian In Name Only). Skeptics love to attack such inconsistencies as if the *lives* of the people define the *teachings* of the faith.

The paper forced me to define "Biblical Christianity" and declare what I had often felt growing up in the American Christian church but had never articulated.

> *Classical Biblical Christianity refers to what is taught by the Bible as the ideal, and not what is accepted or tolerated by*

---

1 Essay by the author, December 9, 1993.

the contemporary "Christian" church and culture.

*Christian thought, like feminist thought, cannot be judged
on the basis of how well it is lived out by its practitioners.
Christian doctrine...is not what "Christians" may actually
do, but rather what the Bible teaches Christians ought to do.
This unfortunate dichotomy includes even male ministers
who are guilty of the male domination and abuse of women
which feminism so rightly seeks to rectify.[1]*

In support of my personal observation, I cited part of a letter from
Lyn Cryderman, the senior acquisitions editor at Zondervan Publishing who, in his rejection letter to *Masculine Holiness,* wrote:

*Even with the clear and sensible teaching on male headship,
men just don't get it. I could mention the names of many
pastors' wives who you know who have been beaten into
submission with the Ephesians and Timothy passages being
used for ammunition. For some reason, no matter how we
say it, the typical evangelical (read: conservative Christian)
male views headship as an excuse to treat his wife in a
manner that is un-Christian.[2]*

Expressing this kind of thinking in a paper to be judged by a secular university professor, who was admittedly liberal in her political
and moral thinking, forced me to look beyond the behavior of those
that raised me to what the Christian faith actually taught.

Of course, the problem I still faced was that I still didn't know exactly what the faith was supposed to teach. It's been said that *you could
prove anything with the Bible,* and clearly, it seemed, each different
Christian denomination was out to prove (or give evidence for) that
adage. This gave credence to the skeptic's claim of hypocrisy within
Christianity, since an absolute definition of Christian teaching was
necessary to universally claim someone wasn't living a Christian life.
In such a situation, which denomination was right?

Some denominations saw nothing wrong with smoking or drinking
alcoholic beverages; others, like Free Methodism, claimed smoking
and drinking were sins. Some fundamentalist sects even decried recreational activities on Sunday as participating in worldly activities and

---

1 Male Representation...essay by the author, December 9, 1993.
2 Lyn Cryderman, personal letter, September 10, 1992.

demanded that Sundays be reserved for reading the Bible and prayer.

In the other direction, the Evangelical Lutheran Church in America and the United Church of Christ are pro-abortion and sponsor hospitals in the Chicago area that not only allow abortions but offer a "Comfort Room" where the parents can hold the baby until it dies. The Comfort Rooms are equipped with…

> …a First Foto machine if parents want professional pictures of their aborted baby, baptismal supplies, gowns, and certificates, foot printing equipment and baby bracelets for mementos, and a rocking chair. Before the Comfort Room was established, babies were taken to the Soiled Utility Room to die.[1]

With such wide spread differences in belief, it was impossible for me to know what was right. But for Dr. Byars' paper I assumed I did know, and I worried that she would challenge me and point out that I could not be so sure that there was such a thing as "Classical Biblical Christianity" since such a definition didn't seem to exist.

But Dr. Byars never challenged my tenuous logic and gave me an "A" for the paper and an "A" for the course. She commented at the end of the paper, "You're doing a good job integrating the ideas covered in class into your personal philosophy and vice versa." While I appreciated the mark and her gracious comment, I wasn't sure she was right.

D URING MY GRADUATE studies I made a friend in Dave Strubler, a Christian businessman working on his doctorate in business communications and organizational development. One day Dave walked into the office of communications professor Dr. Bernard L. Brock (1935-2006) to ask a question about an assignment. Among the stack of books and papers David carried was a copy or Christianity Today. Brock spied the periodical and asked David, "What's that, Christianity Today?"

Somewhat taken off guard, David answered, "Oh, it's like a…ah, Christian intellectual journal."

Brock laughed, "That's an oxymoron, isn't it? Christian intellectual?"

In telling me the story later, David was disheartened at Brock's opinion of Christianity in general. But then I reminded David of our shared vision and why, in part, we had both decided to earn our doc-

---

1 *The Testimony of Jill Stanek, R.N.* (1999) in reference to Christ Hospital in Oak Lawn Illinois. On-Line: www.priestsforlife.org/brochures/deathindeliveryroom.htm

torates in communications. Christians had earned the reputation of defending their faith based on *ideological opinions and not rational*

> **Christians had earned the reputation of defending their faith based on ideological opinions and not rational evidence.**

evidence. We both knew that Christianity was based on faith and reason. We welcomed debate and rational, intelligent arguments.

Ironically and unfortunately, however, we never engaged Brock, who was the university's debate coach, about our faith. Perhaps the reason we avoided Brock was that at the outset of our studies, neither of us had been fully prepared to defend the faith. And who knows how prepared we'd be by the time we were done. Yet, we both believed, that the intellectual effort expended during the journey would better prepare us to not only defend the faith but also showcase the robust nature of Christianity's character.

A S MY ACADEMIC work continued, it came time to write a prospectus, and propose a research question for my dissertation. It had to be an effort that would provide new knowledge to my chosen discipline. In preparation I read dozens of books, and collected a file-drawer full of film criticism. My curiosity was piqued by one of the more famous questions in the film business: "How does a movie connect at the box office?" or "What are the most significant factors that contribute to a movie's popularity and success?"

Famous screenwriter and author William Goldman in his ever-popular book *Adventures in the Screen Trade*, claims "NOBODY KNOWS ANYTHING." Twice he sets the phrase in all caps on lines of their own. He writes "not one person in the entire motion picture field knows for a certainty what's going to work [at the box office]. Every time out it's a guess—and, if you're lucky, an educated one."[1] But, by driving around Beverly Hills, California, and gaping at the mansions that line the streets, it was clear to me that someone knew something, and not just occasionally. How else could the luxurious life styles of even the not so famous be explained?

The common answers to a movie's box office success were many. If you asked Hollywood executives, one big reason was the presence of recognizable names on the marquee, like an A-list actor or director. Another reason was the adaption of an already successful underlying

1 Goldman, William (1983). *Adventures in the Screen Trade*. Warner Books, p 39.

property, like a best selling novel or play. But "getting the film made" (attaching big names to attract investor dollars), and having the audience "make the film" (selling tickets to pay back investors) were two entirely different issues. There were plenty of movies with attached A-list actors or directors or that were based on a successful novel, or play that had miserably failed.

The box office secret offered at the time by Christian pundits was that the more family friendly a movie was, the more money it made. Thus, numbers were cited that claimed to prove that "G" rated movies made more money than "PG" rated movies, which make more money than "PG-13" movies, which made more than "R" rated motion pictures. That made sense to me, especially since the information came from what I considered trustworthy sources.

Preparation for the prospectus forced me to do a lot of reading that centered on the factors that might be predictive of a movie's box office success. When I examined the details in the box office data and compared it to MPAA[1] ratings, I was surprised. What was true then, is true now. Today (2015), of the top 25 all-time domestic grossing films categorized by MPAA rating (not adjusted for inflation), only 3 are rated G, 5 are rated PG, 16 are rated PG13, and only 1 was rated R. That one R-rated film was THE PASSION OF THE CHRIST, which came in at number 25. While the detailed analysis of the numbers are a bit more complicated than what I've just stated, a full analysis still suggests that PG13 movies do better than PG films, which do better than G rated films, which is contrary to what Christian pundits were claiming.

THE RESEARCH

The research I conducted for my doctorate, inadvertently had a major impact on my journey of faith. Since I dedicated a whole book to the topic,[2] it's only right that within this story I devote a few pages to summarizing it.

In reading about movies, I had finally come to the conclusion that there was one critical factor that had not been researched, and that had to do with consistency and truth of a story's moral theme, or what I ended up calling the story's "moral premise."

In the end, my research analyzed six films and their sequels (12

1 Motion Picture Association of America is the major trade association that represents Hollywood studios.

2 Williams, Stanley D (2006). *The Moral Premise: Harnessing Virtue and Vice for Box Office Success.* Michael Wiese Books, Studio City, CA, 196 pgs.

films in all). Each pair featured nearly the same setting, actors, genre, and usually the same writers and director. In five of the pairs, the box office receipts were dramatically different; and one pair of films provided a sort of pseudo[1] control pair, where the box office results were nearly identical. By carefully watching the films and analyzing the scenes in each, I was able to *identify* and *quantify* the overall movie's theme and the theme of each individual scene. When the theme of each individual scene aligned with the overall movie's theme, the film's *validity score* increased. When the theme of an individual scene disagreed with the overall movie's theme, the film's *validity score* decreased. Averaging the consistency of the theme's portrayal gave me a validity value for the film, which I reasoned was related to the audience's acceptance or rejection of what the movie was truly about at a psychological and moral level.

I then *qualitatively* evaluated the moral truth or falsehood of the various themes in terms of Natural Law. For instance, if the theme of the movie involved sex, then scenes that portrayed promiscuity as something good, scored negatively, while scenes that portrayed monogamy as something good, scored positively. Likewise, scenes that portrayed promiscuity as something bad scored positively, and scenes that portrayed monogamy as bad scored negatively.

While promiscuity and monogamy were outwardly portrayed on the screen, what became intriguingly apparent were the correlations such actions had with the character's *motivational values*—the values that a character believes will bring him or her happiness. Promiscuous behavior was usually linked with a character that was motivated by selfish lust or deception, while monogamy was the behavior motivated by sacrificial love and honesty.

In the 12 films of my sample, and in a wide variety of films outside the 12 selected for the study, I began to see a pattern between the internal motivations of the characters and the movie's box office. This was a different kind of analysis—I was considering the character's internal conflict and motivations as primary, where the MPAA rating were determined primarily by what was visible on the screen.

This paralleled the truth of the human condition. The human

---

1 Because my sample of 12 films was less than 32, and because they were not randomly selected, the results of my study were *not statistically significant*. Finding 32 films (randomly selected from a much larger population) was problematic since there were not that many sequels for which box office numbers were available. Thus, my research results only indicate a *probable* correlation.

person is: (1) motivated psychologically by cultivated inner-values, to (2) make decisions of their own choosing, that (3) result in outward action, which (4) leads to some physical consequence that obeys Natural Law, over which the person has no choice. The first three steps are under the control of the person, but the fourth step is controlled by Natural Law.

When these four-steps, as portrayed in the story, followed Natural Law, the movie connected with audiences. If these logical steps were sidestepped, resulting in a moral universe that the audience did not recognize, the movie was not popular. What was true, won at the box office. What was false, failed.

It also became clear that the outward consequence experienced by the character, although it may not have been welcomed, became a metaphor for the character's inward struggle. Thus, what was seen and heard in a movie were symbols for what the story was really about at the root level— the character's moral transformation.

As you might imagine, the more consistent a portrayal of a true moral theme, with all other factors being the same, the movie performed significantly better at the box office.

Here's one example of the correlation. There were two CITY SLICKERS (1 & 2) movies produced, both starring Billy Crystal, the first in 1991 and the second in 1994. Both movies were about three men who leave their homes in Manhattan to go on vacations together out West in search of adventure. The theme of the first movie was about how happiness is found by being true and loyal to your wife and avoiding promiscuity. It sold 29.4 million tickets and was a hit. The second movie was about how happiness would result if you lied to your wife and you came home with a million dollars that belonged to someone else. It sold only 10.4 million tickets and bombed. Greed does not end in happiness.

> **What was seen and heard in a movie were symbols [metaphors] for what the story was really about at the root level—the character's moral transformation.**

I discovered that the movies which bombed repeatedly used narrative arguments that employed logical or linguistic fallacies. For instance, if a character is about to do something illegal and defends it by saying to a friend , "Hey, what can happen?"…and then nothing bad happens as the result of the illegal action, the filmmakers have employed a fallacy called "Ignoring the Counter Evidence." They have not been honest about what the real world demands of persons.

Or, if a character believes that "stealing" is actually "borrowing" and the "borrowing" is justified with a happy ending, then a linguistic fallacy is employed called "equivocation." Audiences subliminally recognize such bad logic or language, and expect the bad motivation and action to be caught and corrected. But when the bad motivation and action is rewarded with a good outcome without negative consequences, the audience registers the scene or combination of actions as untrue, unfair, and not faithful to how the world works.

I found that the ticket sales of such films were dismal. Greed does not foster harmony; promiscuity does not lead to trust; lying does not lead to goodwill. Yet, when filmmakers work such arguments into their otherwise entertaining story, general audiences subliminally reject it, and tell their friends to avoid the movie, and the box office suffers.

In all of this, however, there was a caveat. While in most cases there was a strong and direct correlation between a film's popularity and the truth of the moral premise portrayed, ultimately the judgment about what was true or false is the *audience's* perception of Natural Law. Thus, a film that celebrates promiscuity over monogamy, hostility over love, greed over generosity, and rebellion over respect would need an audience that was attracted to promiscuity, hostility, greed and rebellion.

When I compared the goofball comedies Caddyshack I (1980) with Caddyshack II (1988), I found proof that as much as I wanted God and nature to do the bidding about what was true, it was the audience that determined what was "true," and "false." Caddyshack I's protagonist was played by 25-year old Michael O'Keefe. The movie's moral premise centered on the concept that "rebellion leads to riches." The story thus elevated the "virtues" of promiscuity, hostility, greed and rebellion. Normally, these were all false moral premises. But because it was marketed to adolescent boys who were discovering new hormones every day, it was a huge success with over 15 million tickets sold.

Eight years later along comes Caddyshack II whose protagonist was played by 57-year old Jackie Mason. Clearly this second movie was written with the older generation in mind. Its moral premise centered on how "love leads to forgiveness, and the story elevated the *real* virtues of monogamy, love, generosity, and respect. Sounds good so far, except it was marketed to the same audience as Caddyshack I—adolescent teens. The consequences were dismal. When the teens came to the theater the first weekend they were expecting more of the same from the first movie. But the moral premise had been flipped on them, and they flipped-off the movie. At the same time the older generation ignored Caddyshack II because they thought it was just like Caddyshack I. At the end it sold only 2.7 million tickets. Bomb!

Thus, both movies involved fallacies. In the first movie fallacies like *Appeal to Common Opinion* and *Omission of Key Evidence*[1] were used in the story to argue that promiscuity and greed were acceptable. I rated the movie's moral validity at 32%. Caddyshack I, however was marketed to a niche audience who valued such invalid premises; so, teen boys turned out in droves.

Caddyshack II's story avoided most fallacies and I rated its moral validity at 93%. But, now it was the marketing team who invoked a fallacy called *Inference from a Name or Description*. The name inferred that the second was like the first, but it was morally the opposite. After the first weekend, the teens gave it bad word of mouth, and the older audience stayed away because of the name, convinced it was a rehash of the first movie.

A FTER THREE YEARS of part-time course work I passed the written and oral examinations in December of 1995. Then, after another three years of research and writing, I produced a 750-page dissertation titled *Narrative Argument Validity and Film Popularity*,[2] which I successfully defended on October 20, 1998.

Thus, after six years of intense effort I was excited to get the degree. I had worked hard, learned a lot, and become a better writer. I was proud...in a good way, I thought. But a few days later when I went to the grocery store, I was brought back down to earth when the cashier told me I had to pay for the gallon of milk I had put on the counter.

It was the next spring when I arranged for three copies of my two-volume dissertation to be hardbound in *imitation* red leather. I presented a set to each of my adult children. I said, "I don't really expect you to ever read this. But put them on the shelf and occasionally look at the bright red bindings and remember that you're never too old to learn a few things. Your old man was 52."

Though I considered it inadvertent at first, it became apparent that God was leading me in ways beyond my expectations. Looking back, my dissertation research built a single vehicle that drove me simulta-

---

1 Damer, T. Edward (2001). *Attacking Faulty Reasoning.* Wadsworth/Thomson Learning, Stamford, CT.

2 Williams, Stanley D. (1998). University Microfilm (Number 9915752), Ann Arbor, Michigan.

neously down three different but related roads in my journey. The vehicle was the study of logical and linguistic fallacies, which elucidated my search for a reasonable faith, established a premise for a culturally influencing career, and motivated me to get my life in focus. Having never learned to walk, I galloped down all three.

THE FIRST ROAD revealed itself while writing my dissertation. In it I quote Laurie Beth Jones's 1995 book *JESUS CEO: Using Ancient Wisdom for Visionary Leadership.* It's a classic. In part, my research examined the importance of a protagonist to have a goal, a physical something he or she strives passionately towards—in short, a mission. This, of course, reminded me that I, as the protagonist of my life's story, also needed a mission...something that was clear, unique and would lend guidance at the many turning points in my life's plot.

So, a year later I picked up a copy of another Jones book: *THE PATH: Creating Your Mission Statement for Work and for Life,* along with the companion *Field Guide,* a workbook. Developing a personal mission statement with these tools, derived out of the passions that had driven my life, was euphoric. It was an epiphany. I had discovered what the plot of my life was all about. Here's what I came up with:

To discover and promote divine truth to those within my sphere of influence.

When making any major life decision I ask myself if the activity or direction I face will help or hinder the fulfillment of this mission. And so, when faced with finding a practical use for the dissertation, my mission statement led me to an important and life changing decision.

THE OPPORTUNITY TO drive down the *second road* came about more as a surprise and, assuredly, because of my easily ruffled and impetuous nature. If you recall, my doctoral work was originally intended to usher me across the Hollywood threshold so I could make theatrical movies...at least that was the idea. What actually happened was this.

After completing the dissertation, I tried to get my academic friends in Hollywood to use the moral premise concept in their screenplay writing courses. I had nothing to sell, nor was I looking for an endorsement. The moral premise was nothing I invented, but rather an ancient Natural Law of storytelling. Every other story guru wrote something about it, yet they all called it something different, and seemed to avoid discussing the mechanical crux of the whole idea—that a character's moral values are what determines his or her actions and that, in turn, leads to consequences that are dictated by Natural Law and thus outside the character's control. I was convinced that if writers and directors were just aware of this simple concept, better movies featuring strong redemptive themes would be the result.

MY MISSION: To discover and promote divine truth to those within my sphere of influence.

But, I was ignored. So, being easily ruffled and impetuous, I sat down and wrote a book in 2004-2005.

By e-mail, I submitted the completed manuscript to my favorite Hollywood publisher, Michael Wiese Books (otherwise known as Michael Wiese Productions—MWP), via the company's manager, Ken Lee in Seattle, Washington. Such submissions are notorious for requiring writers to be long on patience and wait months for a reply.

You can understand my surprise when, three days later, I received an e-mail from Michael Wiese, himself (who lives near Lands End, England), informing me he would "love" to publish my book. Editorially, MWP requested very few changes. The biggest change came from my writing partner, Bill Wiitala, who suggested I add a chapter on how experienced writers come to use the moral premise without knowing anything about it. It's Chapter 4: "Storytelling's Natural Law and Processes."

The Moral Premise: Harnessing Virtue and Vice for Box Office Success was released in 2006, and it introduced me to the story consulting industry, something I knew very little about before. I began getting calls to read scripts, give notes on story ideas, consult on major film projects, give workshops, and brainstorm with novelists on new efforts. While most of the projects I have worked on are little known or will never get made, I've had the privilege of working with Will Smith and his company, Overbrook Entertainment, on over a dozen of his movies, half of which have been made and, together, have grossed over a billion dollars.

The consequence of all of this has been a platform in both secular and religious arenas to be a Christian witness to the entertainment industry and to talk both publicly and privately about the anchor of human morality—Natural Law—which is also the anchor of all Christian doctrine.

Indeed, ex-missionary Dr. Frank Allen, in telling me to forget Hollywood and "Get a life!"…was prophetic, even as he was dismissive. I got a life, and although I don't think of myself as a missionary, per se, I've nonetheless been able to teach and lecture about these life changing discoveries to thousands of workshop attendees, readers, social media followers, and private story clients. As filmmakers, novelists and playwrights they have used the guiding principles of the moral premise to promote truth in perhaps the most culturally influencing activity known to human society—the mystery of storytelling.

A GATE TO THE *third road* opened when, as a result of my research, I realized how particular logical and linguistic fallacies had convinced a large number of American Christians to believe some things about the Bible and their faith to be true, when, in fact, they were false. And, ironically, I was one of those persons.

But how and why that fully came to my awareness would sadly take a few more years to sort out as I navigated around a major pothole in the last Evangelical road I was to drive down.

64
Magnet Church

I N 1988, WITH concern that our children (ages 16, 14, and 12) make Christian friends during the impressionable teen years, Pam and I started attending a regional magnet church known as Highland Park Baptist Church (HPBC). The old-timers at the large independent church joked that it wasn't in the city of Highland Park anymore (where it began) nor was it very Baptist, in its theology. But that didn't matter. Things (like theology) changed but the name stayed the same. It was one of the largest Evangelical churches in the Detroit metroplex and it enjoyed a good reputation for Bible teaching and a large, active, and spiritually oriented youth group. Its former pastor was Dr. Joseph M. Stowell, who left in 1987 to be the president of the Moody Bible Institute, which also gave added credibility to HPBC's Evangelical conservative reputation.

HPBC was associated with the Conservative Baptist Association of America, which was not a denomination, but an administrative support group of hundreds of churches across the country. The CBAA's statement of faith was less than 1,000 words, and was worded loosely enough to allow the individual member churches leeway in establishing a teaching doctrine that was more stringent.

HPBC had such a teaching doctrine. It prevented the teaching or promotion of the Pentecostal or Charismatic Gifts of the Holy Spirit. When we were considering becoming members this restriction concerned me. But, the elders made it clear that they took no position on whether tongues, for instance, was of this age or not, but that in order to avoid division they just forbade teaching about it, one way or another. That satisfied me, and we joined and became active members.

A hierarchy of Boards made up mostly of business owners, and managers from large corporations like Ford Motor, General Motors and Chrysler Corporation, expertly administrated HPBC. Consequently the church attracted a high caliber of talent, including dedicated Christian laymen, teachers, sports figures and musicians. In spite of the clientele, however, the church was not considered rich or affluent. It's motivation was Bible teaching, evangelism, and promoting spiritual growth. It was a perfect fit for our sensibilities.

When we began attending, HPBC had no senior pastor. For years after, the Pastoral Board would hire well-known national speakers and preachers to come and fill the pulpit. Each Sunday the sermons were delivered by the best in the country, and I began to collect autographs in my hardbound diary of Sermon Notes. None were super famous, but if they were good speakers I tried to let them know how much I appreciated their sermon by having them sign my notes. It was like attending a national preaching conference with the best and the brightest.

Although our original decision was to spiritually benefit our kids, there were two bonuses for Pam and me, other than the on-going series of great preachers. The first, was a great adult Sunday School class taught by Rev. Al Kuhnle (1930-2008), who was the head of Youth for Christ in S.E. Michigan. To be head of YFC and run monthly rallies with 5,000 teens attending at the Masonic Temple in Detroit, you had to be a sharp wit and fast enough to stay ahead of pop culture, myriad of fads, slang, movies, bands, and jokes. Kuhnle was the man, and he did so with flair, and with compassion for everyone he met, even as he excelled at teaching the Bible. His Sunday School class at HPBC was attended every week by nearly 200 adults. It was always entertaining, Biblically based, and practical, in that order. There's an adage in Hollywood: "Entertain First". Unless there's some entertainment value to get the audience's attention, the message will be lost. Al Kuhnle's priority was Christian evangelization and discipleship. But he knew how to get your attention and keep it. It could be said that we went to HPBC just for Kuhnle's Sunday School class.

THERE WAS A second attraction at HPBC for us adults. Another "Al"—Al Yungton—was a well-known musician and maestro in the Detroit film and commercial scene. I knew him from my professional haunts. He wrote music and jingles, conduced small orchestras, and taught music composition at Wayne State University. Al also scored movies for National PBS television specials.

I forget the event, but in the mid 1980's I tried to book Yungton to do something for one of my productions that was time sensitive. He turned me down because he was already booked. I asked him what he was doing and he said, "I've got church choir rehearsal that night."

To me, at the time, this sounded silly. In my experience church choirs didn't rehearse. Anyone that could mouth the words was welcome to "sing" in the church choir. They just showed up Sunday morning and put on their robes. So, when Al Yungton put the church choir ahead of a paying gig, I took notice.

I asked, "Are you directing the choir?"

"Oh, no," he said. "I'm just one of the singers."

"Do they pay you."

"Good grief, no. Wouldn't think of it."

I wondered. *Why would Al Youngton, of all people, lower himself to sing in a church choir...for free?* I knew he was a Christian, but I could not imagine anything at a church that would get his attention.

Then, in 1988, when Pam and I first attended HPBC, I discovered why—the worship music director, Gary Matthews! Every Sunday behind the pulpit, in addition to a grand piano and five-manual electronic organ with massive speakers, Gary assembled a 30-piece orchestra and a 70-voice choir. Forget the preaching, as good as it could be with the guest speakers. Gary's inspirational music was astounding and alone worth the 20-minute drive on Sunday mornings.

EVENTUALLY THE OFFICIAL Board at HPBC started to do some serious shopping for a senior pastor. They hired a wonderful man with a big heart and a passion for preaching who loved Jesus. He was Rev. LC.

The selection process, which took over a year, curiously revealed that the Official Board had the final approval of the pastor's appointment, which was recommended by the Pastoral Board, in consultation with the Deacon Board and the Christian Education Board. While they wanted a pastor with strong character and pulpit personality, the big concern was finding someone that agreed with all those boards and the church's teaching doctrine.

This discovery caused me concern. While

> **While they wanted a pastor with strong character and pulpit personality, the big concern was finding someone that agreed with all those boards and the church's teaching doctrine.**

I had had my share of disagreements with former pastors, I still considered them to be the spiritual head of a church, much like the Apostles were the spiritual head of the New Testament church. The way the New Testament Church was organized, it was the Apostles who appointed the board of deacons and elders. It was not the board of deacons and elders that appointed the Apostles.

The process seemed backwards, but then what option did they have? It wasn't as if there was a group of Apostles or bishops at HPBC. The only leadership that HPBC had were the HPBC elders and deacons...who were elected by a democratic vote of the membership. If I understand this correctly, then, the spiritual authority of HPBC was the democratic vote of the members. This raised a red flag.

But, I was in no position of authority or influence, so I said nothing and let it slide. In my mind, however, democracy, without the infallible direction by the Holy Spirit, was the downfall of Evangelicalism. Perhaps that's what the boards at HPBC were counting on...the Holy Spirit. But, how could they be sure?

HPBC WAS ARCHITECTURALLY plain. Inside there was no *original* art displayed either in the lobby or auditorium. I still longed for the grand art that graced Lutheran churches. Nonetheless, HPBC seemed to have a heart for art, if not in the glorious music, then in a very large framed, reproduction of Jan Styka's *The Crucifixion* mounted on the lobby wall. It was positioned so that it greeted worshipers as they entered the auditorium for services. My guess is that the reproduction was 13-feet wide by 3-feet tall. It was large enough to engage the viewer, especially if you walked close to it. I often stood in the lobby and stared in contemplation, putting myself on Golgotha with Christ and the company of soldiers and on-lookers, allowing the artwork to pull me in and put me in the mood for worship. At the time I did not realize how big the original was. As I sat down to write this chapter I discovered that *The Crucifixion*, which was originally titled, *Golgotha*, is 195-feet long by 45-feet tall and took Styka 3-years to paint in oils on canvas. It currently hangs in a building built

> **I often stood in the lobby and stared in contemplation, putting myself on Golgotha with Christ and the company of soldiers and on-lookers, allowing the artwork to pull me in and put me in the mood for worship**

for it alone at Forest Lawn Museum in Glendale, California.[1] It's on my pilgrimage list.

A YEAR OR SO after Rev. LC was installed, a Christian painter of some note, and unfortunately whose name I have now forgotten, made a donation to the church in the form of a 24" x 36" oil painting. The painting was a glorious montage of beautifully, detailed faces representing perhaps 20 different ethnic men and women, young and old, dressed in their native garb from various nations around the world. The painting may have had a title like *Faces of the Nations*. Some of the faces were old with deeply etched wrinkles, others represented young people with vivacious smiles, some were laborers and others commoners. The common theme of each face was hope, their eyes bright and looking up as if gazing at their salvation. Because HPBC was deeply committed to missionary work, the painting inspired viewers to identify with and have compassion for the many different nationalities around the world to which the church had sent missionaries. Without explanation, the painting communicated love, compassion, hope, and caring.

Yet, whoever was charged with the painting's display decided the message wasn't clear enough. After a few weeks, the work of art was professionally defaced and transformed into a cheap poster. Someone in authority had directed that the bottom of the painting be covered, as if it was offensive, with block printing. If I remember correctly, the block lettering (also done professionally) read, "GO YE INTO ALL THE WORLD AND PREACH THE GOSPEL - MATTHEW 16:15."

I cannot explain to you how offended I was at the demeaning transformation of a talented artist's work. It reminded me of the clear confusion that Evangelicals had regarding the role and purpose of art. It also reminded me that mountains, flowers, trees and other wonders of nature do not have Scripture plastered across them to remind us of God. To Evangelicals the Word of God only meant literally, *words*—the sense of the *words* (ironically enough) found in Psalms 19:1-4 clearly lost:

> **Mountains, flowers, trees and other wonders of nature do not have Scripture plastered across them to remind us of God.**

The heavens declare the glory of God;

---

1 http://forestlawn.com/glendale/

the skies proclaim the work of his hands.
Day after day they pour forth speech;
night after night they reveal knowledge.

They have no speech, they use no words;
no sound is heard from them.
Yet their voice goes out into all the earth,
their words to the ends of the world.
In the heavens God has pitched a tent for the sun.[1]

IN 1994, WHILE attending HPBC, our family experienced multiple and substantive changes. In March, during Spring Break of her senior year in college, our oldest, Trudy, took a trip to Turkey for a week to visit her boyfriend. Steve was there working with campus Crusade for Christ evangelizing university students in Istanbul. No sooner had Trudy arrived than Steve called me long distance and asked permission to propose marriage to Trudy. I immediately said yes. He was that kind of guy. Besides I knew what Trudy was thinking. [Before they even dated 4 years earlier she told her mom, "I'm going to marry that guy someday."] Steve proposed the next evening on the Bosporus Straits to a very happy young lady. Trudy graduated from Taylor University in May, with a double major in Computer Science and History. She had no idea what she was going to do, but immediately landed a job as the first computer archivist for the country's first Holocaust Memorial Museum in West Bloomfield, Michigan. She and Steve were married December 31 at HPBC.

At the end of March, 1994, Pam and I finally got to take our long forgotten honeymoon, now delayed a quarter of a century. We went big, and flew to Hawaii for a three-island tour. While there, on Easter morning, we drove in the dark to the top of Haleakalā, the 10,000-foot dormant volcano to watch the sunrise. All the way up along Route 378—the steep switch back road that leads to the Visitor's Center at the top—our rental car's fuel gage read *below* empty. I kept thinking that if I ran out of gas before I got to the top I would have to coast down, backwards, in the dark, while looking in the rear view mirror. Prospects were bleak.

But we made it.

As the sun came over the crater's eastern horizon, we stood in the cold mountain air with a small group of other Christians and read

1 Psalm 19:1-4 (NIV)

aloud the Resurrection story from Luke 24.

Going back down we coasted to Kula and into a gas station. *Whew!*

In May 1994, our second child, April, finished her first year of college. This was a major milestone since she had a learning disability. It would take her eight years, but she graduated with a B.A. in literature from Madonna University in 1998 and made the Dean's list her last semester. We were very proud.

The next month, in June 1994, our youngest, Josh, at 6' 10" graduated from high school. Having been heavily recruited to play college basketball, and much to our pleasure, he signed with Navy. Yet he wasn't sure he could make the grade going directly into the Academy. So, along with other athletes, he chose to attend the one-year Naval Academy Prep School (NAPS) in Newport, Rhode Island, beginning August 1, 1994. If he maintained a "C" average at NAPS he would have an automatic appointment to the Academy. He surprised himself (but not us) with a B+ average. The next summer he reported for Plebe Summer at Annapolis.

A FEW YEARS EARLIER, when our kids had all been in the Youth Group at HPBC, I had started meeting early Wednesday mornings to pray with the Youth Pastor SB. We prayed mostly for his ministry and many of the kids in the group by name. This was important to Pam and me. We had gone out of our way to put the kids in a good situation, and I wanted to secure our spiritual investment. Youth Pastor SB and I continued to invite other parents to join us, but they rarely did. Usually it was just the two of us for 45-minutes of sharing and intercession before I had to leave for work. I found Youth Pastor SB to be an alert, articulate, and smart young man with a passionate heart for Christ and the 200 or so teens under his charge at HPBC.

When Pam and I returned home from taking Josh to NAPS in August 1994, I didn't meet with Youth Pastor SB for a couple weeks because he was on a mission trip. He and several chaperones had taken 20 teens to Los Angeles, California where they connected with another youth group from Kansas to work on a building project and evangelism outreach efforts in the inner city. Their host church was John Wimber's Anaheim Vineyard Christian Fellowship. John Wimber was the Evangelical-charismatic church planter and founder of the worldwide Vineyard Movement. Before he was saved and called to the ministry, Johnny Wimber was the keyboard artist for The Righteous Brothers and The Paramours.

One evening at the Vineyard church, the 100 or so youth involved in the project got together for worship and prayer. Suddenly, in the middle of the meeting, RC, one of the HPBC teens who had a history of mental illness and almost did not get to go on the trip because of a rebellious attitude, fell into a convulsive trance of a demonic nature. Youth Pastor SB and others were at a loss for what to do. But the Vineyard youth leader, who was from Latin America, recognized what was happening, took charge of the situation, and subsequently led the group in an exorcism of a demon from RC. The scene was reported to me as if it was right out of a horror movie.

So shocking and unnerving was the experience that the normal ministry activities were put on hold for a day. Youth Pastor SB separated the HPBC teens from the others to spiritually decompress and pray. He took the group to a hillside overlooking Los Angeles. There, in the bright sunshine and fresh air, the group of teens began to pray with only their chaperones from HPBC present. But it happened again. RC fell into another trance and experienced a series of convulsions, this time with vile ranting. Youth Pastor SB and the other teens laid hands on RC, prayed fervently and after an exhaustive period of time, a second demon made its appearance and left.

This was all very new and upsetting for the HPBC youth. They were from a Christian background that frowned on supernatural phenomena. In their experience, reports of such things were cast aside as fraudulent.

When RC's father back in Michigan found out what had happened, he became angry with our senior pastor, LC, for not flying to Los Angeles and "rescuing" his son from the influence of the "crazy" charismatics and an out of control youth pastor. RC's father was a prominent member of HPBC. During the day he was an engineer. But part time, at night, he was a psycho-therapist.

The proof of the spiritual pudding, however, was something else entirely. Where before Evangelical groups found fault with Charismatics because (the Evangelicals claimed) the fruits of the spirit were not present along with the charismatic gifts, now the fruits were evident. One father, who was the chairman of the HPBC School Board (the church ran a successful K-12 school on the property) told me how overjoyed he was at the change in not only his son's life, but in RC, his son's friend. The father referred to the kids as "new persons in Christ" since their return from L.A., with a passion for the Bible and love for each other.

The youth group had came home "fired up" for Jesus. But the adult leadership was quick to dismiss, marginalize and ignore the renewal of the group's faith. The HPBC youth reminded me of Joshua and Caleb who came back from their trip to the West with faith that God had given them the land. But the people sided with the 10 spies who grumbled...and there was a consequence.

The situation at HPBC upset the entire leadership, although I believe that RC's father, the engineer who worked evenings at a psychiatric clinic, engineered up a great deal of the unrest. I had some conversations with him. Visibly upset weeks later, he told me, "This [the exorcism] is not the way it's supposed to work." He revealed that RC had been seeing a psychiatrist for over a year due to RC's earlier attempt at suicide. But the sessions had not helped.

> **The youth group had came home "fired up" for Jesus. But the adult leadership was quick to dismiss, marginalize and ignore the renewal of group's faith.**

Upon their return from L.A., when Pastor LC and the Board of Deacons (yes, that's another board) tried to temper the teen group's enthusiasm with talks that downplayed the charismatic gifts, the blame game began.

You'll recall, HPBC espoused a local doctrine that forbade teaching anything about the charismatic Gifts of the Holy Spirit. Oddly, exorcism did not directly involve the Gifts, although it was likely that some of the Vineyard Church leadership, when praying over RC, were praying in tongues and tried to exercise gifts of healing. But the HPBC youth didn't come back promoting tongues. They were simply on fire for the reality of God's supernatural power in their lives. No doubt the event forced some adults in the church to do some research on John Wimber and the Vineyard Fellowship. They discovered that while Vineyard called themselves "Empowered Evangelicals," they had one foot squarely in the Pentecostal-Charismatic camp.

Ironically, the Classical Pentecostals didn't like John Wimber either. John Wimber's take on the Bible didn't require speaking in tongues as proof of salvation the way classical Pentecostals or the Word of Faith[1] movements did. Consequently, Wimber and others left the charismatic ministry of Calvary Chapel where they had attended and taught (in LA.) and began Vineyard Fellowship.[2]

---

1 Bethesda Missionary Temple grew out of the Word of Faith movement.

2 See Wikipedia article and citations on John Wimber. Recall, it was John Wimber

Back at HPBC, suddenly, the issue was not on what happened in Los Angeles, or on the ministry of the Holy Spirit. Instead the grievance was that Youth Pastor SB had not properly *fulfilled his fiduciary responsibilities* in caring for the youth while in Los Angeles. "He should have known L.A. was a strange place," said one distressed parent.

The concern then became whether or not the youth pastor, with his newfound discoveries of the Holy Spirit, was willing to come fully under the teaching authority of the senior pastor and some combination of the boards. He wasn't. He told me he felt that following the Holy Spirit was more important, and he decided to resign, leaving many of the youth angry with the senior pastor and deacons, and me angry as well.

A week after Youth Pastor SB was forced out, on September 4, 1994, I attended a Sunday evening "Town Meeting" led by Sr. Pastor LC and the chairman of the Deacon Board, who wore a foot cast that caused him to limp wherever he went. Being a man, myself, who was learning about metaphors, the foot cast spoke volumes to my understanding of the situation. Pastor LC made it clear that the issue was *not* what happened in L.A. but that Youth Pastor SB had violated his "fiduciary responsibilities" and was not willing to come under the authority of the Senior Pastor and the Pastoral Board. It was a bold-face misrepresentation of the doctrinal issue they did not want to confront. Youth Pastor SB had become the scapegoat and it wasn't even Passover. In referring to some of our complaints that they needed to deal with the spiritual and doctrinal issues not the fiduciary ones, LC publicly stated in the Town Meeting:

We are not willing to do that.[1]

For a month after this, in my prayer diaries, I pleaded with God for Sr. Pastor LC and the various leaders of HPBC to deal with the spiritual and doctrinal issue and not blame Youth Pastor SB. I spoke with LC several times, and with others, but I was shut down each time and nothing else was done.

But the story wasn't over. On October 22, 1994 I wrote in my prayer diary:

---

that sidetracked our pastor at Northwest Church forcing him to leave the Christian Missionary Alliance denomination and start his own storefront church.

1 Rev. LC, Town Meeting at HPBC September 4, 1994. (Author's prayer diary written at the time.)

*Lord, this will not go away. It will be a shadow over their
ministry until they allow the situation to be fully explored
and discussed, and if there is error on their part to find
restitution for it. From our perspective, the deacons or LC,
or whoever is in charge have lied, and they have blasphemed
your H.S. — and no words or explanation to cover-up or
to exonerate themselves will change it. There is blight on
the ministry of HPBC & it will get worse until they seek
forgiveness.*

While writing this, I reached out to RC, now in his thirties and
*working as a counselor in the human resource department of a munici-
pality.* I asked if he would talk to me about his recollections of the time.
He told me by phone, "No, I would not like to talk about it. That's not
a part of my life that I want to revisit. I'm still processing it, yet today.
Feel free to recount [in your book] whatever you remember." [!]

God would write the last chapter, but He was patient and so the
story would not play out for another three years. In the meantime, my
impatience with Evangelicalism was egged on by two events, otherwise
insignificant, that became symbolic of the scandal of Christianity.

65
Last Straws

WHEN THE QUARTERLY HPBC communion service came around in early 1995, I was still stinging emotionally and theologically from the events described in the last chapter. This particular Sunday, for some reason, I was sitting alone, near the back door of the large church.

HPBC, like most other Evangelical fellowships, celebrated the Lord's Supper every three months. I liked better the Lutheran practice of taking communion every Sunday, but the quarterly tradition had been drilled into me since I was a child. I had also heard that some churches took communion every day of the week. That sounded a bit much, but the daily occurrence was backed-up by one interpretation of 1 Corinthians where Christ is quoted by St. Paul:

> The Lord Jesus, on the night he was betrayed, took bread, and when he had given thanks, he broke it and said, "This is my body, which is for you; do this in remembrance of me." In the same way, after supper he took the cup, saying, "This cup is the new covenant in my blood; do this, whenever you drink it, in remembrance of me." For whenever you eat this bread and drink this cup, you proclaim the Lord's death until he comes.[1]

I had always interpreted the line "do this whenever…in remembrance of me," as meaning, *whenever you think of me*. Yet, it didn't seem realistic to take communion multiple times during the day. So, to me, a compromise of every worship service seemed appropriate.

I suspect these thoughts of having communion every Sunday came

---

1 1 Corinthians 11:23-26 (NIV)

to me after many years of attending Evangelical-preaching services and visually being reminded of Communion every Sunday. Just below the pulpit, regardless of what church we attended, was a beautiful wood table—this was the altar (although we all thought the altar was the railing we knelt at between us and the table.) No one called it an altar in Evangelicalism. They all called it the Communion Table, and it was usually empty, except during communion services. Sometimes there would be an open Bible laid on it.

But one thing was always consistent: Decoratively carved into the table's front panel were these words in all caps: "DO THIS IN REMEMBRANCE OF ME." There it was in bold print every Sunday, a proclamation from Scripture, front and center, right below the pulpit. It was a command of the Lord read a dozen times by every eye in the congregation during every sermon. And it was ignored, except once very 3 months.

> **No one called it an altar in Evangelicalism. They all called it the Communion Table, and it was usually empty.**

Thus, I got the idea that distributing communion more often than once every three months (to the leadership) was a hassle, and to think of communion as a "hassle" was a repugnant concept. But that certainly is what some folks thought as evident by what happened one Sunday.

EVANGELICAL COMMUNION SERVICES were served by ushers who passed plates of unleavened bread chips down each row of pews, followed by a round aluminum tray of 40 little disposable plastic cups filled with grape juice. Congregants never left their seats. Each person took a bread chip and a cup as they were passed. Then, when everyone was served, the pastor prayed, spoke some words of institution, and everyone together consumed first the bread, and then the little cup of juice. I had always tried to enter into the moment during communion and make the ceremony count for something.

One particular Sunday morning, with the bread chip and cup in my hands, I bowed in my pew and visualized Christ on the cross looking down and speaking to me very personally, "I'm dying for you, Stanley. Are you going to make my death worth it?" Often, during this personal ritual, there would be tears of humility at my disloyalty. Then I would consume the elements as a symbol of my death and my re-dedication to make Christ's death worth it.

On this Sunday I did that, then I put the bread chip in my mouth and swallowed, then tipped back the little plastic cup and drank what I thought was going to be pure, unsweetened grape juice straight from the vine—rich and robust. Except, this time, I coughed and almost spit the liquid out of my mouth. It tasted bland, tepid and absent of any sense that it was grape juice. It was disgusting. *What have they done to this?*

Holding the empty little cup between my thumb and index finger, I left my pew, exited the door, and stepped around the corner to the kitchen where the communion trays of little cups were prepared. There on the counter was a two-foot high by one-foot round contraption fashioned out of layers of clear Plexiglas and masses of clear surgical tubing. When a gallon of grape juice was poured into a basin at the top, opening a value allowed the juice to flow down through tubes to automatically fill an entire tray of 40 little cups…all at once—a real time saver. Some ushers were cleaning things up but the contraption—the "wine" dispenser as it was called—was still in place ready for use if needed. One of the ushers saw me come in with a frown on my face and nodded in my direction. I held the empty cup up in my fingers and said, "What's wrong with the communion juice? It tasted insipid."

"Oh," he smiled and gestured at the contraption that looked like a badly designed UFO. "Concentrated grape juice won't flow through the dispenser tubes unless it's diluted. If we didn't dilute the juice, the tubes would gum up and communion could not be served."

I shot back. "Well, why don't you get a squeeze bottle and pour the cups by hand like you did before you had this?"

"Oh, that would take too long. Don't be so upset!"

I said nothing more, but just stared in amazement at this usher and the time saving gadget from hell. I glanced at the usher's wrist. Wrapped around it was a black woven wrist band, popular at the time, with white capital letters that read "W.W.J.D." *Amazing!*

On-line, I found this satirical description of the "Wine" Dispenser:

> *This baby can prepare as many as 240 cups per minute … fill 5,000 to 6,000 communion cups in 20 minutes without any spillage and has been a tremendous asset to our ushers' ministry," according to a satisfied customer. Drive-through communion, anyone?* [1]

---

1 On-line: http://shipoffools.com/gadgets/church/150.html

FOR ME, THERE was still one last straw. On Sunday, April 2, 1995, I left our Sunday School class at the north end of the HPBC complex and walked the long hall to the lobby outside the worship auditorium. As I walked I tried to prepare my heart for worship. When I got to the lobby I slowed my steps. Something was different and my emotions told me it wasn't good. I stopped and looked around. Everything seemed normal as peopled filed through the four sets of doors to the worship space. But I couldn't shake the discontent. I watched people for a moment, shook a few hands of friends…and then…slowly, like a tsunami rolling in from 1,000 miles away, the awareness of what was wrong engulfed me.

> **Slowly, like a tsunami rolling in from 1,000 miles away, the awareness of what was wrong engulfed me.**

The large reproduction of Jan Styka's painting, "The Crucifixion," had been removed from the wall of the lobby between the main doors that led into the auditorium. In its place, what greeted worshipers as they entered for worship, were framed, color photographs of the dozens of missionaries that HPBC supported around the world. Their light pine frames and smiling faces, with brass nameplates under each, were in stark contrast to the dark foreboding crucifixion scene.

I instantly understood what had happened. HPBC was very proud of being a church that supported missionaries. And that's a good thing—supporting missionaries, not being proud about it. There had been a much smaller display of these missionaries' pictures on one side of the lobby. I glanced over at the former space; it was now empty. Was this an example of a good thing taken to extremes becoming a bad thing? No doubt Frank Allen, the missionary pastor, had persuaded the powers that be that missionaries deserve central recognition and celebration of their sacrifice of service. And what better location to put such a sacrificial display than in place of Our Lord's ultimate sacrifice. After all, the smiling faces of happy missionaries was a lot more uplifting than the dark foreboding scene of death at Golgotha.

After worship I tracked down Frank ("Get a life, Stan") Allen, HPBC's missionary pastor, and asked him why the switch was made. He confirmed my thinking, but passed the buck to the obscurity of a committee, saying that the missionaries are a central part of HPBC's ministry and their lives and sacrifice needed to be acknowledged and given their due exposure.

I was dumbfounded. What he didn't say might as well have been shouted from the rooftops. That the missionary's sacrifice was more important than our Lord's sacrifice; and that the missionaries deserved central recognition as we entered into worship...more so than Christ.

In my mind, HPBC replaced an image of Christ's suffering for our salvation with not one, but dozens of pseudo-graven images. This wasn't their explicit intent, such as Aaron's was when he had the Golden Calf made in the wilderness. But the juxtaposition was just as startling. Granted, if you had never seen Styka's Crucifixion painting on the lobby wall next to the worship entrances (or over time, forgotten about it's existence), the replacement of an image representing the one God with images of many little gods would not have made much difference. But it did to me. The shift of adoration from one to the other nearly brought me to tears, except I was too angry. To me, the church had committed a subtle but clear form of idolatry, even as they were probably unaware that they had stepped on the First and Second Commandments, (as Protestants count them).[1]

But there may have been another more subtle reason for the switch. Jan Styka was a *Polish Catholic*. In 1894 when he was commissioned to paint the work, he traveled to Jerusalem to do sketches. Upon his return to Poland before starting the three-year effort, he stopped off in Rome and had his palette blessed by Pope Leo XIII. Was that reason for HPBC to reject the painting? Probably not, although to a few it would be. More likely, "The Crucifixion" painting bothered Evangelicals for the same reason they avoided the display of crucifixes displaying Christ's bloody and battered body attached, and why preachers avoided taking their sermon texts from Romans 5 where Paul reminds us repeatedly of the importance of Christ's death. Evangelicals would prefer not to think about the role and depiction of suffering in redemption, but rather the empty cross that depicted the resurrection, or happy faces exuding joy.

In 1995, the day following April Fools day, was my last day as an Evangelical—a fork in the road along which I took my first steps when I left Taylor Free Methodist. Going forward I no idea what "kind" of Christian I was.

---

1 During the writing of this chapter Pam and I ordered a museum quality, canvas reproduction of Jan Styka's *The Crucifixion*. We stretched and framed it on an ornate gold frame. It now hangs it in our home. The reproduction is six-feet long—one-thirty-second and a-half scale. That means Christ's figure in our painting, which is 1.5-inches tall, in the original is 48-inches.

B UT THE HPBC story was still not over. In 1998, Rev. LC got into a debate with the middle managers that sat on the multiple Boards that ran the church. At issue was, who was the spiritual leader of the church? LC believed he was the spiritual head of the church, and that the Holy Spirit was calling him to focus his teaching ministry in a particular direction. But the Boards disagreed. LC reiterated that he needed to follow the Holy Spirit and not the Board's political process.

Sound familiar?

What goes around comes around. LC was forced out of his position as senior pastor at HPBC, for the very same reason he had forced Youth Pastor SB out. The Boards affirmed their "infallible" right over the spiritual leaders they hired, regarding what the Holy Spirit was saying to the church.

LC left full-time ministry and ended up in Colorado Springs, Colorado selling financial securities to Christian organizations, while teaching the Bible part-time. Today his on-line resume does not mention the eight years he spent at HPBC.[1] That is disappointing because he was a much-loved and appreciated spiritual leader; he demonstrated himself to me to be a man of superior integrity with passion for the things of God. He is missed.[2]

The business with Youth Pastor SB and the Sr. Pastor LC was the last of many experiences that revealed to me the inferior structure upon which Evangelical Christianity depended. Such structures had few, if any, infallible checks or balances. Whoever happened to be in charge from moment-to-moment, that is, whoever had more political clout, determined doctrine. There was no single, dogmatic system of beliefs. Everyone considered themselves to be infallible interpreters of the Bible, or infallibly led by the Holy Spirit.

J UST AFTER REV. LC left, what I predicted in 1994 occurred, but much worse than I anticipated. Recall, on October 22, 1994, I had written in my prayer diary:

---

1 LinkedIn

2 The non-profit investment firm L.C. became associated with states on-line that one of its Core Beliefs is: "Boards can Harm. Board's default to political governance ("the most votes win"), often causing division. Biblically-based Principled Governance is superior." But the link that explains "Biblically-based Principled Governance" is empty. My guess is the Board that runs the firm is divided on its meaning. *Irony is eternal.*

*Lord, this will not go away. It will be a shadow over their
ministry until they...find restitution. [they] have lied, and
they have blasphemed your H.S...There is blight on the
ministry of HPBC and it will get worse until they seek
forgiveness.*

God was patient. He waited nearly four years. But the leadership
did not find restitution for their blasphemy that publicly called "evil"
the good work and fruit of the Holy Spirit.

The church split. Of the seven pastors and school superintendent,
five left and the membership dwindled to less than half its former peak.
When we attended our first grandchild's dedication in the HPBC auditorium three years after the split, attendance was still a fraction of
its former state. On that Sunday, in 2001, white plastic shower curtains had been hung on bare wires and strung across the stage and rear
of the auditorium to give the illusion of a smaller space. To me they
looked like God-sized tears.

IN SPITE OF my problems with HPBC at the end, our initial decision
to attend and become members eventually paid spiritual and practical dividends. Our oldest and youngest children met their future
spouses at HPBC. And, today, all three of our children and ten grandchildren attend HPBC where they are actively participating in various
roles of leadership and all are following the Lord, under a new pastor,
Rev. Brent Slater, who was called to be senior pastor in 2008. Ten years
after LC was forced out, the church's spiritual role in the community
and its attendance have returned to normal levels.

But nothing was normal for me. April 2, 1995 was my last day at
HPBC. Beginning the next day I considered myself a freelance Christian, unattached to a church fellowship. And the very next day, April 3,
1995, I gave up my professional freelance career and joined the Sandy
Corporation to work on the Harley Davidson account. The timing was
nothing short of ironic Providence.

It was about that time when I realized that the four-and-a-half years
I spent freelancing as a writer-producer had allowed me the flexible
schedule for two very important tasks. (1) I started and completed my
course work for my doctorate. And (2), I was free to support and enjoy
Josh's high school basketball career by not missing any of his games,
often shagging balls for him, and in the summers driving him to tournaments around the country. The timing of that, too, was nothing I

planned or sought. It was pure Providence, and it gave me the confidence that my journey of faith, albeit not always what I planned or wanted, was in God's will and plan.

PAM WRITES: *After HPBC replaced Jan Styka's "The Crucifixion" and Stan left HPBC to troll for more churches, pastors, and boards to walk out on...I was mad. He didn't understand that every time we left one church for another, I was ripped away from Christian friends. We had been at HPBC for eight years, the longest we had ever stayed in one church. I told him, "Enough! This time I'm staying here while you get this out of your system. You'll never be satisfied! When you find exactly what you want, I'll visit and see what I think."*

I felt, in my heart, that his goal (whatever it was) was impossible to achieve, and he'd eventually be back. HPBC had become my home. Trudy had found her husband at HPBC, and Josh would find his wife there, although he didn't know it yet. At this time, Trudy was married, and Josh and April were in college, so it wasn't like I had to try to keep our family together on the weekends. So on Sundays, Stan and I went our separate ways.

Part IV
MARTYR

EVANGELICALISM—THAT VESTIGE OF hope and security that dominated my life—had died. Evangelicalism had been unfaithful to reason, logic, and Natural Law. It had succumbed to moral relativism. Each Evangelical pastor alone determined how the Bible was to be interpreted and what was morally right or wrong. Or, if it wasn't the pastor, it was the authority vested in a popularly elected committee—democratic, politically correct, Christianity. There was no standard.

This exegesis philosophy was called into question during Martin Luther's 1521 heresy trial (Diet of Worms) that led to his excommunication. Luther's famous lines, spoken to the emperor's representative and the Secretary of the Archbishop of Trier, Johann Eck, were these:

> Unless I am convinced by the testimony of the Scriptures or by clear reason...I am bound by the Scriptures I have quoted and my conscience is captive to the Word of God. I cannot and I will not retract anything, since it is neither safe nor right to go against conscience.

What Protestants almost never quote in recalling this statement of Luther is Johann Eck's reply, which Evangelical historian Mark Noll does when he suggests that Protestants, especially, need to hear these words:

> For what purpose does it serve to raise a new dispute about matters condemned through so many centuries of church and council?...if it were granted that whoever contradicts the councils and the common understanding of the church must

be overcome by Scripture passages, we will have nothing in Christianity that is certain or decided.[1]

> **If individual Reformers could start their own church with new doctrines, then what was hindering anyone else from coming up with entirely new doctrines?**

Noll then reforms Eck's posit this way, "What if everyone simply followed his or her own conscience? The end result was obvious— 'we will have nothing certain.'"[2]

And with Luther's trial and excommunication began the second splintering of Christianity, leading into hundreds of denominations and thousands of fellowships each with distinct doctrines, and where many reject biblically defined disordered behaviors as sins—e.g. abortion and homosexual acts.

ABORTION IS OKAY

IT WAS DURING this period of time that I began to understand that Protestant ideology had allowed moral relativism to creep into American Christianity and spread like aggressive cancer through culture. It was the actions of "reformers" like Martin Luther, John Calvin, and King Henry VIII who ripped the top off Pandora's box. They proclaimed themselves individually infallible arbiters of doctrine, and through their actions informed Christians that came after them: *"Follow our lead. As individuals you have the power to decide for yourself what is right and wrong."* Starting with the Protestant Reformation, Christians have hid behind the Bible as their authority, willfully picking and choosing which moral truth they liked or disliked.

> **What if everyone simply followed his or her own conscience? The end result was obvious – "we will have nothing certain."**
>
> (Mark A. Noll quoting Johann Eck)

Evidence of such disregard for an infallible arbiter of truth was, to me, blatant. First there was April's research paper. For 1,500 years (from the fourth to the nineteenth century) the proclaimed inspired, inerrant Christian Bible contained 73 books. Then, in the early

---

1 Quoted in *Turning Points: Decisive Moments in the History of Christianity* (1997). Mark A. Noll (Protestant historian at the time, teaching at Wheaton College.) Inter-Varsity Press/Baker books, Grand Rapids, MI, (p.154).

2 Ibid, p155-156.

1800s, Protestants decided the Holy Spirit was wrong for all of Christian history, and independent of the majority of Christendom, ripped out seven of the Bible's inspired writings. The removal of the Deutero-canonical books so late in Christian history by a minority of Christians, destroyed for me the credibility of their claim that Sola Scriptura was valid. (And, never mind that I could never find Sola Scriptura in Scripture. Wouldn't that be a prerequisite?) Dennis Stacey was entirely right. If you didn't like something in the Bible, just rip it out. With a modified Bible, (either by ripping out pages, removing books, or never preaching on passages that challenge your personal doctrine) Sola Scriptura works much better.

> **With a modified Bible, (either by ripping out pages, removing books, or never preaching on passages that challenge your personal doctrine) Sola Scriptura works much better.**

The second obvious evidence of moral relativism in Christianity was the thousands of disagreeing denominations and independent churches, each with their divergent doctrines. *They claimed agreement on the essentials, but that meant their separation was due to the non-essentials. Is there any logic to such a thing?* But, in fact, by attending their services and reading their statements of faith, *it was clear to me that they disagreed on the essentials, things like salvation, what was a sin, confession, baptism, sanctification, life styles, the sacraments and eternal security. You can't get more essential than those.*

Thus, *I had no trouble putting culture's embrace of abortion at the foot of Protestantism, for it was Protestantism that championed the individual rights of American citizens to pursue truth, goodness, beauty, life, liberty and happiness on their own terms.*

At the time I did not understand that the doctrines of Roman Catholicism had never changed. I considered Catholicism to be just another wayward denomination. But it was abundantly and logically clear that when Christian leaders decided on their own to interpret the Bible without some sort of infallible check that avoids a personal and biased interpretation of God's Word, moral relativism became the soup du jour.

> **They claimed agreement on the essentials, but that meant their separation was due to the non-essentials.**

I knew this viscerally because at the time, there were Christian churches that approved of abortion, homosexuality and other grave sins. In so doing they had utterly removed whatever salt, light or authority the Christian church had over society. If individual Reformers could start their own church, and make up their own doctrines, then what was hindering anyone else from coming up with entirely new doctrines?

Indeed, what was going to hinder a man from deciding he was a woman, or that he was his own God? *Forget making a graven image to worship, I've got a mirror.* And, what Protestant church has any logical right to say, 'Wait, you can't do that,' without becoming the pot calling the kettle black? Moral Relativism was ubiquitous.

That was the Scandal of Christianity. And I had no solution, for I saw no infallible source of morality.

IN SHORT, I was a Christian who believed in an absolute moral code and doctrine. But I was without a community of believers I could trust and I had no idea how such an absolute moral code or doctrine could be known with certainty by anyone.

I stood like a warrior-knight on the edge of a dark, foreboding forest. Was I willing to give myself up as a martyr for the truth in what so far had been a fruitless search? I had nowhere to go except to enter the darkness.

66
Interlude

I N ALL MY meanderings through America's Christian landscape, I never gave up on God or the Bible. I did marvel, however, that God had seemingly not given up on *me*. I knew...that He knew...that I was an indolent, intolerant, idealistically lost child, or so I'm sure my mother told Him.

I usually found some out-of-the-way, unknown, church to attend every Sunday, and I even returned to HPBC now and then for some special event of a friend or relative. Thus, I kept in contact with what was going on among various denominations. My tithe, which had always been a minimum of 10% of my gross income, went regularly to a small host of Christian parachurch organizations to which I was close enough to like their mission but not so close that I became upset with their theological stance. Purposeful ignorance can often be...peaceful.

PAM WRITES: I prided myself in talking Stan into attending HPBC for any reason, always hopeful that he'd want to return. But, it always came back to bite me, in the form of an argument. Our fists, in my mind's eye, were pounding against each other, knuckles-to-knuckles. Not fun! One time in the midst of a particularly heated verbal fight over churches, I felt God speak to me, in a fist metaphor. God said, "Quit knocking heads with Stan. He's not going off on his own to hurt or spite you. He is on an honest search, and you are not to oppose him. He needs to follow his heart on this."

Then one of the fists rotated 180-degrees and rested beside the other. God seemed to say, "You are his help-mate for a reason. Come alongside him and help him on his journey." After that, I did try to go with him to a few Sunday church trials. Together we visited United Methodist,

Episcopal, and Presbyterian churches, for their more liturgical worship services. On the independent and contemporary side, we frequented a few seeker or mega-churches and enjoyed their contemporary music and drama.

But I was not feeling what he was, and I missed HPBC.

A ND, ME? I was tired. The passion for attending church was gone. I was simply going to some church service every Sunday out of obedience, not wanting to disregard the assembling of the faithful as the writer of Hebrews commands.[1]

On the other hand, just below the surface, my Christian idealism and faith in God was as fiery as ever. I didn't fully realize how strong it was, however, until I found myself rising up in defense of God (as if I needed to) against Evangelicals who seemed to have dropped common sense and wisdom from their prayer lists.

Four situations come to mind. They upset me, but also spiritually engaged me...although they did nothing to foster benevolent thoughts toward Evangelicalism. They involved a foundation, a suicide, a midnight ride, and a simple college application.

---

1 Hebrews 10:25

67
Why Is It God's Fault?

ROM 1995 TO 1998 I wandered the American Christian landscape like a willing martyr. I was at once beleaguered and desperate. I was an orphan, like Holly in Rumer Godden's *The Story of Holly and Ivy*, looking for "my Grandma's home on Christmas Eve."[1]

Yet, I was free to visit church-after-Christian church of nearly every denomination and independent fellowship to observe and contemplate a few of the broader issues I had been raised to accept without question. One trait particularly intrigued me; it was one that seemed unique to Evangelical and Fundamentalist circles.

From my study of Scripture, I was quite clear on the concept that if something bad happened, it was probably Satan or a human's fault... *and in extremely rare cases mine...(smile)*. But it was never God's fault. I knew that...and pagans knew that. The Bible told me that—God didn't do evil...bad...mistakes...or wrong.[2] But I kept coming across instances where the American Evangelical and Fundamentalist Church told me, in innocuous ways, that for much of what went wrong in our lives God was to blame.

---

1 My company, Full Circle Communications purchased a film option on *The Story of Holly and Ivy*. We went to New York, met with Ms. Godden. Bill Wiitala and a friend wrote a beautiful script. Godden hated it, but Disney liked it. We also met the man who created Jim Henson's Muppet puppets—Kermit Love, who agreed to work with us on the project. Yet, nothing came of the script.

2 c.f. James 1:13, Job 34:12

The Ponzi Scheme

THE FOUNDATION FOR New Era Philanthropy, founded by John G. Bennett Jr., marketed itself to public and private non-profits, including Christian churches and parachurch organizations as a unique opportunity for beneficiary donors to give or invest in charities. A non-profit was told that their investment in the fund would be doubled in three months to a year depending on the size of the contribution. Bennett's story was that there were certain rich donors who would give matching gifts to charities. So, if a church raised $5,000 and deposited it with New Era (rather than in escrow), in a few months time, double the money would be returned to the organization.

On it's face, common sense should have told you this was a Ponzi scheme. And it was.

But many Christian organizations and individuals fell for it and lost a lot of money. In my sphere, two of those organizations were Spring Arbor College and Highland Park Baptist Church.

We had heard through the Spring Arbor College grapevine, that Professor Albert Meyer was causing a fund raising crisis at the school. Meyer was a CPA from South Africa in the U.S. on a work visa. At Spring Arbor, he taught accounting and also worked in the college's bookkeeping department. Because of this latter responsibility he had been advising the administration not to risk any more money in New Era. In 1991, he was convinced something was fraudulent. But the administration had already seen their money double and was upset with Meyer's criticism. When the administration shunned his advice, Meyer went semi-public within Free Methodist Church circles (which is how we found out), thus risking donations to the college, which infuriated his boss.

When Meyer earned tenure in early 1995 and felt his job was more secure, he sent his "Ponzi File" on New Era to the U.S. Securities and Exchange Commission. Within a month, the SEC was asking New Era questions, and in June before the SEC concluded anything, New Era filed for Bankruptcy with $511 million in liabilities and only $80 million in assets. Two years later, in March 1997, Bennett was indicted on 82 counts of fraud, money laundering, and tax code violations. He pleaded "no contest" and went to prison for 12-years. Spring Arbor College lost $6 million, one-fourth of their endowment.

Meanwhile, the Detroit News awarded Meyer one of their 1995 Michigander of the Year Awards, even though he was from South Africa. *Irony lives forever.*

Highland Park Baptist Church lost hundreds of thousands of dollars of their school's endowment in the scheme. In June, I was back at HPBC for a single Sunday, at Pam's insistence, when Pastor LC delivered a sermon during which he told the congregation about the New Era collapse and the money HPBC had lost. The statement carried the impression that the Official Board had approved his remarks, or at least he had reviewed them with the Board and they went along with his assessment.

In plain terms Pastor LC explained that we, as people of God, do not know why these things happen…"we have to trust God and His will and follow him wherever it leads…even in situations like this… that God often leads our lives in ways we do not understand."

In ways we do not understand? Did the leadership not see even in hindsight their error? I kept waiting for the admission of error, or "I'm sorry," or "we ran before we walked," or "we were guilty of simple but noble greed," or at the very least, "we will be more careful next time."

But there was none of that. There was no *mea culpa.* It was all "God's will," or "God's fault."

Driving home that day I dumped my frustrations on Pam about the "guiltless, gutless" American Evangelical Church. But I had to admit that we had both grown up with the ideological belief that Christians were supposed to be perfect; although it was entirely permissible to admit guilt at the altar (rail) in an attempt to get saved (yet) again. The peer pressure to appear and sound perfect and not be rejected by other Christians was subtle but always there. It was the same thing when Prof. Albert Meyer was told to be quiet so Spring Arbor College would not be seen by its supporters as—*Oh my! Jumping Jehoshaphat!*—imperfect, incompetent, or…what's that other term? Oh, yeah…human.

> **Couldn't there be a form of Christianity, I wondered, that embraced the foibles of being human, even openly acknowledging Christians as sinners in constant need of redemption?**

Couldn't there be a form of Christianity, I wondered, that embraced the foibles of being human, even openly acknowledging Christians as sinners in constant need of redemption? Why were we always under pressure to act, look, and proclaim our perfection…even in the face of monumental screw-ups?

Over the years whenever I encountered this mindset I'd flashback to the time, when my mother did not want to go to Sunday evening church with me—an adult—because I was not wearing a suit and tie. Ironically, she was telling me that my worship of God was not based on "faith alone" but on my works (appearance).

I wondered if Professor Bock was right when he challenged David Strubler...that the words "Christianity" and "intellectual" should not be used in the same sentence unless one were inviting mockery.[1]

The Suicide

ONE DAY IN 1997, I got a telephone call from a friend who attended a small Evangelical church across town. He said, "Stan, I have terrible news. Jake, Pete's son, committed suicide this afternoon."

A ton of bricks fell on my chest. "WHAT!?" Pete was a good friend and I knew his son, Jake.

"Yeah, evidently an overdose of his father's pills."

Peter had been in an industrial accident and was on prescription pain medication. They lived on a small farm outside Detroit where they raised horses. Spending an afternoon feeding, or grooming such large and beautiful animals was always a rewarding experience and I enjoyed being there. But Pete was also a close friend and I had spent considerable time with him and his family.

I was more mad than sad over Jake's death. I was mad at the evil that had brought it on and the sadness and emptiness it would bring the family and all of their friends.

A few of us thought back. In retrospect there had been some warning signs but few of us thought seriously about them, even as we ribbed Pete about his "family."

Pete's family *was* his six horses and a pony. They weren't thoroughbreds. Most were retired show horses that Pete had rescued. He loved being the wrangler. And while no one doubted his love for his children, when we were visiting the farm, we never saw any signs of affection toward his two sons or daughter. Oh, he was kind and considerate and thanked them for their work in the barn and for mucking out the run-ins. But I had the sense they were treated more like stable hands than as his flesh and blood. At the same time he babied and fussed over

---

1 Today, David is the Department Chair/Professor of Organizational Leadership, School of Education and Human Services at Oakland University in Michigan.

his horses as if they were his lost prodigal children come home. He hugged them, nuzzled them, fed them treats, and even kissed them.... on the lips (if horses have lips). Around the house were pictures of dad with his horses. But there were no pictures with Pete and his children, except one staid family group portrait taken for the church's pictorial directory.

We'd visited their place from time-to-time for a group barbecue during a holiday or on special occasions. Pete would show off his latest tackle acquisition, or the inventive drain on a water trough, or the vet's latest visit to medicate a mare. Meanwhile, mom, who taught political science at the local junior college, would stew over the grill and direct their daughter in the fixing of the salads. If anyone got close to the grill she'd drill them on her opinion of the latest foreign policy decision by the White House. In other words, the kids were there but left out. It was noticeable, but who would have thought the situation was enough for Jake to do what he did. I was distraught for weeks afterwards.

> **I found the absence of any mention of evil's participation...wrong; and I found it repugnant that the blame for suicide was placed at the feet of the Almighty as "God's will."**

I share all that because it was again at Jake's funeral where I heard those all too famous lines, "We don't know why these things happen. It's God's will, I guess. We have to trust the Almighty with our lives and in our death. God knows what's best for us. We have to accept this as the best thing for us, from a loving God."

There was no culpability on the part of Jake, the culture, the church's ministry to him, nor on the part of Jake's parents. You might argue with me that the funeral sermon was certainly no place to bring up the parents' failures. And, I would certainly agree. But I found the absence of any mention of evil's participation in Jake's death wrong; and I found it repugnant that the blame for Jake's suicide was placed at the feet of the Almighty as "God's will."

Death of a Midnight Rider

IN 1998, WHEN my son Josh was a senior at the U.S. Naval Academy, he came back to the Detroit area and home for Thanksgiving. Another midshipman, a sophomore that Josh knew, also came home for the break. Randy (not his real name) was from a Christian family that Pam also knew from the staff at the Christian school where Pam taught. About midnight, the Sunday after Thanksgiving, and the day before the midshipmen were to return to the academy, Randy was on his way home from a church party. He was riding his motorcycle when he crossed through an intersection and was broadsided by a pickup driven by a drunk driver. Randy died instantly.

At the funeral, which we all attended, along with Randy's family and a number of military personnel, the pastor reassured us that Randy was in heaven and that God loved him, and his guardian angel carried Randy off, etc. And then there was the line I was hoping not to hear: "We don't know why these things happen. But we have the confidence that God is in control. That his will was at work in this tragedy."

For some weeks after that I could not shake the juxtaposition of the contrary theological propositions: "God's will was at work in this tragedy. We had no idea why these things happen. We just have to trust God who loves us."

I was convinced, however, that we *did* know *why* such things happened. In particular:

1. Randy was driving a motorcycle, without a helmet.
2. Visibility at intersections was limited because it was midnight.
3. Randy did not cross the intersection defensively.
4. The driver of the pickup ran a red light.
5. The driver of the pickup was drunk.

And finally, the one reason that I thought should have been front and center.

6. Evil is out to destroy what is good.

Was the failure to mention any of these another example of Evangelicals pretending to be victorious and always in control? Was it God's will that Randy died that night? A funeral is no place to condemn bad or careless behavior of a Christian who has just died, but neither is it a time to blame God.

This was not a religion I wanted much to do with, where the epitome of love and goodness is blamed for evil…even accidental evil.

The Lost Application

IN 1990 OUR oldest daughter, who graduated from high school *cum laude*, applied to Taylor University, a highly respected Evangelical school known for its Christian witness and high academic standards. She applied only to Taylor, because she was sure that's where she wanted to go. So, we were careful to follow all the application rules and timetables.

Because we had mailed everything in ahead of the early deadlines, and had ensured that everything was complete with transcripts and letters of recommendations, we sat back without much of a concern.

The deadline to hear back from Taylor passed, however, and so at Pam's insistence I called the Admission's Office to find out what had happened. After being passed around from one department to the next, the assistant admissions director came on the phone.

She told me that Trudy's application had been held up, perhaps indefinitely, because it was incomplete. I told the woman that was impossible. But she insisted that we had missed the deadline because we had checked that part of the form requesting financial aid, and our paperwork for financial aid had not been included with the application. I told the woman she was wrong because I was the one that completed said financial aid paperwork and stuffed the envelope. She in turn "corrected me" and said I was no doubt mistaken and that we were free to submit to her financial aid papers at some point in the next three weeks but that Trudy would only receive second tier consideration because of missing the first deadline. And, further, it was entirely possible (she was threatening me for being cock sure of myself) that Trudy could be denied entry because of our...ah, mistake.

The disappointing conversation ended, and I passed on the bad news to my family, and then to a few others in our extended family. In my mind I had already determined that I would resend the paperwork (I had copies). But I was worked-up at what I had been told—that I was, evidently, an incompetent robot who was mistaken about spending an hour filling out a form with very private financial information, and then repressing my memory and not including the financial aid paperwork with the application.

The telephone call with the university had occurred late on a Friday afternoon.

On Sunday, my extended adult family (except for Trudy) and friends at church consoled me. They told me it was pretty clear that

Trudy's rejection (which was now inevitable in their minds) was *"God closing the door." "It must be God's will, that she not go to this particular Christian school."* I was told, *"You should just accept God's will in this matter and move on. Have faith that God knows what's best for her life, not her, not you, not now."*

> **Such an attitude did not allow for human incompetence, but rather assigned the incompetence as an example of God's perfection.**

What irked me was that such an attitude did not allow for human incompetence, but rather assigned the incompetence as an example of God's perfection.

On Monday, before I made copies of our financial papers to mail in again, I again called the Taylor admissions office. This time I asked to speak directly to the VP of admissions. When he came on the line I introduced myself (standing up straight and using the lowest voice I could command), explained the situation and my conversation from Friday, and my dissatisfaction with the assumption that I was a lobotomized, neophyte envelope stuffer. I explained that as a boy at home I had worked for my dad stuffing insurance renewal invoices into envelopes, and that because of my competent work, my family enjoyed a reasonable income. I also explained that my part-time job in college was stuffing boxes with funeral announcement envelopes for shipment to funeral homes all over America, and I was sure everyone that needed to get buried did so, on time, because of my anal attention to detail. Would he please look again for the lost financial papers and when he finds them treat my daughter as if her application was received early, and not late?

Two hours later I received a call from the first lady I talked to on Friday, the one that told me I had no business stuffing envelops. Very nicely, as if it was all her idea, she said she found Trudy's financial papers misplaced in the financial aid office, and indeed they had been dated and time-stamped before the original deadline.

It took a while, but four years later Trudy graduated from Taylor University, again with honors, and had maintained her financial aid scholarship all the way through school.

So much for blaming God for our incompetence.

A FTER YEARS OF observing Evangelicalism from within, a pattern emerged. I came to believe that Evangelicals, at a subliminal level, found it difficult to accept that they might be wrong.

In my mind, they too easily politicized theology to save face, and without an overarching authority that held to more altruistic philosophy, the pastor of a church could say just about anything, back it up with a biblical excerpt, and there'd be no way to check if he was right.

What was left was *the individual*. As a human being, it is reasonable that I should only believe in and trust what *I thought* was perfect. I suspected that is a common bias. We were each our own pope, we might say. Why was that? Because, on some issues the Bible was no help at all. It didn't speak directly about Ponzi schemes, running midnight traffic signals, or office protocol, except in general terms that required interpretation. The more I ran into these inconveniences and searched for an answer, I came to see that there was a difference between the *object of our adoration* (which may indeed be perfect), and *our understanding of it* (which would always be imperfect.)

Cosmologist and Christian apologist to the scientific community, Dr. Hugh Ross, points out that *the Bible and Nature, having both originated from a perfect God, will always perfectly agree*. But the human disciplines that explain the Bible and Nature, namely *Theology* and *Science*, are often going to disagree because their theories originate from imperfect human beings.

> **I wondered if the fear of questioning what was considered perfect, namely Christianity, was the basis for not questioning our imperfect interpretation of it.**

I wondered if the fear of questioning what was considered perfect, namely Christianity, was the basis for not questioning our imperfect interpretation of it—our doctrines, rules and creeds.

While I'm confident it wasn't the conscious reason why HPBC removed Jan Styka's foreboding *The Crucifixion* and replaced it with pictures of smiling missionaries, there was perhaps an unconscious effort to remove from sight something that seemed imperfect but was, in fact, perfect—*The Crucifixion,* and put before our eyes something that seemed perfect, but, in fact, was imperfect—happy missionaries.

It was why, as a kid, standing up in testimony services, I dared not give witness to my imperfections and sins, but only talk about my holiness, and acts of righteousness, even if my only righteous act was getting saved ten years earlier. I felt that if I failed at projecting perfection, then Christianity would cease to be perfect in the eyes of others. So, when things did not go according to plans, I would compensate and claim those bad things were part of God's will.

Of course, such a position resulted in mockery from the pagans in my life. I tried to tell them they needed Jesus, but they'd take one look at me and rattle off all the ways in which I was a hypocrite. I was ridiculed, as I noticed many Christians in our culture were.

It took a long time to realize that I wasn't prefect. I was just forgiven.

I also wondered if this was why my mom was so concerned when I happened to go into a Catholic Church with Ned one time when he went to confession. I wasn't supposed to go to confession and tell a priest my sins. I was supposed to go directly to Jesus. Yes, as an Evangelical I was supposed to regularly ask Jesus to forgive my sins. But, it was supposed to be *private*...so that no one else knew I was a sinner... except my mother, of course.

And so, I came to incorrectly recognize that although I was imperfect and a sinner, my imperfection was between God and me and no one else was to know. When imperfect things happened, it was appropriate not to blame my weaknesses, or poor decisions, or even my sin. No, my job was to be a witness for Christ even in the midst of trials and tribulations. I just needed to praise God in my sorrow, and tell everyone that God was in control...that God's will, not mine, was directing everything in my life... even the bad stuff.

> In other words, if my intentions were good, I could never be culpable, and it was God's will that was to blame.

In other words, if my intentions were good, I could never be culpable, and it was God's will that was to blame for the undesirable things that happened due to Natural Law's reluctance to embrace my understanding of the universe.

I wondered if it was God's fault that I was still wandering in search of His Church? Little did I know that I would not have to wonder or wander much longer.[1]

---

1 I cannot resist a related story. When Catholic evangelist and Hollywood screenwriter Barbara Nicolosi was catechizing TV drama show-runner Barbara Hall, Hall expressed concern to Nicolosi that she would be a terrible Christian because of all the sin in her life and her perceived inability to be good. Nicolosi's response was this: "You may become a terrible Christian, but you'll be a great Catholic."

68
The Closest Thing To Me

I N APRIL OF 1997 I was running out of options for new or different places to worship. I think I visited every denomination and independent church this side of hell...except the Quakers (sorry, Bill).

Finally, I was forced to visit the one church closest to my house, if not closest to hell.

Groan! I don't wanna go there.

PAM WRITES: *Just when I thought we'd tried them all, one day Stan declared, "I think I'll try the Catholic Church." I remember exactly what I said. It wasn't a kind inquiry...I was annoyed, "Why would you want to do that?" Going into a Catholic Church was something I knew I never wanted to do. "You go," I said. "I'm going back to Highland Park."*

It was exhaustion and boredom that caused me to walk into St. James Catholic Church in Novi, MI, the closest large church to my house, and the only major church I had ignored in my wanderings. I had avoided it because my experience as a child living in a Catholic neighborhood had convinced me that Catholics were not very good Christians. They attended a ritualistic affair called the Mass, prayed in vain to Mary to save them from hell, swore a lot, didn't have Bibles stacked in every corner of their homes, displayed porcelain idols in their front yards — usually chipped and faded—had a pope that wanted to take over the world, loved authority (a big bug-a-boo for me), and their refrigerators were filled with beer. The idea of walking into a Catholic church made me shudder. But I was worn down and susceptible to groveling in the gutter. So, one Sunday I drove the mile-and-a-half to the place.

St. James looked like a modern, but unpretentious mini-cathedral constructed from bricks instead of marble. Steeply gabled standing-seam metal roofs framed the gable ends that, high up, housed 25-foot diameter stained glass windows. Brick pavers created a wide sidewalk under a similarly peaked wood and brick canopy supported by rounded brick columns that stretched from the parking lot to the four oversized wood carved entrance doors.

As I walked in with hundreds of others I first noticed that no one was carrying a Bible. But I was carrying mine, the biggest one I could find. I was determined to be a witness for Christ especially if I went to a Catholic Church. Secondly, I couldn't help but notice how many were dressed-up, or dressed-down. My mother would have turned over in her grave. The most egregious were teen girls in halter-tops, short-shorts, and flip-flops. It was, in part, a bad scene. I almost turned around and found a fig tree to sit under.[1]

But I also noticed that there were a number of fathers in business casual attire holding babies while they simultaneously opened doors for mom's dragging smartly dressed kids behind.

Passing from the foyer into the nave I was taken aback at the beautiful light oak and pine, open-beam ceiling that jutted heavenward, over a hardwood floor and a sea of chairs neatly forming pews. In the center, hanging from threads from the four central corners of the transept, were tall, slender green banners that floated effortlessly in the cross currents of the room. The inside walls were white, rough-finished cinder-blocks that set off the large stained glass windows, and darker stained wood. On one wall was a large cross with a fully robed Jesus leaning forward off the cross, arms raised in blessing over the congregation, as if he were in the process of being resurrected. The decor was simple and clean, not unlike the plain Free Methodist Churches I had been raised it. But here there was also art, especially in the very large stained glass windows. It was a bold, beautiful place.

As I looked for a seat I noticed all manner of people. There were clearly the well-dressed men in suits and women in hats and dresses. There were also workmen in t-shirts, jeans and work boots, and women in fashionable and unfashionable torn jeans and tire-tread sandals. The children were numerous and noisy but sitting with their moms and

---

1 Read the story of Jonah when he finally went to Nineveh, in Jonah 4.

dads. In the Evangelical churches I had attended, the kids would have been taken to another room for "Junior Church" or the "cry room." But here, there seemed to be a desire to keep the family together when worshipping God, regardless of the noise.

I noticed a couple of nuns in gray and blue habits, a scattering of African Americans, several large Mexican families, and an older Indian couple, the woman in a full sari. *Clearly, here was the world.* When you walked into a Free Methodist Church, or many of the Evangelical churches we attended, you easily got the sense that the congregation had been selected for their homogeneity, not their universality.

I found a seat near the side on an aisle so I could observe the congregation, and in case I chose, make a hasty retreat. Up front on a slightly raised platform was a chair facing the congregation, an altar (i.e. a large communion table centrally positioned) with a white cloth draped over it, and a podium (to one side). An organist and small choir were off to the side on the main floor. There was no balcony.

Soon, the organist spoke into a microphone and announced the number of the opening hymn. As he started to play, without being told, (there was no song leader as every Evangelical Church demanded) the people stood and began to sing. I looked around. The place was full, maybe 700, with more streaming in.

As the congregation sang, a procession came up the center aisle from the back of the church, first a crucifix on a pole with candle bearers to the side, then a man holding a red book high in the air, and finally a vested priest. Thus started my first Catholic Mass. It was so different in many ways—both subtle and obvious—that I spent most of the time just getting my bearings and remembering very little of what was said except for what I recount below.

At the time I was working for Sandy Corporation as the Creative Director over the Harley Davidson Business University account. As I have discussed earlier, a significant part of my job was finding and evaluating good inspirational speakers and trainers. Thus, I was always on the lookout for good talent that could hold an audience's attention and pass on memorable content.

The priest for this, my first Mass, was Rev. James Cronk, whom, after you were introduced, was simply addressed as "Father." (That was one nice thing about Catholicism, that I discovered early on. You never had to remember the name of any priest to show him respect. Just call him "Father.")

Although now, some 18 years later, I don't remember the readings (it was shortly after Easter) or what the homily was about. I do know that I could recite all the basic points of Cronk's talk for a couple of months thereafter. The man had a rare talent. He was able to stand comfortably before the large group of people without pacing or rocking or fidgeting, and without any theatrics or special effects, tell a story, make some points, and segue into the rest of the liturgy as if it were all one seamless whole.

I found out later that Rev. Cronk's pastime (especially, on vacation) was attending Shakespeare plays…in Europe. He didn't come off as an actor, but he had that subtle flair for public speaking that connected with his audience, and tied the entire Mass together in a way that impressed my professional instincts.

At home I recalled the outline of the homily to Pam point by point. This was remarkable, since I do not have a great memory. Often, I would take notes during a sermon. But going to a Catholic Mass I had no expectation of wanting to do so, so I didn't. I knew it wasn't my ability to remember, but rather Fr. Cronk's ability to communicate.

After that first Sunday, I wanted to see and hear this man again. Sounds silly, but remember this was part of my job. To find talent. And Cronk *was talent*, as we say in the entertainment business.

I have to admit, however, that there was another reason. Evangelicals, like myself, had been trained to be attracted to the personality of the person in the pulpit, not the liturgy or even the purpose for the service. Huge Protestant mega-churches are built around such personalities, and when that personality retires or leaves for some reason, the church will shrink to a fraction of its former size.

An example in recent memory was the retirement of Rev. Robert Schuller, who built a large worldwide television ministry. He broadcast "The Hour of Power" from his famous Crystal Cathedral in Garden Grove, California. Shortly after he retired the ministry went bankrupt. Ironically, today, the soaring, glass-paned cathedral designed by American architect Philip Johnson, is owned by the Catholic Archdiocese of Orange County and is the chair (or official church) of the local bishop.

So, early on, Fr. Cronk was the accomplished preacher that drew me back. In his early 50s, about my age, he was shorter and a bit rotund, with a round face and dark hair that circumvented his thinning top. He tended to be jovial but I cannot recall him ever telling a joke. When teaching or preaching the essence of his persona was, "Trust me, I know this is true (and cool) but you may not believe a bit of it. I'm here to help, but only if you want."

THERE WAS ONE other thing Fr. Cronk did, which no doubt contributed to my appreciation of his presentation skills. It had to do with context. Now, what I'm going to explain next I do for folks who have not been to Mass very much. And I certainly didn't understand all of this during my first visit. But I want to share something that did affect me that first Sunday, but it was only much later that I learned enough to be able to explain what caught my attention. So let me jump forward a bit as a matter of explanation.

The Mass is divided into two parts.
1. The Liturgy of the Word, and
2. The Liturgy of the Eucharist.

The Liturgy of the Word is subdivided into four parts:
1. The Biblical Readings
2. The Homily
3. The Profession of Faith (a recitation of the Creed)
4. The Prayers of the Faithful

The Biblical Readings are comprised of four readings: (1) Old Testament, (2) Psalm (which is sung), (3) New Testament Epistle, and (3) Gospel, and all are thematically related. For example, the readings for, July 27, 2014 were:

1 Kings 3:5, 7-12 - where the story is told about the Lord appearing to King Solomon and telling him to "ask something of me and I will give it to you." Solomon asks for *wisdom* and an understanding heart to judge the people rightly. For asking as he did, the Lord *rewards* Solomon not only with *wisdom* greater than anyone else in history, but also with great physical *treasures* and wealth.

Psalm 119 (various verses scattered throughout) - where David proclaims his love for God's law *(wisdom* to govern), which is more precious than *gold and silver*.

Romans 8:28-30 - where Paul instructs the Christians in Rome that all things work together for good for those who love and obey God [practical *wisdom*], and whom God will justify and *glorify*. (Think of how God did this for Solomon and David when they obeyed him.)

Matthew 13:44-52 - where Jesus portrays the Kingdom of Heaven to his disciples as a _treasure_ buried in a field, or a merchant who finds a pearl of great price, and how the _wisdom_ of God is more valuable than _gold and riches_.

After these Scriptures are read, along with moments of silence to let them assimilate in the congregation's minds, Fr. Cronk would leave his chair and the altar, come down to the front of the platform and deliver his extemporaneous homily, presumably on one or more of the Biblical Readings.

Now, recall that the next item on the agenda is the Profession of Faith in which the congregation stands and recites The Nicene Creed. As Cronk finished his homily he would say something like this:

> As Solomon asked God for wisdom and God gave him much more...as David reveled in the perfection of God's laws to guide his life toward all that is good, true and beautiful...as Paul reminds us to trust God in all that happens, both good and bad in our lives...and finally, as Christ pictures for us a buried treasure in the field that is worth selling all we have so we can buy that field, WE BELIEVE...

Cronk would pause for just a moment as he looked out over the congregation. Instantly, on some nonverbal cue, the congregation would stand to its feet and continue in unison with him...

> ...IN ONE GOD, THE FATHER ALMIGHTY, MAKER OF HEAVEN AND EARTH. AND IN ONE LORD JESUS CHRIST..."

It was masterful. The Scripture-Homily-Creed was all as one. But that first Sunday, I was caught off guard. I didn't know the Nicene Creed. I could not have recited it to save my life. But I heard the words clearly come from the mouth of the unshaven, droopy eye-lidded, dude next to me who wore a black Doobie Brothers' T-shirt, worn jeans and dirty cowboy boots. I had to think about that. _Is it possible that this Doobie Dude knows more about the faith than I do? -- Naw!_ Not possible. But he did know the creed...and I did not.

I was impressed—not so much with Tex, although I thought about him off and on for a while—but, with Cronk. I had to go back and hear this guy again.

Family commitments with our children's various activities at HPBC prompted me to attend there with Pam the next few weeks. But soon I went back.

I T WAS SOMETIME in May 1997 that I next attended St. James. I sat a little closer to the front and center. While Fr. Cronk again did his usual masterful job at homiletics, I didn't remember it like I had the first Sunday. This time something else surprised me.

It was the Readings. This second time at Mass was the first time I paid attention to them. Remember, I didn't think Catholics read the Bible. After all, they didn't take their Bibles to church. So, how could they be familiar with Scripture?

About 30-minutes into the worship, it hit me like the 30-pound original edition of the King James Bible…with all 73 books. I was dumbfounded. The first-half of the service was all Scripture. *What!? How could that be?* Did I miss this last time? I thought back. No, they had done the same thing. This was ritual. They did this all the time, probably all around the world, in tens of thousands of Masses everywhere.

After I left Mass that second Sunday, I thought a lot about what I had heard. Walking out to the car I realized that for the Gospel, everyone stood up and sang Alleluia, in respect, as Cronk paraded the red book (*Was that a book of all the Gospels?*) from the altar to the podium before he read from it. I had never done that in an Evangelical church, but standing and praising God for the Gospel before and after it was read each time sure seemed appropriate.

Somewhat jokingly, I mused about hearing more Scripture in the first half of one Mass, than I had heard in a month of Sunday's in the last Evangelical church I had attended.

> **I mused about hearing more Scripture in the first half of one Mass, than I had heard in a month of Sunday's in the last Evangelical church I had attended.**

There, the pastor had read a few verses of Scripture that took about one to two minutes, and then preached on it for 45 minutes. Here, in the Mass, I got about 30 minutes of Scripture and a 10-minute homily. The two services were effectively the opposite, with the greater Biblical emphasis demonstrated *not* by the Bible Evangelical Church but by the "non-bible-reading-ignorant-of-Scripture" Catholic Church.

What's up with that? I had to figure this out.

I DECIDED THAT THE very next Sunday I would go back for Mass the third time. The problem was, I knew that Pam would not like my going, or understanding any explanation I gave. She had been all through this too many times before.

PAM WRITES: *When he told me this, I challenged his plans, quite assertively, which was unusual for me. "Wasn't once enough?"*

He tried to explain but I was not happy. Thankfully he backed off his plans this one time and we avoided an argument. He seemed to waffle about what he was going to do, but I didn't believe it. I sensed that as soon as I left the house for services at HPBC he'd sneak off, go to Mass, and be back before I returned.

And that's exactly what I did, following Christ's command:

Be as shrewd as snakes and as innocent as doves.[1]

When I got to the foyer, Fr. Cronk was there in his vestments, welcoming people as they arrived. I decided to ask a polite question in a small step to get to know him. I approached him.

Cronk stuck out his hand. "Hi, welcome to St. James, what's your name? Are you new here?"

"Hi, I'm Stan Williams. Glad to meet you. Yeah, this is just my third time. Say, I noticed there are a lot of people that come to Mass. How many people came to worship last week? I didn't see an Attendance Board up front."

And that was the first time I heard James Cronk laugh out loud. As if he already knew the answer, he said, "What's an Attendance Board? Count people, you mean? And post the numbers on the front wall?

"Yeah," I said.

Cronk's smile was infectious, and he chuckled so hard that his rotund body bounced. "That's disgusting! Why would we do that? I know the Apostles counted them, 4,000 on one hillside and 5,000 on another, but those were the same guys that were fighting over sitting at Jesus's right

> **"What's an Attendance Board? Count people, you mean? And post the numbers on the front wall? ...That's disgusting!"**
>
> (Fr. James Cronk)

---

1 Matthew 10:16 (NIV)

and left. Christ never told the church to count people. Gracious! But to answer your questions, I have no idea, and I don't want to know."

It dawned on me that I just might be out of my league.

Mary Kochan, my editor, when reading this passage, reminded me of the dangers of counting people. In 2 Samuel 24, and 1 Chronicles 21, Satan incited King David to take a census of Israel, which God allowed. But God was not pleased. David orders his general, Joab, to count the people. But Joab challenges the king, "Why does my lord want to do this? Why should he bring guilt on Israel?" But David overrules, and Joab organizes the census. But "Joab did not include Levi and Benjamin in the numbering, because the king's command was repulsive to him. Counting the people was "evil in the sight of God; so he punished Israel."[1]

The passage in 2 Chronicles about the consequences of counting due to pride is mind-blowing and worth repeating here. It's the story that was no doubt going through Fr. Cronk's mind when I asked if he was counting his people (underlining mine):

> *The Lord said to Gad, David's seer, "Go and tell David, 'This is what the Lord says: I am giving you three options. Choose one of them for me to carry out against you.'" So Gad went to David and said to him, "This is what the Lord says: 'Take your choice: three years of famine, three months of being swept away before your enemies, with their swords overtaking you, or three days of the sword of the Lord—days of plague in the land, with the angel of the Lord ravaging every part of Israel.' Now then, decide how I should answer the one who sent me." David said to Gad, "I am in deep distress. Let me fall into the hands of the Lord, for his mercy is very great; but do not let me fall into human hands." So the Lord sent a plague on Israel, and <u>seventy thousand men of Israel fell dead</u>. And God sent an angel to destroy Jerusalem. But as the angel was doing so, the Lord saw it and relented concerning the disaster and said to the angel who was destroying the people, "Enough! Withdraw your hand." The angel of the Lord was then standing at the threshing floor of Araunah the Jebusite. <u>David looked up and saw the angel of the Lord standing between heaven and earth, with a drawn sword in his hand extended over Jerusalem</u>.*[2]

1 1 Chronicles 21:1-6
2 1 Chronicles 21:9-16.

After reading that I'm afraid to balance my checking account.

A S I SAT through the Mass and watched, listened, and contemplated what I had learned the first two times, I slowly came to the surprising realization that the whole service was about Jesus Christ. All the words, the invocations, the gestures…were not about the saints or Mary, although occasionally they were invoked to pray for us. The Mass didn't focus on parish activities such as bingo or the parish festival. Notices of such activities were left until after Mass.

This discovery was unnerving, and it was in spite of a very deliberate effort to find something that *wasn't* about Christ, or directed to him in worship. A sliver would have sufficed…perhaps that the Mass emphasized some insignificant artifact of the faith like symbols, statues, or prayer clothes, or such. I figured at the very least there would be a reading by a pope that would be elevated to the authority of Scripture. But at the end of every Mass I had not collected one splinter of evidence that the Mass was anything but about Christ. There was nothing that could support my hypothesis without twisting the clear intent of the priest and the liturgy.

> **At the end of every Mass I had not collected one splinter of evidence that the Mass was anything but about Christ.**

In scientific and statistical terms I had applied a *null-hypothesis* to my observations, by attempting to collect evidence that there was *nothing* about Catholicism or the Mass that correlated it to Christianity and the worship of Christ. That I found evidence only to the contrary disproved my null-hypothesis and I had to conclude the Mass was Christian in intent and execution.[1]

In all these observations, however, I have to clarify one thing. I did not believe in the real presence of Christ in the Eucharist. That would be a topic I'd deal with later. Neither was I aware of the criticism leveled by some anti-Catholics who claimed that bread and wine in Catholic Mass was worshipped. I saw all the bowing, genuflecting and even the priest holding the host and cup up proclaiming it to be the Body and Blood of our Lord. But at the time I interpreted all of that as symbolic, not literal. I saw it as very Christ-centered, not bread and wine centered. Such things similarly were said and done in Evangelical commu-

---

1 This is the scientific method at work. Using a null-hypothesis helps to avoid bias evaluations. See Wikipedia on-line.

nion services, too, where the intention was entirely symbolic. The pastor would proclaim that the bread was the body of the Lord, and likewise the little grape juice cups. But there would be subtle words included that indicated the pastor's intention was symbolic. I carried over that understanding, at first, to the Mass.

So, considering my incorrect understanding of the Eucharistic consecration, I finally had to admit that the entire Mass was directed to and about Jesus Christ, with an emphasis on the "to" and not just "about." Indeed the name of Jesus was invoked over 30 times in prayers, Scripture, the homily and the Liturgy of the Eucharist.

> **The entire Mass was directed to and about Jesus Christ, with an emphasis on the "to" and not just "about."**

I reeled in my seat.

One of the things that had always bugged me about many Evangelical services is that God was only invoked during the prayers, rarely did we talk to him during worship. Instead Christ was usually referred to in the third person—e.g. *God is good. Jesus is God. We love Jesus. We worship God. He watches over us.*

But in this third Mass I attended, and I was pretty sure in the first two, all the words were directed in the second person to God and to Jesus—e.g. *God, You are good. Jesus, we acknowledge You as God. We love you, Jesus. We worship You, O God. You watch over and protect us.*

To me this was a big deal. This was worship.

At the same time I took note of the people in the pews (actually, they were chairs) and their attitude. Yes, there were a great many who seemed to be going through the motions without sincerity. But there was an equal number who were devout and deeply involved in what was going on. I also noticed there were books in the pews that people were opening and peering into from time to time. These were missals that contained the liturgy, the Scripture reading, along with the formal prayers, and of course the hymns. I thought, *That's why they didn't bring Bibles to church, books with Scripture were provided in the pockets between every chair.* I still thought Bibles would be a cool thing to have in hand.

By flipping through the missal I discovered that I was not supposed to take communion, unless I was Catholic. I was tempted. I sure wanted to. There was something right about taking communion every Sunday...it was "whenever we remembered Him." But there seemed to be some sort of secret hand signal involved that I was not familiar with.

So, I decided to quietly stay in my seat when others in my row went up. And everybody seemed to go up. The line of communicants was as mismatched as any cattle call for movie extras. As I watched the long lines of people, I thought back to the many times I went forward to the altar to get saved. Unlike Evangelical communion services where everyone stayed in their seats, here, in the Mass, everyone was going forward to receive Christ (literally)

It was about this time that I made the observation that what *I had called* an "altar" from my Evangelical days was actually a "rail" that stretched across the front of the church. Some Catholic churches had rails, but they were called communion rails, not "altars rails," and certainly not "altars." But in Evangelical churches we called the rail an "altar." It suddenly hit me, looking at the table at St. James upon which Fr. Cronk prayed over the communion elements, that the *table*, not the *rail* was the *altar*. I recall a rush of eternal embarrassment at the misunderstanding that came over me. In fact, in Evangelical churches they did have an "altar". It was the table near the pulpit that had the words "Do This In Remembrance of Me" engraved on the front, but the table was almost never used. And, in Evangelical Churches, the preacher was asking us to come to "kneel at the altar." But we never knelt at the "altar," we knelt at the "rail," but never to receive communion but only to confess our sins. The equivocation involved was deep and confusing. Back in St. James and the communion distribution, I realized I was at once intellectually befuddled and spiritually excited.

> **Unlike Evangelical communion services where everyone stayed in their seats, here, in the Mass, everyone was going forward to receive Christ (literally).**

At the end of this third Mass I anxiously walked back to the foyer and looked for Fr. Cronk. He was in the midst of the throng, rapidly shaking hands with people as they left, stopping and chatting with a few. I stood back and waited, rehearsing my pitch. I wanted an extra moment with him.

When the crowd thinned, he caught my eye and I walked over and shook his hand once again. He remembered my name. He looked up at me, and smiled. "Hi, Stan. How did you like Mass?"

"Father Cronk," I said, "I've been a Christian all my life. I was raised in a Bible believing Evangelical home. My heritage has been blessed with preachers and missionaries back generations. My wife and I are both Christians and we're bringing our children up in the Lord."

I paused…then asked my question: "May I take communion with you next Sunday?"

Cronk looked me in the eye and said, "Well, let me ask you something, Stan. Do you believe that the communion elements, what we call The Eucharist, are the real Body, Blood, Soul, and Divinity of Jesus Christ?"

Although I was stunned by the ludicrousness of the question I didn't hesitate, "Of course not. That's ridiculous!"

He didn't hesitate either. He smiled quietly and said simply, "Then we'd prefer you not."

The silence between us seemed deafening.

I was offended—deeply offended—and I quickly walked out of the church.

Fifty feet from my car, I prayed under my breath, "God, what *idiots*! How can that be true? They're nuts."

Three strides later, and 40 feet from my car, my Guardian Angel spoke (in his Tubby the Tuba vice): "Okay, *idiot*, what don't you get? The first Sunday you didn't expect anything challenging, just impersonal ritual. You didn't see that did you? The second Sunday, you didn't expect any reference to the Bible, and you got 30 minutes of Scripture with a very good homily. Hey, remember, you didn't think they even read the Bible. And then today, o-great-one, all-knowing-being that you presume to be, (he always addressed me in "lower-case") you discovered the Mass was not only about Jesus, it was all directed to Him."

> **My Guardian Angel stood between me and my car, glaring: "So what else don't you understand?"**

"So what?" I said.

My Guardian Angel stood between me and my car, glaring: "So what else don't you understand?"

PAM WRITES: When Stan came back from that third Mass, he was clearly upset, but he didn't explain himself. I thought, "Good. Finally the truth came out. It took three times, but at least the man might now see the light of day." I decided to keep quiet and let God work on Stan's heart. Clearly things were looking in my favor. Praise the Lord!

69
Searching

THE REBUFFS, ONLY moments apart, one from Fr. Cronk and the second from my Guardian Angel, threw off my game. I had walked out on Cronk and his church after only three Sundays in May of 1997. Usually, at Evangelical Churches, it took three years, average, for me to stomp away.

For a few days I was convinced that Catholicism was indeed crazy. Sight, smell, taste, touch…all would confirm that even after the hocus-pocus around the altar, the host was still bread and the cup was still wine. (It never occurred to me that I should be happy it wasn't diluted grape juice.) Never mind that first century skeptics looked at Jesus and saw only a human being. Yes, it took the faith of Peter to recognize the incarnate Son of God. But it never occurred to me that faith might also be necessary to recognize the presence of Jesus in The Eucharist.

I did not go back to St. James the next two Sundays. And the following week I left on a business trip.

While passing through the airport bookstore, in one of those rotating racks of large-size paper backs, a title jumped out and grabbed me by the throat: *Why Do Catholics Do That? A Guide to the Teachings and Practices of the Catholic Church,* by Dr. Kevin Orlin Johnson.[1]

Why, indeed!

I bought it.

---

1 Johnson, Kevin Orlin (1994). *Why Do Catholics Do That?* Ballantine Press, 287 pages with index.

O N THE PLANE I scanned the table of contents. This was not a basic primer in Catholic theology. Johnson was an art historian who had merged his academic career with writing religious columns for the secular press. As such, Johnson was more interested with the practice of the faith on the periphery of Catholic culture than dissecting Catholic teaching. This was fine by me. I was not ready for heavy theology. Besides, in spite of the recent rebukes by both a mortal and an immortal being, within minutes of each other, I needed a straight-ahead explanation of temporal things for which I had little knowledge.

In very succinct writing, as you might expect from a columnist, Johnson explored topics like purgatory, how the church makes laws, why the Old Testament is important, decoding symbols, the sign of the cross, the Miraculous Medal, chant, Stations of the Cross, Monks & Nuns, apparitions of Mary, the Rosary, and two dozen other topics.

I turned to Chapter 12, "The Rosary: A Garden of Christian Images." Before I started to read I checked my assumptions—it was another null-hypothesis. *I'm not gullible. I'm a skeptic by nature. None of this has any historic or sensory validity.* I wanted to set up the debate with my presuppositions before Johnson presented his. The Rosary, I reminded myself, was a litany of vain repetitions that dulled the mind into a trance-like state, thus mimicking a religious experience. I figured Johnson would probably explain the benefits of such self-induced trances to Christian meditation. I needed logical reasons for things, not vacuous practices that dulled the mind.

Johnson began the chapter chronicling the invasion of the Middle East by The Turks who were conquering nation after nation and murdering millions and forcing the survivors to convert to Islam.

Pope Pius V Ghislieri called on the princes of Europe to defend themselves and the Church. A big naval battle was brewing off the coast of Greece in the Gulf of Lepanto that pitted the Ottoman Empire against a fleet of the Holy League, made up of ships from European Catholic maritime states. The European fleet of 198 ships, was vastly outnumbered by the Ottoman fleet of 338 ships.[1] But the Pope had asked all of Europe to pray the Rosary on the first Sunday of October in 1571. At the end of the day, known as the Battle of Lepanto, almost all of the Turks were driven to shore or drowned. Europe was saved.

Johnson then flashes back to how the Rosary began, as a devotion with the Lord's Prayer which was repeated as many as 300 times

---

1 On-Line Wikipedia, Battle of Lepanto.

during the day by hermits. Time passed and over 60 different prayers were approved for daily use. Irish monks would count off their prayers by counting the knots on the chord around their waist. Later, Lady Godiva introduced a string of jewels for the same purpose that she donated to a convent and asked that the jewels be placed over the neck of a statue of Mary.

Among many other tidbits of history, Johnson traces the development of the "Hail, Mary!" prayer and how it was purposely composed from Holy Writ as a way of praying with Scripture. The prayer begins with Gabriel's annunciation to Christ's future mother: "Hail Mary, full of grace" and incorporates Elizabeth's greeting to Mary at the Visitation, "Blessed are thou amongst women and blessed is the fruit of thy womb."

Johnson also explains that at the Council of Ephesus in 431, one of the heresies being debated was whether or not Jesus was the Son of God at his birth. The heretics claimed Jesus only acquired his divinity later in life not at conception and not at birth. The people of Ephesus, who were very loyal to Mary, who tradition has it lived in their city with the Apostle John after Christ's death, rioted in the streets whenever anyone tried to deny that Mary was not only the Mother of Christ (a human) but also the Mother of God (the incarnate infant).

So, the council of Ephesus decided to proclaim Mary as the "Mother of God." The move was not intended to elevate Mary, but to protect the divinity of Christ at his conception by the Holy Spirit. Thus, at the end of the "Hail, Mary!" prayer is the line, "Holy Mary! *Mother of God!* Pray for us sinners!"

The heart of the rosary, Johnson said, were the devout contemplations and meditations on scenes from Jesus's life that accompany each recitation of the "Hail, Mary!" prayer. The vocal repetitions become a secondary vocal pacing for what is busily going on in the praying and worshipping mind. Johnson writes:

> *As your fingers count off the beads, you don't think about work or bills or school. You spend time with Christ and his mother—you keep them company, you might say— contemplating the great events of their lives, the turning points in the Cycle of Redemption. You feel the happiness of the Joyful Mysteries, the pain of the Sorrowful, and the triumph of the Glorious.*[1]

---

1 Johnson, page 101.

To me, this was far from vain repetitions. It was profound meditation and required a disciplined and thoughtful mind. The Rosary suddenly made a lot of sense, and I marveled at how Satan had convinced so many Christians to reject this prayerful practice by associating it with Catholicism.

As I sat on the plane I could close my eyes and place myself in the events of the Gospel. At the birth of Jesus, I was a shepherd; at the temple with Simeon, I was sweeping the floor nearby and heard the prophecies; at the wedding in Cana, I was the servant that the filled the jars with water and then served the first cup to the bridegroom. Shivers ran down my spine as I contemplated being there for those events. Over the next few days, I found my mind wandering into these stories and gleaning the emotions and insights gained by standing within feet of Jesus Christ and listening to him. I was startled at the simplicity and mystical nature of the practice.

Then, I began to consider how this remembrance of the stories from the Bible helped develop the faith of the illiterate masses from centuries past. If I was honest about it, I knew that Bibles and books did not exist for most of the history of Christianity. Stained glass in churches reminded the faithful of the Bible events because they had no Bibles or they could not read. So, the Rosary provided a tool which allowed any person to meditate and contemplate the life of Christ, at anytime during the day or night with just their ten fingers. It was ingenious and I was blown away by the power of this tool of prayer, faith building, and Scriptural meditation.

When I got done with the chapter it was like a few scales fell off my eyes. I started the chapter believing the Rosary was some mindless repetitive vain practice, and ended the chapter realizing the Rosary's very powerful role in Christian history.

S UFFICE IT TO say, I read all of Kevin Orlin Johnson's book and still highly recommend it. The book didn't convince me that Catholicism was true, but it did peel away some of the peripheral questions and objections. It also reinforced my belief that I should always be in a state of inquiry, always searching and always open to new knowledge.

Thus, I attended St. James regularly the rest of the summer, and signed up for a weekly class at St. James called RCIA, or Rite of Christian Initiation for Adults. It was mostly for people preparing to become Catholic at the coming Easter Vigil. But I had no plans of becoming Catholic, and I told Pam that. She was upset, of course, that I had attended a Catholic Church even once. Although she continued to attend HPBC, she clearly voiced her concern about my increasing curiosity with the Roman Church.

PAM WRITES: Stan finally explained himself, sort of. He told me of those first three Sundays at St. James. I knew he had heard (1) some meaty homilies. But I was unsure of him finding (2) loads of Scripture in the Mass, and (3) that the Mass was all about Jesus. That seemed a bit far-fetched. He told me he had wanted to take communion but wasn't allowed until he went through RCIA to get the Catholic understanding of it. So, he signed up for RCIA, which didn't start until September, a summer away. He said he didn't want to become Catholic; he just wanted to attend Mass and take communion, if there was a way to do that. In the meantime, he tried to get me to come to a Mass with him. "Just come to Mass," he'd say.

I did attend Mass with him a couple of times. But I was skeptical.

On the second time, however, I remember distinctly the spot where I sat and how all of a sudden I began to sense the presence of the Lord. I looked around the church and my eyes stopped in a corner to the right of the steps going up to the altar. I didn't know at the time that what I was gazing at was the "nave" for the tabernacle containing the holy Eucharist, nor did I know what that meant. But I had known the presence of God before as a Protestant. I thought it strange that I would feel God in this place. But, it did give me some comfort that the Catholic Church might be an okay place to be.

In September Stan started weekly RCIA classes, without me. Each Thursday night he came home excited to tell me all he had learned. I was again mad that he could believe such preposterous things.

A FTER MY THIRD week of RCIA I came home to find Pam sitting at the kitchen table writing a condolence letter to a college chum whose husband had just left the comfort of his wife and home for Mongolia's mountains to become a Buddhist monk. Was she making this up to get my attention, trying to draw a parallel to my own intrepid journey? If so, I'm not sure, "condolences" applied. I was learning way-too-cool mountain-top stuff and I wanted to bring her along on my adventure. Besides, women couldn't become Buddhist monks but they could come to RCIA. I remember pacing back and forth, waving my arms, holding a Bible in one arm, and going on-

and-on about something. I'm sure I looked liked a crazed, one-armed evangelist who had inhaled too much sawdust as I quoted from my *Protestant* translation of Holy Writ.

If I had taken the time to look into her lovely deep brown eyes I probably could have read her livid thoughts.

PAM WRITES: I looked into his bloodshot blue eyes, the ones I fell in love with years before they were bloodshot, and thought: The guy is certifiably nuts...and the priest must be whacko, too. If I don't put a stop to this right away, he'll put a statue of Mary on our front lawn and bow down to it four times a day. Can't have that.

So I lit into him.

After about ten minutes of quoting Bible verses at each other like dueling guitars missing a few strings, he said, "Okay! Okay! Next time, you come to class and argue with the priest!"

He probably flung that out there thinking it was something I would never do. He knows I hate to argue...with anyone but him. Thinking he had me boxed in, he continued, "I don't want to hear your arguments. I'm just telling you what the priest said. Your disagreement is with him and the Church, not with me. Come to class with me or forever hold your peace."

> **The guy is certifiably nuts...and the priest must be whacko, too. If I don't put a stop to this right away, he'll put a statue of Mary on our front lawn and bow down to it four times a day. Can't have that.**

Suddenly, he looked satisfied as if he had finally put a cork in me and there'd be some PEACE! But the peace lasted all of ten seconds.

I said, "Okay, when's the next class? I'm coming!"

He froze.

I continued, "This priest guy of yours clearly does not understand one iota of the Bible. I'll be ready for him."

"How?" He said, "You going to bring your Thompson Chain Reference Bible, the one with all the maps, glossary and study helps in the back?"

"No, I need something more impressive." I thought for a moment. "Wait, I know. I'll bring my red leather Bible, that will impress him."

"Actually it won't. Nobody brings their Bibles."

"Figures!" I said.

"They provide them for everyone in the class."

"Probably some doctored translation," I said. "Well, I'll straighten him out."

I HAD ALWAYS KNOWN Pam to be the shy adapter. Rarely would she feel the need to speak up in public or challenge another person. Avoiding confrontation was her "love language." But recently, in her mind, the crazed "insights" that I had come upon, which had cast a "spell" over me, and drawn me into that "cult" that starts with a capital "C" and rhymes with Communism, was too much for her to bear... and she was transformed.

She came to RCIA all right; rarely did she miss a class from that point on. And, true to her word, she was *loaded for priest*, and not shy about engaging Fr. Cronk in debate or quoting a Bible verse to defend our Evangelical beliefs. I loved it, and I freely participated in the verbal ruckus, switching sides depending on where I thought the advantage was.

> **She came to RCIA all right; rarely did she miss a class from that point on. And, true to her word, she was "loaded for priest."**

You can imagine what effect this had on our class, which was made up mostly of engaged couples, one being Catholic who was hoping the other would soon become one so they could get hitched. Pam and I may have been the only couple in the room that were married. I imagine our frequent and sometimes animated discussions, as a married couple of some 30-years, gave the unmarried couples pause and something to think about. *Is this what we have to look forward to?* Yes, folks, married life has plenty of spice.

PAM WRITES: *I was NOT one to argue. I don't like arguing at all. But I was prepared, I felt, to meet this priest head-on and challenge him on all fronts. I knew my Bible inside and out, and I had Scripture on my side! I was not rude or disruptive, but I did have questions.*

Sometimes I would wait till after class, but for every question I had, Fr. Cronk was a step ahead of me. I could never put him on the defensive. He had a sensible, Biblical response without even having to hesitate or look in a Bible. It totally threw me for a loop.

ME: *Mary couldn't have been a perpetual virgin, be-*

cause Scripture says Jesus had brothers and sisters. Look, right here!

CRONK: "Brothers" was a term used for cousins. They
didn't have words to distinguish between the two.

ME: Peter was not being commissioned as the leader/
pope of the church. Those keys of the kingdom
were given to all of us as his disciples.

CRONK: Look at the audience Jesus was speaking to. It was
Peter alone, and Peter, alone, was told three times
to "feed my lambs, feed my sheep."

One time I thought I'd bring up a very clever concept instead of a
question to prove I knew more about the Bible than he did. At one of our
many churches we had attended, I had been to a Bible study where we
were given an insightful lesson on how Jesus's life paralleled the journey
of the Jews. It went like this:

The Jewish nation began with Abraham being asked by
God to go to a land He did not know, to start a nation that
would follow God. His descendants
in the fourth generation fled to
Egypt to save their lives. After many
generations they were brought out
of Egypt by miracles and signs from
God, across the Red Sea, to be led
to the Promised Land. But, after all
those miracles, they still complained
against God and had to spend 40
years in the wilderness for lack
of faith. Finally, after a plague of
poisonous snakes, they were saved
by looking at a bronze replica of a
snake on a pole and were delivered
safely back into the Promised Land
flowing with milk and honey.

> **Fr. Cronk was
> a step ahead
> of me. I could
> never put
> him on the
> defensive. He
> had a sensible,
> Biblical
> response
> without even
> having to
> hesitate or look
> in a Bible.
> It totally threw
> me for a loop.**

The parallel was that Jesus (like
Abraham) was asked by the Father to go to the earth to
birth a nation that would follow God with their hearts.
After the magi came to worship Jesus, as King of the Jews

at around age 2, his parents fled with him to Egypt (like the Israelites) to save his life from the jealousy of King Herod. After 10 years, when Jesus was 12, they returned to the land of Israel. (The 10 years represented the 10 generations the Jews were in Egypt.) After Jesus's baptism by John (like the Israelites passing through the Red Sea) he was led into the wilderness for 40 days of fasting and prayer and temptation by the devil, (like the Israelites wandered in the wilderness for 40 years). Jesus resisted every temptation to complain or sin against God, the Father. And, in the end was crucified on a pole/tree/cross to save not just the Jews but all mankind who would look upon Him and believe (just like the Israelites looked at the brazen serpent on the cross.) Those who believe will receive eternal life in the Promised Land of heaven.

Figuring that Fr. Cronk really didn't know the Bible, I sought him out after RCIA one evening. "You know," I said, "there is a parallel between Jesus's life and that of the Jews."

He said, "Yup, that's right. The parallels are called "types" or "figures". What happened to the Jews prefigured the life of Christ in many ways. It's the study of typology. Great stuff."

What?! He can't know about this. He couldn't really understand all the things I did about it. So, I asked him more specifically about Egypt and the Red Sea parallels.

He looked at me and said, "Yup, it's all in the reading material I gave you tonight." He took the handout that was in my hands and pointed to a place on page two. "Right here."

I scanned the paragraphs he pointed to...and my eyes bugged out. It was all there. How could he have such a nugget of spiritual insight? I didn't get it at the time. But, I began to understand that perhaps a lot of what we as Protestants knew about God and Scripture may have come from the Catholic Church.

THAT SUMMER AND into the fall when I started RCIA, my reading about Catholicism, Christianity, and the Bible had become insatiable. There was the shelf-full of a dozen Bible translations that I had collected over the years. I had several other shelves filled with a variety of Protestant commentaries including an original 1850 edition of Adam Clarke's famous six volume Bible commentary, in its original bindings. The set belonged to my 1800's circuit-riding grandfather, Jeremiah Williams. I still reference this massive set and find Clarke's research insightful.

I had both Greek and Latin interlinears, and multiple concordances, including a well-broken-in Strong's Exhaustive Bible Concordance, a useful New Englishman's Greek Concordance of the New Testament and Zondervan's Analytical Greek Lexicon —both of which use Strong's word numbering system.

Recall, that I described Strong's Exhaustive Concordance earlier with its 1,807 pages of very small, single-spaced print. I have thought many times that had it not been for the Protestant Reformation and the Protestant reliance on the "Bible Alone," these fantastic Bible study aids would never have been compiled.

Aside from the above assistance to my study, there were five "guide" books that were my initial "print" introduction to Catholicism. They were:

- ► *Surprised by Truth: 11 Converts Give the Biblical and Historical Reasons for Becoming Catholic*, (1994). Patrick Madrid (Ed.) Basilica Press.
- ► *Why Do Catholics Do That?*, (1995). Kevin Orlin Johnson. Ballantine Books.
- ► *Catechism of the Catholic Church*, (1995). The Holy See. Image/ Doubleday Paperback. (Available now is a Revised, hardback edition with additional study helps.)
- ► *On Being Catholic*, (1997). Thomas Howard. Ignatius Press.
- ► *Reclaiming The Great Tradition: Evangelicals, Catholics & Orthodox in Dialogue*, (1997). James S. Cutsinger (Ed.). InterVarsity Press.

You can understand that seeing what I was reading, Pam wasn't buying my line that I was not going to become Catholic. Her intuition told her something different from what my reasoning mind was telling me. We argued, for sure. Consciously, I was not trying to be Catholic, although a lot of what I was reading and hearing was making more sense than the five decades I had spent in Evangelicalism.

M Y DIARY RECORDS a great deal of turmoil that surrounded my life during the summer and fall of 1997, as if I were being intentionally distracted. Pam and I had been working for years to get out of debt and were almost there except for the house mortgage. But, within just a few months of beginning RCIA, I slowly became aware that there was a force at work to deter me.

- ► A man spent 40-minutes in my home examining a computer I was selling. He gave me traveler's checks and took the computer. But the checks turned out to be forgeries. I was out $3,000 and my home violated.
- ► Pam and I tried to sell our house and move aboard a large sailing vessel in order to sail the South Pacific and retrace the adventures of my missionary great uncle, John Williams... minus the cannibals. After some effort and $2,000 we abandoned the idea.
- ► A relative and pastor confessed to adultery and left his ministry. The events eventually led to his divorce. The whole family was shaken.
- ► A business acquaintance of mine asked for a large donation for the Fellowship of Christian Athletes. The check never cleared, and the "friend" disappeared. I was shaken again by evil's presence in my house.
- ► After spending $3,800 to repair an old mini-van for April to get to school, the motor froze on the freeway. Providentially, with friends on board, she coasted safely to a parking lot. But the engine replacement set us back an additional $7,500.
- ► My new computer kept crashing and I lost weeks working on my dissertation.
- ► Pam's car broke down, as did my van. Together the repairs were $2,200.
- ► The refrigerator stopped working. A new one cost $750.
- ► I made an emergency trip to Annapolis, Maryland, to support Josh during a difficult time. Together we attended a Promise Keepers Rally on the Washington Mall. (A choice well worth the cost.)
- ► On two occasions I woke up with chest pains and shortness of breath. Panic trips to the doctor forced a change in diet and exercise.
- ► At the end of all this, in spite of a good job, Pam and I were set back $22,000 on a home equity loan, which created a lot of stress and tension between us.

There was a temptation to think these trials were brought-on by Satan because of my inquiry into Catholicism. But I don't believe that.

Most of this, including the investigation into Catholicism, was the consequence of my natural, ambitious, inquisitive, Type-A personality. My diary is filled with prayers asking for God's guidance and help to re-prioritize my life. Over time he did, and things quieted down. But I had to be constantly vigilant or debt and chest pains threatened.

In the middle of all this, Pam wrote me a kind note with red ink on a green slip of paper. I have it glued in my diary:

> *Stanley,*
>
> *You are a wonderful man. You love the kids and me dearly and you have provided for us in ways including but far above money.*
>
> *You have a beautiful giving heart that the enemy wants you to believe caused us to lose thousands of dollars, and time working on your dissertation. But God is pleased with the choices you made to help others. So, He'll provide the money and work time. I love you so much, my beloved.*
>
> *Pam*

Her tender message made a tremendous impression on me. And although Pam and I were arguing about Catholicism almost daily, and there would be more rough times ahead, the note gave me hope.

I chose to interpret Pam's note as if it came from God.

70
The Scales
Come Off

O N THURSDAY EVENING, November 6, 1997, at Fr. Cronk's regular class, he began to cover the Catholic understanding of The Eucharist. I listened carefully, as this was the heart of what I had been calling "Cronk's Challenge," when he denied my participation in communion months earlier. I evaluated what he had to say and read the Scriptures along with him and the rest of the class, but I had already been investigating this whole idea that was so alien to Evangelical theology—that after the priest's prayers of consecration, the bread and wine miraculously became the Real Presence of Jesus Christ.

The next evening, at home, I sat down in my office to study John 6:41-66, the passage touted by Catholics as proof of Christ's Real Presence in their communion. I still could not believe Catholics held to something so utterly stupid. And yet, there were over a billion that believed it. *Certainly, among that number, there were a few educated and very smart individuals.*

What was utterly incomprehensible to me was that the bread and wine, even after the prayers of consecration still looked and smelled like bread and wine. So, clearly, it was not flesh and blood, as my scientific mind assured me.

That was my null-hypothesis—*The Eucharist was nothing special.*

Thus, I began to study John 6:41-66. Because this was so important to my story, let me insert it below from the NRSV, with **bold** and <u>underlined</u> phrases that revealed to me two interwoven themes, or two interwoven concepts of faith.

The **bold** phrases indicate the first concept of faith, that Jesus came down from heaven—**He was God.** That's something Christians claim they take on *faith*, although to the people of Jesus's time there was no physical evidence in looking at Jesus that he was anything but a man.

The underlined phrases indicate a second concept of faith, that Jesus was truly present under the appearance of the bread and wine—His Real Presence in the elements. That's something that Catholics take on faith, although to me, a Protestant, there was no physical evidence in touching, smelling or tasting the elements that they were anything but simple bread and wine. It is this second concept that I noticed dominated the passage. Here it is:

> 41 *Then the Jews began to complain about him because he said, "I am the bread that came down from heaven." 42 They were saying, "Is not this Jesus, the son of Joseph, whose father and mother we know? How can he now say, 'I have come down from heaven'?" 43 Jesus answered them, "Do not complain among yourselves. 44 No one can come to me unless drawn by the Father* **who sent me;** *and I will raise that person up on the last day. 45 It is written in the prophets, 'And* **they shall all be taught by God.'** *Everyone who has heard and learned from the Father comes to me. 46 Not that anyone has seen the Father except the one* **who is from God; he has seen the Father.** *47 Very truly, I tell you, whoever believes has eternal life. 48* I am the bread of life. *49 Your ancestors ate the manna in the wilderness, and they died. 50* **This is the bread** *that* **comes down from heaven,** so that one may eat of it *and not die. 51* I am the living bread *that came down from heaven.* Whoever eats of this bread *will live forever; and* the bread that I will give for the life of the world is my flesh."

> **What was utterly incomprehensible to me was that the bread and wine, even after the prayers of consecration still looked and smelled like bread and wine.**

> 52 *The Jews then disputed among themselves, saying,* "How can this man give us his flesh to eat?" *53 So Jesus said to them, "Very truly, I tell you,* unless you eat the flesh *of the Son of Man and* drink his blood, *you have no life in you. 54*

*Those who <u>eat my flesh</u> and <u>drink my blood</u> have eternal
life, and I will raise them up on the last day; 55 for <u>my flesh
is true food</u> and <u>my</u> <u>blood is true drink</u>. 56 <u>Those who eat
my flesh</u> and <u>drink my blood</u> abide in me, and I in them.
57 Just as the **living Father sent me**, and I live because of
the Father, so <u>whoever eats me</u> will live because of me. 58
<u>This is the bread</u> that came down from heaven, not like
that which your ancestors ate, and they died. But <u>the one
who eats this bread</u> will live forever." 59 He said these things
while he was teaching in the synagogue at Capernaum.*

*60 When many of his disciples heard it, they said, "This
teaching is difficult; who can accept it?" 61 But Jesus, being
aware that his disciples were complaining about it, said to
them, "Does this offend you? 62 Then what if you were to see
the Son of Man **ascending to where he was before?** 63 It
is the spirit that gives life; the flesh is useless. The words that
I have spoken to you are spirit and life. 64 But among you
there are some who do not believe." For Jesus knew from the
first who were the ones that did not believe, and who was
the one that would betray him. 65 And he said, "For this
reason I have told you that no one can come to me unless
it is granted by the Father." 66 Because of this many of his
disciples turned back and no longer went about with him.*

As I read the passage several times I began to see that *faith was
required to believe that Jesus was God, and that faith was also required
to believe that Jesus was truly present in the elements* distributed by the
priest.

But my scientific mind wanted physical evidence. Blind faith was
not the only thing that led Christians to believe that Jesus was God,
there were the *miracles* and, of course, *his resurrection*. But then I had
not observed any of Jesus's miracles or his resurrection. I trusted in the
eyewitness accounts recorded in Scripture. And I trusted Scripture because *when I applied the truths of what the Bible taught, I saw the physical evidence in the redemption of my life and others around me.* Thus, I
certainly believed in the Bible and particularly in the words of Christ.
My faith in Christ as God was not based on direct observation of Christ
but in the second and third tier *evidence of lives being redeemed after
putting faith in God and the words of the Bible.* The Bible, too, was physical evidence. The Bible, intrinsically, had provided physical evidence

that it contained trustworthy revelation about reality, Natural Law, the universe, and the human condition. Yes, it could be misinterpreted. But even when slightly misinterpreted the Bible gave strong evidence that it was true and trustworthy.

All of that spun through my mind as I began to see the comparison between faith that Christ was God and faith that the consecrated elements were Jesus present with us to the end of time.

I looked over the passage again. There were nine (9) places where Jesus said explicitly or alluded to the idea that he came from heaven. The phrases were clear and unhindered by language:

> I trusted Scripture because when I applied the truths of what the Bible taught, I saw the physical evidence in the redemption of my life and others around me.

- ► I...came down from heaven (41)
- ► I have come down from heaven (42)
- ► The Father sent me (44)
- ► They shall be taught by God (45)
- ► (I) have seen the Father (46)
- ► (indicating himself) This...comes down from heaven (50)
- ► I...came down from heaven (51)
- ► (indicating himself) This...comes down from heaven (50) (58)
- ► ...Ascending to where he was before (62)

But there were double that number of places, nineteen (19), where Jesus says explicitly or alludes to the idea of his true body and blood being in something that his followers will consume. And he makes a repeated point to declare that what he's talking about is *real* and *not symbolic* in the same way that Jesus is really God and not just a symbol of God.

- ► I am the bread (41)
- ► I am the bread of life (48)
- ► (Indicating himself) This is the bread (50)
- ► So that one may eat of it (50)
- ► I am the living bread (51)
- ► Whomever eats of this bread (51)
- ► The bread that I will give...is my flesh (51)
- ► How...his flesh to eat? (52)

- ► Unless you eat the flesh (53)
- ► And drink his blood (53)
- ► Eat my flesh (54)
- ► Drink my blood (54)
- ► My flesh is true food (55)
- ► My blood is true drink (55)
- ► Those who eat my flesh (56)
- ► And drink my blood (56)
- ► Whoever eats me (57)
- ► This is the bread (58)
- ► The one who eats this bread (58)

I wondered, *what could the Jews and some of his disciples have thought of all this?* There were very strict rules against Jews eating flesh that contained blood. With Jesus being a human the idea of eating his flesh and drinking his blood sounded like cannibalism. Certainly, he meant this symbolically and his disciples would have known he meant it symbolically. I looked over the passage yet again. *Why is that not clear?*

It was then I noticed that what his disciples were saying, "This teaching is difficult; who can accept it?" Certainly, I was having a hard time accepting it, if it meant that it was really Christ's flesh and blood.

But Jesus doesn't back down. He chastises his disciples, reinforces what he's been saying, and then says to them in verse 64: "Among you there are some who do not believe." In verse 65 he suggests that if you reject what he's been saying, you're not going to make it to heaven. And in verse 66: "Because of this many of his disciples turned back and no longer went about with him." And, then it registered that Jesus didn't call them back and explain that he was speaking symbolically, which is what I believed as an Evangelical. Instead, Christ let them go—"there are some who do not believe."[1]

> **Faith was required to believe that Jesus was God, and that faith was also required to believe that Jesus was truly present in the elements.**

That bothered me, a lot. I knew the consequences of rejecting something Jesus was trying to get across.

My eyes then drifted over to verse 61,

---

1 Is it just coincidence that this verse's citation is 6:66. cf. Revelation 13:16-18, "the name of the beast or the number of its name...is 666."

which I read again: "Does this offend you?"

Yes, it did.

I stopped reading...and at that moment the rest of world seemed to stop as well. My breathing certainly did.

Then, all of a sudden...I started to cry. I came to faith.

Months earlier, I had been offended by Fr. Cronk for refusing me communion. But now I recognized that I was being offended by Christ for exactly the same reason. I caught my breath and broke out in a cold sweat. I looked at my hands and arms. I was trembling. I was not *surprised* by truth, I was *blown away* by it.

> **I had been offended by Fr. Cronk for refusing me communion. But now I recognized that I was being offended by Christ for exactly the same reason.**

And this verse came to me: "For by grace you have been saved through faith, and this is not your own doing; it is the gift of God."[1]

The upshot of these realizations was that communion in Evangelical services was indeed symbolic. There were two reasons for this. First, they did not have the faith that it could be anything but symbolic. Second, they were theologically correct about its lack of real substance, because an Evangelical pastor is not empowered through proper ordination by a apostolic successor of St. Peter to effect the miracle of transubstantiation at the altar.

[Later research revealed that the valid priesthood capable of effecting this miracle of The Eucharist is present in 23 Catholic Rites, all the various Orthodox Rites and in some priests in the Episcopal and Lutheran churches. *Transubstantiation is by far the vast norm in Christianity.* What is believed by most Protestants and Evangelicals (that communion is not the real sacramental presence of Christ) is not only very recent (last 200 years) but believed by very few.]

When I had recollected my thoughts, I anxiously turned to two other passages of Scripture that I had read and heard many times before. I wondered: *Was this same blatant teaching of His presence in The Eucharist in Christ's words after he prayed over the elements at the Last Supper?*

> *While they were eating, Jesus took bread, and when he had given thanks, he broke it and gave it to his disciples, saying, "Take and eat; this is my body." Then he took a cup,*

---

1 Ephesians 2:8

and when he had given thanks, he gave it to them, saying, "Drink from it, all of you. This is my blood of the covenant, which is poured out for many for the forgiveness of sins.[1]

What'd that say? *"This is my body...this is my blood..."* Oh, wow! Why hadn't I seen that before?

I turned hurriedly to Luke 24 and the story of Jesus on the road to Emmaus. The men he's walking with invite him to dinner. He accepts. When he sits at the table with them read what happens:

When he was at the table with them, he took bread, gave thanks, broke it and began to give it to them. Then their eyes were opened and they recognized him, and he disappeared from their sight.[2]

> **Moments later I realized I was growing faint... I was hyperventilating. These Bible passages had always been there...in my Protestant translations.**

As soon as Christ blesses the bread, he vanishes and leaves the bread behind. He leaves his body in the bread. All of this struck me hard. Moments later I realized I was growing faint...I was hyperventilating. These Bible passages had always been there...in my Protestant translations...but I was blind to them.

One of the critical techniques in Biblical interpretation is not to ignore the context of the "proof texts" you're using. So, I went back to John 6 and decided to read the whole chapter, from the beginning (which is always a bit easier than reading the chapter from the end.)

At the beginning of John 6, Jesus feeds 5,000 men (plus women and children) on a grassy mountainside. As I read this, I was astonished to see the description paralleled the celebration of the Mass, including the supernatural transubstantiation of the food that was brought forward as a gift.

1. In feeding the 5,000, a little boy offers up his five barley loaves and two fish to the Apostles and Jesus. (**In the Mass**, the people bring their offerings of bread and wine to the Deacon and to the Priest who acts as "in persona

---

1 Matthew 26:26-28, NIV
2 Luke 24:30-31 (NIV)

Christi"—in the person of Christ.)

2. In feeding the 5,000, Jesus blesses the food. (**In the Mass**, the priest blesses the bread and wine.)

3. In feeding the 5,000, the loaves and fish supernaturally are changed. They look like loaves and fish, but they are clearly transformed into something supernatural in order to feed all those people. (**In the Mass**, the bread and wine are supernaturally changed.)

4. In feeding the 5,000, to the people sitting on the grass, the loaves and fish have no apparent supernatural texture or taste. They look and taste like bread and fish. But they are clearly not just regular bread and fish to have multiplied supernaturally. (**In the Mass**, to the congregation, the host and cup taste like bread and wine, but through consecration they are supernaturally and sacramentally transformed.)

5. In feeding the 5,000, the disciples gathered the pieces of food that were left over so that nothing was wasted. (**In the Mass**, the left over Hosts that are not consumed are collected and placed in a tabernacle for the next Mass.)

That November Friday evening, all of that ran through my head in an instant. I was transformed like the loaves and fish. I could no longer deny what the Bible and Christ were clearly telling me. The Eucharist was truly the real presence of Christ, just as He had promised to always be with us to the end of time.[1] Yes, he was spiritually with us, but even more miraculously I saw that he was present *physically*, throughout the world, in all the Masses of the world, in his real presence in the Eucharist.

The epiphanies kept rolling in like refreshing waves of a big surf. The phrase, "Christ lives in you"[2] was literally, physically true. Communion in Roman Catholicism wasn't just spiritual but when we eat his body and drink his blood he is literally and physically living within us as well.

---

1 Matthew 28:20
2 Romans 8:10-11, Colossians 1:27, Galatians 2:20

This was all too much. I cried like a baby. It was a watershed of revelation that all this had been in the Bible all this time, so clear, direct, and obvious.

> **I cried like a baby. It was a watershed of revelation that all this had been in the Bible all this time, so clear, direct, and obvious.**

I walked down the hall from my home office to the kitchen where I found Pam again at the table reading. She looked up at me as I held my Bible limply at my side, my eyes red, and a handkerchief wiping my eyes and nose. I gathered my emotions and said: "Pam you were right. I thought you were wrong as you usually are. But this one time, this once, you were right."

I took a long pause to see if she was smiling at my "gracious" compliment. But her eyes narrowed, her lips grew thin and tense. That was not the reaction I was going for.

In as concise a way as I could, I explained all that I had just come to understand...logically, linguistically and biblically...about John 6 and Christ's teaching about The Eucharist. I also went on and tried to explain my astonishment that the passage had always been there, and how I had memorized it as a teenager during Bible quizzing, but that only now had I come to see the obvious..

Then I went for broke: "I'm going to join the Catholic Church, and I am not waiting for you."

If this were a television drama, we'd now cut to a commercial.

But it's not, so we'll reverse camera angles and cut to Pam's point of view.

PAM WRITES: I looked up at him and could see the resolve in his eyes. "You can't do this, Stan," I said. "I thought we were on this journey together. We've been arguing, sure, but only to hone in on the truth, like iron sharpens iron. What about all the other things that we don't understand? Just because you think you understand The Eucharist? That's not enough. There's this Mary thing, and purgatory, and the pope. Why are you being this way?"

But I could see that his understanding of the passage in John about the Real Presence of Christ in The Eucharist, was enough for him. He didn't understand everything, but this was enough for him to take a leap of faith that he had wanted to make for decades...and only now did he see a reasonable landing pad.

ON SUNDAY, TWO days after my John 6 revelation, I found Fr. Cronk again in the foyer greeting parishioners as they came into Mass. I was very much aware that the tables had been turned from the Sunday in May not that many months ago when I walked out on him after he told me I could not take the Eucharist. With all the sincerity I could muster, I told him what had happened Friday night. Then I said, "Can I take communion today, I believe it now. I don't think I can wait."

"Yes, you can," Fr. Cronk said jovially.

"I don't think so, I might die before then," I said.

"You're not going to die before Easter."

"Really?"

"Really! Wait. It will be a special time."

Judith Marchinda

JUDITH MARCHINDA WAS a grace in my life during the next few months. God knew I was too proud to seek out someone like Al Kresta, who I knew had returned to the Catholic Church, or Internet Catholic apologist, Dave Armstrong, who I knew lived near me. My pride had been content to bury itself in books and go to RCIA. God knew I needed daily contact with a Catholic that was living the faith and enjoying it on an hourly basis.

As I've mentioned, I was employed by Sandy Corporation at the time and was the Creative Director for the Harley-Davidson University account. Judith Marchinda was the Project Coordinator who was assigned to help me coordinate the many aspects of the annual training conference. She was a woman two years older than me but by attitude and enthusiasm about 20 years younger. Judith was vibrant and happy; in all aspects she was a well-educated Catholic who was born into the faith and had been raised correctly in it.

She found my journey fascinating, having never met a Protestant that was interested in, of all things, Catholicism. So it happened that during the course of our time together working on Harley, I would ask her questions of a personal faith nature, or she would share with me something that occurred to her about my journey. She was knowledgeable about the Bible, history, the doctrine, and her responses were always pleasant, informed, and faithful.

Without thinking of it as such, she helped to catechize me in an everyday sort of way. She was the living testament, the living example of the famous Deuteronomy passage where God commands His people:

> *You shall teach them [the commands of God] diligently to your sons and shall talk of them as you sit in your house and when you walk by the way and when you lie down and when you rise up.*[1]

Thank you Judith for being faithful to God's call.

---

1 Deuteronomy 6:7 (NIV)

71
You Can't
Sit Together

I N SPITE OF a new tension between us, Pam still came to RCIA with me and occasionally lit into Fr. Cronk. It was fun for me. For once I was not the ornery partner in our marriage.

Every person taking instruction to enter the church was called a catechumen. As soon as possible, during the six months of RCIA instruction, each catechumen was to bring a sponsor to class. The sponsor had to be a practicing Catholic in good standing, who would encourage the catechumen, answer their questions between classes, and stand with them during the Easter Vigil when they came into the church. So, I was tasked with finding such a person.

Years earlier, as I produced films for corporations, I often hired a very smart audio engineer by the name of Ed Wolfrum. In his early days, Ed had attended Catholic seminary. At the same time he became the token white guy at Motown Records where he helped develop the equipment that produced the famous Motown sound. I've seen photographs of Ed sitting at the audio console in his clerical seminary collar surrounded by the likes of the Supremes and Barry Gordy. Eventually, Ed left the seminary, got married, and became well-known for his audio production expertise. Over the years we worked together, Ed chided me in a friendly way for not being Catholic. "Just being a Christian isn't good enough, Stan," he'd say. Over the years we had some fun debates, but strangely I never took anything he said about Catholicism seriously.

Once Ed turned the tables, and hired me. The job was to shoot an endorsement video for a Catholic Conference with the renowned theologian, Fr. John Hardon, a Jesuit and prolific author, who was Ed's confessor. Fr. Hardon was also Mother Teresa's spiritual advisor and traveled frequently from Detroit to India. He was the celebrant at her official, and private, Catholic funeral in Calcutta.

When Ed introduced me to Fr. Hardon, the first thing Hardon said to me, even before "Hello," was, "Who is your patron saint?"

Fr. Hardon was an elderly, stooped over Jesuit. He wore a long black cassock and white collar, his pure white hair was thin and his glasses thick. I said, "I'm not Catholic."

"That doesn't matter. You still need a patron saint," said Hardon. He had to work to look up at me from his stooped posture but he did so with a wryly, confident smile.

I was speechless. I had no idea that I needed a saint.

> **Hardon turned to Ed and said, "Get him a saint, will you? He needs one. Someday he'll be a Catholic."**

Hardon turned to Ed and said, "Get him a saint, will you? He needs one. Someday he'll be a Catholic."

One could claim that Ed was more Catholic than the pope. He (Ed) preferred the Latin Tridentine form of the Mass rather than anything in English. Ed, and his wife Sue, however, were not renegades, but loyal Romans...they just thought that when in Rome...speak Latin.

Ed and Sue attended church with another friend that played an increasing role in all this, Ray Long, Jr.

R AY LONG, JR. and I had maintained a friendship over the years. He was a prolific freelance technical writer and producer, who dabbled in screenplays, one of which was eventually optioned in Hollywood. He lived on a small farm an hour north of Detroit where he, along with his capable wife, Crystal, raised and home schooled their ten children...and the kids, in turn, raised a menagerie of competitive 4-H animals.

Ray had departed my employ years earlier when he and Crystal had started having babies and he wanted a raise, because, as he explained, it was the employer's duty to pay employees according to how many kids they had. (Ray and Crystal had some experience living in French Quebec, Canada, where Catholic social policy was a bit more prevalent than the capitalist mindset found in the U.S.) I refused to give him a raise and he went off to find other work. I've since changed my mind and believe he was right.

Ray was freelancing at Sandy Corporation where I was working at the time, and had heard secretly from Judith Marchinda that I was investigating Catholicism. So, one day, Ray called Ed up on the phone, and said, "Ed, are you sitting down."

"I can be if its necessary, what's up."

"Nothing's up. You better sit down."

"Okay...I'm sitting down."

"Stan Williams is attending RCIA."

There was a long pause during which Ray heard furniture move, and then a loud thud.

"Ray, I just fell on the floor. The chair didn't help."

WHEN I ASKED Ed if he would be my RCIA sponsor, he got excited, claiming that he had been praying for ten years that I would someday be Catholic. He had to drive about 45-minutes one way to get to our classes, but he was there every week and was a constant encouragement through my confirmation.

Now, imagine the setting. Fr. James Cronk, a great liturgist and faithful priest, is teaching our class, but he's not into old school Catholicism like the Latin Tridentine Mass. The 60 individuals were arranged in chairs facing one another, around a square of tables, not unlike a boxing ring.

In the corner to my right, in the petulant Protestant trunks, sat Pam, who thought Fr. Cronk was *too Catholic* and not Christian enough. Pam aptly fulfilled the role of argumentative challenger. Fr. Cronk patiently answered her challenges, knowing that he might never persuade her, but his answers had a chance of being absorbed by the others in the class, who, otherwise, had no interest in making the evening any longer than necessary.

In the corner to my left, in the gold trimmed Tridentine trunks, thick glasses, and a heavy satchel filled with Fr. Hardon's writings and the catechism in Latin, sat Ed Wolfrum, who thought Fr. Cronk *was not Catholic enough*. If Pam wasn't commanding the floor demanding Cronk's attention, Ed would launch an attack for what he thought was weak orthodoxy. One time, in rebuttal to Fr. Cronk's answer, Ed said, "Well that's not what Fr. Hardon says."

To which Cronk chuckled and said, "Who the pope is Fr. Hardon?"

To which I burst out laughing.

I was usually the guy who liked to argue, but here I was with my wife on the right and good friend on the left doing it all for me.

> **"Look, kids. You can no longer sit together. Next week we're going to have to separate you."**

Later, after another equally strange and lighthearted exchange, Cronk looked at the three of us, (Brother Latin Grumpy, Sister Protestant Grumpy, and me, Brother Laughing-Out-Loud-and-not-believing-my-luck), and said, "Look, kids. You can no longer sit together. Next week we're going to have to separate you."

But Fr. Cronk was never angry. He just smiled and (I think) enjoyed our repartee. Then, again, perhaps he smiled because the competitive claims by Ed and Pam kept the two-dozen couples and others around the table awake.

Oh, one more thing.

At the end of every session, Fr. Cronk would scan the room, make eye contact with all of us, and say, "Remember, there will be a test."

72
Easter Vigil
1998

PAM WRITES: It was time to prepare for the Easter Vigil, the night Stan would come into the Church with others from his RCIA class. He would be provisionally baptized and take communion for the first time. But I was not convinced; and there was no way I was going to become Catholic. Ironically, our roles seemed to be reversed from when Bethesda baptized me but wouldn't baptize Stan.

I attended the Easer Vigil Mass with Stan, clearly as a skeptic. I was neither mad nor sad. I was just numb. I had been mad that Stan did not try to help me understand things as he did, but the debates grew stale when he said he couldn't wait for me. This was something he had to do. It was what he had been searching for. I still had questions about Mary and the Eucharist, praying to Saints and Confession, and I could not see past those obstacles.

O N THE EVENING of April 11, 1998, all over the world, Catholics celebrated The Easter Vigil Mass. This would be the night thousands of new Catholics and I would enter the Church and receive the Eucharist for the first time. Fr. Cronk was right: I had not died. So, I stood outside of St. James Catholic Church in Novi, Michigan and watched Fr. Cronk stoke a blazing fire, built in a backyard barbecue grill, and anxiously waited for the evening to begin.

Nearby, an attendant held a three-foot tall pure white Easter Paschal Candle that had never been lit. Fr. Cronk, adorned in white vestments, began.

"In the name of the Father, and of the Son, and of the Holy Spirit."
"Amen!" we all said.
An altar girl held a book for Cronk to read from as he addressed us:

> *Dear brothers and sisters,*
> *On this most sacred night,*
> *in which our Lord Jesus Christ*
> *passed over from death to life,*
> *the Church calls upon her sons and daughters,*
> *scattered throughout the world,*
> *to come together to watch and pray.*
> *If we keep the memorial*
> *of the Lord's paschal solemnity in this way,*
> *listening to his word and celebrating his mysteries,*
> *then we shall have the sure hope*
> *of sharing his triumph over death*
> *and living with him in God.*

Fr. Cronk then extended his hands over the fire and blessed it.

> *Let us pray.*
> *O God, who through your Son*
> *bestowed upon the faithful the fire of your glory,*
> *sanctify this new fire, we pray,*
> *and grant that,*
> *by these Paschal celebrations,*
> *we may be so inflamed with heavenly desires,*
> *that with minds made pure*
> *we may attain festivities of unending splendor.*
> *Through Christ our Lord.*

Again we responded, "Amen!"
After blessing the candle adorned with a cross, A and Ω Greek
letters, and the year (1998), he inserted Paschal nails (pins with embedded incense representing the wounds of Christ) into the candle
around the points of the cross while saying,

> *By his holy--and glorious wounds,--may Christ the Lord--*
> *guard us--and protect us. Amen.*

Fr. Cronk then took an altar candle and lit it in the blazing fire, then
lifted it up and lit the Easter Paschal Candle. The attendant holding the

Paschal Candle then lowered it so those standing nearby could light their processional candles and share it with others around them.

I did not have a candle. The lit candles held by the faithful were a sign of Christ's indwelling in the baptized. As a catechumen I would receive my candle later, after my baptism. (Yes, I was going to get baptized yet again. Can't be too sure or careful about these things.)

Then, without singing, we filed into the darkened church foyer led by the lit Paschal Candle, held high, and the hundreds of processional candles held by the faithful. No one was talking. It was eerie and my skin tingled with just the sound of feet on marble, the smell of beeswax and the radiant glow of the warm candlelight on the wooden beams of the high, steeply peaked ceiling.

We took our seats, the faithful blew out their candles, and in the pitch darkness the Liturgy of the Word began. I had no idea how long this would be. As much as I wanted to receive the Eucharist, I also found meaningful the order and structure of things. "All things in good time," Cronk would often say. There was something about ritual that made the journey robust and satisfying.

The Liturgy of the Word normally took perhaps 30-minutes. That night it took over an hour. The lectors read every reading from the ambo (or podium) by candlelight, as the history of Redemption was recounted. There were seven Old Testament readings, after which a Psalm was sung, and after each Psalm a prayer read by Fr. Cronk. All of this was in a dark church, reminding us of the darkness of time before the coming of the Light of the World.

After the seven readings there was a brief pause. Then bells began to ring...louder and louder...as a procession of bell ringers entered from the back of the nave and proceeded to the front of the church to the choir side of the sanctuary. The candles around the altar were lit, all the lights in the church were turned up to full, and the organ, with all the stops pulled out, led the congregation in singing The Gloria in Excelsis Deo (Glory to God in the Highest). This was a favorite song of mine that was normally sung at the beginning of every Mass right after the general confession and absolution, but had not been sung throughout the 40 days of Lent. To hear it again, with its vigorous melody and spirit brought me to tears, so I closed my eyes and sang with all my heart this great song of worship...not about God, but *to* God.

> *Glory be to God in the highest.*
> *And on earth peace*

to men of good will.

We praise Thee; we bless Thee;
we worship Thee; we glorify Thee.
We give thanks to Thee
for Thy great glory.

O Lord God, Heavenly King,
God the Father Almighty.
O Lord Jesus Christ, the only begotten Son.
Lord God, Lamb of God,
Son of the Father.

Thou that takest away the sins of the world,
have mercy upon us.
Thou that takest away the sins of the world,
receive our prayer.
Thou that sittest at the right hand of the Father,
have mercy upon us.

For thou only art holy,
thou only art the Lord,
thou only art the most high, Jesus Christ.
Together with the Holy Ghost
in the glory of God the Father.

Amen.[1]

When I opened my eyes after singing, they stung a little from the bright lights. Revelations can do that at times—sting.

The lector then read from the book of Romans, about how those of us "who are baptized into Christ Jesus are baptized into his death… so that we too might be dead to sin and alive to God in Christ Jesus." I would be baptized in a few minutes, so the passage struck home.

Then there was yet another Psalm and another prayer.

After a moment of reflection (everything in its own time—the liturgy was never rushed but each moment respected) the organ and a small orchestra sitting next to the choir began a celebratory three-fold *Alleluia!*

Suddenly we were all on our feet singing the Alleluia. I can re-

---

1 This is the Gloria text used in the Mass in 1998, which was revised on the first Sunday of Advent in 2011.

member the profound respect I had for this moment in the Mass, where everyone stood for the reading of the Gospel. We were giving God a standing ovation for the Good News.

Fr. Cronk, having left his chair, took up the Book of the Gospels from the altar, raised it high above his head, and paraded it to the ambo as we continued to sing.

We were coming to a moment that may be insignificant to most, but one that had always meant a lot to me. Upon placing the Book of the Gospels on the ambo, Fr. Cronk's call and our response went like this:

CRONK: The Lord be with you.

WE: And also with you.

CRONK: A reading from the Holy Gospel according to
Mark.

And then there was the poignant moment that made so much sense. As we responded with the next line, we made the Sign of the Cross on our forehead, our lips and our breast.

WE: Glory be to you, O Lord.

The meaning of the three gestures was simple, yet to me sacred. I prayed: "Lord, may your word be ever on my mind +, on my lips +, and in my heart +. Amen."

The reading was from Mark about when Mary Magdalene, Mary the mother of James, and Salome went to the tomb to anoint Jesus's body only to find an angel there telling them he had risen from the dead.

After the Gospel, Fr. Cronk gave a homily. Those of us to be brought into the church out of RCIA sat near the front. He looked us over, and began with these words, "I told you there would be a test. (pause) Actually, there will be two of them. There will be one here and one there. I'll administer the test to you here. But it will be God Almighty who will administer the test to you there. Will you be ready?" He then went on to explain the significance of the night, not just to us catechumens but to all the faithful present, as they relive their own vows and recommit themselves to the sacraments that a few of us would receive tonight for the first time.

There was no creed on this night so I missed Cronk's patented transition to it. But I had other things on my mind. With others I was excused to change into robes for baptism. As we walked out the congregation chanted *The Litany of the Saints*.

It started out like many prayers asking God for mercy and forgiveness...

> *Lord, have mercy. Christ, have mercy.*
> *O Christ, hear us. O Christ, graciously hear us*
> *God the Father of heaven. Have mercy upon us*
> *O God the Son, Redeemer of the world. Have mercy upon us.*

But then all of history unfolded as the congregation invoked Mary, and the Archangels to pray for us, the catechumens...

> *Saint Michael. Pray for us*
> *Saint Gabriel. Pray for us*
> *Saint Raphael. Pray for us.*
> *All ye holy Angels and Archangels. Pray for us.*

Through the building's walls I heard the Church calling on the names of John the Baptist, Joseph (Mary's spouse), and others...begging for them to come to our aid...

> *All ye holy Patriarchs and Prophets. Pray for us.*
> *Saint Peter. Pray for us.*
> *Saint Paul. Pray for us.*
> *Saint Andrew. Pray for us.*
> *Saint James. Pray for us.*

The chant called on the rest of the Apostles, plus Luke, Mark and the other Disciples of the Lord to come witness and beg God for His blessing on us, this night, in St. James Catholic Church...

> *Saint Stephen. Pray for us.*
> *Saint Ambrose. Pray for us.*
> *Saint Augustine. Pray for us.*
> *Saint Nicholas. Pray for us.*

Yes, please pray for us, Saint Dominic, Saint Francis, Priests, Levites, Monks, Hermits...

> *Saint Mary Magdalene. Pray for us.*
> *All ye Holy, Righteous, and Elect of God.*

Intercede for us.
Be thou merciful. Spare us, Lord.
From all evil. Good Lord, deliver us.
From all deadly sin. Good Lord, deliver us.
We beseech thee to hear us, Lord.
O Son of god. Spare us, Lord.

As I pulled the rope belt around my waist, I imagined all those saints, surrounding the baptismal font, suspended in the air like ghostly figures standing on Heaven's vestibule, looking down on us, their hands extended over us in blessing. *Yes, pray for us...we who are about to make solemn vows of obedience to God and to Jesus Christ.*

When I heard the Litany of the Saints and envisioned those saints suspended above us, I felt a *cold shiver* course through my body. Up until that moment I wasn't too sure about the communion of the Saints and praying to them. But at that moment I believed.

P**RAYING TO SAINTS** was one of those Catholic beliefs you didn't have to believe in or even do in order to become Catholic. There were a lot of such teachings (or doctrines) of the church that were not *dogmas*. Dogmas were teachings you had to believe in. But the Church understood that some doctrines took time to assimilate and understand, if ever they could be. So much of Christianity is a mystery. Thus, while *faith* was important to Catholicism, *reason* had an equal place. Among Evangelicals, reason was often given short shrift and I was expected to believe some things to which my reason objected. Catholicism was different. If reason were not a part of the formula, if it was only faith, there was nothing stopping you from becoming Buddhist, Mormon, or embracing any other spiritual fad. *Reason* forced Catholic beliefs to agree with Natural Law, and for that *reason*, my *faith* in Roman Catholicism was strengthened.

> **The church understood that some doctrines took time to assimilate and understand, if ever they could be. So much of Christianity is a mystery.**

Being told that I could *pray* to saints, at first, put me off. *We only pray to God*, I thought. But then, I realized that I had equivocated[1]

---

1 To equivocate is to use the same word, term, or phrase with a different underlying definition or understanding than others are using. The result is

the word "prayer." As an Evangelical, "prayer" was synonymous with worship. I would never worship a saint. But to Catholics, "to pray" does not mean "worship" but rather "talk to" or "request" something of someone alive in heaven. That someone could be God the Father, Jesus Christ, the Holy Spirit, an angel, or one of the many Christians already in heaven who, before God's throne, intercede for us and pray with us to the Trinity.

G ETTING BACK TO the "cold shiver"...hearing The Litany of the Saints as I stood before the baptismal font reminded me of when we produced the musical Y'SHUA a couple hundred pages earlier. In Act 2 of that stage production, I recreated an imagined balcony or vestibule in Heaven, where the patriarchs of the Old Testament listed in Hebrews 11 (Abel, Enoch, Noah, Abraham, Isaac, Jacob, Joseph, and Moses), looked down on Earth and watched the events surrounding the birth of Christ unfold. They came to realize for the first time the meaning behind their many prophecies regarding a coming Messiah. The Litany of the Saints that night was very much like Hebrews 11. And our baptism in a few moments was very well described ian Hebrews 12:

> *Therefore, since we are surrounded by such a great cloud of witnesses, let us throw off everything that hinders and the sin that so easily entangles. And let us run with perseverance the race marked out for us, fixing our eyes on Jesus, the pioneer and perfecter of faith.*[1]

When this realization hit me, I suddenly...very suddenly...understood the Communion of Saints and how we have a relationship with them just as we do with our close friends on earth. We ask our friends to pray for us and intercede for us to Jesus, who intercedes for us to God, and so we ask other Christians, those that have already made it to heaven, to do the same...to intercede for us to God. I wondered if realizations like this would come out of the blue in the months and years to come, after I had come into the Church.

---

miscommunication. I've concluded it is one of the major reasons Christians disagree on points of theology—if they were to avoid equivocation by carefully defining the terms, they would discover they actually agree on many things that now separate them.

1 Hebrews 12:1-2

W HEN WE CATECHUMENS had all donned our robes and cinched our belts, we filed out to the entrance of the nave and stood next to the baptistery font with Fr. Cronk. Here was another enlightening symbol.

I thought back to the many Evangelical and Protestant churches I had attended in my life. In Evangelical churches the baptism tank was architecturally incorporated at the front of the church, often elevated and behind the pastor and choir, so the congregation can see what's happening without turning in their seats. But its location had no meaning otherwise. Some Evangelical Churches claimed that baptism is an important sacrament that needs to be displayed up front to call attention to its importance. Some do public full-immersion baptism in a local river or lake. Other Evangelicals demanded that baptism only be conferred with a particular formula of words and it "has to be with complete immersion…or it's invalid."[1] But no Evangelical Church, and only a few Protestant denominations, will claim baptism as a sacrament that actually imparts the saving

> **Why would it matter how it was done, if it was just a symbol?**

grace of God. Instead, they claim baptism is only symbolic. So, I stood there at the back of St. James' nave wondering how important could it be if it was only symbolic? *Why would it matter how it was done, if it was just a symbol?*

But there I stood, getting ready to be "provisionally" baptized in the Catholic Church that claims baptism, when done with the right disposition of heart and in the right form, is a true Sacrament that literally conveys salvation grace. I checked my own heart. I wanted to do this, of my own free will. I was sorry for my sins and wanted to be cleansed of them all.

In the months I had been attending Mass and RCIA classes, if my observations were half-accurate, there were a lot of Catholics that were just going through the motions. I did not want to be one of them.

I had learned about the New Evangelization. While the Church had spent most of its life preaching the Gospel to nations of non-Christians, it had by its own evaluation, neglected to mature the spiritual growth of its members who now were caught up in modern society. Some surveys indicated that as few as 23% of "baptized" Catholics actually went

---

1 Detroit Church of God in Christ minister challenging Alex Jones on his Catholic conversion in the 2006 trailer for a documentary "Catholic Paradox: The Story of Alex Jones." Alex became a permanent Deacon in the Catholic Church.

to Mass each week. The New Evangelization was the name given to re-evangelizing the "faithful," or those that "have already heard Christ proclaimed."[1]

As I stared at the water in the baptistery I recalled how the Church taught that the Sacraments, like baptism, and communion are efficacious and still impart grace, even to those who do not come with a tender, humble heart. During RCIA, Cronk described how the Children of Israel passed through the Red Sea and were saved physically, which foreshadowed the baptism in the New Testament that saves spiritually. But as St. Paul reminded me, just going through the motions was a deadly enterprise.

> Don't be ignorant of the fact...that our ancestors were all under the cloud and that they all passed through the sea. They were all baptized into Moses...They all ate the same spiritual food and drank the same spiritual drink; for they drank from the spiritual rock that accompanied them, and that rock was Christ. [2]

The cloud was God's literal presence personified in a pillar of smoke and fire that went before, above and behind the Children of Israel as protection and a reminder of whom they belonged to. This was not dissimilar from Christ's presence in the reserved Eucharist that sat in every Catholic Church in a gold tabernacle, with a flame nearby to remind us of the cloud of God's presence, literally. The Children of Israel also partook daily of *Old Testament Sacraments* (my term) when they ate manna and drank water from the rock that also followed them around like the cloud. These were just like the host and cup at Mass.

But then, although these Sacraments were received daily by the Israelites, most did not make it. Paul says...

> Nevertheless, God was not pleased with most of them; their bodies were scattered in the wilderness.

So, the motions alone will never save us. The thought of the baptismal waters, the holy water at the door, or the sprinkling that occurs during Mass sometimes as the priest flings holy water over the congregation, are all things that remind us of our baptism and how its best effect is when we don't take it for granted. Paul's words reminded me to

---

1 On-line. AveMariaPress.com/yearoffaith/what-is-the-new-evangelization/
2 1 Corinthians 10:2

exercise self-discipline and not just go through the motions.

Now these things occurred as examples to keep us from setting our hearts on evil things as they did.[1]

The Litany of the Saints was wrapping up...

Make haste, O God, to deliver me.
Make haste to help me, O Lord.
O God, save thy servants.
That put their trust in thee.

...as I made a mental note that at St. James, as in most Catholic Churches, the baptistery was placed just inside the entrance, because it is through the sacrament of baptism that we enter the Church,[2] if St. Peter's words mean anything.

There was also, just inside the entrance door, a small wall-mounted font of Holy Water. It wasn't required to be a Catholic to use one, so I had already been in the habit of wetting my fingers in the font and crossing myself *In the name of the Father, Son and Holy Ghost.*[3]

After Fr. Cronk blessed the waters in the baptistery with the help of the Paschal Candle, it came time for our test. He would ask questions of the whole group, but my answers would determine if I was ready to be Catholic.

Do you reject Satan? (I do.)

And all his works? (I do.)

And all his empty promises? (I do.)

Do you believe in God the Father, almighty, creator of heaven and earth? (I do.)

Do you believe in Jesus Christ, his only son, our Lord, who was born of the Virgin Mary, was crucified, died, and was buried, rose from the dead and is now seated at the right hand of the Father? (I do.)

Do you believe in the Holy Spirit, the Holy Catholic Church, the communion of saints, the forgiveness of sins, the

---

1 1 Corinthians 10:1-6. (NIV)
2 *Baptism now saves you*, 1 Peter 3:21
3 Matthew 28:19

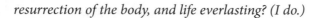

resurrection of the body, and life everlasting? (I do.)

I passed the test.

When it came to my turn, I knelt in the water at the foot of the font's waterfall and Fr. Cronk, using a white porcelain pitcher, poured water over my head three times.

> *Stanley, I baptize you in the name of the Father...*
>
> *And of the Son...*
>
> *And of the Holy Spirit. Amen.*

There was no baritone voice from heaven, nor did a dove alight on my head, but my faith was strengthened by my mere obedience. When I dried off, Ed Wolfrum, my sponsor, gave me my own candle, lit from the Pascal candle that stood guard over the evening.

A S THE THREE-HOUR long Vigil Mass at St. James approached midnight on April 11, 1998, I experienced three sacraments of the Church. (1) I was provisionally[1] baptized with water. (2) I was confirmed in the faith through the anointing of Holy chrism oil. (3) I partook of my first Holy Communion—The Eucharist.

That night at St. James, when it was my turn to take communion, I approached Fr. James Cronk...but I didn't have to ask if I could take communion. He smiled and held up the host for me to see and said, "The body of Christ." I bowed at the presence of Christ and then ate his flesh and drank his blood—Christ *in* me...real presence...real life.

I returned to my pew-chair and began to contemplate what had just happened and how my spiritual life would change. The engraving on the communion table in our Evangelical churches read, "DO THIS IN REMEMBRANCE OF ME". And so, now I remembered:

- ► Fr. Cronk's prayers of consecration over the bread and wine were like the prayers Jewish priests said in the Holy of Holies over the bread on the Table of Showbread—the sacred presence of God.
- ► How Christ transformed the five-loaves and two-fish on the hillside to feed the 5,000 with supernatural food that looked natural to the people.

---

1 I was baptized "provisionally" because no one knew for sure if my earlier baptisms in the FM Church had been valid per Catholic teaching.

- ▶ How Jesus took and blessed the bread at Emmaus and then suddenly disappeared, leaving His sacred presence in the form of bread on the table.
- ▶ Jesus's words, "I am the bread of life, unless you eat my body and drink my blood you will not have life within you."
- ▶ How Christ told us, "Behold I am with you always," which meant The Eucharist that was held in reserve in all the Tabernacles of all the Catholic Churches throughout the world.
- ▶ Pam sensing God's presence in St. James the second time she came to Mass.
- ▶ How the engraving on communion tables in the churches we grew up in had always meant (to me) to take communion every day, and how now I could, at daily Mass in any Catholic Church anywhere in the world.
- ▶ That I no longer had to settle for watered-down grape juice four-times a year. Now, I could take the full-bodied, real flesh and real blood of Jesus everyday as I contemplate his sacrifice for my salvation.
- ▶ Working out with my son Josh in the gym, lifting weights. If we wanted to be strong and well-conditioned, we had to work out more often than four-times a year, or even once a month.
- ▶ How seriously I took Evangelical communion, and how communion now, as a Catholic, suddenly became very serious...because I was literally was ingesting Him so that Christ *could dwell in me.*

THE EVENING WAS like coming home after years of being in exile. Like never before I felt spiritually aware. Yes, there was much more to learn and sort out, but in faith and with reason all that I needed would come.

During my Before Catholic (B.C.) period, I never stayed in a church longer than seven years until something in its teaching or practice appeared inconsistent with the Bible or Natural Law, and I was forced to bolt to save my sanity. Seventeen-years later, in the writing of this book, I still feel as if I'm on my Catholic Honeymoon. That must be some sort of proof, for me at least, that I was always meant to be Roman Catholic.

But that wasn't all I learned from my journey.

73
Prima Facie

IF THERE IS a capstone to my journey of faith, it is here, smack dab in front of me. I've learned that religious institutions (at least the honest ones) attempt to teach their adherents how to live a meaningful and happy life by writing down a code that corresponds to the immutable Natural Laws of the physical universe and the mystical laws of reality beyond our perception...all, of which, are established by God.

The problem is, that when you're dealing with God-things explained by man-things, regular-things freeze-up like the computer I'm writing this book with often does...and the God-thing, like computer code, is so difficult to decipher that you're forced to take up cryptology. (At least that's what I've felt like for most of my life dealing with the Protestant-thing called Christianity.)

This was a big part of the puzzle for me. There were thousands of pieces to the jigsaw puzzle and there was no picture on the cover of the box. I needed a picture, a prima facie,[1] that made sense. Nature made sense to me, and so did the Bible, although neither could be fully understood.

Yes, it was those two things, nature and the Bible. So, for me, a trustworthy religion was going to have to get the correlation between its doctrine (the picture on the box) and the pieces inside the box (representing all the various pieces of the Bible and Nature) and get them to fit together...and make a picture...that was on the box.

Let me step back (hopefully not off a cliff) and explain myself.

1 (pry-mah fay-shah) adj. Latin for "at first look," or "on its face." In law: Refers to the evidence before trial being sufficient to prove the case unless there is substantial contradictory evidence presented at trial. It implies that the case, apparently, is "open and shut." In my use, I mean the evidence is everywhere.

F ROM THE TIME I was the twinkle in my parent's eyes, my belief system was pegged on those things that exhibited the most evidence. (I always liked the Perry Mason scenes where he introduced the murder weapon into evidence. Now we're getting somewhere!)

The evidence I wanted was a prima facie event, a logical, reasoned, ordered system of the visible universe. I liked the ideas of super novas... they stood out as obvious. To me the complexities of the solar system, the immensity of the far flung galaxies, and the intricacies of our microscopic and atomic world were miracles beyond comprehension... although, I *thought* about them a lot.

The lushness of the Earth compared to the cratered, airless surfaces of the nearby planets and our moon, further drove the stake into the moist rich soil that there was someone who loved us, and had our best interests in mind. But it clearly wasn't Milky the Clown, the Teletubbies, or whatever that purple obese thing Barney is.

I wanted something eternal, everlasting, over-powering, omniscient and loving. And, the simplest experiments from Mr. Friend's science class demonstrated that in the absence of intelligent energy put into a system, the system would turn into a pile of garbage faster than a disposal truck could open and close its carnivorous jaws.

Yet the universes (both the large and small kind) were robust miracles of engineering that flourished. That the heavens and the earth and all that is in them declared the glory of God was always and continues to be, for me, a prima facie proof for God.

> **In the absence of intelligent energy put into a system, the system would turn into a pile of garbage faster than a disposal truck could open and close its carnivorous jaws.**

M Y PARENTS INTRODUCED me to the wonders of the next prima facie piece of evidence, the Christian Bible, both the Old and the New Testaments, in sweet smelling Tasmanian leather. Here was a book that also exhibited a logical, reasoned, ordered system of intellectual thought and explanation of *why* the natural world existed, *why* there was suffering in that same beautiful world, *what* the answer was to that suffering, and *what* was beyond the visible world.

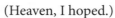

(Heaven, I hoped.)

Indeed, quantum science later gave me theoretical and experimental evidence that the three-dimensional space and the zero-dimension of time in which we physically exist, is not all there is. On that, the Bible and science pointed to the same conclusion—that there are extra dimensions of space and time, surely, and perhaps dimensions of mental telepathy, morality and who but God knows what else.

> **The three-dimensional space and the zero-dimension of time in which we physically exist, is not all there is.**

That the Bible, with its various authors stretched over millennia, all cogently writing about one story, some foretelling later events with great precision, and all with a singular moral premise (of which I eventually wrote the book),[1] is remarkable enough. But add to that the statistical impossibility of the content's internal and external integrity, the literary evergreen quality of the narratives, the epic poetry, the passion and pathos of the epochal story of humanity, conjoined with eternal hope for the future, and the Bible is unsurpassable. How could I not believe in its inerrancy, even with a few pages ripped out by belligerents or argumentative well-meaning bookstore owners?

Yes, so-called "scholars" would point out so-called "Biblical difficulties"—supposed contradictions in the texts or chronologies. Yet, different human perspectives of time or space of the same event easily explain each, as if these "scholars" had never been to a family reunion where Uncle Yatsi brought his customized dictionary to play Scrabble.

ALL OF THIS good stuff, however, gave me a problem. Yes, nature's benevolence and the Natural Laws that kept Earth together, implied the existence of a loving God—an omniscient, omnipotent, omnipresent person who was beyond my universe of space-time, and who came before and caused it all.[2] Not to be outdone, the Bible, with all the attributes of sacredness, went beyond implication of a God, and in explicit detail described His attributes—a quiver full

---

1 The Bible's moral premise is simple: Hating God leads to damnation and death; but loving God leads to blessing and life."

2 "Cause" is a doubtful term in this context, as I have my doubts that linear time (which "cause" implies) exists in God's reality. It makes more sense that in God's "presence" *time* is not a zero dimension that relentlessly marches forward as we experience it, but a three-dimensional concept with volume. But more about that another *time*.

of anger, love, judgment, compassion, grace and mercy...for starters.

But now came the difficulty. Nature's implication and the Bible's explanation needed interpretation. To me, both Nature and the Bible came from the same source, an intelligence that was so far beyond Uncle Yatsi's dictionary, that humanity's ability to comprehend it all began to look like contradictions, not paradoxes. Why? Because human beings have this uncanny avoidance of paradoxes. They either want something obvious (a prima facie) or they don't want it at all. They don't like mysticism or mystical things, unless it lasts no longer than a 60-minute Agatha Christie murder mystery. Then it's okay. Why? Because, afterwards it's no paradox that Colonel Mustard was done in by Miss Scarlet with a revolver in the pantry next to the 1943 bottle of *Richebourg Grand Cru* pickles.

> **Paradox is perhaps the best humanity can do, owing to our innate inability to know much of anything about the universe, let alone everything.**

But paradox is perhaps the best humanity can do, owing to our innate inability to know much of anything about the universe, let alone everything. I was fortunate that I understood, even if the pickle connoisseurs did not, that nature and the Bible had to agree because they have the same author. The disagreements are between the *interpretations* of Nature (i.e. Science) and the *interpretations* of the Bible (i.e. theology). Science and theology are both human endeavors; their sometimes vastly different understandings of humanity's limited knowledge.

That is why I have never respected the concept of *atheism* that declares something does *not* exist when so little is known about what *does* exist—amidst the myriad of evidence that points to *the vastness of the unknown. Atheism's declarative claim of omniscience has only ignorance for evidence.*

> **Atheism's declarative claim of omniscience has only ignorance for evidence.**

THE PROBLEM WAS exacerbated by the many different Christian denominations that all claimed to believe the Bible, but battled bitterly over what they respectfully believed the Bible to be saying. And we're not even talking about the many different Bible translations, which introduces a whole new complexity to the problem of Biblical interpretation, unless you dream in Aramaic, Latin...and in color. Theologians from different Christian sects would use the same book, the same translation, and even read the same verse at the same time...and they would come to different conclusions.

How could that happen?

Do I hear an "Amen!" Can anyone say, "PRIDE!"?

To me, desperately different interpretations of the same book by so-called Christians was always the consequence of sin. Or, as St. Paul wrote to the Romans, "The wages of sin is death." For me, denominationalism is the prima facie scourge of Christianity. It was irrational and directly contrary to at least one particular passage where St. Paul admonishes Christians in Corinth.

> *There are quarrels among you...One of you says, "I follow Paul"; another, "I follow Apollos"; another, "I follow Cephas"; still another, "I follow Christ." Is Christ divided? Was Paul crucified for you? Were you baptized in the name of Paul? I thank God that I did not baptize any of you except Crispus and Gaius, so no one can say that you were baptized in my name.[1]*

> **Yet, the American Christian Church was proudly divided... This was the Scandal of Christianity I faced.**

This was, on its face, wrong. And yet the American Christian Church was proudly divided. Not into four different fellowships, which is what Paul faced, but thousands. This is the Scandal of Christianity I faced, but I knew not what to do about it. I saw no way out of the morass of confusion and pride.

It took a long time (at least 500 pages) for me to discover there was a solution and it was ubiquitous within Christendom. How could I have missed it?

WHEN I FINALLY walked into a Catholic Church it took a while for me to believe that this was the Church that Jesus founded, and that there was nothing in its teaching that contradicted my two prima facie requirements—non-contradiction with nature and non-contradiction with the Bible. To come to that conclusion, I stepped back into my college days and donned the hat Prof. Royal Mulholland asked me to wear that one day when I role

---

1 1 Corinthians 1:11-15 (NIV)

played an empiricist for his Introduction to Philosophy class. In investigating Catholicism, I applied the Scientific Method. Now, a full explanation of that would be too long for this volume. So, for now, a quick overview will suffice.

THE SCIENTIFIC METHOD

SOME CHRISTIANS READING this will want Scripture proof-texts to get them over the hump that I'm not a heretic for claiming that the Scientific Method has some place in Christianity. Okay, in a moment. Hold your angels!

It's instructive to first mention that the Scientific Method was developed over hundreds of years by a great many investigators, and that Catholic scientists like Roger Bacon (a Franciscan Friar), Galileo, and Descartes, are given most of the credit. But the proof text for the Scientific Method as a tool of theology is here, in St. Paul's charge to the Thessalonians:

> *Do not quench the Spirit. Do not treat prophecies with contempt, but test them all; hold on to what is good, reject every kind of evil.*[1]

Don't see it? Well, in a fortnight (depending on how fast you read) on the next pages, we'll get to it. If you go back and review the records of the church councils, beginning with the First Jerusalem Council documented in Acts chapter 15, and expanded a bit in Paul's discussion of his conflict with Peter in Galatians chapter 2, we find this same Scientific Method at work in determining a particular aspect of Christian doctrine—whether or not Gentiles needed to be circumcised before they were allowed into the nascent Church. Here are the four fundamental steps of the Scientific Method as they are found in: a) Thessalonians 5:19-22, b) how the Apostles applied them in the first century Church to determine doctrine regarding the circumcision of Gentile converts to Christianity, and c) how I applied them in my investigation of Catholicism.

---

1 1 Thessalonians 5: 19-22

STEP 1
OBSERVE THE ENVIRONMENT
(COLLECT DATA)

1 Thessalonians 5:19-22: *Do not quench the Spirit. Listen to the prophecies from God.*

First Jerusalem Council: The leaders in Jerusalem listened to the different testimonies of Paul, Barnabas, local believers, and James. They even considered revelation—the miraculous signs and wonders God had done through them among the Gentiles. And, they considered the Natural Law evidence—the pain and difficulty that circumcision would bring to the new believers. They also considered Old Testament Scriptures. In short, the leaders of the Church at Jerusalem understood that the Natural Law given to them and all men through common revelations, and special revelations of the prophets, all emanated from the same source—God. It was all data that had to be considered.

My Investigation of Catholicism: I attended Mass and watched. I listened to what the priests said and what the people did. I read many books. I considered the Bible. I considered what Protestants said of Catholicism. I evaluated my own experience and interactions with Catholics over the years. I sought the Holy Spirit in prayer as I had done my whole life.

STEP 2
FORM HYPOTHESES
(STATE POSSIBLE THEORY)

1 Thessalonians 5:19-22: *Ask,what the Spirit and the prophecies mean in a practical sense. Do not throw out the data acquired through observation, or assume you know what the data means with prideful contempt (paraphrased).*

First Jerusalem Council: The leaders in Jerusalem (and later Paul and Peter) combined their observations, guided by their faith in the Holy Spirit and their reason, of what was observed in Step 1. Peter formed an hypothesis that said the doctrine should not "make it difficult for the Gentiles who are turning to God." And, he added some other suggestions of what the doctrine should contain. Later, after more discussion and comparison of revelations and the Natural Law of the human situation at the time, they wrote a letter with their hypothesized decisions: *"It seemed good to the Holy Spirit and to us not to burden you with anything beyond the following requirements: You are to abstain from food sacrificed to idols, from blood, from the meat of strangled animals and from sexual immorality. You will do well to avoid these things."*

My Investigation of Catholicism: I formed several "null" hypotheses. One stated that Catholicism worshipped, Jesus's mother, Mary. Another stated that there was no evidence in the Bible or history that the consecrated wine and bread during Mass were the substantive, sacramental real presence of Jesus Christ. (And, there were many others.)

STEP 3
EVALUATE APPLICATION
(TEST THE THEORY)

1 Thessalonians 5:19-22: *Test the message from prophecies and those that may come from the Holy Spirit.*

First Jerusalem Council: The leaders in Jerusalem wrote a letter to the believers in Antioch, Syria, and Cilicia explaining their decision about what should be done regarding new Gentile male Christians. And they sent representatives with Paul and Barnabas back to Antioch as witnesses and ambassadors. The result? *"The people read it and were glad for its encouraging message."*

My Investigation of Catholicism: My readings, Bible study, and discussions with priests revealed that my "null" hypotheses were wrong. Catholicism did not teach the worship of Mary. Rather, I discovered that I was committing an equivocation about the word "prayer." Where I used it only as worship, others in the world used it as "request" of non-divine persons, and even earthly magistrates (England). I also discovered there was plenty of biblical evidence for the real presence of Christ in the communion elements, and such was the literal teaching in the *early* church by every one of the Church Fathers I researched.

STEP 4
ESTABLISH DOCTRINE
(CONFIRM THE THEORY AS LAW)

1 Thessalonians 5:19-22: *Hold on to what is good, reject every kind of evil.*

First Jerusalem Council: That the Jerusalem formulation about circumcision was accepted as true is evident by Peter being reprimanded by Paul later in Galatians 2 when Peter acted contrary to his own Jerusalem Council doctrine formulation. And, in fact, the doctrine has been part of the Church since that time without change.

My Investigation of Catholicism: The more I studied Catholicism, the more I saw the consistency of its doctrines with Scripture and the natural world. My many hypotheses that were contrary to Catholic teachings all proved false. My new hypotheses, the ones that proved true, were that Catholicism coincided with Natural Law and the Bible better than any Christian institution to my knowledge.

I HAVE CONTINUED TO look, but within the teachings of the Roman Catholic Church I've yet to find a contradiction, and yet I've found a deep treasure trove of understanding about Natural Law and the human condition that I never knew before.

And, that's why I'm Catholic. It was like jumping out of the apple tree when I was three, and instead of dangling with my feet looking for their footing, I had landed solidly on the ground, with my harness keeping me upright and secure.

Pam's Postscript: From Cancer to Catholicism

PAM WRITES: *So, here we were, after nearly 30-years of marriage, bearing a deep split in our relationship. Spiritually, we were on two different wave-lengths. I never thought that was possible when we came together to say, "I'll love you through thick and thin, for better or worse, sickness or health, richer or poorer." I never envisioned that the one sure foundation of our Christian faith could end up causing such a great divide. How could this be a part of God's plan? We tried to carry on as usual, but around every corner were the issues that divided us. The big question looming was, who had the truth? Pontius Pilate may have had a point, "What is truth?"*

One night we went out to eat and in attempt to have a peaceful date we kept our differences emotionally repressed. As we drove home, I tried to bring up all the Protestant ministers and hymn writers and missionaries who had spread the Gospel message. "They can't all be so off track!" I said. "Why would God allow the Protestant Reformation to occur unless some good could come out of it? Surely, God has blessed this branching off from Catholicism."

I don't remember Stan's reply; I just remember it did not go well. His stinging words pained my heart, and I had to get away. When the car stopped at a stoplight, I got out of the car and slammed the door behind me. As the door swung shut its sharp steel corner left a stinging bruise on my leg. The pain was sudden and intense, but I wasn't going to give in and go back because of a "little" scrape. I walked to a nearby restaurant and called a neighbor on a pay phone to come pick me up and take me home.

Later that night, and for weeks to come, Stan was more tender in his dealings with me. Life went on, but it was bandaged.

*I*N SEPTEMBER, 1998, after 13-years of teaching in a Christian school and subbing for a year in the public system, I started my first full-time teaching job in a public middle school.

Josh was in his senior year at the Naval Academy, and we were invited to Parents Weekend at the end of the month. What a thrill! I took off work for a four-day weekend and drove with Stan to attend the festivities.

When we passed the "Annapolis, Maryland" city limits sign Stan had to make a comment!

"You know," he said, "Maryland was named after Jesus's mother and Annapolis was named after Mary's mother, Anne. Maryland was to become a safe haven for Catholics when they came to the New World! [1]

I thought, how could he know that? I've never heard that before. He made that up! It can't be true! My mind sped ahead. Maryland is just the name of one of our states. I said nothing, but was fuming just under the surface.

Yet, as the weekend wore on, I wondered if he could be right? I began to think of all the cities named after Catholic saints: Saint Louis, San Diego, San Francisco, Saint Paul, San Antonio. Then there were lakes and islands. Near our house was Lake Saint Clair and the Saint Clair River. In Upper Michigan there was Sault Ste Marie and the Saint Mary's River that ran next to Saint Joseph's Island. In the Caribbean there was Saint Lucia, and Saint Maarten. I started to notice, too, for the first time, how many Catholic Churches there were…everywhere we went…always with the tallest spires! But, I couldn't mention any of this to Stan. No way was I going to give him any satisfaction for maybe being right.

Eventually, all these thoughts were buried under the excitement of being with Josh. It was the beginning of the last year he would be schooled at this academically-elite, ethically-sound, physically-challenging,

---

1 Stan's footnote: Some historians claim that Maryland was named after English King Charles I's French Catholic wife, Queen Henrietta Maria. But some Catholics believe that George Calvert, 1st Lord Baltimore, to whom the land was deeded by Charles I, intended the names to honor St. Mary and St. Anne.

leadership-building institution. It didn't get any better than this! We had so much to look forward to...and at that time we didn't know that eight months later, at the culmination of his senior year and Commissioning Week, Josh would marry his high school sweetheart in the Naval Academy Chapel...with crossed swords on the steps leading out, in the whole, beautiful Navy tradition.

I REMEMBER THEIR WEDDING ceremony that following May (1999) as if it were yesterday...and the crossed swords ritual, after the wedding, was just as reverent and emotionally charged.

Josh and Christin exited the chapel...her left arm through his, her right holding a large bouquet of flowers in front. They stopped at the top of the stone steps and smiled at the crowd of well-wishers gathered below. Eight of Josh's academy friends, dressed in their formal white uniforms and carrying steel, ceremonial swords, formed a crossed-swords arch on the steps for Josh and Christin to pass through. As the new Mr. & Mrs. approached the first set of swords, the swords were dropped to form a cross in front of them preventing their progress. One of the swordsmen said, "Pass with a kiss!" Josh and Christin leaned toward each other and kissed...at which point the first set of swords were raised allowing them to step down another two steps, only to be stopped by the second set of swords which were dropped as they approached. This forced them to kiss again. This progressed through another two sets of swords at which point Josh and Christin walked to freedom. Or so those of us watching thought.

But just as they left the last set of swords, Josh's best man, Seth, who was the last sword bearer on Christin's side of the arch, took his sword and, as tradition would have it, swatted Christin hard on the rump and said, "Welcome to the Navy, Mrs. Williams."

But Christin, knowing this was part of the tradition, was prepared. She abruptly let go of Josh's arm, and from underneath her bouquet of flowers pulled a fully loaded water pistol, turned and began shooting Seth with a powerful stream of water directly into his startled and laughing face.

From that moment on it was no longer a question of whether Christin was prepared for the Navy, but whether the Navy was prepared for Christin.

GETTING BACK TO *Parents Weekend in September, 1998, I was visiting the Academy gift shop trying to figure out how many Navy sweaters, jackets and other gifts I could persuade Stan to let me buy, and picturing how to fit most of the store into my closet...*

perhaps, if Stan moved his clothes to the garage.

Suddenly, Stan interrupted me with an alert on his pager...from my doctor...I needed to call the doctor's office right away.

So, I found a pay phone and called. A nurse answered right away and asked me an innocuous question. I said, "Yes, m'aam. I had a lump removed from my neck 3 days ago....No, I can't come in today to see the doctor...Why?...Well, I can't. I'll be out of state for two more days...Yes, I'll make an appointment as soon as I return. What is this about? Why can't you tell me over the phone?"

And so began my experience with the dreaded news of cancer.

When we returned to Michigan I went alone to see Dr. Kushner. He could barely say the "C" word. He kept calling it non-Hodgkin's Lymphoma. I finally asked, "Are you trying to tell me I have cancer? He said, "Yes."

That night Stan and I cried in each other's arms, not knowing what the future held.

In the days that followed, Stan became almost overly protective of me. He started reading up on all the antioxidant food sources, vitamins and minerals, and made sure my diet was full of them. He would take off work to be with me at every appointment and rush me to the hospital if my temperature climbed. He even did this on the day of his PhD graduation when the pain in my calves indicated I had blood clots.

*A*FTER THE FIRST *round of chemotherapy, I found myself often in bed more and had to take a leave of absence from my teaching job—the one I just started. Providentially, it was a job with excellent insurance provisions that carried us through financially. I was also thankful for a very supportive school administrator-principal, who worked with me to provide a wonderful long-term substitute for my beloved students.*

When my hair fell out, I bought a couple of wigs, and Stan shaved his head in an effort to express his solidarity with me. The wigs were quite natural but very uncomfortable to wear all day. Though, I did wear one while teaching, I'd exchange it for a baseball cap or head scarf upon coming home. I never liked the bald look or feel. I was glad it was winter, so I had an excuse to wear a hat.

Occasionally, I would go into school to deliver my lesson plans to my long-term sub. To those who asked, I shared how my faith kept me strong in the midst of the side effects and the pain. Thus, I began to discover who on the teaching staff were Christians and Catholic. As it turned out, the long-term sub who was teaching for me was a wonderful, capable young lady fresh out of college who just happened to be a devout Catholic. She and I got along famously and we had a few personal talks about my questions regarding the Catholic faith.

BY THIS TIME, *God was bringing some articulate Catholic people into our lives, and I began to learn the Catholic view of suffering. As a Protestant, we had always prayed for every pain, disease, and injury "to be gone in Jesus's name."*

As my Catholic acquaintances began to give me a reason for suffering, I started to understand the Lord Jesus in a different light. I saw the crucifix as a beautiful thing, not ugly or disdainful. I saw my own pain and trial as a way to be united to Christ in his suffering, and I willingly joined my suffering with His for the whole world's salvation. Thus, I found myself cooperating with God...all as a consequence of my cancer.

Now, don't think I was some saint. I had my times of complaining and moaning and wondering if ever I'd be well again. There were times of crying when things did not go my way, but God was stripping everything out of my life—even life itself—so that I would be able to listen to Him with fresh, new ears and eyes.

UPON HEARING OF *my cancer, Ray Long Jr. suggested we come to the rectory at Assumption Grotto Catholic Church, and let him pray for me and anoint me with oil.*

STAN WRITES: The parish of The Assumption of the Blessed Virgin Mary Church hails back to 1830 when German immigrants arrived in Detroit. In a bid to avoid the cholera epidemic in the heart of the city, they settled a few miles to the north to live among French Catholics. There they built a small log Catholic Church in the woods. Over the years the buildings were lost to fire, rebuilt and expanded. In 1876, an Our Lady of Lourdes grotto was built in the church cemetery, where outdoor Masses were and are still held today. It's after the Lourdes grotto that the church gets its nickname, "Assumption Grotto." The present Neo-Gothic stone church building was designed by Aloys Frank Herman, and was dedicated in 1929. Today, the second oldest Catholic Church in Detroit is listed in both the Michigan and National Register of Historic Places. Masses are often celebrated in Latin. Several times a year, at feasts like Easter and Christmas, its current pastor, Fr. Eduard Perrone, a respected classical composer and conductor, will hire members of the Detroit Symphony Orchestra and with the Grotto choir celebrate a Mass setting (e.g. musical genre) by Mozart, Beethoven, or others. Not to be missed, and I rarely do.

Ray worked as a technical writer and producer for corporations in a rectory basement office of Assumption Grotto. He also worked for the church as a full-time organist, cantor, EMS First Responder, and occasionally helped Fr. Perrone translate letters and lyrics for an orchestral project Fr. Perrone recorded of the late composer Paul Paray who conducted the Detroit Symphony orchestra for a decade.

*W*HEN WE ARRIVED *at Grotto, we met with Ray in the rectory conference room. There he prayed simply over me, and anointed me with holy oil from the Church. I was humbled that he would do this. In so doing, he introduced us to the St. Joseph Prayer that became a favorite prayer for me to pray for others.*

A few weeks later, Ray called up and said he had discovered that under current Church rules he should not have anointed me with oil, but that it was to be done by a priest. It didn't matter if Pam was Catholic or not, since this was not a sacrament being administered. He asked if we'd return, and we did a few days later.

Being in the rectory and seeing the reverence and yet the simple trust exhibited by Ray and Fr. Matthew, who anointed and prayed over me with the Church's blessings, had a profound impact. I learned that the effect of the prayer wasn't just in the words themselves, nor did the saint (Joseph), who carried our prayer to Jesus, have the power to heal. Rather, the Church's trust was in the power of Almighty God who longed to show us His love and would see us through whatever lay ahead. And, I learned that praying to saints like St. Joseph was not worshipping them, but rather exercising a communion with those who just happened to be in heaven. We were asking them to pray for us as we would ask our friends to pray for us. Except the saints could pray before the throne of Jesus Christ...literally.

Praying the St. Joseph prayer every day also centered my mind on this faithful servant of God and how he was lead by God to protect our Lord during his early years. I wanted to have that saintly faithfulness and obedience in my life—whatever was left of it.

*A*S I PRAYED *and read my Bible, I came to realize that the Catholic Church was founded on the Apostles—as Scripture says and as the Apostles' Creed proclaims—and that the promises* of Christ were given to the Church the Apostles founded. But I still had problems with doctrines like transubstantiation—that the common bread and wine offered at Mass was miraculously transformed on the altar into the sacramental Body and Blood of Jesus.

One day, as I lay in bed praying and recovering from a round of chemo, Stan came into the bedroom and offered me a printout from a website he had found. "Here," he said, "I found these quotes from the Early Church Fathers." There were several pages of quotes that he had compiled. Some of the statements were underlined. One was from Justin Martyr.

> This food we call the Eucharist, of which no one is allowed to partake except one who believes that the things we teach are true, and has received the washing for forgiveness of sins and for rebirth, and who lives as Christ handed down to us. For <u>we do not receive these things as common bread or common drink; but</u> as Jesus Christ our Savior being incarnate by God's Word took flesh and blood for our salvation, so also we have been taught that the food consecrated by the Word of prayer which comes from him, from which our flesh and blood are nourished by transformation, <u>is the flesh and blood of that incarnate Jesus.</u>[1]

All of the quotes supported the Catholic claim of transubstantiation, or the Real Presence of Christ in the bread and wine consecrated during the Mass. I sensed that Stan was coming out of his self-imposed "do not push Catholicism on Pam" cocoon. I liked him in the cocoon. Why did he have to come out like this, always pushing?

"Where did you get these?" I asked.

"The on-line Christian Classics Ethereal Library of the Early Church Fathers."

I was suspicious. "What's that on, some Catholic website?"

"No, " he said. "Actually, it's on Calvin College's website."

Calvin College was a Christian Reformed (Protestant) college in Grand Rapids, Michigan. I knew about the Early Church Fathers, some of who were the disciples of the Apostles themselves. "You mean this stuff is on a Protestant website?"

"Sure is," he said.

Suddenly I was upset with someone other than Stan. Did Protestants

---

1 Justin Martyr, First Apology, Ch. 66, inter A.D. 148-155.

have this information all along and keep it hidden from the rest of us? Was Catholicism tied to the True Early Church in this way? Was this proof that Catholics had not made up this whole idea of transubstantiation, and that it had been part of Christian theology from the very beginning? If that was true, it meant Protestants (especially Evangelicals), and not Catholics, had changed what the Early Church believed—that the Eucharist is the true Body and Blood of Christ.

That was an important milestone in my understanding of the difference between communion in a Catholic Church and communion in an Evangelical Church. A Catholic priest had been ordained in a strict succession of Holy Orders from the Apostles, and the faith of the priest, and the Church at large held that the consecrated bread and wine miraculously became the real presence of Christ. But in Evangelical Churches the pastors were not ordained in a successive line from the Apostles; nor did they have faith in the miracle of the altar. Nor did they have the authority that the sacrament of Holy Orders passed down to priests. Of course, Evangelicals had to believe the elements of communion were only *symbolic of Christ's Body and Blood. That's all the elements in an Evangelical church could be—symbolic.*

With this epiphany, more Scripture made sense to me that I could not have understood except from a Catholic perspective. For instance, 1 Corinthians 10:16: "The cup of blessing that we bless [the cup that the priest prays over at the altar], is it not a participation *in the blood of Christ? The bread that we break, is it not a* participation *in the body of Christ?"*

And there was 1 Corinthians 11:27: "Therefore, whoever eats the bread or drinks the cup of the Lord unworthily will answer for the body and blood of the Lord."

All of this explained something else. I recalled with a rush, the second time I attended Catholic Mass with Stan and I had mystically felt the presence of Christ in the church. Laying there in bed, holding onto these printouts about the Early Church's belief in the Real Presence of Christ in the Eucharist, it dawned on me that indeed, as the Catholic Church taught, Christ was there, at St. James, in the leftover consecrated hosts that after communion had been gathered and reserved in the Tabernacle. The gold-plated Tabernacle at St. James was located in the part of the Church to the right of the altar, the very location I had felt the presence on my second Sunday there. Jesus was there, literally, to be worshipped. Like Jesus said, "I will be with you always, to the very end of the age." [1]

---

1 Matthew 28:20 NIV

Shortly thereafter I went to Fr. Cronk. I had the same questions I had asked in the past, but now I had a mind to listen to his answers and try to understand instead of finding fault. I wanted to come alongside the Catholic Church and embrace Her teachings. When I still couldn't believe some things yet about Mary, Father Cronk told me, "It's okay. You don't have to become Catholic."

"Yes, I do," I protested. "Because now I believe. I know that the Catholic Church is the Church Christ established."

I COULD NOT WAIT *until the Easter Vigil, and Father accommodated me because I had been through RCIA and because of my fragile condition after three rounds of chemo and 21 radiations. I came into the Church after Saturday evening Mass on January 23, 1999. I still did not understand some of the teachings about the Saints and Mary, but I accepted them on faith that God would reveal them to me.*[1]

I offered to be baptized bald so my wig would not get wet. But Fr. Cronk tenderly offered to have the water poured across my forehead as I leaned sideways over the font. It was a beautiful time with only four persons attending with me. One was a teacher from my new school, who I had never seen at St. James, but who providentially happened to be at the Mass just beforehand and asked why I was dressed in white. It was wonderful to have her there to witness the occasion.

As I write this in 2015, my cancer has been in remission for 16 ½ years, and I have lived to see 10 grandchildren born and all but the six-month old baby accept Christ as their Savior and Lord. All of her siblings and cousins are already telling her about Jesus and God's love poured out for us. They love the Lord and are very active in their church (still HPBC) and community, schools and families. I am confident God is leading them on their own journey to His Promised Land.

It has not been easy being Catholic. Our children, their spouses, my parents, my siblings, everyone dearest to me, still does not understand how I could willingly choose to become a part of this One, Holy, Catholic (universal), and Apostolic Church. Our first attempts to try to share our joy ended in a huge rift between us. Many in my family still think that I was brainwashed by Stan. I totally remember how I used to think toward the Catholic Church, too, so I can't fault them. God had to take me down a hard road, a fast track of cancer, to open my eyes. But, I am forever

---

1 After I came into the church I devoured tapes, books, and Catholic radio programs to more fully and deeply understand Catholic teaching. There was so much to absorb since nearly 1,500 years of Christianity preceding the Protestant Reformation had been hidden from me.

grateful.

It also has not been easy, because, as a Protestant, I thought I "knew it all." I knew the Bible inside and out. I could quote whole chapters of the Bible and knew where to find every book and verse, lightening fast!

Of course, we knew Our Bible. It was all we had!

As a Protestant, it was "sola scriptura," the Scripture alone, whereby truth could be obtained from God.

Now, as a Catholic, I felt like a baby Christian. I knew nothing about the Saints (there were thousands of saints to learn from), the holy Sacraments (there are 7 through which God works, performed by an ordained priest or deacon, to impart graces to his people), and the holy Mass (worship directed TO God, not just about Him, and where the holy Eucharist is transubstantiated on the altar). Nor did I know anything about the seven books of the Bible that Protestants had taken out of the canon of Scriptures. I had SO much to learn.

And, then there was the season of Lent, where the passion of Our Lord was emphasized and contemplated on for 40 days! When I first came to Catholicism, I had such trouble just looking at the crucifix. Now I had to think about the terrible things done to Christ every day for over a month! For a while, I just cried at every Mass. Stan did, too. We were overwhelmed at Christ's love for us and that He would leave Himself with us every Mass to consume and dissolve into our own bodies, It was too much to take in.

The weight of living my whole life up to this point without the "personal heart knowledge" of the fullness of the truth of these things made me sad. As a Protestant, my life was all sunshine and joy, but what was I to make of this new lack of joy I went around with? I finally mentioned this in the Confessional to Father Cronk, who gave me encouragement that I would receive back my joy. I would be fine, in time. It was a hard adjustment period for me to become Catholic, but God has taken me one step at a time along with each day's experiences, and I can see, looking back, that nothing has been an accident.

*D*ID MY JOY return? You bet it did. Nearly 15 years ago now, when I was still arguing with Fr. Cronk during RCIA he would tell me, "Come to the Mass. Just come to the Mass," as if that would answer all my questions about the things I didn't understand about the Catholic Church. It didn't make sense to me then, but lately I see the wisdom of his words, and they have come back to find lodging in my soul.

One year and two months ago, I retired from teaching. I decided that one of my priorities would be to attend daily Mass whenever possible. I can't tell you the day or date when something miraculous first occurred, but it was during an ordinary morning Mass, very unexpectedly, the words of the priest suddenly jumped out at me. The first time it happened, it was these words:

Blessed are those who are called to the Supper of the Lamb.

You know that part of the Mass, when the priest holds up the consecrated host? I'd heard it a hundred times. But, at that moment, I knew those words were FOR ME. I had been CALLED. I had been drawn to come to the Mass. The Supper of the Lamb. For so many years, before I was Catholic, I had not been called—50 to be exact. I didn't even know about the Catholic Mass, but now I do and I am...called to it. What a blessing and a joy! And, every time I go to Mass, those same words pop out at me again and again, and fill me with love and joy for the Lamb of God, who called me to come.

The next time the words of the Mass jumped out at me was just as unexpected as before. It happened as the priest said the words of remembrance from Our Lord at the Last Supper with His disciples. The priest was saying: "...taking the chalice, He gave thanks, and gave it to His disciples, saying..." All of a sudden, as the priest looked out at the people and said, "gave it to His disciples,.." I had the thought, "Wait a minute! I'm one of His disciples!" In that moment, I knew Jesus was right there saying those words to me that followed:

Take this, all of you, and drink from it, for this is the chalice of My blood.

I felt like I was right THERE at the Last Supper WITH Jesus. As the priest recites the words that Jesus spoke to His disciples, I am actually hearing JESUS speak those words to me!...as His disciple...NOW, in this current generation. In the Mass, Christ speaks those words TO US!...as His disciples TODAY!

Well, this just kept happening. Words kept jumping at me with more and more meaning each time I went to the Mass. In the Eucharistic prayer, the priest is thanking God the Father through His beloved Son who...

...stretched out His hands as He endured His Passion, so as to break the bonds of death and manifest the resurrection.

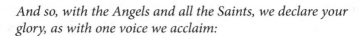

And so, with the Angels and all the Saints, we declare your glory, as with one voice we acclaim:

And I join in...

> *Holy! Holy! Holy! Lord God of hosts.*
> *Heaven and earth are full of your glory.*
> *Hosanna in the highest.*
> *Blessed is he who comes in the name of the Lord*
> *Hosanna in the highest.*

I felt like my voice was being added with all the Heavenly Hosts in giving God praise. Looking up I imagined (no, not just imagined...I knew) I was participating with the Angels and the Saints in heaven to proclaim the holiness and glory of God. I felt that sense of wonder and UNIFYING BOND between heaven and earth during the Mass.

It does not seem to end. Just recently, another phrase in the Mass has grabbed my attention, where the priest prays:

> *Therefore, as we celebrate the memorial of his Death and Resurrection, we offer you, Lord, the Bread of life and the Chalice of salvation, giving thanks that you have <u>held us worthy to be in your presence and minister to you.</u>*

Starting with the word "held" to the end, the words have continued to amaze me, because we are NOT worthy. But, quickly I became aware that God meets us where we are, (as unworthy people) and through Christ's worthiness, seats us with Him to "minister to"/worship Him in the beauty of the Supper of the Lamb/the Mass—the same Mass that has been celebrated around the world and over all the centuries since Christ left His authority and keys of the kingdom with His Apostles, to today!

...Blessed are those who are called—and are still being called—to that Supper!

Come to the Mass. Just come...

I loved my life as a Protestant Christian, and I love even more being a Catholic Christian. I realize everyone else is on a journey through this life, too, and if we are open to God, He will lead us all according to our own response to His call in our lives. But, I will be ever grateful for His call on my life and be willing to tell of His love and saving power. I pray my life will reflect the love He has put into me.

Epilogue: Life's Ironies

Fate or Providence?

ARE THE THINGS that happen to us the consequence of capricious fate or loving Providence? Do we, like the prophet Jeremiah, "curse the day we were born"[1] or are we like Fr. Solanus Casey and say, "Blessed be God in all his designs"?

How we are raised has a great deal to do with whether we see the "glass half full" or "empty on arrival." *I cannot speak for those that are born into slavery and abuse, tyranny or abject poverty.* For me, in spite of the troubles I had with my mother, the glass was always mostly full. As I indicated at the beginning of this memoir, I ascribe my good fortune to the Godly and moral obedience of the generations that came before me.

But my life was not pre-determined by such persons or forces. As smartly as I felt the vice-principal's paddle or my Dad's leather belt attached to the end of my mother's arm, it was clear that free will would be my constant companion. I had a choice to make at every point in my life. Was I going to embrace the spiritual legacy of my past and believe in the benevolent design of providence, or was I going to choose to refute it all and go my own way, just because I could, letting fate determine my life? As I tell my Moral Premise story clients, characters embrace certain values that lead to decisions, which lead to actions. All of that is under the free will of the character. But what comes next is the consequence of Natural Law, over which no character has control.

Thus, if I make wise decisions, I have learned to expect good consequences...eventually. If I make foolish decisions, I have learned to

---

1 Jeremiah 20:14

expect bad consequences...almost immediately.

One of the challenges in life is acquiring the wisdom to make good choices and avoid foolish ones. Discerning the difference between the two is part of the confusion of growing up. I learned you cannot make any choice you want and have God bless it. I had a choice whether to put water in the glass or empty it. I was always trying to fill my glass, but I discovered it was fairly easily to inadvertently knock the glass over.

The difference between fate and providence is tied to one's understanding of nature. If we believe nature is orderly and that the universe exists for our benefit, we're more likely to make decisions that cooperate with nature. But if we think nature is capricious and random, then our decisions will be less responsible and more foolish...because, in the end, we have no say. And yet, gravity is not just a good idea. It's the law. There is, in fact an *up* and a *down*. Obey it and live. Ignore it, and you'll fall to your death the first cliff you come to and decide you want to "jump across the Grand Canyon...flat footed."

Counsel or Headstrong?

M Y DAD GAVE counsel. My Mother was headstrong. Here was another great irony in my life. Opposites attract. Dad would continually encourage me with Scripture, mostly from the Psalms and Proverbs. Mom would "encourage" me with discipline, mostly with my Dad's old belts. Using Dad's belts was her way of involving my otherwise easy going dad in the discipline, since he was never there when she made such decisions.

Dad *encouraged* me with verses from the Old Testament:

> This book of the law shall not depart out of thy mouth; but thou shalt meditate therein day and night, that thou mayest observe to do according to all that is written therein: for then thou shalt make thy way prosperous, and then thou shalt have good success. (Joshua 1:8, KJV)

> Wait on the Lord: be of good courage, and he shall strengthen thine heart: wait, I say, on the Lord. (Psalms 27:14, KJV)

> Trust in the Lord with all thine heart; and lean not unto thine own understanding. In all thy ways acknowledge him,

and he shall direct thy paths. (Proverbs 3:5-6, KJV)

Mom, on the other hand, *threatened* me with verses from the New Testament:

> *All things work together for good to them that love God, to them who are the called according to his purpose. (Romans 8:28, KJV).*

This was flung at me when things didn't go so well for me—she was telling me that the bad consequence I experienced was because I did not love God. But, from my perspective, I just failed to see how *her* will lined up with the Almighty's.

And then there was...

> *Depart from me, ye cursed, into everlasting fire, prepared for the devil and his angels. (Mt. 25:41, KJV)*

Commentary's not needed for that one.

The irony here was that when I was young I knew Mom hated me, and I did my best to return her "affection." But as I grew up, and the more my bruises faded, I came to understand she loved me very much...on some days.

During college, as I've explained, I stayed away from home during the summer, and on college breaks I rarely visited for more than a few days. When Pam and I married, the bonds with my parents were broken, and we could visit my parents in their retirement homes in East Flat Rock, North Carolina or Winona Lake, Indiana with our family for several days and generally get along—except when Mom wanted me to wear a tie to Sunday evening church.

Then, in her old age, she became mentally disabled with dementia, and I could finally spend the entire day with her and get along beautifully. At times, you could see she'd want to argue, but she didn't...and neither did I. I was very thankful to God for these years of her illness. It wasn't terribly debilitating for her, and it allowed me to drive her to her various doctor appointments, and be with her on our trip to India as she allowed me to care for her.

SPEAKING OF INDIA, in 1981 I had the good fortune of escorting my Mother and Aunt Hopie back to their birth place in central India. Growing up, I heard dozens of stories about their lives as children there. At the time of our trip, Mom's mind was not very clear, Aunt Hopie's was. The 10 day trip, as the guests of Becky Bibbee, the head of the Wesleyan Mission that my grandmother worked in for decades, was very fruitful. Remarkably, in spite of her mental incapacity during the trip, Mom would gravitate to the old pianos at the various missions we visited, sit down and site read hymn after hymn, singing many of them in the Hindi dialect she learned as a child. She was headstrong, but her trust in God's providence was ever present.

We visited all the mission churches Edith Willobee started or worked at. The Willobee Sisters sang in Hindi at several services. And old childhood friends they had not seen in 60 years, greeted them over bowls of chicken curry near large black pots that cooked the ingredients on open fires.

On our third day in India, Mom wandered off and got lost in Bombay for eight hours. We missed our train to the interior because of her wandering. We rented a hotel room near where she went missing, made police reports, hired a translator to get on the phone and call around, and I turned over my credit card to cover the bill. Seven hours later, by God's grace, we were told she had been found by a local businessman and taken to the central police station 10 kilometers across the busy city.

It was night when we arrived and were directed to the second floor of a central building in a dimly lit compound. We climbed a set of exterior stairs, stepping over sleeping policeman who were catching shuteye between shifts. Once on the second floor veranda we negotiated more police who were sleeping propped up against the plastered walls. Around a corner we found the opening we were looking for. There was no door to the room, which was illuminated by two large, bare light bulbs that hung from the ceiling on frayed chords. Packed tight in the hot room on this muggy night, a dozen radio operators sat before their boxy, vacuum tube equipment from the 1920s and tried to coordinate police operations across the vast city. Such was their technology that no police station had the ability to call any other police station, except to relay messages through this radio room. Amidst the cacophony of sound and a few smiling faces we found Mom hugging her purse on a wooden bench against one wall. Her curly grey-blonde hair, light skin, and bright blue polyester dress was quite the contrast to the dark skin of the radio operators dressed in military khakis. When she saw us, she jumped up, smiled and said, "Oh, I'm so glad they found you. You were lost for the longest time. Where were you?"

D AD HAD ALWAYS wanted Mom to return and visit India, but she never got around to it. When we finally made the trip, Dad was 95 and in good health. He was still driving his car around Winona Lake, pushing guys 20 years his junior in their wheelchairs around the local nursing home, and handing out Bibles at Gideon events.

Nine days after Mom, Aunt Hopie, and I returned from India, Dad spent part of the morning raking leaves in their small front yard, came in for lunch with my Mom, and then laid down for his regular afternoon nap.

I was at home when I got a phone call from Mom. She said, very unemotionally, as if the newspaper had just been delivered, "Stanley, I think Ben is dead." Dad died during his nap. God just took him. It was time, he had raked the leaves that morning and there was nothing else to do. He was never sick a day in his life, and was only hospitalized at 92 when he fell and broke his thumb. They kept him over night for observation.

We buried Dad next to Edith Willobee. I looked at Mom and she pointed to the vacant plot next to Dad and smiled, "That's where I'll be buried some day."

> *Brothers and sisters, we do not want you to be uninformed about those who sleep in death, so that you do not grieve like the rest of mankind, who have no hope. (1 Thessalonians 4:13, NIV)*

And so, a few years later, she was.

Sure, Mom and Dad made some mistakes in raising me. But they didn't mess up in the most important aspect of my growing up. They taught me, at once, to love and fear God, and to respect the Bible with deep reverence. Consequently, throughout my long sojourn through the American Christian landscape, those values never left me for an instant.

> *Train up a child in the way he shall go, and when he is old he will not depart from it. (Proverbs 22:6, KJV)*

Dad may have been easy going. Mom may have been mean. But neither were malicious or selfish. They were steadfast in their trust, love, and fear of God, and instilling those values on their children. It worked! And I love them for it.

ONG BEFORE I thought of becoming Catholic, you'll recall how Fr. John Hardon asked me, "Who's your patron saint?" To him it didn't matter if I was Catholic or not...I needed someone in heaven interceding for me.

I've thought a lot about Fr. Hardon's question over the years. But it was not until I had to sit down and write this chapter that I came up with an answer. My sponsor, Ed, has tried to persuade me that my patron saint should be Maximilian Kolbe, who was a pioneer in media evangelization. Kolbe is the patron saint of journalists, amateur radio operators, the pro-life movement...and drug addicts.[1] He went to India for a time (and Japan) but returned to Germany in 1936 where he was imprisoned and sent to the concentration camp at Auschwitz. There he died, in the starvation bunker, volunteering his life for another prisoner, who survived and eventually attended Kolbe's canonicalization at the Vatican in 1982. Kolbe was a great man...and he was out of my league.

The irony is, the only person in heaven I've ever prayed to for help... has been my Dad, a Protestant, who will never be canonized. I'm sure he's in heaven, and I'm sure he's praising God and praying for me, if his life here on Earth was any indication. But, can a Protestant be a saint? And, in that is the great irony of Christianity. The Catholic Church says, yes...but not officially, at least not with a capital "S". In the meantime I guess it's *saint* Benji...*Pray for me, Dad, that I don't die like Maximilian Kolbe, but like you.*

Catholic or Protestant?

YOU MAY REMEMBER how I wanted to marry a Christian woman? When Pam finally made the decision to become Catholic I was so excited and thankful that I prayed over-and-over that she'd become a better Catholic than me. I think she has, although I'm not sure how to qualify "better." We both have an intense desire to obey God and work for his Kingdom, through the Church.

Perhaps one final story will confirm this joy and confidence of becoming Catholic...together.

At the beginning of January 1999, I traveled to Ft. Lauderdale, Florida to help run the Harley's Dealer Operations Training for several weeks. By now, Pam had decided to be received into the Church and had scheduled with Fr. Cronk a time to do it—two days after I was to

---

1 Wikipedia, on-line.

return, on Saturday, January 23, 1999 after the Saturday evening Mass.

Prior to my trip to Florida, Pam decided it was time to tell her parents and our children of her decision. As expected, their reception was cold and flooded with discontent.

When I called Pam from my hotel room in Florida on that Sunday afternoon, she said she was about to leave for Highland Park Baptist Church for Sunday evening services. I asked her why she was going there. She explained that she wasn't going to the worship service, but had agreed to meet during the service with her Dad, Trudy (our oldest and articulate daughter), and one of the HPBC pastors. Why? To talk Pam out of becoming Catholic.

Their attempt at cornering Pam, didn't surprise me. But I was angry at the timing. They had waited until the evil antagonist (me) was out of town.

Pam then told me that she had spent over two hours with Ed Wolfrum on the phone earlier that afternoon writing up a defense of the Catholic Church that she intended to read to her deprogrammers. She called Ed's help "a wonderfully insightful apology with Scripture and reason," and that it was "far more thorough" than what she (Pam) would have written.

I was still upset that these close friends and relatives would dare to gang-up on Pam with me 1,300 miles away. But then she told me why it was good that I wasn't there. "This way they will know it's not you brainwashing me, as they've claimed, but it's really me and that I've got the reasons why."

> **I made choices.. But I had no choice over the consequences that Natural Law prescribed.**

And I instantly had this reversal of thought, "I'm not there! It's not me! This is great!"

When we hung up, I, of course, spent some time in prayer for her and then checked my schedule. DOT had scheduled a dealer banquet that night, which neither I nor my instructors needed to attend. Instead, what was on my schedule was dinner with Doug Olsen. Irony of ironies—I almost fell out of my chair.

DOUG OLSEN WAS a presenter I had recruited to speak to the Harley dealers in a workshop about Customer Satisfaction. Doug was a longtime Harley rider and customer. He had ridden all over the country and had been in perhaps 100 different

Harley stores over the years. He was a rider's rider, a true HOG. He had long blonde hair that hung out from under his helmet and...just as important, he was a sought after inspirational speaker. But here's the clincher. I knew Doug because he was the Superintendent for South-field Christian Schools, the K-12 school run by Highland Park Baptist Church. He was the only male in the entire high school building that was allowed to wear his hair below his collar. And he wore it proudly, with his bike often parked outside. Otherwise, he ran a tight ship. Doug was also on HPBC's Official Board.

The Providential scheduling of our dinner (while Pam was meeting back in Michigan with other HPBC staff) reminded me that if I was in God's will I would not have to worry about what came next or when. I have been reminded of this truth time-and-time again. Recently, I came across this passage in the biography of Mother Benedict Duss, OSB, foundress of the Bethlehem, Connecticut Abbey of Regina Laudis:

> *If you do something concrete, that opens the possibilities. You don't know what God is doing on the other side, but He's doing something. You have to keep a sense of obligation on the one hand, and trust on the other.*[1]

As I took the elevator to the lobby of the hotel to meet up with Doug, I shook my head at the irony. Here I was, supposedly out of the HPBC picture for the night. But, this dinner meeting had been set-up a week prior, in part, because Doug had heard I was now Catholic and was curious why. So, here we were, Pam and me, 1,300 miles apart, with no chance to coordinate the evenings engagements, but we would both be meeting with leaders of HPBC...and telling them of our conversion to Catholicism.

The dinner with Doug went smoothly. I thanked him for his participation at DOT. He was paid well for his work, and the dealers loved him and invited him back the next year to give additional workshops and a keynote address. We also talked about Catholicism, and he found my explanations "fascinating and intriguing."

After dinner I was anxious to talk to Pam to hear how her meeting went. We talked that night from 10:10 to 10:30. She reported they had a "pleasant" conversation. The pastor they met with (a man with a doctorate in Old Testament Theology) tried to explain why Catholicism

---

1 Bosco, Antoinette (2007). *Mother Benedict: Foundress of The Abbey of Regina Laudis*. Ignatius Press, San Francisco, 422 pages.

wasn't really a Christian Church. But according to Pam, the reasons were all based on Protestant misunderstandings or straw-man arguments that weren't true in the first place. She said they brought up nothing that wasn't contradicted in Scripture...if one were to take the whole Bible and not twist some proof texts out of context.

In preparing for the session she said she had seen profound things in Scripture that had never made sense before, thus further convincing her of Catholicism's truth.

Pam's meeting with her detractors without me, was a watershed moment. I realized fully that her excitement about being Catholic was genuine, heartfelt, and intellectually rooted. At the same time, we were both excited because, as we joked, we had 2,000 years of Christianity to catch up on. There was much more to learn.

Now, not only had I come home to the historical Christian faith, but so had Pam. We were together and we were one-flesh with Christ in His One, Holy, Catholic, and Apostolic Church.

In The End

THIS MEMOIR BEGAN with a recitation of a premise from Exodus:

> I, the Lord your God... showing love to a thousand generations of those who love me and keep my commandments.[1]

Growing Up Christian submits that the above premise is true and the details and arc of my life support the premise. But, as an ethnographic study, there are holes in my argument. The most obvious is that my life represents a single piece of data, collected over several decades, and therefore any conclusions drawn from it alone are statistically insignificant. The anecdotes of my life cannot be extrapolated to everyone. My life does not represent the masses. I do not identify with the marginalized, neglected, enslaved or abused...even if you include my mother's punishments.[2]

However, in spite of the statistical insignificance of my life, it is still scientific-ethnographic evidence, which can be added to the experience (and evidence) of others to demonstrate that the blessings of God do flow to the "thousandth generation" of those that love God and keep his commandments. I am beholden to my parents and ancestors.

---

1 Exodus 20:5 (NIV)
2 c.f. Proverbs 13:24, 19:18, 22:15, Hebrews 12:6-7 et al

A T THE SAME time, I am not the mechanical precipitant of my ancestors' actions, blessed as they may be. Of my own free will I made choices. I have embraced some values and rejected others, made decisions and took specific actions. But I had no choice over the consequences that Natural Law prescribed, whether they be penalties or rewards.

So, what can I conclude from what has transpired over my short life and the longer history of my ancestors? That *the fear of God, the love of His commandments, and the pursuit of wisdom found in Natural Law will lead to a meaningful, happy, and purpose filled life.*

A M D G

ACKNOWLEDGMENTS

WRITING ABOUT MY journey of faith has been surprisingly therapeutic, and now having completed it, I recommend the effort to anyone who wants to discover or confirm their place in the world. But I am fully aware that I could not have finished the task without the abled and enthusiastic support and inspiration of some wonderful people.

PAM WILLIAMS, MY wonderful, beautiful, and only wife of 46 years laughed, groaned and went through a dozen Precise V5 rolling ball red-ink pens with an extra fine tip in a final attempt to change her flawed husband. Usually I saw the wisdom of her comments and rewrote and rewrote until she was smiling or laughing again. I'm not a confident writer and often I would take her a paragraph or a few pages that didn't seem to make sense to me, although I had just written them. She would drop what she was doing, read, and then we'd discuss "my issues." Her interest, patience and enthusiasm for the project befuddled me at first. But when we were done the effort brought us closer together. I love her deeply and am so grateful God brought us together.

MARY KOCHAN, MY principal editor, chased me for years about writing this book. It began when I wrote a series of articles on the juxtaposition of informal (fallacy) logic and Catholic doctrine for CatholicExchange.com that she edited. She published 26 of those essays, which became the inspiration for this book. Each essay told a story from my past and then focused on a relevant logical or linguistic fallacy I had found in Protestantism but were absent in Catholicism. Mary and I started in on this book with those 26 essays believing we had 26 chapters already completed. But, alas, that was not the case. We liked the stories but we felt the didactic explanation of logic and theology hindered the read. The stories were fun, but the explanations were too heavy. So, with her deft encouragement I rewrote everything and moved most of the propositional, didactic elements into a large file that now sits on my Mac's internal flash drive as "Volume 2." Time will tell if that effort finds its way to my screen again. If it does, the point will be to explain (on the nose) what is imbued between the lines of this book that we have coined "Volume 1." Mary stuck with me for years as this was coddled into shape. I am greatly indebted to her.

BILL WIITALA, MY writing partner of many years, also took several passes at the manuscript, and again, made many valuable suggestions and provided insights. Bill and I have several common friends, and none of them can understand how Bill and I can tolerate each other for more than a few minutes, let alone write screenplays together or spend hours pouring over a manuscript such as this one.

They're perplexed because Bill and I hold opposing political world views; and where I'm driven to know what is absolutely true and how things tick and/or tock, and I demand liturgy, ritual, chants, and encyclical letters (and thus became Catholic), Bill's happy to fellowship with the Quakers, where:

> *All Friends (i.e., Quakers) can agree that outward*
> *statements of belief are an insufficient basis for a life of faith.*
> *Friends aim at an inward knowledge of the Spirit—both*
> *individually and in our Meetings. The core of our faith is our*
> *living relationship with and obedience to God, not merely*
> *the rote recitation of creeds or performance of rituals.*[1]

And, in that statement lies the secret, I think, of our relationship. I agree with it, as does Catholicism. One of the barriers I had to overcome in understanding Catholicism was that it was not like the faith of my childhood where (it appeared) "outward statements of belief" or "going through the motions" or appearances were sufficient. During my journey, I discovered that the Catholic Catechism makes a long case for the proper inward "secret disposition of heart" and the necessity of virtues that spring from a "habitual and firm disposition to do the good." Thus the Quaker's "inward knowledge of the Spirit... [that leads to] relationship with and obedience to God" seems to be

---

1 www.quakerinfo.org/quakerism/beliefs

identical to the Catholic concept of a "supernatural disposition that perfects the soul itself to enable it to live with God, [and] to act by his love."[1] I think that kind of agreement on the level of virtues is why Bill and I get along.

But how one gets to that "inward knowledge" or "habitual disposition" is where Bill and I differ. Our makeups require different disciplines. Here's an interesting example. When Bill read the chapter on Bill Gothard and the Institute of Basic Youth Conflicts, he told me that he and his wife had, before they met, each attended the Bill Gothard seminars—he in Detroit, Nancy in Los Angeles. During their courtship they both expressed their distaste for the regimented, legalistic Binder of rules Gothard had fashioned for living the perfect Christian life. They had both witnessed how such a system of suggestions could become a narrow list of rules by which a person's spirituality could be unfairly judged. They wanted nothing to do with such a culture. So they vowed to encourage each other's spirituality in other ways and avoid judgments based on the massive list of dos and don'ts that Gothard's teachings inspired. As a symbol of this belief, they gathered their IBYC notebooks and other Gothard materials and ceremoniously torched them.

When I heard that I laughed out loud. Because of my upbringing, much of which is distilled in this book, I totally understood why they had torched Gothard's materials, and I could find no fault in it. As for Pam and me? We still have much Gothard's materials and find it useful.

In the end, I not only bless Bill's friendship but I long for his inner quiet.

JAN SWEDORSKE WAS the instigator, proctor and assistant writing instructor for a two-year long Story Structure Symposium I led for Catholic high school home-schoolers from the Ann Arbor area who wanted to learn to write screenplays or novels. I enjoyed them and have become their fans as they've now all entered college. Related to the current work, Jan tirelessly reviewed later drafts of the book and my many revisions, and provided numerous helpful suggestions. She also pointed out a number of unresolved story threads that I subsequently tied up. Her assistance in many things make me look more "together" than I really am. Thank you, Jan, and Mike, her diligent husband!

---

1 Catechism of the Catholic Church paragraphs 682, 1803, 2000.

KELLY NIETO HAS become a close creative comrade in our battle against the laissez-faire attitude toward the Arts in Christianity. Kelly's a brilliant creative mind and the creator and producer behind the Broadway-styled musical show "The Cross and The Light," on which I've had the privileged of helping her a little. (She's also a former Miss Michigan and Talent competition winner at the Miss America Pageant.) Kelly and I are both convinced that it is only through the pursuit, development and execution of good Art that God can communicate his heart to his people. Without the communication Arts, presentations of the Gospel become cold and academic. With presentations of the Gospel that engage both heart and soul, mind and emotions, there's a chance that people will understand the fullness of God's passionate love for us and respond with the commitment of obedient lives. (So much for our bully pulpit.) I thank Kelly for her great suggestions in the artistic nuances of helping Growing Up Christian to press. She also stars as the wacky Bible Bookstore clerk in video trailers for this book. (Yes, I know "Art" is capitalized...it's a proper noun in our lexicon.)

DAVE ARMSTRONG, FORMER Protestant who is now the author of numerous books on Catholicism, and one of the best online Catholic apologists, was gracious enough to look over some of the theological sections of the book. I was wise enough not to try to send this to the Detroit Archdiocese's official censor, a wonderful theologian that Dave and I both know and respect. Since this book does not pretend to teach Catholic doctrine, any theological missteps are entirely my own. And if you have a question about Catholicism, Dave's large website (Biblical Evidence for Catholicism) is a great place to start: www.patheos.com/blogs/davearmstrong/.

IMUST ALSO THANK several friends who have encouraged me over the years, by their example, to do more writing. There is **Bonnie Virag**, a neighbor I met through the recommendation of my cable guy (no kidding). Bonnie wrote a great memoir titled *The Stovepipe* about her horrific upbringing in the Canadian foster care system. It's a beautiful read and the book you're now holding was styled, in part, after Bonnie's effort.

Michael Mahony, is a retired Information Technology guru, who is originally from Ireland, but has lived in South Africa since 1975. I've never met Michael, but once upon a time he purchased something from my distribution company, Nineveh's Crossing, and wrote me about it. We struck up a friendship via email. Years ago Mike began to write about his journey of faith in a series of seven books on Catholic theology titled *One of Us*. Published by South African Catholic Online Publishing, the series is comprehensive and an intellectual examination of Christendom. The handsome volumes are written and laid out in South Africa, then uploaded to Amazon's Createspace, where they're printed in Kentucky (USA) for distribution here in the U.S.

And I can't forget **Tamera Alexander**, a friend, client and best selling Historical Christian Novelist from Nashville. I've helped Tamera structure some of her recent novels, and in exchange she's encouraged me to do my own writing. She wants me to write a couple of novels, but I had to get this one out first. Tammy, God bless you.

FINALLY, I WOULD be amiss if I didn't thank a small contingent of very loyal Nineveh's Crossing customers and fans of my writing over the years. They generously provided financial support which paid for Mary's editing. They are **Linda Capp, Sheryl Collmer, Judith Oebrink, Deacon Louis Feté, Adam Lennon, Mwaura Chege, Teresa Dearing, L. Marie Caddell, L. Marie Chong, Kerrie Summers, Arthur Reynoso,** and **Fr. Adrain Head.** Thank you! May your names be written in the book of life, and your sponsorship of this tome not held against you when you enter the Pearly Gates.

—SW

Author's Highlights

For my readers who like an electronic reader app's ability to capture your highlights and put them neatly into a text file, I've taken the presumptuous liberty of capturing "your" highlights on these pages. They're actually my favorite sidebars that litter this memoir. If these aren't your favorites and you'd like to suggest deletions (or additions) please let me know. In the meantime, as Woody Allen would say, "Here's the Author's Message(s)" with page numbers, no less. Sorry there are so many, but I had a lot on my mind.

xvi	*God showered me with His blessings because those that preceded me had kept His commandments.*
23	*My challenge was to figure out which of their rules were Natural Laws and which were made by mankind for less than infallible purposes.*
31	*Miraculous answers to prayer only had to happen once in a while to impress me that God and his angels were listening.*
62	*It was inconsistent that our Free Methodist preachers would proclaim that salvation was a free gift, and then demand a list of mandatory behaviors to maintain membership in the Church.*
108	*Evangelicalism existed for the purpose of saving dweebs like me...so I could save other dweebs like you. It was very utilitarian.*
121	*Is it possible that the arts... are intended by God to make the unseen visible, and the mystical known?*
159	*Was the purpose of faith to help us do the work? And if we put all our effort into faith and not the work, would we be any earthly good? Faith without works seemed like an ironic death.*
175	*I came to believe that Absolute Truth was knowable, and that it wasn't found in the concept of faith alone, or in Scripture alone, but also relied on the careful observation of the universe (i.e. Reason).*

210	It made little sense for Protestants to say Scripture interprets itself and then in the same breath claim, "we need a new translation."
222	Something was tragically wrong with the system that prevented Christians from being of one mind and worshipping together.
240	A virtue taken to extremes becomes a vice.
247	I just didn't believe that the Holy Spirit was schizophrenic; at least I couldn't find that in the Bible.
252	Words meant something, and their definitions and interpretations could not be subject to personal interpretations without endangering missions and lives.
305	Dennis's Bible customizing trick made me think — Indeed! Where's the trustworthy authority to interpret the infallible Bible? Really! How do we know who's interpretation is right?
331	Wasn't it time for preachers to put getting saved on the back burner and make spiritual maturity a priority?
348	My trust in what Protestant Bible scholars had led me to believe for 40 years evaporated quickly.
388	Christians had earned the reputation of defending their faith based on ideological opinions and not rational evidence.
304	My MISSION STATEMENT: To discover and promote divine truth to those within my sphere of influence.
402	Mountains, flowers, trees and other wonders of nature do not have Scripture plastered across them to remind us of God.
418	What if everyone simply followed his or her own conscience? The end result was obvious — "we will have nothing certain."
419	With a modified Bible, (either by ripping out pages, removing books, or never preaching on passages that challenge...) Sola Scriptura works much better.

419   *They claimed agreement on the essentials, but that meant their separation was due to the non-essentials.*

420   *If individual Reformers could start their own church, and make up their own doctrines, then what was hindering anyone else from coming up with entirely new doctrines?*

431   *I wondered if the fear of questioning what was considered perfect, namely Christianity, was the basis for not questioning our imperfect interpretation of it.*

432   *In other words, if my intentions were good, I could never be culpable, and it was God's will that was to blame for the undesirable things that happened due to Natural Law's reluctance to embrace my understanding of the universe.*

460   *I trusted Scripture because when I applied the truths of what the Bible taught, I saw the physical evidence in the redemption of my life and others around me.*

479   *The church understood that some doctrines took time to assimilate and understand, if ever they could be. So much of Christianity is a mystery.*

489   *Paradox is perhaps the best humanity can do, owing to our innate inability to know much of anything about the universe, let alone everything.*

489   *Atheism's declarative claim of omniscience has only ignorance for evidence.*

516   *I made choices...but I had no choice over the consequences that Natural Law prescribed.*

516   *The fear of God, the love of His commandments, and the pursuit of wisdom found in Natural Law will lead to a meaningful, happy, and purpose filled life.*